SAINTS

The Story of the Church of Jesus Christ in the Latter Days

Volume 3

Boldly, Nobly, and Independent

1893–1955

Published by
The Church of Jesus Christ of Latter-day Saints
Salt Lake City, Utah

saints.ChurchofJesusChrist.org

Cover art by Greg Newbold
Cover design and interior layout by Patric Gerber

Library of Congress Cataloging-in-Publication Data
Names: The Church of Jesus Christ of Latter-day Saints, issuing body.
Title: Saints : the story of the Church of Jesus Christ in the latter days. Volume 3, Boldly, nobly, and independent, 1893–1955.
Other titles: Story of the Church of Jesus Christ in the latter days
Description: Salt Lake City : The Church of Jesus Christ of Latter-day Saints, 2022. | Includes bibliographical references and index. | Summary: "The third volume in a four-volume series recounting the history of The Church of Jesus Christ of Latter-day Saints"— Provided by publisher.
Identifiers: ISBN 9781629726496 (paperback) | ISBN 9781629738123 (ebook)
Subjects: LCSH: The Church of Jesus Christ of Latter-day Saints—History—19th century. | Mormon Church—History—19th century | The Church of Jesus Christ of Latter-day Saints—History—20th century. | Mormon Church—History—20th century.
Classification: LCC BX8611 .S235 2022 | DDC 289.309/034-dc23
Printed in the United States of America
10 9 8 7 6 5 4 3 2 1

SAINTS

THE STORY OF
THE CHURCH OF JESUS CHRIST
IN THE LATTER DAYS

The standard of truth has been erected.
No unhallowed hand can stop the work from
progressing; persecutions may rage,
mobs may combine, armies may assemble,
calumny may defame, but the truth of God will
go forth boldly, nobly, and independent till it
has penetrated every continent, visited every clime,
swept every country, and sounded in every ear,
till the purposes of God shall be accomplished and
the great Jehovah shall say the work is done.

—Joseph Smith, 1842

CONTRIBUTORS

SAINTS
THE STORY OF THE CHURCH OF JESUS CHRIST
IN THE LATTER DAYS

Church Historian and Recorder
Executive Director, Church History Department
Elder LeGrand R. Curtis Jr.

Assistant Executive Director,
Church History Department
Elder Kyle S. McKay

Managing Director, Church History Department
Matthew J. Grow

Director, Publications Division
Matthew S. McBride

Managing Historian
Jed Woodworth

Product Manager
Ben Ellis Godfrey

Editorial Manager
Nathan N. Waite

VOLUME 3
BOLDLY, NOBLY, AND INDEPENDENT
1893–1955

General Editors
Scott A. Hales
Angela Hallstrom
Lisa Olsen Tait
Jed Woodworth

Writers
Scott A. Hales
Angela Hallstrom
Melissa Leilani Larson
Dallin T. Morrow
James Perry

Editors
Kathryn Tanner Burnside
Leslie Sherman Edgington
Alison Kitchen Gainer
Petra Javadi-Evans
Catherine Reese Newton
R. Eric Smith
Nathan N. Waite

CONTENTS

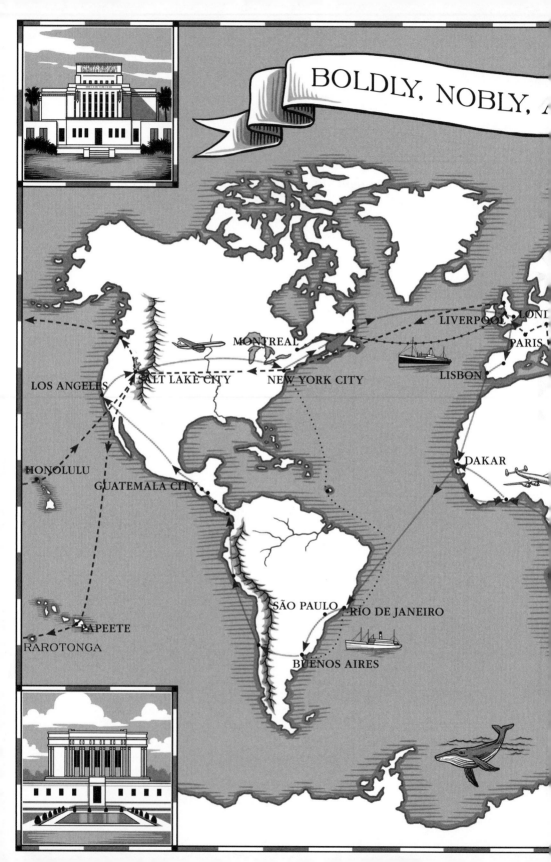

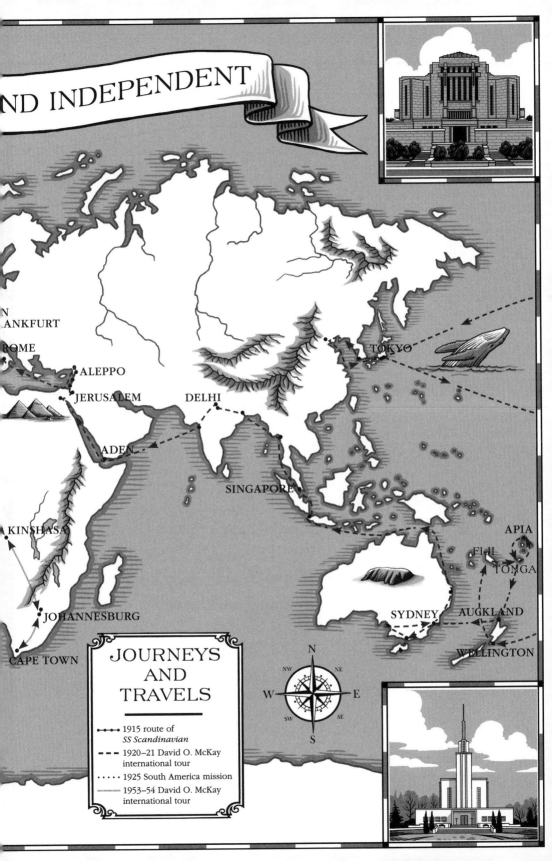

ND INDEPENDENT

FRANKFURT
ROME
ALEPPO
JERUSALEM
DELHI
TOKYO
ADEN
SINGAPORE
KINSHASA
APIA
FIJI
TONGA
JOHANNESBURG
SYDNEY
AUGKLAND
CAPE TOWN
WELLINGTON

JOURNEYS AND TRAVELS

●━━● 1915 route of
SS Scandinavian

- - - 1920–21 David O. McKay
international tour

· · · · 1925 South America mission

▭▭▭ 1953–54 David O. McKay
international tour

N
NW   NE
W   E
SW   SE
S

PART 1

—◆—

A Firm Basis

1893–1911

"This Church will stand, because it is
upon a firm basis. . . . The Lord has shown it
to us by the revealing principle
of the Holy Spirit of light."

Lorenzo Snow, April 1900

1893–1911

TRONDHEIM

LIVERPOOL
LONDON   ROTTERDAM   BERLIN
EXETER   GÖTTINGEN
        PARIS
        BERN

Boundaries 1893

CARDSTON   C A N A D A

                    SHARON
CHICAGO   PALMYRA   BOSTON
SALT LAKE CITY
            WASHINGTON, DC

U N I T E D   S T A T E S

COLONIA JUÁREZ

M E X I C O

            C U B A
            HAVANA

CHAPTER 1

A Brighter and
a Better Day

Evan Stephens and the Tabernacle Choir had the opportunity of a lifetime. It was May 1893, and the World's Columbian Exposition had just opened in Chicago, a booming metropolis in the midwestern United States. For the next six months, millions of people from around the world would come to the exposition. There were six hundred sprawling acres to explore, filled with grassy parks, shimmering lagoons and canals, and gleaming ivory-colored palaces. Everywhere visitors turned at the fair, they heard beautiful concerts, breathed in enticing new aromas, or beheld awe-inspiring exhibits from forty-six participating nations.

If you wanted to get the world's attention, Evan knew, you could find no bigger stage than the world's fair.[1]

As the conductor of the choir, he was eager to perform in the Grand International Eisteddfod, a prestigious Welsh singing competition to be held at the fair that fall. He and many choir members were Welsh or of Welsh descent and had grown up steeped in the musical traditions of their homeland. Yet the competition was more than a chance to celebrate their heritage. Performing in Chicago would give the Tabernacle Choir—the premier singing group of The Church of Jesus Christ of Latter-day Saints—the perfect opportunity to put their talent on display and introduce more people to the Church.[2]

Time after time, misinformation about the Saints had brought them hardship and conflict with their neighbors. Half a century earlier they had fled to the Salt Lake Valley, far from their harassers. Yet peace had been fleeting, especially after the Saints began openly practicing plural marriage. In the decades that followed, the United States government waged an unrelenting campaign against plural marriage, and critics of the Church deployed every means to destroy its public image and portray the Saints as a crude, unenlightened people.

In 1890, Church president Wilford Woodruff issued the Manifesto, an official statement calling for the end of plural marriage among the Saints. Since then, the federal government had eased its opposition to the Church. Change was slow, however, and misunderstandings persisted. Now, at the century's end, the Saints wanted to give the world a true picture of who they were and what they believed.[3]

As eager as Evan was to have the choir represent the Church at the fair, he very nearly had to pass up the opportunity. A financial crisis had just struck the United States, crippling Utah's economy. Many choir members were poor, and Evan did not want them to use their income for the journey. He also worried that they were not ready for competition. Although they had sung like angels at the recent Salt Lake Temple dedication, they were still a choir of amateurs. If they were no match for the other choirs, they could embarrass the Church.[4]

In fact, earlier that year Evan and the First Presidency of the Church had decided not to enter the contest after all. But then the Eisteddfod had sent representatives to Salt Lake City. After listening to the choir sing, the representatives informed George Q. Cannon, first counselor in the First Presidency, that the Saints could win the competition.

Turning to Evan, President Cannon asked, "Do you think our choir has a fair chance?"

"I do not think we can win the contest," Evan replied, "but we can make a fine impression."[5]

That was enough for President Cannon. Other Saints, also hoping to represent the Church well, had already left for Chicago. Leaders of the Relief Society and Young Ladies' Mutual Improvement Association would be speaking at the fair's Congress of Representative Women, the largest assembly of women's leaders ever held. B. H. Roberts, one of the seven presidents of the Seventy, hoped to speak about the Church at the Parliament of Religions being held at the fair.

At the First Presidency's request, the choir began rehearsing immediately—and scrambling to find a way to fund the trip. Evan needed to do the impossible, and he had less than three months to do it.[6]

THAT SPRING, THE ECONOMIC crisis hampering the Tabernacle Choir was also threatening the Church with financial ruin.

Six years earlier, at the height of its antipolygamy campaign, the United States Congress had passed the Edmunds-Tucker Act, authorizing the confiscation of Church property. Worried the government would seize their donations, many Saints had stopped paying tithing, greatly reducing the Church's main source of funding. To cover its losses, the Church had borrowed money and invested in business ventures to provide enough funds to keep the Lord's work moving forward. It also took out loans to cover the cost of finishing the Salt Lake Temple.[7]

On May 10, 1893, the First Presidency asked apostle Heber J. Grant to travel east immediately to negotiate new loans to relieve the Church's financial burdens. In Utah, banks were failing and agricultural prices plummeting. Soon the Church would not be able to pay its secretaries, clerks, and other employees.[8] Since Heber was the president of a Salt Lake City bank and had many friends in the finance industry, Church leaders hoped he could secure the money.[9]

Once Heber agreed to go, President Cannon gave him a blessing, promising that angels would assist him. Heber then caught a train for the East Coast, the weight of the Church resting on his shoulders. If he failed, the Church would default on its loans and lose the trust of its creditors. It would then be unable to borrow the money it needed to stay running.[10]

Soon after arriving in New York City, Heber renewed several loans and borrowed $25,000 more. He then pursued another loan, ultimately securing an additional $50,000. But his efforts were not enough to keep the Church financially afloat.[11]

As the days went by, he struggled to find more lenders. The crisis had frightened everyone. Nobody wanted to issue loans to an institution already deep in debt.

Heber began losing sleep. He worried his health would fail before he fulfilled his mission. "I am over six feet high and weigh but 140 pounds," he noted in his journal, "so there is not much surplus for me to draw on."[12]

ON THE MORNING OF May 19, Emmeline Wells was anxious. At ten o'clock, she and other leaders of the Relief Society would be speaking about their organization to the World's Congress of Representative Women at the Chicago World's Fair.[13]

She hoped their speeches would correct harmful stereotypes about women in the Church. Since most of the Church's two hundred thousand members lived in the American West, few people had ever met a Latter-day Saint woman. What people knew about them usually came from books, magazines, and pamphlets that spread false information about the Church and characterized its women as uneducated and oppressed.[14]

When ten o'clock arrived, the room's eight hundred seats were not all filled. Although the Relief Society session had been well advertised, other important sessions were happening at the same time, drawing away people who might otherwise have come to hear the Utah women speak. Emmeline recognized a few faces in the audience, many of them Saints who came in support. She did, however, spot one important audience member who was not a Latter-day Saint: reporter Etta Gilchrist.[15]

Ten years earlier, Etta had written a novel condemning plural marriage and the Saints. But since then, she and Emmeline had found common cause in advocating for women's voting rights, leading Emmeline to publish one of Etta's articles on suffrage in the *Woman's Exponent,* a newspaper Emmeline edited in Utah. A positive report from Etta would certainly help the Saints' reputation.[16]

The session opened with a performance of Eliza R. Snow's hymn "O My Father." Relief Society general president Zina Young and other leaders then delivered short addresses about the work of the Relief Society and the history of the Church. The speakers included women who had come to Utah as pioneers as well as those who were born in the territory. When Emmeline spoke, she praised the sophistication of Utah's women writers and described the Relief Society's many years of experience in grain storage.

"If ever there is a famine," she told the audience, "come to Zion."[17]

Before the meeting ended, Emmeline called Etta to the platform. Etta rose and took a seat beside Zina. She shook hands with each of the women from Utah, touched that they would treat her kindly after she had once belittled them.

Etta's report on the Relief Society meeting appeared in the newspaper a few days later. "The Mormons are apparently a most religious people," she wrote. "Their faith in their religion is marvelous."

Describing the welcome she received from the Saints, she added, "This one meeting was to me worth coming to Chicago for."

Emmeline was grateful for the compliment.[18]

As banks and businesses in Utah failed, nineteen-year-old Leah Dunford worried about her family. They were not wealthy, and her mother, Susa Gates, a daughter of Brigham Young, had sold precious land so Leah could study health and fitness at a summer school held on Harvard University's campus in Cambridge,

Massachusetts. Leah was not sure she should go. Was it right, she wondered, to benefit from her mother's sacrifice?[19]

Susa wanted Leah to attend the summer school, no matter the expense. At the time, many young Latter-day Saints were leaving Utah to study at prestigious universities in the eastern United States. Susa had studied at the summer school the previous year, and she hoped her daughter would have a similarly good experience. She also thought that one of the students she met there, a young Norwegian Latter-day Saint named John Widtsoe, would be an ideal match for Leah.[20]

Worries about money aside, Leah was eager to further her education. Her mother believed that young Latter-day Saint women needed a good education and career training. Until recently, plural marriage had made a covenant marriage available to virtually any Latter-day Saint woman who desired it. But Leah's generation, the first to reach adulthood after the Manifesto, no longer had that guarantee—or the guarantee of financial support that marriage brought women at that time.[21]

Though educational and career possibilities were expanding for women in many parts of the world, parents in the Church often worried that these opportunities would lead their daughters to marry husbands outside the Church and leave the faith. For this reason, leaders in the Young Ladies' Mutual Improvement Association had begun emphasizing that young women should

develop strong testimonies and make important decisions prayerfully.[22]

Susa, in fact, had already encouraged Leah to fast
and pray about her relationship with John Widtsoe.
Susa's marriage to Leah's father, who was a heavy drinker
at the time, had ended in divorce. She yearned for her
daughter to have a happy marriage to a righteous young
man. Of course, Leah had yet to meet John in person.
So far, they had only exchanged a few letters.[23]

In June 1893, Leah traveled to Harvard, a distance
of more than two thousand miles, with four other
women from Utah. They arrived late at the house
where John and the other Latter-day Saint students
lived, so they did not have time to meet the young
men. The next morning, though, Leah noticed a quiet
young man sitting in a corner by himself. "I guess
you're Brother Widtsoe," she said to him. "I heard my
mother talk about you."

She had always imagined John as a tall, strapping
Scandinavian. Instead, he was short and slight. What on
earth did her mother see in him?

Thoroughly unimpressed, Leah ignored John until
dinnertime. When the housekeeper recruited John to
carve the meat, Leah thought, "At least he's useful." Then,
after everyone knelt to bless the food, John offered the
blessing. His prayer went straight to Leah's heart.

"There's the man," she told herself.[24]

After that, Leah and John were almost always together. One afternoon, while wandering together in a

park, they stopped on a small hill overlooking a pond. There John told Leah about his childhood in Norway and his youth in Logan, Utah.

It soon started to rain, so they took shelter in a nearby tower, and Leah went on to tell John about her life. They then climbed to the top of the tower and talked for another hour and a half about their hopes for the future.[25]

John Widtsoe was in love with Leah Dunford, but he did not want to admit it. When she first came to the school, he wanted to ignore her. He was too busy and not interested in romance at this stage in his life. He had big plans for his future. Leah was a distraction.

But he liked how she could play several instruments and talk lightly or seriously depending on the occasion. He liked that she helped the housekeeper clean up when everyone else sat and did nothing. More than anything else, he liked her ambition.

"She has a desire to do something in the world," he wrote to his mother, Anna, in Salt Lake City. "She will be one of Utah's leading women in education."

By his calculations, he would need at least two or three years to pay off his Harvard debts. He would then need four years for graduate school in Europe—and another four years to pay off that debt. Then he would need at least three more years to earn enough money to even consider marrying Leah.[26]

John was also still sorting out his own religious beliefs. He had faith in Jesus's purity and goodness. When he first came to Harvard, he had also received a strong spiritual witness that God had helped him pass his entrance exams. But he was less sure about the Church. Earlier that year, he had written to his mother with questions he had about the Church and its leaders. The letter had so distressed Anna that she had written back immediately, certain he had lost his testimony.[27]

In his next letter, John had tried to explain himself. Like some other Saints his age, he grappled with doubts. Church leaders had always taught him that he lived in the last days, when the Lord would deliver His people from their enemies. But over the last three years, he had watched the Saints set aside plural marriage and grow bitterly divided over politics. He now questioned whether the Saints would ever succeed in building Zion.

"Everything seems to have gone against expectations," he had told his mother.

In his letters home, John had also tried to explain that it was not enough for him to simply believe something. He had to know why he believed it. "It is of no use to say that 'I believe it' and think no more about it," he had written. Still, he continued to pray for greater understanding of things pertaining to the Church.[28]

Then, on July 23, he had a powerful spiritual experience. A Methodist woman attended the Latter-day Saint students' Sunday service, and John was asked to give an impromptu sermon. Surprised, he stood up, unsure what he should say. He quickly decided to talk about the personality of God, hoping his words would help the visitor understand what the Saints believed. As he spoke, he did not get flustered or repeat himself, as he sometimes did when speaking in public. Instead, he preached a clear, intelligible sermon for more than thirty minutes.

"I felt God's Spirit help me," he wrote to his mother. "I have never known so much about God and His personality."[29]

After the meeting, John spent the rest of the day with Leah. As they talked, John told her he wanted her to visit his mother. He had already told Anna so much about Leah. Now he wanted them to meet in person.[30]

As MIDNIGHT APPROACHED ON September 1, 1893, Heber J. Grant lay wide awake in a New York City hotel room. Earlier that day he had received a terrifying telegram. Zion's Savings Bank and Trust Company, the Church's most important financial institution, was on the verge of failure. So too was the State Bank of Utah, where Heber served as president. If he did not wire money to the banks the next day, they would not be able to open for business. Both Heber's and the Church's reputation with creditors would be damaged, perhaps forever.

Heber tossed and turned for hours. Earlier that year, George Q. Cannon had promised that angels would help him. More recently, Joseph F. Smith, the second counselor in the First Presidency, had promised him success beyond his expectations. But now Heber could not imagine anyone loaning him enough money to save the banks.

He prayed for help, pleading with God as tears streamed from his eyes. Finally, around three o'clock in the morning, he fell asleep, still unsure how he would solve this dilemma.[31]

He awoke unusually late. Since it was Saturday, the banks would close at noon, so he needed to hurry. Kneeling in prayer, he asked the Lord to find someone willing to loan him $200,000. He said he was willing to make any sacrifice, including giving the lender a hefty commission on the loan.[32]

After the prayer, Heber felt cheerful, sure the Lord would help him. He decided to visit John Claflin, the head of a large mercantile company, but John was not in his office. With time running out, Heber caught a train to the city's financial district, hoping to visit another bank. On the way, he became absorbed in a newspaper and missed his stop. Exiting the train, he walked along aimlessly. When he came upon the office of another acquaintance, he stepped inside. There he ran into John Claflin, the very man he wanted to see.

Knowing Heber's predicament, John agreed to loan the Church $250,000, provided he receive a 20 percent commission.[33] Despite the high cost, Heber could see that the Lord had answered his prayers.[34] He wired money to Salt Lake City immediately.

The funds arrived just in time to save the foundering banks.[35]

"PAY NO ATTENTION TO your competitors until you have sung," Evan Stephens told the members of the Tabernacle Choir. "Simply be calm."

It was the afternoon of September 8. The choir had finished their final rehearsal for the Eisteddfod. In a few hours, the singers would take the stage to perform the three musical numbers they had practiced nearly every day that summer. Evan was still not sure they could win, but he would be satisfied if they did their best.[36]

The choir, in company with the First Presidency, had arrived in Chicago five days earlier. To meet the requirements of the competition, Evan had trimmed the choir down to two hundred and fifty singers. When their star soprano, Nellie Pugsley, had a baby weeks before the concert and did not think she could perform at the fair, arrangements were made for her sister to care for the baby while Nellie sang.[37]

Funding the trip during an economic depression proved as challenging as getting the choir ready to sing. Choir leaders first tried raising money from Salt Lake City's businessmen. When that failed, the choir decided to hold several concerts, hoping ticket sales would cover costs. They held two concerts in Utah and four more in major cities between Salt Lake City and Chicago.[38]

The concerts were a financial success, but they were a strain on the singers' voices. The choir had continued to prepare in Chicago, drawing hundreds of spectators to their rehearsals at the Utah Building, a large exhibition hall displaying goods and artifacts from the territory.[39]

After their final rehearsal, Evan and the singers assembled in the basement of the concert hall. As they waited for their turn to perform, John Nuttall, the choir's secretary, offered a prayer, reminding each singer that she or he represented the Church and its people at the fair.

"Enable us at least to reflect credit upon Thy work and Thy people," he prayed, "in our endeavor to represent them here before the world—a world that mostly deems us as ignorant and uncultured."[40]

When the choir's turn came, Evan took his place at the conductor's podium. The hall was full of around ten thousand people, almost none of them members of the Church. In times past, a Latter-day Saint could expect to be heckled in front of such an audience, but Evan sensed no enmity from them.

Once the singers arranged themselves onstage, the hall went silent. The choir then sang the opening words of Handel's "Worthy Is the Lamb":

> *Worthy is the Lamb that was slain,*
> *and hath redeemed us to God by his blood,*
> *to receive power, and riches, and wisdom,*
>   *and strength,*
> *and honour, and glory, and blessing.*

Their voices were strong, and Evan thought they sounded splendid. When the choir finished the number, the audience erupted in applause. The choir then sang two more numbers, and though Evan could hear the weariness in some of their voices, they finished well and exited the stage.[41]

"We have done the very best possible," Evan told the First Presidency afterward. "I am satisfied."

Later, when the results were announced, the Tabernacle Choir took second place, finishing only half a point behind the winner. One of the judges said the Saints should have won the competition. Yet President Cannon believed the choir had achieved something greater. "As a missionary enterprise it is likely to be a success," he noted, "for it will give thousands of people the opportunity of learning a little truth about us."[42]

Evan was likewise pleased with all his singers had accomplished. News about the "Mormon choir" winning a prize at the World's Fair appeared in newspapers across the globe. He could not have asked for a better reward.[43]

THE DAY AFTER THE concert, President Woodruff spoke about the Saints during a formal banquet at the fair. "Come and see us," he said, his voice strong. "If you have not already been to Salt Lake City, you are all welcome." He also invited ministers of other faiths to speak in the city. "If there is not room in the churches," he said, "we will give you our tabernacle."[44]

The prophet returned to Utah ten days later, cheered by the kindness the Saints had received in Chicago. The only incident that marred the Church's experience at the fair occurred when organizers of the Parliament of Religions resisted B. H. Roberts's efforts to speak about the Church at their assembly. Their actions were a sad reminder that prejudice against the Church still existed, yet Church leaders believed that people across the nation were beginning to see the Saints in a new light.[45] The warm reception the Relief Society and the Tabernacle Choir had received at the fair offered hope that the persecutions of the last sixty years were coming to an end.[46]

At a small meeting in the Salt Lake Temple on October 5, the evening before the Church's general conference, the First Presidency and the Quorum of the Twelve Apostles partook of the sacrament together.

"I feel deeply impressed," George Q. Cannon said, "that a brighter and a better day is dawning upon us."[47]

CHAPTER 2

As We Prove Ourselves Ready

While the Saints in the United States enjoyed a season of goodwill, a missionary named John James faced hecklers in South West England. At one meeting, a man claimed that the Saints in Utah were murderers. At another, someone said the missionaries had come to England to seduce young women and carry them off as plural wives. A short time later, someone else tried to convince a crowd that John and his companions did not believe in the Bible—even though they had been preaching from it during the meeting.

At one gathering, a man interrupted the missionaries to say he had been to Salt Lake City and seen two hundred women herded into a shed, where Brigham Young himself had come to select as many wives as he wanted. John, who had been born and raised in Utah, knew the story was ludicrous. But the crowd refused to listen to his rebuttal.

Most of what these critics claimed to know about the Church, John suspected, came from William Jarman. William and his wife, Maria, had joined the Church in England in the late 1860s. A short time later, they emigrated to New York with their children and Emily Richards, Maria's apprentice in a dressmaking business—who, unknown to Maria, was pregnant with William's child. Eventually the family moved to Utah, where William married Emily as a plural wife and started a dry goods business with supplies he apparently stole from his employer in New York.

Life in Zion did not change William's ways. He proved to be an abusive husband, and both Maria and Emily divorced him. He was also charged with grand larceny, which landed him in prison until the courts dismissed the case. He became disillusioned with the Church, began earning a living lecturing against it, and returned to England. Often, he moved audiences to tears with a heart-wrenching story that accused the Saints of murdering his oldest son, Albert.[1]

By the time John James arrived in Great Britain, William had been on the lecture circuit for years. He had published a book criticizing the Church, and his followers sometimes attacked missionaries. In one town, some of William's followers had hurled stones at the elders, striking one in the eye.[2]

Despite the danger, John was determined to spread the gospel in Great Britain. "We have met with much opposition from men who have heard Jarman," he reported to mission leaders. "I think we have ably met them on every hand and intend to continue holding meetings."[3]

"JARMAN IS STILL LECTURING against us and using the foulest language," apostle Anthon Lund wrote to his wife, Sanie, in Utah. As the newly called president of the European Mission, headquartered in Liverpool, England, Anthon was well aware of the threat William Jarman posed to the work of the Lord. Many missionaries dismissed the lecturer as a madman, but Anthon believed he was a cunning critic whose deceptions were not to be underestimated.[4]

Having joined the Church in Denmark as a boy, Anthon also understood how difficult it was to be a Latter-day Saint in Europe. When facing opposition to their beliefs, Saints in Utah could find assurance and strength in large communities of fellow believers. But on the other side of the Atlantic, eight thousand Latter-day Saints were spread throughout western Europe and Turkey. Many Saints were recent converts attending tiny branches that often depended on missionaries for leadership and moral support. When men like Jarman attacked the Church, these branches were particularly vulnerable.[5]

Anthon had seen the difficulties branches experienced firsthand as he visited Great Britain, Scandinavia, and the Netherlands in the summer and fall of 1893. Even in England, where the Church was strongest, Saints struggled to rally together when they lived far from each other. Sometimes missionaries would stumble upon Saints who had lost contact with the Church for twenty or thirty years.[6]

Elsewhere in Europe, Anthon found similar problems. He learned that a popular pastor was lecturing against the Church in Denmark. In Norway and Sweden, Anthon met missionaries and Church members who sometimes encountered opposition from local governments or other churches. In the Netherlands, Saints struggled because they had almost no Church literature in their language besides the Book of Mormon.

Across the continent, Saints were dedicated to the gospel. But few of the branches were really thriving, and Church membership was dwindling in some areas.[7]

For decades, European Saints had gathered to Utah, where the Church was better established. But the United States government, hoping to halt the spread of plural marriage among the Saints, had shut down the Church's Perpetual Emigrating Fund in the late 1880s, stopping the Church from loaning money to poor Saints who wanted to move to Utah. More recently, the worldwide economic crisis had thrown many Europeans deeper and deeper into poverty. Some Saints who had been saving money to emigrate were forced to abandon their plans.[8]

United States immigration officials were also strict about whom they let into the country. Since some

people still feared that European Saints were coming to Utah to practice plural marriage, Church leaders directed emigrants to cross the Atlantic in small
companies to avoid attracting attention. Shortly after
Anthon arrived in Europe, in fact, the First Presidency
had censured him for sending a group of 138 Saints to
Utah. Send no more than 50 emigrants at a time, they
cautioned him.[9]

Not having the resources or authority to conduct
a large-scale emigration, Anthon rarely spoke publicly
about the gathering. But in private he encouraged Saints
to emigrate if they could afford it. In late November,
after returning to England, he met an elderly woman
who had saved enough money to travel to Utah. He
advised her to settle in Manti, not far from where his
own family lived.

"She could work in the temple," he thought, "and
enjoy her old days."[10]

MEANWHILE, LEAH DUNFORD WAS back in Salt Lake
City, writing long letters to John Widtsoe at Harvard
University. As promised, she went to see his mother,
Anna, a forty-four-year-old widow who lived south of
the Salt Lake Temple. During the visit, Anna showed
Leah a bookshelf John had made. Surprised by the
scholar's carpentry skills, Leah said, "Good, I will have
something to tease John about now."

"Oh," Anna said, "you write him, do you?"

"Yes," Leah said, suddenly worried that Anna might object. But Anna said she was glad John had a friend like Leah.[11]

Having completed her course in health and fitness, Leah was thinking about continuing her education at a university in the midwestern United States. Her mother had consulted with Joseph F. Smith and George Q. Cannon, though, and believed it best not to send her off alone to a place where the Church was not established.

Disappointed, Leah enrolled instead at a Church-run school in Salt Lake City, taking classes in natural science and chemistry from James E. Talmage, the president of the school and the most respected scholar in the Church. While Leah enjoyed her classes and learned many things from her professors, she envied John's opportunities at Harvard.

"Oh, I wish I were a man," she told him. "Men can do anything on earth, but if women think of anything but waiting on men, or cooking their meals, 'they are out of their sphere.'"

She found immense support from Professor Talmage, who told Leah he wished more young women aspired to teach at Church schools. John also lent his support. "Your determination to devote yourself to the good of others I cannot too highly praise," he wrote. "I shall give you all the help I can by faith and prayer."[12]

One Sunday in December 1893, Anna Widtsoe came to Leah's house for a visit. She spoke about her conversion in Norway and her early experiences in the

Church. "We had such a lovely visit," Leah informed John. "I feel so selfish and unworthy when I hear how much some people have sacrificed for their religion."

Leah lamented that Saints her age often seemed more interested in making money than in progressing spiritually. To fortify the rising generation, the Church had established the Young Ladies' and Young Men's Mutual Improvement Associations in the 1870s. Young people in these organizations usually met on a week-night to study the gospel, develop talents and good manners, and enjoy one another's company. The or-ganizations also published two magazines, the *Young Woman's Journal* and the *Contributor,* and manuals to help youth leaders prepare lessons on the scriptures, Church history, health, science, and literature.[13]

Young men could also look forward to missionary service to help them grow spiritually. But this opportu-nity was not officially available to women. Young adult women could serve their neighbors through mem-bership in the Relief Society, but Leah's generation tended to view it as an old-fashioned organization for their mothers. For additional spiritual strength, Leah usually worshipped with her local congregation, fasted regularly, and sought out other opportunities to study the gospel.

On New Year's Eve, Leah attended a special meet-ing with the girls in her mother's Sunday School class in Provo. Zina Young and Mary Isabella Horne, who had both belonged to the Relief Society in Nauvoo, visited the class and spoke of the early days of the Church and Joseph Smith's prophetic call.

"We had a spiritual feast," Leah told John. One by one, every girl in the room shared her testimony. "It was the first time I ever bore my testimony or spoke to a crowd on a religious subject," she wrote. "We all enjoyed it so much."[14]

ON THE FIRST DAY of 1894, George Q. Cannon awoke full of gratitude to the Lord for his family's well-being. "We have food, raiment, and shelter," he wrote in his journal. "Our houses are comfortable, and we need nothing to add to our physical comfort."[15]

The previous year had been good for the Church. The Saints had dedicated the Salt Lake Temple, the Relief Society and Tabernacle Choir had met with success at the Chicago World's Fair, and the Church had narrowly avoided financial ruin. In late December, the United States House of Representatives had also granted Utah Territory permission to apply for statehood, bringing the Saints one step closer to a goal they had been chasing since 1849.

"Who could have dared to predict such a thing concerning Utah?" George had written in his journal. "No power but that of the Almighty could have effected this."[16]

As the new year unfolded, however, George and other Church leaders faced new problems. On January 12, the U.S. government returned around $438,000 of what it had confiscated from the Church under the Edmunds-Tucker Act. Unfortunately, the restored funds were not enough to pay off the Church's loans. And as grateful as Church leaders were for the money, they believed the government had returned less than half of what it had taken from the Saints.[17]

With money still scarce, the First Presidency continued to take out loans to fund Church operations. Hoping to create stable jobs and bring revenue to the territory, the Church also invested in several local businesses. Some of the investments helped Saints find work. Other investments were unsuccessful, further adding to the Church's debt.[18]

In early March, Lorenzo Snow, the president of the Quorum of the Twelve Apostles, sought the First Presidency's advice on how to perform the temple work for his immediate ancestors. He was specifically interested in sealing children to parents who had not embraced the gospel during their lives.[19]

The first sealings of children to parents had occurred in Nauvoo. At the time, several Saints whose parents were not members of the Church chose instead to be sealed by adoption to Church leaders. They believed that doing so would ensure them a place in an eternal family and connect the community of Saints together in the next life.

After the Saints arrived in Utah, adoption sealings and child-parent sealings were not performed until the

St. George Temple was dedicated in 1877. Since then, many more Saints had chosen to be sealed by adoption into the families of apostles or other Church leaders. In fact, the usual practice of the Church was to not seal a woman to a man who had not accepted the gospel while alive. This meant a Latter-day Saint widow at that time could not be sealed to her deceased husband if he had never joined the Church. The practice could sometimes be painful to bear.[20]

George had been uncomfortable with adoption sealings for many years. As a young man in Nauvoo, he had been sealed by adoption into his uncle John Taylor's family, even though his parents had been faithful Church members. Other Church members had also chosen to be sealed to apostles rather than their own faithful Latter-day Saint parents. George now believed this practice had created some clannishness among the Saints. And in 1890, he and his siblings canceled their sealing to the Taylor family and were sealed instead to their own deceased parents in the St. George Temple, affirming the bonds of natural affection within their family.[21]

As the First Presidency discussed the case of Lorenzo's family, George proposed a possible solution. "Why not have his father and his brothers sealed to his grandfather," he asked, "and then have his grandfather and his brothers and sisters sealed to their parents, and so on back as far as possible?"

Wilford Woodruff and Joseph F. Smith seemed pleased with George's proposal. Both men harbored their own concerns about adoption sealings. Yet President Woodruff was not ready to endorse any changes to the practice. George held out hope that the Lord would soon reveal His will on the subject.[22]

"The fact is, there has not been much known about this doctrine of adoption," George observed in his journal. "It is our privilege to know concerning these things, and I trust the Lord will be kind to us and give us knowledge."[23]

ALBERT JARMAN, THE SON of the Church's most vocal critic in England, had not been the victim of a grisly murder. In the spring of 1894, he was serving a mission in Great Britain, and his presence was proof that his father was not telling the truth.[24]

When Albert first arrived in the mission field, he had wanted to confront his father immediately. But mission president Anthon Lund could see that Albert was not ready to face off against someone so sly and shrewd. He sent the young man to London instead, encouraging him to study the gospel and prepare himself against his father's attacks. In the meantime, President Lund advised, "Write him a nice letter."[25]

Albert wrote to his father as soon as he was settled in London. "My dear father," he began, "I do sincerely hope and pray that you may ere long see the error of telling the people that the Mormons murdered your son."

"You are now getting along in years, and I feel very much pained when I read and hear people repeat what you have said," he continued. "I would be pleased to shake a repentant father by the hand, and proud to own and respect you once more."[26]

As Albert waited for his father's reply, he preached and taught in London. "I am studying to the best of my knowledge," he informed his mother, Maria Barnes. "I am not much of a preacher as yet, but I hope to be one before I come home."

Albert soon received a short, hurried reply from his father. "You had better come down," William wrote in a letter. "I shall be pleased to see you."

Knowing how violent William could be, Maria was anxious for her son. But Albert told her not to worry about his father harming him. "He won't have the power," Albert reassured her. Mostly, he was eager to speak with William or any other relatives he had in England.

"I want to be able to bear my testimony to them," he wrote, "if God will so desire me to do."[27]

BACK IN SALT LAKE City, Wilford Woodruff announced to his counselors and the Quorum of the Twelve Apostles that he had received a revelation on the law of adoption. "I have felt we are too strict in regard to some of our temple ordinances," he declared on the eve of the April 1894 general conference. "This is especially the case in regard to husbands and parents who are dead."

"The Lord has told me that it is right for children to be sealed to their parents, and they to their parents just as far back as we can possibly obtain the records," he continued. "It is also right for wives whose husbands never heard the gospel to be sealed to those husbands."

President Woodruff believed they still had much to learn about temple ordinances. "God will make it known," he assured them, "as we prove ourselves ready to receive it."[28]

The following Sunday, at general conference, President Woodruff asked George Q. Cannon to read a passage from section 128 of the Doctrine and Covenants to the congregation. In the passage, Joseph Smith spoke of Elijah turning the hearts of the fathers to the children and the hearts of the children to the fathers in the last days. "The earth will be smitten with a curse," the prophet Joseph had declared, "unless there is a welding link of some kind or other between the fathers and the children."[29]

President Woodruff then returned to the stand. "We have not got through revelation," he declared. "We have not got through the work of God." He spoke of how Brigham Young had carried on Joseph Smith's work of building temples and organizing temple ordinances. "But he did not receive all the revelations that belong to this work," President Woodruff reminded the congregation. "Neither did President Taylor, nor has Wilford Woodruff. There will be no end to this work until it is perfected."

After noting that the Saints had acted according to all the light and knowledge they had received, President Woodruff explained that he and other Church leaders had long believed the Lord had more to reveal about temple work. "We want the Latter-day Saints from this time to trace their genealogies as far as they can, and to be sealed to their fathers and mothers," he declared. "Have children sealed to their parents, and run their chain through as far as you can get it."

He also announced an end to the policy that prevented a woman from being sealed to a husband who had died without receiving the gospel. "Many a woman's heart has ached because of this," he said. "Why deprive a woman of being sealed to her husband because he never heard the gospel? What do any of us know with regard to him? Will he not hear the gospel and embrace it in the spirit world?"

He reminded the Saints of Joseph Smith's vision of his brother Alvin in the Kirtland Temple. "All who have died without a knowledge of this gospel, who would have received it if they had been permitted to tarry," the Lord had taught, "shall be heirs of the celestial kingdom."

"So shall it be with your fathers," President Woodruff said of those in the spirit world. "There will be very few, if any, who will not accept the gospel."

Before closing his sermon, he urged the Saints to ponder his words—and seek out their kindred dead. "Brethren and sisters," he said, "let us go on with our records, fill them up righteously before the Lord, and carry out this principle, and the blessings of God will attend us, and those who are redeemed will bless us in days to come."[30]

CHAPTER 3

The Path of Right

Anthon Lund was visiting branches of the Church in Germany when word of Wilford Woodruff's revelation on sealings arrived in the European Mission. "This revelation will give joy to many hearts," he exclaimed when he learned the news.[1]

The new practice had special significance for several elders in his mission. Ever since the Lord revealed to Joseph Smith that Saints could perform essential ordinances for the dead, Church members had been researching their ancestors and performing ordinances on their behalf. Some elders, the sons of immigrant Saints, had come to Europe hoping to gather more information about their ancestors from relatives and archives.[2]

Now, after President Woodruff's revelation, their research took on added purpose. Many Saints throughout the Church, in fact, had grown more eager to research their family lines in order to seal generations together in an unbroken chain. Apostle and Church historian Franklin Richards even planned to organize a Church-supported genealogical library.[3]

With hard economic times plaguing Europe and the United States alike, though, many European Saints had little hope of emigrating to Utah, the only place with temples where they could perform these ordinances for their ancestors. The financial crisis in the United States was making it all but impossible for Saints who did come to Utah to find work, and Church leaders worried that immigrants would flee the territory in search of employment. Financial disappointments had already led some of them to leave the fold.[4]

In July 1894, Anthon learned how dire the situation was in Utah. In an urgent letter to the European Mission, the First Presidency reported that the Church's financial burdens had become almost unbearable as more and more wards and stakes turned to the Church for monetary aid.

"In view of this state of things existing among us," the First Presidency wrote, "we deem it wisdom to instruct you to discourage emigration for the time being."[5]

The First Presidency, in making this request, was not ending the gathering of Israel. For over forty years, the Saints had earnestly sought to carry out the revelations commanding them to gather together. Missionaries had urged new converts from across the globe to move to Utah and be near the Lord's house. Yet that practice could not continue until the economic situation improved.[6]

"We constantly pray for the gathering of Israel and rejoice to see the Saints come to Zion," the First Presidency wrote, but added, "Great wisdom must be exercised in order that the best interests of gathered as well as ungathered Israel might be best conserved."

Until conditions improved in Utah, the presidency instructed, Anthon was to strengthen the Church in Europe. "Let the Saints, one and all," they wrote, "regard it as their moral and religious duty to do all they possibly can to assist the missionary elders in building up branches and maintaining them."[7]

Anthon immediately sent copies of the letter to mission leaders, directing them to follow its counsel.[8]

ON JULY 16, 1894, THE United States Congress and President Grover Cleveland authorized the people of Utah to draft a state constitution. The First Presidency rejoiced later that day when they received a telegram from the Church's allies in Washington: "Statehood bill signed. Your people are free; and this ends our labor."[9]

When the Saints had first petitioned for a state government in 1849, the federal government granted them a territorial government instead. As citizens of a territory, the people of Utah were not allowed to choose a governor or other high government officials. Rather, they had to rely on the president of the United States to appoint officials for them. This system had led to many conflicts between the Saints, other Utahns, and the U.S. government over the years. It also barred Saints from holding some government offices. Under a state government, the people of Utah would finally be able to govern themselves.[10]

But the labor in Utah was just beginning. As delegates met in Salt Lake City to write the constitution, Emmeline Wells and other women leaders wrote a petition asking that the new constitution restore suffrage, or voting rights, to Utah's women. Although most states and territories in the United States barred women from voting, Utah had granted suffrage to female citizens in 1870. Then, seventeen years later, the Edmunds-Tucker Act had revoked the right in order to weaken the Saints' political power in the territory.[11]

The act had outraged Emmeline and other women in Utah, leading them to organize women's suffrage associations throughout the territory. They also continued working with other national and international suffrage organizations to fight for all women's right to vote.[12] For Emmeline, suffrage and other rights had a sacred purpose. She believed that freedom was a principle of the gospel of Jesus Christ. The Relief Society urged its members to be self-reliant and develop their abilities. In Church meetings, women also voted on ecclesiastical matters. Why should they not enjoy the same privilege in the public sphere?[13]

Yet women's suffrage was a hotly debated issue, dividing even Church leaders.[14] People who disagreed with women's suffrage usually claimed that women were too emotional to make political decisions. They argued that women did not need to vote when they had husbands, fathers, and brothers to represent them at the ballot box.[15] Elder B. H. Roberts, who was serving as a convention delegate, believed similarly. He also opposed including women's suffrage in the constitution because he believed it might make the document too controversial to receive approval from Utah voters.[16]

A constitutional convention opened in Salt Lake City in the spring of 1895. Since nonvoters were barred from participating officially in the proceedings, the women recruited the husband of one of the suffragists to present their petition to the delegates.[17]

On March 28, B. H. spoke about the issue at the convention. "While I concede that a majority of the people of this territory are in favor of woman suffrage," he stated, "there is nevertheless a large number who are not in favor of it, and are bitterly opposed to it, and will vote against this constitution if it contains a provision granting it."[18]

Two days later, Orson Whitney, a longtime bishop in Salt Lake City, addressed the convention on behalf of the suffragists. He declared that it was woman's destiny to participate in government, and he urged the delegates to support women's suffrage. "I regard it as one of the great levers by which the Almighty is lifting up this fallen world, lifting it nearer to the throne of its Creator," he said.[19]

In an editorial for the *Woman's Exponent,* Emmeline also voiced her disagreement with opponents of women's suffrage. "It is pitiful to see how men opposed to woman suffrage try to make the women believe it is because they worship them so, and think them far too good," she wrote. "The women of Utah have never failed in any time of trial of whatever name or nature, and their integrity is unquestioned."[20]

During the April 4 Relief Society meeting at general conference, Emmeline again spoke about women's suffrage, confident the delegates at the convention would include it in the new state constitution. The next speaker, Jane Richards, invited the women in the room who supported suffrage to stand up. Every woman in the room rose to her feet.

At Emmeline's request, President Zina Young then led the women in prayer, asking for the Lord's blessing on their cause.[21]

WHILE WOMEN IN UTAH Territory petitioned for the vote, Albert Jarman traveled from London to South West England to bear testimony to his father. He hoped to change William's mind about the Church and put an end to his harmful lecturing. He believed his words, presented in a clear and understanding manner, could do his father good, if only he would listen.[22]

Albert found William living comfortably in a city called Exeter. He was in good health, although his full head of white hair and bushy beard made him appear older than he was. More than a decade had passed since they had seen each other, and at first William still seemed suspicious of Albert's identity.[23] After returning to England, William claimed, he had heard a rumor about Albert's murder and wrote the First Presidency about it. When they did not respond, he said, he had assumed the worst.[24]

After meeting face to face, though, Albert was able to convince him of his error.[25] President Lund's counsel that Albert study the gospel before trying to match wits with William had been wise. After reuniting with his father, Albert could tell he was an intelligent man.[26]

But William was not unkind or abusive toward him. The winter of 1894–95 was harsh in England, aggravating respiratory problems Albert had developed. William let him stay in his family's home to recuperate until the weather improved. His wife, Ann, also did all she could to help Albert get well.[27]

During his stay, Albert tried to bear testimony to his father, without success. At these times, Albert could not tell if his father deliberately lied about the Church or if he had said absurd things so often that he had come to believe them.[28]

One day, William told Albert he was willing to stop attacking the Saints if the Church paid him £1,000. For this small price, he said, he would publicly admit that he was wrong about the Saints and never enter a lecture room to criticize the Church again. Albert passed the proposal on to President Lund, but the First Presidency rejected it.[29]

Unable to change his father's mind about the Church, Albert left Exeter after a few weeks. Before they parted, he and William went to a photographer's studio to have portraits taken together. In one photograph, William sat at a table, his right hand pointing to a page in an open book, while Albert stood behind him. In another, the two men stood side by side as father and son. Behind William's whiskers was the trace of a smile.[30]

THE CONSTITUTIONAL CONVENTION IN Salt Lake City ended in May. To the joy of Emmeline Wells and countless others in Utah, the delegates voted to include women's suffrage in the constitution.[31]

After the convention, B. H. Roberts remained active in politics, despite his full-time Church responsibilities. His speeches against women's suffrage had been unpopular across the state. Yet his reputation as a preacher and lecturer remained strong in and out of the Church. In September, two months before the next election, Utah Democrats nominated B. H. as their candidate for the United States House of Representatives.[32]

For decades, Church leaders had often held important government positions in Utah. The Saints had also voted as a bloc, sometimes sacrificing their individual political beliefs to preserve the Church's influence in the territory. But after the Saints split into different political parties in the early 1890s, Church leaders had become more sensitive about keeping matters of church and state separate, recognizing that not everyone in Utah had the same political opinions. At that time, the First Presidency and Quorum of the Twelve Apostles agreed that general authorities should not influence voters by speaking publicly about politics.[33]

During the constitutional convention, however, the First Presidency had temporarily suspended this counsel, allowing B. H. and other general authorities to serve as delegates. When B. H. later received the Democratic Party's nomination, he did not think he was wrong to accept it. Nor did he notice any objections from the First Presidency. Apostle Moses Thatcher felt the same way when the Democrats nominated him to run for the U.S. Senate.[34]

At the October 1895 general priesthood meeting, however, Joseph F. Smith publicly rebuked the two men for accepting the nominations without first consulting the members of their quorums. "We have the living oracles in the Church, and their counsel must be sought," he reminded the congregation. "The moment a man in authority decides to do as he pleases, he steps on dangerous ground."[35]

In his remarks, President Smith did not criticize B. H.'s political beliefs. Rather, he reaffirmed the Church's political neutrality as well as its policy that full-time

Church leaders should focus their time and efforts on their ministry. After the meeting, however, members of the Republican Party seized on the reprimand to attack B. H.'s campaign. Since Joseph F. Smith was a Republican, many Democrats accused him of using his position in the Church to injure their party.[36]

A short time later, in a newspaper interview, B. H. spoke of his respect for Church authority and stopped short of accusing the First Presidency of trying to hurt his campaign. Yet he insisted on his right to seek political office, despite the First Presidency's objections, because he believed he had violated no Church rules. Later he spoke more brazenly. At a political rally, he condemned men who used their influence in the Church to sway voters.[37]

On Election Day, Republicans across the country won landslide victories against Democrats like B. H. Roberts and Moses Thatcher. And voters in Utah approved the new constitution with its provision granting voting rights to women.

B. H. tried to put on a cheerful face in public. He and his party knew someone had to lose. "It seems to have fallen to our party this time," he said.

But inside he felt the sting of his defeat.[38]

ON JANUARY 4, 1896, UTAH became the forty-fifth state in the United States of America. In Salt Lake City, people fired off gun salutes and blew whistles. Bells rang out across the crisp, blue sky as people crowded the streets, waving flags and banners.[39]

Heber J. Grant continued to worry about his friends B. H. Roberts and Moses Thatcher, though. Both men refused to apologize for not consulting their priesthood leaders before seeking public office, leading the First Presidency and the Twelve to conclude that they were putting their political careers ahead of their Church service. The First Presidency also believed that B. H. had unfairly criticized them and the Church in some of his political speeches and interviews.[40]

On February 13, the First Presidency and a majority of the Twelve met in the Salt Lake Temple with B. H. and other presidents of the Seventy. During the meeting, the apostles asked B. H. about his statements against the First Presidency. B. H. affirmed everything he had said and done, taking none of it back.

As the meeting unfolded, Heber's heart grew heavy. One by one, the leaders pleaded with B. H. to humble himself, but their words had no effect. When Heber stood to address his friend, emotion overwhelmed him, choking his words.

After each apostle and seventy spoke, B. H. stood and said he would rather lose his place in the presidency of the Seventy than apologize for what he had done. He then asked the men in the room to pray that he not lose his faith.

"Will you pray for yourself?" asked apostle Brigham Young Jr.

"To tell the truth," said B. H., "I do not feel much like it now."

When the meeting ended, Heber offered a closing prayer. B. H. then tried to leave the room, but Heber caught hold of him and embraced him. B. H. broke free and stalked away, his expression hard.[41]

A few weeks later, on March 5, the First Presidency and the Quorum of the Twelve Apostles again met with B. H. and found him unchanged. President Woodruff gave him three weeks to reconsider his position. If he remained unrepentant, they would release him from the Seventy and prohibit him from using the priesthood.[42]

The following week, Heber and his fellow apostle Francis Lyman arranged to meet privately with B. H. As they talked, B. H. told the apostles that he would not change his mind. If the First Presidency needed to find someone to take his place in the presidency of the Seventy, he said, they were free to do so.

B. H. put on his coat and started to leave. "I want you to know that the action that is to be taken against me is causing me the deepest sorrow," he said. "I do not want you to think that I fail to appreciate all that I am going to lose."

Heber noticed tears in his friend's eyes, and he asked him to sit down. B. H. then spoke of times when Church leaders had slighted him in public and preached in favor of the Republican Party. For two hours, Heber and Francis responded to his concerns and pleaded with him to change his course. Heber felt as if he and Francis were being blessed to know what to say.

When they finished speaking, B. H. told his friends that he wanted to think about his situation that night and get back to them with his decision in the morning. Heber then took leave of his friend, praying the Lord would bless him.[43]

The next morning B. H. sent a short letter to Heber and Francis. "I submit to the authority of God in the brethren," it read in part. "Since they think I am wrong, I will bow to them, and place myself in their hands as the servants of God."

Heber made a copy of the letter immediately and ran across the street to President Woodruff's office.[44]

ABOUT TWO WEEKS LATER, in the Salt Lake Temple, B. H. Roberts apologized to the First Presidency, admitting his error in not seeking permission to run for political office. He was sorry if anything he had said in public had caused rifts among the Saints, and he promised to make amends for any offense he gave.

He also said that during his conversation with Heber J. Grant and Francis Lyman, thoughts of his ancestors softened his heart.

"I am the only male representative in the Church on my father's side, and also on my mother's side," he said, "and the thought of losing the priesthood and leaving my ancestors to rest without a representative in the priesthood worked very strongly upon my feelings."

"I went to the Lord and received light and instruction through His Spirit to submit to the authority of God," he continued. "I express to you my desire and prayer that I may be able to make such satisfaction, and pass through whatever humiliation you may see proper to put upon me, in the hope of retaining at least the priesthood of God, and to have the privilege of doing the work for my fathers in this holy house."[45]

The First Presidency accepted B. H.'s apology. Ten days later, under the direction of President Woodruff, George Q. Cannon drafted a statement clarifying the Church's position on its leaders' involvement in politics. He then presented the statement to the First Presidency and general authorities of the Church for their approval.[46]

The following day, at the April 1896 general conference, Heber J. Grant read the statement to the Saints. Every general authority of the Church had signed it except Anthon Lund, who was still in Europe, and Moses Thatcher, who had refused to reconcile with the First Presidency and his fellow apostles.

Called the "Political Manifesto," the statement affirmed the Church's belief in the separation of church and state. It also required all general authorities who committed themselves to full-time service in the Lord's work to secure the approval of their quorum leaders before seeking or accepting any political office.[47]

At the conference, B. H. Roberts urged the Saints to sustain their ecclesiastical leaders, and he testified of the enduring work of the Lord. "In this dispensation, the unfailing word of God has been pledged to the stability of the work, notwithstanding the imperfections of the people," he declared.

"Even though some might have stumbled in the darkness," he said, "they might still return to the path of right, taking advantage of its unerring guidance to the good of salvation."[48]

CHAPTER 4

A Great Amount
of Good

On May 31, 1896, Susa Gates spoke in Salt Lake
City at the first combined conference of the general
Young Ladies' and Young Men's Mutual Improvement
Associations. The two organizations had long held annual and quarterly conferences of their own. But in
recent years, many young men had stopped attending
their meetings regularly, leading some YMMIA leaders
to propose breathing new life into their organization by
merging with the YLMIA.[1]

YLMIA general president Elmina Taylor and her officers disliked the idea. While some Mutual Improvement
Associations had already combined successfully at the
ward level, the general YLMIA was thriving, and its
leaders wondered if combining was in the best interest
of the young women. They ultimately decided against

merging, but they agreed that more combined activities with the YMMIA, including this new annual conference, could be beneficial.[2]

For the first conference, MIA leaders divided the program equally between speakers from their organizations. Susa, the second to last on the program, encouraged her listeners to have good character and live righteously. The experience was somewhat new for Susa, since women in the Church at this time did not usually speak to mixed audiences except to bear testimony. Now she and other leading women had the opportunity to preach to both men and women in the same setting.[3]

After the conference, Susa talked with her friend and former classmate Joseph Tanner, who was the president of the Agricultural College in Logan. As they chatted, Joseph asked if Leah, who had just graduated from the University of Utah, was still in love with John Widtsoe. John had recently finished his degree in chemistry at Harvard and was now a member of Joseph's faculty.

Susa did not know how to answer Joseph's question. John had been avoiding her daughter ever since he returned home. When Leah recently wrote him to get his advice on whether she should return east to study home economics at Pratt Institute, an esteemed college in New York City, John had replied with a curt, indifferent letter.[4]

"Do what will be for your own good in the long run," he had told her. He then expressed regret that they had fallen in love so young. As much as he wanted to marry Leah, he did not want her to be a poor man's wife. His education had left him about $2,000 in debt, and most of his small teaching salary went to support his mother and younger brother.[5]

Leah had written back immediately. "We can't live without money, I am aware, but for heaven's sake don't let it figure in your love," she responded. "If I love you, then I love you whether you own thousands or whether you owe thousands."[6]

John did not change his mind, and Leah departed for the Pratt Institute in September 1896. She traveled with her friend Donnette Smith, who was studying at Pratt to become a kindergarten teacher. Before the young women left, Donnette's father, President Joseph F. Smith, blessed Leah to hold on to her faith in the face of temptation, promising that her testimony would grow stronger than ever before.[7]

In New York City, Leah and Donnette had experiences their mothers' generation could hardly have imagined. Latter-day Saint women from that older generation, like other American women at the time, had usually received only a grade-school education. Some did go east to study medicine and midwifery, but most married young, had children, and helped establish homes and family businesses in their settlements. Many had never traveled outside Utah Territory.[8]

Leah and Donnette, by contrast, were single young women living in a large boardinghouse in a bustling city more than two thousand miles from home. On weekdays, they attended classes at Pratt and socialized with people from different backgrounds and faiths. And on Sundays they attended church in a tiny branch of about a dozen Saints.[9]

Leah and Donnette resolved to live their religion faithfully. They prayed together on Sunday and read the Book of Mormon every night before bed. "My testimony of the truth of our gospel grows stronger every day," Leah wrote her mother. "I can see the force of Brother Smith's blessing."[10]

Unlike at home, they also had opportunities to talk about their faith with people who knew little about Latter-day Saints. They befriended two art students, Cora Stebbins and Catherine Couch, who showed some interest in the Church. One day, Leah and Donnette had a chance to talk with them about the temple and the Book of Mormon. Leah explained how Joseph Smith found and translated the gold plates. She also spoke about the Book of Mormon witnesses, continuing revelation, and the organization of the Church.

"You never saw such interested girls in your life," Leah later wrote to her mother. "They sat here for two solid hours before we realized how time was passing."[11]

ON OCTOBER 13, 1896, MĀORI Latter-day Saint Mere Whaanga went to the Salt Lake Temple to perform baptisms for ten deceased friends from New Zealand, her homeland. Since moving to Salt Lake City earlier that year, she and her husband, Hirini, had become known for their diligent temple attendance. Like many Saints from outside the United States, the Whaanga family had immigrated to Utah to be closer to the temple and its ordinances. And as the only endowed Māori, they served as a link between their people and the house of the Lord.[12]

There were only four temples in the world, so Saints who lived outside the United States could send the names of deceased loved ones to relatives in Utah to perform the temple work for them. When Mere and Hirini were baptized in 1884, however, they had no relatives in Utah. Soon they felt a deep, powerful desire to come to Zion and attend the temple.[13]

From the beginning, their children and grandchildren had opposed their plan to move. Utah was seven thousand miles away from Nuhaka, their village on the eastern coast of New Zealand's North Island. Hirini had important responsibilities as a branch president and a leader of the Ngāti Kahungunu tribe of Māori. And Mere was her parents' only living daughter. Yet the Whaangas' longing for Zion had grown stronger every day.[14]

In prior decades, Saints from the Pacific Islands had not been strongly encouraged to migrate to Zion. And by the time Mere and Hirini were contemplating the move, Church leaders had already begun discouraging all Saints outside the United States from gathering to Utah, where jobs were scarce and immigrants could become disillusioned. The First Presidency granted permission for a small number of Māori to come, though, after the mission president in New Zealand vouched for their industry and capability.[15]

Mere and Hirini came to Utah in July 1894 with a few members of their extended family. They settled in Kanab, a remote town in southern Utah, where Hirini's young nephew Pirika Whaanga had moved a few years after Hirini and Mere's baptism. The family expected to adapt well to southern Utah's warm climate, but when Mere saw the dry, stark landscape, she broke down and cried. A short time later, she received word from New Zealand that her mother had passed away.[16]

As time went on, the family's situation did not improve. A missionary they had known in New Zealand persuaded Hirini to invest money in a poor business venture. After hearing rumors of the scheme, the First Presidency sent William Paxman, a former mission president in New Zealand, to help Mere and Hirini move to an area where their neighbors would not take advantage of them.[17]

The Whaangas were now settled in their home in Salt Lake City. They attended reunions of the Zion's Māori Association, an organization of returned elders from the New Zealand Mission, and met every Friday evening with a few members of the group. The First Presidency also authorized them to perform temple work for the deceased relatives of all Māori Saints in New Zealand.[18]

Though she was illiterate when she came to Utah, Mere taught herself to read and write so she could study her scriptures and write letters to her family. Hirini also wrote encouraging letters to relatives and friends, doing what he could to strengthen the Saints back home. In New Zealand, the Church was growing among European inhabitants and Māori alike. Dozens of branches were spread throughout the country, with priesthood quorums, Relief Societies, Sunday Schools, and Mutual Improvement Associations.[19]

Yet many New Zealanders were still new to the faith. Some missionaries, after hearing the rumors of the Whaanga family's ill treatment in Kanab, worried the news might shake Māori Saints' faith in the Church. Already, exaggerated accounts of what happened were spreading to New Zealand. If such rumors went unchecked, the mission could face a crisis.[20]

THE FOLLOWING YEAR, ELIZABETH McCune, a wealthy Latter-day Saint from Salt Lake City, took a trip to Europe with her family. While visiting the United Kingdom, where her son Raymond was serving a mission, she and her daughter Fay often helped the elders share the restored gospel.

One day, in late June 1897, she and Fay went to London's Hyde Park to sing with a choir of missionaries. Queen Victoria was celebrating sixty years on the throne, and preachers from all over Britain had come to the park to hold open-air meetings and compete for the souls of those celebrating in the city.

Elizabeth and Fay took their place among the missionaries, and Elizabeth quietly congratulated herself and the choir as more and more people gathered around them. Then a well-dressed man with an eyeglass approached and peered at them.

"Oh dear! Oh dear!" he exclaimed. "What a horrible noise they do make in our park!"[21]

His words made Elizabeth check her pride in the choir's performance. Yet it did not stifle her desire to share the gospel. Before leaving Utah, Elizabeth had received a blessing from Lorenzo Snow, promising her she would be an instrument of the Lord during her travels.

"Thy mind shall be as clear as an angel's when explaining the principles of the gospel," he had blessed her.[22]

Elizabeth wanted to do all she could to help with missionary work. Her son had begun his mission holding meetings in parks and streets in central England. By then, William Jarman had resumed lecturing against the Saints. Though he was no longer telling the crowds that his son Albert had been murdered, he continued to provoke attacks on missionaries, forcing elders to turn to the police for protection. Some of the missionaries in Raymond's area were injured by mobs.[23]

Elizabeth often accompanied the missionaries in London, holding their hats and books during meetings. She also felt a burning desire to preach. Although she could not be called on a mission, she could imagine herself being commissioned of God and having quiet religious chats with people in their homes. In fact, she thought female missionaries might attract more attention than the young elders and therefore help the work move forward.[24]

A few months after singing in Hyde Park, Elizabeth attended the semiannual Church conference in London. During the morning session, Joseph McMurrin, a counselor in the mission presidency, denounced William Jarman's criticism of the Saints. He took particular issue with William's habit of making unflattering statements about Latter-day Saint women.

"We have with us just now a lady from Utah," he announced. "We are going to ask Sister McCune to speak this evening and tell you of her experience in Utah." He then encouraged everyone at the conference to bring their friends to hear her speak.[25]

The announcement startled Elizabeth. As much as she wanted to preach, she worried about her inexperience. "If we only had one of our good woman speakers from Utah," she thought, "what good she might do!" The missionaries promised to pray for her, and she resolved to ask her Father in Heaven for help as well.[26]

Word quickly spread that Elizabeth was going to speak that evening. Anticipating a large crowd, the elders set up extra seats in the hall and opened the gallery. As the hour of the meeting neared, people filled the room to capacity.[27]

Elizabeth said a silent prayer and took the stand. She spoke to the crowd about her family. She had been born in England in 1852 and emigrated to Utah after her parents joined the Church. She had traveled throughout the United States and Europe. "Nowhere," she testified, "have I found women held in such esteem as among the Mormons of Utah."

"Our husbands are proud of their wives and daughters," she continued. "They give them every opportunity to attend meetings and lectures and to take up everything which will educate and develop them. Our religion teaches us that the wife stands shoulder to shoulder with the husband."[28]

When the meeting ended, strangers shook Elizabeth's hand. "If more of your women would come out here," someone said, "a great amount of good would be done."

"Madam," said another man, "you carry truth in your voice and words."[29]

ON SEPTEMBER 7, 1897, JOHN Widtsoe waited outside a faculty meeting at Brigham Young Academy in Provo. Earlier that day, Leah Dunford had reluctantly agreed to see him after the meeting. She was now a domestic science instructor at the academy, teaching what she had learned from her year at Pratt Institute. John was on his way home after a work trip through the deserts of southern Utah, and he had stopped in Provo to mend his relationship with Leah.[30]

John was still worried about his debts, but he loved Leah and wanted to marry her. They had all but stopped writing each other, though. In fact, a young, unmarried mission president Leah met in New York was about to propose to her.[31]

The faculty meeting was supposed to end at 8:30 that evening, but it did not conclude until an hour later. Leah then kept John waiting another hour while she attended a committee meeting for a student event. When that meeting finally ended, John walked Leah home.

As they walked, he asked her if he could see her the next day. "You can't see me at all," Leah replied. "I will be busy until five o'clock."

"Well," John said, "I might just as well go home in the morning then."

"Why, certainly," Leah said.

"I guess I will stay over," John said, "if I might see you in the evening."[32]

The next evening, John picked Leah up at the academy in a horse-drawn buggy, and they drove out to a spot north of town. He told her he was ready for a serious relationship, but she was not as ready as he was. She told him he had a year to prove his love. She didn't care how he did it. But she would not make up with him before then.

The night was clear, and John parked the buggy at a place overlooking the valley. Gazing at the bright moon, they talked frankly about the many times they had offended each other over the last four years. They tried to understand why their relationship had taken such a sour turn. Before they knew it, they were no longer gazing at the moon but at each other.

At last, John put his arm around Leah and asked her to marry him. Her determination to make him prove himself melted away, and she promised to marry him once their school terms ended—as long as her parents agreed to the union.[33]

SINCE LEAH'S MOTHER WAS traveling through Idaho on YLMIA business, John spoke to Leah's father first. A Salt Lake City dentist, Alma Dunford at first thought John had come to see him about his teeth. But once John explained his purpose, Alma's eyes teared up and he spoke of his love and admiration for Leah. He gave his consent to the marriage, expressing trust in his daughter's decision.[34]

Leah, meanwhile, wrote to her mother about the engagement and received an unhappy response. "The man you have chosen has plenty of ambition," Susa told Leah. "Not to do good and build up Zion—but to acquire fame, add new laurels to his own brow, and make you follow in his wake, your own future usefulness narrowed down to him and his selfish wants."[35]

Unsettled, John also wrote to Susa. She responded one month later, granting her consent to the marriage but also repeating her criticism of his apparent lack of devotion to the Church.[36]

The letter stung John. As a scientist, he did yearn for honor and recognition in his field. And he had dedicated much of his time and talents to advancing his career. Yet even while wrestling with his faith at Harvard, he had never shirked his responsibilities in the Church. He knew he had a duty to use his knowledge and training to benefit Zion.[37]

Susa seemed to expect more from him. Her generation of Saints—and her parents' generation—believed that personal ambition was incompatible with building up the kingdom. John had managed so far to balance his scientific career with his calling as a counselor and teacher in his elders quorum. But his dedicated Church service was not widely known outside his local congregation in Logan.[38]

"I have not been called to be a bishop," he acknowledged to Leah, "or a president of a stake, or any stake officer, or a president of seventies, or an apostle, or any of the high offices in the Church which occupy a man's whole time."

"This I can say, honestly," he declared, "that I stand today ready to do anything the Church will ask of me. Let the work assigned to me be ever so humble, I will do it cheerfully."[39]

Leah did not need convincing. It had been John's simple prayer, offered that first day at Harvard, that first attracted her to him. But Susa needed more time with John to know his heart and his faith.[40]

That December, the Gates family invited John to spend Christmas with them. During that time, something in John's everyday words and actions impressed Susa, reminding her why she had brought him and Leah together in the first place. "I have always fancied you were narrow and selfish," she told John after the visit, "but some of your expressions while with us have dispelled that notion."

She had no more fears about the wedding. "I feel in my spirit the testimony that all is well," she wrote.[41]

CHAPTER 5

An Essential Preparation

As her ship steamed into the port of Liverpool, England, twenty-one-year-old Inez Knight spotted her older brother William on the docks, waiting in a crowd of fellow missionaries. It was April 22, 1898. Inez and her companion, Jennie Brimhall, were coming to the British Mission as the first single women set apart as "lady missionaries" for the Church. Like Will and the other elders, they would be preaching at street meetings and going door to door, spreading the restored gospel of Jesus Christ.[1]

The decision to call women as missionaries was partly a result of Elizabeth McCune's preaching the year before. After seeing Elizabeth's effect on audiences, mission leader Joseph McMurrin had written to President Woodruff. "If a number of bright and intelligent women were called on missions to England," he reasoned, "the results would be excellent."[2]

The First Presidency agreed. Louisa Pratt, Susa Gates, and other married women had served successful missions alongside their husbands, though without official mission calls. Leaders in the Relief Society and YLMIA, moreover, had been good ambassadors for the Church at venues like the World's Fair of 1893. And many young, unmarried women had gained experience teaching and leading in YLMIA meetings, preparing them to preach the word of God.[3]

After reuniting with Will, Inez walked with him and Jennie to the mission headquarters, a four-story building the Saints had occupied since the 1850s. There they met President McMurrin. "I want each of you to understand that you have been called here by the Lord," he said. As he spoke, Inez felt for the first time the great responsibility resting on her shoulders.[4]

The next day, she and Jennie accompanied President McMurrin and other missionaries to Oldham, a manufacturing town east of Liverpool. In the evening, they formed a circle on a busy street corner, offered a prayer, and sang hymns until a large crowd formed around them. President McMurrin announced that a special meeting would be held the following day, and he invited everyone to come and hear preaching from "real live Mormon women."

As he said this, a sick feeling crept over Inez. She was nervous about speaking to a large crowd. Still, as she stood among the missionaries in their silk hats and black suits, she had never been prouder to be a Latter-day Saint.[5]

The next evening, Inez trembled as she waited for her turn to speak. Having heard terrible lies about Latter-day Saint women from William Jarman and other critics of the Church, people were curious about her and the other women speaking at the meeting. Sarah Noall and Caroline Smith, the wife and sister-in-law of one of the missionaries, addressed the congregation first. Inez then spoke, despite her fear, and surprised herself by how well she did.

Inez and Jennie were soon assigned to labor in Cheltenham. They went door to door and frequently testified at street meetings. They also accepted invitations to meet with people in their homes. Listeners usually treated them well, although occasionally someone would mock them or accuse them of lying.[6]

Efforts to correct false information received a boost when James E. Talmage, the English-born Latter-day Saint scholar, traveled throughout the United Kingdom to give public lectures on Utah, the American West, and the Saints. The lectures were held in well-known halls and attracted hundreds of people. As he spoke, James used a device called a stereopticon to project high-quality images of Utah onto a large screen, giving audiences a vivid picture of the state's people and places. After one presentation, a man left saying, "That was vastly different to Jarman's lecture."[7]

Inez and Jennie, meanwhile, hoped to see more women serving missions. "We feel that the Lord is blessing us in our attempts to allay prejudice and spread the truth," they reported to mission leaders. "We trust that many of the worthy young women in Zion will be permitted to enjoy the same privilege we now have, for we feel that they can do much good."[8]

AROUND THE TIME INEZ Knight and Jennie Brimhall left for England, Hirini Whaanga arrived in Wellington, New Zealand, as a full-time missionary. The First Presidency had issued the call at the beginning of 1898, and Hirini responded immediately. "I shall make all necessary preparation," he told the presidency, "and will endeavor to magnify my calling as an elder in The Church of Jesus Christ of Latter-day Saints."[9]

Hirini's mission call, like those of the single female missionaries, marked a milestone in the history of the Church. Although Māori "home missionaries" had sometimes assisted the elders in New Zealand, Hirini was the first Māori called into full-time service. The call came after Benjamin Goddard and Ezra Stevenson, two former missionaries to New Zealand, recommended that President Woodruff send Hirini on a mission. As one of the most beloved and respected Māori in the Church, Hirini could do a great work among his people, including gathering their genealogy and testifying of the sacred work he and his wife, Mere, were performing in the Salt

Lake Temple.[10] With exaggerated reports of their family's hardships in Kanab creating unrest among some Māori Saints, he could also give a true account of his experiences in Utah.[11]

Aware of the Whaanga family's financial struggles, members of the Zion's Māori Association promised to pay for Hirini's mission. The Salt Lake City Eleventh Ward also held a benefit concert to raise money for him.[12]

Leaving his family in Utah, Hirini traveled to New Zealand with other new missionaries. Now seventy years old, he was decades older than all of his companions. Ezra Stevenson, who had recently lost his wife and only child, led the group as the new mission president. He had served as the secretary of the Zion's Māori Association just prior to his call and spoke Māori well. None of the other new American missionaries could speak the language.[13]

The day after arriving in New Zealand, Hirini and his companions attended a conference about fifty miles northeast of the city of Wellington. Knowing Hirini would be there, many Māori Saints made an extra effort to attend. They and the other New Zealand Saints met the missionaries with a brass band and led them down the street to the conference. There the new arrivals were greeted with a Māori ceremonial dance called the haka.

Tears flowed freely for the rest of the afternoon. The Saints enjoyed a meal, and Hirini's relatives shook hands with him and pressed their foreheads and noses against his in a traditional Māori greeting. The mission president then led Māori Saints to a nearby porch, where they gathered around Hirini and gave speeches to welcome him back to the North Island. They did not retire until after two o'clock in the morning.[14]

The next day, Hirini preached to the Saints about Joseph Smith, priesthood authority, and the work of the Zion's Māori Association. He also asked the Saints to gather their genealogies and have temple work done for their dead.[15]

Following the conference, the Saints returned to their homes, and Hirini and Ezra began their tour of the mission.[16]

IN THE SPRING OF 1898, tensions between the United States and Spain arose after an American battleship exploded off the coast of Havana, Cuba. Newspapers blamed Spain for the explosion and ran heart-wrenching stories about the Cubans' struggle for independence from Spanish rule. Across the United States, indignant citizens called on Congress to intervene in Cuba's behalf.[17]

In Utah, Church leaders were divided over going to war with Spain. Aside from outfitting the Mormon Battalion for the Mexican-American War of 1846–48, the Church had never encouraged Saints to enlist in the military during armed conflicts. George Q. Cannon favored action against Spain, but Joseph F. Smith lamented the war fever sweeping the nation. In the *Woman's*

Exponent, Emmeline Wells published pieces supporting and opposing war.[18]

No Church leader was more vocal in his opposition to war than apostle Brigham Young Jr. "The mission of the gospel is peace," he declared at a meeting in the Salt Lake Tabernacle, "and the Latter-day Saints should strive to create and maintain it." Calling the rising conflict "a chasm that had been dug by uninspired men," he urged young Saints not to enlist in the armed forces.[19]

Whenever controversies arose in the Church, Wilford Woodruff would usually turn to his counselors, George Q. Cannon and Joseph F. Smith, and ask, "Well, brethren, what do you think of this?" But after learning what Brigham Jr. had said, the prophet quickly censured him. The Church had only recently mended its relationship with the United States, and President Woodruff did not want prominent Church leaders appearing disloyal to the nation.

"Such remarks were very unwise and ought not to have been made," he said. "We are now a part of the nation, and we are under obligation to do our share with the rest of the citizens of the government."[20]

The United States declared war on Spain on April 25, 1898, the day after Brigham Jr.'s speech, and the *Deseret Evening News* published an editorial affirming the Saints' loyalty to the United States. "Not lovers of war, nor given to bloodthirstiness, they are nevertheless firmly and steadfastly with and for Our Country in every just cause," it declared. Soon, more than six hundred

Utahns enlisted in the U.S. armed forces to fight in the war, which lasted just a few months.[21]

Around that time, Wilford's health began to decline. And in early June, George Q. Cannon suffered a minor stroke. At the invitation of friends of the Church in California, the two men traveled to San Francisco, hopeful its mild climate would help them rest and recover. There they consulted with doctors, visited friends, and met with the local branch of Saints.[22]

On August 29, Wilford and George took a carriage ride through a park beside the Pacific Ocean. As they watched waves roll in from the sea and break against the shore, Wilford talked about his time as a missionary in the early days of the Church. He recalled sharing the gospel with his father and stepmother, who were baptized just before his first child was born.

He and George had met for the first time a year and a half later. Wilford had been a young apostle on his first mission to England. George had been a thirteen-year-old boy with a fondness for books.

Now, sitting side by side nearly sixty years later, they spoke of the gospel and the happiness it brought them. "What delightful labor we have had," they agreed, "in bearing testimony to the work of God."[23]

THREE DAYS LATER, ON September 2, George sent a telegram from San Francisco to Joseph F. Smith in Salt Lake City:

*President Woodruff is dead. He left us at 6:40
this morning. Break the news to his family.
He slept peacefully all night and passed away
without movement.*[24]

Lorenzo Snow was at his home in northern Utah when he learned of the prophet's passing. He immediately caught a train for Salt Lake City, anxious about the future. As the senior apostle, he knew he would likely become the next president of the Church. Six years earlier, in fact, President Woodruff had spoken to Lorenzo about the Lord's will for him as the next prophet.

"When I go, I want you, Brother Snow, not to delay but organize the First Presidency," he had said. "Take George Q. Cannon and Joseph F. Smith for your counselors. They are good, wise, and men of experience."[25]

But Lorenzo was worried about taking on the office, especially when he thought about the state of Church finances. Despite the efforts of Heber J. Grant and others, the Church was still mired in debt, and some people were speculating that it owed at least a million dollars to creditors. Lorenzo himself feared the debt was as high as three million.[26]

In the days following President Woodruff's death, Lorenzo directed Church business as president of the Quorum of the Twelve Apostles. Yet he felt deeply inadequate. On September 9, the day after the funeral, Lorenzo met with the Twelve. Still feeling unequal to the calling, he proposed stepping down as president of the quorum. The apostles, however, voted to continue sustaining him as their leader.[27]

One evening, around this time, Lorenzo sought the will of the Lord in the Salt Lake Temple. He felt depressed and discouraged about his new responsibilities. After changing into his temple clothing, he pleaded with the Lord to enlighten his mind. The Lord answered his prayer, clearly manifesting that Lorenzo needed to follow President Woodruff's counsel to reorganize the First Presidency immediately. George Q. Cannon and Joseph F. Smith were to be his counselors.

Lorenzo did not tell his fellow apostles about his revelation. Instead, he waited, hoping they would receive the same spiritual witness about what to do.[28]

The quorum met again on September 13 to discuss Church finances. With President Woodruff gone, the Church no longer had a trustee-in-trust to handle its temporal business. The apostles knew this responsibility would eventually fall on the next Church president. But the Quorum of the Twelve Apostles had always waited more than a year before organizing a new First Presidency. For the time being, they needed to authorize someone to carry out Church business until the Saints sustained a new president.

As the apostles discussed solutions to the problem, Heber J. Grant and Francis Lyman suggested simply organizing a new First Presidency. "If the Lord should manifest to you, President Snow, that it was the proper thing to do now," Francis said, "I am prepared to not only vote for a trustee-in-trust but for the president of the Church."

The other apostles embraced the idea quickly. Joseph F. Smith proposed that they appoint Lorenzo as the new president, and everyone sustained the motion.

"It is for me to do the very best I can, and depend upon the Lord," Lorenzo said. He then told the apostles about the revelation he received in the temple. "I have not mentioned this matter to any person, either man or woman," he said. "I wanted to see if the same spirit which the Lord manifested to me was in you."

Now that the apostles had received the witness, Lorenzo was ready to accept the Lord's call to serve as the next president of the Church.[29]

ONE MONTH LATER, AT the October 1898 general conference, the Saints sustained Lorenzo Snow, George Q. Cannon, and Joseph F. Smith as the new First Presidency.[30]

President Snow made repairing the Church's financial situation his first priority as president. He carried out a plan approved by Wilford Woodruff before his death to sell long-term, low-interest bonds to help cover the Church's immediate expenses. He organized an audit committee to assess Church finances and instituted a new accounting system. He also sought to generate new revenue by having the Church take full ownership of the *Deseret News,* which had previously been in private hands.[31]

These efforts improved the Church's financial footing, but none of it was enough. At the April 1899 general conference, President Snow and other Church leaders preached on tithing, a law the Saints had not kept diligently since the government seized significant Church assets more than a decade earlier. The prophet also counseled the Saints not to go into debt themselves.

"Wear your old hats until you can pay for a new one," he said. "Your neighbor may be able to buy a piano for his family, but wait till you can pay for one before you get one."[32]

He also instructed local leaders to spend Church funds wisely. "There might be circumstances that would justify our going into debt, but they are comparatively few," he said. "As a rule, it is wrong."[33]

One morning early in May, President Snow was sitting in bed when his son LeRoi came into the room. LeRoi had just returned from a mission to Germany and was working as his father's personal secretary. The prophet greeted him and announced, "I am going to St. George."[34]

LeRoi was surprised. St. George was in the southwestern corner of the state, three hundred miles away. To get there, they had to take the train as far south as it would go, then travel the rest of the way by carriage. It would be a long, demanding trip for an eighty-five-year-old man.[35]

They left later that month, traveling with several friends and Church leaders. When they arrived in

St. George, dusty and weary from the journey, they went to the home of stake president Daniel McArthur, where they were to stay the night. Curious, the stake president asked why they had come.

"Well," President Snow said, "I don't know what we've come to St. George for, only the Spirit told us to come."[36]

THE NEXT DAY, MAY 17, the prophet met with the Saints in the St. George Tabernacle, a red sandstone building several blocks northwest of the temple. He had been restless the night before, but he looked strong and alert as he waited for the meeting to begin. He was the first speaker, and when he stood to address the Saints, his voice was clear.[37]

"We can scarcely express the reason why we came," he said, "yet I presume the Lord will have somewhat to say to us." He had not been to St. George in thirteen years, and he spoke of how pleased he was to see the Saints in town placing the kingdom of God over the pursuit of wealth. He urged them to listen to the voice of the Spirit and heed His words.

"To go to heaven we must first learn to obey the laws of heaven," he told them, "and we shall approach God's kingdom just as fast as we learn to obey His laws."[38]

During the sermon, President Snow paused unexpectedly, and the room went utterly still. His eyes brightened, and his countenance shone. When he opened his mouth, his voice was stronger. The inspiration of God seemed to fill the room.[39]

He then spoke on tithing. Most of the Saints in St. George were full-tithe payers, and the prophet acknowledged their faithfulness. He also noted that the poor were the most generous tithe payers. But he lamented that many other Saints were reluctant to pay a full tithing, even though the recent financial crisis had ended and the economy was improving. He wanted all Saints to observe the principle strictly. "This is an essential preparation for Zion," he said.[40]

The next afternoon, President Snow spoke again at the tabernacle. "The time has now come," he announced to the congregation, "for every Latter-day Saint who calculates to be prepared for the future and to hold his feet strong upon a proper foundation, to go and do the will of the Lord and to pay his tithing in full. That is the word of the Lord to you, and it will be the word of the Lord to every settlement throughout the land of Zion."[41]

ON HIS RETURN TRIP to Salt Lake City, President Snow stopped in villages and towns along the way to testify of the Lord's revealed will. "We have been educated in the law of tithing for sixty-one years but have not yet learned to observe it," he told the Saints in one town. "We are in a fearful condition, and because of it the Church is in bondage. The only relief is for the Saints to observe this law." He challenged them to obey the law fully and promised the Lord would bless them for their efforts. He also declared that tithe paying would now be a firm requirement for temple attendance.[42]

When he arrived in Salt Lake City, he continued to urge the Saints to pay tithing, promising that the Lord would forgive their past disobedience to the law, sanctify their land, and keep them from harm. On July 2, he spoke about the law at a meeting with general authorities, general Church officers, stake presidencies, and bishops in the Salt Lake Temple.[43]

"The Lord has forgiven us for our carelessness in paying our tithing in the past, but He will forgive us no longer," he declared. "If we do not obey this law, we will be scattered as were the Saints in Jackson County."

Before the close of the meeting, the prophet called on everyone to stand up, raise their right hands, and pledge to accept and keep the law of tithing as the word of the Lord. "We want you to be diligent in obeying this law," he told the Saints, "and see that the word is conveyed to all parts of the Church."[44]

CHAPTER 6

Our Wish and Our Mission

Hirini Whaanga's face brightened as a group of Māori Saints welcomed him and his fellow missionaries to their village, Te Horo, on New Zealand's North Island. Māori Saints loved Hirini as a grandfather, and they were proud of his work as a full-time missionary. Whenever he visited their settlements, they greeted him and his companions with the same familiar phrase: "Haere mai!" *Come in!*

In Te Horo, some people believed the rumors about the Whaangas' mistreatment in Utah. Some of them had even heard that Hirini died. Brushing these stories aside, Hirini asked, "Do I look as though I am dead? Do I look as though I am ill-treated?"[1]

The missionaries held a two-day conference with Saints from the ten branches in the area. When it was his turn to address the congregation, Hirini felt inspired to speak about the salvation of the dead. Afterward, most of the Saints in the congregation gave him the names of their deceased ancestors so he and his family could perform their temple work.[2]

Soon after the conference, Hirini traveled with mission president Ezra Stevenson and two other missionaries to a remote village called Mangamuka. Missionaries had been ordered out of the village a few years earlier and warned never to return. Hirini had a relative who lived there, though, so they decided to call on him.

The missionaries approached Mangamuka cautiously. When they asked for Tipene, Hirini's relative, they were told to wait outside the village. The welcome was far less friendly than those they received elsewhere on their journey, and Hirini was discouraged.

After a while, Tipene emerged from the village and tearfully embraced Hirini. They then had a meal together, and Tipene took the missionaries to a comfortable dwelling. The mood in the village became more friendly, and the elders were invited to speak to those who had gathered.

Before he spoke, Ezra assured his listeners that he had not come to condemn them but to invite them to share in the truth of his message. The congregation listened with interest, and several men responded favorably to his words. Hirini also spoke, preaching boldly until midnight, when his companions went to bed. He then went on talking well into the early hours of the morning.[3]

Ezra and one of the other elders had to leave that morning, but the villagers invited Hirini and the remaining missionary, George Judd, to teach them more. The missionaries stayed four days, held five meetings, and baptized two young men. Hirini and George then preached in other villages, baptizing eighteen more people by the time they rejoined Ezra a few weeks later.[4]

Hirini continued traveling with the mission president, instructing the Saints and collecting their genealogies. Often, as Ezra listened to Hirini preach, he marveled at his friend's ability to engage Māori audiences. "He bears a strong testimony and impresses the people," Ezra wrote in his journal. "He knows just how to get at the Māori feeling, so much better than we do."[5]

In April 1899, Hirini received an honorable release from his mission. A newspaper report announcing his return to Salt Lake City praised his labors in New Zealand. "A great impetus has been given to the work in that far distant land," it read. "In every district genealogical information was obtained and the faith and zeal of the Māori Saints has been strengthened and increased."[6]

THAT SPRING, JOHN WIDTSOE was studying chemistry at the University of Göttingen in central Germany. His work at the Agricultural College in Logan led him to research carbohydrates, and at Göttingen he was able to study under the leading scientist in his field. Now he was only months away from completing his doctorate degree.

John had married Leah Dunford in the Salt Lake Temple on June 1, 1898, two months before the couple moved to Europe. Before leaving, John was set apart as a missionary to Europe by Leah's uncle Brigham Young Jr., authorizing him to preach the gospel when he was not pursuing his education. Since Germany was renowned for its conservatories, Leah's seventeen-year-old sister, Emma Lucy Gates, joined them to study music. As of April 2, 1899, John and Leah were also the proud parents of a baby girl, Anna Gaarden Widtsoe, named for John's mother.[7]

Although John was still supporting his mother and younger brother, Osborne, who was serving a mission in Tahiti, he and Leah could afford to live in Europe thanks in part to a generous financial award from Harvard. Göttingen was an old university town surrounded by tree-topped hills and acres of farmland. As the only Latter-day Saints in the city, John, Leah, and Lucy held their own sacrament meetings and gospel study. Occasionally, missionaries in the German Mission would come to Göttingen to visit them.[8]

The Church in Germany had about a thousand members. There were German translations of the standard works as well as a twice-monthly Church magazine, *Der Stern*. But only five German Saints held the Melchizedek Priesthood, and growth was slow.[9] Many Germans were skeptical of churches from foreign lands, and missionaries were frequently banished from cities. Saints sometimes had to meet in secret or endure police surveillance.[10]

In late spring, Lucy left to study at the Berlin Conservatory of Music. Her grandmother Lucy Bigelow Young came from Utah to live as her chaperone. When John finished his thesis, he, Leah, and baby Anna joined them in Berlin. He then began studying for his doctoral exam, the last step in completing his degree. He also took a six-week trip to Norway and Denmark to preach the gospel, visit relatives, and research his genealogy.[11]

Having not been in Norway since he moved from the country at age eleven, John thrilled to be around more family. "I have had an excellent time with my mother's folks," he wrote Leah in September. "I was received royally and treated like 'somebody.'"[12]

When John returned to Germany, he traveled back to Göttingen to take his exam while Leah and the baby stayed in Berlin. His professors seemed optimistic about his success, but John worried about disappointing them.

"I have laid the matter in the hands of the Lord," he wrote Leah on November 20, the day of the exam. "If I do not get it, which God forbid, I shall have no self-reproach. The fasting and prayers of you all cheers me more than I can tell you."[13]

When the time of his examination arrived, John went before a board of more than a dozen professors, each prepared to interrogate him about his research. John did his best to answer their questions to their satisfaction. When they finished two or three hours later, they sent him out of the room while they decided his fate.

Later that evening, after she finished her fast, Leah received a telegram from John. "Magna by God's grace," it read. She knew just what it meant. John had passed his exam and completed his doctorate with honors, magna cum laude.[14]

A FEW WEEKS LATER, on December 4, 1899, B. H. Roberts waited nervously in Washington, DC, to take his oath of office as Utah's newly elected representative in the United States Congress. Stacked at the front of the chamber of the House of Representatives were twenty-eight rolls of paper, each about two feet in diameter. On them, B. H. knew, were the names of seven million people who did not want him to be there.[15]

Three years after losing the election of 1895, B. H. had run for Congress again, this time with the consent of the First Presidency.[16] His campaign was a success, but critics of the Church immediately seized on the victory to undermine the Saints' emerging image as a law-abiding, patriotic, monogamous people. Protestant ministers and women's organizations led the assault, warning people far and wide that B. H., a polygamist Church leader who had fathered children with a plural wife after the Manifesto, was coming to Washington to champion plural marriage, corrupt public morals, and extend the political power of the Church.[17]

As outrage over B. H.'s election grew, editor William Randolph Hearst joined in the fray. Eager to use the

controversy to boost sales of his New York City newspaper, Hearst published scathing articles about B. H.
and the Church, portraying both as threats to American
morals. The petition of seven million names on the floor
of the House chamber, in fact, had been assembled by
Hearst's newspaper to pressure lawmakers into denying
B. H. his seat in Congress.[18]

Shortly after noon, B. H. was summoned to take his
oath of office. As he walked to the front of the chamber, a congressman stood up and calmly motioned to
exclude B. H. from the House because of his plural
marriages. Another congressman seconded the motion.
"He is a polygamist," the man said, "and his election is
an assault upon the American home."[19]

The following day, B. H. tried to assure lawmakers
that he had no desire to use his new position to defend
plural marriage. "I am not here to advocate it," he told
them. "There is no occasion for championing that cause.
It is a question that is settled."[20]

Unconvinced, the House assigned a special committee of congressmen to review B. H.'s case and the
nature of his plural marriages. They were particularly troubled that he had continued living with his
plural wives and having children with them. When
the committee presented evidence of these relationships, B. H. insisted he had not openly defied the law.
Many Latter-day Saint men continued to live discreetly
with plural wives they married before the Manifesto,
and they did not believe that doing so violated their

agreement to obey the laws of the United States from that time forward. Yet the committee disagreed, and on January 25, 1900, an overwhelming majority of the House of Representatives voted to exclude him.[21]

B. H.'s dismissal from the House of Representatives made the front pages of newspapers across the country. In Utah, the First Presidency admired B. H.'s bold defense of his principles in Washington, but they regretted the backlash his election set off against the Latter-day Saints. The American press had again turned a critical eye on the Church.[22]

Although some of what the newspapers reported was inaccurate, they were correct on the basic point: plural marriage still existed in the Church. And it was not simply that men and women maintained their plural marriages after the Manifesto.[23] Having lived, taught, and suffered for plural marriage for more than half a century, many Saints could not imagine a world without it. In fact, some members of the Twelve—acting with the approval of George Q. Cannon, Joseph F. Smith, or their intermediaries—had quietly performed new plural marriages in the eight years since the Manifesto. During that time, four of the apostles had also married plural wives themselves.

Saints who married after the Manifesto did so believing the Lord had not completely renounced plural marriage but had simply removed the divine command for the Saints to sustain and defend it as a practice of the Church.[24] In the Manifesto, moreover, Wilford Woodruff had advised the Saints to submit to antipolygamy laws in the United States. He had said nothing in the document about the laws of Mexico or Canada, however. Most of the new plural marriages occurred in those countries, and a small number had been performed in the United States.[25]

Now, amid the fallout over B. H. Roberts's election, Church leaders began to see the harm in consenting to a polygamous Saint running for federal office. It was not something they intended to do again.[26]

IN APRIL 1900, ZINA Presendia Card, the daughter of Relief Society general president Zina Young, returned home to Cardston, Canada, after spending several weeks with her seventy-nine-year-old mother in Salt Lake City. During the visit, she and her mother had traveled to the Oneida Stake in southern Idaho to speak at a Relief Society conference.

"She stood the trip fine, and spoke like an angel to her sisters," Zina Presendia reported in a letter to her younger sister Susa Gates. "I am so proud of her."

Yet Zina Presendia fretted about her mother's advanced age. Cardston was about seven hundred miles from Salt Lake City. If her mother's health took a sudden turn for the worse, Zina Presendia might not be able to see her again before she passed away.[27]

Back in Cardston, Zina Presendia resumed her responsibilities as president of the Alberta Stake's YLMIA.

Fourteen years had passed since President John Taylor had asked her husband, Charles Card, to lead a group of polygamous Saints to Canada. Since then, the Saints had established a dozen settlements in southern Alberta. The Cardston Stake was founded in 1895, with Charles as president. Although the era of Latter-day Saint colonization had drawn to a close, new families and businesses continued to move to the area, helping to build up the Church.[28] Now there were many young Saints coming of age in the area, and Zina Presendia was deeply concerned about them.

Cardston was relatively isolated, but its young people were not immune to such ills as gambling and alcohol abuse. Some adults in town, she knew, were setting bad examples for the younger generation.[29]

Also, it was clear that Latter-day Saint youth in Cardston and other communities needed to be taught more about chastity. Before the Manifesto, young women had more opportunities to marry and often did so at an earlier age. Now, however, the rising generation tended to marry later, and some, particularly women, did not marry at all. This meant that more young people were expected to remain chaste for longer periods of time.[30]

Zina Presendia addressed these problems at a joint meeting of the Cardston Ward's YLMIA and YMMIA in early May. "The pleasures of a moment often bring sorrow for life," she warned the youth. "We should seek for humility and charity and do to others as we would wish to be done by."[31]

That spring and summer, she also attended several meetings of the Cardston Ward YLMIA. The association met every Wednesday afternoon. Mamie Ibey, the twenty-three-year-old president of the ward association, often conducted the meetings while others taught lessons. Every other month, the young women also held a testimony meeting, giving each member of the group a chance to bear witness to her peers.[32]

All through the year 1900, the *Young Woman's Journal* published a twelve-part series of lessons called "Ethics for Young Girls." Every month a new lesson appeared, each designed to help young women discern right from wrong. Among the topics covered were honesty, self-control, courage, chastity, and reverence. A series of questions followed each lesson, prompting the young women to review and discuss the material.[33]

Zina Presendia believed regularly attending the MIA could shore up the youth and influence their actions for the better. At the meetings, the young women were encouraged to stand apart from worldliness and error. "We should never be ashamed of the truth," Zina Presendia taught them, "nor to own that we are Mormons."[34]

She also urged their parents to guide them along the path of righteousness. Earlier that year, while visiting a stake in Idaho, she heard her mother repeat something Joseph Smith had taught the Relief Society in Nauvoo: "Plant good ideas into the minds of the children. They notice our example." Zina Presendia believed this truth applied in Cardston as well.

"We should set good examples for our children," she reminded other leaders in July, "take them to our arms and our heart, and teach them to shun all evil."[35]

ON THE AFTERNOON OF December 10, 1900, George Q. Cannon saw the Hawaiian Islands for the first time since his mission there in the 1850s. At age twenty-three, he had been the youngest of the ten original Latter-day Saint missionaries sent to the islands. Now, as a counselor in the First Presidency, he was returning to commemorate the fiftieth anniversary of their arrival and the beginning of the Church in Hawaii.[36]

A few hours after spotting the islands, George and his fellow passengers docked at Honolulu on the island of Oahu. He stayed the night with Hawaiian Latter-day Saints Abraham and Minerva Fernandez and spent the following day at a reception with about a thousand Saints at a meetinghouse. Some in attendance had been baptized by George during his mission. Others were the children and grandchildren of people he had taught.[37]

George awoke the next morning, December 12, uneasy about speaking to the Hawaiians at the anniversary celebration. As a young missionary, he had been admired for his skill in speaking and writing Hawaiian. But he had seldom used it since coming home, and now he worried that his clumsiness with the language would disappoint the Saints.[38]

The celebration was held in a brand-new theater in Honolulu. Local Church leaders had recruited a fine orchestra, two choirs from Honolulu and Laie, and other musical groups. At a nearby government building, the Saints had also prepared an enormous feast of Hawaiian dishes and invited everyone in the community to come. To George, it seemed the entire city was joining in the celebration.[39]

When the time came for George to speak, he began his talk in English, recalling the earliest days of his mission, when several of his companions abandoned the work and the islands' English-speaking inhabitants showed no interest in the gospel. "It was then that I protested," George recounted, "and declared myself determined to stay in these islands and labor among its people."[40]

As he spoke, George felt the Spirit rest powerfully upon him. Hawaiian words suddenly came back to him, and his uneasiness slipped away as he began speaking in the language. The Hawaiian Saints were at once astonished and delighted. "How wonderful," someone said, "that he should remember our language all these long years!"[41]

The celebration continued into the next day, and George once again addressed the Saints confidently in their language. "I feel today more than ever the ties that bind the people of God together," he told them. "Where people come to believe in the gospel and go down into the waters of baptism, they grow to love one another."[42]

George spent a little more than three weeks with the Saints in Hawaii. While on the island of Maui, he visited the town of Wailuku, where he had his first success as a missionary. The town had changed almost beyond recognition, but he easily found the home of his friends Jonathan and Kitty Napela, both of whom had passed away decades earlier. The Napelas were like family to George, and Jonathan had been his fellow translator of the Hawaiian Book of Mormon.[43]

As he visited the islands, George made many new friends, including Tomizo Katsunuma, a Japanese man who had joined the Church while studying at the Agricultural College of Utah. He also met lifelong Saints who, despite their faithfulness, had never received the ordinances of the temple. Touched by their situation, he urged them to live worthy to enter the temple and exercise faith that the Lord would inspire His prophet to bring temple blessings to them.[44]

On the day of George's departure, hundreds of Saints and a local band met his carriage at the wharf in Honolulu. As a final gesture of their love, some twenty children and elderly Saints rushed forward and covered him in colorful lei. He then climbed aboard his ship, and the band struck up a farewell tune.

Gazing back at the Saints on the dock, George knew he would never forget them. "Aloha nui," they called out to him, expressing their love and farewell. "Aloha nui."[45]

"A NEW CENTURY DAWNS upon the world today."

The voice of LeRoi Snow echoed throughout the Salt Lake Tabernacle as he read the opening words of a message his father, Lorenzo Snow, had written to the nations of the earth.[46]

It was January 1, 1901, the first day of the twentieth century. The weather outside was bitterly cold, but more than four thousand people had left the warmth of their homes that morning to commemorate the occasion in a special service with the prophet, other general authorities, and the Tabernacle Choir. The Tabernacle itself was decorated for the occasion, and strung across the organ pipes was a cluster of electric lights spelling the word "Welcome."[47]

Sitting on the stand, not far from where LeRoi stood, was President Snow himself, his voice ravaged by a severe cold. With the other Saints in the room, he listened keenly as LeRoi read the message. Simply titled "Greeting to the World," it reflected on the astounding scientific discoveries and technological advancements of the last hundred years and expressed President Snow's optimism for the coming century.

In the message, he called upon world leaders to forsake war and seek the "welfare of humanity" instead of the "enrichment of a race or the extension of an empire." He declared, "The power is in your hands to pave the way for the coming King of Kings, whose dominion will be over all the earth." He urged them to promote peace, put an end to oppression, and work together to end poverty and uplift the masses.

He also called on rich and poor alike to seek better, more charitable ways of living. "The day of your redemption draweth nigh," he told the poor. "Be provident when in prosperity." To the rich, he counseled generosity: "Unlock your vaults, unloose your purses, and embark in enterprises that will give work to the unemployed and relieve the wretchedness that leads to the vice and crime which curse your great cities and that poison the moral atmosphere around you."

He testified of the Lord and His restored gospel. "He will assuredly accomplish His work," President Snow declared, "and the twentieth century will mark its advancement."

Finally, he blessed the people of the world, wherever they might be. "May the sunshine from above smile upon you," he said. "May the light of truth chase darkness from your souls. May righteousness increase and iniquity diminish as the years of the century roll on. May justice triumph and corruption be stamped out."

"Let these sentiments, as the voice of the 'Mormons' in the mountains of Utah, go forth to the whole world," he declared, "and let all people know that our wish and our mission are for the blessing and salvation of the entire human race."[48]

CHAPTER 7

On Trial

Early in 1901, Joseph F. Smith began shouldering more Church responsibilities in the First Presidency as George Q. Cannon's health worsened. In March, George and his family went to the California coast, hoping its ocean breezes would revive him. Joseph, meanwhile, tried to rally his friend from afar.

"My lifelong associations with you in the work of the ministry," he wrote to George, "have bound my heart, my soul, my love and sympathies to you in the cords of affection as strong as the love of life, which cannot be broken."[1]

George's health continued to decline, however. His sons sent regular reports on their father's failing health to Salt Lake City, so Joseph was not surprised when a telegram announcing George's death arrived on April 12.

Still, he felt the loss keenly. "He was both a humble and a great man, a mighty chieftain in the councils of his brethren," Joseph reflected in his journal that day. "All Israel will mourn his death."[2]

Amid his grief, Joseph turned his attention to his expanded role in the First Presidency.[3] That year, he and President Lorenzo Snow assigned three apostles to lead missionary efforts in key parts of the world. They called Francis Lyman to preside over the European Mission, John Henry Smith to revitalize the mission in Mexico, and Heber J. Grant to lead the first mission to Japan. Wanting to expand the Lord's work to other parts of the world, Church leaders also contemplated sending missionaries to South America and constructing a small temple for the colonies of Saints in Arizona and northern Mexico. The Church was still in debt, however, and nothing immediate came of these plans.[4]

The Saints mourned two more deaths that year. In August, Relief Society general president Zina Young collapsed while visiting her daughter, Zina Presendia Card, in Canada. Zina Presendia rushed her mother back to Utah, where she died peacefully in her Salt Lake City home. Throughout her life, Zina had been an example of placing the kingdom of God before all else.[5]

"Each day makes me rejoice more in the grandeur of the principles which we believe in," she had told the Relief Society in Cardston two weeks before her death. "The greatness of our blessings is beyond expression.

There is nothing compared to the blessings we enjoy through our reliance on God."[6]

Two months later, President Snow was overcome with sudden illness. Several apostles faithfully attended to him and at Joseph F. Smith's request knelt around his bed to pray in his behalf. He passed away a short time later.

At President Snow's funeral, Joseph eulogized him and his unwavering witness of truth. "With the exception of the prophet Joseph," he declared, "I don't believe any man ever stood upon this earth who bore a stronger, more clear-cut testimony of Jesus Christ."[7]

A few days later, on October 17, 1901, the Quorum of the Twelve Apostles sustained Joseph F. Smith as the sixth president of the Church. He called John Winder of the Presiding Bishopric and Anthon Lund to be his counselors. The apostles then laid their hands on Joseph, and John Smith, his older brother and the Church patriarch, set him apart.[8]

THE SAINTS SUSTAINED THE new First Presidency at a special meeting in the Salt Lake Tabernacle on November 10, 1901. "It is our duty to take hold of the work vigorously, with full determination and purpose of heart to carry it on, with the help of the Lord and in accordance with the inspiration of His Spirit," President Smith told the congregation. With a new century dawning, he wanted to give Church members hope for the future.

"We have been driven from our homes, maligned and spoken evil of everywhere," he said. "The Lord designs to change this condition of things and to make us known to the world in our true light—as true worshippers of God."[9]

At the meeting, President Smith also called on the Saints to sustain Bathsheba Smith as the fourth general president of the Relief Society. It was the first time the priesthood quorums were asked to give their sustaining vote for a new Relief Society general presidency.

"It was very gratifying to women interested in the advancement of the sisters," observed Emmeline Wells, "to see the uplifted hands of all the several quorums of the holy priesthood raised to sustain them."[10]

Seventy-nine years old, Bathsheba was one of the few founding members of the Nauvoo Relief Society still living. After joining the Church at age fifteen, she had gathered with the Saints first in Missouri and then in Nauvoo. In 1841 she married apostle George A. Smith and later served as an ordinance worker in the Nauvoo Temple. She had been an active worker in the Relief Society, most recently as Zina Young's second counselor in the general presidency.[11]

Two months after the Saints sustained her, Bathsheba issued a greeting of love and goodwill to all Relief Society members. "Dear sisters, seek to bind your society with hoops of love and union," she declared. "Let us go forth at this hour with renewed resolutions to take up the work of relief and improvement."[12]

With her counselors, Annie Hyde and Ida Dusenberry, she advocated serving the poor and needy and promoted grain storage and silk production. To raise funds for relief work, she encouraged society members to collect donations by holding bazaars, concerts, and dances. She sent delegates to national women's organizations and helped women train to be nurses and midwives. She also began gathering funds and making plans for a "Woman's Building" across the street from the Salt Lake Temple, on land Lorenzo Snow had set apart for the organization before his death.[13]

Like their predecessors, Bathsheba and her counselors believed it was important to visit with individual Relief Societies. They often relied on the wives of mission presidents to visit Relief Societies in Europe and Oceania. But they themselves or members of the Relief Society general board tried to visit Latter-day Saint women in the western United States, Mexico, and Canada at least twice a year. Because the Church had dozens of stakes in this region, making it more difficult to visit everyone, they called six additional women to assist in the work.[14]

During their visits to stakes, Relief Society leaders noticed a lack of interest among younger women. Because many of these women were new mothers, the general presidency encouraged stake Relief Societies to make their meetings more appealing to the younger generation. Relief Societies at this time did not follow a set curriculum, so Bathsheba instructed the stakes to design their own education classes for mothers. She asked that each Relief Society draw on the life experiences of its older members while also studying scientific books on child-rearing, which interested the new generation of women. Soon the *Woman's Exponent* began publishing course outlines to help stakes develop their programs.[15]

In August 1903, Bathsheba sent thirty-year-old Ida Dusenberry to Cardston to help Zina Presendia Card and local Relief Society presidencies prepare mothers' classes. Ida instructed them to take charge of the program and use Church magazines and other Church publications in their lessons.

"How far in a scientific way are we to study in our mothers' classes?" Zina Presendia asked.

As a college-educated kindergarten teacher and school administrator, Ida was eager to infuse the mothers' classes with the latest ideas on parenting. Yet she understood that the older Relief Society sisters had much to offer from their own experience.

"We want you to take up needs of a mother and her duty to her children in a general way," she explained. "We may learn many good practical things from each other."[16]

WHILE IDA DUSENBERRY WAS visiting Cardston, her older brother Reed Smoot was preparing for a political battle in the United States Senate. A junior member of the Quorum of the Twelve Apostles, Reed had been elected to the Senate earlier that year after receiving the First Presidency's permission to run.[17] His wife, Allie, also supported his desire to serve in the Senate, certain he could do much for the people of Utah. "I am very anxious for you to succeed," she told him, "and feel like God will bless us both and help us."[18]

Predictably, Reed's victory sparked outrage and protests.[19] The Church had struggled to improve its public image after B. H. Roberts's election to the House of Representatives in 1898 provoked a national backlash against the Saints. The Church had since opened a Bureau of Information on Temple Square to help people learn more about the Saints. The bureau was staffed by volunteers, many of them from the YMMIA and YLMIA, who distributed Church literature and answered questions about the Church and its beliefs. So far, they had welcomed thousands of visitors to Salt Lake City with accurate information about the Church. Yet their work did little to change the minds of the Church's fiercest opponents in and out of Utah.[20]

Reed's most aggressive critics were members of the Salt Lake Ministerial Association, a group of Protestant businessmen, lawyers, and clergymen from Utah. Shortly after the election, they formally petitioned the Senate to deny Reed his seat. Their petition claimed that the First Presidency and the Quorum of the Twelve Apostles wielded supreme political and economic authority over the Saints and demanded absolute obedience from them. They also asserted that Church leaders still preached, practiced, and supported plural marriage, despite the Manifesto. These factors, they concluded, made the Saints undemocratic and disloyal to the nation.

The members of the Ministerial Association feared that Reed would use his position as an apostle in the Church to promote plural marriage and protect those who practiced it. One member even accused Reed, a monogamist, of practicing plural marriage in secret. He warned that Reed would be a pawn of the First Presidency, wholly subject to their direction.[21]

Senate leaders reviewed the petitions and appointed a committee of thirteen senators to conduct a hearing into the Ministerial Association's claims. Yet they also permitted Reed to take his oath of office, allowing him to serve as a senator at least until the committee finished its hearing.[22]

Although the threat of investigation loomed over the Church, Joseph F. Smith believed that Reed should keep his apostleship and his Senate seat, confident that he could do more good in Washington than anywhere else. President Smith saw the investigation as a chance to help people better understand the Saints and their beliefs.[23]

Since Reed had never practiced plural marriage, he did not fret about the committee's investigation into his personal life. But he worried about how the Church would fare during the hearing. Rumors about new plural marriages abounded in Utah, and doubts about the Church's commitment to abandoning the practice lingered in the public mind since B. H. Roberts's election. As a leader in the Church, Reed had to answer for Church policies. He knew the committee would investigate post-Manifesto plural marriages thoroughly. He also expected the senators to question him and other witnesses about the Church's involvement in politics and the Saints' loyalty to the United States.[24]

If the committee proved that the Church promoted lawbreaking, Reed could be stripped of his seat, and the Saints' reputation would suffer.

On January 4, 1904, Reed submitted a rebuttal to the committee, formally denying the Ministerial Association's accusations. He hoped to focus the committee's attention on him and his conduct. But when he met with the committee one week later, it was clear the senators were determined to investigate the Church. And they were especially eager to question Joseph F. Smith and other general authorities about their political influence over the Saints and the continuation of plural marriage after the Manifesto.

"Senator Smoot, you are not on trial," the committee chairman told him. "It is the Mormon church that we intend to investigate, and we are going to see that these men obey law."[25]

On February 25, 1904, the Senate committee subpoenaed Joseph F. Smith to testify at the Smoot hearings. He left for Washington, DC, two days later, confident the Church could withstand the coming scrutiny. Reed had warned him, though, that senators would ask about every aspect of his home life and demand details about his plural marriages. As president of the Church, he would also be asked about his role as prophet, seer, and revelator to the Saints. The committee would want to know what influence he and his revelations would have on Reed and his actions in the Senate.[26]

On the first day of questioning, March 2, the committee room was packed with senators, lawyers, and witnesses. Members of women's organizations opposed to Reed's election were also present. At the chairman's request, President Smith took a seat across from him at a long table. His gray hair and long beard were neatly combed, and he wore a simple black coat and gold-rimmed glasses. Pinned to his lapel was a small portrait of Hyrum Smith, his martyred father.[27]

Robert Tayler, the lawyer representing the Ministerial Association, opened the inquiry with questions about President Smith's life. Turning his attention to revelation and its influence on the individual decisions of Church members, the lawyer then asked the prophet to explain when Church members might be obligated to obey revelation from the Church president. If he could get the prophet to admit that all members were required to obey his revelations, Tayler could show that Reed Smoot was not truly free to make his own decisions in the Senate.

"No revelation given through the head of the Church ever becomes binding and authoritative," President Smith told him, "until it has been presented to the Church and accepted by them."

"Do you mean," asked Tayler, "that the Church in conference may say to you, Joseph F. Smith, the president of the Church, 'We deny that God has told you to tell us this'?"[28]

"They can say that if they choose," the prophet replied. "Every man is entitled to his own opinion and his own views and his own conceptions of right and wrong, so long as they do not come in conflict with the standard principles of the Church."[29]

As an example, he noted that only a portion of Saints had practiced plural marriage. "All the rest of the members of the Church abstained from that principle and did not enter into it, and many thousands of them never received it or believed it," he said, "but they were not cut off from the Church."[30]

"You have revelations, have you not?" questioned the committee chairman. He was asking when a revelation from the Lord's prophet would be considered a fundamental doctrine of the Church, something a faithful Latter-day Saint like Reed Smoot would feel obliged to obey.

President Smith chose his words deliberately. He had often received personal revelation through the Holy Ghost. As the prophet, he had also received inspired direction for the Saints. But he had never received a revelation for the entire Church in the Lord's own voice—the kind of revelation found in the Doctrine and Covenants.

"I never said I had a revelation," he told the chairman, "except so far as God has shown to me that so-called 'Mormonism' is God's divine truth. That is all."[31]

PRESIDENT SMITH CONTINUED ANSWERING questions until the committee adjourned late that afternoon. When the hearing resumed the next day, the committee focused their questions more and more on plural marriage and the Manifesto. While he sought to respond accurately to their questions, President Smith avoided disclosing what he and other Church leaders knew about new plural marriages. He knew Congress would condemn him and the Church if this information came to light in the investigation.[32]

Furthermore, his guarded answers to the committee's questions were based on his understanding that Saints who practiced plural marriages after the Manifesto did so at their own risk. For this reason, he believed the Manifesto had not forbidden him and his wives, or any other plural couples, from discreetly continuing to honor their sacred temple marriage covenants to each other.[33]

When Robert Tayler asked him if he thought it was wrong to continue living with a plural wife, President Smith said, "That is contrary to the rule of the Church and contrary as well to the law of the land." But he then spoke openly of his refusal to abandon his large plural family. "I have cohabitated with my wives," he said. "They have borne me children since 1890."[34]

"Since that was a violation of the law," said Tayler, "why have you done it?"

"I preferred to face the penalties of the law rather than abandon my family," the prophet replied.[35]

Trying to root out the names of men who had married plural wives after the Manifesto, the senators asked him about the marriages of the apostles and several other members of the Church. The chairman of the committee also asked President Smith if he himself had performed any plural marriages after the Manifesto.

"No sir, I never have," the prophet replied. He then followed his response with a carefully worded statement designed to prevent further scrutiny. "There have been no plural marriages solemnized by and with the consent or by the knowledge of The Church of Jesus Christ of Latter-day Saints," he said.

"Since the Manifesto?" a senator asked.

"I mean that, of course," President Smith clarified. In making this statement, he was not denying the existence of post-Manifesto plural marriages. Rather, he wanted to draw a subtle distinction between practices the Church and its councils sanctioned and those that individual Church members chose to follow according to their consciences. The Saints had indeed sustained the Manifesto in 1890, so the plural marriages performed by Church leaders had taken place without the consent of the Church as a whole.

"If an apostle of the Church had performed such a ceremony," another senator asked, "would you consider that being with the authority of your Church?"

"If any apostle or any other man claiming authority should do any such thing as that," President Smith
said, "he would not only be subject to prosecution and
heavy fine and imprisonment in the state under the
state law, but he would also be subjected to discipline
and excommunication from the Church by the proper
tribunals of the Church."[36]

AFTER COMPLETING HIS TESTIMONY, which lasted five
days, President Smith felt he had followed divine guidance in the witness chair. "I firmly believe the Lord did
the best He could with the instrument through whom
He had to work," he stated.[37]

Still, his testimony provoked public outcry when
it was published in the newspapers. People across the
United States were shocked to learn that President Smith
still lived with his five wives. They also doubted his
credibility and sincerity as a witness and denounced
Church leaders as liars and lawbreakers.[38]

"An avalanche of unfavorable public sentiment
is now sweeping over us as a community," the First
Presidency's secretary confided to a friend, "and about
the only thing we feel like doing just now is to button
up our coat collar, turn our back to the storm, and
patiently wait."[39]

While the Senate hearing continued in
Washington, DC, the prophet returned to Salt Lake
City, resolved to take steps to restore confidence in him

and the Church. He had assured the committee that Church officials would discipline Saints who performed new plural marriages in violation of the Manifesto. He was now bound to give the Senate stronger proof that he and the Saints were serious about stopping new plural marriages.[40]

On April 6, 1904, the last day of general conference, he stood at the pulpit of the Tabernacle and read a new official statement on plural marriage in the Church. "Inasmuch as there are numerous reports in circulation that plural marriages have been entered into, contrary to the official declaration of President Woodruff," he said, "I hereby announce that all such marriages are prohibited."

The statement did not condemn the two hundred or so couples who had entered into plural marriage after the Manifesto or censure those who had continued to live with their plural families since that time. Yet it declared that new plural marriages were forbidden from now on, even outside the boundaries of the United States. "If any officer or member of the Church shall assume to solemnize or enter into any such marriage he will be deemed in transgression against the Church," President Smith said, "and will be liable to be dealt with according to the rules and regulations thereof and excommunicated therefrom."[41]

After reading the statement, which became known as the Second Manifesto, President Smith urged the Saints to be united in their support of this new declaration and restore the government's confidence in them. Where the

Manifesto had revealed that the Church was no longer under the command to practice plural marriage, this new statement acted to stop new plural marriages from that time forth.[42] He hoped it would put an end to claims that Church members were not law-abiding citizens.

"I want to see today," he said, "whether the Latter-day Saints representing the Church in this solemn assembly will not seal these charges as false by their vote."

As a body, the Saints in the Tabernacle raised their arms to the square and sustained his words.[43]

CHAPTER 8

The Rock of Revelation

During the spring of 1904, John Widtsoe followed the Smoot hearings from afar. His friend and mentor Joseph Tanner, now serving as the superintendent of Church schools and a counselor in the Sunday School general presidency, was one of several Saints summoned to testify before the Senate committee. Since Joseph had married plural wives after the Manifesto, he refused to submit to the investigation and instead fled to Canada.

"I do not feel at all alarmed," he wrote to John in late April, signing the letter with an alias. "When the Smoot case is decided, we shall have rest perhaps for a while."[1]

Like other Saints, John believed the Smoot hearings were simply another trial of faith for the Church.[2] He and Leah Widtsoe were back in Logan. Along with their daughter, Anna, they had a son, Marsel, and a baby on the way. Another son, John Jr., had died in February 1902, a few months before his first birthday.

The rest of the Widtsoe family was far away. John's mother, Anna, and her sister Petroline Gaarden had left Utah to serve a mission in Norway, their homeland, in 1903. In a letter to Leah, John's mother described their work. "We have met many old friends and talked with them about the gospel, many who never have had a conversation with a Latter-day Saint before," she wrote. "We are trying to knock on the door of 'tradition,' but it is not easy work to get it open."[3]

John's younger brother, Osborne, meanwhile, had recently completed a mission in Tahiti and was now studying English literature at Harvard.[4]

Leah worked at home with the children and served on her stake Young Ladies' Mutual Improvement Association board. She also wrote monthly lessons on home economics for the *Young Woman's Journal*. Each lesson was part of a yearlong course that young women in the Church could study and discuss in their YLMIA meetings. Leah approached each lesson scientifically, drawing on her university training to teach her readers about cooking, home furnishing, first aid, and basic medical care.[5]

John taught chemistry at the Agricultural College, ran the school's experiment station, and studied ways to improve farming in Utah's dry climate. His work took him to rural towns all around the state as he taught farmers how to use science to raise better crops. He also served as president of his ward Young Men's MIA and as a member of the stake Sunday School board. Like Leah, he wrote regularly for the Church magazines.

John had sympathy for young Saints who struggled, as he once did, to reconcile gospel knowledge with secular learning. More and more people were embracing the idea that science and religion were at odds with each other. Yet John believed that science and religion were both sources of divine, eternal principles and could be reconciled.[6]

Recently, he had begun publishing a series of articles called "Joseph Smith as Scientist" in the *Improvement Era,* the official magazine of the YMMIA. Each article explained how the restored gospel anticipated some major discovery of modern science. In his article "Geological Time," for instance, John explained how passages from the Book of Abraham accommodated scientific views that the earth was much older than the six thousand years some biblical scholars estimated. In another article, he identified parallels between aspects of the controversial theory of evolution and the doctrine of eternal progression.[7]

The series was a success. President Joseph F. Smith, who served as editor of the *Improvement Era,* sent a personal letter praising the series. His only regret was that he could not pay John for the work. "Like some of the rest of us," he wrote, "you will, for the present at least, have to accept your pay in the knowledge that you have done good work for the benefit of the boys and girls of Zion."[8]

"Our situation seems most serious now," apostle Francis Lyman wrote in his journal. Joseph F. Smith's testimony at the Reed Smoot hearing had done little to resolve the Senate committee's concerns about the existence of post-Manifesto plural marriages in the Church. Nor did it help the Saints' case that apostles John W. Taylor and Matthias Cowley, acting on the advice of Church leaders, made themselves scarce soon after the Senate committee summoned them to testify at the hearings. Like Joseph Tanner and other Church members, both men had married plural wives after the Manifesto. The two apostles had also performed many new plural marriages and encouraged Saints to keep the practice alive.[9]

As president of the Twelve, Francis had resolved that each man in the quorum should comply with the newly issued Second Manifesto. He had sent letters to several apostles, advising them of the First Presidency's determination to implement the proclamation. "It is well that we shall understand this important matter alike and govern ourselves accordingly," he wrote, "that there shall be no dissensions or disputations among us."[10]

Later, President Smith assigned Francis to make sure that no more plural marriages took place in the Church. Since the late 1880s, some apostles had been authorized to perform sealings outside of temples for outlying areas.

In September 1904, President Smith declared that all
sealings must now take place in temples, thus making
it impossible for Saints to enter into legitimate plural
marriages in Mexico, Canada, or elsewhere. Francis
promptly informed the apostles of this decision.[11]

In December, President Smith sent Francis to persuade John W. Taylor to testify at the Smoot hearings.
Francis found John W. in Canada and encouraged
him to follow the prophet's counsel. At last, John W.
agreed to testify and began preparing to travel to
Washington.

That night, Francis went to bed, his mission a success. But at three o'clock in the morning he awoke
trembling. The thought of John W. testifying at the hearings troubled him. John W. was deeply committed to
plural marriage. If he revealed that he had performed
post-Manifesto plural marriages, it would embarrass
the Church and ruin Reed Smoot's chances of serving
in the Senate.

A quiet, peaceful feeling settled over Francis
as he considered advising John W. *against* going to
Washington. He asked the Lord to confirm that this
was the correct course to take. A gentle sleep overtook
him, and he dreamed that he saw President Wilford
Woodruff. Surprised and full of emotion, he called out
President Woodruff's name and threw his arms around
him. He then awoke, confident that his change of mind
was right. He sought out John W. immediately and told
him about the dream. John W. was ready to leave for

Washington, but he was relieved when Francis counseled him not to go.[12]

Francis returned to Salt Lake City a short time later. Joseph F. Smith approved of his work in Canada, yet the question remained of what to do with the two apostles. President Smith knew he needed to demonstrate that the Church was firmly committed to ending plural marriage. To satisfy the Senate committee, he would have to formally distance John W. and Matthias from Church leadership, either by disciplining them or by asking them to resign. He relished neither option.[13]

Church leaders were split on how to handle the crisis. In October 1905, however, advisers to Reed Smoot warned them that time was running out for the Church to act. While testifying before the Senate committee earlier that year, Reed had promised that Church authorities would investigate the charges made against John W. and Matthias. Six months later, no investigation had taken place, and now some senators were questioning Reed's honesty. To postpone an investigation any longer would signal to the world that Church leaders were acting in bad faith when they claimed to be actively opposing polygamy.[14]

The two apostles were summoned to Church headquarters, and over the next week, the Twelve met day after day to discuss what to do. At first, John W. and Matthias defended their actions, drawing a distinction between the Church's formal withdrawal of support for plural marriage and their individual choice to continue entering into new marriages. Neither man fully sustained the Second Manifesto, however, a position now incompatible with good standing in the Church.

Ultimately, the quorum asked the two apostles to sign resignation letters. At first, John W. refused to resign. He accused his quorum of giving in to political pressure. Matthias responded more mildly, but he too was reluctant to comply. In the end, though, both men wanted what was best for the Church. They signed the papers, willing to sacrifice their place in the Twelve for the larger good.[15]

"It was a very painful and serious ordeal," Francis wrote that day in his journal. "We were all very sorely distressed over it." John W. and Matthias left the meeting with the goodwill and blessings of their brethren. But while the Twelve allowed them to retain their Church membership and apostleship, they were no longer members of the quorum.[16]

TWO MONTHS LATER, ON the morning of December 23, 1905, Susa Gates climbed into a carriage in Vermont, in the northeastern United States. The prophet Joseph Smith had been born exactly one hundred years earlier on a farm about three miles to the east, in the tiny village of Sharon. Now Susa and around fifty Saints were going to the farm to dedicate a monument to his memory.[17]

Leading the group was President Joseph F. Smith. With the Smoot hearings still in progress, he remained under the constant scrutiny of government officials and newspaper reporters. Earlier that year, the *Salt Lake Tribune* had published his testimony at the Smoot hearings alongside editorials casting doubt on his prophetic call and personal integrity.

"Joseph F. Smith has publicly denied that he receives revelations, or ever has received revelation, from God to guide the Mormon church," read one editorial. "How far ought the Mormons to follow that kind of leader?"[18] The editorials left some Saints confused and full of questions.

As Joseph Smith's nephew, Joseph F. Smith had personal reasons for coming to Vermont. Yet the dedication would also give him another opportunity to speak publicly about the Church and testify of the divine work of the Restoration.[19]

Once Susa and the party were situated in their carriages, they set out for the dedication ceremony. The farm was at the top of a nearby hill, and the steep country roads were muddy with thawing snow. Local workers had hauled the one-hundred-ton monument along the same roads, piece by piece. At first, they had simply planned to pull the load with draft animals. But when a team of twenty strong horses could not budge the stone, workers spent nearly two grueling months dragging the monument up the hill with a horse-drawn system of ropes and pulleys.[20]

Nearing the farm, the party gasped as they rounded the final bend in the road. Ahead of them was a polished granite obelisk reaching 38½ feet into the sky—a foot for each year of Joseph Smith's life. Beneath the obelisk was a large pedestal with an inscription bearing testimony of the prophet's sacred mission. The words of James 1:5, the scripture that had inspired him to seek revelation from God, graced the top of the pedestal.[21]

Junius Wells, the monument's designer, met the party at a cottage built on the foundation of the site where Joseph Smith was born. Upon entering the house, Susa admired the flat, gray hearthstone, which the builders had preserved from the original home. Most of the Saints who had known the prophet personally were now dead. But this hearthstone was an enduring witness of his life. She could imagine him playing beside it as a toddler.[22]

The service began at eleven o'clock. As he dedicated the memorial, President Smith gave thanks for the Restoration of the gospel and asked a blessing on the people of Vermont who supported the monument's construction. He set the site apart as a place where people could come to meditate, learn more about Joseph Smith's prophetic mission, and rejoice in the Restoration. He likened the foundation of the monument to the Church's foundation of prophets and apostles, with Jesus Christ as the chief cornerstone. He also compared its base to the rock of revelation on which the Church was built.[23]

In the days that followed, Susa, Joseph F. Smith, and other Saints took a short tour of Church sites in the eastern United States. Under President Smith's direction, the Church had begun purchasing several sites sacred to its history, including the Carthage jail, where his father and uncle had been killed. Other Church historic sites in the eastern states remained out of the Church's hands, although their owners generally gave the Saints permission to tour them.[24]

In Manchester, New York, the group walked reverently through the woods where Joseph Smith had seen his first vision of the Father and Son. During the prophet's life, he and other Saints had occasionally testified publicly of his vision. But in the decades after Joseph's death, Orson Pratt and fellow Church leaders had emphasized its central role in the Restoration of the gospel. An account of it now appeared as scripture in the Pearl of Great Price, and missionaries frequently referred to it in their discussions with people outside the Church.[25]

A profound sense of awe rested over Susa and her companions as they pondered the sacred event. "Here the boy kneeled in absolute faith," Susa reflected. "Here, finally, earth's fountains burst, and truth, the sum of existence, swept down on the beams of direct revelation."[26]

Later, as they headed back to Utah, President Smith led a small testimony meeting aboard the train. "'Tis not I, nor any man, not even the prophet Joseph Smith, who stands at the head of this work, directing and leading it," he told them. "It is God, through His Son, Jesus Christ."

The message stirred Susa, and she was awed by the love of the Savior for God's children. "Men are men, and therefore weak!" she noted. But Jesus Christ was Lord of all the world.[27]

WHILE THE SAINTS CELEBRATED the dedication of the Joseph Smith memorial, Anna Widtsoe and Petroline Gaarden were still in Norway, preaching the gospel. More than two years had passed since the sisters left Utah. Their mission call had been unexpected, but not unwelcome. They had both been eager to return to their homeland to share their faith in the restored gospel with relatives and friends.[28]

Anthon Skanchy, one of the missionaries who taught Anna the gospel in the 1880s, was president of the Scandinavian Mission when the sisters arrived in July 1903. He assigned them to work in the area of Trondheim, Norway, where Anna had lived when she joined the Church. From there, the sisters took a boat to their home village, Titran, on a large island off Norway's west coast. Anna was apprehensive when she arrived on the island. Twenty years earlier, people in Titran had turned their backs on her for joining the Church. Would they accept her and her religion now?[29]

Word quickly spread that the sisters had returned as Latter-day Saint missionaries. At first, no one—friend or family—would give them a place to stay. Anna and Petroline persisted, and eventually some people opened their doors.[30]

One day, the sisters visited their uncle Jonas Haavig and his family. Everyone seemed guarded, ready to debate the sisters about their beliefs. Anna and Petroline avoided the topic of religion, and the first night ended without conflict. But the next morning, after breakfast, their cousin Marie began asking the sisters difficult questions about the gospel, trying to provoke an argument.

"Marie," Anna said, "I was determined not to speak to you about religion, but now you'll listen to what I have to say." She bore a forceful testimony, and Marie listened in silence. But Anna could tell that her words had no effect. She and Petroline left the house later that day, heartbroken over what had happened.[31]

The sisters soon returned to Trondheim, but they went back to Titran several times over the next two years. The people grew more welcoming as time went on, and Anna and Petroline were eventually invited into every home in town. Their service in other parts of Norway was also challenging, but the sisters were grateful they had experience in Church service before they left for their mission.

They were also grateful that they spoke Norwegian before they arrived. "We take our part more on all occasions than the young missionaries who can't speak the language, neither when they come nor when they go home," Anna informed John in a letter.[32]

As happy as missionary work made Anna, she missed her family in Utah. John, Osborne, and Leah wrote regularly. In the summer of 1905, John reported that he lost his job at the Agricultural College when the school administration ousted him and two other faithful Church members from the faculty. Brigham Young University, the new name for Brigham Young Academy in Provo, immediately hired him to run its chemistry department. Since its founding in 1875, the school had grown into the Church's preeminent institution of higher learning, and John gratefully accepted the job.

Osborne, meanwhile, graduated from Harvard and accepted a position as head of the English department at Latter-day Saints' University in Salt Lake City.[33]

"God has been good with us," Anna told John in a letter. "I believe we have been able with the Lord's help to do something good. We have seen much fruit of our labor here, and I hope and pray to God that we may also be assisted by Him in the new year as in the year past."[34]

In January 1906, mission leaders assigned Anna and Petroline to remain in Trondheim to finish their mission among family members and do genealogical research. Their relatives were still not interested in the gospel. But the sisters no longer sensed hostility and suspicion from them. They took comfort in this change. They had done their part to serve the Lord in Norway.[35]

THAT SUMMER, EUROPEAN SAINTS learned that President Joseph F. Smith was taking a brief tour of their continent. The news thrilled eleven-year-old Jan Roothoff, especially when he heard that the prophet's first appearance would be in the Netherlands, where Jan lived. The boy was too excited to talk about anything else.

Several years earlier, Jan had caught a disease that infected his eyes and made him sensitive to light. His mother, Hendriksje, a single parent, kept him out of school and tried to make him as comfortable as possible by hanging curtains so he could play in the dark. But he eventually went blind, and doctors told his mother that he would never regain his sight.

Jan now wore bandages over his eyes to protect them from the light. But he knew that if anyone could heal his eyes, it was a prophet of God. "Mother, he is the most powerful missionary," he said. "All he has to do is look into my eyes and I will be well."[36]

Jan's mother believed that the Lord could heal him, but she was reluctant to encourage him to seek President Smith's help. "The president is very busy just now," she replied. "There are hundreds of people who want to see him. You are only a boy, my son, and we must not intrude."[37]

On August 9, 1906, Jan and his mother attended a special meeting in Rotterdam, where President Smith spoke to about four hundred Saints. As Jan listened to him speak, he tried hard to picture the prophet. Before losing his eyesight, Jan had seen a photograph of President

Smith, and he remembered his kind face. Now he could hear kindness in the prophet's voice as well, even though he had to wait for a missionary to translate the words into Dutch before he understood them.[38]

President Smith spoke about the power of missionaries. "It is their business to come to you and to show you the greater light," he said, "that your eyes may be opened, that your ears may be unstopped, that your hearts may be touched with a love for the truth."[39]

Jan's faith did not waver. After the meeting, his mother led him to a doorway where President Smith and his wife Edna were greeting the Saints. "This is the president, little Jan," Hendriksje said. "He wants to shake hands with you."

Taking him by the hand, President Smith lifted away Jan's bandages. He then touched the boy's head and peered into his inflamed eyes. "The Lord bless you, my boy," he said. "He will grant you the desires of your heart."

Jan did not understand President Smith's English, but his eyes had already begun to feel better. When he arrived home, he could not suppress his joy. He tore off his bandages and looked toward the light. "See, Mother," he said. "They are healed. I can see well!"

His mother hurried to him and tested his vision in every way she could imagine. Jan could indeed see just as well as he could before the disease.

"Mama," said Jan, "the president's name is Joseph F. Smith, isn't it?"

"Yes," his mother said. "He is a nephew of the prophet Joseph."

"I shall pray for him always," Jan said. "I know he is a true prophet."[40]

AFTER LEAVING ROTTERDAM, JOSEPH F. Smith and his party traveled east to Germany, where around three thousand Saints lived. The Swiss-German Mission was the fastest-growing mission in the Church. Yet Germany's religious freedom laws did not recognize the Church or protect it from persecution, which was on the rise after scandalous reports of the Smoot hearings reached Europe. Some German ministers, stung by the loss of members from their congregations, worked with the press to turn public opinion against the Saints. The police drove missionaries out of towns and kept Church members from meeting together, administering the sacrament, or using the Book of Mormon or other latter-day scriptures.[41]

After stopping in Berlin to meet with local Church members, missionaries, and a small group of American Latter-day Saints studying music in the city, President Smith and his party traveled south to Switzerland. At a conference in Bern, the prophet counseled the Saints to submit to their local governments and respect the religious beliefs of others. "We do not wish to force our ideas on the people but to explain the truth as we understand it," he said. "We leave it to the individual to accept it or not." He taught that the message of the restored gospel was peace and freedom.

"One of its most glorious effects on people," he said, "is that it frees them from the bands of their own sins, cleanses them from sin, brings them into harmony with heaven, makes them into brothers and sisters under the covenant of the gospel, and teaches them to love their fellow human beings."[42]

President Smith closed his sermon with a prophecy of future days: "The time will yet come—maybe not in my days or even in the next generation—when temples of God that are dedicated to the holy ordinances of the gospel will be established in diverse countries of the earth."

"For this gospel must be spread across the whole world," he declared, "until the knowledge of God covers the earth like the waters cover the great deep."[43]

CHAPTER 9

Struggle and Fight

When Joseph F. Smith returned from Europe in September 1906, Reed Smoot's future as a United States senator was still uncertain. At the general conference five months earlier, Francis Lyman had publicly announced the resignations of apostles John W. Taylor and Matthias Cowley. Joseph Tanner was also released from his leadership positions.[1]

The resignations, along with the recent death of apostle Marriner Merrill, had left three vacancies in the Quorum of the Twelve Apostles, which were filled by George F. Richards, Orson F. Whitney, and David O. McKay.[2]

The announcement of the resignations seemed to have a positive effect on many of Reed's colleagues in the Senate. "From all that I can hear," Reed had reported to

Church leaders, "the senators, generally, have taken the action of the last conference as an evidence of good faith on the part of the Church, and especially of President Joseph F. Smith."[3]

That was not true of the members of the Senate committee assigned to the investigation, however, most of whom remained suspicious of the Church. After closing their investigation, they voted to recommend removing Reed from office.[4]

The full Senate finally considered the matter in February 1907, four years after Reed's election first sparked an outcry. The committee had documented more than three thousand pages of testimony from upward of one hundred witnesses, hostile and friendly. As the senators reviewed this record, they also considered their personal interactions with Reed, who had gained the respect of many in Washington, DC. Theodore Roosevelt, the president of the United States, was his staunch supporter and strongly urged the Senate to vote in his favor. When the senators finally ruled on the matter, they voted to disregard the committee's recommendation and permit Senator Smoot to retain his seat.[5]

Within a few days, Joseph F. Smith wrote to congratulate Reed and thank the senators for their fair-minded decision. He wished others could become better acquainted with the Saints. "If this could be done, the current misunderstanding and widespread misrepresentation of The Church of Jesus Christ of Latter-day Saints," he wrote, "would forever cease."[6]

A few weeks later, President Smith opened the April 1907 general conference with more good news. "The tithes of the people during the year 1906 have surpassed the tithing of any other year," he said. "Today The Church of Jesus Christ of Latter-day Saints owes not a dollar that it cannot pay at once. At last we are in a position that we can pay as we go."

He praised the Saints' faithfulness and commented, "We do not have to borrow any more, and we won't have to if the Latter-day Saints continue to live their religion and observe this law of tithing."[7]

After his sermon, President Smith invited Orson F. Whitney to read a public statement the First Presidency and the Twelve had prepared about Latter-day Saint beliefs and values. The statement responded to many of the charges made against the Church and its members during the Smoot hearings. But it also provided the Saints with an official summary of basic gospel principles and practices. "Our religion is founded on the revelations of God," the declaration affirmed. "The gospel we proclaim is the gospel of Christ, restored to earth."

The statement characterized the Saints as an honest, open-minded, intelligent, and pious people. It also testified of their devotion to home and family, including monogamous marriage. "The typical 'Mormon' home is the temple of the family," it stated. "The 'Mormon' people have bowed in respectful submission to the laws enacted against plural marriage."

The declaration also explained the principles of individual agency, tithing, and priesthood leadership. And it attested to the Saints' patriotism, allegiance to earthly governments, and commitment to the separation of church and state. "We desire to live in peace and confidence with our fellow citizens of all political parties and of all religions," it proclaimed.

The restored gospel sought to uplift society, the declaration stated, not destroy it. "Our religion is interwoven with our lives, it has formed our character, and the truth of its principles is impressed upon our souls," it read.[8]

After Elder Whitney finished reading the declaration, Francis Lyman voiced support for it on behalf of the Quorum of the Twelve Apostles. At the invitation of President Smith, the congregation then voted unanimously to adopt and sustain its message.[9]

ON APRIL 16, 1908, JANE Manning James, one of the earliest Black Latter-day Saints, passed away in her Salt Lake City home. She had come to the Salt Lake Valley with her husband and children in September 1847 as part of the first company of Saints to follow Brigham Young's advance company west.[10] Since then, she had become a well-known presence in the city. She was proud of her eighteen grandchildren and her seven great-grandchildren. She and her brother Isaac went to Church meetings in the Salt Lake Tabernacle and often attended reunions of the Church's "old folks" and pioneers.[11]

Her funeral was held in the Salt Lake City Eighth Ward meetinghouse. The chapel was crowded with Jane's friends, both Black and white, who came to remember her life. The room was filled with flowers to honor Jane's faith and goodness of heart.

Jane's friend Elizabeth Roundy read a short autobiographical sketch that Jane dictated to her a few years earlier. Jane had been born free at a time when slavery was still legal and Black people throughout the world were often treated as social inferiors. Her autobiography told the story of her conversion in the eastern United States, her family's nearly eight-hundred-mile walk to Nauvoo, and her experiences living with and working for the prophet Joseph Smith's family. It also recounted how Emma Smith had twice invited Jane to be adopted into her and Joseph's family.[12]

Near the end of her autobiography, Jane bore a fervent testimony. She had been widowed, had outlived all but two of her children and ten of her grandchildren, and was nearly blind by then, yet she affirmed, "The Lord protects me and takes good care of me in my helpless condition, and I want to say right here that my faith in the gospel of Jesus Christ as taught by The Church of Jesus Christ of Latter-day Saints is as strong today, nay, it is, if possible, stronger than it was the day I was first baptized."[13]

President Joseph F. Smith spoke at the funeral. Over the years, Jane had sometimes sought his help in receiving temple ordinances for herself and her deceased family members. She particularly longed to receive the endowment and be sealed to a family.[14] But since the early 1850s, the Church had restricted Saints of African descent from holding the priesthood or receiving any temple ordinance except baptism for the dead. Explanations for the restriction varied, but they were speculative, not the word of God. Brigham Young had promised that all Saints, regardless of race, would one day receive all the ordinances and blessings of the gospel.[15]

Like other Black Saints, Jane had done baptisms for her kindred dead. She had also asked to be endowed and then be sealed by proxy to Walker Lewis, one of the few Black Saints to hold the priesthood before the restriction took effect. On later occasions, she asked to be sealed by adoption into the family of Joseph Smith. But each time she petitioned for an endowment or sealing, Joseph F. Smith or another Church leader had upheld the Church's restriction.[16]

With the help of Relief Society general president Zina Young, however, Jane had received permission from Church leaders to be joined for eternity with Joseph Smith's family. In response to her request, they had prepared a vicarious ceremony that joined Jane to the family as a servitor. Zina Young had acted as Jane's proxy in the ceremony while Joseph F. Smith stood in for the prophet Joseph Smith.[17]

Although she felt dissatisfied with the ceremony, Jane had continued faithful. "I pay my tithes and offerings, keep the Word of Wisdom," she said. "I go to bed early and rise early. I try in my feeble way to set a good example to all."[18]

In 1902, Jane asked Patriarch John Smith, Joseph F. Smith's older brother, when she would be allowed to receive her endowment. "Be patient and wait a little longer," he had said, assuring her that the Lord had His eye on her. He promised that the Lord "would be far better to her than ever she had dreamed." To the end of her life, she retained a hope that she might one day receive all temple blessings.[19]

Following the funeral, Jane was buried in the Salt Lake City Cemetery. "Few persons were more noted for faith and faithfulness than was Jane Manning James," the *Deseret News* eulogized. "Though of the humble of the earth, she numbered friends and acquaintances by the hundreds."[20]

IN JULY 1909, THE *Salt Lake Tribune* began publishing lists of men who had allegedly entered into new plural marriages since the Manifesto. The lists alarmed the First Presidency and Quorum of the Twelve Apostles. Joseph F. Smith immediately appointed apostles Francis Lyman, John Henry Smith, and Heber J. Grant to investigate the matter and discipline Saints who had violated the Church's policy on plural marriage since the Second Manifesto.[21]

The investigation lasted more than a year and re-sulted in the excommunication of two men who had recently entered into or performed new plural mar-riages. The First Presidency also sent a letter to all stake presidencies, directing them to instruct bishops to dis-cipline violators of the Second Manifesto. "We hold that anyone violating this important rule and action not only commits an individual transgression but dishonors the Church as well," they wrote.[22]

Around this time, *Pearson's,* a popular magazine in the United States, published a series of articles criti-cizing the Church. Drawing on the *Salt Lake Tribune's* lists of new plural marriages, the articles accused the Church of dishonesty and corruption. Joseph F. Smith also learned that another popular magazine, *Everybody's,* planned to run a similar series written by Frank Cannon, son of George Q. Cannon.[23]

Frank was a former senator from Utah and had once been an adviser to the First Presidency. But his hard drink-ing, extramarital affairs, and other wrongdoing had driven a wedge between him and Church leaders. After the death of his father, he became a bitter critic of the Church and Joseph F. Smith, and his former standing among the Saints gave his words the appearance of credibility.[24]

When they learned about Frank's plans, Joseph F. Smith and Anthon Lund wrote immediately to the editor of *Everybody's,* warning him that Frank's writings were false and unworthy of attention. But magazine editors at the time were often eager to print scandalous stories and exposés, and the editor promptly began publishing Frank's articles. Soon, subscriptions to the magazine poured in from across the country.[25]

Frank was not the first former Latter-day Saint to attack the Church publicly. Ezra Booth, John C. Bennett, T. B. H. and Fanny Stenhouse, and William Jarman had all tried to damage the Church with their writing. Still, the popularity of Frank's series was disheartening.

Once again, the Church was facing a crisis of public opinion.[26]

A HANDFUL OF LATTER-DAY Saint students and missionaries from the Swiss-German Mission cheered as Emma Lucy Gates appeared for her second curtain call at Berlin's Royal Opera House. Since first coming to Germany with John and Leah Widtsoe a decade earlier, Lucy had become a rising star in European opera, and it was her first time singing in the famous hall. She did not disappoint her audience.

From the stage, Lucy could feel the faith and support of her fellow Saints, who were tucked away in the top gallery. They called her their "Utah Nightingale." Many of them had been praying for her success that night, and some of them had fasted for her.[27]

The newspapers praised her performance. "The training in her voice leaves nothing to be desired," one reviewer wrote, "and the fine, clear-cut technique showed the real musical art."[28]

While some reviews noted Lucy's imperfect German, none mentioned her home state or religion. Opposition to the Church was still on the rise in Germany and other parts of Europe, so Lucy had kept her membership secret from the Royal Opera House. Most German Saints were harassed in their communities, and missionaries were frequent targets of fines, banishments, arrests, and imprisonments.[29]

Lucy's voice teacher, Madame Blanche Corelli, had urged her to conceal her religion for the sake of her career. Writing home, Lucy told her mother, Susa Gates, that she reluctantly identified as a Protestant at the Royal Opera House. Lucy did not want to hide her faith, but she would not allow someone's prejudice to define her future.[30]

Susa supported her choice, noting that she had spoken to President Smith about it, and he believed it was all right for her to keep her religion private. Her father, Jacob Gates, also gave his support. "You are doing it for a good purpose," he wrote, "and not because you are ashamed of what you know to be true."[31]

In the summer of 1910, German opposition to the Church worsened, leaving Lucy afraid to worship publicly with the Saints in Berlin. Police in the city had recently arrested twenty-one Latter-day Saint missionaries, tourists, and students. When officials released them from jail eighteen hours later, the prisoners were banished from the city as "undesirable foreigners." Only a few students were permitted to remain, provided they did not attend church or preach the gospel.[32]

In September, after missing three weeks of church meetings, Lucy longed to worship with other Saints and partake of the sacrament. She suggested holding small sacrament meetings for the American Saints in Berlin, as she had done with Leah and John in Göttingen. Since all religious meetings had to be officially registered in the city, though, the small group met in secret.

At their meetings, the American Saints partook of the sacrament, sang hymns, and bore testimony. Lucy had brought several Church books with her to Berlin, including the scriptures. So at their second meeting, they studied the Doctrine and Covenants and spent an hour discussing the doctrine of resurrection.

"Now *please* do not publish this around," Lucy cautioned her mother in a letter describing the meetings. The German government monitored the news coming out of Salt Lake City. If an article about their secret meetings appeared in a Utah newspaper and the Berlin police took notice of it, Lucy and her friends would be in serious danger.

"We can be put in jail," she wrote. "So please, all be careful that read this."[33]

IN JANUARY AND FEBRUARY 1911, *McClure's* magazine in New York City published a two-part article on post-Manifesto plural marriage under the title "The Mormon Revival of Polygamy." With the appearance of these articles, three of the most widely circulated magazines in the United States were now publishing attacks on the Church. The articles had an audience of millions.[34]

The *McClure's* article estimated that between 1,500 and 2,000 plural marriages had taken place in the twenty-one years since the Manifesto. The number was actually about 260, but that did not slow the author down. "There seems no immediate likelihood that the practice will die out," he opined. In fact, he believed there were enough young people entering new plural marriages to keep the practice thriving for at least another fifty years.[35]

The article caught the eye of New York City journalist Ike Russell, who had grown up in the Church in Utah. He was a grandson of apostle Parley P. Pratt, and his wife's uncle was the mission president in New York City. Ike had left the faith as a teenager, but he followed news from Utah and had an affection for the Saints.[36]

Ike was irritated that so much in the *McClure's* article was untrue or misleading. One page had pictures of seven apostles who had married plural wives after the Manifesto. Its caption read, "The Church has not excommunicated one of them for violating the revelation." In fact, five of the men had already passed away, and the other two were John W. Taylor and Matthias Cowley, who were no longer in the quorum. The article also failed to mention that all but one of the apostles pictured had since been replaced by monogamists.[37]

Ike wrote to the editor of *McClure's* about the many errors in the article. He also wrote letters to other magazines, but the editors largely ignored him.[38]

He then felt prompted to try something else. One of the articles in *Pearson's* claimed that former U.S. president Theodore Roosevelt had made a deal with Church leaders to secure votes during a recent election. If Ike could get Roosevelt to deny the claim in a letter, he could use it to discredit the article.

Ike sat down and began typing. "I am writing in the hope that you will be so good as to assist me in an effort I am making to have the record made more straight."[39]

MEANWHILE, IN ENGLAND, APOSTLE and European Mission president Rudger Clawson learned that the British government was launching an investigation into Latter-day Saint missionary work. Aware of the German efforts to banish missionaries from their cities, some lawmakers wondered if Britons should do the same. Although a few British journalists argued for religious tolerance of the Saints, many people in the United Kingdom continued to see missionaries as representatives of a foreign church who taught strange ideas and lured British women into plural marriage.[40]

Critics of the Church fed these fears, eroding the good work Latter-day Saint women had done as missionaries to correct misconceptions. Following the example of William Jarman, who was still giving occasional lectures, another former Latter-day Saint from the United States was touring the country with a withering account of his experiences in the Church. Other critics were publishing antagonistic literature and leading opposition against the Saints.[41]

In early 1911, Rudger wrote to British Home Secretary Winston Churchill, promising to cooperate with the government. "In case of any investigation," he noted, "we stand ready and willing to render you whatever assistance we can." Churchill began an inquiry into the Church and its missionary work soon after. "I am treating it in a serious spirit," he told Parliament.[42]

Opposition to the Church in Britain remained steady into the spring. One Sunday in April, a group called the Liverpool Anti-Mormon Crusade started a riot in the town of Birkenhead, where around thirty Saints were meeting in a hall. Spurred on by a crowd, some of the rioters rushed a group of police gathered outside the hall. Others threw stones at its windows.

As the violence escalated, the officers tried arresting those causing trouble, but the rioters fought back. Some in the mob gave the missionaries a letter demanding that they leave Birkenhead within seven days.

"I will give no heed to it," said Richard Young, the presiding missionary at the conference.

"You are willing to take the consequences?" one of the mob asked.

"Yes," he said.[43]

Local newspapers published stories about the riot and the mob's ultimatum, and many people were eager to see what would happen next. Rudger worried that the missionaries would be physically harmed if they remained in the town. But after counseling with Richard and the other missionaries, he agreed they should stay. If the elders abandoned Birkenhead, what would stop mobs from trying to force missionaries out of other towns and villages?[44]

Rudger designated the following Sunday as a day of prayer and fasting for the missionaries. When the day arrived, the elders in Birkenhead gathered for their first public meeting since the riot. The police came and formed a line in front of the hall. A crowd of around five thousand people soon assembled, and members of the mob paraded past the police with a brass band. The crowd cheered the mob, but no violence broke out.

The elders' defiance of the mob impressed some observers. "It seemed to change the tone of newspaper articles concerning us," Rudger reported to the First Presidency. "For the time being at least, the air seems to be cleared of the spirit of abuse and malice towards the Latter-day Saints."[45]

During this time, Winston Churchill continued his investigation into the Church. Across the country, police questioned the families of young women who had joined the Church and emigrated to Utah, and government representatives attended worship services. No one found evidence that the Church or its missionaries were causing harm. Satisfied, Churchill concluded that there was no reason to expel missionaries, and he recommended no legal action against the Saints.[46]

IN UTAH, JOSEPH F. SMITH received a copy of a long letter Theodore Roosevelt had written to Ike Russell, refuting claims that he had struck a deal with the Saints to get Utah's vote. "The accusation is not merely false," Roosevelt informed Ike, "but so ludicrous that it is difficult to discuss it seriously."[47]

Joseph knew Ike wanted to publish the letter in *Collier's,* a magazine with a circulation of about one million readers. Reed Smoot also urged Joseph to do something about the attacks. "Without action," Reed warned, "I doubt whether we can escape an investigation." But so far Joseph had done little to respond to the magazine articles.[48]

Then, in early April 1911, he telegrammed Reed to ask if any eastern newspaper would publish an official response from the Church. Reed contacted the newspapers immediately, but he received no promises. Ike, meanwhile, arranged for Theodore Roosevelt's letter to appear in *Collier's.* Pleased, Joseph had the letter and the Church's response to the magazine articles published as pamphlets and distributed to prominent citizens throughout the United States and Great Britain.[49]

Still, new magazine articles about the Church continued to appear. In March, a fourth magazine, *Cosmopolitan,* had launched a series of three articles comparing the Church to a viper that was poised to strike at hearth and home. Like the other magazines, it claimed the Church still promoted plural marriage.[50]

Around this time, Francis Lyman heard reports that John W. Taylor and Matthias Cowley had recently married new plural wives and performed more plural marriages. He and his committee met with both men individually. John W. was headstrong at his meetings. He had indeed married another plural wife in 1909, yet he refused to admit or deny the fact.[51] For his part, Matthias acknowledged he had done wrong. In the end, the Twelve excommunicated John W. and forbade Matthias from using priesthood authority.[52]

After the former apostles were disciplined, Joseph F. Smith traveled to Washington, DC. While there, he met with a reporter at the home of Reed and Allie Smoot. The reporter asked about politics, Church finances, and other issues normally raised in negative articles about the Church. But most of his questions were about plural marriage. Joseph responded frankly to his questions, eager to correct the misinformation circulating through the magazines.

"Polygamy among the Mormons is now absolutely frowned upon and forbidden by the Church," Joseph declared.

"How could it be shown that polygamy now is absolutely forbidden by the Mormon church?" asked the reporter.

"The best evidence that we seriously and conscientiously are fighting polygamy," Joseph replied, "is shown by the fact that Mr. Taylor, formerly an apostle of the Church and a member of the governing council, has been excommunicated."[53]

The interview appeared in the newspaper a few days later, and it was soon followed by other favorable articles about the Saints. "I hear nothing but good reports from your visit here," Reed told Joseph. "I believe it has done an immense amount of good."[54]

The magazines soon lost interest in publishing critical articles about the Church. Later that summer, Joseph wrote to Ike Russell, reflecting on the recent uproar. "We believe that public opinion will change," he observed. "We have had to struggle and fight our way through from the beginning, and we expect nothing else but opposition of one kind and another until victory shall be won."[55]

PART 2

—◦◆◦—

In the Midst of the Earth

1911–1930

"I believe that the cause of Zion is sacred
in the sight of the Lord,
that His eye is upon His people
and that His power is working in their
midst and in the midst of the earth
for the accomplishment of His purpose."

Joseph F. Smith, October 1916

1911–1930

STOCKHOLM

GLASGOW

COPENHAGEN

LIVERPOOL

LONDON

LIÈGE

PRAGUE

VERDUN

PARIS

Boundaries 1914

SARAJEVO

AINTAB

ALEPPO

EL PASO

COLONIA JUÁREZ

UNITED STATES

COLONIA DUBLÁN

MEXICO

SAN MARCOS

MEXICO CITY

CHAPTER 10

Give Me Strength

In the fall of 1911, Alma Richards returned to Brigham Young University with the goal of going to the 1912 Olympic Games in Stockholm, Sweden. Alma was a twenty-one-year-old high jumper from Parowan, a small town in southern Utah. Before going to BYU the previous year, he had known next to nothing about the Olympics. Then his coach told him he had a shot at competing in the games.

"If you will train consistently for a year and half," he said, "you will make the team."[1]

At first, Alma thought his coach was joking. He was naturally athletic, but he was taller and heavier than most high jumpers. And he did not have much experience or training in the sport. Rather than scissor kicking or rolling his body horizontally over the high jump bar, as most jumpers did, he would launch himself awkwardly into the air, curling up in a ball as he flew.

But he put his coach's words to the test. He trained regularly and began excelling in local athletic competitions. Soon he had become a champion throughout Utah.[2]

Sporting events were becoming popular among young people across the world, and many high schools and colleges in Utah sponsored athletic teams for both boys and girls. Yet, for many years, Mutual Improvement Associations did not include sports in their activities. The Young Men's MIA, in fact, normally centered its meetings on studying religious or academic subjects from a manual, to the disappointment of many young men.[3]

Protestant groups in Salt Lake City, meanwhile, had begun using a popular gymnasium run by the Young Men's Christian Association, or YMCA, to attract young Latter-day Saints to their Sunday schools. Alarmed, Church leaders decided to provide similar opportunities. They began holding sporting competitions during the annual conjoint MIA conferences and encouraged stake and ward leaders to let the youth use meetinghouse amusement halls for "light gymnasium work." In 1910, the year Alma entered BYU, the Church opened the Deseret Gymnasium, a three-story recreational facility one block east of Temple Square.[4]

With Young Ladies' MIA attendance still outpacing the YMMIA's, Church leaders also recognized that the current program was not reaching the young men. The realization came amid efforts to define and clarify the duties of the Church's auxiliaries and priesthood quorums. In 1906, a newly formed "correlation committee," consisting of representatives from the Church's auxiliaries, determined that Aaronic Priesthood meetings were to include doctrinal instruction for the young men. YMMIA meetings, on the other hand, would cultivate the boys' minds and bodies. This meant introducing many of the young men to athletics and outdoor activities.[5]

Eugene Roberts, Alma's coach and the director of physical training at BYU, was a respected advocate for sports in the Church. Like many others in his day, he believed that technology and city living had advanced too quickly in the nineteenth century, cutting young men off from the refining influence of physical activity and the natural world. Idealizing the lives of the Latter-day Saint pioneers, he encouraged young men to emulate their work ethic and religious fervor.

"No one can read of their physical hardships and religious trials without being fired with admiration," he wrote in a 1911 issue of the *Improvement Era.* "The pale, city-bred boy, who has never camped on the desert, nor seen the wilds, who has never tramped over the hills, nor 'roughed' it, cannot truly sympathize with the struggles of his father."[6]

Eugene and YMMIA leaders urged the Church to adopt a program modeled on the newly created Boy Scout movement, which taught young men to develop high moral standards and strengthened them physically and spiritually through camping, hiking, and other outdoor activities. Another advocate of Scouting, YMMIA board member Lyman Martineau, encouraged youth leaders to introduce the boys to physical recreation. "If properly organized and controlled," he declared, "these activities afford wholesome recreation and promote pluck, courage, enthusiasm, spiritual and moral purpose, and temperate habits."[7]

Alma Richards himself was proof of these words. His desire to excel in his sport led him to keep the Word of Wisdom at a time when the principle was encouraged but not strictly required in the Church. In abstaining from alcohol and tobacco, he trusted the Lord's promise that those who followed the Word of Wisdom would "run and not be weary" and "walk and not faint."[8]

In the spring of 1912, Eugene told Alma that he was ready for the Olympic tryouts. "You are one of the fifteen best high jumpers in the world," he said, "and one of the seven best in the United States." To cover Alma's travel to the tryouts, he prevailed on BYU to award the young athlete a generous grant. He wanted to accompany Alma himself but did not have enough money for the trip.

Even before leaving Utah, Alma felt anxious and lonely. Eugene came to see him off with words of encouragement and support. Before Alma boarded the train, Eugene handed him an inspirational poem to give him strength and faith in tough times.[9]

A few weeks later, the news arrived in Utah: Alma had made the Olympic team. He was on his way to Sweden.[10]

IN MID-1912, MORE THAN four thousand Latter-day Saint settlers in northern Mexico found themselves in the middle of a revolution. The previous year, rebel forces had ousted Mexico's longtime president, Porfirio Díaz. But another uprising had since broken out against the rebel victors.[11]

Junius Romney, the thirty-four-year-old stake president in northern Mexico, declared that the Saints would not abandon their homes, despite the conflict. Since taking refuge in Mexico during the antipolygamy raids of the 1880s, the Saints had generally stayed out of Mexican politics. But now many rebels viewed them as foreign invaders and frequently raided their prosperous cattle ranches.[12]

Hoping to weaken the rebels, the United States forbade the sale of weapons and ammunition to Mexico. Senator Reed Smoot, however, persuaded U.S. president William Howard Taft to send additional weapons to the Saints in northern Mexico to help protect their settlements. But rebel leaders soon learned about the shipment and demanded that the Saints surrender their firearms.

Knowing the First Presidency wanted to prevent any harm from befalling the Saints, Junius and other Church leaders in the region negotiated with the rebels to let the Saints keep their firearms for self-defense. The rebel leaders also promised not to disturb the settlements.[13]

On July 27, however, a rebel general named José Inés Salazar summoned Junius to his headquarters along with Henry Bowman, a local Church leader and businessman. He told Junius and Henry that he could no longer keep rebel forces from attacking the Saints. Alarmed, Junius reminded the general that he had given both verbal and written assurances that the rebels would not harm the settlements.

"Those are mere words," the general said, "and the wind blows words away." He then informed Junius and Henry that the colonies would have to surrender their weapons.

"We do not feel justified in giving up our arms," Junius said. There were some two thousand rebels in the area with five or six cannons they could use against the colonies. If the Saints gave up their weapons, they would be defenseless.[14]

The general was unmoved, so Junius explained that he had no authority to order the Saints to surrender their private property. Hearing this, General Salazar stepped out of the room to discuss the matter with one of his officers, Colonel Demetrio Ponce.

Once they were alone, Henry said, "Brother Romney, I feel it is unwise to anger the general." He could see that Junius was fuming, and he did not want the conflict to escalate.

"My mind is made up," Junius said. "When Salazar comes back, I am going to tell him what I think of him if it is the last act of my life!"

Soon General Salazar returned to the room with Colonel Ponce. "Evidently the general has not succeeded in making clear what he wished to convey," the colonel said, rubbing his palms together. "What the general wishes you to do is simply to suggest such action to them and they will do it!"

"I will not make any such suggestion," Junius said. He knew the Saints would feel betrayed if he asked them to surrender their only means of defense.

"Unless your guns and ammunition are delivered here to me by 10 a.m. tomorrow," General Salazar warned, "we will march against you."

"Is that your ultimatum?" Junius asked.

"That is my ultimatum!" the general said. "I will come and get the guns no matter where I have to go for them."

Junius was shocked that the general was willing to attack the settlements without restraint. "You would invade our homes and take our guns by force?" he said.

"We will consider you as our enemies," General Salazar said, "and will declare war on you immediately."[15]

THAT NIGHT IN COLONIA Juárez, one of the larger Latter-day Saint settlement in northern Mexico, seventeen-year-old Camilla Eyring listened as her father described the danger looming over her family.

The rebels were seizing the Saints' weapons and leaving them defenseless, he said, so Church leaders had decided to evacuate the women, children, and elderly from the settlements. They would journey 150 miles to

El Paso, Texas, just north of the United States border. The men would stay to protect the houses and livestock.[16]

Colonia Juárez was the only home Camilla had ever known. Three generations of her family had lived in the colonies in Mexico after her grandfathers moved there to escape prosecution for practicing plural marriage. Since that time, Colonia Juárez had blossomed into a community of dozens of Latter-day Saint families, with beautiful apple orchards and fine brick buildings.

Camilla was the oldest of eleven children. Her father, the husband of two wives, operated a large cattle ranch where she sometimes helped make cheese. He employed native Mexicans, whose families she had come to love. She attended school with her friends at the large Juárez Academy schoolhouse, where she learned both English and Spanish. On warm days she would put on one of her old dresses and head with her friends to a swimming hole made by the Piedras Verdes River. Now, as she prepared to leave her home, she was uncertain when—or if—she would return.[17]

Each family member packed only what could be carried in a single shared trunk. The rest they had to hide from the rebels. Camilla stowed her school papers and other keepsakes in hard-to-find places in the house. Her father, meanwhile, pried up the floorboards of the front porch and concealed one hundred quarts of blackberries, which Camilla and her siblings had helped their mother bottle earlier that day. The family's precious silver, linens, and dishes went into the attic.[18]

The next morning, July 28, the family loaded their trunk onto a buggy and rode ten miles to the nearest train depot. Dozens of other families waited outside the station, their arms laden with bundles and suitcases. Nearby, a group of rebels on horseback lined up in formation, their guns and bayonets drawn.

When the train arrived, the Saints packed themselves into the cars. A railroad company had sent every available train car to help with the evacuation. Some cars were windowless boxcars or dingy cattle cars. Camilla, her mother, and her siblings were placed in a car for third-class passengers. Clutching their bundles and bedding, they huddled together on hard benches. It was a hot summer day, and flies buzzed around them. Camilla felt like a sardine in a can.[19]

The train soon left the depot and headed north to Colonia Dublán, the largest settlement of Saints in the area, to take on more passengers. Once the Dublán Saints boarded the train, the passengers numbered around a thousand. Baggage was piled high throughout the cars.

The train traveled northeast all day and all night. Some of the railroad track had been damaged during the revolution, forcing the train to travel at a crawl. Camilla was terrified that rebels would hold up the train and rob the passengers.

The train arrived safely in El Paso just as the sun was rising. At the train depot, residents of the city met the Saints with cars and trucks and transported them across town to a vacant lumberyard set aside for the refugees. Camilla and her family were brought to a large, dusty corral with several stalls where families could set up camp. Camilla's family piled into one stall and hung blankets up for privacy. A nauseating stench hung over the place. Swarms of flies were everywhere.

People from the settlements continued to arrive at the lumberyard throughout the day, and reporters and photographers came to interview them and take pictures. Locals also came to the yard from town. Some offered help, while others peeked into the campsites to get a look at the Saints.

Camilla was embarrassed. "We're just monkeys in a cage," she thought.[20]

ALMA RICHARDS'S EYES HURT as he peered at the high jump bar. It was the third day of the 1912 Olympics. The sun over Stockholm's new brown-brick stadium was unbearably bright, irritating an eye infection that had plagued Alma for weeks. When he was not jumping, he wore an old, droopy hat to shade his eyes. But now that his turn had come again, he stepped to the side of the field and tossed his hat into the grass.[21]

The running high jump competition had begun with nearly sixty athletes from dozens of nations. Only he and a German jumper named Hans Liesche remained. Hans was the best jumper Alma had ever seen. He had performed effortlessly, clearing each of his jumps on the first try. Alma, on the other hand, had struggled to clear the bar all day. Now the bar was set at nearly six feet, four inches, higher than anyone had ever jumped in Olympic competition. No one, not even Alma's teammates, expected him to clear the bar.[22]

As Alma prepared to jump, his mind raced. There he was, representing his country at the greatest athletic competition in the world. Yet he felt weak, as if the whole world were resting on his shoulders. He thought of Utah, his family, and his hometown. He thought of BYU and the Saints. Bowing his head, he silently asked God to give him strength. "If it is right that I should win," he prayed, "I will do my best to set a good example all the days of my life."[23]

Raising his head, he felt his weakness slip away. He threw his shoulders back, walked up to the starting line, and crouched into position. He then skipped forward in a burst of energy and leapt into the air, tucking his knees beneath his chin. His body barreled forward and sailed over the bar with inches to spare.

On the sidelines, Hans Liesche suddenly looked nervous as he warmed up for his jump. Alma ran in circles to keep his legs limber. If Hans cleared the bar, as Alma was sure he would, the bar would be raised even higher, and Alma would have to jump again.

When Hans launched into his first jump, he fell on the bar and sent it crashing to the ground. Frustrated, he returned to the field and made a second jump. Once again, he knocked the bar off its pegs.

Alma could see that his competitor was losing composure. Just as Hans squared up for his final attempt, a pistol fired nearby, signaling the start of a race. Hans waited for the runners to cross the finish line and then prepared to jump. Before he could, though, a band began playing, and he refused to start. Finally, after nine minutes, an official prodded him to hurry along. With nothing left to do but jump, Hans bounded forward and threw himself into the air.

Once again, he failed to clear the bar.[24]

Joy washed over Alma. The competition was over. He had won the gold medal and set an Olympic record. Hans came over and heartily congratulated him. Others soon joined in the praise. "You have put Utah on the map," one man said.

James Sullivan, an official on the American Olympic team, was especially impressed with Alma's coolness under pressure and wholesome lifestyle. "I wish we had a hundred clean fellows like you on our team," he said.[25]

Within days, newspapers across the United States praised Alma's victory, crediting his success in part to his religion. "They call the winner of the great jump 'the Mormon giant,' and he deserves the title," one reporter wrote. "He is a self-made athlete, and his winning of world renown comes after years of endeavor and a determination inherited from the men who established the Mormon religion and made the desert blossom."[26]

One of Alma's friends, meanwhile, teased him about praying before his winning jump. "I wish you wouldn't laugh," Alma quietly responded. "I prayed to the Lord to give me strength to go over that bar, and I went over."[27]

ON AUGUST 15, 1912, SISTERS Jovita and Lupe Monroy tended their family store in San Marcos, Hidalgo, Mexico. The small town was nestled in the heart of the country, far from the revolutionary violence in the north. That day, two young, well-dressed American men entered the store, ordered a soda, and politely asked the sisters if they knew where Señor Jesús Sánchez lived.

The sisters knew the old man well, and they gave the visitors directions to his house. Since Señor Sánchez was not a Catholic, some people in town were wary of him. But he was friends with Rafael, Jovita and Lupe's older brother.

Later, when the sisters had a chance to speak with Señor Sánchez, they asked him who the young men were.

"They are missionaries," he replied. Some thirty years earlier, he had joined The Church of Jesus Christ of Latter-day Saints. But the Church's mission in central Mexico had not taken root, despite its promising start, and had closed less than a decade after his baptism. The mission had since reopened, and over sixteen hundred Mexican Saints now lived in the region. Missionaries were traveling the countryside searching for longtime Church members like him.[28]

"When the missionaries come again," the sisters told Señor Sánchez, "bring them to our house so we can ask them questions."

A few months later, Señor Sánchez came to the store and introduced Jovita and Lupe to two missionaries, Walter Ernest Young and Seth Sirrine. As Catholics, the sisters had many questions about how the elders' beliefs differed from theirs. They especially wanted to know why the missionaries did not believe in infant baptism. Señor Sánchez let the sisters borrow his Bible so they could read more about the principles the missionaries taught. Afterward, whenever Jovita and Lupe could spare a minute, they would study its pages.[29]

In March 1913, Señor Sánchez fell ill. The Monroy sisters helped his family attend to him. As his condition worsened, Jovita and Lupe sent for the missionaries to give him a blessing, but they were laboring in another town and could not come immediately. By the time they arrived, Señor Sánchez had died. The elders held a funeral service for him and preached a sermon on resurrection. About a dozen people attended the service, including Jovita and Lupe's widowed mother, Jesusita Mera de Monroy, who invited the missionaries to have dinner with the family that evening.

Jesusita was not happy that her daughters had continued speaking with the missionaries, especially after Jovita and Lupe had stopped attending Mass. At night, she would ask God to stop the missionaries from coming to San Marcos so they would not lead her daughters astray. But at dinner, she treated the missionaries kindly. Before they ate, one of the missionaries asked if he could offer the blessing. Jesusita agreed, and she was moved by his prayer. After the meal, the elders sang the hymn "O My Father," which moved her even more.[30]

Two months later, Lupe took her older brother and sister, Rafael and Natalia, to a conference of Saints near Mexico City, where the Church was more established. About a hundred people attended the conference.

The siblings heard talks on peace and brotherhood, the Holy Ghost, apostasy, and the Restoration. They also met the mission president, Rey L. Pratt, who had grown up in the Latter-day Saint settlements in northern Mexico. The conference impressed the Monroys. Before returning to San Marcos, Rafael had a dream that he was preaching everything he had learned at the meeting.

A few weeks after the conference, President Pratt and Elder Young visited the Monroys in San Marcos. They spent a day with the family, relaxing at their home and listening to the sisters play music. In the evening, Elder Young preached about baptism, and President Pratt spoke about the first principles and ordinances of the gospel.

The next day, June 11, 1913, Jovita, Lupe, and Rafael agreed to be baptized. To avoid drawing the attention of suspicious neighbors, the siblings led President Pratt and Elder Young to a secluded grove along a nearby river. There they found a shoulder-deep spot in the river where they could perform the ordinance.

After the baptisms, President Pratt and Elder Young confirmed the siblings by the water's edge. President Pratt took pictures of the group with Elder Young, and everyone returned to town for dinner.

It was a happy day.[31]

CHAPTER 11

Too Heavy

On the evening of August 6, 1914, Arthur Horbach, a seventeen-year-old Latter-day Saint in Liège, Belgium, took cover as German artillery rained down on his city.[1] Earlier that summer, a Serbian nationalist had assassinated the heir to Europe's Austro-Hungarian Empire, provoking war between Austria-Hungary and the Kingdom of Serbia. Soon allies of both nations joined in the fight. By early August, Serbia, Russia, France, Belgium, and Great Britain were at war with Austria-Hungary and Germany.[2]

Belgium, originally a neutral nation, entered the conflict when German troops launched an invasion of France through Belgium's eastern border. The city of Liège posed the first significant obstacle for the invading army. Twelve forts surrounded the city, and at first they had kept the Germans at bay. But the assault was unrelenting. Thousands of troops assailed the forts, and the Belgian defenses began to crumble.

German troops soon breached the Belgian line and captured Liège. Attackers swept through the city, looting homes, burning buildings, and shooting civilians.[3] Arthur and his mother, Mathilde, somehow evaded the troops. The fifty or so other Saints in Liège were all in danger, just like Arthur, but it was the missionaries serving in the city that kept coming to his mind. He spent much of his time with the missionaries and knew them well. Had they been hurt in the attack?[4]

Days passed. Arthur and his mother lived in terror of the German troops and the heavy artillery bombarding the uncaptured forts. Latter-day Saints were scattered throughout the city, with several branch members huddled together in a cellar. A group of soldiers had moved into the rented hall where the branch normally met. Fortunately, Tonia Deguée, an elderly member of the Church who spoke fluent German, quickly gained the trust of the invading soldiers and persuaded them not to damage the hall or its furniture.[5]

Eventually, Arthur learned that the elders were safe. The American consulate in Liège had ordered them to evacuate the city on the first day of the bombing, but road blockades had kept them from getting word of their removal to Arthur or anyone else.[6]

Missionaries across continental Europe, in fact, were leaving their fields of labor. "Release all German and

French missionaries," President Joseph F. Smith had cabled European mission leaders, "and exercise due discretion about transferring all missionaries from neutral as well as belligerent countries to United States missions."[7]

Arthur felt the loss of the missionaries immediately. In the six years since he and Mathilde joined the Church, their branch had depended on missionaries for priesthood leadership. Now the only priesthood holders in the branch were a teacher and two deacons—one of whom was Arthur himself. He had received the Aaronic Priesthood less than a year earlier.[8]

After Liège fell into German hands, the branch all but stopped meeting together. The soldiers who occupied their meeting hall moved on, but the landlord refused to let the branch meet there. Every day was a struggle for survival. Food and everyday supplies became scarce. Hunger and misery pervaded the city.

Arthur knew that everyone in the branch longed to gather for prayer and comfort. But without a meetinghouse and someone authorized to bless the sacrament, how could they resume functioning as a branch?[9]

AS WAR SPREAD THROUGH Europe, Ida Smith wondered how she could help the British soldiers leaving for the battlefield. She and her husband, apostle Hyrum M. Smith, had moved to Liverpool with their four children about a year earlier. Hyrum, the oldest son of Joseph F. Smith, was serving as president of the European Mission.

Ida supported the work, but she had decided not to take an active part in missionary labor—or any service outside their small branch of the Church—while she still had young children at home.[10]

One afternoon, though, Ida saw a notice written by Liverpool's lady mayoress, Winifred Rathbone, calling on women's organizations in the city to join other female volunteers throughout Great Britain in knitting warm clothes for soldiers. Ida knew that hundreds of thousands of British soldiers, including some Latter-day Saints, would desperately need the clothes to survive the coming winter. But she felt useless.

"What can I do to assist this woman?" she asked herself. "I have never knit a stitch in my life."[11]

A voice then seemed to speak to her: "Now is the time for the Relief Societies of the European Mission to step to the front and offer their services." The words impressed Ida deeply. Liverpool's Relief Society was small—eight active members, at most—but the women could do their part.[12]

With the help of the mission secretary, Ida arranged to meet with Winifred the next day. Her heart raced prior to the meeting. "Why do you go to the lady mayoress and offer your services with a handful of women?" she scolded herself. "Why don't you go home and mind your own business?"

But Ida swept the thought away. The Lord was with her. In her hand she carried a tiny card printed with information about the Relief Society and its purpose.

"If I can just hand her this card," she told herself, "I am going."[13]

The lady mayoress's office was in a large building that served as the headquarters for her charity work. Winifred received Ida graciously, and Ida's nervousness quickly subsided as she told the lady mayoress about the Relief Society, the Church, and the small Liverpool Branch. "I have come to offer our services in helping to sew or knit for the soldiers," she explained.[14]

Having delivered her message, Ida was about to leave, but Winifred stopped her. "I would like you to go through our building," she said, "and see how our work is carried on." She led Ida through seventeen large rooms, each filled with a dozen or so women hard at work. She then brought Ida into her private office. "This is the way we keep our records," she said, showing her a ledger. "Everything you do for us will be recorded in this book as work being done by the Relief Society of The Church of Jesus Christ of Latter-day Saints."

Ida thanked her. "We will do the best that we can," she said.[15]

That fall, the Relief Society in Liverpool knitted. They also recruited their friends and neighbors to help. After a week, they numbered around forty knitters. Ida herself learned to knit and began work on several large mufflers. At the request of the Relief Society general presidency in Salt Lake City, Ida's husband set her apart as the president of the Relief Societies in the European Mission. With continental Europe unsafe for travel, she began traveling throughout Britain to organize new Relief Societies, train their members, and recruit them to knit for the soldiers. Ultimately, the women created and distributed some twenty-three hundred handmade articles of clothing.[16]

Ida and other Relief Society members received letters and commendations from important officials all over Great Britain. "If all the women's organizations in Great Britain would work like the Latter-day Saint women are doing," one woman wrote, "our soldiers would want for nothing."[17]

"THE REPORTS OF THE carnage and destruction going on in Europe are sickening and deplorable," President Joseph F. Smith wrote Hyrum M. Smith on November 7, 1914. Two months earlier, French and British troops had stopped the advance of German forces in a bloody battle at the Marne River in northeastern France. More battles had followed, but neither side had succeeded in striking a decisive blow. Now the armies were hunkered down in a spider's web of defensive trenches across the French countryside.[18]

The war was spreading throughout eastern Europe, into Africa and the Middle East, and as far away as the islands in the Pacific Ocean. Newspaper accounts of the conflict brought to President Smith's mind the Lord's 1832 revelation on war. "Then war shall be poured out upon all nations," it foretold. "And thus, with the sword and by bloodshed the inhabitants of the earth shall mourn."[19]

On Sunday, January 24, 1915, the prophet called on Church members in the United States and Canada to contribute to a relief fund for needy European Saints. "This is the most direct manner of reaching those members of the Church who are in need of help," he declared.[20] In response, more than seven hundred wards and branches collected money and sent donations to the office of the Presiding Bishopric of the Church. The money was then sent to the mission office in Liverpool for Hyrum to distribute among the European Saints, regardless of which side they supported in the war.[21]

A few months later, President Smith traveled with presiding bishop Charles W. Nibley to inspect a more peaceful corner of the world: the Church's six-thousand-acre farm in Laie, Hawaii.[22] In Honolulu, the two men met up with apostle and United States senator Reed Smoot, who had come to the islands with his wife, Allie, to improve her health and visit the Hawaiian legislature. Along with Abraham and Minerva Fernandez, who had hosted George Q. Cannon during his final visit to the islands, they traveled to Laie and enjoyed a celebratory feast with four hundred Saints.[23]

Over the next few days, as President Smith visited with Church members and toured the farm, he was pleased to see the Hawaiian Saints thriving spiritually and temporally. Nearly ten thousand Saints now lived on the islands. The Doctrine and Covenants and the Pearl of Great Price had recently been published in Hawaiian. More than fifty Latter-day Saint meetinghouses dotted the islands, and Laie itself had a Church-owned school. The Saints in Laie had also beautified their yards and streets with flowers and sturdy trees.[24]

The Church was expanding in other parts of Oceania as well. The Book of Mormon and other Church materials were now available in Māori, Samoan, and Tahitian. The Tahiti Mission had a printing press and published its own Church periodical in Tahitian, *Te Heheuraa Api.*[25] In Tonga, the Church was once again taking root after being closed to missionary work for more than ten years. Saints in Australia, Samoa, and New Zealand worshipped in strong branches with Relief Societies, Sunday Schools, and choirs. In 1913, the Church also opened the Māori Agricultural College in Hastings, New Zealand. The school trained young men in farming and other vocations.[26]

On June 1, their last evening in Laie, President Smith walked with Bishop Nibley and Elder Smoot to a meetinghouse at the top of a low hill overlooking the town. The meetinghouse had stood there since 1883. Its name, *I Hemolele,* meant "Holiness to the Lord," the same biblical phrase that appeared on the exterior of the Salt Lake Temple.[27]

Just outside the building, President Smith mentioned to Elder Smoot that he and Bishop Nibley had been discussing the possibility of building an endowment house or a small temple in Laie, since the Church in Hawaii was on strong footing. He suggested moving *I Hemolele* to another location so a temple could be built on the site.[28]

Elder Smoot favored the idea. Earlier that week, after attending the funeral of an elderly Saint who had received his endowment years ago in Utah, he'd had a similar thought. For most of its history, the Church had built temples near large populations of Saints. But in 1913, President Smith had dedicated a site for a temple in Cardston, Alberta, Canada, where there were now two stakes. It was the first time plans had been laid to build a temple for Saints who lived far from the main body of the Church.[29]

"Brethren," President Smith said to his companions, "I feel impressed to dedicate this ground for the erection of a temple to God, for a place where the peoples of the Pacific Isles can come and do their temple work." He acknowledged that he had not consulted the Quorum of the Twelve Apostles or the other members of the First Presidency on the matter. "But if you think there would be no objection to it," he said, "I think now is the time to dedicate the ground."

Elder Smoot and Bishop Nibley were enthusiastic about the idea, so the prophet offered the dedicatory prayer on the spot.[30]

BY THE SUMMER OF 1915, the Mexican Revolution no longer posed much of a threat to the Church's colonies in northern Mexico. Many families had returned to their homes in the colonies and were living in relative peace. Meanwhile, some of the colonists, including Camilla Eyring and her family, chose to remain in the United States.[31]

But conditions were different in San Marcos, where Rafael Monroy now served as the president of a branch of around forty Saints. On July 17, a group of rebel troops overran the village, set up headquarters in a large house at the center of town, and demanded that Rafael, a prosperous rancher, provide them with beef.[32]

Hoping to appease the troops, Rafael gave them a cow to slaughter. The rebels were Zapatistas, or followers of Emiliano Zapata, one of several rebel leaders vying for control of Mexico's government. For months, the Zapatistas had been battling the forces of Venustiano Carranza, or the Carrancistas, in the area around San Marcos. Following the counsel of mission president Rey L. Pratt, Rafael and his fellow Saints had tried to stay out of the fight, hopeful the armies would leave them in peace. Until the rebels arrived, San Marcos had been a haven for Saints displaced by the violence in central Mexico.[33]

Among the Saints in San Marcos were Rafael's mother, Jesusita, and wife, Guadalupe, who had both been baptized in July 1913. President Pratt, who had left for the United States, continued to assist the branch from afar.[34]

After Rafael delivered the cow, some of his neighbors began talking to the rebels. One neighbor, Andres

Reyes, was unhappy about the growing number of
Saints in the area. Many Mexicans opposed foreign
influences in their country, and Andres and others in
town resented the Monroys for leaving their Catholic
faith to join a church widely associated with the United
States. The fact that the oldest Monroy sister, Natalia,
had married an American only made the town more
suspicious of the family.[35]

Hearing this, the soldiers followed Rafael back to
his house and arrested him just as he was sitting down
for breakfast. They ordered him to open the family store,
claiming that he and his American brother-in-law were
colonels in the Carrancista army who were hiding weapons to use against the Zapatistas.

At the store, Rafael and the troops found Vicente
Morales, another Church member, doing odd jobs.
Believing he was also a Carrancista soldier, the troops
arrested him and began ransacking the store as they
searched for weapons. Rafael and Vicente pleaded
their innocence, assuring the troops that they were
not the enemy.

The soldiers did not believe them. "If you do not
give us your weapons," they said, "we will hang you
from the highest tree."[36]

WHEN THE ZAPATISTAS FORCED Rafael out of the
house, his sisters Jovita and Lupe ran after them. Jovita
reached the soldiers first, but they ignored her entreaties.

Lupe arrived just in time to see the rebels seize her sister. "Lupe," Jovita cried, "they are arresting me!"

By now, a crowd had formed around Rafael and Vicente. Some people were holding ropes in their hands and shouting, "Hang them!"

"What are you going to do? My brother is innocent," Lupe said. "Tear down the house if you need to, and you won't find any weapons."

Someone in the crowd called out to arrest her too. Lupe dashed to a nearby tree and clung to it as tightly as she could, but the rebel soldiers grabbed her and easily tore her away.[37] They then returned to the Monroy house and arrested Natalia.

The rebels took all three sisters to their headquarters and held them in separate rooms. Outside, some people told the soldiers that Rafael and Vicente were "Mormons" who were corrupting the town with their strange religion. The soldiers had never heard the word before, but they took it to mean something bad. They brought the two men to a tall tree and slung ropes over its strong limbs. Then they placed nooses around their necks. If Rafael and Vicente would abandon their religion and join the Zapatistas, the soldiers said, they would be freed.

"My religion is dearer to me than my life," Rafael said, "and I cannot forsake it."

The soldiers pulled the ropes until Rafael and Vicente dangled from their necks and passed out. The rebels then released the ropes, revived the men, and continued to torture them.[38]

Back at the store, the rebels kept up their search for weapons. Jesusita and Guadalupe insisted there were no weapons. "My son is a peaceful man!" Jesusita said. "If it weren't so, do you think that you would have found him in his home?" When the soldiers again demanded to see the family's weapons, the Monroys held out copies of the Book of Mormon and Bible.

"Those aren't weapons," the rebels said.

In the afternoon, at the Zapatista headquarters, the rebels put the Monroy siblings together in the same room. Lupe was shocked at Rafael's appearance. "Rafa, you have blood on your neck," she told him. Rafael walked to a sink in the room and washed his face. He looked calm and did not seem angry, despite everything that had happened.

Later, Jesusita brought her children food. Before she left, Rafael handed her a letter he had written to a Zapatista captain he knew, seeking his help to prove his innocence. Jesusita took the letter and went looking for the captain. The Monroys and Vicente then blessed their meal, but before they could eat, they heard the clatter of footsteps and weapons outside the door. The soldiers called for Rafael and Vicente, and the two men exited the room. At the door, Rafael asked Natalia to come out with him, but the guards pushed her back inside.

The sisters looked at one another, their hearts pounding. Silence settled over them. Then gunshots split the night.[39]

HYRUM M. SMITH FELT AN incredible weight on his shoulders as he contemplated the situation in Europe. As European Mission president, he had promptly followed the First Presidency's directive and pulled missionaries out of Germany and France soon after the war began. But he had been unsure what to do with missionaries in neutral countries or areas without fierce fighting, like Great Britain. The First Presidency had given him few instructions on how to proceed. "We leave the question for you to decide," they had written.[40]

Hyrum had met twice with the elders in the mission office to discuss the right course of action. After some discussion, they had agreed to release only missionaries in continental Europe, leaving the missionaries in Great Britain to finish their missions as planned. Hyrum had then written to mission presidents on the continent, instructing them and their assistants to remain at their posts to maintain the Church in their areas. The rest of the missionaries were to evacuate.[41]

Now, one year later, newspapers were filled with stories about the Germans attacking British naval and passenger ships. In May 1915, a German submarine torpedoed the *Lusitania,* a British ocean liner, killing nearly twelve hundred civilians and crew. Three months later, the Germans sank another British ocean liner, the *Arabic,* off the coast of Ireland. On board the ship was a returning missionary who nearly died in the attack.

As the man responsible for arranging passage for missionaries and emigrating Saints crossing the Atlantic, Hyrum struggled to know how best to respond to the crisis.[42] Many of the American missionaries in Britain were so eager to return home that they were willing to take any risk to get there. Emigrating Saints, likewise, often put their desire to gather to Utah ahead of their personal safety.

To complicate matters, the Church had contracted with a British shipping company to handle all Church-related travel across the Atlantic. Unable to see an honest way out of the contract, Hyrum believed the mission office could not legally book passage for Saints on American ships, even though they were deemed safer because the United States was not at war with Germany.

On August 20, 1915, he wrote to the First Presidency about the dilemma. He had already booked passage for several missionaries and emigrating Saints on the *Scandinavian,* a British-Canadian ship departing Liverpool on September 17. But now he questioned if he should let them go.

"To bear the responsibility alone is almost too heavy for my shoulders," he wrote. "I most humbly plead that you will counsel me upon this matter, so that I may feel that I am acting entirely in harmony with your wishes."[43]

A week before the *Scandinavian* was scheduled to leave, Hyrum received a cable from the First Presidency:

"Emigrants coming in belligerent ships must assume personal responsibility." If Saints chose to travel under a British flag, then they did so at their own risk.[44]

Hyrum weighed his options carefully. The First Presidency clearly did not want to encourage Saints to travel on ships that could be attacked. Yet the safer American ships were not available to Saints unless they chose to travel independently of the Church. And even if they did so, the high price of passage on an American ship might prohibit them from making the voyage.

"I feel loath to risk our Saints on the ocean," he wrote in his journal. But he knew he had to do something. "Inasmuch as we are not instructed *not* to proceed," he wrote, "we will go on with it and trust in the Lord."[45]

On September 17, 1915, Hyrum said farewell to four missionaries and thirty-seven emigrants on the *Scandinavian*.[46] Then all he could do was wait for word of its safe arrival at its destination.

CHAPTER 12

This Terrible War

The *Scandinavian* and its passengers arrived safely in Montreal in late September 1915. Hyrum M. Smith then suspended Atlantic crossings for Church members while he and the First Presidency determined the safest way to transport missionaries and emigrants. After the German government agreed to stop attacking British ocean liners, Hyrum resumed sending Saints on British ships until the spring of 1916, when he felt impressed to place Saints only on ships from neutral nations.

"The risk of their traveling on belligerent ships is too great," he wrote in his journal, "and I cannot afford to longer carry the responsibility of taking such risks."[1]

In Liège, Belgium, meanwhile, Arthur Horbach and his fellow Saints labored to keep their small branch together. Chaos had enveloped Belgium as German troops stormed the country. They killed civilians, tormented prisoners, pillaged and burned homes and towns, and punished all forms of resistance. Night and day, drunken soldiers terrorized the cities. No one was safe from violence.

For the first ten months of the German occupation, the Liège Branch hardly dared to meet for worship. But in the spring of 1915, after months of lying low, Arthur and the branch's two other priesthood holders, Hubert Huysecom and Charles Devignez, decided to try holding regular meetings again.

Marie Momont, an older woman in the branch, opened her home to the Saints. After a few weeks, the meetings moved to the home of Hubert and his wife, Augustine. Their house was larger and situated halfway between Liège and its neighbor Seraing, making it an ideal gathering place for Saints from both cities. As a teacher in the Aaronic Priesthood, Hubert held the highest priesthood office in the city, and he took charge of the branch. He also served as president of the Sunday School.[2]

Arthur was appointed branch secretary and treasurer, making him responsible for maintaining the records and accounts. He and a Church member from Seraing also assisted Charles Devignez in teaching Sunday School classes. Three women in the branch, Juliette Jeuris-Belleflamme, Jeanne Roubinet, and Guillemine Collard, oversaw the Primary. The branch also started a small library.

Soon the Liège members made contact with a Latter-day Saint elder and priest living in Villers-le-Bouillet, a little town over twenty miles away. The two men visited the branch once a month, giving the Liège Saints a chance to partake of the sacrament and receive priesthood blessings.

Suffering hunger, misery, and privation, some Saints in Liège grew discouraged and lashed out against others in the branch. Then, that summer, the European Mission office began sending funds to relieve the poor and needy. Despite the hardships, most Saints in the branch paid their tithing, and as the dark days persisted, they leaned on the restored gospel, the Spirit of the Lord, and one another.

They also continued to share the gospel with their neighbors, some of whom were baptized amid the chaos. Still, the branch missed the stability they had enjoyed before the invasion.[3]

"During this terrible war we have seen the power of the Almighty manifested many times," Arthur reported. "The branches are in good condition, but we long for the return of the missionaries."[4]

ON APRIL 6, 1916, THE first day of the Church's annual general conference in Salt Lake City, President Charles W. Penrose spoke about the Godhead. He and the other members of the First Presidency often received letters about doctrinal disputes among Church members, most of which were easily resolved. But lately the presidency had become troubled by questions about the identity of God the Father.

"There still remains," President Penrose noted in his talk, "an idea among some of the people that Adam was and is the Almighty and Eternal God."[5]

Such a belief stemmed from some statements Brigham Young had made during the nineteenth century.[6] Critics of the Church, in fact, had seized on President Young's statements to claim that Latter-day Saints worshipped Adam.[7]

Recently, the First Presidency had tried to clarify the doctrine about the Godhead, Adam, and the origins of humankind. In 1909, they published a statement drafted by apostle Orson F. Whitney on "The Origin of Man," which affirmed truths about the relationship between God and His children. "All men and women," they declared, "are in the similitude of the universal Father and Mother, and are literally the sons and daughters of Deity." It also stated that Adam was a "preexistent spirit" before receiving a mortal body on earth and becoming the first man and the "great progenitor" of the human family.[8]

They had likewise commissioned Church leaders and scholars to publish new doctrinal books for use in Sunday School classes and priesthood quorum meetings. Two of these works, John Widtsoe's *Rational Theology* and apostle James E. Talmage's *Jesus the Christ,* presented the Church's official teachings on God the Father, Jesus Christ, and Adam. Both books clearly distinguished

God the Father from Adam while also emphasizing how the Atonement of Jesus Christ overcame the negative effects of Adam's Fall.[9]

Now, as President Penrose addressed the Saints in general conference, he identified several verses of ancient and modern-day scripture to show that God the Father and Adam were not the same being. "God help us to see and understand the truth and to avoid error!" he implored at the conclusion of his words. "And don't let us be too strong in our feelings in regard to our opinions of matters. Let us try to be right."[10]

Shortly after the conference, the First Presidency and the Quorum of the Twelve Apostles agreed that the Saints needed a definitive statement on Deity. That summer, Elder Talmage helped them draft "The Father and the Son," a doctrinal exposition on the nature, mission, and relationship of God the Father and Jesus Christ.[11]

In the statement, they testified that God the Father was Elohim, the spirit parent of all humanity. They declared that Jesus Christ was Jehovah, the firstborn of the Father and the elder brother of all women and men. Since He had carried out His Father's plan for Creation, Jesus was also the Father of heaven and earth. For this reason, the scriptures often referred to Him by the title of Father to describe His unique relationship to the world and its people.

The First Presidency also explained how Jesus was a spiritual father to those who were born again through His gospel. "If it be proper to speak of those who accept and abide in the gospel as Christ's sons and daughters," they declared, "it is consistently proper to speak of Jesus Christ as the Father of the righteous."

Finally, they articulated how Jesus Christ acted on behalf of the Father in serving as a representative of Elohim. "So far as power, authority, and Godship are concerned," they stated, "His words and acts were and are those of the Father."[12]

On July 1, "The Father and the Son" appeared in the *Deseret Evening News.* That same day, Joseph F. Smith wrote to his son Hyrum M. Smith in Liverpool, eager for him to share the new statement with the Saints abroad. "This is the first time this task has been undertaken," he noted. "I hope you will approve of it and will have it very carefully printed."[13]

THAT SUMMER, IN NORTHEASTERN France, the German and French armies were locked in another bloody stalemate, this time outside the heavily fortified town of Verdun. Hoping to break the resolve of the French, the German army had bombarded the town's defenses and attacked with hundreds of thousands of troops. The French met them with heavy resistance, and months of futile trench warfare followed.[14]

Among the German infantrymen fighting at Verdun was forty-year-old Paul Schwarz. A bill collector and sewing machine salesman from western Germany, Paul had been drafted into the army the previous year. At the time, he was serving as president of a small branch of the Church in a town called Barmen, where he lived with his wife, Helene, and their five young children. Paul was a calm, peace-loving man, yet he believed it was his duty to serve his country. Another Melchizedek Priesthood holder had been called to take his place in the branch, and before long, Paul was at the battlefront.[15]

At Verdun, the terrors were constant. Early in the battle, the Germans assailed the French lines with artillery before sending troops with flamethrowers to clear the way for the advancing infantry column. But the French were stronger than the Germans expected, and casualties on both sides numbered in the hundreds of thousands.[16] In March 1916, soon after Paul's regiment arrived at Verdun, their commander was killed in action. Paul remained unscathed. Later, while transporting grenades, barbed wire, and other war materials to the front, he felt inspired to move to the head of his company. He quickly hurried up the line, just before a plane dropped bombs on the spot where he had been marching.[17]

Other Latter-day Saint soldiers he knew were not so fortunate, a reminder that God did not always spare the faithful. The previous year, the Church's German-language magazine, *Der Stern,* reported that eighteen-year-old Hermann Seydel had been killed on the war's eastern front. Hermann was from Paul's branch. "He was an exemplary young man and a devoted member of the Church of Jesus Christ, whose memory shall live on in all who knew him," his obituary read.[18]

Before the war, Paul had always been eager to share the gospel. Both he and his wife had gained testimonies of the Restoration after reading missionary pamphlets. Now Helene sent him Latter-day Saint tracts, which he passed out to the men in his unit. The soldiers would often read the tracts to pass the time before the next attack. It even inspired some of the men to pray.[19]

The battle at Verdun—and countless battles on other fronts of the war—carried on through 1916. Troops huddled in the dark, filthy trenches, fighting battle after hellish battle across the mud and wire of "No Man's Land," the desolate killing ground between the armies. Paul and other Latter-day Saint soldiers on both sides of the conflict clung to their faith, finding hope in the restored gospel as they prayed for an end to the strife.[20]

AS WAR RAGED THROUGHOUT Europe, the revolution in Mexico continued unabated. In San Marcos, the Zapatista troops who had occupied the town one year earlier were gone. Yet the memory of their violence still scarred the Monroy family and their Church branch.

On the night of the Zapatistas' invasion of San Marcos, Jesusita de Monroy had been on her way to speak with a rebel leader, hopeful that he could help her free her imprisoned children, when she heard the fateful gunshots. Hurrying back to the prison, she found her son Rafael and fellow Latter-day Saint Vicente Morales dead, victims of the rebel bullets.

In anguish, she shouted into the night, her cries loud enough for her daughters to hear in the room where they were being held.

Nearby, someone said, "What a brave man!"

"But what did they find in his house?" someone else asked.

Jesusita could have answered that question. Zapatistas had searched for weapons on her son's property, and they had found nothing. Rafael and Vicente had been innocent.

The next morning, she and Rafael's wife, Guadalupe, persuaded the rebel commander to release her three daughters, Natalia, Jovita, and Lupe. The women then went to retrieve the remains of Rafael and Vicente. The Zapatistas had left the bodies outside, and a large crowd of townspeople had formed around them. Since no one seemed willing to help carry the bodies back to the Monroy house, Jesusita and her daughters enlisted the few men who worked on Rafael's ranch to assist them.

Casimiro Gutierrez, whom Rafael had ordained to the Melchizedek Priesthood, conducted a funeral service at the house. Afterward some women from town, including some who had spoken out against the Saints, appeared guiltily at the door and offered their condolences. The Monroys found no comfort in their words.[21]

Jesusita had struggled to know what to do next. For a time, she contemplated moving away from San Marcos. Some of her relatives invited the family to live with them, but she declined their offer. "I cannot resolve to do so," she told mission president Rey L. Pratt in a letter. "We will not be well looked upon for the present, as in these little towns there is no tolerance nor freedom of religion."[22]

Jesusita herself wanted to move to the United States, perhaps to the border state of Texas. Yet President Pratt, who was overseeing the Mexican Mission from his home in Manassa, Colorado, cautioned her against moving to a place where the Church was not well established. If she found it necessary to move, he further counseled her, she should find a place among the Saints with a good climate and a chance to earn a living.

President Pratt also encouraged her to remain strong. "Your faith," he wrote, "has been one of the greatest inspirations of my life."[23]

Now, a year after her son's death, Jesusita was still living in San Marcos. Casimiro Gutierrez was the president of the branch. He was a sincere man who wanted to do what was best for the branch, but he struggled at times to live the gospel and lacked Rafael's talent for leading people. Fortunately, other Saints in the branch and the surrounding area ensured that the Church remained strong in San Marcos.[24]

On the first Sunday in July 1916, the Saints held a testimony meeting, and each member of the branch bore witness of the gospel and the hope it gave them. Then, on July 17, the anniversary of the killings, they met together again to remember the martyrs. They sang a hymn about the Second Coming of Jesus Christ, and Casimiro read a chapter from the New Testament. Another branch member compared Rafael and Vicente to the martyr Stephen, who died for his testimony of Christ.[25]

Guadalupe Monroy also spoke. After the Zapatistas had been driven from the region, one of the rival Carrancista captains had promised her that he would seek revenge on the man who was responsible for her husband's execution. "No!" she had told him. "I do not want another unfortunate woman to cry in loneliness as I do." She believed that God would serve justice in His own time.[26]

Now, on the anniversary of her husband's death, she testified that the Lord had given her strength to endure her pain. "My heart feels joy and hope in the beautiful words of the gospel for those who die faithful in keeping its laws and commandments," she said.[27]

Jesusita likewise remained a pillar of faith for her family. "Our sorrows have been grievous," she assured President Pratt, "but our faith is strong, and we will never forsake this religion."[28]

BACK IN EUROPE, MEANWHILE, apostle George F. Richards replaced Hyrum M. Smith as the president of the European Mission.[29] Before Ida Smith returned with her husband to the United States, she wrote a grateful farewell to her Relief Society sisters in Europe.

"In the past two years we have seen a great re-awakening of interest in the Relief Society cause," she wrote. "There is every reason to hope that the work will continue to increase and become more and more a power for good."

Under her leadership, the Relief Society had grown to more than two thousand women across Europe. Many local units thrived as never before, combining their efforts with the Red Cross and other organizations to relieve the poverty and suffering of their neighbors during wartime. By the end of her mission, Ida had organized sixty-nine new Relief Societies.

Now she hoped they would extend their influence even further. "The field in which to labor is extensive," she wrote, "and I hope that all the sisters will take advantage of every opportunity to make themselves known and their influence felt in as wide a circle as possible." Knowing the war had deprived branches of missionaries and priesthood leaders, she specifically encouraged the women to find time to distribute missionary tracts.

"This has been done in a few instances with splendid effect," she wrote. "Many doors have been opened for the preaching of the gospel in this way."[30]

In the fall of 1916, President Richards supported the efforts of local women to serve as missionaries in the towns and cities where they lived. He instructed mission leaders to call "lady missionaries," sustain them in conferences, set them apart, and give them missionary certificates. He also recommended giving women branch responsibilities, such as praying and speaking in

190

sacrament meetings, that had been done by men prior to the war.[31]

In Glasgow, Scotland, more than a dozen women, including the branch Relief Society president, Isabella Blake, were called on local missions. Isabella had great respect for Ida Smith. Following her example, Isabella and her Relief Society had worked with other churches to provide clothing for soldiers and sailors. When they sent items to the front lines, they attached messages of sympathy and cheer for the troops. They also comforted the many grief-stricken women in Glasgow who had lost loved ones in the war, praying all the while for the end of the terrible conflict.[32]

Ida had once told Isabella, "Whatever you do, always keep alive the spiritual side." Isabella tried to keep this advice in mind as she shouldered her responsibilities. All the new missionaries had day jobs, and some of them were wives and mothers. Isabella herself had five children and was expecting a sixth. What free time they had—on their weekly half day off from work or on Sundays—they spent distributing tracts, teaching the gospel, holding Relief Society meetings, or offering service such as visiting wounded soldiers in hospitals.[33]

Like other female missionaries before them, the women in Glasgow succeeded in reaching people who were suspicious of the American elders. The working-class neighborhoods of their city were a fruitful field for the gospel message. And as a local convert herself, Isabella could testify of her own experience with the gospel. As she spoke with the people of her city, Isabella found them to be kind and anxious to find the truth.

"We alone—a little handful of people in this densely populated world—have had this knowledge revealed to us, of the renewal of the family relation on the other side," she testified. "We know that the Lord has opened up the way for us, that by complying with His requirements, the wife will be restored to her husband and the husband to his wife, and they will again be one in Christ Jesus."[34]

The good spirit among the Glasgow Saints contributed to their success. Working together with the few men remaining in their branch, Isabella and her fellow missionaries brought back many people who had left the Church. The Relief Society also went from holding two meetings a month to four. Isabella especially appreciated their testimony meetings. "Some nights we feel loath to close them," she reported.

The accomplishments of the Glasgow Branch and its newly called missionaries made Isabella wish the Church were better established in the city. "If we had a little church here of our own, that could be kept for the sole purpose of worshipping God in and performing baptisms," she wrote mission headquarters, "I believe it would be the finest branch in the British Mission."[35]

CHAPTER 13

Heirs of Salvation

In January 1917, Susa Gates traveled to New York City to visit a sick friend, Elizabeth McCune, who served with her on the Relief Society general board. Elizabeth and her husband, Alfred, had moved to New York that winter so Alfred could conduct business in the city. When Susa learned about her friend's illness, she came at once to help her recuperate. By the time she arrived, however, Elizabeth was already on the mend. Still, she urged Susa to stay and keep her company. While there, Susa could use the city's libraries to conduct genealogical research, which had become an all-consuming part of her Church service.

In Denmark fifteen years earlier, Susa had fallen gravely ill while attending a meeting of the International Council of Women. She sought a blessing from apostle

Francis Lyman, the president of the European Mission at the time, who blessed her not to fear death and promised that she had a work to do in the spirit world. But then, midway through the blessing, he paused for about two minutes. "There has been a council held in heaven," he finally told Susa, "and it has been decided you shall live to perform temple work, and you shall do a greater work than you have ever done before."[1]

After recovering from her illness, Susa had dedicated herself to genealogy and temple work. She became active in the Genealogical Society of Utah, a Church-run organization created after Wilford Woodruff's 1894 revelation on temple sealings. She began working in the Salt Lake Temple, teaching genealogy classes, and writing a weekly column on family history for the *Deseret Evening News*.

When Susa and Elizabeth McCune became members of the Relief Society general board in 1911, they made genealogy and temple work a new priority for the women of the Church. They visited wards and branches in the United States and Canada and trained Saints to do research on their ancestry. Susa also wrote genealogy lessons for the *Relief Society Magazine,* and, at the request of the general board, she was currently writing a reference book to aid Saints in their family history work.[2]

While in New York City, Susa researched McCune family names at the library as well. She also did her best to give Elizabeth all the love and attention she could offer.

The day before Susa was scheduled to return home, Elizabeth felt well enough to attend a Relief Society meeting at the Eastern States Mission headquarters in the city. Susa spoke to the women about genealogical research. Even though the number of Latter-day Saint women in New York City was small, she felt the Spirit powerfully among them.[3]

On her return trip, Susa stopped in two other cities to visit the Saints. After one meeting, a branch president stopped to speak with her. "I always enjoy the testimonies of the aged," he said, "and love to hear an old person speak of their experiences."

Susa laughed inside. "You are an *aged person,* Susa, do you hear?" she told herself. She was sixty years old, but she still had years ahead of her—and so much more work to do.[4]

"WE ARE LIVING IN critical times," Joseph F. Smith acknowledged as he opened the Church's April 1917 general conference. Newspapers throughout Utah were filled with alarming reports of German aggression against the United States.[5] For the past two and a half years, the United States had remained neutral in the war. But Germany had recently renewed its policy of unrestricted submarine warfare, making American ships vulnerable to attack. German officials had also sought an alliance with Mexico, creating a pathway to attack the United States from the south. In response, the U.S. Congress had authorized President Woodrow Wilson to declare war on Germany.[6]

Standing at the pulpit of the Salt Lake Tabernacle, President Smith understood that many Saints in the congregation were anxious and fearful. He encouraged them to seek for peace, happiness, and the well-being of the human family. "If we do our duty today, as members of the Church and as citizens of our state," he said, "we need not greatly fear what tomorrow may bring forth."[7]

President Wilson formally declared war later that day. Nearly five thousand young men from Utah—most of them Latter-day Saints—soon enlisted.[8] Many women in the Church joined the Red Cross to serve as wartime nurses. American Saints who could not enlist in the armed forces supported their country in other ways, such as by purchasing government-issued "Liberty Bonds" to help fund the war. Betty McCune, Elizabeth's daughter, learned to operate and service an automobile and became an ambulance driver. Elder B. H. Roberts of the Seventy volunteered to serve as one of three Latter-day Saint chaplains in the army.[9]

Shortly after general conference, Joseph F. Smith traveled to Hawaii and observed the progress on the temple in Laie. Under the direction of foremen Hamana Kalili and David Haili, workers had already completed the outside of the temple and were now busily finishing its interior. Built from reinforced concrete and lava rocks from the nearby mountains, the Hawaii Temple was cross-shaped and had no steeple. Cement sculptures of scriptural scenes, cast by Utah artists Leo and Avard Fairbanks, adorned the outside of the building.[10]

In October, a month before his seventy-ninth birthday, the prophet told the Saints that he was beginning to feel old. "I think I am just about as young as I ever was in my life in spirit," he told them, "but my body gets tired, and I want to tell you, sometimes my poor old heart quivers considerably."[11]

His health continued to decline as the year came to an end, and he began seeing a doctor regularly at the start of 1918. Around the same time, his son Hyrum became ill as well. Sixteen months had passed since the end of Hyrum's tenure as president of the European Mission, and during that time he had been healthy and strong. Still, Joseph was anxious about his welfare. Hyrum had always occupied a special place in his heart, and Joseph found immense joy in his son's service and devotion to the Lord. He even reminded Joseph of his own father, the patriarch Hyrum Smith.[12]

Hyrum's sickness became more serious with each passing day. He felt severe pain in his abdomen, a sign he had appendicitis. His friends urged him to go to the hospital for an operation, but he refused. "I have kept the Word of Wisdom," he said, "and the Lord will take care of me."

On January 19, the pain became almost unbearable. Hyrum's wife, Ida, notified Joseph immediately, and he prayed earnestly for his son's recovery. Apostles Orson F. Whitney and James E. Talmage, meanwhile, joined Hyrum at his bedside and watched over him during the night. A group of doctors and specialists, including Dr. Ralph T. Richards, Joseph's nephew, also attended him.

After examining the patient, Dr. Richards feared that Hyrum had waited too long to seek medical help, and he pleaded with him to go to the hospital. "There is only one chance in a thousand if you go now," he warned Hyrum. "Will you take it?"

"Yes," Hyrum said.[13]

At the hospital, the doctors took two x-rays and decided to remove Hyrum's appendix. During the procedure, Dr. Richards discovered that the appendix had ruptured, spreading toxic bacteria throughout Hyrum's abdomen.

Hyrum survived the procedure, but Joseph remained weak with anxiety and spent the afternoon lying down, unable to eat. Hyrum seemed to gain strength that evening, which lifted Joseph's spirits. Filled with gratitude and relief, he returned to his duties as Church president.

Then, three days after Hyrum's surgery, Joseph received a telephone call from the hospital. Despite many prayers and the careful work of the doctors, Hyrum had passed away. Joseph was speechless. He needed Hyrum, and the Church needed Hyrum. Why was his life not spared?

Overcome with grief, Joseph poured out his anguish in his journal. "My soul is rent asunder," he wrote.

"And now what can I do! Oh! What can I do! My soul is rent, my heart broken! Oh! God help me!"[14]

A CLOUD OF SORROW hung over the Smith family in the days after Hyrum's death. There were Saints questioning his decision not to go immediately to the hospital. "If he had gone when first spoken to," some said, "he might have lived." Presiding bishop Charles Nibley, a close friend of the family, agreed. Hyrum's faith in the Word of Wisdom was well intentioned, he noted, but the Lord had also provided skilled men and women who were scientifically trained to care for the body.[15]

Seeking comfort in their loss, the Smiths gathered at the Beehive House, Brigham Young's old home where Joseph F. Smith lived. Being together eased some of their sadness and gave the family a chance to rejoice in Hyrum's honorable and faithful life. But everyone remained stunned by his death.[16]

Ida, his widow, was speechless with grief. She and Hyrum had been married for twenty-two years. During that time, Hyrum would sometimes say, "Now, look, if I ever die first, I'm not going to leave you here very long."[17] He meant it as a playful expression of love and affection. Neither he nor Ida could have known how soon and unexpected his death would be.

On March 21, 1918, Hyrum's forty-sixth birthday, Ida invited his closest friends over to her house for a small party to remember his life. As they reminisced about their friend, sometimes telling humorous stories, the conversation turned heartfelt. Orson F. Whitney, who had long been a friend to Hyrum and Ida, recited a poem about God's perfect plan for His children.

> *Sometime, when all life's lessons have been*
> *learned,*
> *And sun and stars forevermore have set,*
> *The things which our weak judgment here have*
> *spurned,*
> *The things o'er which we grieved with lashes wet,*
> *Will flash before us out of life's dark night,*
> *As stars shine most in deeper tints of blue;*
> *And we shall see how all God's plans were right,*
> *And what most seemed reproof was love*
> *most true!*

Ida loved the poem, and she told Orson that its message was one she had longed to hear since Hyrum's death. But the evening was a strain on her emotions. When the guests gathered around the dining table, she could not help but cry when she saw the vacant chair where Hyrum usually sat.[18]

One of her few consolations was knowing she and Hyrum would have one more baby. She had learned that she was pregnant shortly after her husband's death. She immediately invited her older sister Margaret to move in with her to help with the other four children, whose ages ranged from nineteen to six years. Margaret accepted her invitation.

Ida's health was good all summer, yet she acted as if she were preparing for her own death. "There's nothing wrong with you," Margaret would tell her. "You're going to live."[19]

Yet, as the end of her pregnancy drew near, she seemed convinced she would not live long after the birth of her child. While visiting with her mother-in-law, Edna Smith, Ida spoke as though she was anxious to be with Hyrum in the spirit world. She said they could do important work together on the other side of the veil.[20]

On Wednesday, September 18, Ida delivered a healthy baby boy. Afterward, she told her mother that Margaret would raise him. "I know I am going home to Hyrum and will have to leave my children," she said. "So please pray for my baby and for my lovely children. I know the Lord will bless them."[21]

The following Sunday, Ida felt as if Hyrum was at her side all day. "I heard his voice," she told her family. "I felt his presence."[22]

A few days later, her nephew burst into his family's home. "I just saw Uncle Hyrum go into Aunt Ida's house," he told his mother.

"That's ridiculous," his mother said. "He's dead."

"I saw him," the boy insisted. "I saw him with my own eyes."

Mother and son walked over to the Smith house, just a few doors down. There they found out that Ida was gone. She had died earlier that evening from heart failure.[23]

JOSEPH F. SMITH'S FAMILY DID not immediately tell him about Ida's passing, afraid the news would crush him. He had grown more frail since Hyrum's death, and he had rarely appeared in public over the last five months. On the day after Ida's death, however, family members brought her newborn son to Joseph, and he wept as he blessed the baby and named him Hyrum. The family then told him about Ida.

To everyone's surprise, Joseph received the news calmly.[24] So much suffering and pain had descended on the world lately. The daily newspapers contained horrific reports on the war. Millions of soldiers and civilians had already been killed, and millions more had been maimed and wounded. Earlier that summer, the soldiers from Utah had arrived in Europe and witnessed the unrelenting brutality of the war. And now more young Latter-day Saints were preparing to join the fight, including some of Joseph's sons. His son Calvin, in fact, was already on the front lines in France, serving with B. H. Roberts as an army chaplain.

A deadly strain of influenza had also begun taking lives throughout the world, compounding the pain and heartache of the war. The virus was spreading at an alarming rate, and Utah was only days away from shutting down its theaters, churches, and other public places in hopes of stopping the wave of disease and death.[25]

On October 3, 1918, Joseph sat in his room, reflecting on the Atonement of Jesus Christ and the redemption of the world. He opened his New Testament to 1 Peter and read about the Savior preaching to the spirits in the spirit world. "For this cause was the gospel preached also to them that are dead," he read, "that they might be judged according to men in the flesh, but live according to God in the spirit."

As he pondered the scriptures, the prophet felt the Spirit descend upon him, opening his eyes of understanding. He saw multitudes of the dead in the spirit world. Righteous women and men who had died before the Savior's mortal ministry were joyfully waiting for His advent there to declare their liberation from the bands of death.

The Savior appeared to the multitude, and the righteous spirits rejoiced in their redemption. They knelt before Him, acknowledging Him as their Savior and Deliverer from death and the chains of hell. Their countenances shone as light from the presence of the Lord radiated around them. They sang praises to His name.[26]

As Joseph marveled at the vision, he again reflected on the words of Peter. The host of disobedient spirits was far greater than the host of righteous spirits. How could the Savior, during His brief visit to the spirit world, possibly preach His gospel to all of them?[27]

Joseph's eyes were then opened again, and he understood that the Savior did not go in person to the disobedient spirits. Rather, he organized the righteous spirits, appointing messengers and commissioning them to carry the gospel message to the spirits in darkness. In this way, all people who died in transgression or without a knowledge of the truth could learn about faith in God, repentance, vicarious baptism for the remission of sin, the gift of the Holy Ghost, and all other essential principles of the gospel.

Gazing upon the vast congregation of righteous spirits, Joseph saw Adam and his sons Abel and Seth. He beheld Eve standing with her faithful daughters who had worshipped God throughout the ages. Noah, Abraham, Isaac, Jacob, and Moses were also there, along with Isaiah, Ezekiel, Daniel, and other prophets from the Old Testament and Book of Mormon. So too was the prophet Malachi, who prophesied that Elijah would come to plant the promises made to the fathers in the hearts of the children, preparing the way for temple work and the redemption of the dead in the latter days.[28]

Joseph F. Smith also saw Joseph Smith, Brigham Young, John Taylor, Wilford Woodruff, and others who had laid the foundation of the Restoration. Among them was his martyred father, Hyrum Smith, whose face he had not seen in seventy-four years. They were some of the noble and great spirits who had been chosen before mortality to come forth in the latter days and labor for the salvation of all God's children.

The prophet then perceived that the faithful elders of this dispensation would continue their labor in the next life by preaching the gospel to the spirits who were in darkness and under the bondage of sin.

"The dead who repent will be redeemed, through obedience to the ordinances of the house of God," he observed, "and after they have paid the penalty of their transgressions, and are washed clean, shall receive a reward according to their works, for they are heirs of salvation."[29]

When the vision closed, Joseph pondered all that he had seen. The next morning, he surprised the Saints by attending the first session of the October general conference despite his poor health. Determined to speak to the congregation, he stood unsteadily at the pulpit, his large frame shaking from the effort. "For more than seventy years I have been a worker in this cause with your fathers and progenitors," he said, "and my heart is just as firmly set with you today as it ever has been."[30]

Lacking the strength to speak of his vision without being overcome by emotion, he merely alluded to it. "I have not lived alone these five months," he told the congregation. "I have dwelt in the spirit of prayer, of supplication, of faith, and of determination, and I have had my communication with the Spirit of the Lord continuously."

"It is a happy meeting this morning for me," he said. "God Almighty bless you."[31]

ABOUT A MONTH AFTER the fall general conference, Susa and Jacob Gates went to the Beehive House to pick up a box of apples from the Smith family. When they arrived, Joseph F. Smith called for Susa to join him in his sickroom, where he had lain bedridden for weeks.

Susa did her best to comfort him, as he had comforted her family in the past. But she was discouraged about her Church service.[32] Aside from Elizabeth McCune, who had donated a million dollars to the Genealogical Society of Utah the year before, few women on the Relief Society general board seemed enthusiastic about family history or temple work. In fact, some board members had proposed abandoning monthly Relief Society genealogy lessons, which stake Relief Society leaders had recently criticized for being too difficult and not spiritual enough.[33]

"Susa," Joseph said as they spoke, "you are doing a great work."

Embarrassed, Susa replied, "I am certainly busy enough."[34]

"You are doing a great work," he insisted, "greater than you know anything about." He told her that he loved her for her faith and devotion to the truth. He then asked his wife Julina to bring him a paper. As she did so, Jacob and a few other people joined them in the room.

With everyone gathered, Joseph asked Susa to read the paper. She took it and was astonished by what she read. As a prophet, Joseph had always tried to be cautious when speaking about revelation and other spiritual matters. But here, in her hands, was an account of a vision he had seen of the spirit world. He had dictated the revelation to one of his sons, apostle Joseph Fielding Smith, ten days after general conference. Then, on October 31, the First Presidency and

Quorum of the Twelve had read the vision and fully endorsed its content.

As Susa read the revelation, she was moved that it mentioned Eve and other women serving alongside the prophets in the same great work. It was the first time that any revelation she knew of spoke of women laboring with their husbands and fathers on the Lord's errand.

Later, after saying goodbye to Joseph and his family, Susa felt blessed for having read the revelation before it had been made public. "Oh, it was a comfort to me!" she wrote in her journal. "To know the heavens are still opened, to have Eve and her daughters remembered, and above all—to have this given at a time when our temple work and workers and our genealogy need such encouragement."

She could hardly wait for Elizabeth McCune to read it. "It is a view or vision of all of these great ones laboring on the other side for the salvation of the spirits in prison," she told her friend in a letter. "Think of the impetus this revelation will give to temple work throughout the Church!"[35]

ON NOVEMBER 11, 1918, THE armies in Europe agreed to an armistice, ending four years of war. The influenza pandemic, however, continued to spread, eventually leaving millions of victims in its wake. In many places, the rhythms of everyday life ceased. People began wearing cloth masks over their noses and mouths to protect themselves and prevent the spread of the virus. Newspapers regularly published the names of the dead.[36]

A week after the cease-fire, Heber J. Grant decided to check on Joseph F. Smith at the Beehive House. Heber was now the president of the Quorum of the Twelve Apostles, the next man in line to lead the Church. He was not eager to take on the responsibilities of the Church president. He had hoped and prayed that Joseph would live twelve more years—long enough to celebrate the one hundredth anniversary of the Church. Even now he did not believe that Joseph would die.

At the Beehive House, Joseph's son David met him at the door and invited him to come speak with his father. Heber hesitated, however, not wanting to disturb the prophet.

"You had better see him," David said. "It may be your last chance."[37]

Heber found Joseph lying in bed, awake and breathing heavily. Joseph took his hand and pressed it firmly. Heber looked into his eyes and saw the prophet's love for him.

"The Lord bless you, my boy," Joseph said. "You have got a great responsibility. Always remember this is the Lord's work and not man's. The Lord is greater than any man. He knows who He wants to lead His Church and never makes any mistake."[38]

Joseph released his hand, and Heber stepped into a side office and wept. He went home, ate his evening meal, and then returned to the Beehive House to see Joseph one more time. Anthon Lund, Joseph's counselor in the First Presidency, was there with Joseph's wives and several of his sons. Joseph was in great pain, and he asked Heber and Anthon to give him a blessing.

"Brethren," he said, "pray that I may be released."

Joined by Joseph's sons, they placed their hands on his head. They spoke of the joy and happiness they had shared while laboring with him. And then they asked the Lord to call him home.[39]

CHAPTER 14

Fountains of Light
and Hope

After leaving Joseph F. Smith's bedside, Heber J. Grant returned home. He could not sleep, so he read and reread President Smith's most recent conference talk, weeping as he thought of the dying prophet. As a boy, he had thrilled whenever Joseph F. Smith, then a young apostle, spoke to his ward. Even now, Heber was in awe of the president's preaching. He believed his own sermons paled in comparison.

Heber fell asleep just after six thirty the next morning. When he awoke, he learned that President Smith had died of pneumonia.[1]

Family and friends of the prophet gathered at the cemetery a few days later. With influenza spreading throughout Utah, the state board of health had banned all public gatherings, so the mourners held a private graveside service.[2] Heber honored his friend with a short tribute. "He was the kind of man I'd like to be," he said. "No man that ever lived had a more powerful testimony of the living God and of our Redeemer."[3]

On November 23, 1918, the day after the funeral, the apostles and presiding patriarch set Heber apart as Church president, with Anthon Lund and Charles Penrose as his counselors.[4] While his friends expressed confidence in his leadership, Heber had reservations about following in President Smith's footsteps. Although he had served in the Quorum of the Twelve Apostles since the age of twenty-five, Heber had never served in the First Presidency. President Smith, on the other hand, had served as a counselor for decades prior to his calling as Church president.[5]

Joseph F. Smith's presidency had also been full of successes. Church membership nearly doubled during his administration and was now approaching five hundred thousand. He started a general reform of priesthood quorums, clarifying the duties of Aaronic Priesthood offices and standardizing meetings and lessons for Church quorums and organizations.[6] He had also helped people see the Church in a better light by giving interviews to the press and addressing controversies over past practices and teachings of the Church. And in 1915, he started "home evenings," asking families to set aside one evening each month for prayer, singing, gospel instruction, and games.[7]

Overwhelmed by this legacy, Heber lost more and more sleep. To ease the burden of his new calling, he and his counselors delegated some of President Smith's many leadership responsibilities to others. Heber served as president of the General Church Board of Education, as President Smith had, but he called apostle David O. McKay to be general superintendent of the Sunday School. He also appointed apostle Anthony Ivins to lead the Young Men's Mutual Improvement Association.[8] But since Heber had years of experience as a businessman in banking and insurance, he chose to oversee Church-managed companies himself.[9]

Still, he remained anxious. At the insistence of friends and fellow Church leaders, he and his wife, Augusta, took a vacation to the California coast. There Heber was able to sleep well for the first time since President Smith's death. When he and Augusta returned to Salt Lake City a few weeks later, he was rested and ready to get back to work.[10]

During the early months of 1919, the influenza pandemic kept Heber from addressing the Saints as often as he would have liked. More than a thousand Church members had already perished from the flu, and Heber and his counselors decided to postpone general conference to the first week in June out of concern for public health. They could also take comfort in knowing that President Smith had introduced inspired practices that would protect the Saints' health once they began holding regular sacrament meetings again.

Throughout most of the Church's history, for instance, the Saints had drunk from a common cup when partaking of the sacrament. But in the early 1910s, as information about germs became better known, President Smith had recommended individual sacrament cups made of glass or metal. Heber could see the health benefits of such an innovation in fighting infectious diseases.[11]

In November, after the pandemic had eased its grip on the world, Heber traveled to Hawaii to dedicate the temple in Laie. Once again, he could not help comparing himself to President Smith, who had spoken the people's language and understood their customs.[12]

The temple was filled to overflowing for the dedication. For many people, the day's events were the culmination of years of earnest prayers and faithful service. Saints who had moved to the Hawaiian colony at Iosepa, Utah, to be closer to the Salt Lake Temple had now left the settlement and returned to their homeland to worship and serve in the new temple.

Like his predecessors, Heber had prepared the dedicatory prayer beforehand. As he dictated the prayer to his secretary, he had felt the inspiration of the Spirit. "It is so far above any of my usual prayers," he told Augusta, "that I do thank the Lord with all my heart for His aid to me in preparing it."[13]

Standing in the celestial room, he spoke gratefully of Joseph F. Smith, George Q. Cannon, Jonathan Napela, and others who had established the Church in Hawaii. He asked the Lord to bless Church members in the Pacific Islands with the power to secure their genealogies and perform saving ordinances for their dead.[14]

Afterward, Heber wrote his daughters about the experience. "I had considerable anxiety and fear that there might be a falling off in the inspiration in our meetings in comparison to what would have been the case had President Smith been present with us," he admitted. "I feel now, however, that there was no occasion for my anxiety."[15]

WHILE HEBER J. GRANT WAS in Hawaii, Relief Society general secretary Amy Brown Lyman returned from speaking at a conference of professional social workers. Over the last three years, she had attended similar conferences to learn the latest methods for helping the poor and needy. She believed new approaches could help improve the charitable work done by the Relief Society, which had lately relied more and more on outside organizations, like the Red Cross, to assist struggling Saints.[16]

Amy had become interested in social work years earlier when her husband, Richard Lyman, was studying engineering in Chicago. At the time, many reform-minded citizens in the United States championed scientific remedies for poverty, immorality, political corruption, and other social problems. Amy worked with several charity groups while in Chicago, and they inspired her to do similar work in Utah.[17]

The Relief Society general board had since appointed Amy to lead the Church's newly formed Social Service Department to oversee aid to needy Saints, train

Relief Society members in modern relief methods, and coordinate with other charitable organizations. This appointment overlapped with Amy's service on the Church's Social Advisory Committee, which was made up of members of the Twelve and representatives from each Church organization and which sought to improve the morals and temporal well-being of Church members.[18]

After returning from the conference on social work, Amy tried to practice what she had learned. But not everyone on the Relief Society general board was so enthusiastic. Since some social workers were paid, Susa Gates believed that it commercialized something that should be voluntary. She also worried that social work would replace the Church's revealed pattern for carrying out charitable service, with bishops having stewardship over collecting and dispensing aid to the needy. But what concerned her most was that social work seemed to focus on temporal welfare rather than on the spiritual growth of God's children, a cornerstone of the Relief Society's message.[19]

The board considered the views of both Susa and Amy and ultimately agreed on a compromise proposal. They did not think organizations like the Red Cross should take the lead in caring for needy Saints when it was the Relief Society's sacred duty to do so. Yet they approved of training ward Relief Societies in modern social work methods, employing a limited number of paid social workers, and reviewing each request for assistance to ensure that aid was being distributed appropriately. Bishops were still ultimately responsible for deciding where fast offerings went, but they would coordinate their efforts with Relief Society presidents and social workers.[20]

Beginning in 1920, Relief Society members studied a monthly course on social work. The Social Advisory Committee also organized a six-week summer institute at Brigham Young University to train new social workers. Nearly seventy representatives from sixty-five stake Relief Societies attended the institute. They learned how to assess the needs of an individual or family and determine the best way to help. Amy oversaw the institute's classes on health, family welfare, and related topics. The institute also recruited an authority on social work from New York City to give lectures.

When the course ended in July 1920, the women were able to receive six hours of college credit for completing it. To Amy's satisfaction, they could now return to their local Relief Societies and share what they learned, improving the organization's work among the Saints.[21]

THREE MONTHS AFTER THE summer institute, President Grant announced that apostle David O. McKay would be traveling throughout Asia and the Pacific to learn more about the needs of the Saints in those areas. "He will make a general survey of the missions, study conditions there, gather data concerning them, and in short, obtain general information," President Grant told the

Deseret News. Hugh Cannon, a stake president in Salt Lake City, would serve as Elder McKay's companion on the journey.[22]

The two men left Salt Lake City on December 4, 1920, and stopped first in Japan, home to about 130 Saints. They then toured the Korean Peninsula and visited China, where Elder McKay dedicated the land for future missionary work. From there they visited the Saints in Hawaii and observed a flag-raising ceremony performed by Hawaiian, American, Japanese, Chinese, and Filipino children from the Laie Mission School, one of dozens of small Church-owned schools Elder McKay planned to observe during his travels.[23]

The ceremony inspired the apostle, who had a special interest in Church schools.[24] President Grant had recently called him to be commissioner of Church education, a new position that complemented his work as Sunday School superintendent. As commissioner, Elder McKay managed the Church's educational system, which was undergoing many changes.

For more than thirty years, the Church had operated stake-run academies in Mexico, Canada, and the United States as well as mission-run schools in the Pacific. Within the last decade, however, young Saints in and around Utah had begun attending free public high schools in great numbers. Since these schools did not provide religious instruction, many stakes had set up a "seminary" near a local high school to continue providing religious education to Latter-day Saint students.

The success of the seminary program prompted Elder McKay to begin closing the stake academies. Yet he still believed the Laie school and other international mission schools, including the Juárez Stake Academy in Mexico, were doing essential work and should continue to receive Church support.[25]

From Hawaii, they traveled to Tahiti and then to New Zealand's north island, Te Ika-a-Māui. There they caught a train to the town of Huntly, not far from a large pasture where Māori Saints were holding their annual Church conference and festival. No apostle had ever visited New Zealand before, and the Saints turned out by the hundreds to hear Elder McKay speak. Two large tents and several smaller tents had been set up in the pasture to accommodate everyone.

When Elder McKay and President Cannon arrived at the conference, Sid Christy, a grandson of Hirini and Mere Whaanga, ran out to meet them. Sid had grown up in Utah and only recently moved back to New Zealand. He led both men toward the tents. As he did so, they heard welcoming cries of "Haere Mai! Haere Mai!"[26]

The following day, Elder McKay addressed the Saints in one of the large tents. While many Māori Saints spoke English, he worried that some people in the congregation would not understand him, and he expressed regret that he could not speak to them in their own language. "I am going to pray that while I speak in my own tongue, you may have the gift of interpretation and discernment," he said. "The Spirit of the Lord will bear witness to you of the words that I give you under the inspiration of the Lord."[27]

As the apostle spoke about unity in the Church, he noted that many Saints were listening attentively. He saw tears in their eyes, and he knew that some of them had been inspired to understand the meaning of his words. When he finished, his interpreter, a Māori named Stuart Meha, rehearsed the main points of the sermon for the Saints who did not understand it.[28]

A few days later, Elder McKay spoke again at the conference. He preached on vicarious work for the dead. Now that a temple had been built in Hawaii, the New Zealand Saints had better access to temple ordinances. But Hawaii was still thousands of miles away and could not be visited without great sacrifice.

"I have no doubt in my heart but what you will get a temple," he told them. He wanted the Saints to prepare themselves for that day. "You must be ready for it."[29]

IN EARLY 1921, FORTY-NINE-YEAR-OLD John Widtsoe was nearing the end of his fifth year as president of the University of Utah. After being ousted from the Agricultural College of Utah in 1905 and teaching briefly at Brigham Young University, he had returned to the Agricultural College as its new president. He was then appointed president of the University of Utah in 1916, so he and Leah moved with their three children to Salt Lake City.

When they first came to the city, John's mother, Anna, his aunt Petroline, and his brother, Osborne, lived near one another. Osborne, who was married with two children, was the head of the English Department at the university.[30]

But their time together was short-lived. Anna became sick in the spring of 1919. When her condition worsened in the summer, she called John and Osborne together. "The restored gospel has been the great joy of my life," she told her sons. "Please bear that witness for me to all who will listen."

She died a few weeks later with her sister, children, and grandchildren at her side. Heber J. Grant, who had served as European Mission president during Anna's mission to Norway, spoke at the funeral. As John thought about his mother's life, his heart swelled with gratitude for her.

"She was self-sacrificing beyond expression in behalf of her own and those who needed help," he recorded in his journal. "Her devotion to the cause of truth was almost sublime."[31]

Just eight months later, Osborne suffered a sudden cerebral hemorrhage. He passed away the next day. "My only brother died," John grieved. "I am left very much alone."[32]

On March 17, 1921, one year to the day after Osborne's funeral, John learned that apostle Richard Lyman had been trying to reach him all morning. John immediately called him on the telephone. "Come to my office without delay," Richard said urgently.[33]

John left at once and met Richard at the Church's new administration building.[34] They then crossed the street to the Salt Lake Temple, where the First Presidency and Quorum of the Twelve Apostles were in a meeting. John sat down with them, unsure why he was there. As a member of the YMMIA general board, he often met with members of the Church's highest councils. But this was the regular Thursday meeting of the First Presidency and the Twelve, and he was not usually invited to it.

President Grant, who led the meeting, discussed a few items of Church business. He then turned to John and called him to fill a vacancy in the Twelve left by the recent death of Anthon Lund. "Are you willing to accept the call?" President Grant asked.

Time suddenly seemed to stop for John. Thoughts of the future flashed through his mind. If he accepted the call, he knew, his life would be the Lord's. His academic career would fall by the wayside, despite the years he had dedicated to it. And what about his personal limitations? Was he even worthy of the call?

Still, he knew the gospel had claim on his life. Without further hesitation, he said, "Yes."[35]

President Grant ordained him immediately, promising him more strength and power in God. He blessed John for listening to his mother's counsel and always being humble and able to discern between worldly wisdom and the truths of the gospel. And he spoke of the work John would do as an apostle. "When you travel in the different stakes or in the nations of the world," the prophet promised, "you shall have the love and confidence of the Latter-day Saints and the respect of those not of our faith with whom you may come in contact."[36]

John left the temple, ready to start a new phase in his life. It would not be easy. He and Leah still had debts, his oldest children were ready to serve missions, and he would be trading his university salary for the modest living stipend general authorities received for their full-time service. But he was determined to give all he had to the Lord.[37]

Leah too was willing. "My life will be quite different, I realize, and I could, if I would let myself, dread the many necessary separations," she told President Grant a short time later, "but I hail with delight the chance to work not only for my people as I have done in the past, but more directly with them."

"There is no regret in my heart," she added, "for any change of finances, or of public work, or of daily duties that may come to me as the wife of a man who has been called to this great service."[38]

SUSA GATES WAS ECSTATIC when she learned about her son-in-law's call to the Quorum of the Twelve Apostles. Her early fears that John would place his career over his family and Church were long gone, replaced by a deep and abiding love for him and his devotion to Leah, their children, and the restored gospel.

Full of advice, she wrote John a long letter, expressing her hopes for his new ministry. She was still worried about changes happening in the Relief Society and other Church organizations. "The world is in a spiritually starving condition today," she told John. She believed more and more people in the Church were seeing salvation as a matter of intellectual and ethical development rather than spiritual progress.

She urged her son-in-law to awaken spiritually dormant men and women, who already had the "seed of eternal life" planted in them. "It is for you to cultivate it, master agriculturist that you are," she wrote. "For after all, there lies in each of these souls a tiny, deep pool of truth and love of God which needs only a little clearing away of the underbrush of mental inactivity to well up into fountains of light and hope."[39]

John's call came at a time when Susa felt her own influence in the Church slipping away, especially as Amy Lyman and others continued to lead the Relief Society in new directions. Hoping to breathe new life into the organization, some members of the Relief Society board had even quietly urged Heber J. Grant to release Emmeline Wells as Relief Society general president.

Now ninety-three years old, Emmeline was the only Church officer still living who had known the prophet Joseph Smith. Physically frail and in poor health, she was often bedridden, many times leaving Clarissa Williams, her first counselor, to conduct Relief Society business at board meetings.

Heber's counselors and the Quorum of the Twelve Apostles likewise believed that the Relief Society needed new leadership. Yet Heber was reluctant to release Emmeline, and he pleaded for patience. All Relief Society general presidents since Eliza R. Snow had served until death. And he loved and admired Emmeline. When his mother was president of the Salt Lake City Thirteenth Ward Relief Society—a position she held for thirty years—Emmeline had been her secretary. Heber's wife Emily, who had died over a decade earlier, was a member of the Wells family, and Heber felt a deep connection with them. How could he think of releasing Emmeline?[40]

After counseling further with members of the general board, however, the First Presidency and the Twelve decided it was in the Relief Society's best interest to release Emmeline. Heber personally extended the release to Emmeline at her home. She received the news calmly, but it hurt her deeply.[41] The next day, at the Relief Society's spring 1921 conference, Clarissa Williams was sustained as the new Relief Society general president. Most of the members of the general board were also released and new members were called in their stead.[42]

Susa was one of the women who remained on the general board after the reorganization. She believed President Grant had been right to release Emmeline, yet she was wary about what would come next. On April 14, 1921, at the first meeting of the new board, Clarissa announced several changes to the organization.

The most significant was Amy Lyman's appointment as managing director of the activities of the Relief Society, giving her charge over all activities within its departments, including the *Relief Society Magazine.* Susa retained her place as editor of the periodical, but at Clarissa's direction, the position became an annual appointment. Susa's future with the magazine was no longer guaranteed.

Troubled by the changes, Susa wondered if they had anything to do with her inability to see eye-to-eye with Amy on social services.[43]

Six days later, Susa visited Emmeline, who was now spending more time in bed and often wept over her release. Her daughters Annie and Belle remained at her side constantly, trying to comfort her. Susa did her best to cheer her old friend. "Aunt Em," she said, "everybody loves you."

"I hope they do," Emmeline replied. "If they don't, I can't help it."[44]

She died peacefully on April 25, and Susa wrote a glowing tribute for the *Improvement Era.* She praised Emmeline's many years as a poet, an editor of the *Woman's Exponent,* and a staunch advocate for women's suffrage, which had recently been written into law in the United States Constitution. But Susa saved her greatest praise for Emmeline's work in grain storage, an assignment Emmeline first received from Brigham Young in 1876. Relief Society grain, Susa noted, had aided suffering people around the world.

"The dominant characteristic of Mrs. Wells's life was her supreme will," she wrote. "Her ambitions were high, her purposes lofty; but in and through them all ran the thread of truth to her testimony, which preserved her, and which made of her a light set upon a hill."[45]

CHAPTER 15

No Greater Reward

Throughout 1921, Heber J. Grant received letters from David O. McKay and Hugh Cannon about their world travels. After meeting with Saints in Samoa in May, the two men visited Fiji, returned to New Zealand, and visited Australia. They then made stops in Southeast Asia and continued on to India, Egypt, Palestine, Syria, and Turkey.[1]

While in the war-torn city of Aintab, Turkey, they met some thirty Armenian Latter-day Saints preparing to flee their homes. In the last decade, countless Armenians, including the local branch presidency and other Latter-day Saints, had been killed in communities like Aintab. Saints in Utah had fasted for them, and the First Presidency had sent money for their relief. But the violence had since escalated, making it increasingly dangerous for the Armenian Saints to remain in the country.[2]

With great difficulty and much prayer, mission president Joseph Booth and local leader Moses Hindoian secured passports for fifty-three people. The Saints then set out for Aleppo, Syria, more than seventy miles to the south, where another branch of the Church met. Their journey took four days, but the refugees pushed on through constant rain and arrived safely at their destination.[3]

In his final report to the First Presidency, submitted after his return to the United States, Elder McKay praised the Saints around the world. He was enthusiastic about Church schools and recommended supplying them with better teachers, textbooks, and equipment. Expressing concern about the challenges facing mission presidents, he proposed giving only the strongest leaders that assignment. He also recommended that general authorities travel more frequently to support the Saints abroad.[4]

The prophet agreed with Elder McKay's conclusions. In the past, Church members had found strength by gathering to Utah. But the days of leaders urging the Saints to move to Zion had passed. Since the end of the world war, in fact, many Saints had left Utah's small towns, seeking better employment in larger cities across the United States. More and more, Church members everywhere looked to local branches and missions for the support earlier Saints had found in wards and stakes in the American West.[5]

During a trip to Southern California in early 1922, Heber was impressed by the size of Church branches in and around Los Angeles. "The California Mission is growing by leaps and bounds," he proclaimed at the April 1922 general conference. Soon the Saints in the area would be ready to form a stake.[6]

Yet Heber knew Church members needed more than a strong congregation to remain true to the faith. Times were changing, and like others of his generation, he worried about society becoming more secular and permissive.[7] Wary of dangerous influences, he encouraged young Saints to participate in the Church's Mutual Improvement program. The MIA promoted faith in Jesus Christ, Sabbath keeping, church attendance, and spiritual growth as well as thrift and good citizenship. It also encouraged the youth to keep the Word of Wisdom, a principle Heber had taught frequently since he became Church president.[8]

"If we can make Latter-day Saints of the boys and the girls who attend our Mutual meetings," he declared, "then these associations will have justified themselves, and we will have the blessings of Almighty God upon our labors."[9]

Not all aspects of modern life troubled Heber. On the evening of May 6, 1922, he and his wife, Augusta, participated in the first evening program of KZN, a Church-owned radio station in Salt Lake City. Radio was new technology, and the station house was little more than a rickety shack made from tin and wood. But with a flash of electricity, its operators instantly broadcast messages a thousand miles in every direction.

Holding the large radio transmitter to his mouth, Heber read a passage from the Doctrine and Covenants about the resurrected Savior. He then bore a simple testimony of Joseph Smith. It was the first time a prophet had proclaimed the restored gospel across the airwaves.[10]

LATER THAT MONTH, IN a meeting about the future of the *Relief Society Magazine,* Susa Gates could feel that more changes were coming. She had edited the magazine since it replaced the *Woman's Exponent* in 1914. From the beginning, she wanted it to be "a beacon light of hope, beauty, and charity." Yet she knew the fate of the magazine was ultimately out of her hands.[11]

As the months passed, Relief Society general president Clarissa Williams and her secretary, Amy Brown Lyman, were taking a greater role in the magazine's production, inserting articles about social work and the Relief Society's collaboration with charitable organizations outside the Church. Susa did not doubt Amy's sincerity in championing social service. Rather, she feared that Amy was allowing the Church to become too entangled with the world.[12]

Susa prayed hard to view the situation differently, but her disapproval of the new approach to Relief Society work kept her from seeing the good Amy accomplished. The Red Cross and other charities now referred all cases concerning Latter-day Saints to the Relief Society. Many cases involved needy Saints who had lost contact with the Church after leaving their rural wards to find work in the city. To care for these Saints, the Relief Society often worked hand in hand with public and private medical, educational, and employment agencies.[13]

Clarissa had also recently consulted with Amy and the general board on an effort to reduce the number of Latter-day Saint women and infants who died during labor and delivery. The Relief Society had long focused on women's health, and childbirth was a vital concern during this time. The mortality rate for mothers and babies in the United States was high, leading Congress to provide funds to organizations that supported expectant mothers.

Even before these funds became available, the Relief Society general board worked with the First Presidency to establish a maternity home in Salt Lake City and provide medical supplies for expectant mothers in more remote areas. To fund the program, the Relief Society used money it had received from selling grain to the U.S. government during the war.[14]

Unable to reconcile herself to the Relief Society's new methods and administrative changes, Susa resigned from the general board and the *Relief Society Magazine*. "I am leaving my work with a love for my co-laborers," she told the board, "and trust they will extend the same love to me."[15]

Never one to be idle, Susa turned to other pursuits. Earlier that year, she had criticized Edward Anderson, editor of the *Improvement Era,* for writing Church history that hardly mentioned women. In response, Edward recommended that she compose a history of Latter-day Saint women. Susa had already written a history of the Young Ladies' MIA, so the project appealed to her. The First Presidency liked the recommendation as well, and Susa soon began writing.[16]

Apostle and Church historian Joseph Fielding Smith, son of President Joseph F. Smith, invited Susa to work on her history at a table in the Historian's Office. A short time later, he brought her across the hall to Elder B. H. Roberts's office. It had a desk, a typewriter, a washstand, two chairs, and shelves full of books and papers.

Since Elder Roberts was in New York serving as president of the Eastern States Mission, Elder Smith said, she could use the office—and B. H. would never need to know.

"I thank thee, Father!" Susa exclaimed in her journal. "Help me comply with my instructions!"[17]

ON NOVEMBER 17, 1922, ARMENIA Lee completed her tenth year as president of the Alberta Stake YLMIA in Canada. Her administration had been full of challenges as she traveled by horse and buggy through all kinds of weather to visit young women and their leaders. Winters were extremely cold in Alberta, requiring great stamina and courage for those who ventured outdoors. Nevertheless, she would don her warmest clothing, all but smother herself in quilts and wool robes, and head out into the snow and ice.

It was hazardous work, but she loved it.

Originally from Utah, Armenia was nineteen when she married William Lee, a widower with five young children. They had moved to Canada after William found work at a store in Cardston. The move was difficult on Armenia, but she and William started a new life in the small town. They had five more children together, started a mortuary business, and moved into a four-room home. Then, in 1911, a few months shy of their tenth wedding anniversary, William suffered a stroke and died. Armenia was not yet thirty years old when she became a widow with ten children in her care.[18]

William's death was sudden and shocking, but Armenia felt the Lord's Spirit comfort her, helping her to say, "Thy will be done." The experience was sacred and undeniable. "I know there is a future life, without a doubt," she testified, "and that family ties stretch into eternity."[19]

Armenia was called to lead the stake YLMIA less than two years after William's death.[20] At the time, the YLMIA, which was open to young women age fourteen and over, was undergoing many changes. A few months before Armenia's call, a stake in Salt Lake City had organized the first of many summer camps for young women in the Church. Like the Young Men's MIA, the YLMIA had begun seeing recreation as a way to develop character.

At first, young women leaders considered joining an outside organization for girls, just as the YMMIA had adopted the Boy Scout program. But Martha Tingey, YLMIA general president, and her board decided to develop their own program instead.[21]

Martha's counselor Ruth May Fox had suggested the name for the program: Bee-Hive Girls. The beehive had long been an important symbol of hard work and cooperation for the Saints in Utah. But it wasn't until board member Elen Wallace read a book called *Life of the Bee,* which detailed how bees worked together to build hives, that the leaders saw how the symbol applied to their organization.

Soon young women across the Church were organized into "swarms" under the leadership of a "bee keeper." To advance through the program, from "Builder in the Hive" to "Gatherer of the Honey" to "Keeper of the Bees," young women earned achievements in religion, home, health, domestic arts, outdoor recreation, business, and public service.[22]

Armenia and her counselors had begun promoting the Bee-Hive Girls program in the summer of 1915, and soon the wards in Cardston were forming swarms of eight to twelve girls. One year later, Armenia spoke to the Bee-Hive Girls and young men in the stake about the importance of temple work. The temple in Cardston was under construction, and each of them would have a chance to do temple work when it was completed. Such work was a privilege, she told them.[23]

Now, six years later, the temple was nearly ready to dedicate. Set atop a hill at the center of town, the white granite structure had a pyramid-shaped roof and rows of square columns around it. Like the temple in Hawaii, it had no spires stretching to the sky. Instead, it sat squarely and majestically on its foundation, as solid and immovable as a mountain.[24]

ELDER JOHN WIDTSOE GRIPPED his satchel as he stepped off a train at Waterloo Station in London. It was about noon on July 11, 1923, and the station was crowded and unbearably hot.[25]

He had come to Europe with fellow apostle Reed Smoot. Since the war, Scandinavian nations had been slow to let missionaries return, so President Grant asked Reed to use his position as a United States senator to petition the governments of Denmark, Sweden, and Norway on behalf of the Church. Because John was Norwegian and knew several European languages, he was called to join Reed on the mission.[26]

As John marched down the railroad platform, he heard a familiar voice cry out, "Here he is!" Then he felt his breath escape him as his twenty-year-old son, Marsel, wrapped him in a solid embrace.[27]

Marsel, who had been serving in the British Mission for the past year, rode with his father and Senator Smoot to the hotel. Marsel had been a good student and athlete as a young man. And John believed the mission had only improved him. "He is thoroughly in love with his work," John later wrote to his wife, Leah. "All in all I found him good company—a healthy, thoughtful, intelligent, affectionate, ambitious boy who intends to make the most of his life."[28]

After spending a few days in England, John and Reed traveled to Scandinavia with David O. McKay, who had been called as president of the European Mission about a year after returning from his world tour. As usual, misinformation about the Church lay at the heart of government restrictions against it.

In Denmark, their first stop, Reed sat for an interview about the Church with a major newspaper. Their meetings in other nations, which included audiences with the Lutheran archbishop in Sweden and the king of Norway, were also productive. John credited Reed's reputation for their success. Twenty years after his controversial election, the senator had become an influential lawmaker who enjoyed a close friendship with the president of the United States.[29]

At the end of their assignment, John reported to the First Presidency that he and Reed had garnered good press for the Church and convinced many European leaders that their policies against missionary work were outdated.[30] But the experience had left him pensive. After one tiring meeting, John came upon a bronze statue of Jöns Jacob Berzelius, a renowned Swedish chemist whom he admired.

Sitting down near the statue, John wondered what might have happened if he too had devoted himself entirely to science instead of returning to Utah to help educate the Saints and serve in the Church. "How I would have reveled in the life of a Berzelius," he wrote Leah later that evening, "for I know that with God's help I would have succeeded greatly."

Instead, John had given up his profession and abandoned much of his scientific research to serve as an apostle of Jesus Christ. Yet he did not regret his new path, despite the sadness he felt in burying old dreams.

"I cannot talk here of these things that fly through my soul," he told Leah. "Only the promise of life hereafter could justify some things."[31]

ON AUGUST 25, 1923, NOT long after the two apostles returned from their mission to Scandinavia, a special train carrying Heber J. Grant, nine apostles, and hundreds of Saints from Salt Lake City and other parts of the Church arrived in Canada for the dedication of the Cardston Alberta Temple. The visitors quickly overwhelmed the town, which scarcely had room for everyone. Yet the Canadian Saints gladly went out of their way to accommodate their guests.[32]

Amid the excitement of the day, Armenia Lee had an interview with apostle George F. Richards and her longtime stake president, Edward J. Wood, who had been called as the president of the new temple. Armenia and Edward had been friends for many years. After her husband's death, she had often gone to him for counsel and advice. They had worked together as stake leaders, and Edward had become like a brother to her.

Once the meeting began, Elder Richards asked Armenia if she would be willing to serve as matron of the new temple. If Armenia accepted the position, she would be required to select and supervise female temple workers, counsel women receiving their ordinances for the first time, and attend to myriad other duties.

Armenia was at once dazed and honored by the call. "I will accept the position in all humility, and do my best," she said.[33]

The following day, Anthony Ivins of the First Presidency set Armenia apart inside the temple. Then, at ten o'clock in the morning, she attended the first session of the dedication. Kneeling at an altar in the celestial room, President Grant offered the dedicatory prayer, asking God to sanctify the temple and bless those whose lives it would touch. He also called down a special blessing on the young people of the Church, who were so dear to Armenia's heart.

"Keep the youth of Thy people, O Father, in the straight and narrow path that leads to Thee," he prayed. "Give unto them a testimony of the divinity of this work as Thou hast given it unto us, and preserve them in purity and in the truth."[34]

The temple opened for ordinance work a short time later. In recent years, President Grant had looked for ways to increase temple participation. In 1922, he had asked a committee of apostles to study how to shorten endowment sessions, which could last up to four and a half hours. Temples now held multiple daily sessions and began offering evening sessions to accommodate Saints who could not attend during the day. Church leaders also ended a practice of having Saints come to the temple to receive a healing baptism or blessing, reasoning that it could interfere with regular ordinance work.[35]

One unexpected change was a modification of the temple garment. The existing garment pattern, which stretched to the ankles and wrists and had string ties and a collar, was ill-suited for the types of clothing worn in the 1920s. Recognizing that the symbolism of the garment was more important than the style, the First Presidency instructed that a shortened and simplified garment be made available.[36]

Since Armenia's duties as matron occupied much of her time, she was released as stake YLMIA president. Her time with the young women was a cherished part of her life, and she missed working with them. Yet she found new joy in greeting the young women she had known from the MIA as they came to the temple to receive their endowments and be sealed for time and eternity to their husbands.[37]

At the invitation of the editors of the *Young Woman's Journal,* Armenia published her feelings on being released after years of service in the YLMIA. "How I love the youth of Zion!" she wrote. "I ask for no greater reward than that which has come to me in seeing our girls grow and develop into womanhood, true to their heritage."[38]

CHAPTER 16

Written in Heaven

When Anna Kullick's brother Ernst Biebersdorf told her about his Latter-day Saint friends at work, she was intrigued. Their beliefs reminded her of a dream her mother had back in Germany, before Anna and Ernst had moved with their families to Buenos Aires, Argentina, in the early 1920s.

A deeply religious woman, Louise Biebersdorf had seen a beautiful place in her dream. Although she was not permitted to go there, she was told she would get there someday through two of her children. In the same dream, she learned that the true church would come from America.[1]

Anna and Ernst soon began attending Latter-day Saint meetings in Buenos Aires with Ernst's friends, whose names were Wilhelm Friedrichs and Emil Hoppe.[2]

After Parley Pratt's brief mission to Chile in 1851, the Church had sent few missionaries to South America and had no official presence on the continent. Wilhelm, Emil, and their families, in fact, had joined the Church in Germany and brought its teachings to Buenos Aires when they and thousands of other Germans—including the families of Anna and Ernst—had emigrated to Argentina to escape hard economic times brought on by the recent world war.[3]

On Sundays, the Saints met in a small room at Wilhelm's residence. Since neither Wilhelm nor Emil had priesthood authority to bless the sacrament, the meetings were primarily a time for scripture study and prayer. Lacking an organ, the group sang hymns while Wilhelm's son played the mandolin. The Saints also met at seven o'clock on Thursday evenings to study the Bible at Emil's house. As the congregation grew, the group began holding a Sunday school, where they studied from a German copy of James E. Talmage's *Articles of Faith*. Soon Anna was paying tithing, which Wilhelm sent to Church headquarters in Salt Lake City.

Eager to share the restored gospel, Wilhelm wrote and distributed tracts and advertised Church meetings in local German newspapers. He also wrote articles and delivered lectures on a variety of gospel topics. But he could not speak Spanish, the primary language in Argentina, which limited his efforts. Still, German-speaking people would occasionally turn up at his door, curious about what they had read regarding the Saints.[4]

By the spring of 1925, Anna was ready to be baptized. At first, her husband, Jacob, had been against her going to Church meetings, but he soon started attending. Their three teenage children were also becoming interested in the gospel. Anna's brother Ernst and his wife, Marie, were eager to join the Church as well, but there was no one in Argentina who had the authority to administer the ordinance.

As interest in the Church grew, the believers began meeting in three different locations throughout the city. Their faith inspired Wilhelm. "They have a testimony of the authenticity of this work, and desire to be baptized, as soon as opportunity affords," he wrote Church leaders in Salt Lake City.[5]

Wilhelm soon received a response from the presiding bishop of the Church, Sylvester Q. Cannon. "We have taken up with the First Presidency the matter of sending missionaries to the Argentina, but so far nothing definite has been decided," he wrote. "However, we are making inquiry with regard to suitable men who can speak the German and Spanish languages."[6]

The news offered hope to Anna, Ernst, and their families. Soon everyone wanted to know when they could expect missionaries in their country.[7]

AROUND THIS TIME, MANY white Americans were growing unsettled by changes happening in the United States. Millions of African Americans and immigrants were moving to northern U.S. cities to escape discrimination and find better employment. Their presence alarmed many working-class whites, who were afraid of losing their jobs to the newcomers. As resentment grew, hate groups like the Ku Klux Klan, which used secrecy and violence to brutalize Blacks and other minorities, gained members across the country.[8]

Heber J. Grant watched the spread of hate groups with dismay. Decades earlier, Klan members had sometimes assaulted missionaries in the American South. Such attacks on Saints had stopped, but recent reports of the Klan's actions were no less troubling.

"The number of whippings, murders, and the mob violence laid at the door of this organization make a sad page in the history of the South," the president of the Southern States Mission wrote President Grant in 1924. "There have been no convictions for these crimes. The spirit of lawlessness and violence that has swept over the South is exactly the same as that which inspired the Gadianton robbers."[9]

Throughout the 1920s, hate groups fed on widespread racism, which could be found in every region of the United States and in other areas of the world. In 1896, the U.S. Supreme Court had ruled that state laws allowing the separation of white and Black Americans in schools, churches, restrooms, railroad cars, and other public facilities were legal. Furthermore, popular novels and films demeaned Black people and other racial, ethnic, and religious groups with harmful stereotypes.

Few people, in the United States or elsewhere, believed Black and white people should mingle socially.[10]

In the Church, wards and branches were officially open to all people, regardless of race. Yet not all congregations agreed. In 1920, Black Latter-day Saints Marie and William Graves were welcome and fully integrated members of their branch in California. When Marie visited a branch in the southern United States, however, she was asked to leave because of the color of her skin. "I never had nothing to hurt me like that in all of my life," she wrote in a letter to President Grant.[11]

To prepare the earth for the Lord's return, Church leaders knew the restored gospel must be taught to every nation, kindred, tongue, and people. For decades, the Saints had actively preached among other people of color—including Native Americans, Pacific Islanders, and Latin Americans. But centuries-old obstacles, including racism, stood in the way of taking the gospel to all the world.

In the case of Marie Graves, the First Presidency did not ask the congregation to integrate, for fear that challenging racial codes like those in the South put both Black and white Saints at risk. Nor did Church leaders encourage active proselytizing among Black communities, since the Church restricted priesthood ordination and temple blessings from people of African descent.[12]

Some people in the Church sought exceptions to this practice. During his visit to the Pacific Islands, Elder David O. McKay had written to President Grant, asking if an exception could be made for a Black Latter-day Saint who had married a Polynesian woman and together raised a large family in the Church.

"David, I am as sympathetic as you are," President Grant had responded, "but until the Lord gives us a revelation regarding that matter, we shall have to maintain the policy of the Church."[13]

Beginning in the early 1900s, Church leaders taught that any Saint known to have Black African ancestry, however small, would be restricted. Yet the uncertainty about some Saints' racial identity created inconsistencies in how the restriction was applied. Nelson Ritchie, the son of a Black woman and a white man, knew little about his parents' history when he and his wife, Annie, a white woman, joined the Church in Utah. He had light skin, and many of his children were thought to be white. When two of his daughters were ready for marriage, they entered the temple and received the endowment and sealing ordinances.

Later, however, when Nelson and Annie desired to be sealed in the temple, their bishop questioned Nelson about his ancestry. Nelson told him what he understood about his parents, and the bishop took the case to the First Presidency and Quorum of the Twelve Apostles, who sent the question back to the bishop to decide. In the end, the bishop affirmed that Nelson and Annie were good Latter-day Saints, but he declined to issue Nelson a temple recommend because of his ancestry.[14]

While many Saints shared the racial prejudice of the time, most disapproved of organizations that used secrecy, lawlessness, and violence to oppress others. After the Ku Klux Klan spread to Utah in the early 1920s, President Grant and other Church leaders denounced it in general conference and used their influence to stop it. Few Church members ever joined the group. When a Klan leader sought a meeting with Church leaders, President Grant refused the request.[15]

"It is beyond my comprehension," the prophet noted in April 1925, "how people holding the priesthood will want to associate themselves with the Ku Klux Klan."[16]

IN MID-1925, HEBER J. GRANT and others around the world were captivated by the case of John Scopes, a high school science teacher who had been brought to trial in the southern United States for teaching that humans and monkeys evolved from a common ancestor.[17]

The Scopes trial exposed a great divide among Christian churches. Some "modernist" Christians believed that the Bible should not be treated as an authority on scientific questions. Science provided a more reliable guide to understanding the natural world, they reasoned, and teachers like Scopes ought to be able to teach evolution in the schools without fear of punishment. "Fundamentalist" Christians, on the other hand, saw the Bible as God's final and absolute truth. For them it was blasphemy to claim that humankind, God's highest creation, evolved from less-sophisticated life-forms.[18]

Heber had great respect for modern science and for scientists like apostles James E. Talmage and John Widtsoe, who had excelled in their fields while retaining faith in the restored gospel. Like them, he was open to the discovery of new truths outside of scripture, and he had faith that science and religion could ultimately be reconciled.[19]

But he worried about young Latter-day Saints who had abandoned their faith while studying science at colleges and universities. As a young man, he had been ridiculed by a scientist for believing in the Book of Mormon. The man pointed to the passage in 3 Nephi in which God's voice was widely heard among those who had survived the destruction at the time of Christ's Crucifixion. The scientist said it was impossible for a voice to carry so far and anyone who believed otherwise was a fool. Years later, after the invention of radio proved that voices could travel great distances, Heber felt vindicated.[20]

During the Scopes trial, Heber and his counselors decided to publish a condensed version of "The Origin of Man," the essay issued by the First Presidency in 1909.[21] Rather than condemn the teaching of evolutionary theory, as fundamentalists did, the essay affirmed the biblical teaching that God created male and female in His own image. It also declared the unique restored doctrine that all people once lived as spirit children of God before they were born on earth and that these spirit sons and daughters had grown and developed over time.

"Man, as a spirit, was begotten and born of heavenly parents, and reared to maturity in the eternal mansions of the Father," the First Presidency testified.

The statement ended by emphasizing another kind of change over time—one that looked far into the future. "Even as the infant son of an earthly father and mother is capable in due time of becoming a man," it declared, "so that undeveloped offspring of celestial parentage is capable, by experience through ages and eons, of evolving into a God."[22]

Three days after the First Presidency published its statement, the jury in the Scopes trial issued a verdict. John Scopes was found guilty and ordered to pay a $100 fine.[23] After that, when people wrote to Heber asking for the Church's view on evolution, he sent them a copy of the First Presidency's statement. He did not have to tell people what to believe. Truth could be judged by its fruits, he said, as Jesus had taught in the Sermon on the Mount.[24]

WHEN LEN HOPE WAS about seventeen years old, he spent two weeks attending a Baptist revival near his home in Alabama, in the southern United States. At night, the young Black man would come home from the revival, lie down in the cotton fields, and look up at the heavens. He would beg God for religion, but in the morning the only thing he had to show for his effort was clothing wet with dew.

One year later, Len decided to be baptized in a local church. Soon after, though, he dreamed that he needed to be baptized again. Confused, he started reading the Bible—so much so that he worried his friends. "If you don't stop reading so much, you will go crazy," they said. "Already the asylum is full of preachers."

Len did not stop reading. One day, he learned that the Holy Ghost could lead him to truth. At the advice of a preacher, he retreated to the woods to pray in an old empty house hidden in a tangle of bushes. There he wept for hours, pleading with God for the Holy Ghost. In the morning, he was ready to go without food or drink until he received the gift. But then the Spirit prompted him not to do so. Only someone with authority from God could confer the Holy Ghost on him.

A short time later, as Len waited for an answer to his many prayers, a Latter-day Saint missionary gave his sister a tract about God's plan of salvation. Len read it and believed its message. He also learned that Latter-day Saint missionaries had authority to confer the gift of the Holy Ghost on those who accepted baptism.

Seeking out the elders, Len asked if they would baptize him.

"Yes, gladly," said one of the missionaries, "but if I were you, I would read a little more."[25]

Len got copies of the Book of Mormon, Doctrine and Covenants, Pearl of Great Price, and other Church books—and soon read them all. But before he could be baptized, he was drafted to fight in the world war. The army shipped him overseas, where he served bravely at the front. Then, after returning home to Alabama, he was baptized by a local Church member on June 22, 1919, and finally received the gift of the Holy Ghost.[26]

A few nights after his baptism, a mob of white men came to the house where he was staying and called out for him. "We just want to talk to you," they said. In their hands were rifles and shotguns.

Len stepped outside. He was a Black man in the American South, where armed mobs sometimes en-forced racial segregation with violence. They could injure or kill him on the spot and may never have to answer for their crime.[27]

Someone in the mob demanded to know why Len had joined the Latter-day Saints. It was legal for Blacks and whites to worship together in Alabama, but the state also had a strict set of segregation laws and unwritten social codes to keep the races separate in public set-tings. Since nearly every Latter-day Saint in Alabama was white, the mob saw Len's baptism as a challenge to the region's deeply rooted color line.[28]

"So, you went over to the waters and learned a few things," the man continued, referring to Len's army service. "Now you want to join the whites."

"I was investigating the Church long before I went to war," Len finally said. "I found it was the only true church on earth. That is why I joined it."

"We want you to go and have your name scratched off the record," the mob said. "If not, we will hang you up to a limb and shoot you full of holes."[29]

The next morning, Len attended a conference of fellow Saints in the area and told them about the mob's threat. He knew he was taking a risk by coming to the meeting, but he was willing to die for his newfound faith.

"Brother Hope, we could not scratch your name off if we tried to," Church members reassured him. "Your name is in Salt Lake City and also written in heaven." Many of them offered to help Len if the mob ever came after him again.[30]

But the mob never returned. Len soon married a woman named Mary Pugh in 1920, and they moved to Birmingham, a large city in central Alabama. Mary's uncle, a Baptist pastor, predicted that she would join the Church before the year was over.

Mary read the Book of Mormon and gained a testimony of its truth. It took a little longer than predicted, but after five years of marriage she decided to join the Church. On September 15, 1925, the Hopes went with two missionaries to a secluded spring near Birmingham. Mary was baptized without incident, finally becoming a Latter-day Saint, like her husband.[31]

"I couldn't be anything better," she told her uncle, "and I can see no better church."[32]

MEANWHILE, IN BUENOS AIRES, Anna Kullick and her family welcomed apostle Melvin J. Ballard and his companions, Rey L. Pratt and Rulon S. Wells of the Seventy, to their city. The First Presidency had sent the three general authorities to Argentina to dedicate South America for missionary work, establish a branch of the Church, and preach the gospel in German and Spanish to the residents of the city. The Kullicks had waited months for someone to come. The missionaries were the only ones on the South American continent who had the proper authority to baptize them into the Church of Jesus Christ.[33]

Elder Wells spoke German well, and Elder Pratt spoke fluent Spanish. But Elder Ballard spoke neither language and seemed overwhelmed by his new surroundings. Everything about Buenos Aires—the language, the warm December air, the stars in the southern sky—was unfamiliar to him.[34]

The missionaries spent their first days in Argentina visiting with the German Saints in the city. They held meetings in the home of Wilhelm Friedrichs and attended a Book of Mormon class in the home of Emil Hoppe. Then, on December 12, 1925, they baptized Anna, Jacob, and the couple's sixteen-year-old daughter, Herta. Anna's brother Ernst and his wife, Marie, were also baptized, as was Wilhelm Friedrichs's adopted daughter, Elisa Plassmann. The next day, the missionaries ordained Wilhelm and Emil as priests and Jacob and Ernst as deacons.[35]

Two weeks later, on Christmas morning, the three missionaries went to the Parque Tres de Febrero, a well-known city park with wide green lawns, blue lakes, and serene groves of weeping willows. Finding themselves alone, the men sang hymns and then bowed their heads while Elder Ballard dedicated the continent for the Lord's work.

"I do turn the key, unlock and open the door for the preaching of the gospel in all these South American nations," he prayed, "and command to be stayed every power that would oppose the preaching of the gospel in these lands."[36]

Once the South American Mission was officially open, the missionaries and members worked together to share the gospel with their neighbors. Herta Kullick, who knew Spanish, sometimes shared the gospel with her Spanish-speaking friends at school. Elder Ballard and Elder Pratt, meanwhile, went door to door to distribute tracts and invite people to Church meetings. The work was tiring. The missionaries often had to travel long distances across open fields or on muddy roads in all kinds of weather.[37]

In January 1926, Elder Wells returned home because of ill health, so Herta became responsible for helping Elder Ballard and Elder Pratt communicate with the German Saints. Elder Ballard would prepare a message for the Saints in English, Elder Pratt would translate it into Spanish, and Herta would translate the Spanish into German. It was a complicated—and sometimes very funny—process, but the missionaries were grateful for her help.[38]

During their meetings, the missionaries often presented slideshows using a projector they brought from the United States. Thinking her friends might take an interest, Herta invited them to attend the shows. Soon, nearly a hundred young people—most of them Spanish speakers—were appearing at the Saints' rented meetinghouse, and the elders organized a Sunday school to teach them.[39]

Parents of the youth, curious about what their children were learning, started meeting with the Saints as well. At one meeting, more than two hundred people crowded the meetinghouse to see slides about the Restoration and hear Elder Pratt teach in their native language.[40]

Six months after Elder Ballard, Elder Pratt, and Elder Wells came to Buenos Aires, a permanent mission president and two young missionaries arrived to carry on the work in their place. The new president, Reinhold Stoof, and his wife, Ella, had joined the Church in Germany just a few years earlier. One of the missionaries, J. Vernon Sharp, spoke Spanish, ensuring that both German-speaking and Spanish-speaking South Americans would be able to hear the gospel in their own language. Not long after they arrived, the mission had its first Spanish-speaking convert, Eladia Sifuentes.[41]

On July 4, 1926, just before he was to return to the United States, Elder Ballard bore his testimony to a small congregation of Argentine Saints. "The work will go slowly for a time, just as an oak grows slowly from an acorn," he declared. "It will not shoot up in a day as does the sunflower that grows quickly and thus dies."

"Thousands will join here," he prophesied. "It will be divided into more than one mission and will be one of the strongest in the Church."[42]

CHAPTER 17

Spared for Each Other

As the Church continued to spread throughout the world, President Heber J. Grant wrestled with the future of Church education. The cost of operating Church schools had risen tenfold over the last twenty-five years. Some efforts, like replacing the expensive stake academy system with the seminary program, had saved money. But Brigham Young University, Latter-day Saints' University, and other Church colleges were growing. If these institutions wanted to offer the same quality of education as the University of Utah and other local state-sponsored schools, they would need more money than tithing funds could provide.[1]

The expense troubled the prophet constantly. "Nothing has worried me more since I became president," he told the General Church Board of Education in

February 1926. Brigham Young University alone wanted to spend more than a million dollars to expand its campus. "We can't do it," President Grant declared. "That's all."[2]

Some board members, sharing the prophet's concern, wanted the Church to close all its colleges and universities, including BYU. But apostles David O. McKay and John Widtsoe, who had both attended Church schools and served as commissioner of Church education, countered that young adults needed Church schools for the important religious education they provided.

"The schools were established for the influence they would have upon our children," Elder McKay said at a board meeting in March. He believed Church colleges and universities were crucial for molding young people into faithful Latter-day Saints.

Elder Widtsoe agreed. "I know the value in Church schools in making a man," he said. "I think the Church would make a great mistake if it did not maintain an institution of higher learning."[3]

Around this time, President Grant's counselor Charles W. Nibley met with William Geddes, a Church member from Idaho, just north of Utah. William's daughters Norma and Zola were among a handful of Latter-day Saints attending the University of Idaho. Their small branch met in a shabby, rented hall where locals sometimes held dances on Saturday nights. When Norma and Zola would show up for Church the next morning, the place reeked of cigarette smoke, with trash and empty liquor bottles littering the floor.[4]

William wished there were a better meetinghouse for his daughters near the school. "The university can never attract Latter-day Saint students," he told President Nibley, "unless there are better facilities."[5]

President Grant and the board of education considered the situation in Idaho as they discussed the future of Church education. They decided to continue to fund Brigham Young University while gradually withdrawing support from most of the Church's other colleges. The Church would also start providing religious education to students by extending seminary to the university level. The board saw the University of Idaho as a testing ground for the new program. All they needed was someone who could move to Moscow, the small town where the university was located.[6]

In October, the First Presidency met with Wyley Sessions, a former agricultural agent for the University of Idaho who had just returned from serving as president of the South African Mission. They had recommended him for a position at a local sugar company, but as they spoke with him about the job, President Nibley stopped midsentence and turned to the prophet.

"We're making a mistake," he said.

"I'm afraid we are," President Grant agreed. "I haven't felt just right about assigning Brother Sessions to the sugar company."

The room went silent for a minute. Then President Nibley said, "Brother Sessions, you're the man for us to send to the University of Idaho to take care of our boys and girls who are attending the university there, and to study the situation and tell us what the Church should do for Latter-day Saint students attending state universities."

"Oh no, brethren," Wyley said. "Are you calling me on another mission?" His assignment in South Africa had lasted seven years and left him and his wife, Magdalen, almost penniless.

"No, Brother Sessions, we're not calling you on another mission," the prophet chuckled. "We're giving you a fine opportunity to render a splendid service to the Church." He added that it would be a professional opportunity—a paid position.

Wyley stood up sadly. President Nibley moved toward him and took him by the arm.

"Don't be disappointed," he said. "This is what the Lord wants you to do."[7]

SNOW BLANKETED SALT LAKE City on New Year's Day 1927, but brilliant sunshine flooded the Widtsoe home, keeping the cold at bay.[8] Normally, fourteen-year-old Eudora was the only child living at home, but the whole family had gathered for the holidays, and Leah was delighted to have her children near her.

Marsel, now twenty-four, was engaged to be married and only months away from graduating from the University of Utah. Soon he hoped to attend Harvard University, like his father, and probably study business administration.[9] His older sister, Ann, meanwhile, had recently married Lewis Wallace, a young Latter-day Saint lawyer, and moved with him to Washington, DC. A bout of homesickness had brought her back to Utah, however, and Leah was worried about her. Still, both Leah and John were grateful for the Lord's kindness and mercy to their family.[10]

As the new year progressed, John returned to his duties in the Twelve, and Leah spent her spare time helping her mother with a new writing project.[11] For years, Leah had watched Susa gather information and jot down stories about her father, Brigham Young, with the goal of one day publishing his biography. But some time ago, Leah had noticed that while her mother was still making progress on other writing projects, like her history of Latter-day Saint women, she was no longer working on the biography.

"Mother, what about the book about your father?" Leah asked her one day. "Aren't you writing it anymore?"

"No, he is too big for me," Susa had replied. "If you are standing beside a mountain, you can't really describe the mountain, for you're too near to see it."

"Nevertheless, you have it to do," Leah had insisted. "Someday you must write that book about your father, and I'll be glad to help you with it."[12]

Since then, Susa had written two hulking manuscripts on Brigham Young and recruited Leah to help her shape them into a single, coherent biography. Leah found the work hard and sometimes tediously slow, but she knew her mother needed her help. Susa was a natural writer, with a strong mind and determined voice. Yet Leah added polish and structure to her prose. Working together at Susa's house, they made a good team.[13]

On the morning of May 23, 1927, Leah's routine came to a sudden halt when a letter arrived from Preston, Idaho, where Marsel was teaching seminary. Recently, after helping a stranded motorist on the side of the road, Marsel had caught a severe cold. Although his friends believed he was getting better, his temperature was running high. Pneumonia could settle into his lungs and put his life at risk.[14]

Leah caught a train to Preston within the hour and was soon at Marsel's side. The next day, his temperature dropped a few degrees, giving Leah hope he would recover. But after he improved no further, her fears returned. John joined her in Preston, pleading with the Lord to spare Marsel's life. He called one of his friends, a doctor, to attend the young man. Other friends gave Marsel priesthood blessings or sat up with him at night.

Exhausted, Leah collapsed on May 27. That night, however, Marsel showed signs of recovery. His fiancée, Marion Hill, arrived the next morning. Marsel's lungs seemed to clear, and his temperature dropped again. But later that day, his breathing grew heavy and his body swelled. Leah remained at his side with John and Marion all afternoon. Hour after hour passed, but he did not get better. He died later that evening.[15]

Leah was inconsolable. Death had taken four of her children already. Now her only surviving son, whose future had seemed so bright and certain at the start of the new year, was gone.[16]

THAT SPRING, SOME SIXTEEN hundred miles east of Salt Lake City, eight-year-old Paul Bang was preparing for baptism. He was the sixth of ten children—four girls and six boys. They lived in an L-shaped room behind a grocery store their parents owned and operated in Cincinnati, Ohio, a bustling city of more than four hundred thousand people in the midwestern United States. To maintain some privacy, the family had divided the room into quarters with the aid of curtains. But no one really had any privacy. At night, they would sleep on foldout beds that took up so much space a person could hardly move around the room.[17]

Paul's father, Christian Bang Sr., was from Germany. When he was a small boy, his family had moved to Cincinnati, where many German immigrants had settled during the nineteenth century. In 1908, Christian married Rosa Kiefer, whose parents were also German immigrants. Three years later, Rosa's friend Elise Harbrecht gave Rosa a Book of Mormon, and she and Christian read it with interest. After a year of meeting with missionaries, they were baptized in a Jewish bathhouse because the nearby Ohio River was frozen.[18]

The branch in Cincinnati was like many branches of the Church in the eastern United States. The city had once been home to a thriving congregation of Saints, but it had shrunk over the years as more and more Church members gathered to Utah. By the time Paul's parents joined the Church, Latter-day Saints were a curiosity in the area. When missionaries baptized a boy in 1912, hundreds of people came down to the river to gawk at him. The newspaper printed an article about the baptism the following day, advising readers that missionaries were in the area.

"A strong attempt will be made to secure many converts openly," it read.[19]

After joining the Church, Paul's parents attended services with the missionaries and a few other Saints in a small, rented hall. One Church member soon moved to Utah, another died, and two quit coming to meetings. Christian and Rosa thought about gathering to Utah as well, but they decided to stay in Ohio since their families and business were there.[20]

Like other branches far from Salt Lake City, the Cincinnati Branch benefited when more seasoned Church members moved into its boundaries. Soon after the Bangs joined the Church, a Latter-day Saint couple from Utah, Charles and Christine Anderson, moved to Cincinnati and began going to church with them.

The Andersons had been endowed and sealed in the temple and had spent many years serving in wards and stakes in the American West. They were among the many Saints who had left Utah to seek opportunities elsewhere. Born in Sweden, Charles had invented a new kind of mop and had come east to manufacture it. He knew nothing about Cincinnati except that it was a large city and a prosperous business center. Nonetheless, the president of the Southern States Mission immediately called him to reorganize and lead the branch. Paul's father became his first counselor.[21]

It was not an easy time to be a Latter-day Saint in Cincinnati. News articles and demonstrators had railed against the Church in the area for years. Once, the local paper had even called Cincinnati a "battleground of the war against the spread of Mormonism in America" when Frank Cannon, the apostate son of George Q. Cannon, had held a rally in the city.[22]

Still, despite the opposition, Paul's parents worked hard to raise their children in the gospel. They attended their weekly church meetings and served faithfully in the small branch. Each morning, his father would call everyone together for family prayer and a recitation of the Lord's Prayer, a common practice among German Christians. On Mondays, his mother would often have the missionaries over for dinner. The family and missionaries would sit at a large table in a kitchen connected to the back of the store. Since Paul's mother never threw anything usable away, she would cook up the store's old food, being careful to trim away the rotten parts of any fruit, vegetable, or meat before she served it. His father would then insist that the missionaries eat to bursting.[23]

The Bangs also made sure each of their children was baptized at age eight.[24] On June 5, 1927, Paul and four other people were baptized at a place called Anderson's Ferry along the Ohio River. His parents, President Anderson, and some of his friends were there to celebrate the occasion.

There were no gawking crowds there to witness the event, and no newspaper articles. But an account of the baptism did appear in the *Liahona, the Elders' Journal,* the official magazine of the Church's North American missions. Paul's name even appeared in print.[25]

WYLEY AND MAGDALEN SESSIONS did not receive a warm welcome when they got to the University of Idaho. Moscow was in the northern part of the state, where few Church members lived. Many people had come to the region to farm its rich soil or to seek their fortune in the mining and lumber industries. These residents were suspicious of the Church, and Wyley's presence set them on edge.

"Who is this fellow, this man Sessions?" some people asked. "What's his duty up here? What's he want to do?"[26]

Had Wyley been asked the last two questions directly, he would have had no clear answers. The First Presidency had instructed him to help the Latter-day Saint students at the school, but how he would do that was entirely up to him. He knew the students needed regular religious instruction and a new place to meet. But aside from his work as a mission president, Wyley had no experience with religious education. He had studied agriculture in college. If the students wanted to learn about fertilizer, he could teach them. But he was no Bible scholar.[27]

Soon after arriving in Moscow, Wyley and Magdalen enrolled in the university's graduate school to further their education and become more acquainted with the school and its faculty. Wyley studied philosophy and education, took some classes in religion and the Bible, and began writing a thesis on religion at state universities in the United States. Magdalen, meanwhile, took classes in social work and English.

Wyley and Magdalen found an ally in C. W. Chenoweth, the head of the philosophy department, who was concerned about the absence of religious education in state universities. He had been a chaplain in the world war and now served as a pastor at a church near Moscow. "If you're coming onto this campus with a religious program," he told Wyley and Magdalen, "you had better be prepared to meet the competition of the university."

With Dr. Chenoweth's encouragement, the Sessionses drew up plans for a seminary-like program for Latter-day Saint students at public universities. They based the program on religious education programs at other universities and were careful to honor the separation of church and state. Their religion classes needed to meet the state's standards for university-level courses, but the program also had to be completely independent of the school itself. When the Church constructed a building for classes, it had to be off campus.[28]

Knowing the university would not support the new program as long as local leaders remained suspicious of him and the Church, Wyley joined the chamber of commerce and a civic group so he could meet important community members. He found that local business leaders, ministers, and faculty had formed a committee to keep an eye on him and make sure he was not trying to assert the Church's influence over the university. Fred Fulton, an insurance agent, led the committee. Whenever Wyley attended chamber of commerce events, he would sit beside Fred and try to make friends with him.

At one meeting, Fred said to Wyley, "You son of a gun, you're the darndest fellow." He then confessed to his role in the committee. "Every time I see you," he said, "you come in here so darn friendly that I like you better all the time."[29]

The town soon warmed to the Sessions family. With Wyley's help, the Church found property near the campus and purchased it for the Saints' student center. Wyley and a Church architect then worked with the university and chamber of commerce to design the building and approve and oversee its construction. In the fall of 1927, Wyley began teaching religion classes, and the university agreed to grant college credits to students who took them. Magdalen, meanwhile, organized a series of social activities for Latter-day Saint students like Norma and Zola Geddes.[30]

One day, while Wyley was walking with Jay Eldridge, the faculty dean, they passed the property for the Church's new student center. "You were pretty smart to get that land," Dr. Eldridge told Wyley. He asked what the Church intended to name its new program. "You can't call it the seminary," he said. "You've spoiled that, anyway, with your high school seminaries."

"I don't know," said Wyley. "I haven't really thought about it."

Dr. Eldridge stopped. "I'll tell you what the name is," he said. "What you see up there is the Latter-day Saint Institute of Religion."

Wyley liked the recommendation, and so did the General Church Board of Education.[31]

IN SEPTEMBER 1927, LEAH Widtsoe felt spiritually, mentally, and physically exhausted. The sudden death of her son Marsel had plunged her into a dark depression. "I really wonder if life is worthwhile," she told John one day. "If it were not for your love I know it would not be."[32]

Marsel had been buried on May 31 in the Salt Lake Cemetery. The next day was Leah and John's twenty-ninth wedding anniversary, and they had spent it trying to clean up after the funeral. Friends and family visited often in the weeks and months that followed, but even with their support and love, healing was slow to come.[33] They could take joy in the news that their daughter Ann was expecting a child. Yet Ann was also unhappy in her marriage, so she decided to stay in Utah with her parents rather than return to her husband in Washington, DC.

Leah's depression turned most days into a struggle. John's Church assignments kept him traveling as much as ever, but when he was home, he was frequently at her side, making her life bearable. "I pray that we may be spared for each other," she told him that summer. "With you I can fight any battle!"[34]

Ann's baby, John Widtsoe Wallace, arrived on August 8, 1927, making Leah and John grandparents.[35] One month later, Harold Shepstone, an English news-paperman, met Leah's mother during a visit to Salt Lake City. Susa told him all about the biography she and Leah were writing about Brigham Young, and he asked to look at it. Susa gave him a copy of the manuscript, and he agreed to help her find a publisher.

"It will make a most interesting reading," he said, "but, of course, it will have to be greatly condensed."[36]

All this good news was not enough to lift Leah's spirits. Susa invited Leah to join her on a trip to California, perhaps hoping a visit to the coast would cheer her up.[37] But almost as soon as they purchased tickets, President Grant called John to be the new president of the European Mission. John was in a daze for the rest of the day, and he hardly slept that night. The European Mission was one of the oldest and largest missions in the

Church, and the president had responsibility for managing nine other mission presidents who were stationed in countries spreading across thousands of miles—from Norway to South Africa. Normally an apostle with more experience was called to lead it.[38]

Leah welcomed the new call, even though it would pull her away from her home and loved ones in Utah. The last year had been a nightmare, and she could use a change in her life. Reminders of Marsel were everywhere, and moving to Europe would give her space to grieve. John, in fact, believed that President Grant had been inspired to call them on a mission to help them cope with the loss of their son.[39]

Preparation consumed the next two months.[40] As Leah packed, she thought about Harold Shepstone and the Brigham Young biography. Determined to hold Harold to his word to help her find a publisher, she packed the manuscript.[41]

On November 21, Leah and John were set apart for their missions. They then returned home to say goodbye to John's aunt Petroline, who was now seventy-four years old. Leah and John had offered to take her to Europe with them, but she did not think she was strong enough to go. Yet she was happy that John had a chance to return to Europe and teach the gospel, as she and his mother had done twenty years earlier.

Later that day, a crowd saw Leah, John, and their daughter Eudora off at the railroad station. Susa gave them a letter to open on the train. "I shall follow you in

your journey, and in the great work you will both accomplish," she wrote. "Auntie and I will both be on the
depot platform when you come home, serene, smiling,
rejoiced in the return of our best beloved children."

She also urged Leah to prepare herself for the
many difficulties sure to surround her on the mission.
"Our Father must Himself be ruthless at times," she
wrote, "when experience is to be gained by His children
through sorrow, poverty, and struggle."[42]

CHAPTER 18

Any Place on Earth

In December 1927, Reinhold Stoof, the president of the South American Mission, was ready to leave Argentina—if only briefly.

When Reinhold came to Buenos Aires eighteen months earlier, he had expected to work mainly with German-speaking immigrants. But the Germans in the city were spread out and hard to find, making it difficult to do missionary work among them. If the Church was to grow like an oak in South America, as Elder Melvin J. Ballard had prophesied, Reinhold and his small band of missionaries would need to take the gospel to Spanish speakers.[1]

As a German-born Saint who hardly knew a word of Spanish, Reinhold started studying the language almost immediately. Yet he still felt responsible for the

Germans on the continent. He knew there were large German-speaking immigrant communities in neighboring Brazil. In fact, before returning to the United States, Elder Ballard had recommended sending missionaries to these communities to gauge their interest in the gospel.

Reinhold was aware of a few German Saints already living in Brazil, and he believed they could help establish branches of the Church in their towns and cities. With work among German immigrants slowing down in Buenos Aires, the time seemed right to visit Brazil.[2]

On December 14, Reinhold left a missionary in charge of the work in Argentina and traveled to Brazil with an elder named Waldo Stoddard. They stopped first in São Paulo, one of Brazil's largest cities, where they hoped to find a Church member who had moved there after serving in the Swiss-German Mission. But their search was unsuccessful, and the city itself proved too challenging for missionary work. São Paulo had many German immigrants, but as in Buenos Aires, they were scattered throughout the city.[3]

A week later, Reinhold and Waldo traveled to a smaller city called Joinville, in southern Brazil. The city had been founded by immigrants from northern Europe in the 1850s, and many people who lived there still spoke German. The people were kind and seemed interested in the gospel. Reinhold and Waldo distributed tracts and held two meetings in the city. On both occasions, more than a hundred people attended. The elders found similar interest when they preached in other towns in the area. On their last day in Joinville, they were invited to administer to two sick women.

After spending three weeks in and around Joinville, Reinhold returned to Argentina thrilled by what he found in Brazil. "Working among the Germans in Buenos Aires will always be good," he informed the First Presidency, "but is nothing compared with a work among the Germans in Brazil."

He wanted to send missionaries to Joinville immediately. "I was always an optimist in my life, but never too enthusiastic not to see the shadows and hindrances," he admitted. "And yet I repeat: This South Brazil is the place!"[4]

AROUND THE TIME REINHOLD Stoof returned from Brazil, John and Leah Widtsoe arrived in Liverpool, England, to begin their mission. They immediately enrolled Eudora in a local high school and settled into their new lives. Leah embraced the change. She had never served a mission nor devoted so much time to work outside her home, and every day brought new experiences. Missionary work came naturally to her, and she enjoyed serving alongside John, whose career and church assignments had often kept them apart.[5]

Nearly thirty years had passed since they had come to Europe for John's education. In that time, the Church had changed remarkably throughout the continent. The end of large-scale emigration to Utah meant that some twenty-eight thousand Saints now lived in Europe, almost half of them German-speaking. Hostile critics like William Jarman had also faded from view, and many newspapers now published fair-minded reports of Church conferences or remarked favorably on the good deeds of the Saints.[6]

Yet, as Leah and John visited branches throughout the continent, they sensed some indifference and frustration among the Saints. Some ordinances of the Church, like patriarchal blessings and temple worship, were unavailable in Europe. And since the Church had stopped promoting emigration efforts, few European Saints could ever hope to participate in these ordinances.[7]

Other factors were hindering progress. Missionaries coming from America were younger and more inexperienced than their predecessors. Many of them could hardly speak the language of the mission, yet in most cases, missionaries were put in charge of congregations—even in places where there were strong, capable members who had been in the Church for decades. Relying on modest tithing revenues, these branches usually rented meeting halls in run-down parts of town, making it difficult to attract new members. A lack of Relief Societies, Primaries, Mutual Improvement Associations, and Sunday Schools also made the Church less appealing to Latter-day Saints and potential Church members alike.[8]

Leah, like John, was eager to serve the European Saints. Her primary responsibility was to direct Relief

Society work in Europe, and soon after arriving in England, she began writing Relief Society lessons on the Book of Mormon for the coming year. In her first message to the Relief Society in the British Isles, published in the *Millennial Star,* she acknowledged their distance from Church headquarters but expressed her view that Zion was not a single location.

"After all, where is Zion?" she asked. "Zion is the 'pure in heart,' and that may be any place on earth where men choose to serve God in fullness and truth."[9]

As Leah and John traveled around the mission, learning more about how to help the people of Europe, their thoughts kept returning to their son Marsel. It was hard for John to visit the area where his son had served faithfully. Yet he took comfort from an experience he had shortly after Marsel's death, when the young man's spirit came and assured him that he was happy and busy with missionary work on the other side of the veil. The message had given John courage to face life without his son.[10]

Leah also drew strength from this assurance. Previously, knowing that Marsel was cheerfully laboring in the spirit world had not been enough to pull her from her depression. But the mission changed her perspective. "The knowledge that our son is busy over there as we are here in the same great cause gives me an added spur to increase my activity and zeal," she wrote in a letter to a friend in Utah. Marsel's death was still a painful memory, but she found hope and healing in Jesus Christ.

"Nothing but the gospel could make such an experience bearable," she testified. And now her faith in the healing power of the Lord was unshakable. "It has stood the test," she wrote. "It works."[11]

IN LATE MARCH 1929, rain and wind battered the home of Bertha and Ferdinand Sell in Joinville, Brazil. For Bertha, the storm could hardly have come at a worse time. She and Ferdinand, both second-generation German immigrants, supported their seven children by selling milk around the city. Since Ferdinand had suffered an accident leaving him unable to deliver the milk to their customers, it was Bertha's job to make the deliveries, come rain or shine. Never mind that she had asthma.[12]

On this day, Bertha spent hours on her feet, making delivery after delivery despite the terrible weather. She returned home weary, but after entering the house, she caught sight of a scrap of newspaper on the table. She picked it up and asked, "Where did this newspaper come from?" No one in her family knew.

The paper had an advertisement for a Latter-day Saint meeting that night in Joinville. "How interesting! I've never heard about this church," she said to her husband. "All of us are invited to go there."

Ferdinand was not interested. "What are we going to do at a meeting with strangers?" he asked.

"Let's go," Bertha insisted.

"You are tired," he said. "You've already walked so much today. It's better for you not to go." Besides, there was her health to consider. What if she overexerted herself getting to the meeting?

"But I want to go," she said. "Something whispers to me that I need to go."[13]

Ferdinand at last gave in, and he and Bertha walked into town with a few of their children. The streets were thick with mud from the day's rain, but the family arrived at the meeting in time to hear two German-speaking missionaries, Emil Schindler and William Heinz, speak about the restored gospel of Jesus Christ. The elders had come to Joinville six months earlier with President Reinhold Stoof, who had returned to Brazil to start a branch in the city.

While some ministers in town had tried to turn people against them, the missionaries had been quick to defend their beliefs. They had distributed tracts and presented well-attended slideshows about the Church. They now held regular evening meetings and a Sunday school for around forty students. Still, no one in Joinville had joined the Church.[14]

When the meeting ended, everyone said "amen" and left the hall. As Bertha stepped outside, she had a sudden asthma attack. Ferdinand rushed into the building and called to the missionaries for help. Emil and William came at once and carried Bertha back inside. They placed their hands on her head and gave her a priesthood blessing. She soon recovered and walked back outside, smiling.

"They said a prayer for me," she told her family, "and now I am better."[15]

The missionaries helped the family back to their house, and Bertha immediately told her neighbors what had happened. "Of this I am sure," she said to her friends. "The Church is true." She was so happy. She could feel the truth of the gospel.

The next day, Bertha sought out the missionaries to tell them that she now wanted them to baptize her and her children.

Over the next two weeks, the elders visited the family and taught them lesson after lesson about the restored gospel. Ferdinand and the oldest daughter, Anita, did not want to join the Church at that time. But Emil and William baptized Bertha and four of her children—Theodor, Alice, Siegfried, and Adele—on April 14 in the nearby Cachoeira River. They were the first Latter-day Saints baptized in Brazil.

Soon Bertha's friends and neighbors were attending meetings with her, and before long, a branch of The Church of Jesus Christ of Latter-day Saints was established in Joinville.[16]

THAT SAME SEASON, IN Cincinnati, Ohio, the Presbyterian church put a small brick chapel up for sale in early 1929. The chapel was about seventy years old and was on a side street at the north end of the downtown area. Although not as grand as other churches or synagogues in the city, it had a beautiful arched entryway, an ornate tower, and several large windows facing the street.[17]

The chapel quickly caught the eye of Charles Anderson, the Cincinnati Branch president, and his counselors, Christian Bang and Alvin Gilliam. Like many branch presidents in the Church, Charles had long wanted to find a permanent meetinghouse for his congregation. At the time, ward and branch leaders throughout the Church were eager to build or purchase meetinghouses with modern heating, indoor plumbing, and electric lights. While Charles had fond memories of all the old stores and other rented halls the Cincinnati Branch had met in over the years, he knew they were only temporary homes for the Saints. Sooner or later, the branch would grow too big or a lease would end, and the Saints would have to find another place to meet.[18]

The cycle was tedious. Charles had always tried to secure the nicest, most respectable hall he could find. For many years, the Church was not well regarded in the city, and some people had flatly refused to rent to Latter-day Saints. Charles and the branch had worked to change perceptions about the Church by holding street meetings, staging free concerts and plays, and inviting people to worship with them on Sunday. These efforts were somewhat successful, and finding new meeting halls had become easier. But the frequent moving from street to street hindered the Saints' ability to attract converts in the city.

Recognizing the problem, the local mission president had counseled Charles to begin looking for a permanent chapel for the Cincinnati Saints. The branch now numbered around seventy people, most of them young working-class women and men who had grown up in the area. They were new to the Church, and many of them were the only members in their families. The branch provided them with priesthood quorums, a Relief Society, a Sunday School, a Primary, and an MIA to help them grow in the gospel. All they needed now was a home.[19]

Once Charles and his counselors made an offer on the Presbyterian chapel, the mission president came to Cincinnati and inspected the property. He approved the purchase and worked with Charles to secure funding from Church headquarters to acquire and renovate the building.[20]

Some Presbyterian ministers, meanwhile, were outraged when they learned that Latter-day Saints were purchasing the chapel. In the past, Presbyterians in Cincinnati had taken part in efforts to criticize and discredit the Church. How could the congregation think of selling its chapel to the Saints?

A few influential Presbyterians in Cincinnati supported the sale, content to know the chapel would remain a place of worship. But the ministers tried everything in their power to prevent the Saints from making the purchase. When their efforts failed, they asked Charles to complete the transaction through a middleman so the public records would not show that the Presbyterians had sold their chapel to the Latter-day Saints. Charles was hurt by the request, but he ultimately arranged to have the property transferred first to a lawyer and then to the Church.[21]

Spring soon turned into summer, and the branch began counting down the days until renovations on the building were finished. The dedication of the chapel promised to be a grand event. In a matter of months, the Cincinnati Saints would finally have a place they could call their own.[22]

MEANWHILE, IN THE CITY of Tilsit in northeastern Germany, forty-five-year-old Otto Schulzke was one of the few locally called branch presidents on the European continent.

Otto was a short man who worked in a prison and had a reputation for being stern.[23] Earlier that year, about a month before receiving his call, he had offended half the branch when he spoke out too sharply during an MIA lesson. Some people left the meeting crying. Others responded sarcastically to him. The missionaries, who were leading the branch at the time, simply seemed annoyed with him.

In fact, before being transferred to another city, the missionaries had worried about Otto becoming branch president. "No one will support him," they told each other.[24]

But the elders underestimated the older, more experienced man. His family's devotion to the Church was well known in the area. Years earlier, his father, Friedrich Schulzke, had heard terrifying stories about "Mormon" missionaries, so he had prayed fervently that they would always stay far away from his home and family. And when "Mormon" missionaries eventually showed up at his door, he chased them away with a broomstick.

Some time later, Friedrich met two young men who introduced themselves as missionaries from The Church of Jesus Christ of Latter-day Saints. They invited him to a meeting, and he was so impressed by what he heard that he invited the elders to preach in his home. When they arrived, however, he was startled to see one of them carrying a Book of Mormon, and he knew at once that they belonged to the very church he was trying to avoid. Still, he reluctantly let them speak, and before long he knew they were messengers from God.

One year later, he and his wife, Anna, joined the Church, and Otto and some of his siblings soon followed their example.[25]

When the war began in 1914, the missionaries left the area, and Friedrich had become the new branch president. Although he did not hold the Melchizedek Priesthood, he had served effectively in the calling. His branch would gather at his home, and together they would study the gospel and learn about the wonderful things the Lord had in store for them. Whenever he became overwhelmed by his responsibilities, he would kneel down and ask the Lord for help.[26]

Otto had also served as a branch president once before, shortly after the war. At the time, the Tilsit Branch was still recovering from the devastation, and many people had drifted away from the Church. Otto, as gruff as he was, certainly did not seem like the best person to revive the branch, but he rose to the occasion. During his first year as president, twenty-three people in Tilsit had joined the Church.[27]

Otto's first experience as president lasted only a few years before missionaries returned to the area and took charge of most branches. Now, with Elder Widtsoe's desire to make the branches in Europe more self-sustaining and self-governing, Otto and other local Saints were being called to lead again.[28]

But the question remained: Would the Saints in Tilsit accept his leadership, as they had in the past? Or would they refuse to support him, as the missionaries predicted?

The branch had many faithful Saints—around sixty or so members attended meetings each week—and they were eager to serve the Lord. But after being led by young missionaries, they might not respond well to a strict, older man who had little tolerance for nonsense.

As a branch president, after all, Otto expected the Saints to live the gospel. And he was not afraid to tell them so.[29]

CHAPTER 19

The Gospel of the Master

On Monday, September 9, 1929, lightning shattered a utility pole when a severe storm ripped through Cincinnati, Ohio. The strike sent a surge of electricity down a wire and into the newly renovated Latter-day Saint chapel at the north end of town. Some wiring insulation caught fire, flooding the building with smoke. Firefighters soon arrived, but the damage was done.

At first, the Cincinnati Branch worried that the fire had destroyed the building's wiring. With the chapel's dedication less than a week away, the Saints would have neither time nor money to repair any extensive damage. But after an inspection, they discovered that the wiring was salvageable. They went to work at once to repair and replace wires, and soon the building was back in working order.[1]

As the dedication day neared, more and more people seemed to take notice of the Church. On September 12, Christian Bang, the branch's first counselor, took time away from his grocery store to give an interview to a local newspaper. The reporter knew the Saints had once been the subject of controversy, and Christian was willing to clarify misconceptions the public had about the Church.[2]

"The Church has outgrown many prejudices in the past decade," he told the reporter. "People are beginning to put aside age-old ideas and recognize the ideals for which we stand."

"What is your stand on polygamy now?" the reporter asked.

"That is a dead issue," Christian said. "We are strictly orthodox in our belief. We believe in tithing, and practice it, although our elders and counselors do not receive any salary for their services."[3]

Three days later, reporters turned out again for the dedication of the chapel. The joy of the Saints was unmistakable. About four hundred people, including missionaries from the surrounding area, crowded into the chapel for the meeting. Apostle Orson F. Whitney, whose grandparents Newel and Elizabeth Ann Whitney had joined the Church in Ohio nearly a century earlier, had come from Salt Lake City to offer the dedicatory prayer.[4]

Perhaps no one was more enthusiastic that afternoon than branch president Charles Anderson. Together with the Bang family and other early branch members, he and his wife, Christine, had labored long and hard to grow their branch in Cincinnati. When it was his turn to speak to the congregation, he recounted the many challenges that came with purchasing and renovating the meetinghouse.

"We worked night and day to get it in condition for the dedication," he declared, "and no one could be prouder than we are today."[5]

In his sermon, Elder Whitney recounted Joseph Smith and Oliver Cowdery's 1836 vision of the Savior in the Kirtland Temple, a powerful reminder of Ohio's sacred history. As the apostle spoke, the Spirit of God rested upon him, and when he finished recounting the vision, he began to pray.

"Almighty God, our Heavenly Father," he said. "May all who enter this house feel the influence of the Spirit of God. Reward those who have contributed of their means for its completion. Manifest the power of God in this chapel."

He asked a blessing on the members of the Cincinnati Branch, the missionaries and mission leaders who served them, and all those who lived nearby. "Pour out Thy Spirit upon those who are here assembled," he prayed, "and accept of this, our offering."

A feeling of peace and quiet rested over the Saints in the chapel. Before returning to his seat, Elder Whitney said, "I feel that Mormonism from this time on will be better understood and be received with a kindlier feeling by the people of Ohio."[6]

ON NOVEMBER 1, 1929, HEBER J. Grant reminisced in his journal about the day he replaced apostle Francis Lyman as president of Utah's Tooele Stake. The year was 1880, and Heber had been just a few weeks shy of his twenty-fourth birthday. President John Taylor and his counselors, George Q. Cannon and Joseph F. Smith, were in town for the stake conference, and Elder Lyman hosted them and Heber at his home.

During the visit, someone—Heber could not remember who—had prayed for "thine aged servant, President Taylor." The word "aged" did not sit well with the prophet, who was about to turn seventy-two years old. When the prayer was over, he asked, "Why didn't you pray for my youthful counselors?" Heber could still remember the annoyance in his voice.

Now, nearly half a century later, Heber was about to turn seventy-*three* years old. "I am afraid I would feel a little shocked if someone were to pray for 'thine aged servant President Grant,'" he wrote in his journal. He felt just as young as he did when he was forty—and even more healthy.

"The fact that we do not seem to get old in spirit is to me one of the evidences of the immortality of the soul," he noted.[7]

Normally Heber would have gathered his children and their families together for his birthday. But his daughter Emily had died from complications with childbirth a few months earlier, and his heart was not yet ready for a family party. Instead, he was preparing to visit the stakes in Arizona, just south of Utah.[8] Shortly before his death, Brigham Young had asked for two hundred volunteers to settle in Arizona. Since that time, the Saints had established dozens of settlements across the state, and Church members could now be found in high positions of civic responsibility. In 1927, Heber had dedicated a temple there to serve them as well as the Saints in nearby areas, including northern Mexico.[9]

Heber was also looking forward to a much larger celebration. The Saints would soon commemorate the one hundredth anniversary of the organization of the Church. With nearly seven hundred thousand Church members in almost eighteen hundred wards and branches throughout the world, the celebration would be a global event. For more than a year, a small committee led by apostle George Albert Smith had been planning an extravaganza to coincide with the April 1930 general conference. Heber had followed their preparations and provided occasional feedback.[10]

He left for Arizona on November 15 and spent the next ten days visiting with Saints and basking in their love. Over the last eleven years, his feelings of inadequacy had faded. He had not disappointed the Church, as he feared he would, nor failed to live up to previous Church presidents. Instead, as the Church moved toward its second century, it was growing and flourishing.[11]

As Church president, Heber had witnessed a technological revolution that carried general conference and other gospel messages across the airwaves. Now, every

Sunday evening, people living hundreds of miles from Salt Lake City could tune in to KSL, the Church's radio station, to hear leaders and teachers giving addresses on gospel subjects.[12] What was more, in July 1929, the Tabernacle Choir had begun a weekly radio broadcast through a New York City network. The program was an instant success across the country, and millions of listeners became better acquainted with the Church through the choir.[13]

Heber had also used his influence as Church president to encourage the Saints to teach and serve one another in their wards and branches. When he was young, Sunday meetings had been a time for Saints to listen to prominent men preach and teach. But under his direction, wards and branches had become the center of Church activity. Everyone was now expected to serve. Men, women, and youth taught classes, participated in quorum and class presidencies, and gave talks in sacrament meeting.[14] Many Saints were also called as stake missionaries to seek after Church members who had stopped attending.[15] And, for the first time, wards and stakes were sending groups of youth to the temple to perform baptisms for the dead.[16]

Believing the Church would be known by its fruits, Heber had urged the Saints to live clean lives. Over and over, he challenged them to keep the Word of Wisdom with exactness, abstaining from alcohol, coffee, tea, tobacco, and other harmful substances earlier generations of Saints had sometimes used. He made obedience to the Word of Wisdom mandatory for temple attendance and missionary service and pleaded with the Saints to pay full tithes and give offerings.[17]

On the morning of his seventy-third birthday, Heber amused high school students in Snowflake, Arizona, with stories about his efforts to master marbles, baseball, penmanship, and singing. He had told these stories many times over the years to inspire persistence and excellence, and his listeners never seemed to tire of them.[18]

As the day wore on, Heber's bright eyes, strong voice, and firm step were proof of his excellent health and stamina. No one who saw him could tell that he had traveled across a good portion of the state the previous day, stopping eight times to speak to gatherings along the way.[19]

THAT SAME AUTUMN, IN northeastern Germany, the Saints in the Tilsit Branch met every Sabbath morning for Sunday School. To help the meeting run smoothly, branch president Otto Schulzke did everything he could to assist the Sunday School superintendent. If something needed to be done, from conducting meetings to leading the music, Otto would do it. Now more and more people were coming out to class each Sunday, including people who were not members of the Church.

Nine-year-old Helga Meiszus, one of the many children who attended Sunday School, liked President Schulzke, despite his sternness. He and his family had been a part of her life for as long as she could remember.

After she was born, he was the one who had blessed her in church.[20]

Helga's family was a mainstay in the Tilsit Branch. Her maternal grandmother, Johanne Wachsmuth, had first met missionaries many years earlier. But it was not until the family moved to Tilsit and encountered some local Saints that they had begun attending MIA and other Church meetings. At first, Helga's grandfather was suspicious of the Saints, but he eventually joined the Church along with Helga's mother, grandmother, aunts, and uncle. Helga's father had also been baptized just before she was born, but neither he nor her grandfather attended Church very often.

Helga enjoyed going to Sunday School. Someone was always playing the organ five minutes before the meeting started. It used to be Helga's aunt Gretel, but she had emigrated to Canada in 1928 with the hope of one day making it to Utah.[21] Now another woman in the branch, Sister Jonigkeit, played the prelude music.[22]

The Tilsit Sunday School followed the same order of exercises as every other Sunday School in the Church. Meetings opened with a hymn, an opening prayer, and another hymn. Priesthood holders then administered the sacrament for the benefit of the children who did not attend sacrament meeting later in the evening. The Sunday School then recited a scripture together and practiced singing.[23]

Helga's uncle Heinrich once led the singing lessons, but he had also emigrated to Canada some months after

Gretel. Now President Schulzke often led the lessons. One of the songs Helga knew well was "Abide with Me; 'Tis Eventide," which she would sing when the sirens went off at the nearby paper factory where her father worked. Anytime she heard the sirens, she knew something bad had happened at the factory, and she worried about her father.[24]

When singing practice ended, the Sunday School hung curtains to divide the hall into separate classrooms for adults, youth, and children. In wards, children's Sunday School was divided in two classes, one for younger children and one for older. In small branches like Tilsit's, however, all children met together in one class.[25]

Around fifteen children attended class with Helga. Each week they learned about God and His works, faith in Jesus Christ, the Second Coming, the mission of Joseph Smith, and other gospel subjects. Often children who were not members of the Church would attend the classes. Between Church meetings, Helga sometimes attended Lutheran meetings with her school friends and sang old Lutheran hymns. But her heart was always with the Latter-day Saints.[26]

When their Sunday School class ended, Helga and the other children would gather again with the older Saints to hear closing remarks. They sang a hymn and said a prayer, and then the class adjourned until sacrament meeting later that evening. Erika Stephani, the Sunday School secretary, recorded each meeting in her minute book.[27]

"The past year has developed such an unexpected amount of work for me," Leah Widtsoe told a friend in December 1929. "I have had time for little else than chasing all over the face of Europe with my husband, visiting and instructing our people, and supervising the welfare of our 750 young men who are in these lands acting as missionaries."[28]

She was not complaining. She loved the work.[29] So far, she and John had witnessed many important changes in the Church in Europe. More and more local Melchizedek Priesthood holders were serving as branch presidents, giving missionaries more time to share the gospel with those who had never heard it. Branches were also finding better places to meet. In July 1929, Church members in the eastern German town of Selbongen had finished building a meetinghouse, the first Latter-day Saint chapel in Germany. The Saints in Liège and Seraing in Belgium, as well as the Saints in Copenhagen, Denmark, were also building chapels. And that summer, John had traveled to Prague, Czechoslovakia, where a small group of Saints lived, and dedicated that country for missionary work.[30]

Still, as rewarding as mission life was, it could be taxing. The work was intensive, and both Leah and John were losing weight. Concerned about their health, Leah had begun carefully monitoring their diets, relying on her university training in nutrition to ensure that they ate healthy foods. She had also taken an interest in the health of the European Saints.

During her first year in the mission, she noticed that many people ate cheap imported foods that provided few nutrients for the body, resulting in serious health problems. In January 1929, she began publishing a series of Relief Society lessons on the Word of Wisdom in the *Millennial Star.* At a time when discussions about the Word of Wisdom often emphasized what to avoid, Leah's lessons drew on her knowledge of scripture and nutritional science to explain how eating whole grains, fruits and vegetables, and other healthy foods recommended by the Word of Wisdom could make a person stronger physically, mentally, and spiritually.

In her first Word of Wisdom lesson, Leah paraphrased Doctrine and Covenants 88:15 to remind readers that spiritual and physical health were intertwined. "The spirit and the body constitute the soul of man," she reminded readers. "Indeed, the true gospel must include bodily health and vigor since the body is but the tabernacle of the spirit which dwells within the body and is the direct offspring of our heavenly parents."[31]

She and John had also encouraged the European Saints to do genealogical work. "There are no temples at present in Europe in which the Saints may perform the actual ordinances of the gospel," John acknowledged in a September 19, 1929, article in the *Millennial Star.* "Therefore," he wrote, "the main activity in these lands must be the gathering of genealogy."

Leah began writing genealogy lessons for the European Saints, and John devised an exchange program to help them participate in temple work. He asked every branch to start a genealogy class to help Saints research their family histories, prepare pedigree charts, and identify names for proxy ordinance work. These names would then be sent to Saints in the United States, who would perform the temple work for them. In exchange for this service, the Saints in Europe would conduct genealogical research for American Saints who could not afford to travel across the Atlantic.[32]

At this time, Leah and John worked with Harold Shepstone, the English newspaperman, to find a publisher for her mother's biography of Brigham Young. Susa trusted Leah and John to make whatever cuts were needed to get the manuscript ready for publication. She told Leah, "The best thing is to use it for the building up of the kingdom of God."

Susa also insisted that Leah share authorship with her. "I am not going to be satisfied to have my name only appear on the history of my father," she wrote Leah. "You will never know, for I could not put into words, the help you have been to me in that and in all my writing in the last few years."

In December, Harold notified John and Leah that a major British book company had agreed to publish the biography.[33] The news was an answer to the family's prayers, and it came at the end of a busy but rewarding year.

Leah could not be more satisfied working as a missionary alongside John. "We are not anxious to come home, except to see our dear ones and friends," she wrote in a letter around this time. "I feel as though I'd like to end my days on a mission—trying actively to spread the glorious truths of the gospel of the Master."[34]

ON THE MORNING OF Sunday, April 6, 1930, President Heber J. Grant awoke at five o'clock, ready for the historic day ahead of him. Outside, the streets around Temple Square in Salt Lake City were radiant with colorful bunting and banners to celebrate the one hundredth anniversary of the organization of the Church.[35]

Over the past week, tens of thousands of Saints had been pouring into the city to take part in the festivities. Hotels were filled to capacity, and many Salt Lake City residents had opened their homes to accommodate the visitors. Nothing this big, save the dedication of the Salt Lake Temple, had ever occurred in the city.[36]

Major newspapers and magazines across the world were already reporting on the centennial. Anyone who strolled down South Temple Street, moreover, could see B. H. Roberts's new six-volume history of the Church's first hundred years on display in the window of Deseret Book, the Church's bookstore. When first organized in upstate New York, the Church had hardly attracted any notice. Now the *Deseret News* was estimating that publicity for the centennial had reached some 75 million people in the United States alone. President Grant's portrait was featured that week on the cover of *Time,* one of the most popular newsmagazines in the United States. The article that accompanied it was respectful—even complimentary—of the work of the Church.[37]

The opening session of general conference, the premier event of the centennial celebration, began at ten o'clock. Since seating in the Tabernacle was limited, Church leaders had issued special tickets for the session and extended the conference one additional day so more people could attend in person. They also organized overflow meetings in the nearby Assembly Hall and in several other buildings throughout the city.

For Saints living farther away, KSL radio broadcast the conference throughout Utah and its neighboring states, allowing Saints for hundreds of miles to listen to the proceedings. Saints in more distant parts of the world, who could not receive the broadcast, were instructed to gather at the same time for smaller centennial celebrations patterned after the celebration in Salt Lake City.[38]

President Grant's heart was brimming with gratitude as he opened the conference by reading an address prepared by the First Presidency. Weeks earlier, he and his counselors had sent the address to the stakes and missions in the Church, instructing them to translate it, if necessary. "At this hour," he announced, "all over the world this message will be read by our people."

In the address, President Grant and his counselors testified powerfully of the Restoration of the gospel, the mortal ministry of the Savior, and His redeeming sacrifice. They spoke of the persecution of the early Christians and the centuries of religious confusion that followed their trials. They then bore testimony of the Book of Mormon, the restoration of the priesthood and the organization of the Church, the gathering of Israel, the commencement of temple work for the living and dead, and the Second Coming of Jesus Christ.

"We exhort our brethren and sisters to put their houses in order, that ye may be prepared for that which is to come," they said. "Refrain from evil; do that which is good. Visit the sick, comfort those who are in sorrow, clothe the naked, feed the hungry, care for the widow and the fatherless."[39]

After the Saints sustained the general authorities of the Church, President Grant waved a handkerchief in the air and led the congregation in the Hosanna Shout. In their own centennial celebrations, hundreds of thousands of Saints throughout the world performed the sacred rite as well, shouting praises to God and the Lamb in their native tongues.[40]

Crowds returned to the Tabernacle that evening for the first performance of *The Message of the Ages,* a lavish pageant tracing the sacred history of the world. The production engaged a thousand actors to re-create events from the scriptures and Church history while singers and musicians performed hymns and selections from some of the greatest musical compositions of all time. The colorful costumes were well crafted, aiming for historical accuracy. The actor playing Joseph Smith wore a collar once owned by the prophet himself.[41]

As the sun went down on the celebration, the Church illuminated each of its seven temples with powerful new floodlights. The grandeur of the buildings shone brilliantly against the dark of night, exhibiting their beauty and solemnity for miles in every direction. And in Salt Lake City, the gleaming statue of the angel Moroni, with his golden trumpet raised high above the crowds, seemed to be calling Saints from far and wide to rejoice in the magnificent centennial.[42]

PART 3

In the Heat of Battle

1930–1945

"In the quiet hours, in the heat of battle,
and through the hazards of the day;
in times of temptation, of sorrow, of peace
and of blessing, let us pray always . . .
for strength to endure to the end."

Heber J. Grant, December 1942

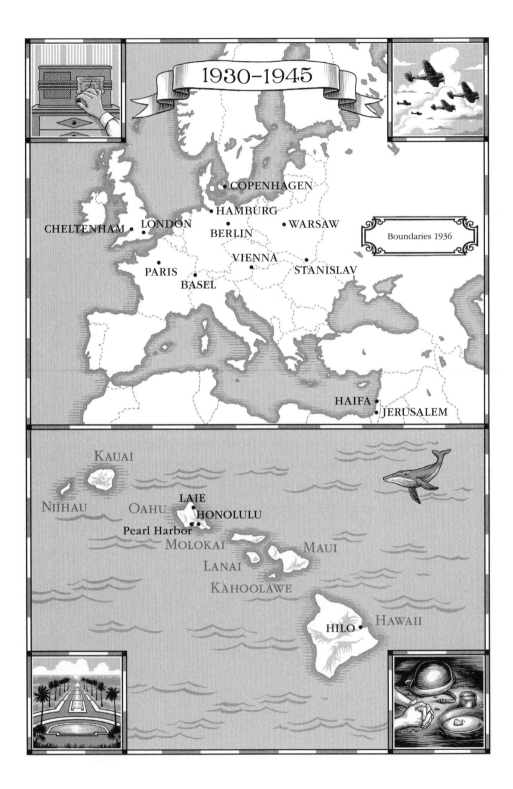

CHAPTER 20

Hard Times

Shortly after graduating from Utah State Agricultural College, twenty-two-year-old Evelyn Hodges turned down a paid position as a schoolteacher to volunteer as a social worker for the Relief Society Social Service Department in Salt Lake City.[1]

Her parents were not pleased. Although very active in the Relief Society, her mother did not think social work was the sort of thing her daughter should do. And her father simply wanted her to remain on the family farm in Logan.

"I have one living daughter, and I ought to be able to support her," he said. "Stay at home. Get a master's degree, get a doctor's degree—anything you want to. But stay home."[2]

Evelyn finally struck a deal with her parents. She would volunteer for nine weeks as a social worker. If the Relief Society did not offer her paid work by then, she would come back home.

On her first Saturday in Salt Lake City, Evelyn reported at the home of Amy Brown Lyman, the first counselor in the Relief Society general presidency and the director of Relief Society Social Service. Amy did not meet her at the door. Instead, Evelyn found her on the second floor of the house, sitting cross-legged in the middle of a bed, absorbed in a sewing project. She wore a rumpled dress and had sewing supplies strewn all about her.

Amy's appearance and aloofness unsettled Evelyn. She wondered if she had made the right decision in coming to Salt Lake City. Did she really want to work for this woman?[3]

Over the next nine weeks, Evelyn discovered that she did. Her job as a caseworker for about eighty families took her all over the city, and she came to know its streets and alleyways well. At first, she was timid about speaking with strangers, but she soon found joy and satisfaction in helping people in need. When her parents came to take her home after her nine weeks were over, she despaired. The Relief Society still had not offered her a job.

Evelyn had been back in Logan for three days when she received a call from Amy. A Relief Society social worker had just accepted a job at a nearby hospital, and Amy wanted to know if Evelyn could take her place.

"Oh yes," Evelyn said. She did not even ask how much Amy would pay her.

Evelyn's father was away at the time, and he was disappointed when he found out she had accepted the job in his absence. She did not want to upset him, but she was committed to her new career.[4]

Back in Salt Lake City, Evelyn worked directly with local bishops who referred widows, disabled people, unemployed families, and others in desperate circumstances to the Relief Society.[5] Under the bishop's supervision, she would help develop a relief plan for each situation. She would also coordinate with wards and the local government to provide money for the needy from fast offerings, Relief Society funds, and county-run charities.

According to Church guidelines at the time, people were encouraged to get help from the government before turning to the Church, so many of the families Evelyn worked with received help from both sources. The assistance was usually small, however, and she always asked her clients what additional help relatives, friends, or neighbors could provide.[6]

In October 1929, a few months after Evelyn returned to Salt Lake City, the stock market in the United States crashed. At first, plummeting stock prices in far-off New York City did not seem to affect Evelyn's caseload. By the spring of 1930, in fact, the economy seemed to be recovering from the crash.[7]

But the recovery was short-lived. Individuals and businesses with large debts could not repay them. People began spending less money, reducing the demand for goods and services.[8] Utah was hit especially hard. Its economy, which depended heavily on mining and farm exports, was already struggling when the stock market crashed. Once prices dropped on all basic commodities, producers could not turn a profit or pay workers, and many people quickly found themselves out of a job. To make matters worse, fewer people had money to give to charitable organizations to help the needy. Tithing and other Church donations also declined.

Not long after the Church's centennial celebration, Evelyn began seeing more families who could not make ends meet. Fear was taking root in their hearts.[9]

ON THE EVENING OF May 19, 1930, William and Clara Daniels welcomed South African Mission president Don Dalton into their home in Cape Town. The Daniels family was hosting a "cottage meeting" to discuss a chapter from James E. Talmage's *Jesus the Christ*. William and Clara's adult daughter, Alice, was there too.[10]

The Danielses had been holding Monday night meetings in their home since 1921. The gatherings offered a refuge from the racial tension they experienced all around them. In Cape Town, churches and schools were segregated, with Blacks and "Coloureds," or people of mixed race, attending one place and whites another. But skin color did not bar worshippers from the Danielses' cottage meetings. William and Clara, who had

Black and southeast Asian ancestry, welcomed anyone who wanted to attend. President Dalton and the missionaries who often attended the meetings were white.[11]

William had first learned about the restored gospel from his sister Phyllis, who had joined the Church with her husband and moved to Utah in the early 1900s. A few years later, in 1915, William had met a Latter-day Saint missionary whose sincerity and selfless devotion to the gospel caught his attention.[12]

Not long after taking an interest in the Church, William had visited Utah to learn more about the Latter-day Saints. What he saw impressed him. He admired the faith of Church members and appreciated their devotion to Jesus Christ and the New Testament. He also met twice with President Joseph F. Smith, who told him that the time had not yet come for men of African descent to receive the priesthood.

The prophet's words troubled William. Although the Protestant church he attended in South Africa was segregated, it did not bar him from serving as an elder in his congregation. If he joined the Latter-day Saints, he would not be able to hold a similar office. President Smith, however, gave William a blessing promising that he would hold the priesthood one day, even if it was in the next life. The blessing touched William and gave him hope. He was baptized in Utah and soon returned home to South Africa.[13]

Since then, William had worshipped in Cape Town's Mowbray Branch alongside white members. At the branch, he bore his testimony and offered prayers. He also helped raise money for a new organ at the meetinghouse.[14] He and Clara, who had joined the Church a few years after his baptism, also took a special interest in the missionaries. The couple often hosted meals to welcome new missionaries, bid farewell to departing elders, and celebrate birthdays and holidays. To help the young men feel welcome at his home, William would sometimes play the Unites States national anthem on his record player or organize games of baseball.[15]

But not everyone in the branch was welcoming. William had recently learned that some members would not accept his family in full fellowship. And President Dalton had been told of visitors who stopped showing interest in the Church when they observed the mixed-race congregation in Mowbray.[16]

Once, William told Clara that he was thinking about leaving the Church. "Listen," she had replied, "you've been over to Salt Lake City and been baptized." Why give it up now?[17]

Clara's words, along with the Monday night cottage meetings, had given him strength to keep the faith, despite his concerns. On this evening in the spring of 1930, after the Danielses and their guests took turns reading from *Jesus the Christ,* they discussed the Savior calming the storm-tossed sea.

The passage reminded them to turn to Christ in moments of trial. Human power was often limited. But Christ could deliver all with a simple command: "Peace, be still."[18]

310

HAILSTONES THE SIZE OF pigeon eggs pelted the Swiss-German Mission home in Basel, Switzerland, on the afternoon of June 24, 1930. For the last week, John and Leah Widtsoe had been lodging in the house, training mission presidents and their wives on the needs and responsibilities of missionaries. Every day had been marked by long meetings and engaging discussions about the Church in Europe. The heavy rattle of the hail was a rare intrusion on the conference.[19]

Leah had never been busier on her mission. She was in charge of training the mission presidents' wives to help the European Saints organize Relief Societies, Young Ladies' Mutual Improvement Associations, and Primaries in their districts and branches. Since Church leaders were advising Saints to remain in their homelands to build up Zion around the world, Leah believed that local Saints needed to take a leading role in these organizations.[20] In some branches, missionaries were serving as presidents of combined Mutual Improvement Associations. But Leah asked that every branch have a YLMIA with a local president, two counselors, a secretary, and as many aides as were necessary.

Furthermore, a mission president's wife was not expected to supervise every organization personally. She was only one woman and could not do all the work effectively. In fact, if she did not delegate responsibilities to local leaders, she would greatly hamper the organizations. Leah wanted mission leaders to inspire and train the European Saints to be leaders in their own right.[21]

On June 27, Leah spoke to the women about the need for stronger YLMIAs in Europe. The YLMIA was divided into two programs, the Bee-Hive Girls and Gleaner Girls. The Bee-Hive Girls was now a three-year program for any young woman fourteen and older. Once she completed her Bee-Hive work, a young woman joined the Gleaner Girls, a less-structured program designed to prepare her for adulthood. The Bee-Hive Girls already had two thousand girls participating in Europe, and Leah urged the women to promote the program throughout the missions.[22]

She also announced that YLMIA general president Ruth May Fox had recently authorized her to create a European edition of the Bee-Hive Girls handbook. The current manual was designed to strengthen young women through various indoor and outdoor activities. Yet some of the content in the book was tailored too specifically to young women in the United States, making it unsuitable for other parts of the world. Leah presented her ideas for the new handbook to the mission presidents' wives, and they offered advice on how to adapt the manual to meet the needs of young women in Europe.[23]

After the conference, Leah wrote to the First Presidency about her work. "I feel that some measure of success may fairly be reported," she noted. "The women in each mission are sensing more and more their need for growth and their responsibility for carrying forward their share of Church activity."

She understood that there was still room for improvement. "The people haven't yet learned to support each other in office," she wrote. "They must learn it here as at home." Over the next year, she planned to emphasize the importance of supporting the local officers and leaders of the Church.

"Every day this past year I have put in a full working day with scarcely an hour's letup," she added. But she had never felt better. "I feel much younger and am a far happier woman than when I came," she wrote. "For this I am grateful to Heavenly Father first, then to you, our leaders and friends."[24]

THAT FALL, IN TILSIT, Germany, ten-year-old Helga Meiszus was baptized in the River Memel. It was cold, but the sky overhead was beautiful, all lit up with stars. As Helga came out of the water, she could hardly contain the joy she felt to be a member of The Church of Jesus Christ of Latter-day Saints.[25]

It was an eventful time in her life. She had decided to attend a new school, and at first she was excited for the change. The school was close to home, and many of her friends and neighbors would be there. But she soon regretted her decision. Her teacher, Miss Maul, did not seem to like her.

One day, Helga was asked to submit a form providing the school with her personal information. When Miss Maul reviewed the form, she scoffed when she saw that Helga was a Latter-day Saint. Although more Church members lived in Germany than any other country outside the United States, they were not well known or highly regarded.

"This is not a religion," Miss Maul told Helga. "This is a sect, and a bad one!"[26]

The word "sect" stung Helga. She was not used to being treated badly because of her religion, so she went home and told her mother what Miss Maul had said. Her mother simply took out a piece of paper and wrote a letter to the teacher, reminding her that it was none of her business what church Helga and her family attended.

A short time later, Miss Maul came to class with the principal. All the girls stood up, and Miss Maul approached Helga, who was near the front of the classroom.

"There she is," she said, pointing a finger at Helga. "She belongs to that awful sect."

The principal stood there for a while, staring at Helga as if she were a monster. Helga held her head high. She loved her religion and was not ashamed of it.[27]

After that, many of Helga's friends quit playing with her. When she walked to or from school, students sometimes threw rocks or spat at her. Once, after returning home from class, Helga realized she had forgotten her coat. She hurried back to school and found her coat right where she had left it. But when she picked it up, she saw that someone had blown their nose in it.[28]

Helga's classmates continued to bully her, but whenever they did, she would silently sing a song she had learned at church, and it would give her strength. In English, its title was "I Am a Mormon Boy," but in the German translation it applied to all Latter-day Saint children:

A Mormon child, a Mormon child,
I am a Mormon child;
I might be envied by a king,
For I am a Mormon child.[29]

ON JANUARY 30, 1931, EVELYN Hodges and other Relief Society social workers in Salt Lake City stood at the second-story windows of the Presiding Bishop's Building, where Relief Society Social Service had its offices. On the street below, nearly fifteen hundred demonstrators were marching north toward the Utah capitol to ask the legislature to help the state's rising number of unemployed people.[30]

Gazing down at the demonstrators, Evelyn was surprised that they did not look angry or militant. They carried two American flags along with signs and banners urging other workers to join them. Many of the demonstrators were dragging their feet and hanging their heads in resignation. If anything, they looked sad.[31]

Before the hard times began, Evelyn had worked mainly with people who were unemployed because of poor health or disability. Now she was seeing more and more willing workers who simply could not find jobs.

Some of them were skilled laborers. Others were college students or university graduates. Many of them had lost a sense of self-worth and did not want to ask for help.[32]

One man she spoke to had provided for his wife and children for years. They lived in a comfortable home in a good neighborhood. But now he could not find a job, and his family was growing desperate. Weeping, he admitted to Evelyn that the only food left in the house was flour and salt. It clearly pained him to ask for money to help support his family, but what choice did he have?[33]

Evelyn dealt with cases like this regularly. And as the economy worsened, the Relief Society could not afford to employ more than five social workers at a time, leaving Evelyn swamped with work. Often, she could do little more than quickly assess a person's situation before filling out a form to provide basic food items, assistance with a month's rent, or a little bit of coal in the winter.[34]

Relief Society general president Louise Y. Robison and her counselors met regularly with the Presiding Bishopric to organize welfare efforts among the Saints. Similarly, bishops and Relief Society leaders worked together to identify struggling people in their wards and provide for their basic needs. Local governments and some businesses also sought creative ways to keep workers fed and employed. A county-run warehouse dispensed free food in Salt Lake City. The city government created temporary jobs, like shoveling snow or chopping wood, to make work for more than ten thousand unemployed men.

Still, Church and community leaders were quickly realizing that their combined efforts and resources were not enough to deal with the economic crisis.[35]

Evelyn soon found herself putting in even longer hours with Amy Brown Lyman and the other Relief Society social workers. Sometimes the days never seemed to end. Weekdays and weekends often blended together. Since social work records were confidential, Evelyn tried to work on cases only in the office. But as her responsibilities increased, she carried records home in a briefcase so she could work on Saturday afternoons or Sundays.

The demands of Evelyn's career were exhausting, and they took a toll on her health. But she could not forget the sad faces of the downtrodden men and women marching toward the state capitol. The legislature had largely ignored their pleas and refused to offer benefits to the unemployed. Now the image of their hopelessness and despair was stuck in her mind. She wanted to cry whenever she thought of it.[36]

CHAPTER 21

A Keener Understanding

In the spring of 1931, John and Leah Widtsoe left Europe for a few months to visit family, meet with Church leaders, and attend general conference. Their daughter Ann was waiting for them at the train depot in Utah. In their absence, she had reconciled for the time being with her husband, and she was now expecting her third child. Leah's mother, Susa Gates, was also there, ready to welcome them home, as she promised to do when they left three years earlier. Her seventy-fifth birthday was in two days, and John and Leah had arrived just in time for a celebration at the home of Leah's sister Emma Lucy and her husband, Albert Bowen.[1]

Sadly, John's aunt Petroline had died two years earlier after a long illness. Ann and Rose, the widow of

John's brother, Osborne, had been at her bedside when she passed.[2]

While John was in Utah, his schedule was full of meetings with Church leaders. The First Presidency and Quorum of the Twelve Apostles were handling a difference of views between apostle Joseph Fielding Smith and B. H. Roberts, who was now the senior member of the First Council of the Seventy. Elder Roberts had written "The Truth, The Way, The Life," an eight-hundred-page manuscript detailing the plan of salvation. He wanted the Church to adopt it as a course of study for Melchizedek Priesthood quorums.[3] But Elder Smith had voiced serious concerns about certain ideas in the manuscript.

At the heart of his unease was Elder Roberts's effort to harmonize the scriptural account of the Creation with scientific theories about the origins of life.[4] Elder Roberts believed that fossil evidence proved humanlike species had lived and died on the earth for millions of years before God placed Adam and Eve in the Garden of Eden.[5] Elder Smith, however, argued that such beliefs were incompatible with scripture and Church doctrine. He believed these species could not have existed before Adam's Fall introduced death into the world.

In a speech to the Genealogical Society of Utah, Elder Smith had vigorously denounced Elder Roberts's ideas, although he did not mention him by name. Elder Roberts, in turn, had written to the First Presidency, seeking to know if Elder Smith's speech represented the official position of the Church on the subject or if it was simply the apostle's opinion.[6]

The Twelve invited both men to present their views to the council. The apostles then submitted a report to the First Presidency, who carefully reviewed both sides of the dispute and prayed to know how to resolve it.[7]

Having recently published his own book on reconciling science and religion, John had reflected deeply on the matter. He believed Church leaders needed to help young Saints develop faith in Jesus Christ amid new and modern ideas. Many religious people were wary of science, he reasoned, because they confused facts with interpretations. He was reluctant to rely solely on science to resolve controversy, since scientific understanding was subject to change and often overlooked religious concepts like prayer and revelation. But he was equally cautious about depending on any interpretation of scripture that did not take into account how the revelations and sacred writings came to be.

"I think our wisest plan is to do as we have done these many years," he told apostle Melvin J. Ballard privately. "Accept all well-established and authenticated facts and refuse to base our faith on theories, whether scientific or theological."[8]

On April 7, the day after general conference, the First Presidency called the Twelve and other general authorities together to settle the dispute. John listened as the presidency expressed their view that both Elder

Smith and Elder Roberts should drop the matter. "Both parties make the scripture and the statements of men who have been prominent in the affairs of the Church the basis of their contention," they observed. "Neither has produced definite proof in support of his views."[9]

The First Presidency reminded the quorums of Joseph Smith's teaching: "Declare the first principles, and let mysteries alone, lest you be overthrown."[10] They warned that preaching personal opinions as if they were Church doctrine could cause misunderstanding, confusion, and division among the Saints. "When one of the general authorities of the Church makes a definite statement in regard to any doctrine," they said, "whether he express it as his opinion or not, he is regarded as voicing the Church, and his statements are accepted as the approved doctrines of the Church."[11]

They urged the men to preach the core doctrine of the restored gospel. "While we magnify our calling in the realm of the Church," they said, "leave geology, biology, archeology, and anthropology, no one of which has to do with the salvation of the souls of mankind, to scientific research." As far as the origins of life were concerned, they had no more to say than the First Presidency had already said in their 1909 statement, "The Origin of Man."[12]

In John's mind, the presidency's words settled the matter. He and the other Church leaders in the room, including Elder Roberts and Elder Smith, sustained the decision and agreed to no longer discuss in public the question of humanlike life before Adam.[13] Still, Elder Roberts could not bear to remove the topic from "The Truth, The Way, The Life." In the end, he set the manuscript aside, unpublished.[14]

LATER THAT YEAR, IN Cape Town, South Africa, William and Clara Daniels and a dozen other Latter-day Saints sang a hymn together, as they did every Monday when they met for gospel discussions at the Daniels home. Yet this was not just another cottage meeting. Mission president Don Dalton had called them together for a special conference.

After Clara offered an opening prayer, William told the story of his conversion and the beginnings of their small meetings. "We first studied *Book of Mormon Ready References,* and we are now studying *Jesus the Christ,*" he reflected. "I have received much knowledge and can tell many people much about the gospel."[15]

Clara also bore her testimony, expressing thanks for her membership in the Church. "I hope that the Lord will help us to remain steadfast," she said.[16]

Several others shared their testimonies, and then President Dalton addressed the group. "I feel sure that the Lord is at the head of this work," he said, "and if we live the commandments, the Lord will not withhold anything." He spoke of the brother of Jared in the Book of Mormon, who lived so close to the Lord that nothing was kept from him. "It will be the same way with us," he testified. "I know that if I am faithful, I will see wonderful things."[17]

President Dalton still worried about the way some members of the Mowbray Branch treated members of mixed race like the Danielses. In handling such cases, the First Presidency had advised him, he should consider the feelings of all Saints. Racial tension was a problem that must be treated with great care to avoid offending Black or white Church members, they wrote.[18]

Knowing and admiring William's faithfulness, President Dalton wanted to give his labors official recognition. "I feel that a branch should be formed here," he announced at the cottage meeting. "Brother Daniels should have the privilege to perform a specific labor. I know that by his diligence the barrier will be lifted, and he will be a leader in Israel."

William was then called to serve as the branch president, Clara as Relief Society president, their daughter, Alice, as Relief Society secretary and branch clerk, and their friend Emma Beehre as Clara's counselor. President Dalton then laid his hands on William's head and set him apart for his new calling. He did not ordain William to the priesthood, so William could not administer the sacrament or set branch members apart in callings. But his new responsibilities would give him greater opportunities to serve and grow in the Church.

"I have been thinking of a name for this branch," said President Dalton. "I should imagine that the name should be 'the Branch of Love.'"[19]

At their next Monday gathering, William asked Clara and other newly called branch leaders to share their thoughts about their new responsibilities. "I find it a bit difficult," Clara confessed, "and know the Lord will help me in my work, as the same Lord has helped the first sister that started the Relief Society."[20]

As leaders of the branch, William and Clara continued to care for the missionaries, who attended the branch meetings along with white visitors from the Mowbray Branch. William also made sure that Alice kept careful minutes so copies could be sent to Salt Lake City. He did not want the Love Branch to be forgotten.[21]

BACK IN THE UNITED States, thirteen-year-old Paul Bang became the Cincinnati Branch's newest deacon on February 14, 1932. Boys his age had been receiving the Aaronic Priesthood since the late 1800s, when deacons chopped wood for the poor, stoked fires to heat meetinghouses, and performed other acts of service in their wards and branches. It was not until President Joseph F. Smith introduced Aaronic Priesthood reforms in the early twentieth century, though, that ordaining young men to priesthood offices became routine. After that, young deacons began taking a larger role in the branch and its meetings.[22]

Now, in addition to caring for the chapel and grounds, Paul could pass the sacrament, collect fast offerings, carry messages for the branch president, and assist widows and other needy Saints.[23] Like other deacons in the Church, he was also expected to understand and explain each of the Articles of Faith, obey the Word of Wisdom, say opening and closing prayers, pay tithing, and know the story of the restoration of the Aaronic Priesthood.[24]

Paul was not given the chance to carry out some of these new responsibilities right away. For decades, adult men had passed the sacrament, and many people throughout the Church remained uneasy about letting boys perform this role. In Cincinnati, the sacrament was always blessed and passed by two adult men, sometimes Paul's older brothers Chris and Henry.[25]

Still, if Paul's new priesthood responsibilities did not keep him busy enough, his many chores at his parents' grocery store made up the difference. He liked working at the store. It opened every morning at six o'clock and did not close until eleven o'clock at night. He tended the counter, stocked and straightened shelves, and kept the wooden floor swept and oiled. When his brother Chris cut meat, Paul would scatter sawdust on the floor to absorb the mess. He would then scrub the cutting blocks with an iron brush once Chris finished his work. After school, Paul would load up boxes and baskets with grocery orders and make deliveries around the neighborhood.[26]

When the economic depression hit, Cincinnati was in the middle of a construction boom. Work had just begun on a nearly six-hundred-foot skyscraper and a massive new train terminal. These projects, along with a diverse local economy, helped the city weather the worst of the crisis. Yet wages were dropping and unemployment ran high.[27]

The Bangs lived in a poor neighborhood where white immigrants like their family lived, worked, played, and studied side by side with African Americans, Jews, and other ethnic groups. Once the city fell on hard times, many of the Bangs' usual customers could not afford to pay their grocery bills. Rather than turn aside customers, Paul's father often gave groceries away or let people buy on credit. But his kindness and generosity could not keep the family business safe from the Depression, and in April 1932, he filed for bankruptcy. Even so, he refused to close the store or stop helping his neighbors.[28]

The Cincinnati Saints carried on amid the economic decline. Hoping to encourage activity among Aaronic Priesthood holders, the Presiding Bishopric had recently asked branches and wards throughout the Church to begin commemorating the restoration of the Aaronic Priesthood each year. On May 15, 1932, four recently ordained priests in the Cincinnati Branch, all of them nineteen or older, spoke in sacrament meeting on the history and growth of the Aaronic Priesthood. Charles Anderson, the branch president, also spoke, as he usually did at the end of sacrament meeting.[29]

Paul did not have an active part in the program, but more opportunities to serve would come. Attendance at the branch rarely exceeded fifty people, so odds were good that his parents or one of his older siblings was giving a talk, singing with the choir, saying a prayer, or otherwise assisting at any given meeting.[30] His brother Henry, in fact, had recently offered the closing prayer at three sacrament meetings in four weeks. And on the day when he was not saying the closing prayer, he gave a talk.[31]

Paul was a Bang, so it was only a matter of time before the branch put him to work.

IN UTAH, MEANWHILE, RELIEF Society social worker Evelyn Hodges had much to worry about as the world plunged deeper and deeper into the Depression. Her father, who had once pleaded with her to stay home so she would not have to work, had fallen on hard times after products from his farm in Logan stopped selling. Evelyn knew how to help him apply for Church and state relief, but he was not interested.

"I can get a job," he had told her at the start of the Depression. "I know I can get a job."

Evelyn had her doubts. Every day in Salt Lake City she spoke to people who said the same thing. "If I can just get down to Los Angeles," they would tell her, "I can get a job." In Utah, one in every three workers was unemployed, and no one was hiring. But Evelyn knew the situation was not much better in California or anywhere else in the United States. She tried to explain that jobs were scarce everywhere, but some families she worked with did not believe her.[32]

By the summer of 1932, she had good reason to hope that change was on the way. After the U.S. government created a program to provide financial aid to states and businesses, officials in Utah quickly enlisted Relief Society Social Service to help the state apply for a federal loan. Evelyn and Amy Brown Lyman spent hours gathering statistics and individual case files to document the deprivation in the state. They then took their research to the state capitol, where lawmakers used it in their successful bid for federal assistance for Utah.[33]

Evelyn learned from Amy as they toiled together. Amy was straightforward and often brusque when speaking to the social workers. While Evelyn liked Amy's outspokenness, she had to admit it sometimes chafed. Amy did not hesitate to criticize her when she made a mistake. But Evelyn knew that Amy was not punishing her. Amy simply did not feel she had the time to be subtle or diplomatic. She expected everyone in the Social Service office, herself included, to give everything they had to the work. For that, Evelyn had come to love and admire her.[34]

The federal relief funds arrived in Utah in August 1932, bringing hope to many despairing Saints. Once again, the state called on the Relief Society for help, and Amy and her social workers soon played a key role in distributing the aid.

With most local Church and government relief funds running out, many of the bishops Evelyn worked with were eager for their needy ward members to receive assistance from the federal government. Yet there were Church members who worried about the Saints becoming dependent on government aid. Some people resisted seeking Church relief because they did not want their bishops, who were often neighbors and friends, to know about their situation. Others did not want to feel the stigma of dependency when they went to church.

Dependency continued to spread, however. Government leaders in the United States had underestimated the economic collapse, and the funding they offered did not provide permanent relief to the American people. The economy continued to spiral downward, taking hope with it. Every day more people were losing their jobs and then their homes. Evelyn often saw two or three families living together in a small house.

And still her own family struggled. When her father's efforts to support the family failed, he had tried selling some property, but no one was buying. Finally, he let Evelyn send him thirty dollars a month from her own earnings. He was happy for the help.[35]

As the Depression worsened, and Evelyn witnessed more and more misery in Salt Lake City, she saw an opportunity for greater compassion and growth in the community. "If we can emerge from this struggle with a keener understanding of the needs of human beings," she believed, "society will be better for suffering through this one."[36]

ACROSS TOWN, PRESIDENT HAROLD B. Lee of Salt Lake City's Pioneer Stake knew he too had to do something to help people get through the Depression. At thirty-three years old, he was one of the youngest stake presidents in the Church, so he did not have as much life experience as other men in his position. But he knew that around two-thirds of the 7,300 Saints in his stake were either wholly or partially dependent on financial assistance. And when people were starving, there was little opportunity to feed them spiritually.[37]

Harold called his counselors together to discuss how to help the Saints under their care. From studying the Doctrine and Covenants, they knew the Lord had commanded the early Saints to establish a storehouse "to administer to the poor and needy."[38] For decades, wards throughout the Church had operated small "bishop's storehouses" to collect and redistribute offerings of food and other items for the poor. Although the Church had transitioned to cash-only tithing in the 1910s, storehouses still existed in some wards and stakes.[39] The Relief Society general presidency, which had operated stores and granaries to assist Saints in times of need, likewise ran a storehouse to provide the poor with clothing and other household items.[40] What if the Pioneer Stake did something similar?

A relief program soon took shape, one that would also help the Saints be more self-sustaining. With the assistance of the bishops, Harold's stake would establish a storehouse supported by tithing and donations.

Rather than dispense items freely, the program would allow unemployed Saints in the stake to work at the storehouse or on other relief projects in exchange for food, clothing, fuel, or other necessities.[41]

After consulting with his counselors, Harold submitted the plan to the First Presidency and received their approval. He then presented it to the bishops of his stake at a special meeting and invited them to discuss it. Right away, one bishop asked a question that was doubtless on the minds of many Church members: If the Lord promised to provide for His people, why were so many faithful, tithe-paying Saints destitute?

Harold did his best to answer, reminding the bishops that the Lord relied on them to carry out His work. "The promises of the Lord are in your hands, and the way and the means of fulfilling these must be up to you," he said. He then urged the bishops to do all they could to make the storehouse a success, testifying that the promised blessings of the Lord would be fulfilled.[42]

To help carry out the plan, Harold and his counselors recruited one of the bishops, Jesse Drury, to manage the storehouse. Many Saints in Jesse's ward had been hit hard by the Depression. Jesse himself had lost his job, and he and his family were now barely getting by on government relief.[43]

Earlier that year, however, Jesse and his counselors had decided to do something to provide extra food and work for their ward members. Just south of the ward boundary was a plot of fertile, unused land.

The bishopric approached the owners, and they agreed to let the ward cultivate the land in exchange for paying the taxes on the property. Two neighboring wards in the Pioneer Stake soon joined the effort, and together they found farmers and county leaders who were willing to donate seeds and supply irrigation water. They also purchased vegetable plants at discounted prices and acquired some farm equipment and horses from people who supported their project.[44]

Now, at Harold's direction, Jesse led a group of unemployed Church members as they converted an old warehouse into a stake storehouse. They installed a cannery and opened a general store. There was also storage on separate levels and space for handling donated clothing.[45]

By the summer of 1932, the storehouse was ready to open. Harold, Jesse, and the rest of the Pioneer Stake observed a special day of fasting to commemorate the event, bringing their fast offerings to the building's opening ceremony. Some women and men in the stake were put to work at the storehouse while others traveled across the valley to work on farms and orchards.[46]

Soon, a wave of produce rolled in. There were hundreds of bushels of peaches, thousands of sacks of potatoes and onions, tons of cherries, and much more. In return for their labor, stake members could enjoy a share of the harvest. Enough was left over that the Relief Society canned some of the surplus for the following winter. Women also exchanged labor for nonperishable necessities by mending old clothes and collecting used shoes.[47]

At the end of the year, Harold could see that the Lord was blessing the Saints in the Pioneer Stake. While many of them had faced adversity over the past year, they had remained firm in the conviction that God would help them in their struggle. What was more, they were ready and willing to work together for the benefit of the needy, despite the devastation wrought by the Depression.[48]

CHAPTER 22

Eternal Reward

On the morning of May 17, 1933, John and Leah Widtsoe awoke to their first view of the Holy Land. From their train window, they saw a barren, rock-strewn plain punctuated by cultivated fields and orchards. John, who had spent years studying the science of farming in deserts, was fascinated by the landscape. "Intensely interesting," he wrote in his journal.

After returning to London in the fall of 1931, the Widtsoes had resumed their responsibilities in the European Mission. They were now on their way to Haifa, a city on the eastern coast of the Mediterranean Sea, to set apart a man named Badwagan Piranian and his wife, Bertha, to lead the Church's Palestine-Syrian Mission.[1] The mission, which would soon oversee four branches in the region, was one of the smallest in the Church.

Badwagan was Armenian, like most Saints in the Middle East, and Bertha was Swiss. Both had joined the Church in the last decade.[2]

At first, Leah had not planned on going to Palestine with John. The economic depression had spread across the globe, devastating communities that were still recovering from the world war. The Widtsoes' finances were low, and a cross-continent trip would not be cheap. But John had insisted that Leah come with him.

"We've done everything in life together, and this trip must be no exception," he had said. "We'll get out of the 'financial hole' somehow."[3]

After arriving in Haifa, the Widtsoes met the Piranians and their sixteen-year-old daughter, Ausdrig. John was impressed with the new president. A fluent speaker of Armenian and German, Badwagan also had some knowledge of Turkish, Russian, and English. "Brother Piranian," John reported, "is an intelligent, industrious, sincere man."[4]

Leah was equally impressed with Bertha. She had a firm testimony of the gospel and was eager to learn how to help the women in the mission participate more fully in their Relief Societies and YLMIAs. Leah believed these organizations were essential for building up the Church in the area. "If these women can be made active and happy through the Relief Society or Bee-Hive and Gleaner Girl programs," she thought, "they are going to become much more capable proselyters for the truth."

Leah sometimes felt like she had to move mountains to persuade mission presidents' wives to let local women run their own organizations. But as Bertha and Leah worked together, Bertha's desire to do the right thing and be a good leader shone. By the time John and Leah were ready to leave Haifa, Leah knew that Bertha would do excellent work.[5]

From Haifa, Leah and John traveled to Tel Aviv and then to Jerusalem. They planned to take a walking tour to the Western Wall, the last remnant of the ancient temple in Jerusalem. After arriving at their lodging, though, John received a stack of mail and began reading two telegrams silently. Their contents were deeply distressing, but Leah was in good spirits, so he set the mail aside and they left the hotel.

The tour took them along old, crooked streets and through colorful bazaars crowded with people. At the Western Wall, they observed Jewish women and men praying and mourning over the destruction of the temple centuries earlier. As Leah looked on, she noticed some visitors slipping prayers written on scraps of paper between the stones in the wall.

That evening, they watched the sun set from the Mount of Olives, not far from the garden where the Savior had suffered for the sins of all humankind. John was still preoccupied by the telegrams and was not enjoying himself, but Leah was thrilled to be in the sacred city.

Later, after returning to their room, John finally told Leah what was troubling him. The telegrams he had received were from President Heber J. Grant, who had written to tell them that Leah's mother had died on May 27, the day after they had left Haifa. John had delayed telling Leah because she had been so cheerful when they arrived in Jerusalem, and he could not bear to shatter her happiness.[6]

The news shocked Leah. She knew Susa had not been feeling well, but she had no idea the illness was so serious. Her mind turned suddenly dark and defiant. Why did she have to be so far away when her mother died? She had been looking forward to reuniting with her and telling her about her experiences on the mission. Now everything had changed. Her joy was gone.[7]

Full of grief, she struggled through the night and the next day. The only comfort she had was thinking of her mother, who had devoted so much time to temple work, joyfully reuniting with her deceased loved ones. She remembered a lighthearted poem Susa had written some time ago:

> *When I have quit this mortal shore*
> *And "mosey" round this earth no more*
> *Don't mourn, don't weep, don't sigh, don't sob*
> *I may have struck a better job.*

On June 5, Leah sent a letter to President Grant, thanking him for the kindness he had always shown Susa. "Mother's life was full of years and rich accomplishment," she wrote. "I pray that Mother's children, each of us, may love and live for the truth as she has done."[8]

LATER THAT YEAR, IN South Africa, William Daniels was faithfully attending to his duties as president of Cape Town's Love Branch. Though he could not perform priesthood ordinances, he could preside at the Monday evening meetings, conduct branch business, counsel the Saints under his care, and attend mission leadership conferences with other branch presidents in South Africa.

One day, William became seriously ill. He was sure the sickness would pass quickly, so he did not immediately ask the missionaries for a blessing. His health worsened, however, and his doctors grew concerned. He was nearly seventy years old, and his heart was weak.

Six weeks passed before William finally contacted the mission home to request a blessing. President Dalton was not there, so another missionary came to administer to him. After the blessing, William felt better for a while, but the sickness eventually returned. This time President Dalton was able to come and give him a blessing.

Concerned for William's life, President Dalton brought his wife, Geneve, and their children to comfort their friend. When President Dalton saw William's condition, he wept. The family knelt around the bed, and five-year-old George Dalton offered a prayer. Then President Dalton anointed William's head with oil and gave him a blessing. He promised William he would be able to return to worship with the Cape Town Saints again.

A few weeks later, President Dalton returned to the city and found William well enough to travel. Together they went to the Mowbray Branch Sunday School, where the Saints invited William to speak to them. With some help, he climbed the stand and bore his testimony of the healing power of faith. After the meeting, everyone in the room, young and old, shook hands with him. And soon he was able to return fully to his duties in the Love Branch.

William rejoiced in the missionaries and the healing blessings he had received from them. "I feel more blessed than the king with all his wealth," he once told the branch. "I thank the Lord for the privilege of having those good people in my home, and for the faith I have in the elders for anointing me."[9]

After his health improved, William wrote down his testimony for the mission newspaper, *Cumorah's Southern Messenger.* As he reflected on his experiences in the Church, he recounted his conversion, his life-changing visit to Salt Lake City, and his recent experience with the power of the priesthood.

"My testimony is that I know Joseph Smith to have been a latter-day prophet of God," he testified, "and that the restored gospel contains nothing but the teachings of Christ Himself."

"I know that God lives and hears and answers prayers," he wrote. "Jesus is the resurrected Redeemer and verily the Son of our true and living personal Father in Heaven."[10]

NOT LONG AFTER HIS mother-in-law's death, John Widtsoe received a letter from President Grant. "Speaking of your return, I wish you would write me with absolute frankness," it read. "Don't hesitate to tell me if you would prefer to come home to be here with your loved ones. You have filled a first-class mission."

John did not know how to respond. On the one hand, he and Leah had already served for six years—twice as long as other recent European Mission presidents. John also knew their family in Utah missed and needed them, particularly now that Susa was gone.[11]

On the other hand, he and Leah felt at home in Europe and enjoyed missionary service. Leah would certainly miss the work. Her mark on the Church in Europe could be seen everywhere. She had strengthened local women's organizations, encouraged a more faithful observance of the Word of Wisdom, and made Relief Society lessons relevant to a European audience. She had just completed her European edition of the Bee-Hive Girls handbook, which had significantly simplified and adapted the MIA program to meet the needs of young women throughout the continent.[12]

The mission was also facing new challenges. As the economic downturn spread worldwide, tithing revenue in Europe plummeted, and some branches lost their meeting halls, unable to pay the rent. The Depression drastically reduced the number of missionaries who could afford to serve, and many families needed their sons at home to help provide. In 1932, only 399 men had been able to accept mission calls, compared with a high of 1,300 missionaries per year in the 1920s. With the missionary force so diminished, would it be best for the Church if John and Leah, who had so much practical experience in Europe, continued to lead the European Mission?

John told President Grant that he and Leah were content to leave the matter in the prophet's hands. "I have always found the Lord's way better than mine," he wrote.[13]

On July 18, John received a telegram stating that apostle Joseph F. Merrill had been called to replace him as president of the European Mission. Although it would be difficult to leave, John and Leah felt good about the decision. By September, they were busily preparing for their departure, with Leah managing business at the mission home in London while John made a trip to the European continent to survey conditions one last time.[14]

John's final stop was a visit to the mission office in Berlin, Germany. Adolf Hitler had been appointed Germany's chancellor earlier that year, and his Nazi Party was tightening its hold on the nation. The First Presidency, concerned about these events, had asked John to report on the state of the country and whether the missionaries in Germany were safe.

John himself was closely watching Hitler's ascent to power and its effect on Germany. Many Germans were still chafing after losing the war fifteen years earlier, and they deeply resented the harsh sanctions imposed on them by the victors. "The political nerves of the German people are laid bare," John informed the First Presidency. "I hope when the boil is ready to break, the poison may be drained off instead of diffusing itself throughout the whole social structure."[15]

After arriving in Berlin, John was struck by how much it had changed in the decades since he was a student there. The city had the air of a military camp, with symbols of Hitler and the Nazi Party everywhere, including in the mission office. "The Nazi flag hangs on the wall," John informed the First Presidency, "not I hope in acceptance of all that the present government is doing in Germany, but as an evidence of the fact that we uphold the lawful government of the country in which we dwell."

As John spoke with the presidents of the two missions in Germany, he felt reassured that the Church was not in immediate danger in the country. The Gestapo— the Nazi secret police—had examined the records of the mission office in Berlin, as well as the books of several branches, but so far they seemed satisfied that the Church was not trying to undermine their government.[16]

Still, John feared that Hitler was leading the German people into another war. Already local Saints were preparing to take charge of the branches and watch over Church members should trouble arise. And John advised mission presidents to make plans to move the missionaries out of Germany within two or three hours, if necessary. He also thought it would be wise for the First

Presidency to limit the number of missionaries going to Germany in the future.

After two days of meetings, John left the Berlin office to travel back to London. He took a familiar path along Unter den Linden, a street in the heart of Berlin named after the linden trees lining the walkways. As he made his way to the railway station, a large company of soldiers came into view, rigidly goose-stepping through the city to replace the soldiers currently on guard.

All around them, thousands of Hitler's supporters crowded the streets, wild with enthusiasm.[17]

IN THE SPRING OF 1934, Len and Mary Hope, the African American Saints who had joined the Church in Alabama, were living on the outskirts of Cincinnati, Ohio. The couple had moved their family to the area in the summer of 1928 to find new work, and Len had quickly secured a steady job at a factory. They now had five children and another on the way.[18]

Cincinnati was a northern city bordering a southern state, and most areas of the city were as strictly segregated as any place in the South. Because they were Black, the Hopes were not allowed to live in certain neighborhoods, stay in certain hotels, or eat at certain restaurants. Theaters designated separate seating for Black patrons. Some schools, colleges, and universities in the city either barred Black students or greatly limited their educational opportunities. Several religious denominations had white congregations and Black congregations.[19]

When the Hopes first arrived in town, they attended meetings with the Cincinnati Branch. Since there was no Churchwide policy on racial segregation, wards and branches sometimes created their own policies based on local circumstances. At first, it seemed the Cincinnati Branch might welcome the family. But then a group of members told branch president Charles Anderson that they would stop attending meetings if the Hopes kept coming.

Charles liked Len and Mary, and he knew it would be wrong to ask them not to attend church. He had moved to Cincinnati from Salt Lake City, where the small population of Black Saints attended church side by side with their white neighbors. But he also knew that racism ran deep in the Cincinnati area, and he did not think he could change how people felt.[20]

The branch boundaries had recently been redrawn, bringing many southern Saints within Charles's stewardship. But it was not just southern Saints who objected to the Hopes coming to church. Some longtime branch members whom Charles had known for years had also voiced fears that integrating the branch would give local critics of the Church a new reason to deride the Saints.[21]

With a heavy heart, Charles went to the Hopes' home and told them the branch members' objections. "This is the hardest visit that I have ever made to anyone in my life," he admitted. He promised to help the family stay connected to the Church. "We will do everything we can," he said. "We will make a special trip out here each month to bring the sacrament to you and have a Church service in your home."

Heartbroken over Charles's decision, Len and Mary stopped attending church except for district conferences and other special events. On the first Sunday of every month, they held a testimony meeting in their home for missionaries and any other branch member who wanted to come and worship with them. The family also enjoyed informal visits from local Saints.[22] The Hopes lived in a cozy four-room house with a large front porch and white picket fence. It was located in a predominantly African American neighborhood about ten miles north of the branch meetinghouse, and a streetcar from Cincinnati could bring visitors to within a mile's walk.[23]

At their monthly Sunday meetings, the Hopes partook of the sacrament and bore their testimonies, oldest to youngest. Sometimes the talented Hope girls sang or played the piano. After every meeting, the Hopes served a delicious meal with foods such as roast turkey, corn bread, potato salad, and other home-cooked dishes.[24]

Among the Saints who visited the Hopes were Charles and his counselors, Christian Bang and Alvin Gilliam. Sometimes Christine Anderson and Rosa Bang joined their husbands on visits. Branch clerk Vernon Cahall, his wife, Edith, and branch members Robert Meier and Raymond Chapin also came, often with their families.[25] Sister missionaries, who taught Primary classes in the homes of several branch members, held Primary classes for the Hope children as well. Elizabeth, the oldest Bang daughter, would sometimes help. Occasionally, the Hopes would visit with missionaries or members of the branch at other places, like the Cincinnati Zoo.[26]

On April 8, 1934, Mary Hope gave birth to a boy. In the past, the Hopes always made sure their babies were blessed, and this time was no different. Two months after little Vernon's birth, Charles Anderson and the branch clerk came to the Hopes' home for another sacrament meeting. Afterward, Charles gave the boy a blessing.[27]

When he bore his testimony, Len often recounted his conversion to the restored gospel. He knew that he and Mary had been extraordinarily blessed since coming to Cincinnati. While the Depression had left many of their neighbors out of work, he had not lost a day's labor. He did not make much money, but he always paid a full tithe.

He also expressed faith in the future. "I know I cannot have the priesthood," he once said, "but I feel in the justice of God that someday this will be given to me, and I will be allowed to go on to my eternal reward with the faithful who hold it."

He and Mary were willing to wait for that day. The Lord knew their hearts.[28]

MEANWHILE, IN TILSIT, GERMANY, fourteen-year-old Helga Meiszus could not help noticing how much had changed in her town since the Nazis took power. She used to be scared to walk home from church at night because so many people were loitering in the street. The economy was bad, and many people were out of work and had nothing to do. They were probably not dangerous, but Helga was always afraid that they would try to hurt her.

Then Hitler came and the economy improved. Jobs were no longer scarce, and the streets felt safe. What was more, people started feeling proud to be German again. Hitler was a forceful speaker, and his passionate words inspired many with the idea that Germany could emerge once again as a powerful nation that would endure for a thousand years. When he spouted lies, spoke of conspiracies, and blamed Jews for Germany's problems, many people believed him.

Like others in their country, German Latter-day Saints held a variety of opinions about Hitler. Some supported him, while others were wary of his rise to power and his hatred of Jews. Helga's family was not very political and did not openly oppose the Nazi Party. Yet her parents thought Hitler was the wrong leader for Germany. Her father, in particular, disliked being forced to use "Heil Hitler" as a greeting. He insisted on using the traditional "good morning" or "good day" instead—even if others disapproved.

Helga, however, was afraid not to say "Heil Hitler" or raise her hand in the Nazi salute. What if someone saw her refuse? She could get in trouble. She was so afraid of standing out, in fact, that she sometimes tried not to think about Hitler at all, worried the Nazis could somehow read her mind and punish her.

Still, she enjoyed the pageantry of the Nazi Party. There were Nazi dances and uniformed troops parading down the street. The Nazis wanted to instill nationalism and loyalty in the youth of the country, so they often used recreation, stirring music, and other forms of propaganda to attract them.[29]

Around this time, Helga became a Bee-Hive Girl in what the Church had recently renamed the Young Women's Mutual Improvement Association. Under the guidance of an adult leader, members of her class set goals and earned colorful seals to place in their German-language edition of the Bee-Hive Girls handbook. Helga cherished her manual, making it her own by coloring its black-and-white illustrations and using a pen or pencil to mark her completed goals with an *X*.

Helga marked off dozens of goals as she worked through the handbook. She named the accomplishments of five great musicians, went to bed early and rose early, bore her testimony at three fast and testimony meetings, and identified the most important ways the Church's teachings differed from other Christian creeds. She also chose a Bee-Hive name and symbol for herself. The name she picked was *Edelmut,* German for "nobleness." Her symbol was the edelweiss, a small, rare flower that grew high in the Alps.[30]

One day, Helga came home excited. Representatives from the Nazi Party's youth movement for young women—the Bund Deutscher Mädel, or League of German Girls—were recruiting in the neighborhood, and many of Helga's friends were joining.

"Oh, Mutti," Helga told her mother. "I would like to go and belong to the group." The league offered all kinds of lessons and activities and published their own magazine. There was even talk of ski trips, subsidized by the government. The girls wore sharp-looking white blouses and dark skirts.

"Helgalein, you are a Bee-Hive Girl," her mother said. "You don't need to belong to that group."

Helga knew her mother was right. Not joining the League of German Girls would once again set her apart from her friends. But the Bee-Hive program was helping her achieve righteous goals and be a better Latter-day Saint. Neither Hitler nor his league could do that.[31]

CHAPTER 23

All That Is Necessary

On February 6, 1935, fifteen-year-old Connie Taylor and other members of the Cincinnati Branch waited at their meetinghouse to receive a patriarchal blessing from James H. Wallis.

For much of the last century, patriarchal blessings had been given only to adult Saints, who often received blessings from more than one patriarch in their lifetime. In recent years, however, Church leaders had begun encouraging teenagers like Connie to receive their blessing as a way to strengthen their faith and receive direction for their lives. Church leaders also clarified that Saints should receive only one patriarchal blessing.[1]

Brother Wallis, a convert from Great Britain, had been called by the First Presidency to give patriarchal blessings to Saints in outlying branches of the Church.

He had recently completed a two-year mission to Europe, where he gave more than fourteen hundred blessings, and he was now on assignment to bless the Saints in the eastern United States and Canada. Since it was a rare opportunity for anyone in Cincinnati to receive a patriarchal blessing, he had been working long hours to ensure that every eligible branch member got the chance.[2]

When Connie's turn for a blessing came, she took a seat in the Relief Society room. Brother Wallis then placed his hands on her head and called her by her full name: Cornelia Belle Taylor. As he spoke the blessing, he assured her that the Lord knew and watched over her. He promised her guidance through life as she sought the Lord in prayer, shunned evil, and obeyed the Word of Wisdom. He urged her to take a greater interest in the activities of the Church, using her talents and intelligence to become a willing worker in the kingdom of God. And he promised that she would go to the temple one day and be sealed to her parents.

"Doubt not this promise," the patriarch told her. "In due time of the Lord, His Holy Spirit will touch the heart of thy father, and through its influence he will see the light of truth and will share in thy blessings."[3]

As comforting as those words were, they required great faith. Connie's father, a cigar maker named George Taylor, was a loving, kindhearted man, but the family he came from hated Latter-day Saints. When Connie's mother, Adeline, first expressed interest in the Church, he had refused to let her join.

But one day, when Connie was around six years old, a car struck her father while he was crossing the street. As he lay in the hospital, recuperating from a broken leg, Adeline once again prodded him to let her join the Church, and this time he agreed. His feelings continued to soften, and he had recently let Connie and her brothers be baptized. But he himself had shown no interest in joining the Church or attending meetings with his family.[4]

Not long after her patriarchal blessing, Connie began participating regularly in the branch's efforts to share the gospel with their neighbors.[5] To make up for the decline in missionaries during the Depression, Saints across the world were often called into part-time service close to home. In 1932, Cincinnati Branch president Charles Anderson organized a tracting society to keep the work moving forward in the city.[6] Since Sunday School was in the morning and sacrament meeting was in the evening, Connie and other youth usually spent an hour or so in the afternoon knocking on doors and talking to people about the restored gospel.[7]

One of her companions in the tracting society was Judy Bang. Lately, Judy had begun going on dates with Connie's older brother, Milton. He and Judy did not have much in common, aside from their Church membership, but they had fun together. Connie herself had recently gone on her first date—with Judy's older brother Henry. But she did not like Henry as much as she liked his handsome younger brother Paul, who was her same age.[8]

In March, Judy told Connie that Paul wanted to ask her to go with him to an MIA roller-skating party. Connie waited all that evening for Paul to ask her, but he never did. The next day, a few hours before the party, Henry asked Milton to ask Connie if she would go skating with Paul. It was a roundabout way to ask her on a date, but she agreed.

Connie and Paul enjoyed skating together. Afterward, some of the youth piled into Henry's car and drove to a nearby restaurant for a bowl of chili. "I had a grand time with Paul," Connie wrote that night in her journal. "Better than I expected."[9]

Later that spring, Connie received a written copy of her patriarchal blessing, reminding her once again of the promises she had received. "This blessing, dear sister, will be a guide to thy feet," it read. "It will show thee the way to walk so that thou wilt not stumble in the dark but be enabled to fix thine eyes upon eternal life."[10]

With so much happening in her life, Connie needed the Lord's direction. When she joined the Church, she made up her mind to always do right. She believed the gospel was a shield. If she went to God and asked Him for his help, He would bless and protect her throughout her life.[11]

MEANWHILE, IN SALT LAKE City, stake president Harold B. Lee was sitting in the office of the First Presidency. He saw himself as a rather inexperienced farm boy from a small town in Idaho. Yet here he was, face-to-face with Heber J. Grant as the prophet asked his opinions on providing for the poor.

"I want to take a leaf out of the Pioneer Stake's book," President Grant announced.[12]

He and his counselors, J. Reuben Clark and David O. McKay, had been watching Harold's work closely.[13] Almost three years had passed since the start of the Pioneer Stake's ambitious relief program. During that time, the stake had created multiple jobs for the unemployed. Saints had picked peas, made and mended clothes, canned fruits and vegetables, and constructed a new stake gymnasium.[14] The stake's storehouse served as the hub of activity, with Jesse Drury overseeing the complex operation.[15]

At the same time, the First Presidency had become deeply concerned about the number of Church members relying on public funds. They were not opposed to Saints accepting government relief when they had no money for food or rent. Nor were they opposed to Church members receiving help through federal public works projects.[16] But as Utah became one of the states most dependent on government aid, the presidency worried that some Church members were accepting funds they did not need.[17] They also questioned how long the government could keep funding its relief programs.[18]

President Clark urged President Grant to provide the Saints with an alternative to federal assistance. Believing that some government relief programs led to idleness and despondency, he called for Church members to take responsibility for one another's care, as the Doctrine and Covenants instructed, and work for the assistance they received when possible.[19]

President Grant had additional concerns. Since the start of the Depression, he had received letter after letter from good, hardworking Latter-day Saints who had lost their jobs and farms. He often felt powerless to help them. Having grown up poor himself, he knew what deprivation was like. He had also spent decades of his life deep in debt, so he was sympathetic to others in similar straits. In fact, he was now using his own money to help widows, family members, and complete strangers pay their mortgages, remain on missions, or meet other obligations.[20]

But he knew that his efforts, as well as the efforts of well-meaning government programs, were not enough. He believed the Church had a duty to take care of its poor and unemployed, and he wanted Harold to draw on his experience with the Pioneer Stake to devise a new program—one that would enable the Saints to work together for the relief of those in need.

"There is nothing more important for the Church to do than to take care of its needy people," President Grant said.[21]

Harold was stunned. The thought of organizing and developing a program for the entire Church was overwhelming. After the meeting, he steered his car through a nearby canyon park, his mind reeling as he drove deeper into the hills above Salt Lake City.

"How can I do it?" he wondered.

When the road ended at the edge of the park, he shut off the engine and wandered through the trees until he found a secluded spot. He knelt and prayed for guidance. "For the safety and blessing of Thy people," he told the Lord, "I must have Thy direction."[22]

In the silence, a powerful impression came to him. "There is no new organization necessary to take care of the needs of this people," Harold realized. "All that is necessary is to put the priesthood of God to work."[23]

In the days that followed, Harold sought the advice of many experienced, well-informed people, including apostle and former senator Reed Smoot. He then spent several weeks creating a preliminary proposal, complete with detailed reports and charts outlining his vision for a possible Church relief program.[24]

When Harold presented his plan to the First Presidency, President McKay thought it was feasible. Yet President Grant hesitated, unsure if the Saints were prepared to carry out a program of such magnitude. After the meeting, he sought guidance from the Lord in prayer, but he received no direction.

"I am not going to move," he told his secretary, "until I feel certain of what the Lord wants."[25]

WHILE PRESIDENT GRANT WAITED for the Lord's guidance on a relief program, he traveled to Hawaii to organize a stake on the island of Oahu.[26] Fifteen years had passed since he had dedicated the temple there, and much had changed. The temple grounds had once been barren and scrubby. Now they were vibrant with bougainvillea trees in full bloom and cascading pools framed by gently waving palm trees.[27]

The Church in Hawaii was likewise flourishing. In the eighty-five years since the first Latter-day Saint missionaries docked at Honolulu, Church membership on the islands had grown to more than thirteen thousand Saints, half of whom lived on Oahu. Attendance at Church meetings had never been higher, and the Saints were eager to be part of a stake. The Oahu Stake would be the Church's 113th stake and the first organized outside North America. For the first time, Saints in Hawaii would have bishops, stake leaders, and a patriarch.[28]

After visiting with the Saints, Heber called Ralph Woolley, the man who had supervised the construction of the Hawaii Temple, as the stake president.[29] Arthur Kapewaokeao Waipa Parker, a native Hawaiian, would serve as one of his counselors.[30] Men and women with Polynesian and Asian ancestry were also called to the stake high council, Relief Society presidency, and other leadership positions.[31]

The diversity of Hawaii's Church members impressed the prophet.[32] Previous missionary efforts had focused on native Hawaiians, but the gospel net was widening. In the 1930s, people of Japanese descent made up more than a third of Hawaii's population. Many other people in Hawaii had Samoan, Māori, Filipino, and Chinese ancestry.[33]

The prophet established the new stake on June 30, 1935. A few days later, he attended a dinner with Japanese Church members. The small group had been meeting weekly to study in a Japanese-language Sunday School class.[34] During dinner, Heber listened as the Saints performed music on traditional Japanese instruments. He also heard the testimonies of Tomizo Katsunuma, who had joined the Church as a student at the Agricultural College in Utah, and Tsune Nachie, a seventy-nine-year-old Saint who had been baptized in Japan and later emigrated to Hawaii in the 1920s so she could work in the temple.[35]

The food, music, and testimonies took Heber back three decades to when he had served as the first president of the Japanese Mission. He had always been disappointed with his work in Japan. Despite his whole-hearted efforts, he had never succeeded in learning the language, and the mission saw only a few converts. Later mission presidents had also struggled, and Heber closed the mission a few years after becoming Church president, still wondering what else he might have done to make the mission a success.[36]

"To the end of my life," he once observed, "I may feel that I have not done what the Lord expected of me, and what I was sent there to do."[37]

As Heber met the Japanese Saints and learned more about their Sunday School, he realized that Hawaii might be key to launching a new mission to Japan. While in Honolulu, he'd had the opportunity to confirm two newly baptized Japanese members. One of these Saints, Kichitaro Ikegami, had been teaching the Sunday School for two years before his baptism. The impressive young man was a devoted father and an influential businessman on Oahu.[38]

It struck Heber that he had now confirmed more Japanese Saints in Hawaii than he had during his entire mission to Japan.[39] Perhaps, when the time was right, these Saints could be called on missions to Japan and help the Church take root in that land.[40]

EVERYDAY LIFE CONTINUED TO change around Helga Meiszus. Early in 1935, Adolf Hitler had publicly announced that Germany was strengthening its military power, violating the treaty it had signed at the end of the world war. The nations of Europe did little to curtail his power. With the help of his minister of propaganda, Hitler was bending Germany to his will. Enormous rallies showcasing Nazi strength attracted hundreds of thousands of people. Pro-Hitler radio programs, nationalistic music, and the Nazi swastika were everywhere.[41]

Changes were occurring in the Church as well. While the Bee-Hive Girls continued to meet, the government had disbanded the Church's Boy Scout program in Germany to encourage more young men to join the Nazi Party's youth groups. Nazi hatred for Jews had also led the government to forbid churches from using words associated with Judaism. *Articles of Faith* was banned for containing the words "Israel" and "Zion." Other Church literature, including a tract called *Divine Authority,* was outlawed for seeming to challenge Nazi power.[42]

Church leaders in Germany had resisted some of these efforts, but they ultimately encouraged the Saints to adapt to the new government and refrain from saying or doing anything that would put the Church and its members in danger.[43] With the Gestapo seemingly everywhere, the Saints in Tilsit knew that any hint of rebellion or resistance could find its way back to the secret police. Most German Saints stayed out of politics, but there was always the fear that someone in the branch was associated with the Nazis.

The safest thing to do, many members of the branch believed, was to act the part of loyal, obedient Germans. A single instance of disloyalty from a branch member could put everyone at risk of Nazi retaliation.[44]

Helga found comfort, safety, and friendship among the other youth at church, including her brother Siegfried and cousin Kurt Brahtz. The branch often put on programs with acting and music or hosted lively parties with tables full of potato salad, German sausages, and streuselkuchen, a tasty crumb cake.[45] The youth usually spent the entire Sabbath day together. After attending Sunday School in the morning, they would go to the home of a Church member, like Helga's aunt or grandmother. If there was a piano, somebody would sit down and play while everyone sang from the Church's German hymnbook.

Later, after sacrament meeting, they would find their way to the house of Heinz Schulzke, the teenage son of branch president Otto Schulzke, to talk, laugh, and enjoy each other's company. President Schulzke had become like a second father to Helga and the other youth. He had high expectations for them, often exhorting them to repent and keep the commandments. But he also told many stories and had a wry sense of humor. Whenever someone came into church late and everyone turned around to see who it was, he would say, "I will tell you when a lion is coming in—you don't have to turn around."[46]

Helga also looked to her grandmother for comfort and guidance. Johanne Wachsmuth could be stern, like Otto Schulzke, and she was not quick to spoil her grandchildren. She was a deeply religious woman who knew how to speak with her Father in Heaven. Whenever Helga stayed at her grandparents' house, Johanne expected her to kneel in prayer beside her.

One night, Helga was mad at her grandmother and refused to pray. Rather than leaving Helga alone, Johanne insisted that they pray together.

Helga relented, and as she knelt on the hard floor, her bitterness melted away. Her grandmother was her friend, the one who had taught her how to talk with God. Afterward, Helga was grateful for the experience. It felt good to know that she had not let anger take hold of her heart.[47]

IN FEBRUARY 1936, TEN months after his initial meeting with the First Presidency, Harold B. Lee once again found himself in their office. President Grant was ready to move forward on a relief plan for needy Saints. A recent survey of wards and stakes, conducted by the Presiding Bishopric, revealed that nearly one in five Saints was receiving some form of financial assistance. Few of them were turning to the Church for help, however, partly because the federal government had dramatically increased the amount of aid given to states in recent years. The Presiding Bishopric believed the Church could assist all needy members if every Latter-day Saint did his or her part to care for the poor.[48]

President Grant and his counselors asked Harold to revise his earlier proposal. They recruited Campbell Brown Jr., the director of the welfare program for a local copper mine, to assist him.[49]

Over the next few weeks, Harold worked night and day, analyzing the statistics, counseling with Campbell, and reconsidering the previous plan. Then, on March 18, they took the revised proposal to President McKay and walked him through every detail.[50] According to the new plan, the stakes of the Church would be organized into geographical regions, and each region would have its own central storehouse stocked with food and clothing. These items would be procured with fast offering or tithing funds, or generated by work projects, or received through "in-kind" tithing donations. If one region had a surplus of a particular item, it could trade with another region for items that it needed.

Regional councils of stake presidents would manage the program, but much of the responsibility for maintaining it would fall on the bishoprics, ward Relief Society presidencies, and newly created ward employment committees. Members of the employment committee would maintain a record of all ward members' employment status, to be updated weekly. They would also organize work projects and assist members with other forms of relief.[51]

The plan called for the Saints to receive assistance in exchange for labor, just as the Pioneer Stake had done. Participants in work projects would meet with their bishop to discuss their need for food, clothing, fuel, or other necessities, and then a representative from the Relief Society would visit the home, assess the family's circumstances, and fill out an order form to be presented at the stake storehouse. Saints would receive aid according to their individual circumstances, meaning that two people might work the same amount of time in one day but receive a different amount of food or supplies, depending on family size or other factors.[52]

When Harold and Campbell finished their explanation, they could see that President McKay was pleased.

"Brethren, now we have a program to present to the Church," he exclaimed, slapping the table with his hand. "The Lord has inspired you in your work."[53]

CHAPTER 24

The Aim of the Church

President Heber J. Grant and his counselors moved quickly to implement Harold B. Lee's relief program. On April 6, 1936, they announced the plan at a special meeting for stake presidencies and ward bishoprics. Several days later, President Grant appointed Harold to serve as managing director of the program, instructing him to work with apostle Melvin J. Ballard and a central supervisory committee.[1]

The Church's primary goal for the next few months was to ensure that by October 1, every needy family in the stakes had enough food, clothing, and fuel to last the winter. President Grant also wanted to put unemployed Saints back to work to boost morale, restore lost dignity, and achieve financial stability.

To accomplish these goals, he and his counselors asked the Saints to pay a full tithe and increase their fast offerings. They also instructed local Relief Society and priesthood leaders to assess needs and create work projects to provide aid for people in their wards. And as much as possible, the Church itself would provide work opportunities such as improving and repairing Church properties.

"No pains must be spared to wipe out all feeling of diffidence, embarrassment, or shame on the part of those receiving relief," the First Presidency declared. "The ward must be one great family of equals."[2]

During the first week of May, President Grant traveled to California to create a new stake and speak to the Saints about the new relief program.[3] Since the organization of the Los Angeles Stake in 1923, thousands of Saints had moved to California seeking warmer weather and better work. Moreover, the state had several fine universities, and many Latter-day Saints had thrived at these institutions. In 1927, Church leaders organized a stake in San Francisco, followed by one in nearby Oakland a few years later. Now the Church had more than sixty thousand members in nine stakes throughout the state.[4]

President Grant spent his first evening in Los Angeles speaking with the president of the new stake and meeting with local Saints about the relief program. When he awoke the next morning, however, he had temples, not the relief plan, on his mind. He and Church leaders had long contemplated building more temples outside of Utah in areas with large numbers of Saints. They had recently decided to build a temple in Idaho Falls, a small city in southeastern Idaho. Now he felt impressed that the Church needed to build a temple in Los Angeles.[5]

The Depression was becoming less severe, and the Church had the financial means to build two temples while also carrying out the relief program. It was free of debt and was operating on sound financial practices. The Church's significant investment in sugar, begun in the early 1900s, was also paying dividends. President Grant did not think the new temples needed to be as elaborate and costly as the Salt Lake Temple. Rather, he envisioned modest-sized temples that met the needs of the local Saints.[6]

For the time being, though, establishing the new relief plan would be the Church's top priority. Already, objections to the program were surfacing. Some Saints chafed at the heavy new workload it demanded of wards and stakes. Wasn't the faithful payment of tithing and fast offerings enough to care for needy Church members? They also worried that the payment of tithing "in kind"—by contributing goods to local storehouses—created additional costs in handling and storage. Others felt that, as tax-paying citizens, they were entitled to government relief if they qualified for it, even if they did not necessarily need it.[7]

President Grant knew the program would have its critics, but he urged Harold to proceed with the work.

Much depended on the next six months. If the relief plan was to succeed, the Saints would have to work together.[8]

MEANWHILE, IN MEXICO, FIFTY-ONE-YEAR-OLD Isaías Juárez was fighting to keep the Church from fracturing in his country. As a district president, he had been leading the Saints in central Mexico since 1926, when religious and political unrest led the Mexican government to expel all foreign-born clergy, including American Latter-day Saint missionaries, from the country. Taking counsel from Rey L. Pratt, the exiled mission president and a general authority of the Church, Isaías and other Mexican Saints had quickly filled vacant Church leadership roles, keeping the local branches from collapsing.[9]

Now, ten years later, the Church in Mexico faced new problems. After Elder Pratt's unexpected death in 1931, the First Presidency called Antoine Ivins of the First Council of the Seventy to take his place as mission president. Although Antoine had grown up in the Latter-day Saint colonies in northern Mexico and studied law in Mexico City, he was not a Mexican citizen and could not legally minister in the country. As a result, he worked mainly with Mexican Americans living in the southwestern United States.[10]

The Saints in central Mexico were troubled by the mission president's absence, especially when local concerns required immediate attention. The Church, for instance, needed to build more meetinghouses since

Mexican law prohibited people from holding religious services in private homes or other nonreligious buildings. Yet the local Church leaders did not have the authority or resources to resolve this problem themselves.[11]

Feeling abandoned, Isaías and his counselors, Abel Páez and Bernabé Parra, held meetings with other concerned Saints in 1932 to discuss what to do. At these meetings, which came to be called the First and Second Conventions, the Saints resolved that it would be best if a Mexican citizen served as their mission president. During the Mexican Revolution, many of them had sided with leaders who fought against foreign powers for the rights of indigenous Mexicans, and they were frustrated with foreign political leaders who governed from a distance and seemed to ignore their needs.[12]

The Conventionists drafted letters lobbying for this change and mailed them to Church headquarters. The First Presidency responded by sending Antoine Ivins and Melvin J. Ballard to Mexico City to speak with Isaías and the other petitioners. The two visitors assured them that the First Presidency would find an inspired solution to their leadership dilemma. But Antoine also chastened them for directly petitioning the First Presidency without first consulting him.[13]

When Antoine's term as mission president ended, the First Presidency called Harold Pratt, Rey Pratt's younger brother, to replace him. Born in the Mexican colonies, Harold could serve freely in the country, and he soon moved the mission headquarters to Mexico City.

Still, some Church members bristled under his close supervision. Other Saints were deeply disappointed that he was not culturally and ethnically Mexican. They wanted a mission president who could understand the everyday lives and needs of the people he served.[14]

In early 1936, the First Presidency decided to split the Mexican Mission at the national border, removing a portion of the southwestern United States from mission boundaries. This news gave some Saints hope that an ethnic Mexican would serve as the new mission president. But when Harold Pratt retained his position, a group of disappointed Saints decided to hold a third convention.

At the head of the effort were Abel Páez and his uncle Margarito Bautista. Margarito took immense pride in his Mexican heritage—and in the belief that he was a descendant of Book of Mormon peoples. He thought the Mexican Saints could govern themselves, and he resented the interference of leaders from the United States.[15]

Isaías sympathized with Abel and Margarito, but he urged them not to hold the convention. "Church organization," he reminded Abel, "is not based on petitions of the majority." When plans for the Third Convention went forward anyway, Isaías sent a letter throughout the mission, discouraging Church members from attending.

"The cause is noble," he wrote, "but the form of proceeding is out of order because it violates the principle of authority."[16]

On April 26, 1936, one hundred and twenty Saints assembled in Tecalco, Mexico, for the Third Convention. At the meeting, they voted unanimously to sustain the First Presidency. Believing that Church leaders in Salt Lake City had misunderstood their previous letter, they decided they needed to submit a new petition clearly calling for a mission president of their own "raza y sangre"—race and blood. The Conventionists then voted unanimously to present Abel Páez as their choice for an experienced indigenous president of the Mexican Mission.[17]

After the meeting, Isaías worked with Harold Pratt to reconcile with Abel and the Conventionists, but their efforts failed. In June, Conventionists drafted an eighteen-page petition to the First Presidency. "We very respectfully ask that you grant us two things," they wrote. "First, that our Church grant us a mission president who is Mexican, and second, that our Church accept and authorize the candidate we choose."

Isaías could do nothing more to keep the Conventionists from submitting the petition. At the end of the month, they sent it with 251 signatures to Salt Lake City.[18]

On October 2, 1936, President Heber J. Grant opened general conference with a progress report on the relief plan, now known as the Church Security Program. By the first of the month, he reminded the

Saints, the Church had wanted every needy, faithful Saint in its stakes to have ample food, fuel, and clothing for the coming winter.

Although only three quarters of the stakes had met the goal, he was pleased with the promptness and efficiency the Saints had shown over the last six months. "More than fifteen thousand persons have performed labor on various stake and ward projects," he reported. "Hundreds of thousands of work hours have been furnished by the people to this necessary and praiseworthy purpose."[19] They had harvested grain and other crops, collected clothing, and made quilts and bedding in abundance. Employment committees had helped as many as seven hundred people find jobs.

"The aim of the Church is to help the people to help themselves," President Grant told the assembled Saints. "We must not contemplate ceasing our extraordinary efforts until want and suffering shall disappear from amongst us."[20]

Two months after the conference, a film crew came to Salt Lake City to make a short documentary about the security program for *The March of Time,* a popular news series shown in movie theaters across the United States. The filmmakers shot footage of Salt Lake City landmarks and everyday Latter-day Saints working the land and operating Church storehouses and workshops. With the cooperation of President Grant and other Church leaders, the crew also filmed discussions and meetings about the security plan.[21]

Now that the Saints were better prepared to weather the cold season, the prophet's attention again turned to temples. That winter, the Church was given land for a temple along the Snake River in Idaho Falls, Idaho, where a strong community of devout Saints lived.[22] President Grant then returned to Los Angeles to visit the stakes there and follow his prompting to build a temple in the city.

In California, he found Church members working hard to implement the security program. As an urban center, Los Angeles posed challenges to the plan, which depended on farming and other rural activities to provide work for unemployed Saints. So the California stakes had adapted the program to their region. They canned fruit from the state's abundant orchards, and as the Church continued to grow in the area, Saints who needed assistance labored as construction workers on new meetinghouses.[23]

Still, the Saints in California struggled to meet the goal of increasing their fast offerings. Speaking to the members of the Pasadena Stake, northeast of Los Angeles, President Grant emphasized the importance of this sacrifice. "No want would exist among our Church members," he promised the congregation, "if once each month all Latter-day Saints would abstain from two meals and give the sum saved thereby into the hands of the bishop, for distribution to the needy."[24]

When he was not meeting with the Saints, President Grant visited prospective temple sites. He found many suitable places, but each time he showed interest in buying, the owners would ask for significantly more money than he thought the land was worth.[25] The best site he found was a beautiful twenty-four-acre lot located along the main thoroughfare between Los Angeles and Hollywood. He made an offer on the property, but he received no response from the owner before he had to return to Salt Lake City.

The next day, he received a telegram from a bishop in Los Angeles. The owner of the lot had accepted the Church's offer. The prophet was overjoyed. "We have the best site in the entire country," he told J. Reuben Clark.[26]

The news came just as *The March of Time* debuted in movie theaters, bringing positive nationwide attention to the Saints' efforts to help the poor.[27] A few weeks before the film's premiere, a theater in Salt Lake City had hosted a private screening for Church and city leaders. President Grant was still in California at the time, so he missed the event. But David O. McKay had been able to attend, and he had high praise for the film.

"It was a beautiful movie," he exclaimed. "The picture is so excellent and so masterfully presented that every man, woman, and child in the Church should be grateful for it."[28]

AROUND THIS TIME, THE rift between Mexico's Third Convention and the Church continued to widen.[29]

After receiving the Conventionists' petition, the First Presidency responded with a lengthy letter, reiterating the importance of following standard procedures of Church government in all parts of the world.

"If this were not so," the presidency declared, "there would soon grow up in the Church different practices, and these would lead to different doctrines, and in the end there would be no order in the Church."[30]

They urged the Conventionists to repent. "The time may come when a mission president of your own race will be appointed," they wrote, "but this will only be when the president of the Church, acting under the inspiration of the Lord, shall determine so to do."[31]

Santiago Mora Gonzáles, a branch president in central Mexico, met with other Third Conventionists in November 1936 to discuss the best way to respond to the First Presidency's letter. Some Conventionists, including Santiago, were disappointed by the letter but wanted to abide by the First Presidency's decision. Others were outraged.

Margarito Bautista, who sat near Santiago at the meeting, jumped up from the table. "This is an injustice!" he exclaimed. He wanted the Conventionists to reject the authority of Harold Pratt once and for all. "He is no longer our president," Margarito declared. "Our president is dear Abel!"

Santiago was alarmed. Earlier that year, he had asked Margarito what would happen if Church leaders did not agree to the Conventionists' petition. Margarito had assured him that whether or not they got the answer they desired, they would continue to support Harold as mission president and hope he would take the issues they raised into consideration. Now it seemed the Conventionists were calling for outright rebellion.

"This is not what we agreed upon," Santiago told his friend.

"Yes, but this is an injustice," Margarito said.

"Well, then," said Santiago, "we are not keeping our word."

That night, Santiago returned home and talked with his wife, Dolores. "What should we do?" he asked. "I don't want to be an element of opposition for the work of the Church."

"Think it over well," Dolores said.[32]

A short time later, Santiago met with more than two hundred Conventionists to discuss the way forward. Many of them were as angry over the First Presidency's letter as Margarito was. Yet they were also troubled over rumors that Margarito was courting plural wives, a practice he had seen as a young convert in the Mexican colonies. When Conventionists discovered these rumors were true, they agreed that his behavior was unacceptable and ejected him from the organization.[33]

Santiago was disturbed that Margarito, one of the chief instigators of the Convention, had gone astray. After attending a few more meetings, Santiago began telling his wife and other Conventionists that he would no longer continue with the group. He and other disillusioned

Conventionists soon met with Harold, told him of their desire to rejoin the main body of the Church, and asked what they needed to do to return.

"Well," Harold said, "there is no condition for you brethren. You continue being members. You are members of the Church."[34]

Santiago continued to serve faithfully as president of his branch. The Third Convention remained a relatively small movement among the Saints in Mexico, but it still drew hundreds of Church members into its ranks. After more efforts at reconciliation failed, Convention leaders sent another letter to the First Presidency, declaring their intentions to fully reject the mission president's leadership.

Church leaders in Mexico responded a short time later, excommunicating Abel Páez, Margarito Bautista, and other Convention leaders in May 1937 for rebellion, insubordination, and apostasy.[35]

THAT SPRING, IN THE eastern United States, eighteen-year-old Paul Bang was busily serving in the Cincinnati Branch. In addition to being a priest in the Aaronic Priesthood, he was branch clerk, a secretary in the MIA, and a local missionary.

Every Sunday he and other local missionaries would go door-to-door in the city, sharing the gospel. One of his companions, Gus Mason, was old enough to be his father and tried to keep a close eye on him. On their first day working together, Paul had knocked on a door by himself and was invited in to give a gospel message. Gus, meanwhile, was frantically walking up and down the streets searching for him. After that, they knocked on doors together.[36]

Paul liked talking to people about the Church. Unlike young men in Utah, he was surrounded by people who did not share his beliefs. He enjoyed studying the restored gospel and taking notes on what he learned. In his spare time, he read the scriptures and other Church books, including Nephi Anderson's *A Young Folk's History of the Church* and James E. Talmage's *Jesus the Christ* and *Articles of Faith.* He usually studied these books while tending the store on Sunday afternoons, when few people stopped in to make purchases.[37]

Paul and his girlfriend, Connie Taylor, were practically inseparable at Church meetings and MIA activities.[38] Alvin Gilliam, who had replaced Charles Anderson as branch president in early 1936, encouraged Paul and Connie's relationship. Over the last ten years, the branch had more than doubled in size, thanks in part to young Saints getting married, staying in the branch, and raising families.

The Depression had also uprooted many people, physically and spiritually, resulting in some growth from local converts or Saints moving to Cincinnati from economically strapped places like Utah or the American South. Others had come from even farther, including a family of German Saints from Buenos Aires, Argentina.

Recently, Paul's sister Judy had married Stanley Fish, a young man from Arizona who had returned to Cincinnati after serving his mission there.[39]

On June 6, 1937, Paul, Connie, and other members of the branch traveled more than a hundred miles to hear President David O. McKay at a mission conference in a neighboring state. Paul and Connie paid close attention as President McKay spoke to the congregation about the sacredness of courtship and marriage. That night, before Paul dropped Connie off at her family's apartment, she told him for the first time that she loved him.[40]

A short time later, President Gilliam spoke to Paul about going on a full-time mission. Not every worthy young man was expected to serve such a mission at that time, and if Paul went, he would be the first full-time missionary to serve from the Cincinnati Branch.[41] Paul was not sure if he should go. The Church certainly needed his help, given the shortage of missionaries during the Depression. But he also had his family and the store to think about. His older brothers had already moved away from home, and he knew his parents depended on him.[42]

Ultimately, Paul decided not to serve a full-time mission. He continued as a branch missionary, and on August 1, two days after preaching at a street meeting, he baptized six people in a swimming pool. In the fall, President Gilliam and Northern States Mission president Bryant Hinckley called Connie to be a branch missionary as well.[43]

Before long, Paul and Connie were heading into the streets together, passing out Church literature and preaching to anyone who would listen. For Connie's nineteenth birthday in May 1938, Paul surprised her with a Bible and a copy of *Jesus the Christ*—two books she could use in her new calling.

For a while he also joked about getting her an engagement ring. But they still had a year of high school to go—and neither of them was quite ready for marriage.[44]

CHAPTER 25

No Time to Lose

On the evening of March 11, 1938, Hermine Cziep gathered her three children around a radio in their small, one-room apartment just outside Vienna, Austria. Kurt Schuschnigg, the Austrian chancellor, was broadcasting an address to the nation. German troops had massed along the border between their countries. Unless the Austrian government agreed to accept the *Anschluss*—the union of Germany and Austria under Nazi rule—the German army would take their land by force. The chancellor had little choice but to resign and ask the country to submit to a German invasion.

"And so I take leave of the Austrian people," he declared. "God protect Austria!"

Hermine began to cry. "Now we aren't Austria anymore," she told her children. "It is Satan's work.

Force begets force, and what the Nazis have is not good."[1]

Over the next two days, few people openly resisted Adolf Hitler's army as the Germans entered the country and took over the police force. Hitler had been born in Austria, and many Austrians supported his desire to unite all German-speaking people in a powerful new empire called the "Third Reich," even if it meant giving up national independence.[2]

Hermine's husband, Alois, shared her wariness of the Nazis. He had been president of the Vienna Branch for over four years, and Hermine served alongside him as Relief Society president. The branch was small, with only about eighty members, and some of them were staunch supporters of Hitler and the *Anschluss*. Other branch members, especially those with Jewish heritage, viewed Hitler's rise to power with fear and apprehension. But the Saints in Vienna were still a family, and the Czieps did not want the Nazis to divide them.[3]

When Hermine and Alois joined the Church as young adults, it had created a rift between them and their parents. Alois's father, a devout Catholic, had effectively disowned his son, telling him in a letter that he must renounce his association with the Latter-day Saints. "If you decide not to heed my words," his father wrote, "I shall not speak to you again in this life, and what you write to me will end up burned in the fire." His father had since died, and although Alois now had a good relationship with his siblings, he knew the pain of a fractured family.[4]

Other Vienna Saints had experienced similar rejection, and many younger couples in the branch looked to the Czieps as parents. Since Hermine did not usually have money for streetcars, she would walk across the city several times a week to visit women in the branch. When someone from the branch had a baby, Hermine would bring the family food, help with cleaning, and take care of the older children. Alois, meanwhile, traveled by bicycle, often heading out to attend to branch business after finishing work at seven o'clock each night.[5]

Three days after Chancellor Schuschnigg's speech, red and white Nazi banners with black swastikas lined Vienna's streets. Since Alois worked for a large German company, he and his coworkers were ordered to leave the shop to form a "guard of honor" as Hitler and his troops paraded through the city. As Alois stood in the crowd, he could barely see Hitler's gray convertible as it rolled down the street, surrounded by police cars and armed soldiers in crisp uniforms. All around Alois the people cheered, raising their right arms in the Nazi salute.

The next day, Alois joined thousands of his fellow citizens as they crowded into the Heldenplatz, or "Hero's Square," just outside Vienna's Hofburg Palace. Hitler strode onto the palace balcony and declared, "I can announce before history the entry of my homeland into the German Reich."[6]

As the crowd surged, shouts of "Heil Hitler!" filled the square. Alois realized he was witnessing a pivotal moment in history. How these events would affect the Saints in Vienna remained unclear.[7]

ON THE OTHER SIDE of the world, twenty-three-year-old Chiye Terazawa was discouraged. For nearly a month, she had been serving as a Japanese-speaking missionary in Honolulu, Hawaii. Although her parents were from Japan, she had been born and raised in the United States and did not speak Japanese. In fact, as she studied the language with other missionaries, she often berated herself for not picking it up more quickly. Almost every day was a struggle, and she pleaded with God to loosen her tongue.[8]

Nearly three years had passed since President Heber J. Grant felt prompted to open a mission among Hawaii's large Japanese population. While he and his counselors had been eager to resume missionary work among Japanese speakers, one former mission president to Japan advised against it. He believed too many cultural barriers stood in the way of success.

Still, President Grant had pressed ahead with the plan, convinced that a Japanese-language mission in Hawaii could establish strong branches of Japanese speakers who could then share the gospel with friends and family in Japan.[9] In November 1936, he called Hilton

Robertson, who had also been a mission president in Japan, to open the mission. President Robertson and his wife, Hazel, moved to Honolulu, and three elders from the United States soon joined them.[10] Chiye then arrived in early February 1938.

Despite her struggles with the language, Chiye was an enthusiastic missionary. She was the first full-time Japanese American missionary to serve in the Church, and the gospel was a treasured part of her life. Neither of her parents were members of the Church, but they had lived for many years among the Saints in southeast Idaho. Before her mother passed away in the influenza pandemic of 1918, she had asked Chiye's father to send Chiye and her five siblings to Church meetings.

"You can't raise them by yourself," Chiye's mother had told him. "The Church will be their mother so you can be their father."[11]

And the Church had done its part well, both in Idaho and then in California after the family moved there. Before Chiye left for her mission, the Saints in her stake had thrown her a farewell party with speeches by local leaders, a tap dancer, a string quartet, and an orchestra for dance music.[12]

As the only single sister missionary in the mission, Chiye usually worked with Sister Robertson. Since neither of them spoke much Japanese, they often taught other English speakers. President Robertson also called Chiye to organize a Young Women's Mutual Improvement

Association in the mission and serve as its president. The assignment was daunting, but she received some advice on how to organize an MIA when Helen Williams, the first counselor in the YWMIA general presidency, visited the islands.

Chiye chose her counselors and decided on leaders for the Bee-Hive Girls and Gleaner Girls. She also worked closely with Marion Lee, the elder assigned to lead the young men, to plan the mission's first MIA meeting.[13] Although the organization was for the youth of the Church, MIA meetings were open to people of all ages. It would be an evening of traditional Japanese songs, dancing, and storytelling from local Saints and friends of the branch. Marion would speak on the purpose and aim of the MIA, and Chiye would talk about the history of the YWMIA program.

They scheduled the meeting for March 22. Chiye was nervous that no one would come. Marion worried that the program they had planned would be too short. His companion said there was nothing to worry about. "The Lord will provide," he promised.

When the time came to start the meeting, some people had not yet arrived, but Chiye and Marion decided to begin without them. The missionaries opened with a song and offered a prayer. Kay Ikegami, the Sunday School superintendent, then showed up with his family. A short time after that, another family arrived. By the end of the meeting, more than forty people had assembled, including every one of Chiye's fellow leaders in the MIA.

One man even sang three songs, filling out the program and alleviating any fear about a short meeting.

Chiye and Marion were relieved. The mission's MIA was off to a promising start. "God has opened up the way," Chiye reported in her journal. "I only hope that we can make it a success."[14]

THAT SUMMER, J. REUBEN CLARK of the First Presidency prepared to speak at an annual gathering of Latter-day Saint seminary, institute, and college religion teachers.

President Clark, a former lawyer and diplomat, was a strong proponent of education. Like many religious people of his generation, he worried about secular trends replacing religious beliefs in the classroom. He was especially bothered by biblical scholars who emphasized Jesus's moral teachings over His miracles, Atonement, and Resurrection. Throughout his adult life, he had seen friends, coworkers, and even fellow Latter-day Saints become so absorbed in secular ideas that they abandoned their faith.[15]

President Clark did not want the same thing to happen to the rising generation of Saints. The Church's three colleges, thirteen institutes, and ninety-eight seminaries were founded to "make Latter-day Saints." Yet he worried that some teachers at these schools missed opportunities to nurture faith in the restored gospel of Jesus Christ when they refrained from bearing testimony, supposing it would bias their students' pursuit of truth. He believed that the youth of the Church needed a religious education, grounded in the foundational events and doctrine of the Restoration.[16]

On the morning of August 8, 1938, President Clark met with the teachers at Aspen Grove, a beautiful canyon retreat tucked away in the mountains near Provo, Utah. As he stood to speak, a rainstorm blew through the area, battering the lodge where he and the teachers were assembled. Undeterred, he told his audience that he intended to speak frankly on behalf of the other members of the First Presidency.

"We must say plainly what we mean," he said, "because the future of our youth, both here on earth and in the hereafter, as also the welfare of the whole Church, are at stake."

He identified the fundamental doctrine of the restored gospel. "There are for the Church, and for each and all of its members, two prime things which may not be overlooked, forgotten, shaded, or discarded," he said. "First—that Jesus Christ is the Son of God, the Only Begotten of the Father in the flesh."

"The second," he continued, "is that the Father and the Son actually and in truth and very deed appeared to the Prophet Joseph in a vision in the woods."

"Without these two great beliefs," he declared, "the Church would cease to be the Church."[17]

He then spoke of the importance of teaching these principles to students. "The youth of the Church are hungry for things of the Spirit," he said. "They want to gain testimonies of their truth."[18]

He believed a personal testimony of the gospel ought to be the first requirement for teaching the gospel. "No amount of learning, no amount of study, and no number of scholastic degrees can take the place of this testimony," he said. Furthermore, he declared, "You do not have to sneak up behind this spiritually experienced youth and whisper religion in his ears. You can come right out, face-to-face, and talk with him. You do not need to disguise religious truths with a cloak of worldly things."

As rain beat against the windows of the lodge, President Clark urged the teachers to help the First Presidency improve religious education in the Church.

"You teachers have a great mission," he testified. "Your chief interest, your essential and all but sole duty, is to teach the gospel of the Lord Jesus Christ as that has been revealed in these latter days."[19]

After the speech, some teachers objected to the course the First Presidency had charted for Church education, believing it restricted their freedom to teach as they thought best. Others welcomed its emphasis on teaching foundational truths and bearing personal testimony. "I am anxious to carry forward the work," commissioner of Church education Franklin West told President Clark. "I promise you that you will see marked and rapid improvement."[20]

A few months later, the seminary program introduced a new class for its students: "The Doctrines of the Church."[21]

388

IN FEBRUARY 1939, CHIYE Terazawa learned that her mission president was planning to transfer two sister missionaries to another area of Hawaii. The news rattled her. With her YWMIA going so well in Honolulu, she did not want to leave. Who would be transferred, she wondered, and where would they go?[22]

The mission now had four sister missionaries, all of them living and working together in Honolulu. President Robertson, however, had recently organized branches of Japanese Saints on Maui, Kauai, and the Big Island of Hawaii. The sisters he selected for the transfer would be responsible for working with the elders to build up one of these branches from its earliest stages.[23]

On March 3, 1939, President Robertson called Chiye and her companion, Inez Beckstead, into his office. He told them he was sending them to Hilo, a city on the Big Island. Chiye felt many emotions at once, and she could not help crying. She was happy and relieved that she no longer had to fret about staying or going. But she would miss working closely with the Robertsons and the Japanese Saints on Oahu.

A few days later, Chiye and Inez said goodbye to a crowd of missionaries and Japanese Saints at the harbor in Honolulu. Several women draped the companions with beads and lei. Kay Ikegami gave them some money for the trip. Longtime Japanese Saint Tomizo Katsunuma presented them with postage stamps.[24]

One person not at the docks was Tsune Nachie, the beloved temple worker from Japan, who had died a few months earlier. The elderly woman was widely known as the "mother of the mission," and she had become a dear friend and mentor to Chiye over the past year. In the hours after Sister Nachie's death, in fact, the Robertsons had asked Chiye to help them prepare her body for burial. Sister Nachie would have loved to know that two sister missionaries were going to Hilo. Some years earlier, she herself had served a local mission there.[25]

Chiye and Inez arrived at Hilo on the morning of March 8, somewhat seasick but ready to work. Hilo was much smaller than Honolulu. Chiye and Inez could see no hotels or restaurants in the town, aside from a café along the waterfront. The Hilo Branch was about five months old, and normally around thirty-five people— most of them investigators—attended Sunday meetings. The elders had already organized a Sunday School and an MIA program for the young men, but there was no YWMIA or Primary. Chiye agreed to lead the young women while Inez served as the Primary president.[26]

The two missionaries moved into the basement of a boardinghouse for women and found plenty of opportunities to improve their Japanese. One of the first things they did was ask administrators and teachers at a local Japanese elementary school if they could speak to the students about Primary. At the time, missionaries used Primary as a way to acquaint children and their families with the Church. Since the activities were fun and promoted simple Christian values, they attracted children of many faiths. Chiye and Inez made a good impression on the school, and before long, dozens of children were attending Primary on Wednesday afternoons.[27]

That spring, the sister missionaries decided to have the children perform *The Happy Hearts,* a musical play the Primary general board had commissioned for Primary festivals throughout the Church. In the play, a king and queen of an imaginary land teach children why unpleasant things like rain, eating vegetables, and early bedtimes are in fact good for them.[28]

When Chiye and Inez were not knocking on doors, studying, or meeting with investigators, they could often be found practicing songs, sewing costumes, assembling props, or pleading with parents to send their children to play practice. The Hilo Saints and the elders helped as well, rounding up the absent children, making sets, and assisting with rehearsals.[29]

Nine days before the performance, the rehearsal was a disaster. "What a mess," Chiye wrote in her journal. "But I do believe it will be all right. At least here's hoping."[30]

Later rehearsals went better, and as the day of the performance neared, everything started to come together. The missionaries advertised the festival in the newspaper and finished sewing and mending costumes. Tamotsu Aoki, a local businessman who was investigating the Church with his family, agreed to serve as master of ceremonies.[31]

On the morning of the performance, Chiye woke up early and helped gather flowers, ferns, and other plants to decorate the meetinghouse stage. Then, as the Saints and elders set up chairs and arranged the scenery, she rushed to get the children in costume and makeup in time.

By seven o'clock in the evening, about five hundred people had gathered for the performance. To Chiye's relief, the children played their parts well. She and Inez were thrilled that so many people had come to the meetinghouse to support the Primary.[32] At the end of the musical, they all listened as the young cast sang in unison:

Where is the Land of Happy Hearts?
Here and ev'ry where!
There are wide and shining roads for you,
Or a little lane or a trail will do,
To lead you surely there.[33]

IN THE SUMMER OF 1939, eleven-year-old Emmy Cziep and her siblings, fifteen-year-old Mimi and twelve-year-old Josef, were enjoying a vacation in Czechoslovakia, a country just north of their home in Vienna, Austria.

The children and their parents, Alois and Hermine, had visited family there several summers since the death of Alois's father. They stayed with two of Alois's brothers, Heinrich and Leopold, and their families in Moravia, a region in the central part of the country.[34]

Like Austria, Czechoslovakia was Nazi-occupied territory. Shortly after the *Anschluss,* Hitler's army had seized the Sudetenland, a Czechoslovak border region with a large number of ethnic Germans. Although many Czechoslovaks wanted to defend their country, the leaders of Italy, France, and Great Britain hoped to avoid another large-scale war in Europe and had agreed to the annexation. In exchange, Hitler pledged to refrain from any further invasions. Within a few months, however, he had broken his agreement and seized the rest of the country.[35]

To Emmy, the conflict seemed far away. She loved being with her extended family. She enjoyed playing cops and robbers with her cousins and splashing around with them in a nearby stream. When her parents had to return to Austria partway through the summer, she and her siblings stayed in Czechoslovakia a few weeks more.

On August 31, 1939, the Cziep children were just sitting down to lunch when their uncle Heinrich burst into the room, his face flushed. "You have to go now!" he exclaimed. "There is no time to lose!"

Emmy was confused and frightened. Her uncle told them that Hitler seemed to be planning something. Orders had been issued to close borders, and the one o'clock train passing through their town could be their last chance to return to Vienna. Catching the train might be impossible, he said, but the children had to try if they hoped to get home to their parents.

Earlier that morning, Emmy and her siblings had put all their clothing in a tub of soapy water for washing. Their aunt and uncle helped them wring out their clothes before tossing them, still wet, into a suitcase. Then they dashed to the train station on foot.

The station was a mass of frantic people, all of them jostling to get out of the country. Emmy and her siblings crammed themselves into the train and immediately found themselves surrounded by scores of hot, sweating passengers. Emmy could barely breathe. When the train stopped at villages along the route, people threw themselves at the train's windows, screaming and trying to climb in, but there was no room.[36]

It was dark when the train finally pulled into Vienna. Full of tears, the Cziep family rejoiced that they were back together.

Instead of returning to the tiny apartment where Emmy had spent her whole life, they went to a new apartment on Taborstrasse, a beautiful street in the center of town. For years, Alois and Hermine had wanted to find a better home for their growing family, but their low income, a housing shortage, and political controls over assigning apartments had made that impossible. Then the economy improved after the *Anschluss,* and business increased fivefold at the company where Alois worked.

With the help of a Church member who worked for a Nazi official, Alois and Hermine had applied for a new apartment and received one with three bedrooms, a kitchen, a bathroom, and a living room. It was also much closer to the branch meetinghouse—a forty-five-minute walk, rather than the two hours they were accustomed to.[37]

Sadly, the good fortune came at the expense of Jews who had once been the main occupants of Taborstrasse. Not long after the *Anschluss,* the Nazis and their followers had vandalized Jewish businesses, burned synagogues, and arrested and deported thousands of Jewish citizens. Many Jews with means to flee the country abandoned their homes, leaving apartments open for families like the Czieps to occupy.[38] Other Jews remained in the city, including some Saints with Jewish heritage in the Vienna Branch. And they were growing ever more fearful for their lives.[39]

On September 1, Emmy and her family spent their first night together in their new apartment. While they slept, one and a half million German troops invaded Poland.[40]

CHAPTER 26

War's Foul Brood

On August 24, 1939, eight days before the invasion of Poland, the First Presidency ordered 320 North American missionaries in the British, French, West German, East German, and Czechoslovak Missions to evacuate to Denmark, Sweden, Norway, or the Netherlands—whichever neutral country was closest.[1] Apostle Joseph Fielding Smith, who had been visiting the Saints in Europe that summer with his wife, Jessie, stayed in Denmark to coordinate the evacuation from Copenhagen.[2]

After receiving the order to leave, Norman Seibold, a twenty-three-year-old missionary from Idaho serving in the West German Mission, saw to it that all the North American missionaries in his district immediately left the country. Then, instead of going straight to the Netherlands, he made his way to the mission home in Frankfurt.

When he arrived, Norman found his mission president, Douglas Wood, sick with worry. President Wood had sent telegrams instructing all missionaries to evacuate, but lines of communication throughout Germany were overwhelmed. Only Norman and a handful of missionaries had confirmed receiving the message. And to make matters worse, government officials in the Netherlands had barred any noncitizens from entering the country unless they were only passing through. Now dozens of missionaries were likely stranded in western Germany with useless train tickets to the Netherlands and no money to purchase new ones.[3]

President Wood and his wife, Evelyn, were leaving to oversee the evacuation of a group of elders who had already arrived at the mission home, and they needed someone to stay in Germany to locate the remaining missionaries.

"It will be your mission to find them and see that they get out," President Wood told Norman. "Follow your impressions entirely. We have no idea what towns these thirty-one elders will be in."[4]

Late that night, Norman left Frankfurt on a crowded train, heading north along the Rhine River. He had tickets to Denmark and money for any missionaries he came across—if only he knew where to find them. And he had to hurry. The German government had just announced that the military needed the railways to transport soldiers, so seats would soon be scarce for any civilian traveling by train.

When the train stopped in the city of Cologne, Norman felt he should exit, and he elbowed his way out of the passenger car. The station was swarming with people, so he climbed onto a baggage cart to see above the crowd. But he did not recognize any missionaries. Then he remembered the "missionary whistle"—the tune to "Do What Is Right," which was familiar to everyone in the mission. Norman had little talent for music, but he pursed his lips and whistled the first few notes as best he could.[5]

People immediately took notice, and soon Norman saw a missionary and a local German Saint coming toward him. He continued to whistle, and more elders and an older missionary couple found him as well. He sent the missionaries to safety, and then he boarded a train to another city.

A few hours later, in the city of Emmerich, Norman found more missionaries. As he gave them money from the mission president, he attracted the attention of a police officer, who seemed to think the missionaries were trying to smuggle cash out of Germany. The officer demanded that they turn over their money and tell him what they were doing. When Norman refused to cooperate, the officer grabbed him and threatened to take him to the city authorities.

Norman usually listened to the police, but he did not want to go with the officer into the city. "You'd better unhand me," he said, "or there might be a fight."

By then a crowd had formed, and the officer glanced at the people nervously. He let go of Norman and took him to a military official at the train station to explain who he was and what he was doing. The official listened to Norman's story, saw no reason to detain him, and even wrote a letter of explanation for him to give to anyone else who might stop him during his travels.[6]

Norman continued on, stopping to look for missionaries whenever the Spirit directed him. At one remote town, hardly anyone was standing on the railway platform, and it seemed silly to look for missionaries there. But Norman felt he needed to get off the train, so he decided to go into town. He soon came to a small restaurant and found two elders drinking apple juice purchased with the last coins in their pockets.[7]

After days of searching, Norman had located seventeen missionaries. To get to Denmark, he and his companions had to catch trains commandeered for troop transport, bluffing conductors and avoiding policemen all the way. When Norman arrived in Copenhagen, one day after the invasion of Poland, every North American missionary in the German missions was safe.

The next day, September 3, France and Great Britain declared war on Germany.[8]

"THE LONG-THREATENED AND DREADED war has broken out," President Heber J. Grant announced at the October 1939 general conference. For years, he had watched with alarm and apprehension as Hitler led

Germany down a violent and dangerous path, unleashing misery and bloodshed on the world. Now the Axis powers, led by Nazi Germany, were locked in combat with the Allied nations under the United Kingdom and France.

"God is grieved by war," President Grant told the Saints. "He will hold subject to the eternal punishments of His will those who wage it unrighteously." The prophet urged the leaders of the world, and all people everywhere, to seek peaceful solutions to their differences.

"We condemn all of war's foul brood—avarice, greed, misery, want, disease, cruelty, hate, inhumanity, savagery, death," he declared. It pained the prophet to think of the millions of people suffering and grieving because of the conflict. Many thousands of them were Latter-day Saints, and some were already in harm's way. He said, "We earnestly implore all members of the Church to love their brethren and sisters, and all peoples, whoever and wherever they are, to banish hate from their lives, to fill their hearts with charity, patience, long-suffering, and forgiveness."[9]

In the weeks and months after general conference, thoughts of war weighed heavy on the prophet's mind. He wrote to his daughter Rachel in December about the unnecessary loss of life. "It makes my heart ache," he wrote. "It does seem as though the Lord ought to wipe off the earth people who create and start wars, like Hitler."[10]

In the winter of 1940, President Grant traveled to Inglewood, a neighborhood in Los Angeles, where the Saints looked forward to hearing from him at their stake conference. As he arrived at the chapel, he felt dizzy and found it difficult to speak. When he stepped out of the car, his legs were unsteady, and he struggled to make his way to the door of the meetinghouse. The dizziness seemed to pass soon after he took his seat on the stand. Still, he asked to be excused from making his remarks.

Later, after a nap, he felt strong enough to speak at the conference's afternoon session. Standing at the podium, he addressed the Saints for nearly forty minutes. But that night, when he tried several times to get up, he nearly fell. The following morning, his left side felt numb and he could not raise his arm or move his fingers on that side. When he tried to stand, the strength in his left leg was gone. His tongue felt thick, and words slurred together when he spoke.

With the help of his family and friends, President Grant went to a nearby hospital, where doctors found that he had suffered a stroke.[11] He spent the next few months in California, slowly recovering his strength and movement. His doctor cautioned him to rest more, eat better, and avoid any strenuous activity. By April, the prophet was well enough to return to Salt Lake City.

"I have been good and lazy carrying out the doctor's instructions," he informed his daughter Grace shortly after his return. "I do not know how long I can keep it up."[12]

ON JUNE 28, 1940, THE war in Europe was far from the minds of the Saints in Cincinnati, Ohio. That evening, twenty-one-year-old Connie Taylor heard the opening notes of Wagner's "Bridal Chorus," her cue to start walking down the aisle of the Cincinnati Branch meetinghouse. The chapel was full of family and friends, all gathered to celebrate her marriage to Paul Bang.[13]

Connie and Paul had been engaged for just over a year. They wanted to be sealed together, but like many Latter-day Saint couples living far from a temple, they had decided first to be married civilly in the meetinghouse chapel.[14]

As Connie made her way to the front of the room, she saw her father sitting among the guests. At weddings in the United States, fathers traditionally walked their daughters down the aisle. But since her father had trouble walking, her brother Milton walked with her instead. Connie was just glad her father was there. Her patriarchal blessing had promised that he would someday enjoy the blessings of the gospel with her. That day had not yet come, but he had attended a sacrament meeting once on Easter Sunday, and that was a good sign.[15]

After Connie joined Paul at the front of the chapel, their branch president, Alvin Gilliam, performed the ceremony. For many people in the room, the evening marked the end of an era. Aside from the next Sunday's meetings, the wedding was the last time the Cincinnati Branch would gather in the little chapel they purchased eleven years earlier. The old building was falling apart, so the growing branch had recently sold it and purchased land north of the city to build a new meetinghouse.[16]

The newlyweds left the next afternoon for Niagara Falls, New York, in Paul's father's truck. They took three baskets of food from the family grocery store, some clothes, and around sixty dollars in cash.

On their way, Connie and Paul visited the Kirtland Temple. The building was now used as a meetinghouse for the Reorganized Church of Jesus Christ of Latter Day Saints. The temple door was locked when they arrived, but a man with a key opened the building and let them spend an hour touring it on their own. They explored every inch of the temple, including the steeple, where they looked out on the tiny village where hundreds of faithful Saints had lived more than a century earlier.[17]

From Kirtland, they moved on to Niagara Falls. The resort town was a popular honeymoon destination on the border of the United States and Canada, but the war in Europe had put everyone on alert. Although the United States had not entered the conflict, Canada was part of the British Commonwealth and had declared war on Germany after the invasion of Poland. Before Connie and Paul could cross into Canada, border inspectors carefully checked them over to make sure they were not spies.

After touring Niagara Falls, the couple drove a hundred miles east to Palmyra and Manchester, New York.[18] Over the years, the Church had acquired several historic sites in the area, including the Hill Cumorah, the Sacred Grove, and the frame home of Lucy and Joseph Smith Sr. Recognizing the sites' potential for missionary work, the Church had begun opening them to visitors and advertising their historical and spiritual significance on roadside signs. In the early 1920s, under the direction of B. H. Roberts, mission-wide conferences were held on the Hill Cumorah, and they had since developed into an annual pageant open to the public.[19]

While in Manchester, Connie and Paul stayed the night in the Smith home for a small fee. They climbed the Hill Cumorah and thought about the gold plates being buried there for so long. At the crest of the hill was a new monument of the angel Moroni, and they paused to take pictures of it and appreciate the magnificent view of the surrounding area. Later, they took a walk through the Sacred Grove, enjoying the holiness and beauty of the place. Before leaving, they knelt together in prayer.[20]

The newlyweds made a short visit to Washington, DC, where they attended a service in a massive marble meetinghouse the Church had dedicated in 1933. The Church had experienced significant growth in the city since 1920, when apostle Reed Smoot and a small group of Saints had organized a branch there. In fact, shortly before Paul and Connie's visit, apostle Rudger Clawson had organized a stake in Washington, calling forty-year-old Ezra Taft Benson as president.[21]

After a few days in Washington, Connie and Paul returned to Cincinnati, where they settled into a drafty apartment not far from the Bang family's grocery store. They had spent all but one penny of their money on their honeymoon, but Paul still had a job with his father. In a few years, after they saved some money, they could take an even longer road trip—this time to Salt Lake City and the temple.[22]

ON A COLD DECEMBER night in 1940, the menacing drone of Nazi bomber planes filled the sky above Cheltenham, a town in South West England. The German air force, the Luftwaffe, had been bombarding Great Britain with relentless air raids for six months. Attacks had first focused on air bases and ports, but the bombers had since moved into civilian areas in London and beyond.[23] Cheltenham was a peaceful place with beautiful parks and gardens. Now it was a target.

Nellie Middleton, a fifty-five-year-old Latter-day Saint, lived in the town with her six-year-old daughter, Jennifer. To prepare her home against air strikes, she had used her modest wage as a dressmaker to furnish an area in her basement as a shelter, complete with food, water, oil lamps, and a small iron bed for Jennifer. Following instructions from the government, Nellie had also covered her windows with netting to catch flying shards of glass in the event of an attack.[24]

Now, all over Cheltenham, bombs were whistling through the air and crashing to the ground with a thunderous roar. The terrifying noise grew ever closer to

Nellie's home until a tremendous explosion on a nearby street rattled her walls, shattering the windows and filling the netting with razor-sharp glass.

In the morning, the streets were filled with rubble. The bombs had killed twenty-three people and left more than six hundred homeless.[25]

Nellie and the other Cheltenham Saints did their best to endure after the attack. When British Mission president Hugh B. Brown and other North American missionaries left the country nearly a year earlier, the small branch and others like it struggled to fill callings and run Church programs. Then the local men went away to war, leaving no priesthood holders to bless the sacrament or formally administer branch business. Before long, the branch was forced to disband.

An older man named Arthur Fletcher, who held the Melchizedek Priesthood, lived about twenty miles away, and he rode his rusty bicycle to visit the Cheltenham Saints whenever he could. But most of the time it was Nellie, the former Relief Society president in the Cheltenham Branch, who took responsibility for the spiritual and temporal welfare of the Saints in her area. With the branch closed, the Church members could no longer meet in the rented hall they used on Sundays, so Nellie's living room became the place where the Relief Society prayed, sang, and studied *Jesus the Christ* and *Articles of Faith* together.[26]

Nellie also ensured that her daughter learned about the gospel. She had been nearly fifty and unmarried when she adopted Jennifer. Now the little girl joined the women when they met to study, and they were careful to discuss the gospel in a way that Jennifer could understand. Nellie and other Relief Society sisters also took Jennifer along when they visited the sick or the elderly. No one in the branch had a telephone or a car, so they made their visits on foot, bringing a pot of jam or a bit of cake along with a message.[27]

But once the sun set, all visiting ceased. To make it harder for German bombers to see their targets, towns and cities across the United Kingdom disconnected streetlights and shut off illuminated signs. People draped their windows with dark cloth and unscrewed the light-bulbs in their entryways.

In Cheltenham, the Saints retreated to their homes. Any glimmer of light could put them and their neighbors at risk.[28]

THE FOLLOWING YEAR, VIENNA Branch president Alois Cziep was finding his calling more and more difficult. The war had severed the usual channels of communication between Church headquarters and branches in Axis-occupied areas. *Der Stern,* the mission's German-language magazine, had ceased publication. The acting mission president, a German member named Christian Heck, was doing his best to keep the Church functioning amid the chaos. Alois did the same for his branch.

While the physical destruction and devastation of the war had not yet reached Austria's borders, Alois knew the British Royal Air Force had attacked German cities. The Soviet Union was now at war with the Third Reich as well. Like Great Britain on the other side of the conflict, Austria was under nighttime blackout orders to protect against enemy aircraft that might be circling overhead.[29]

Most of the men in the Vienna Branch had been drafted for the German army when the war began. Since Alois had lost an eye to disease some years earlier, he was exempt from military service. And despite the rising challenges, he was fortunate to have two counselors, several young Aaronic Priesthood holders, and his wife, Hermine, to assist him. As Relief Society president, Hermine carried much of the emotional burden of women in the branch, who were often overwhelmed, lonely, and afraid—especially if they received news that their loved ones had been taken prisoner or killed in battle.

Hermine would encourage them to trust in God and carry on, and she tried to do the same.[30]

Even as the branch grew smaller after the start of the war, divisions among its members continued, despite Alois's efforts to steer meetings away from politics. Once, at the beginning of a Church meeting, a visitor from Germany offered a prayer for Adolf Hitler. "Brother," Alois said after the man finished, "in this place we do not pray for Hitler."

With Nazi Party members and sympathizers in the branch, Alois often had to be more careful about what he said. Informers and spies could be anywhere, ready to denounce him and his family to the government. While he and Hermine believed in honoring the law of the land, sometimes doing so was painful.[31]

Two members of the branch, Olga Weiss and her adult son Egon, were Jewish converts who served in the branch each week with their musical talents. But when the Nazis invaded Austria, the Weisses knew they had to leave the country or risk falling prey to the regime's violent anti-Semitism. Even though the family no longer practiced Judaism, the Nazis considered them "racially Jewish" because of their ancestry.

Some months after the German annexation of Austria, the Weisses wrote urgent letters to the First Presidency and former missionaries they knew, hoping to find someone who could help them and a few of their relatives emigrate to the United States. "Conditions here are terrible for us Jewish people," Egon wrote in his letter. "We must get away from here."[32]

Like many people throughout the world, President Grant had received conflicting reports about Hitler's hostility toward Jews and the extent of the danger they faced in Germany. The prophet had denounced such anti-Semitism publicly and privately.[33] Yet Church leaders were unable to help the Weisses or any other European individuals hoping to emigrate. U.S. law, they observed, no longer allowed religious organizations to sponsor immigrants, and for many years the Church had declined all requests for such assistance.[34]

As the war in Europe escalated, the First Presidency frequently expressed dismay that the U.S. government did not permit them to help migrating refugees. When President Grant and his counselors received letters such as Egon's, they could do little more than respond with sympathy, sometimes recommending organizations that they hoped could help.[35]

In September 1941, Egon and Olga were still in Vienna. The Nazis were at that time requiring all Austrian Jews to identify themselves by wearing a yellow Star of David on their clothing. When Nazi officials discovered that Jews were coming to meetings at the Vienna Branch, they ordered Alois to forbid them from attending. If he refused, the Saints would be evicted from their meeting place.

Alois decided he had to comply with the demand. Conflicted and full of regret, he met with the Weisses and told them they could no longer attend meetings. But he and other branch members continued to visit the family faithfully—until, one day, Olga and Egon were nowhere to be found.[36]

CHAPTER 27

God Is at the Helm

Come to my house tonight. I want you to hear something," sixteen-year-old Helmuth Hübener whispered to his friend Karl-Heinz Schnibbe. It was a Sunday evening in the summer of 1941, and the young men were attending sacrament meeting with their branch in Hamburg, Germany.

Seventeen-year-old Karl-Heinz had many friends in the branch, but he particularly enjoyed spending time with Helmuth. He was smart and confident—so intelligent that Karl-Heinz had nicknamed him "the professor." His testimony and commitment to the Church were strong, and he could answer questions about the gospel with ease. Since his mother worked long hours, Helmuth lived with his grandparents, who were also members of the branch. His stepfather was a zealous Nazi, and Helmuth did not like being around him.[1]

That night, Karl-Heinz quietly entered Helmuth's apartment and found his friend hunched over a radio. "It has shortwave," Helmuth said. Most German families had cheaper radios provided by the Nazi government, with fewer channels and limited reception. But Helmuth's older brother, a soldier in the German army, had brought this high-quality radio home from France after Nazi forces conquered the country in the first year of the war.[2]

"What can you hear on it?" asked Karl-Heinz. "France?"

"Yes," Helmuth said, "and England too."

"Are you crazy?" Karl-Heinz said. He knew Helmuth was interested in current events and politics, but listening to enemy radio broadcasts during wartime could get a person thrown in jail or even executed.[3]

Helmuth handed Karl-Heinz a document he had written, filled with news about the military successes of Great Britain and the Soviet Union.

"Where did you get this?" Karl-Heinz asked after reading the paper. "It can't be possible. It is completely the opposite of our military broadcasts."

Helmuth answered by switching off the light and turning on the radio, keeping the volume down low. The German army worked constantly to jam Allied signals, but Helmuth had rigged up an antenna, allowing the boys to hear forbidden broadcasts all the way from Great Britain.

As the clock struck ten, a voice crackled in the dark: "The BBC London presents the news in German."[4] The program discussed a recent German offensive in the Soviet Union. Nazi papers had reported the campaign as a triumph, without acknowledging German losses. The British spoke frankly of both Allied and Axis casualties.

"I'm convinced they're telling the truth and we're lying," Helmuth said. "Our news reports sound like a lot of boasting—a lot of propaganda."

Karl-Heinz was astonished. Helmuth had often said that Nazis could not be trusted. He had even engaged in political discussions on the subject with adults at church. But Karl-Heinz had been reluctant to believe his teenage friend over the words of government officials.

Now it seemed that Helmuth had been right.[5]

ON DECEMBER 7, 1941, KAY Ikegami and his family waited for their Japanese Sunday School to begin at a small chapel on King Street in Honolulu, Hawaii. When Kay first began attending the class with other Japanese American Saints, it had been small. But after the organization of the Japanese Mission in Hawaii four years earlier, the number of Japanese Sunday Schools had grown to five in Honolulu alone. Kay was the superintendent of the Sunday School that met on King Street.[6]

There were fewer people than usual in class this morning. As they waited for the meeting to start, Jay C. Jensen, who had replaced Hilton Robertson as president of the Japanese Mission, rushed through the door. "Japan is attacking Pearl Harbor," he said.

Kay's face went ashen. "Oh no," he said. "It can't be true."[7]

Although born in Japan, Kay had lived in the United States since he was a child, and his own children had been born there. The thought of his native country attacking the nation he and his family called home was deeply disturbing.[8]

At eight o'clock that morning, President Jensen had been attending another Japanese Sunday School that met near Pearl Harbor, a large U.S. naval base near the city. Outside, planes were flying back and forth in formation, and some of them were dropping bombs. He had assumed the U.S. military was conducting training maneuvers, so he did not think twice about the commotion. When he returned home, though, his wife, Eva, rushed outside and told him Pearl Harbor was under attack.

Doubtful, he had turned on the radio—only to learn that she was right. "Keep off the streets!" a radio announcer had warned. Japanese planes were still in the air and dropping bombs. But he and Sister Jensen were worried about Kay and his Sunday School, so they had rushed to King Street.

"Hurry home and take cover," President Jensen told Kay. The class quickly broke up and everyone fled the building. A short time later, a bomb landed just one hundred yards away, setting several structures on fire.[9]

In the days that followed, the United States declared war on Japan and its ally Germany, ending American neutrality in the conflict. The government placed Hawaii under strict martial law, closed public schools, censored newspapers, and screened all outgoing mail. Everyone on the islands was subject to a curfew, but Japanese people who were not U.S. citizens were required to be home each night by eight o'clock, one hour earlier than all other residents. The government also banned the use of the Japanese language in public.[10]

During this time, Kay's fifteen-year-old son, David, was unsettled by the sudden change in his family's life. "The days are all dead," he wrote in his journal. "I wish there was school once again." He tried to get to his school building, hoping to retrieve a library book from his locker, but soldiers were blocking the road.

Worried about future attacks from Japan, people on the island began constructing small underground shelters for protection against enemy bombs. Kay and his wife, Matsuye, asked David to help them build a shelter in their backyard. They started digging a trench for the shelter a little over a week before Christmas. The labor was hard and slow, especially when they had to remove rocks from the ground. After recruiting more help, the family was able to finish building the shelter on Christmas morning.

David was relieved the backbreaking work was over, yet he struggled to enjoy the rest of the holiday. "You can't get in the spirit because of the war," he lamented.[11]

A few weeks had passed since the bombing, bringing no further attacks. But it was hard not to look to the sky, searching for planes marked with the Japanese emblem of the rising sun.[12]

ONE SUNDAY EVENING, BACK in Germany, Karl-Heinz Schnibbe and Rudi Wobbe waited for Helmuth Hübener to arrive for sacrament meeting at the Hamburg Branch.[13] For the past few months both Karl-Heinz and fifteen-year-old Rudi had been helping Helmuth distribute anti-Nazi flyers around the city. As a branch clerk, Helmuth had the branch typewriter at his house so he could write letters to Latter-day Saint soldiers, and he often used it to produce the flyers, which had bold headlines like "They Are Not Telling You Everything" or "Hitler, the Murderer!"[14]

Distributing the flyers was high treason, a crime punishable by death, but the young men had so far evaded the authorities. Helmuth's absence from church was troubling, however. Karl-Heinz wondered if perhaps his friend was sick. The meeting went on as usual until branch president Arthur Zander, a member of the Nazi Party, asked the congregation to remain in their seats after the closing prayer.

"A member of our branch, Helmuth Hübener, has been arrested by the Gestapo," President Zander said. "My information is very sketchy, but I know that it is political. That is all."[15]

Karl-Heinz locked eyes with Rudi. The Saints seated near them were whispering in astonishment. Whether they agreed with Hitler or not, many of them believed it was their duty to respect the government and its laws.[16] And they knew any open opposition to the Nazis from a branch member, however heroic or well intentioned, could put them all in danger.

On the way home, Karl-Heinz's parents wondered aloud what Helmuth could possibly have done. Karl-Heinz said nothing. He, Rudi, and Helmuth had made a pact that if one of them should get arrested, that person would take all the blame and not name the others. Karl-Heinz trusted that Helmuth would honor their pact, but he was afraid. The Gestapo had a reputation for torturing prisoners to get the information they wanted.[17]

Two days later, Karl-Heinz was at work when he answered a knock at the door. Two Gestapo agents in long leather overcoats showed him their badges.

"Are you Karl-Heinz Schnibbe?" one of them asked.

Karl-Heinz said yes.

"Come with us," they said, leading him to a black Mercedes. Karl-Heinz soon found himself squeezed in the back seat between two agents as they drove to his apartment. He tried to avoid incriminating himself as they questioned him.

When they finally arrived at his home, Karl-Heinz was grateful that his father was at work and his mother at the dentist. The agents searched the apartment for an hour, flipping through books and peering under beds, but Karl-Heinz had been careful not to bring any evidence home. They found nothing.

But they did not let him go. Instead, they put him back inside the car. "If you lie," one of the agents said, "we will beat you to a pulp."[18]

That evening, Karl-Heinz arrived at a prison on the outskirts of Hamburg. After he was shown to his cell, an officer with a nightstick and pistol opened the door.

"Why are you here?" the officer demanded.

Karl-Heinz said he didn't know.

The officer hit him in the face with his key ring. "Do you know now?" he yelled.

"No sir," Karl-Heinz answered, terrified. "I mean, yes sir!"

The officer beat him again, and this time Karl-Heinz gave in to the pain. "I allegedly listened to an enemy broadcast," he said.[19]

That night Karl-Heinz hoped for peace and quiet, but the officers would not stop throwing open the door, turning on the lights, and forcing him to run to the wall and recite his name. When they finally left him in darkness, his eyes burned with fatigue. But he could not sleep. He thought of his parents and how worried they must be. Did they have any idea he was now a prisoner?

Weary in body and soul, Karl-Heinz turned his face to his pillow and wept.[20]

IN FEBRUARY 1942, AMY Brown Lyman sat before a microphone in the dimly lit Salt Lake Tabernacle, preparing to record a special message for the one hundredth anniversary of the Relief Society. Only a handful of people were there to witness her recording, and her thirty years as a Relief Society leader had given her plenty of opportunities for public speaking. But this was a new experience, and she was nervous.[21]

Amy had been set apart as Relief Society general president on January 1, 1940, just a few weeks before Heber J. Grant suffered his stroke. Since then, President Grant's health had continued to improve.[22] Yet the safety and well-being of people around the world had never been more precarious. War had spread to virtually every part of the globe as the United Kingdom, the United States, the Soviet Union, China, and their allies fought against the forces of Germany, Italy, Japan, and their allies.[23]

As American soldiers prepared to fight overseas, the U.S. government asked its citizens at home to sacrifice in support of the war effort. In January, the First Presidency announced that Church organizations like the Relief Society should cancel all stake conventions in Canada, Mexico, and the United States to reduce expenses and save fuel.[24]

For this reason, Amy was recording her message rather than delivering it in person. Originally, she and other Relief Society leaders expected to throw a grand centennial celebration in March 1942, the anniversary of the first Relief Society in Nauvoo. The Relief Society had also planned to hold a three-day conference in April, sponsor nine performances of a pageant called *Woman's Century of Light,* and host a concert of fifteen hundred "singing mothers" in the Tabernacle.[25]

After those events had been called off, the Relief Society general board encouraged individual wards and branches to hold their own small gatherings and consider planting a "centennial tree" as a way to commemorate the occasion instead.[26]

The board had also decided to send a twelve-inch phonograph record containing Amy's words as well as a brief message from President Grant to all Relief Societies in the United States, Mexico, and Canada. Although the war made it difficult to send the recordings to women in other nations, the Relief Society planned to send records to them once conditions improved.[27]

When the time arrived to give her speech, Amy spoke clearly into the microphone. "Even though the shadows of war hang heavy over many lands," she said, "this hundredth birthday is not forgotten." She then spoke of the tremendous work of the Relief Society, its history of service and faith, and the challenges of the present day.

"In 1942, as we begin a new Relief Society century," she said, "we find the world full of tumult and trouble. It is evident that people everywhere will have to make sacrifices—sacrifices the like and extent of which many have never dreamed."

"In these trying times Relief Society women will not be found wanting," she continued, "and they will never doubt but that finally knowledge and peace will triumph over ignorance and war."[28]

After finishing her speech, Amy was grateful she was able to communicate with women who lived thousands of miles away—women who could not have attended the conferences and pageants in Salt Lake City, even in peacetime.

Amy had expected 1942 to be a year of Churchwide rejoicing for the Relief Society. Instead, it was sure to be a year of sacrifice, suffering, and the acceptance of new responsibilities. Still, as her message went out to the women of the Relief Society, she urged them to trust in the Lord and labor in His cause.

"Let us this day rededicate ourselves to our own special work and mission," she said, "and to the advancement of the gospel of our Lord and Master, Jesus Christ."[29]

MEANWHILE, IN TILSIT, GERMANY, twenty-one-year-old Helga Meiszus supported the war effort by delivering streusel cakes to soldiers and visiting wounded men on Sundays between her Church meetings. One day, while visiting a nearby hospital, she met a wounded Latter-day Saint soldier named Gerhard Birth. Soon she was receiving letter after letter from him.

Although they had met only once, Gerhard invited Helga to come to his hometown and spend Christmas with his family. At first, she did not think she should accept the invitation. Then her brother Siegfried, who worked with her at a local eyeglasses shop, changed her mind. "They are members of the Church, and they invited you," he said. "Why don't you?"[30]

So Helga went and enjoyed getting acquainted with Gerhard and his large family. The young man was clearly in love with her, but she did not see their relationship developing into something more.[31] Faced with war and an uncertain future, young people often rushed into marriage. If Helga did the same, she and Gerhard would likely have little time together before he was sent back to the front. And the war was not going well for Germany. Hitler had invaded the Soviet Union in June 1941, but a few weeks before Christmas, the Soviet army and a harsh Russian winter had repelled the Nazis at Moscow.[32]

Soon after Helga returned to Tilsit, she received a letter from Gerhard, this time proposing marriage. She wrote back, laughing off his proposal. But in his next letter, he assured her of his sincerity. "Let's be engaged," he wrote.

Helga was reluctant at first, but she eventually accepted his offer. She liked and admired Gerhard. He was the oldest of eleven children and was devoted to his parents and the Church. He also had a fine education, plenty of ambition, and an excellent singing voice. She could see them sharing a good life together.

One Sunday a short time later, Helga returned home from a Church meeting to find a telegram from

Gerhard in her mailbox. He had been called back to the front, and his train would be passing through Tilsit, of all places, on its way to the Soviet Union. Gerhard wanted to meet her at the train station and then get married in town.

The thought of going alone to the station to meet a soldier embarrassed Helga, so she asked a friend named Waltraut to go with her. On the appointed day, they found Gerhard at the station with a group of soldiers. He seemed happy to see her, but she greeted him with a simple handshake. Helga then turned to Waltraut, perhaps hoping she would ease the awkward reunion, but Waltraut had disappeared, leaving them alone.

Gerhard received permission to remain in Tilsit a few days while his unit headed off to the front. On February 11, 1942, he and Helga went to the courthouse to get married. It was cold but beautiful outside, and as they walked, they could hear the snow crunching beneath their feet. At the courthouse, family members and friends from the branch joined them for the ceremony.

The following Sunday, Gerhard sang a solo at church. The Tilsit Branch was much smaller now that many of the men had been drafted into service. Helga's own father had been drafted soon after the invasion of Poland, though he had since come home. Her brother Siegfried was old enough to fight, though, and soon her brother Henry would be as well.

As Helga listened to Gerhard sing, she was moved. "Life's pleasures soon will pass away," the words of the hymn reminded the small branch. "Its joys at best are only few."

After the meeting, Helga took her husband to the train station, and they said goodbye. Gerhard wrote her almost every day for a month and a half. Then, a few weeks after his letters stopped, she received the news that he had been killed in action.[33]

THAT APRIL, PRESIDENT J. REUBEN Clark stood before a small general conference audience in the Assembly Hall at Temple Square. Because of travel restrictions, only general authorities and stake presidencies attended the meeting in person. Saints who lived in Utah and the surrounding area could listen on the radio, while those who lived farther away had to wait for the talks to be published and distributed in the Church's conference report. Saints who lived in some war-torn nations, meanwhile, would have no access to the talks at all. Still, President Clark felt that his message, delivered on behalf of the First Presidency, should speak directly to all Latter-day Saints, no matter where they lived.

"In the present war, righteous men of the Church in both camps have died, some with great heroism, for their own country's sake," he declared.[34] His son-in-law Mervyn Bennion was one who had lost his life during the Japanese attack at Pearl Harbor just four months earlier. President Clark loved Mervyn like one of his own children, and his death had shaken him deeply.

But as difficult as Mervyn's death had been, President Clark had been consoled by the Spirit in his grief, and he knew he could not succumb to feelings of anger, malice, or revenge.[35]

"Woe will be the part of those who plant hate in the hearts of the youth and of the people," he said. "Hate is born of Satan; love is the offspring of God. We must drive out hate from our hearts, every one of us, and permit it not again to enter."

He then quoted from section 98 of the Doctrine and Covenants: "Therefore, renounce war and proclaim peace." Strife between nations should be settled peacefully, he declared. "The Church is and must be against war."[36]

The conflict had caused heartache and suffering in the lives of Saints around the world and impeded the Church's growth. The Saints in Europe and the missionaries who served among them had spent the two decades since the last war spreading the gospel and building up the Church. Now many branches were struggling to stay together.

The Saints in the United States struggled as well, though not to the same degree. Government rationing of gasoline and rubber restricted how often the Saints could meet together. All men between the ages of eighteen and sixty-four had to register for military service. Soon far fewer young people were available for missionary service, and Church leaders limited full-time missionary work to North and South America and the Hawaiian Islands.[37]

As much as the First Presidency opposed war, they also understood that Latter-day Saints had a duty to defend the countries where they lived. And despite the painful loss of his son-in-law to a sudden enemy attack, President Clark emphasized that Saints on both sides of the war were justified in answering the call of their respective nations.

"This Church is a worldwide Church. Its devoted members are in both camps," he said. "On each side they believe they are fighting for home, and country, and freedom. On each side, our brethren pray to the same God, in the same name, for victory. Both sides cannot be wholly right; perhaps neither is without wrong."

"God will work out in His own due time and in His own sovereign way the justice and right of the conflict," he declared. "God is at the helm."[38]

CHAPTER 28

Our United Efforts

In the spring of 1942, industries across the United States were throwing their support behind the war effort. In Cincinnati, factories supplied machine parts and engines. Other companies in the city produced blackout curtains, parachutes, and radio transmitters. At grocery stores, like the one the Bang family operated, items were carefully rationed as more and more goods went toward feeding and outfitting soldiers.[1]

Once everyday materials became scarce, Paul and Connie Bang wondered if the Cincinnati Branch would be able to build their new meetinghouse. After selling their old chapel, the Saints had moved their meetings to a rented room in a nearby YMCA facility. Paul and Connie were members of the branch's building committee, and they had been raising money for the new meetinghouse since before the war. But now, with so many shortages, the committee had little hope of proceeding with their plans until the fighting was over.[2]

Around this time, Paul and his brother-in-law Milton Taylor were thinking about taking their families to the temple. Everywhere they turned, the war was pulling families apart. Husbands and wives, sons and daughters were leaving home to serve their country. As young men in their twenties, Paul and Milton had registered for military duty and could be drafted into war at any time. Amid such great uncertainty, eternal marriage and temple covenants provided assurance to them and their young families.[3]

One day, Paul and Milton learned that their friend Vaughn Ball, a member of the Cincinnati Branch from Salt Lake City, wanted to take a trip to Utah. If the Bangs and Taylors drove to Utah with him, they could fulfill their dream of being endowed and sealed in the temple. And by traveling together, they could save on costs.[4]

The only problem was finding a way to get there. Nearly two years had passed since Paul and Connie Bang's wedding, and they now had a ten-month-old daughter, Sandra. Milton and his wife, Esther, also had a young daughter, two-year-old Janet.[5]

Milton knew a man who had a reliable car with enough seating, and he agreed to rent it to them. While previous generations of Saints had gone west by wagon, handcart, or train, the Bangs, Taylors, and Vaughn Ball would be driving a 1939 DeSoto Touring Sedan.[6]

The group left for Utah the last week of April. Since gas was not nearly as scarce as rubber amid the wartime ration, the group could make their cross-country trip in good conscience, provided they drove slowly to avoid wearing out the tires too quickly.[7]

As the DeSoto headed across the United States, the travelers benefited from the many paved roads and service stations that had appeared over the last thirty years. At night they stayed at roadside motels, where they always managed to persuade the owners to let them stay for a few dollars less than the advertised price.

Aside from Vaughn, no one in the car had been so far west before, so the changing landscape was new to them. They enjoyed the scenery until the Rocky Mountains appeared and the roads became steeper and more treacherous. Vaughn loved riding up and over the beautiful mountain passes, but everyone else seemed terrified that the craggy slopes would give way and bury them alive. They were relieved when they arrived safely in the Salt Lake Valley.[8]

In the city, Paul, Connie, and Sandra stayed with the mother of Marion Hanks, a missionary who was serving in Cincinnati, while the Taylors stayed with Vaughn Ball's mother. Both families visited Temple Square several times, taking pictures of the buildings and monuments on the site. They also visited Charles and Christine Anderson, who had led the Cincinnati Branch for more than two decades. The Andersons had immense love for the two couples and had long hoped to see them sealed.[9]

On May 1, Paul and Connie entered the Salt Lake Temple with Milton and Esther. After receiving their endowment, the couples were taken to one of the temple's five sealing rooms. Apostle Charles A. Callis, who had once served as the mission president over Cincinnati, took each couple in turn and sealed them together while President Anderson served as a witness. Janet and Sandra were then brought into the room, dressed in white, and sealed to their parents.[10]

A few days after their sealings, Paul, Connie, Milton, and Esther returned for another endowment session. As Paul and Connie walked through the temple's many rooms and hallways, they marveled at its size and beauty. They were thrilled to be there, secure in the knowledge that they and their daughter were sealed together for time and all eternity.[11]

THAT SPRING, NEAR THE Hague, Netherlands, thirty-seven-year-old Hanna Vlam said goodbye to her husband, Pieter, as he headed to the train station. For the past two years, Nazi Germany had occupied the Netherlands. As a former officer in the Dutch navy, Pieter was required to register with Nazi officials regularly, and he was now headed to a city near the German border to do so.

"I'll see you again tomorrow," he told Hanna before leaving.[12]

The German invasion had taken Hanna and Pieter by surprise. Hitler had promised not to invade the

Netherlands, a neutral nation, and Pieter had believed it. Then, one night in May 1940, the sound of warplanes dropping bombs had shaken them out of bed. Pieter had quickly dressed in his uniform and left to help defend his country. But after five days of fighting, the Dutch military had surrendered to Germany's overwhelming force.[13]

Living under Nazi rule was difficult. Pieter lost his military commission, but he had secured a civilian job to support his family. The German occupiers allowed the Dutch Saints to continue meeting as long as Nazi officials could listen in on what they said. And the Saints had to meet during the daytime to comply with blackout restrictions. As the second counselor in the Netherlands Mission presidency, Pieter spent nearly every weekend traveling with President Jacob Schipaanboord and first counselor Arie Jongkees, both fellow Dutchmen, to visit branches throughout the country.[14]

Tragedy had come to the Vlams in March 1941, when a train had struck and killed their four-year-old daughter, Vera. Hanna and Pieter's only consolation was knowing that she was theirs for eternity. When Vera was just a baby, the Vlams and their three children had been sealed together in the Salt Lake Temple on their way home from a military assignment in Indonesia. That knowledge helped them cling to their covenants and find solace in the dark days that followed.[15]

On the morning Pieter left to register with Nazi officials, Hanna could not have expected their separation to last any longer than his weekend trips with the mission presidency. But later that day, their oldest daughter, eleven-year-old Grace, burst through the door.

"Is it true?" she cried. Rumors were flying that the Nazis had arrested the former military personnel who had shown up for registration, she told her mother. They had been herded into cattle cars and were on their way to a prison camp.

Hanna was too shocked to speak. The next day, she received a notice in the mail confirming that Pieter had been taken to Germany. He was now a prisoner of war.[16]

As the weeks slowly passed, Hanna prayed for peace and strength. She asked the Lord to watch over her husband and keep him safe. After nearly six weeks of waiting for news, she finally received a small card from Pieter, his handwriting cramped to fill every bit of space.

"I am well in body and spirit," Pieter wrote. The Nazis were holding him at a prison called Langwasser in the German city of Nuremberg, and although the guards treated him and his fellow prisoners poorly, he was getting by. "My thoughts are constantly with all of you," he wrote. "In my mind, I embrace you tightly, my dear Hanny."

He asked Hanna to send him some food and his scriptures. Hanna could not be sure if the books would pass the Nazi censors, but she determined she would at least try.

"Be courageous," Pieter urged her. "God will bring us together again."[17]

ON JULY 5, 1942, DAVID Ikegami attended a conference of the Japanese Mission in Hawaii's Oahu Stake Tabernacle. For David, this Sunday meeting was different from most. Not only would he be ordained to the office of a teacher in the Aaronic Priesthood, but he had been asked to speak during the first session of the conference. With more than two hundred people attending, it would be much larger than the Sunday School gatherings he was accustomed to.[18]

David based his talk on Doctrine and Covenants 38:30: "If ye are prepared ye shall not fear." Nearly seven months after the attack on Pearl Harbor, fear and uncertainty still hovered over Hawaii. The United States military had taken over hotels and fenced in beaches with barbed wire. Soldiers enforced the strict curfew, and people who violated it risked being shot. David's school had started classes again, but he had to carry a gas mask with him, and the students often performed drills to prepare for air raids and gas attacks.[19]

As Japanese Americans, David and his family also had to endure the growing suspicions of their non-Japanese neighbors. Some people, including many government and military officials, assumed without any evidence that Japanese Americans would try to undermine the American war effort out of ancestral loyalty to Japan. Beginning earlier that year, the U.S. government had even begun relocating more than one hundred thousand Japanese American men, women, and children from their homes in California and other

West Coast states to internment camps in interior states like Utah.[20]

The government did not carry out such widespread internments in Hawaii, where almost 40 percent of the population was of Japanese descent. But officials detained around fifteen hundred members of the Japanese community who were in powerful positions or deemed suspicious. And most of these detainees became prisoners in camps on the islands.[21]

To show his loyalty to the United States and assist in the war effort, David had joined a volunteer group called the Kiawe Corps to build trails and clear thickets of spiky kiawe trees for military camps. His father, meanwhile, had begun working with his assistants in the Japanese Sunday School to organize a fundraiser for U.S. servicemen, whose ranks included members of their own Sunday School.[22]

When David stood at the pulpit during the mission conference, he shared words from Elder John A. Widtsoe's most recent general conference address. "Fear is a chief weapon of Satan in making mankind unhappy," the apostle had taught the Saints, reminding them that those who lived righteously and unitedly had no need to fear. "There is safety," he had declared, "wherever the people of the Lord live so worthily as to claim the sacred title of citizens of the Zion of our Lord."[23]

In the weeks following the mission conference, David's father continued raising money for American soldiers. Called "We're United for Victory," the fundraiser provided means for a committee of fifty Japanese men on the island to print thousands of invitations and donation envelopes to distribute among their friends and neighbors. Within a few months, they had collected $11,000. Military leaders on the islands expressed appreciation for the money, which would be used to purchase books, phonograph language courses, and two movie projectors and screens to help raise the morale of the soldiers.[24]

The Saints of the Japanese Mission were glad to help. Their patriotism and loyalty were displayed clearly on the invitations distributed throughout the community. "We desire to do everything we can to help secure the freedom and liberty we love," they read. "The servicemen will be made happy through our united efforts."[25]

A FEW MONTHS LATER, in a prison in Hamburg, Germany, Karl-Heinz Schnibbe waited to stand trial for treason. Shortly after his arrest, he had seen his friend Helmuth Hübener in a long, white holding room with dozens of other prisoners. The prisoners had all been ordered to keep their noses to the wall, but as Karl-Heinz walked past, his friend tilted his head, grinned, and gave a little wink. Helmuth, it seemed, had not incriminated him. The young man's bruised, swollen face suggested that he had been beaten severely for holding out.[26]

Not long after that, Karl-Heinz also saw his friend Rudi Wobbe in the holding room. All three boys from the branch had been arrested.

During the first few months of his imprisonment, Karl-Heinz endured interrogation, threats, and beatings at the hands of the Gestapo. The interrogators could not imagine that Helmuth Hübener, a seventeen-year-old boy, could be behind such a conspiracy, and they demanded to know the names of the adults involved. Of course, there were no adult names to offer.[27]

On the morning of August 11, 1942, Karl-Heinz changed from his prison uniform into a suit and tie sent from home. The suit hung on his thin frame like it might on a hanger in the closet. Then he was brought to the People's Court, infamous in Nazi Germany for trying political prisoners and handing down terrible punishments. That day, Karl-Heinz, Helmuth, and Rudi would stand trial for conspiracy, treason, and aiding and abetting the enemy.[28]

In the courtroom, the defendants sat on a raised platform facing the judges, who were draped in red robes adorned with a golden eagle. For hours, Karl-Heinz listened as witnesses and Gestapo agents detailed evidence of the boys' conspiracy. Helmuth's flyers, full of language denouncing Hitler and exposing Nazi falsehoods, were read aloud. The judges were enraged.[29]

At first, the court focused on Karl-Heinz, Rudi, and another young man who had been one of Helmuth's coworkers. Then they turned their attention to Helmuth himself, who did not appear intimidated by the judges.

"Why did you do what you did?" one judge asked.

"Because I wanted people to know the truth," Helmuth replied. He told the judges that he did not think Germany could win the war. The courtroom exploded in anger and disbelief.[30]

When it was time to announce the verdict, Karl-Heinz was shaking as the judges returned to the bench. The chief judge called them "traitors" and "scum." He said, "Vermin like you must be exterminated."

Then he turned to Helmuth and sentenced him to death for high treason and aiding and abetting the enemy. The room fell silent. "Oh no!" a visitor to the courtroom whispered. "The death penalty for the lad?"[31]

The court sentenced Karl-Heinz to five years in prison and Rudi to ten. The boys were stunned. The judges asked if they had anything to say.

"You kill me for no reason at all," Helmuth said. "I haven't committed any crime. All I've done is tell the truth. Now it's my turn, but your turn will come."

That afternoon, Karl-Heinz saw Helmuth one last time. At first, they shook hands, but then Karl-Heinz wrapped his friend in an embrace. Helmuth's large eyes filled with tears.

"Goodbye," he said.[32]

THE DAY AFTER THE Nazis executed Helmuth Hübener, Marie Sommerfeld learned about it in the newspaper. She was a member of Helmuth's branch. He and her

son Arthur had been friends, and Helmuth had thought
of her as a second mother. She could not believe he
was gone.[33]

She still remembered him as a child, bright and
full of potential. "You will yet hear something really
great about me," he told her once. Marie did not think
Helmuth was boasting when he said it. He had simply
wanted to use his intelligence to do something mean-
ingful in the world.[34]

Eight months earlier, Marie had heard about Helmuth's
arrest even before the branch president's announcement
over the pulpit. It had been a Friday, the day that she
normally helped Wilhelmina Sudrow, Helmuth's grandmother, clean the church. When she entered the chapel,
Marie had seen Wilhelmina kneeling before the pulpit,
her arms outstretched, pleading with God.

"What is the matter?" Marie had asked.

"Something terrible has happened," Wilhelmina
replied. She then described how Gestapo officers had
shown up at her door with Helmuth, searched the apartment, and carried away some of his papers, his radio,
and the branch typewriter.[35]

Horrified by what Wilhelmina was telling her,
Marie had immediately thought of her son Arthur, who
had recently been drafted into the Nazi labor service
in Berlin. Could he have been involved in Helmuth's
plan before he left?

As soon as she could, Marie had traveled to Berlin
to ask Arthur if he had participated in any way. She

was relieved to learn that, although he had occasionally listened to Helmuth's radio, he had no idea that Helmuth and the other boys were distributing anti-Nazi materials.[36]

Some branch members had prayed for Helmuth throughout his imprisonment. Others were angry at the young men for putting them and other German Saints in harm's way and jeopardizing the Church's ability to hold meetings in Hamburg. Even Church members who were not sympathetic to the Nazis worried that Helmuth had put them all at risk of prison or worse, especially since the Gestapo were convinced that Helmuth had received help from adults.[37]

Branch president Arthur Zander believed he had to act quickly to protect the members of his branch and prove that Latter-day Saints were not conspiring against the government. Not long after the boys' arrest, he and the interim mission president, Anthon Huck, had excommunicated Helmuth. The district president and some branch members had been angered by the action. Helmuth's grandparents were devastated.[38]

A few days after Helmuth's execution, Marie received a letter he had written to her a few hours before his death. "My Father in Heaven knows that I have done nothing wrong," he told her. "I know that God lives, and He will be the proper judge of this matter."

"Until our happy reunion in that better world," he wrote, "I remain your friend and brother in the gospel."[39]

For months, Pieter Vlam wondered why the Lord had allowed the Nazis to lock him up in a prison camp, far from his family.

The dilapidated barracks in the camp were infested with lice, fleas, and bedbugs, and Pieter and the other prisoners sometimes ventured outside to rest on a small patch of grass. One day, as they lay looking up at the sky, a man asked Pieter if they could talk about spiritual matters. He knew Pieter was a Latter-day Saint, and he had questions about the world beyond this one. Pieter began teaching him the gospel.[40]

Soon, other prisoners sought Pieter's spiritual guidance. The guards would not allow the men to talk in large groups, so Pieter would take two men at a time, one on each side, and go on walks around the camp. Not all the men believed what Pieter taught, but they appreciated his faith and gained a better understanding of the Church.[41]

After spending a few months in the German camp, Pieter and his fellow Dutch officers were transferred to Stalag 371, a prison camp in Nazi-occupied Ukraine. Their new quarters were in a frigid stone building, but conditions there were somewhat better than what the men had endured in Germany. Feeling stronger in body and spirit, Pieter continued to take walks with anyone interested in what he was teaching. He walked so much that he wrote home to his wife, Hanna, asking if she would send him some new wooden shoes to replace his battered footwear.[42]

Before long, a group of around ten men encouraged Pieter to organize a Sunday school, and he agreed. Since the Nazis forbade such meetings, they gathered secretly in an empty building in a far corner of the camp. They covered the window with an old blanket and found a soapbox to use as a pulpit. Miraculously, the scriptures and songbook Hanna had sent to Pieter after his arrest had passed the censors without being confiscated. Pieter taught from the Bible and Book of Mormon, but the group did not dare to sing. Instead, Pieter read hymns aloud. At the conclusion of their meetings, the men would slip out the door one by one to avoid detection.[43]

A Protestant minister at Stalag 371 eventually noticed men walking and talking with Pieter. He took each of them aside, showed them a booklet full of distortions about the Church, and told them Pieter was deceived. Rather than persuading them to abandon Pieter and his teachings, however, the minister's efforts only made the men more curious about the restored gospel.

After reading the booklet, a man named Mr. Callenbach decided to join the group. "I do not want to be converted," he told Pieter. "I only came to hear the story from you."[44]

One Sunday, Pieter decided to teach the principle of fasting. He told the men they should give the little cup of beans they received that day to someone else.

"If you cannot sleep in the night," Pieter said, "you should pray to God and ask Him if the things you heard from me are true."[45]

The following Sunday the men stood to share their testimonies. Mr. Callenbach was the last to speak. With tears in his eyes, he recounted his experience with fasting.

"That night I had been very hungry," he said. "Then I remembered what Mr. Vlam had said about prayer." He told how he prayed earnestly to know if the things Pieter taught were correct. "An indescribable feeling of peace came over me," he said, "and I knew that I had heard the truth."[46]

CHAPTER 29

'Tis Eventide

On a quiet November night in 1943, Nellie Middleton heard her doorbell ring. It was dark outside, but she knew enough not to have the lights on when she opened the door. Nearly three years had passed since German bombs had first fallen near her home on St. Paul's Road in Cheltenham, England, and Nellie continued to darken her windows at night to keep herself and her daughter, Jennifer, safe from air raids.

With her lights out, Nellie opened the door. A young man was standing on her front step, his face in shadow. He extended his hand and quietly introduced himself as Brother Ray Hermansen. His accent was undeniably American.[1]

A lump came to Nellie's throat. After their branch disbanded, she and other women in Cheltenham had rarely had a chance to take the sacrament.[2] The United States had recently sent troops to England, however, to prepare for an Allied offensive against Nazi Germany.[3] Once it had occurred to Nellie that some of the American soldiers stationed in her town might be Latter-day Saints who could bless the sacrament, she had asked her stepsister, Margaret, to paint a picture of the Salt Lake Temple and place it in town. Below the picture was a message: "If any soldier is interested in the above, he will find a warm welcome at 13 St. Paul's Road."[4]

Had this American seen her poster? Did he have authority to bless the sacrament? Nellie shook his hand and welcomed him inside.

Ray was a twenty-year-old Latter-day Saint soldier from Utah and a priest in the Aaronic Priesthood. Although he was stationed ten miles away, he had heard about the Salt Lake Temple painting from another Church member and obtained leave to visit the address. He had walked to Nellie's home on foot, which was why he had arrived after dark. When Nellie told him about her desire to take the sacrament, he asked her when he could come to administer the ordinance to her.

On November 21, Nellie, her daughter, and three other women welcomed Ray to their Sunday meeting. Nellie opened the meeting with prayer before the group sang "How Great the Wisdom and the Love." Ray then blessed and passed the sacrament, and all four women bore testimony of the gospel.[5]

Soon other Latter-day Saint soldiers heard about the meetings at St. Paul's Road. Some Sundays, Nellie's living room was so full that people had to sit on the staircase. Since communication remained open between Allied nations, the Saints in Cheltenham were not cut off from Church headquarters in Utah. And the British Mission continued to publish the *Millennial Star* during the war, providing the Saints with lesson materials and news articles to discuss at their meetings.

One of the most significant news items in the *Millennial Star* at this time was the call of Spencer W. Kimball and Ezra Taft Benson to the Quorum of the Twelve Apostles. Both men had been stake presidents outside of Utah when President Grant called them as apostles, and both had ties to the British Mission. Heber C. Kimball, Elder Kimball's grandfather, had opened the mission in 1837. Elder Benson, meanwhile, had served in the mission in the early 1920s.[6]

During meetings with the soldiers, Nellie could tell how much they missed their families. Since the military censored outgoing mail, loved ones often had no idea where their soldiers were stationed. Nellie began writing letters to the soldiers' families, describing how wonderful it was to have their brother, son, husband, or fiancé in her home. She included her address on the envelope as a clue to where the soldiers were located.[7]

In one letter to a soldier's wife, Nellie wrote, "I know how much you must miss your husband and how you look and long for news. But I want to tell you, you would have been so proud if you had heard him speak of you and of the Church."

"I feel that as long as we do our best," Nellie wrote, "the Lord will continue to bless us. We have had so much of His kind care and protection, and even among all this misery and destruction, we feel so thankful for all our blessings."[8]

AROUND THIS TIME, THIRTY-YEAR-OLD Mary dos Santos visited her aunt Sally's farm near the town of Santa Bárbara d'Oeste in the state of São Paulo, Brazil. Sally had been meeting with Latter-day Saint missionaries from the United States, and she suggested that Mary meet with them as well. Mary was not very religious, and she was not at all interested in a new church. But she agreed to let the young men visit her and her husband, Claudio, as long as they promised not to talk about religion.

Later, when the missionaries visited Mary's house in the city of São Paulo, she and Claudio found them to be both interesting and amusing. They stayed for four hours and only spoke about the Church to mention an English class they taught every Thursday. Mary's grandfather had been born in the United States and emigrated to Brazil after the American Civil War, so Mary had grown up speaking English at home. But Claudio, a Portuguese-speaking Brazilian who knew only a little English, was interested in the class. He thought learning more English might help him advance in his career.

Before Claudio attended his first class, Mary warned him to be careful. "Go to the English class, nothing more," she said. "Do not pay any attention to whatever comes before or after!"

Claudio did not take her advice. After class, he stayed for an activity where local Church members and their friends acted in skits and enjoyed music. Claudio loved anything musical, but he was especially drawn to the good spirit of the meeting and the people.

After he came home, Mary wanted to know more about the class. "How was it?" she asked.

"Marvelous!" he said. He told her about the activity. He was already looking forward to going back.

Mary did not like that he had stayed after the class ended, but she supported him as he returned week after week. One day he persuaded her to go with him, and she enjoyed the activities as well. Before long, both of them became interested in the restored gospel of Jesus Christ.[9]

The Church in Brazil was still in its infancy at the time. On the recommendation of South American Mission president Reinhold Stoof, the Brazilian Mission had been created as a German-speaking mission in 1935. Three years later, however, Brazil's president implemented laws to weaken the influence of foreign governments and promote national unity. One of these laws prohibited the use of any language other than Portuguese, the country's official language, in public meetings, including church services.[10]

Although the Saints received police permission to hold some meetings in German, the missionaries began turning their attention to Brazil's Portuguese speakers, many of whom seemed eager to meet with them. And in 1940, the Church published a Portuguese edition of the Book of Mormon.[11]

The language restrictions, meanwhile, continued to frustrate Brazil's German-speaking Saints. These frustrations only intensified in the summer of 1942, when German submarines attacked Brazilian ships. Brazil declared war on Germany, and German-language missionary work came to a halt.[12] While some German-speaking members turned against the Church and its predominantly American leadership, many remained committed Latter-day Saints.[13]

In the São Paulo Branch, where Mary and Claudio attended meetings and activities, a handful of Portuguese-speaking and German-speaking Saints worshipped together.[14] But there was a problem with leadership. Missionaries had typically led the branches in Brazil, and there were now fewer missionaries because of the war. The Brazilian government had also imposed a ban on new foreign missionaries entering the country. When mission president William Seegmiller arrived in 1942, more than sixty North American elders had been serving in Brazil. Now, in early 1944, the last remaining missionaries were scheduled to fly home, and there were very few Portuguese-speaking priesthood holders in Brazil to fill vacant leadership positions.[15]

Claudio's English lessons stopped once the missionaries returned to the United States. But not long after
the classes ended, he and Mary received a visit from
President Seegmiller's wife, Ada. After chatting a while,
she said, "You know, those missionaries, they would be
very happy if you were baptized."

The couple did not agree that night to be baptized, but they decided to start attending Sunday meetings. Their interest in the gospel grew until, shortly
after the new year, they decided to join the Church. On
January 16, 1944, Mary and Claudio were baptized by
the Seegmillers' son Wan only a few days before he left
the country to serve in the U.S. military.[16]

A FEW WEEKS INTO the new year, Helga Meiszus Birth
learned of the death of her cousin Kurt Brahtz, a soldier
in the German army who had recently been wounded in
the Soviet Union. Growing up, she and Kurt had been like
brother and sister, and she wept as she thought of him and
her late husband, Gerhard, another young victim of the
war. For a while she was inconsolable. Then she forced
herself to stop. "I'm crying for myself," she said.[17]

A short time later, while attending a district conference near her home, Helga met with Paul Langheinrich,
the second counselor in the mission presidency. As
they talked, Paul asked, "Sister Birth, how would it
be for you to go on a mission?" Helga considered the
question. With most of the young men off at war, sister

missionaries were desperately needed. Serving a mission during wartime would not be easy, though, and she would have to get special permission to move to Berlin. Still, she wanted to help the Lord's work, so she told Paul she was willing to serve.

Months passed, and no mission call came. During that time, she worried more and more about her younger brother Siegfried, who had been drafted into the army. She was sure something had happened to him. When she finally received a letter from him, he was in an army hospital in Romania. A bomb had shattered his body, mangling his knee and hip. "Helga," he wrote, "the war is over for me." He died a few days later.[18]

The branch held a memorial for Siegfried the following month. Helga's aunt Nita from Hamburg came to Tilsit for the service, joining Helga, her grandparents, and her aunt Lusche. As they left the memorial together, Lusche grabbed Helga's arm and said, "Why don't you come and stay with me?"

"I can't," Helga said. She had already promised Nita and her grandparents that she would stay with them that night.

"Come home with me," Lusche pleaded. "I cooked so much pea soup!"

Helga felt something inside pulling her toward Lusche. "OK," she said.

That night, after climbing into bed at Lusche's house, Helga saw a blinding flash of light. She knew at once that it was a flare from an Allied bomber, illuminating a target. She and Lusche scrambled down to the cellar as air raid sirens wailed outside.[19]

Helga was no stranger to raids. The year before, shrapnel from an enemy bomb had struck her in the head and stomach. Her entire body had gone numb, and she believed she was going to die. "I will see Gerhard," she had thought.[20]

Now, as the walls rattled with the force of multiple explosions, Helga did not think she would leave the cellar alive. Huddled together, she and her aunt sang a hymn she sometimes turned to when she felt scared:

O Savior, stay this night with me;
Behold, 'tis eventide.

Finally, the house stood still and quiet. The next morning, a man Helga knew from work knocked on Lusche's door. "Hurry! Hurry! Hurry!" he urged.[21]

Helga followed the man to the street where her grandparents lived. Their apartment building had been completely flattened by Allied bombs. Horrified, Helga watched as volunteers searched through the rubble for survivors. Nearby were the bodies of the dead, covered in blankets. Helga searched among them, but her grandparents and aunt were not there.

Workers continued picking through the wreckage of the building. After a few weeks, they found the missing bodies.[22]

Helga could not understand why God had allowed such a thing to happen. Her grandmother had been a faithful member of the Church, and her testimony had anchored Helga's own. "Did they really have to die this way?" she wondered.

Then, one night, she had a dream of her grandparents and aunt. In the dream, she understood that their deaths had come quickly, without suffering. Helga also found comfort in knowing they had died together.

A short time later, she received a call to serve in the mission office in Berlin. She was happy to leave Tilsit. It did not occur to her that she might never see it again.[23]

NOT LONG AFTER CLAUDIO and Mary dos Santos were baptized in São Paulo, Brazil, mission president William Seegmiller asked Claudio if he would like to be an elder. Claudio was surprised, but he said yes. Having attended church for only a few months, he was not exactly sure what it meant to be an elder. He knew all the missionaries were called "Elder," and they were remarkable young men who dedicated their lives to God. If that was what being an elder meant, that was what he wanted to be.[24]

The following Sunday morning, just before Sunday School, President Seegmiller ordained Claudio to the office of elder in the Melchizedek Priesthood. When he finished, he said, "Now we are going to prepare the sacrament and set up for Sunday School."

Claudio was a little bewildered. Everything was happening so quickly, and he did not fully know what he was doing. But he followed the president's instructions and performed his first priesthood responsibility.

That evening, during the branch's sacrament meeting, President Seegmiller recruited Claudio's help again, this time to interpret for him as he spoke to the Saints in English. Claudio was still learning English and had never interpreted before, but he agreed to try.[25]

At the start of the meeting, President Seegmiller asked the Saints to sustain Claudio's ordination. To Claudio's surprise, he understood President Seegmiller clearly, and he easily conveyed the words in Portuguese.

President Seegmiller then told the congregation about a letter he had written to the First Presidency one year earlier. It had expressed his fear that the Church in Brazil did not have enough worthy Portuguese-speaking men who could be ordained to the priesthood and support the branches. He now felt ashamed for having written the letter.

"Today Brother Claudio was ordained an elder," he said. "Will you sustain him as the first Brazilian branch president of São Paulo?"

Claudio was stunned as he interpreted the words. He thought of his inexperience. "What knowledge do I have?" he wondered. He knew the story of Joseph Smith, but he had never read the Book of Mormon. The only thing he had to offer was enthusiasm for the restored gospel. Maybe that was all the Lord needed from him.

He looked out on the congregation and saw the Saints raise their hands in support of his call. He felt honored. Maybe he didn't know much, but he was will-ing to work.[26]

Claudio's responsibilities began immediately. He took charge of Sunday meetings and blessed the sacrament. A missionary had taught Claudio to read music, and he soon developed a repertoire of around twenty hymns on the organ so he could accompany the São Paulo Saints. At first, he had only one counselor to assist him, but the two men did their best to juggle work and family responsibilities as they ministered to Saints scattered throughout the enormous city.

Despite his inexperience, Claudio trusted that God had a purpose for calling him to lead the branch. "If it is the true Church, if there is a God in charge, He had to select someone," he told himself. "He had to choose someone with enthusiasm that could receive authority and do the work."[27]

ACROSS THE ATLANTIC, NELLIE Middleton and her daughter, Jennifer, were still holding sacrament meetings with soldiers and local Saints in Cheltenham, England. War had been a part of Jennifer's life for nearly five years—almost as long as she could remember. Now, at ten years old, she was used to food rationing, air raid sirens, and her gas mask, which she carried everywhere she went in a special case her mother had made.[28]

She was also used to being the only child at Church meetings. She loved the adult Latter-day Saints

454

in Cheltenham and had befriended many of the soldiers who came into her home to worship. But she yearned to be fully united with them—to be a baptized member of The Church of Jesus Christ of Latter-day Saints.

Jennifer had wanted to be baptized as soon as she was old enough, but there was no baptismal font in Cheltenham, and with the war going on she and her mother had never had a chance to travel to another city. During the summer of 1944, however, Hugh B. Brown, who had led the British Mission until the war forced him to leave, was called to return to England to oversee the local missionaries, members, and seventy-eight branches throughout the country. When he came to meet the sisters in Cheltenham, he collected their tithes, which Nellie had kept in a tin box.[29]

Jennifer was impressed by the tall mission president standing in her living room. He bent down and shook her hand.

"President," Nellie said, "I don't know what to do with this child. She wants to be baptized, and we can't travel."[30]

President Brown said he could arrange for them to ride a military train to the city of Birmingham, some fifty miles north. There they would have access to a baptismal font.

Jennifer asked Arthur Fletcher, an elderly man who lived in a nearby branch, to perform the baptism and Harold Watkins, an American soldier she knew, to confirm her.[31] The baptism was set for August 11, 1944. They would all travel to Birmingham together.

When the day arrived, Jennifer stood on the train platform wearing a new, emerald-green traveling outfit her mother had made for the occasion. Since the Church had recently begun asking people to wear white for baptisms, Nellie had also sewn another dress for the ordinance, fashioned from a beautiful old piece of embroidered white cotton.[32]

The train belched clouds of steam as it rolled up to the platform. The stationmaster gave the order to board, but Harold Watkins had not yet arrived. Jennifer squeezed onto the train packed with soldiers, all the while scanning the crowd for her friend. She did not want to leave without him.

Suddenly, a soldier riding a rusty bicycle careened onto the platform. He had his cap shoved in one pocket and his tie in the other. It was Harold! He threw down the bicycle and jumped on the train just as it began to move. Jennifer let out a cheer.

Breathless, Harold told them his story. That morning, the camp's commanding officer had ordered all men to be confined to their barracks. But Harold had promised to confirm Jennifer, and he knew he had to leave—no matter the risk. At the last minute, he sneaked out of camp, found an old bicycle resting against a wall, and rode the six miles to the train station as fast as he could.

Jennifer and the rest of the group made it safely to Birmingham. Two young women from the area came to the service to support Jennifer. One of them spoke about how a person getting baptized was like a ship finally setting forth on the voyage of life. Grateful for the chance to finally call herself a member of the Church, Jennifer was ready to begin her own journey.[33]

THAT SUMMER IN SALT Lake City, seventeen-year-old Neal Maxwell entered an army recruitment office and volunteered to go to war. He had been waiting for his chance to join the service ever since the fighting started. Though he was not old enough to be eligible for the draft, he did not want to wait any longer.[34]

So much was happening. On June 6, 1944, more than 160,000 Allied forces had stormed the beaches in northern France in what came to be called "D-Day." After that fierce battle against the Nazi defenses, the Allies had secured a foothold in continental Europe and begun pushing their way to Germany. Neal hoped the invasion meant the Allies were gaining the upper hand. He wanted to be a part of ending the war as soon as possible.[35]

Neal reported for duty in September. His parents, Clarence and Emma, struggled to understand why he wanted to rush off to war. Their anxiety increased when they learned he would be in the army infantry.[36] His assignment would likely place him in combat on the front lines.

Neal arrived for basic training with a book called *Principles of the Gospel* packed among his gear. The book, which Church leaders had prepared especially for Latter-day Saint servicemen, contained information about the doctrine of the Church, instructions for administering priesthood ordinances, a selection of hymns, and general advice for military service. "We pray that the Lord will give you courage and fortitude to do your duty fully," the First Presidency had written in the introduction, "and to acquit yourselves honorably wherever your lot is cast."[37]

Once training began, Neal could see he had much to learn. Other recruits seemed older and more experienced than he was. Growing up, he had often been self-conscious about his appearance. He was too short to play on the high school basketball team, so he had turned to raising pigs in the agricultural club. Severe acne had left his face scarred, adding to his insecurity. He had gained some confidence, though, as the coeditor of the school newspaper.[38]

Neal wrote home often during training, his letters full of youthful bravado. Since the attack on Pearl Harbor, filmmakers in Hollywood had supported the United States military by producing action-packed movies that idealized the war and the American men who fought it. Neal believed the army was molding him into a tough, resilient fighter. He wrote home about shooting rifles and hiking twenty miles at a time. "Our sergeants are overseas vets, and they spare no punches," he informed his parents. When training was over, he told them, "I'll be a real man."[39]

At times, though, he was shocked by the behavior of some of the soldiers around him, and he expressed new appreciation for growing up in a humble, gospel-centered house. "Our home was heaven," Neal wrote to his mother. "Now I realize how swell and grand you and Dad have been."[40]

Neal's training ended in January 1945, and he was assigned to fight the Japanese at the fierce Pacific Front. A few days before his departure, he spoke with his mother on the telephone. She told him she knew an officer who might have a way for him to fulfill his military duty without having to fight.

"Maybe," she said, "you don't have to go overseas."

"Mom," Neal replied. "I want to go." He knew it was hard for her to say goodbye, but he had a duty to perform.[41]

CHAPTER 30

Such Grief

The winter of 1944–45 was unbearably cold in Europe. Allied forces were advancing on Germany, fighting battle after battle in the frigid snow. Hitler tried to launch one final offensive against the American and British forces on the western front, but the assault only exhausted his already-weary army. Soviet troops, meanwhile, dominated the eastern front as they pushed deeper and deeper into Nazi-held territory.[1]

In Berlin, Helga Birth struggled to stay warm in the office of the East German Mission. The original office had caught fire during a bombing a year earlier, so now the mission was headquartered in the apartment of second counselor Paul Langheinrich and his wife, Elsa. Bombs had destroyed the apartment windows, so Helga and the other missionaries covered the empty frames with blankets to keep the cold out. There was no heat or warm water. Food was scarce, and sleep was hard to come by when air raid sirens wailed at night.

With the city virtually under siege, the missionaries could not safely go out and preach. But the acting East German Mission presidency, made up of local Church members, were responsible for all the Saints in the mission. The mission president, Herbert Klopfer, and most of the office staff were away on military assignments, though, so Helga and other women helped maintain mission records and stayed in contact with thousands of German Saints whose lives had been disrupted by war.[2]

Already, most of Helga's family and friends had left Tilsit as the Soviet military pushed through Germany's eastern cities. Her father and youngest brother, Henry, had been drafted into the army, and her mother had found refuge at a cousin's farm. Other Saints in Tilsit, meanwhile, had held together as long as they could, sharing what little food and clothing they had with one another. Branch president Otto Schulzke and his family had lost their home in a bombing, escaping with only their lives. When the branch met for the last time, they shared a meal and listened once more to President Schulzke.[3]

Given her many losses, Helga was grateful to have found a place among the Saints in Berlin. But by mid-April 1945, the Soviet military had powered through eastern Germany and now surrounded the city. On a rainy Sunday morning in the city, Helga gathered to worship with a small group of Saints. Bombs and street skirmishes had rattled neighborhoods throughout the night, and few Church members had come to the meeting. Paul Langheinrich spoke about faith. Helga was weary, but the Spirit strengthened her. She thought of the Savior's words in the book of Matthew: "For where two or three are gathered together in my name, there am I in the midst of them."[4]

After the meeting, Paul invited Helga to join him and the branch president, Bertold Patermann, on a visit to another branch in the city. Paul wanted to make sure the members were safe after the night's attacks.

It took Helga, Paul, and Bertold an hour to walk to the branch meetinghouse. As they got closer to the building, they saw blood in the streets and an air battle raging overhead. They pressed on, making their way to the safety of the Church building. Suddenly the blasts of artillery shells erupted behind them. Remaining calm, they continued down the street and found the Church building empty. One of its walls had taken a direct hit, reducing the side of the chapel to rubble. It looked as if someone had tried to sweep up the debris, only to stop mid-task.

Helga and her two companions checked on a few Church members living nearby and then decided to return to the mission home. Once they were back in the streets, they felt wholly exposed. The sky was still seething, and shells continued to whistle and burst around them. Fighter planes swooped low over the streets, and

462

gunfire tore up beautiful old buildings and bridges, hurling shards of stone and brick into the air.

Seeking whatever cover they could find, Helga, Paul, and Bertold slipped into buildings and under doorways. Once, the only protection they could find was under a leafless tree, its branches brown and spindly. Finally they came to a blown-out bridge with only a tiny strip intact. Helga was not sure she could cross.

"Sister Birth, don't be scared," her companions said. She knew they were on God's errand, and that gave her confidence. Trusting them, she grasped a handrail and crossed the bridge, her soul filled with calm assurance as they made their way home.[5]

IN THE DAYS THAT followed, Helga and the other missionaries living at the Langheinrichs' apartment rarely went outside. Stories spread that Soviet soldiers had already captured parts of the city, and Bertold warned the missionaries of the terrible things happening outside. They needed to do everything possible to remain safe.

As chaos enveloped the streets, some Saints sought refuge at the mission home. One woman arrived in a state of shock after her husband had been shot in the stomach and died. With Paul's help, Helga and the others prepared abandoned rooms for anyone who came to them for help.

On Saturday, April 28, the small group of Saints gathered in fasting and prayer. As they knelt and prayed for strength and protection, Helga was overwhelmed with gratitude to be surrounded by faithful Saints amid so much terror.

By the time the fast ended, Soviet soldiers were everywhere in the streets around the mission office. Fighting still raged in Berlin, but the Soviet military was already working to restore order and essential services to the occupied parts of the city. Many soldiers did not bother the German civilians, but some soldiers were looting buildings and assaulting German women. Helga and the other missionaries feared for their safety, and the men in the mission office took turns keeping careful watch.[6]

Then, on May 2, Helga awoke to a strange kind of stillness. There had been no bombings that night, and she had slept straight through until morning. Adolf Hitler had taken his own life two days earlier, and the Soviet army had hoisted a hammer-and-sickle flag over the city. With Berlin now in Soviet hands, and other Allied forces seizing more German territory every day, the war in Europe was coming to an end.[7]

Helga tried to put her thoughts in writing in her missionary journal. "PEACE! That's what everybody is saying," she wrote. "I don't have any particular feelings in my heart. We have imagined something quite different in connection with the word 'peace'—like joy and celebration—but nothing of the kind is evident."

"Here I sit, isolated from my relatives," she continued, "not knowing what has happened with the rest." So many of her loved ones—Gerhard, her brother Siegfried and cousin Kurt, her grandparents and aunt Nita—were dead. She had no idea how to contact her mother and father, and so much time had passed since anyone had heard from her other brother, Henry, that she could only imagine the worst.[8]

That Sunday, the Saints gathered again for a prayer meeting. Helga's missionary companion, Renate Berger, shared a verse from the Doctrine and Covenants. It spoke of gratitude in the face of mortal tribulation:

> *And he who receiveth all things with thankfulness shall be made glorious; and the things of this earth shall be added unto him, even an hundred fold, yea, more.*[9]

THE ALLIES CELEBRATED "VICTORY in Europe Day" on May 8, 1945. Neal Maxwell cheered the news, as did other American soldiers battling to capture the Japanese island of Okinawa. But their celebrations were subdued by the reality of their own situation. With kamikaze pilots attacking the Okinawa harbor and artillery fire blazing on the island's hills, the American troops knew their part in the fight was far from over.

"This is real war," Neal thought. The battlefront was far less glamorous up close than what the newspapers and movies had led him to believe. It filled him with a dull, sick feeling.[10]

The Battle of Okinawa was quickly becoming one of the most ferocious battles in the Pacific. The Japanese commanders believed the island was their last defense against an American invasion of Japan's mainland, so they had decided to leverage all their military might to defend Okinawa.[11]

Neal and the soldiers with him were assigned to a division as replacements. On May 13, he wrote home to Utah. He was not allowed to tell his parents the specifics of his assignment, but he assured them of his well-being. "I'm all alone as far as spiritual companions are concerned, except for One," he wrote. "I know He is always with me."[12]

Neal was in a mortar squad assigned to fire explosive shells at enemy positions hidden inland. As he and his fellow soldiers trudged single file toward a hill called Flat Top, the Japanese began firing in their direction. The men all hit the dirt and stayed still until they felt it was safe. Then everyone stood up—except a large man named Partridge, who had been marching just in front of Neal.

"Come on, get up," Neal said to him. "Let's get going." When the man still did not move, Neal realized he had been killed by a piece of shrapnel.[13]

Shocked and horrified, Neal was in a daze for hours. The closer he got to the battlefield, the more the scarred landscape looked lifeless and barren. The dead bodies of Japanese soldiers lay strewn on the ground. Neal had been warned that the area could be rigged with land mines. Even if the ground beneath his feet did not explode, rifle fire split the air above his head.

Neal took a position in a foxhole, and after days of back-and-forth warfare, heavy rains turned the scorched landscape into a quagmire. Neal's foxhole filled with mud, making rest nearly impossible as he tried to sleep standing up. Meager military rations did little to stave off hunger, and the water he received came up the hill in five-gallon tanks and always tasted of oil. Many men drank coffee to mask the water's foulness, but Neal wanted to be obedient to the Word of Wisdom and refused. He did his best to gather rainwater, and on Sundays, he used water he saved and a biscuit from his rations for the sacrament.[14]

One night in late May, three enemy shells exploded near Neal's mortar position. Up until then, the Japanese had not been able to find the location of his squad. But now it seemed the artillerymen had triangulated his position and were closing in. When another shell exploded just a few feet away, Neal feared the next one would find its target.

Leaping from the foxhole, he took cover against a knoll. Then, realizing he was still in danger, he scurried back to the hole to await whatever came next.

In the mud and darkness, Neal got on his knees and began to pray. He knew he did not deserve any special favors from God, and that many righteous men had died after offering fervent prayers during battle. Still, he pleaded with the Lord to spare his life, promising to dedicate himself to God's service if he survived. He had a smudged copy of his patriarchal blessing in his pocket, and he thought of a promise it contained.

"I seal you up against the power of the destroyer that your life may not be shortened," the blessing read, "and that you may not be deprived of fulfilling every assignment that was given unto you in the preexistent state."

Neal finished his prayer and looked up into the night sky. The shattering explosions had ceased, and all was quiet. When the shelling did not resume, he felt in his soul that the Lord had preserved his life.[15]

Not long after, Neal wrote a few letters to his family back home. "I'm so lonely for you, sometimes I feel like crying," he said. "All I have to do is be worthy of my patriarchal blessing, your prayers, and my religion. But time and so much action hang heavy on a man's soul."

"I can say only God prevented my death at times," he wrote. "I have a testimony no one can crumble."[16]

BACK IN EUROPE, THE war was over for Hanna Vlam and other Dutch Saints. On the day Germany surrendered, she and her children joined their friends and neighbors in the town square to sing and dance. They made a huge bonfire of the blackout material that had hung in their windows, watching happily as the reminders of darker days went up in flames.

"Thanks, thanks, O Lord," Hanna thought. "Thou hast been good to us."

Now that the fighting was done, many people in concentration camps and prisons were set free. Hanna had corresponded with her husband during his imprisonment, and she had reason to believe that he had remained safe. Still, she knew she could not truly celebrate the war's end until Pieter was at home where he belonged.

On a Sunday evening in early June, Hanna glanced out the window and saw a military truck stop in front of her house. A door on the truck opened and Pieter stepped out. Hanna's neighbors must have been watching too, because they came running to her front door. She did not want to open it to a crowd, so she waited for Pieter to come in on his own. And when he walked through the door, she welcomed him joyfully.

Soon the Vlams' neighbors placed flags up and down the street to celebrate Pieter's safe return. Hanna and Pieter's twelve-year-old son, Heber, saw the flags and ran to the house. "My father is home!" he cried.

When darkness fell, Hanna lit a candle she had saved for the night of Pieter's homecoming. The Vlam family sat in the flickering light, listening as Pieter told them of his liberation.[17]

Months earlier, when Soviet forces had pushed the Germans from Ukraine, Pieter and the other prisoners of Stalag 371 were transferred to a new prison, north of Berlin. It was dirty, cold, and infested with vermin. The drone of Allied planes filled the air, and the sky turned blood red from the fires that burned all over the city.

One day in April, a prisoner had shouted to some Soviet soldiers as they rumbled past the prison in a giant tank. The soldiers stopped, turned the tank around, and smashed through the barbed wire fencing, liberating Pieter and his fellow prisoners. Before they parted ways, Pieter gave a priesthood blessing to all who wanted one. Some of the prisoners who studied the gospel with him returned home and joined the Church.[18]

Now, together with his family, Pieter felt he had a taste of heaven. It was as if he was reuniting with loved ones on the other side of the veil, and he rejoiced in the sacred ties that bound them together for eternity.[19]

BY THE FIRST WEEK of August 1945, Neal Maxwell was in the Philippines, training for an invasion of mainland Japan later that fall. The United States had captured Okinawa in June, and while more than seven thousand American soldiers had died, the Japanese had suffered truly staggering losses. More than one hundred thousand of their soldiers and tens of thousands of civilians had lost their lives in the battle.[20]

In a letter to his family, Neal wrote soberly, his former bravado gone. He wanted nothing more than for the fighting to stop. "I have a strong desire to destroy this thing that causes such grief," he said of war. He believed the message of Jesus Christ could bring lasting peace, and he longed to share it with others. "That's an opportunity I want more than ever," he wrote.[21]

After leaving the front lines, Neal began participating in gatherings of Latter-day Saint servicemen from a variety of units. While still on Okinawa, he had been thrilled at the thought of finally worshipping again with other members of the Church. But when he finally had a chance to attend a meeting, he realized that men he expected to see were not there. The chaplain, a Latter-day Saint named Lyman Berrett, gave a comforting talk, but the whole time Neal kept one eye on the door, waiting to see friends walk through it. Some never did.[22]

During this time, Neal found out that President Heber J. Grant had passed away. In the five years since his stroke, President Grant had met regularly with his counselors and had spoken several times at general conference.[23] He had never fully recovered, though, and on May 14, 1945, he had succumbed to cardiac failure at the age of eighty-eight. George Albert Smith was now the president of the Church.[24]

In early August, Neal and the rest of the soldiers in the Philippines learned that an American plane, acting on direct orders from the president of the United States, had dropped an atomic bomb on the Japanese city of Hiroshima. Three days later, another plane dropped a similar bomb on the city of Nagasaki.

When Neal heard about the bombings, he was filled with joyful hope that he and his fellow soldiers would not need to invade the Japanese mainland. He later realized how self-centered his reaction had been. More than one hundred thousand people, most of them Japanese civilians, perished in the blasts.[25]

After Japan surrendered on September 2, 1945, the world war was officially over. Neal was still going to

Japan, though, as a member of the Allied occupation. In the meantime, his superiors had noticed his writing talents and given him a special assignment to compose letters of comfort and condolence to the families of fallen soldiers.

"The memory of black days sorta hangs over a guy," Neal wrote his family, "especially when you write letters of condolence to the bereaved ones of your buddies." While he was honored by the responsibility, he did not relish it.[26]

Neal and nearly one million Latter-day Saints around the world now faced a new future as they grappled with how to rebuild after experiencing so much grief, deprivation, and overwhelming loss. In President Grant's final public address, read aloud by his secretary at the April 1945 general conference, he had offered the Saints words of comfort and perspective.

"Into many of our homes sorrow has come," he said. "May we be strengthened with the understanding that being blessed does not mean that we shall always be spared all the disappointments and difficulties of life."

"The Lord will hear and answer the prayers we offer to Him and give us the things we pray for if it is for our best good," he declared. "He never will and never has forsaken those who serve Him with full purpose of heart, but we must always be prepared to say 'Father, Thy will be done.'"[27]

PART 4

—◆—

Crowned with Glory

1945–1955

"Our mission in the world is to save souls, to bless them,
and to place them in a condition that they may go back
into the presence of our Father,
crowned with glory, immortality, and eternal life.
Let kindness, joy, and peace characterize our
efforts, and be a blessing to our Father's children
wherever it may be our privilege to roam."

George Albert Smith, July 1945

CHAPTER 31

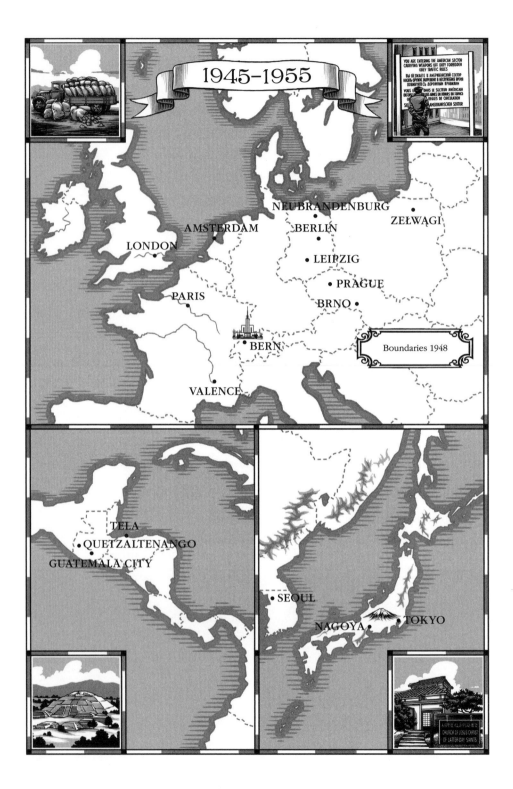

The Right Track

The Salt Lake Tabernacle was quiet and still on the afternoon of October 7, 1945, as George Albert Smith stood to address the Saints at general conference. He had spoken many times in the Tabernacle during his four decades as an apostle, but this conference was his first time speaking to the entire Church as the prophet of the Lord.

He had just returned from dedicating the Idaho Falls Temple in southeast Idaho, a reminder that the latter-day work was moving forward. But he knew that Saints across the globe were suffering after years of deprivation and war. And they now looked to him for guidance and reassurance.

"This world might have been free from its distresses long ago," President Smith told his audience, "if the children of men had accepted the advice of Him who gave His all." He reminded the Saints of the Savior's invitation to love their neighbors and forgive their enemies. "That is the spirit of the Redeemer," he declared, "and that is the spirit all Latter-day Saints should seek to possess if they hope someday to stand in His presence and receive at His hands a glorious welcome home."[1]

Among Church members, President Smith was known as a kind, peace-loving leader. When he was a younger man, he had composed a personal creed to guide his life. "I would not seek to force people to live up to my ideals but rather love them into doing the thing that is right," he wrote. "I would not knowingly wound the feeling of any, not even one who may have wronged me, but would seek to do him good and make him my friend."[2]

Now, as he looked to the future, President Smith was especially concerned about helping Saints whose lives had been shattered by war. Earlier that year, he had asked the Church Welfare Committee to create a plan for sending food and clothing to Europe. Shortly after the October conference, he met with several apostles to discuss shipping the goods overseas as soon as possible.[3]

Sending aid to Europe was no straightforward task. The Church needed help from the United States government to coordinate relief efforts with so many countries. To work out the details, President Smith traveled to Washington, DC, with a small group of Church leaders.[4]

They arrived in the nation's capital on a cloudy morning in early November. Among their many meetings with government officials and European ambassadors was an appointment with Harry S. Truman, the president of the United States. President Truman welcomed the Church leaders graciously, but he warned them that it did not make sense financially to ship food and clothing to Europe when its economy was bad and currencies unreliable. "Their money isn't any good," he told President Smith.[5]

The prophet explained that the Church did not expect to be paid. "Our people over there need food and supplies," he said. "We want to help them before winter sets in."[6]

"How long will it take you to get this ready?" President Truman asked.

"We are ready right now," the prophet said. He described the stores of food and supplies the Saints had gathered, along with over two thousand quilts sewn by Relief Societies during the war. The Church simply needed help transporting these goods to Europe.

"You are on the right track," President Truman said, shocked at the Saints' preparedness. "We will be glad to help you in any way we can."[7]

Before leaving, President Smith told President Truman that the Latter-day Saints were praying for him. The prophet gave him a leatherbound copy of *A Voice of Warning,* a missionary tract written by apostle Parley P. Pratt in 1837.

It struck President Smith that during Elder Pratt's life-time, the Saints were barely surviving. They never could have sent aid across the ocean to thousands of struggling people. But over the past century, the Lord had taught the Saints how to be ready for times of distress, and President Smith was happy they could now act quickly.[8]

As THE CHURCH PREPARED to ship aid to Europe, Helga Birth continued her service as a missionary in Berlin. Germany was still in disarray months after the war. Both the city of Berlin and the country as a whole had been divided into four zones, each controlled by a different occupying nation. Since the war had left most German Saints homeless, they often sought help from Helga and the other missionaries at the mission home. Herbert Klopfer, the acting mission president in east-ern Germany, had died in a Soviet prison camp, so his counselors, Paul Langheinrich and Richard Ranglack, led efforts to minister to the refugees.

Needing more space to house these Saints, the two men received permission from military leaders to move the mission home to an abandoned mansion in the American-controlled zone in western Berlin. Helga's hometown of Tilsit, meanwhile, was in a part of Germany under Soviet control, and she had no idea how to find her father and mother or her brother Henry, who was missing in action. Nor could she easily learn the where-abouts of friends and former branch members.[9]

In the fall of 1945, Helga received a letter from her aunt Lusche. More than a year had passed since they survived the air raid that killed Helga's grandparents and aunt Nita. Now, Helga learned, the Soviet army was holding Lusche and other German refugees in a deserted castle near the German-Polish border. The Soviet authorities had decided to release them, but only if they had relatives who could take them in. Helga quickly wrote back, inviting her aunt to live at the mission home.

Lusche arrived in Berlin a short time later with a woman named Eva, a distant relative who had been imprisoned with her. Both women looked hollow and emaciated. Helga had experienced much hunger and suffering during the war, but her aunt's stories of torture and deprivation shook her soul. Eva's baby girl had died of cold and starvation, and Lusche had considered taking her own life.[10]

Other Latter-day Saint refugees found their way to the mission home as well, and Paul Langheinrich found places for them to stay. Soon, upward of one hundred people were being housed and fed under one roof. Yet Helga's father, mother, and brother were nowhere to be found.

American soldiers who had been missionaries in Germany visited the mission home often. One soldier brought sandwiches to share, made with fluffy white bread from the United States. Helga eagerly devoured a sandwich, but it hardly relieved the relentless hunger plaguing her and her housemates. At times they went days without eating. When Helga managed to purchase or scavenge a meal, the old potatoes and watered-down milk provided little nourishment. She was so weak that some days she could not get out of bed.[11]

Good news came in January 1946, when a letter arrived from her father, Martin Meiszus. He had lost his left eye during an air raid near the end of the war and spent some time in a refugee camp in Denmark. Now he was back in Germany, living in the city of Schwerin, about 130 miles from Berlin.[12] Paul and other mission leaders had been traveling around Germany for several months, searching for displaced Saints and helping them band together to survive. Since they were already planning to visit Schwerin, they invited Helga to join them.[13]

On the crowded train, Helga struggled to stay warm as frigid winter air blasted through the broken windows. In her hands she gripped a small box containing a few pieces of American chocolate. The candy was scarce, so she had decided to save it for her father. Still, she sometimes held the chocolate to her nose just to inhale its delicious aroma.

In Schwerin, Helga was overjoyed to see her father again. He was surprised when she gave him the chocolate, and he tried to share it with her. "Kindchen," he said. *Dear child.*

"No, Dad," Helga said. "I've had so much to eat." And it was true—she no longer felt hungry. She was too full of happiness.[14]

ON THE OTHER SIDE of the world, Neal Maxwell's division in the United States Army was part of the occupying force on mainland Japan. During the war, the country had been devastated by thousands of air raids and the atomic bombs dropped on Hiroshima and Nagasaki. Neal had expected the Japanese to welcome him as a conquering hero. But over three hundred thousand Japanese civilians were dead, and his soul was wrenched by seeing what the war had cost the people.[15]

Neal was now serving as a first sergeant over a company of about three hundred unruly and demoralized men, many of whom wanted nothing more than to go home. Although Neal was only nineteen years old, his superiors had decided he was the right man to bring order to the group. Neal was not so sure.[16]

"I do many things here that require such mature judgment I shiver when I think of the responsibility," he wrote in a letter to his parents. "Way down underneath I'm just a kid, so homesick and young that he doesn't know what to do."[17]

Still, he found ways to succeed as a leader and win the respect of some of the men. He often turned to his Father in Heaven, seeking help. Many nights, he would wander alone outside to pray, finding closer communion with God under the star-studded sky.[18]

He also found strength among fellow Latter-day Saint soldiers. Throughout the war, Church leaders had encouraged Saints in the military to meet together, take the sacrament, and provide spiritual support to one another. In postwar Japan, as well as in Guam, the Philippines, and other places around the world, hundreds of Latter-day Saint servicemembers met together.

These groups often had unexpected missionary experiences. Soon after the war ended, Latter-day Saint servicemen in Italy were granted an audience with Pope Pius XII at the headquarters of the Catholic Church. They told the pope about the Savior's visit to the Western Hemisphere and presented him with a copy of the Book of Mormon.[19]

In Japan, meanwhile, local Saints who had not attended church in years sought out the servicemember groups and participated in their meetings. Under the new occupation government, the Japanese were free to explore their spiritual beliefs, and some Latter-day Saint soldiers invited their Japanese friends to learn about the Church. Soon, American soldiers like Neal sat side by side with their former enemies, partaking of the sacrament and learning together about the gospel of Jesus Christ.[20]

Neal had many months of military service to complete before he could return home. But his experiences on Okinawa, and now on Japan's mainland, solidified his desire to serve a mission as soon as he possibly could.[21]

"There is a field of men ripe for the gospel who are just as Christian as ourselves," he wrote to his family back home, "but have a great need of the gospel to guide them."[22]

BACK IN GERMANY, PAUL Langheinrich contacted the head of the Soviet forces in Berlin. Thousands of Latter-day Saint refugees were now living in Soviet-occupied areas, and Paul was concerned for their welfare. "Because of Hitler's unfathomable actions," he wrote, "many of our members are now on the highways, without home or homeland, banished and cast out."

Paul asked the commander for permission to purchase food and transport it to these Saints. As a former genealogical researcher for the German government, he also felt prompted to ask if he could search for caches of important records, which the Nazis had hidden in remote areas of the country to protect them from damage or theft. Since German Saints would someday need these records to do temple work for their ancestors, Paul wanted to preserve them.

"These records are of no value to you," he wrote the commander. "For us, they are priceless."[23]

A week later, Paul received permission to buy whatever food Church members needed. And as far as the genealogical records were concerned, if the Saints could find them, they were free to keep them.[24]

Paul eventually learned about a collection of documents at Rothenburg castle, southwest of Berlin. On a frigid day in February 1946, he and sixteen local missionaries hiked up an icy road to the old castle, which stood at the top of a mountain. Once inside, the men found piles of parish registers, microfilm, and books containing German genealogies.[25]

A number of the registers were centuries old and contained thousands of names and dates, some written in beautiful German script. Long scrolls depicted family trees illustrated in vivid color. Much of the cache was in good condition, although some of the records were covered with ice and snow and did not look salvageable.[26]

Once Paul and the missionaries secured the records, all that remained was to safely convey them down the mountain. Paul had arranged for a rented truck and trailer to pick up the records and carry them to a railroad car on its way to Berlin. But as time passed, the truck did not arrive.[27]

A missionary finally appeared, trudging up the mountainside. The truck was stranded partway up, its tires spinning against the icy roads.[28]

Paul decided it was time to pray. He asked three missionaries to walk with him into the woods, and they pleaded for the Lord's help. At the moment they said "amen," they heard the sound of an engine and saw the truck rounding the curve.

The driver told Paul he had detached the trailer to make it to the castle. He intended to turn the truck around and leave, but Paul persuaded him to stay and help them transport as many records as possible down the slippery road. Without the trailer, though, the truck was not big enough to transport all the records. If they wanted to get everything out in time to meet the freight car the following day, the ice on the road would have to melt. Once again, Paul and the missionaries turned to God in prayer.[29]

A warm rain fell that night. When Paul woke in the morning, the roads were free of ice. He also learned that the freight car had been delayed by a few days, giving the missionaries the time they needed to load up every salvageable item. Paul could not deny God's role in the marvelous manifestation, and he was grateful to be an instrument in His hands.

Once the last of their cargo reached the railway station, Paul and the men said a final prayer. "We have done our part," they prayed. "Now, dear God, we need Thee to take this freight car to Berlin.[30]

ON MAY 22, 1946, ARWELL Pierce, president of the Mexican Mission, stood with President George Albert Smith on top of the Pyramid of the Sun, a popular historic site just northeast of Mexico City. The stone pyramid, which had once been the center of an ancient city that came to be known as Teotihuacán, rose over two hundred feet into the air and offered spectacular views of the surrounding landscape. Although President Smith was now in his late seventies, he had climbed the pyramid's many stairs with relative ease, joking with Arwell and the missionaries who were with them.[31]

Arwell was happy the prophet had come to Mexico. It was the first time any Church president had toured the mission, and the visit meant a great deal to the local Saints. For the last decade, the Church in Mexico had been split between the main body of Saints and

485

the twelve hundred people who had joined the Third Convention. President Smith's visit offered a real chance for reconciliation—something Arwell had diligently sought over the past four years.[32]

When Arwell became president of the Mexican Mission in 1942, the schism between the Third Conventionists and the other Saints in Mexico ran deep. When Arwell was set apart by the First Presidency, J. Reuben Clark had charged him with trying to heal the breach.[33]

At first, the Conventionists were suspicious of the new mission president. Like his predecessors, Arwell was a U.S. citizen, and the Conventionists did not receive him warmly. Instead of trying to force them to see the error of their ways, Arwell decided to earn their trust and friendship.

He began attending Third Convention meetings and developed a friendship with Abel Páez, the leader of the organization, as well as other Conventionists. The more time he spent with them, the more he thought that reunification was possible. The Conventionists still kept their faith in the core doctrine of the restored gospel. They continued to administer Church programs, and they believed in the Book of Mormon. If he could help them see all they were missing by separating themselves from the body of the Saints, he believed they would return. But he would have to proceed carefully.

"We haven't done much good in the past with harsh methods," he informed the First Presidency. "Let us hope that kindness and sane, patient reasoning may do some good."[34]

Under the First Presidency's direction, Arwell led efforts to build or remodel several chapels in Mexico, addressing a shortage that had troubled Conventionists when they first broke from the Church. He also met often with Abel to encourage him to seek a reconciliation. "What you here in Mexico really need is a stake organization," he told Abel and the Conventionists. "We cannot have a stake in Mexico until we are more united."[35]

He reminded Abel that the Conventionists were forgoing temple blessings. In 1945, the first Spanish-language endowments took place in the temple in Mesa, Arizona. Although many of the Mexican Saints could not afford a trip to Mesa, Arwell said he believed there would someday be temples in Mexico that Abel and so many other Conventionists could enter.[36]

One day, Arwell received a phone call from Abel. He and a few other Third Convention leaders wanted to meet with him to discuss a reconciliation. The men talked for nearly six hours. Eventually, after recognizing ways they had erred, Abel and the others decided to appeal to the First Presidency to be readmitted as members of the Church. President Smith and his counselors reviewed the request and decided that if Conventionists were willing to sever their relationship with the group and sustain the president of the Mexican Mission, they could again be members of the Church of Jesus Christ.[37]

Now, as Arwell toured the mission with President Smith, they spoke with Conventionists who wanted to return. "There has been no rebellion here," President Smith observed, "only a misunderstanding."[38]

On May 25, 1946, Arwell took President Smith to the Ermita Branch in Mexico City. More than a thousand people, many of them members of the Third Convention, crowded into the small chapel and an overflow pavilion to hear the prophet speak. Some Conventionists worried that President Smith would condemn them, but instead he spoke of harmony and reunion. Afterward, most Conventionists committed to return fully to the Church.[39]

A few days later, at a meeting of nearly five hundred Saints in the city of Tecalco, Abel thanked President Smith for coming to Mexico. "It is our purpose to follow the leadership and instructions of the general authorities of our Church and the president of the Mexican Mission," he told the congregation. "We are following a prophet of the Lord."[40]

CHAPTER 32

Brothers and Sisters

On a cool Sunday evening in August 1946, Ezra Taft Benson and two traveling companions drove a military jeep along the eerily quiet streets of Zełwągi, Poland. Rough roads and heavy rains had vexed the travelers all day, but the foul weather had finally cleared up as the men neared their destination.

Zełwągi had once been part of Germany and had been known as Selbongen. National boundaries had shifted after the war, however, and much of central and eastern Europe had come under the influence of the Soviet Union. In 1929, the thriving Selbongen Branch had built the first Latter-day Saint meetinghouse in Germany. But after six years of war, the Saints in the village were barely surviving.[1]

Elder Benson had come from the United States earlier that year to oversee the Church's distribution of relief throughout the European Mission. He had been a member of the Quorum of the Twelve Apostles for less than three years, but he had extensive experience in Church and government leadership. At forty-seven, he was young and healthy enough to handle a grueling travel schedule through several European nations.[2]

But no experience had prepared him for the horrors now surrounding him. Since coming to Europe, he had witnessed the ruins of war from London to Frankfurt and from Vienna to Stockholm.[3] At the same time, he could see the European Saints banding together to help each other and rebuild the Church in their countries. On a visit to the mission home in Berlin, he was impressed by the mountains of genealogical records Paul Langheinrich and others had recovered, even as they worked to provide food, clothing, fuel, and shelter for more than a thousand Saints in their care.[4]

He also saw how the aid from the Church was making a difference throughout western Europe. Under Belle Spafford, the newly called Relief Society general president, women in wards and stakes in the United States, Canada, and Mexico had coordinated massive efforts to gather clothing, bedding, and soap for the European Saints.[5] A Relief Society in Hamilton, Ontario, donated a bundle of children's sweaters, suits, and underwear knitted with cast-off material from a clothing factory. A Relief Society in Los Angeles, meanwhile, contributed to

490

the effort by making more than twelve hundred articles of clothing and volunteering nearly four thousand hours for the Red Cross.[6]

But in much of Germany and in eastern European nations like Poland, where Soviet-influenced governments resisted Western aid, Saints continued to go without necessities.[7] The fact that Elder Benson was in Poland at all felt like a miracle. With no telephone lines operating, he and his associates had struggled to contact officials who could help them secure paperwork to enter the country. Only after much prayer and repeated contact with the Polish government was the apostle able to obtain the necessary visas.[8]

As the jeep neared the old meetinghouse in Zełwągi, most of the people in the streets scattered and hid. Elder Benson and his companions stopped the vehicle in front of the building and climbed out. They introduced themselves to a woman nearby and asked if they had found the Latter-day Saint chapel. The woman's eyes filled with tears of relief. "The brethren are here!" she cried in German.

Immediately people came out from behind closed doors, crying and laughing with joy. The Zełwągi Saints had been out of contact with general Church leaders for three years, and that morning many of them had been fasting and praying for a visit from a missionary or Church leader.[9] Within a few hours, about a hundred Saints gathered to hear the apostle speak.

Many of the men in the branch had been killed or deported as prisoners of war, and the Saints who remained were downhearted. Since the war's end, some Soviet and Polish soldiers had terrorized the town, plundering homes and assaulting residents. Food was rationed, and people often paid outrageous prices for whatever extra nourishment they could get on the black market.[10]

That evening, while Elder Benson spoke to the Saints, two armed Polish soldiers entered the chapel. The congregation stiffened with fear, but the apostle motioned for the soldiers to take a seat near the front of the room. In his talk, he emphasized the importance of liberty and freedom. The soldiers listened attentively, remained in their seats for the closing hymn, and departed without incident. Afterward, Elder Benson met with the branch president and left food and money for the Saints, assuring them more aid was on the way.[11]

A short time later, Elder Benson wrote the First Presidency. He was encouraged to see the Church's aid reaching Church members in Europe but worried about the difficulties the Saints still faced.

"Perhaps the many benefits of the great Church welfare program to these and our other Saints in Europe shall never be known," he wrote, "but many lives have undoubtedly been spared, and the faith and courage of many of our devoted members greatly strengthened."[12]

AROUND THIS TIME IN Austria, eighteen-year-old Emmy Cziep awoke at five thirty in the morning, ate a single piece of bread for breakfast, and started her one-hour walk to Vienna General Hospital. It had been seven years since her harrowing rail journey out of Czechoslovakia, and now she was studying to become an X-ray technician. Because Vienna, like Berlin, was an occupied city, Emmy often passed Soviet soldiers on the road to the hospital. But medical workers were respected, and she believed her Red Cross armband offered her some protection from harassment.[13]

Vienna had been the site of violence and terror during the war, yet Emmy's parents, Alois and Hermine, had continued to lead branch and Relief Society meetings. Alois now served as district president over the Church's five branches in Austria, and he and Hermine worked hard to help their fellow Saints. Most people in Vienna, including Emmy, had emerged from the war traumatized and on the verge of starvation. Emmy's brother, Josef, had served for a time in the German army, surviving capture and torture by Soviet soldiers after the war.[14]

Emmy's training at the hospital was one of the few things in her life that could give her hope. Another was a recent visit to Vienna by Elder Benson, who had brought much-needed cheer to the Saints in Austria. Emmy's family had felt honored to have him stay at their home. In the evening, the apostle had asked Emmy to play hymns for him on the piano, and she had felt uplifted by his presence.[15]

Some months after Elder Benson visited, the Church's aid shipments arrived in Austria, and by 1947,

Alois was overseeing the distribution of hundreds of cases of clothing, cracked wheat, beans, peas, sugar, oil, vitamins, and other essentials. Emmy herself received many wonderful items, including beautiful dresses with notes from the giver pinned to them.[16]

Latter-day Saints elsewhere in Europe were aiding each other as well. The Nordic nation of Finland, which Elder Benson had recently dedicated for missionary work, was home to three branches of Saints. When Church members in neighboring Sweden found out that these branches were in need, they sent boxes of food, clothing, and bedding.[17]

In Vienna, a few days before Emmy's final exams at the hospital, her father asked for her help. Many children in Austria were undernourished and needed medical attention they could not get in Vienna. Since Switzerland had remained neutral in the war, Church members there had more resources, and they offered to take young Latter-day Saint children from Austria into their homes for three months to nurse them back to health.

Alois had a group of twenty-one children who needed care, and he wanted Emmy to help him take them to Switzerland. Emmy agreed to go, knowing she would be returning to Vienna within a few days to take her final exams.

During the journey to Switzerland, the train was so crowded that some of the children had to sit on the floor or in the luggage space above the seats. When it began to rain, the cardboard covering the windows did little to keep water from seeping inside. Many of the children were uncomfortable and missed their parents, so Emmy did her best to soothe them.

After a long night with little sleep, Emmy, her father, and the children arrived in Basel, Switzerland. They were greeted by the mission president and his wife, Scott and Nida Taggart, along with members of the local Relief Society, who presented the boys and girls with oranges and bananas.

The next day the Swiss families brought the children into their homes, and Emmy bade them farewell.[18] Before she could return to Vienna, however, President Taggart invited her to remain in Basel to serve as a missionary. "The Lord needs you," he said.

Emmy was stunned. She had never thought of serving a mission before. And what about her exams at the X-ray institute? If she stayed, she would not be able to finish her training, nor would she get a chance to say goodbye to her loved ones back home. In Switzerland, she would be surrounded by strangers who had not endured bombings, starvation, heartache, and death. Would they be able to understand her?

Despite these concerns, Emmy felt the answer to President Taggart's question settle on her heart. "If the Lord wants me to stay," she said, "I will."

That night, about a month shy of her nineteenth birthday, Emmy Cziep was set apart to serve in the Swiss-Austrian Mission.[19]

IN THE SPRING OF 1947, a year and a half after reuniting with her father, Helga Birth was no longer a missionary in Berlin. Nor was she known as Helga Birth. Now she was Helga Meyer, married to a German Latter-day Saint named Kurt Meyer. They lived in Cammin, a rural town about eighty miles north of Berlin, and had a baby boy, Siegfried, named after Helga's brother who had died in the war.

Helga first met Kurt when he visited the East German Mission home in early 1946. A soldier in the German military, he had returned home at the end of the war only to learn that when the Soviet army had swept through his hometown, his parents had drowned themselves to avoid being taken prisoner or killed.[20]

At the time Kurt came to the mission home, he was not an active Latter-day Saint, but he was interested in returning to church. Not long after meeting Helga, he proposed to her.

Helga did not know how to respond. Ever since the death of her first husband, Gerhard, people had been encouraging her to marry again. She was not eager to rush into another marriage, though. She was not in love with Kurt, and she did not want to move to his hometown of Cammin, where the nearest branch of the Church was a train ride away. Part of her wanted to emigrate to Utah.

But she was not ready to leave Germany yet—at least not until she and her father found her mother. Marrying Kurt would allow Helga to remain in Germany and have some stability in life. Kurt already had a house in Cammin, not far from a lake full of fish. If she married him, neither she nor her father would go without shelter or food.[21]

With few choices available, Helga decided to accept Kurt's proposal and the security it offered. They married in April 1946, and almost a year later their son was born.

Then, late in the spring of 1947, Helga and her father received news that her mother was alive. After being driven out of Tilsit, Bertha Meiszus had evaded capture by the advancing Soviet forces and walked for days, half-frozen, until she reached a boat that took her to a refugee camp in Denmark. She had been there for two years before she finally made contact with the family. Soon she too was living with them in Cammin.[22]

One day, around this time, some Soviet troops came to Helga's door. With the lake nearby, soldiers stopped at the house once or twice a week to demand fish from her. The troops had a reputation for brutality, and Helga had heard stories of them committing rape and other acts of violence in Cammin. The sound of the soldiers' car approaching her house always frightened her.[23]

Helga let the troops in, as usual. They had vodka, and the commander was clearly drunk. He took a seat at her table and said, "Frau—come, sit." The soldiers ordered Kurt to join them, but then they largely ignored him.

Helga sat down beside the commander, and he asked her to have a drink.

"I do not drink," Helga said.

"Give it to her, give it to her," prodded the soldiers' chauffeur, a cruel-looking German.

Helga was afraid. Drunken men could be unpredictable. But she said, "No, I'm not drinking."

"If you do not drink," the commander said forcefully, "I will shoot you!"

"Well, then," Helga said, throwing her arms out, "you will have to shoot."

A few moments passed. "Do you belong to some religion?" the commander asked.

"I'm a Mormon," Helga said.

The commander and his soldiers stopped threatening her after that. The next time he came to her house, the commander patted her on the shoulder and called her a "good Frau," but he did not ask her to sit with him. He seemed to admire her strength and respect her for standing up for her beliefs.

Before long, she and the soldiers were friends.[24]

A FEW MONTHS LATER, in July 1947, Saints from across Austria met in Haag am Hausruck, a town some 140 miles west of Vienna. Since July marked the one hundredth anniversary of the pioneers' arrival in the Salt Lake Valley, district president Alois Cziep wanted the Austrian Saints to gather for a celebration, as many Church members were doing around the world. Haag am Hausruck was near where the first branch of the

Church in Austria had been organized in 1902, and it provided an ideal venue.

More than 180 Saints came to the event—too many for the local branch's meetinghouse to accommodate—so Church leaders rented a large room in a nearby hotel and constructed a temporary stage. The three-day celebration featured speeches, musical performances, and a play depicting scenes of early Church history and the entrance of the pioneers into the Salt Lake Valley.

On Sunday the Saints met in a gravel pit, where they set up a platform for the speakers and hauled out an organ to accompany their singing. Perched on a rocky ledge behind the platform was a seven-and-a-half-foot-tall replica of the Salt Lake Temple. Kurt Hirschmann, a member of the Frankenburg Branch, had spent several months crafting the intricate replica from cardboard packing boxes that had once contained welfare supplies from Salt Lake City.

Neither Alois nor most of the Saints at the celebration had been to the temple. With Europe in disarray and the nearest temple thousands of miles away, all they could do was imagine what the experience of being endowed and sealed to their families would be like. But that did not stop Alois from recognizing the importance of temple covenants or feeling the Spirit as the Saints spoke, sang, and bore testimony.[25]

As night fell, the group lit a bonfire that bathed the cardboard temple spires in a warm, flickering light. Alois closed the meeting by speaking of the faith of the early missionaries in Austria, likening them to the pioneers of 1847. "How thankful we should be for the gospel, the priesthood, and all the splendid opportunities given us in this Church to work out our salvation and even exaltation," he said.

By the end of the meeting, the light from the bonfire had dimmed, so a Latter-day Saint soldier from the United States jumped into his jeep, turned on the headlights, and again illuminated the temple against the night sky.

The Austrian Saints lifted their voices together, the words of the pioneer hymn "Come, Come, Ye Saints" ringing up toward heaven:

Gird up your loins; fresh courage take.
Our God will never us forsake;
And soon we'll have this tale to tell—
All is well! All is well!

Surrounded by his brothers and sisters in the gospel, Alois was sure the hymn had never been sung with more conviction.[26]

WHILE SAINTS AROUND THE world celebrated the pioneer centennial, former prisoner of war Pieter Vlam was serving as a full-time missionary in the Netherlands Mission. As part of his new calling, Pieter had moved about thirty miles away from his home to lead the Church's branch in Amsterdam. His wife, Hanna, and their three children remained at home.

The Amsterdam Branch had suffered terribly under the Nazi occupation. The city had been on the brink of starvation before its liberation. Had it not been for Ruurd Hut, Pieter's predecessor, many branch members would have succumbed to hunger. Ruurd had vowed to do everything in his power to keep the Saints under his care from starving. He had collected money from branch members and purchased food, which the Relief Society cooked and distributed among the hungry Saints.[27]

Still, the Netherlands was in a deplorable state after five years of occupation. More than two hundred thousand Dutch people had died during the war, and hundreds of thousands of homes had been damaged or destroyed. Many Saints in Amsterdam and other cities in the Netherlands were bitter toward the Germans—and toward fellow Saints who had cooperated with the occupiers.[28]

To help unify the Saints, the mission president, Cornelius Zappey, encouraged branches to supplement their food supplies by starting potato-growing projects using seed potatoes from the Dutch government.[29] Pieter and his branch soon rented a piece of land in Amsterdam, and men, women, and children worked together to plant potatoes and other vegetables. Other branches in the Netherlands also started potato patches wherever they could find a spot, growing potatoes in backyards, flower gardens, vacant lots, and road medians.[30]

Near harvesttime, Cornelius held a mission conference in the city of Rotterdam. Having met with Walter Stover, the president of the East German Mission, Cornelius knew that many Saints in Germany suffered from severe shortages of food. He wanted to do something to help, so he asked local leaders if they would be willing to give a portion of their potato harvest to the Saints in Germany.

"Some of the most bitter enemies you people have encountered as a result of this war are the German people," he acknowledged. "But those people are now much worse off than you."

At first, some Dutch Saints resisted the plan. Why should they share their potatoes with the Germans? They did not think Cornelius understood how terrible the Germans had been to them in the war. Although he had been born in the Netherlands, the mission president had spent most of his life in the United States. He did not know what it was like to lose his house to German bombs or watch his loved ones starve to death because German occupiers had taken their food.[31]

Cornelius still believed the Lord wanted the Dutch Saints to help the Germans, so he asked Pieter to visit branches throughout the Netherlands and encourage them to support the plan. Pieter was an experienced Church leader whose unjust imprisonment in a German camp was well known. If the Dutch Saints loved and trusted anyone in the mission, it was Pieter Vlam.

Pieter agreed to help the mission president, and as he met with the branches, he alluded to his hardships in prison. "I've been through this," he said. "You know that I have." He urged them to forgive the German people. "I know how hard it is to love them," he said. "If those are our brothers and sisters, then we should treat them as our brothers and sisters."

His words and the words of other branch presidents moved the Saints, and the anger of many melted away as they harvested potatoes for the German Saints. Disagreements within the branches did not disappear, but at least the Saints knew they could work together going forward.[32]

Cornelius, meanwhile, worked to secure permits to transport the potatoes to Germany. At first, the Dutch government did not want to export any food from the country. But Cornelius kept petitioning them until they relented. When some officials tried to stop the shipment plans, Cornelius told them, "These potatoes belong to the Lord, and if it be His will, the Lord will see that they come to Germany."

Finally, in November 1947, Dutch Saints and missionaries met in The Hague to load ten trucks with more than seventy tons of potatoes. A short time later, the potatoes arrived in Germany for distribution among the Saints. East German Mission president Walter Stover also purchased truckloads of potatoes to add to the supplies.[33]

Word of the potato project soon reached the First Presidency. Amazed, second counselor David O. McKay said, "This is one of the greatest acts of true Christian conduct ever brought to my attention."[34]

CHAPTER 33

Our Father's Hand

Whthe thirty-six-year-old Martha Toronto headed into town to shop for her family and the half dozen or more missionaries living in the Czechoslovak Mission home, she sometimes felt like she was being watched. In the spring of 1948, she had been living in Prague with her husband, mission president Wallace Toronto, for about a year. During her first six months in the city, Martha had worked hard to help the Czechoslovak Saints rebuild the Church in a country still reeling from seven years of Nazi occupation. Then, in February 1948, Soviet-backed communists in the government had staged a coup, forcing all noncommunist leaders out of power.

The coup was part of an emerging "cold war" between the Soviet Union and its former allies. The communist government in Czechoslovakia was generally suspicious of religious groups, and the Church had come under special scrutiny because of its ties to the United States. Government spies and citizen informants now monitored Church members and missionaries, and many Czechoslovaks seemed wary of the Torontos and other Americans. Martha would occasionally see a curtain in a nearby house flick open as she walked by. And once, a man had followed her thirteen-year-old daughter, Marion, home from school. When she turned to look at him, he hid behind a tree.[1]

Martha had experience living under a suspicious and controlling regime. She and Wallace had led the Czechoslovak Mission once before, beginning in 1936, a few years after they were married. At first, the Torontos had been relatively free to preach the gospel. But by early 1939, the Nazi regime had seized control of the country and began harassing Church members and imprisoning some missionaries. When the war broke out a short time later, Martha, Wallace, and the North American missionaries were forced to evacuate the country, leaving behind more than a hundred Czechoslovak Saints.[2]

Wallace had placed the mission in the hands of twenty-one-year-old Josef Roubíček, who had joined the Church only three years earlier. As acting mission president, Josef held meetings and conferences, sent frequent letters to the Saints in the mission, and did what he could to strengthen their resilience and faith.

From time to time, he reported to Wallace on the state of the mission.[3]

Not long after the war's end, the First Presidency called Wallace and Martha to resume their duties in Czechoslovakia. Given the challenges of living in war-torn Europe, Wallace left for Prague in June 1946, promising to send for the family as soon as things were more stable. At times, Martha had wondered if her children would be better off if she remained with them in Utah, but she did not want them to go years without seeing their father. After a year-long separation, the Toronto family had finally reunited.[4]

As a mission leader, Martha directed Relief Society work, took care of the missionaries, and enjoyed seeing recent converts gather in the mission home for Mutual Improvement Association activities each week. But with the communist government keeping a close eye on her family and the Church, she had every reason to expect that life in Czechoslovakia would become more difficult.

Before Martha left the United States, President J. Reuben Clark of the First Presidency had set her apart for her mission. "The problems that will come to you," he had said, "will be numerous and of an unusual kind." He promised she would have the strength to meet them and blessed her with patience, charity, and long-suffering.[5]

Martha clung to his words as she and her family did the Lord's work.

MEANWHILE, FAR FROM THE turmoil in Europe, thirty-one-year-old John O'Donnal knelt beside a tree in a secluded corner of a botanical garden near Tela, Honduras. For the last six years, John had been operating a rubber station in the neighboring country of Guatemala, and he enjoyed it whenever his work brought him to the beautiful garden. For someone who had grown up in the Latter-day Saint colonies in the desert lands of northern Mexico, the peaceful spot, with its extraordinary array of flora and fauna, was a tropical paradise.[6]

Yet John's mind was troubled. He and his wife, Carmen, had fallen in love shortly after he started working in Central America. Since Carmen was a Catholic, they were married by a priest of her church. At the time, though, John had a strong feeling that she would one day share his faith in the restored gospel. He longed to be sealed to her in the temple and often talked with her about the Church, which had no official presence in Guatemala. Carmen did not seem interested in changing her religion, however, and John tried hard not to pressure her.

"I don't want you to join my church just because you want to please me," he told her. "You have to work for your testimony."

Carmen liked much of what John taught her about the Church, but she wanted to be sure the restored gospel was right for her. She had not been allowed to read the Bible as a child, and she did not grasp the importance of the Book of Mormon at first. "Why in the world do I have to read this book?" she asked John. "It doesn't mean anything to me."[7]

John did not give up. On a trip to the United States, he talked to her about eternal marriage as they visited Mesa, Arizona, where the nearest temple was located. No matter how much he shared the restored gospel with her, though, she could not seem to receive a testimony.

Part of the problem, John knew, was opposition from her family and friends, some of whom spoke poorly of the Church. Carmen was not a devout Catholic, but she still valued the traditions she had grown up with. And John regretted that he himself was sometimes slack in living his religion, especially around friends and colleagues who were not members of the Church. It was sometimes a struggle to be so far from any organized branch of Saints. He was grateful for his early years in northern Mexico, where he had been surrounded by the good examples of his parents and other Church members.[8]

In late 1946, John had visited President George Albert Smith in Salt Lake City and urged him to send missionaries to Guatemala. President Smith listened with interest as John spoke of the country's readiness for the gospel. He and his counselors were already consulting with Frederick S. Williams, the former president of the Argentine Mission, about expanding missionary work in Latin America.

Not long after the meeting, the First Presidency had announced their decision to send missionaries to Guatemala. "We are not sure as to when this can be done," they told John, "but we trust in the reasonably near future."[9]

Four missionaries had arrived at the O'Donnals' home in Guatemala City several months later, just after the borders of the Mexican Mission were enlarged to include Guatemala, Costa Rica, El Salvador, Honduras, Nicaragua, and Panama. Two of the elders moved on to Costa Rica, but the other two began holding meetings with John, Carmen, and their two small daughters.

The missionaries also set up a Sunday School and Primary—and even recruited Carmen's sister Teresa as a Primary teacher. Though Carmen attended Church meetings with John, she was still reluctant to get baptized. In fact, by the time John knelt down in the botanical garden, the missionaries had been in Guatemala for nearly a year, and so far no one in the country had joined the Church.

As John prayed, he opened his soul, pleading with Heavenly Father to forgive his sins and shortcomings. He then prayed for Carmen in her struggle to gain a testimony. It seemed as if the adversary had done all he could over the last five years to keep her out of the Church. When would she receive her answer from the Lord?[10]

WHILE JOHN O'DONNAL PRAYED in Honduras, Emmy Cziep was working hard as a missionary in Switzerland. In addition to regular missionary duties, she assisted mission president Scott Taggart with his German-language correspondence and translated lesson materials from English to German. Although she did not know English before her mission, she had developed skill in the language by poring over old *Improvement Era* magazines and carrying a dictionary wherever she went.[11]

In the summer of 1948, a government official informed Emmy that she could no longer renew her visa and would have to return to Vienna in three months. Emmy missed her family, but she had little desire to live in Austria under the influence of the Soviet Union, which still occupied parts of her city and her country. There was a chance she could get a temporary job as a domestic worker in Great Britain, but nothing was certain. She thought often of the proverb "Trust in the Lord with all thine heart; and lean not unto thine own understanding."[12]

One day, Emmy met two sister missionaries from the British Mission who were visiting Switzerland before returning home. Both women were from Canada and did not speak German, so Emmy interpreted for them. As they chatted, Emmy told them of her reluctance to return to Vienna. One of the missionaries, Marion Allen, asked Emmy if she would be willing to emigrate to Canada instead of Great Britain. While most Church members in Canada lived near the temple in Cardston, Alberta, branches of Saints could be found across the vast country, from Nova Scotia in the east to British Columbia in the west.

Emmy thought she had little chance of emigrating to North America. Austria had not yet signed a neutrality treaty, and its citizens were considered enemy aliens to Allied nations. Nor did Emmy have any family or friends in Canada or the United States who could sponsor her or guarantee her employment.[13]

A few weeks later, though, President Taggart received a telegram from Marion's father, Heber Allen, asking if Emmy would be interested in moving to Canada. Marion had told him of Emmy's plight, and Heber had reached out to a contact in the Canadian government who could help her get approved for immigration. Heber was willing to offer Emmy a job and a place to stay at their home in Raymond, a small town near Cardston.

Emmy immediately agreed. As she prepared to leave, her parents, Alois and Hermine, got a one-day pass to the Swiss border to say goodbye. Emmy knew it took faith for her parents to let their twenty-year-old daughter live among strangers in an unknown land, not knowing if they would see each other again.

"Wherever you are going, you are never alone," her parents told her. "There is your Heavenly Father to watch over you." They urged her to be a good citizen and stay close to the Church.[14]

Later, during her voyage across the Atlantic Ocean, Emmy's heart grew heavy as she thought of her close-knit family, the members of the Vienna Branch, and her beloved Austria. She began to weep, thinking that if she had the power to turn the ship around, she just might do it.

Two returning elders from the Czechoslovak Mission were sailing with Emmy, and they made the difficult trip more bearable. In between bouts of sea-sickness, each young man proposed marriage to Emmy, but she turned both of them down. "You just haven't been around girls for two years," she told them. "As soon as you get home, you'll find a real nice one and settle down."[15]

When the ship arrived in Nova Scotia, the two elders were allowed immediate entrance to the country, but Emmy was ushered to a fenced-in holding area with scores of other emigrants. Some of them, Emmy learned, were orphaned children from German concentration camps.

The Nazis had begun using such camps in the 1930s to imprison political dissidents and anyone else they deemed inferior or dangerous to their regime. After the war started, the Nazis continued to apprehend these people, ultimately murdering hundreds of thousands of them. Nazi anti-Semitism also turned genocidal as the regime systematically imprisoned and murdered millions of Jews in concentration camps. Two-thirds of European Jews died in the Holocaust, including Olga and Egon Weiss, the Jewish-born mother and son who had joined the Church and worshipped with Emmy's family in the Vienna Branch.[16]

In Canada, Emmy waited an entire day while government officials placed her and other emigrants into language groups and then questioned them, one by one.

Knowing some emigrants were sent back to Europe because their papers were not in order, or because they did not have enough money, or simply because they were ill, Emmy prayed that she could pass the inspection. When the official took her passport and stamped it, her heart almost leaped out of her chest for joy.

"I am free, in a free country," she thought.[17]

AROUND THIS SAME TIME, in Guatemala City, Carmen O'Donnal had much to think about. She had just received a letter from her husband, John, who was in Honduras on business. While he was away, he wanted her to ask God if The Church of Jesus Christ of Latter-day Saints was true, if Joseph Smith was a prophet, and if the Book of Mormon was the word of God. "Pray about it," he pleaded. "I want my wife to be sealed to me for the eternities, and my children too."

Carmen had already prayed about these things many times before. And praying was especially difficult—even upsetting—when John was away from home. A terrible spirit would surround her, and she would experience alarming displays of Satan's power. The thought of making another attempt without him nearby frightened her.

Still, one night she decided to try again. She put her two daughters to bed and then knelt to pray in her bedroom. Immediately the powers of darkness returned. She felt as if the room were full of thousands of jeering faces who wanted to destroy her. She fled the room and climbed the stairs to the second floor, where the missionaries lived. She told the elders what had happened, and they gave her a blessing.

When Carmen opened her eyes, she felt calmer. "For some reason, Satan is trying to destroy me," she realized. The adversary clearly did not want her to gain a testimony of the restored gospel. Why else would he work so hard to disrupt her prayers? All at once, she knew she had to be baptized.[18]

The next few months were busy for the O'Donnals. After John returned from Honduras, he and Carmen always prayed together. She continued to attend sacrament meetings and other Church gatherings, gaining greater understanding of the gospel. At a testimony meeting with Arwell Pierce, the president of the Mexican Mission, she stood up and said a few words. Others in turn shared their testimonies, and they wept together as the Holy Ghost touched and inspired them.[19]

On November 13, 1948, the missionaries held a baptismal service for Carmen, her sister Teresa, and two others, Manuela Cáceres and Luis Gonzalez Batres. Since the rented hall where they held church had no font, some friends agreed to let John and the missionaries perform the baptisms in a small swimming pool south of the city.[20]

One week later, Mary White and Arlene Bean, two missionaries from the Mexican Mission, arrived to organize a Relief Society in Guatemala City. Carmen was called to be the Relief Society president, and she

and the missionaries held meetings on Thursday afternoons. Most of the women who came were not
members of the Church. One, a middle-aged university
professor, was bothered at first that someone as young
as Carmen was leading the society.

"I don't know why in the world you called this
young lady to be president," she told the missionaries.

Carmen felt bad. She could not help agreeing with
the woman. Why hadn't the professor or another older
woman been called as president?

"Well, you don't have to feel like that, because you
didn't ask for this job," the sister missionaries told her.
"You were the one called to do it."

Since the Relief Society had no manuals, Carmen
improvised lessons and activities. In February 1949,
two women, Antonia Morales and Alicia Cáceres, joined
the Church. A few weeks later, Carmen called them
and Gracie de Urquizú, a woman interested in the
Church, as members of her presidency. The women
were presented at a meeting with twenty-one sisters—
their best-attended meeting yet.

Everyone there was happy and ready to learn.[21]

IN THE SPRING OF 1949, President George Albert Smith
often woke to the sound of barking seals and the rhyth-
mic churn of the Pacific Ocean. The prophet had come
to California in January to inspect the Los Angeles
Temple site. The war and relief efforts in Europe had

delayed the project, and Church leaders now wanted to move forward with construction. After a few busy days of meetings, President Smith had begun to feel ill. His condition worsened, and doctors diagnosed a blood clot in his right temple.[22]

The condition proved not to be life-threatening, but President Smith had struggled to regain his strength. When the doctors finally released him from the hospital, he remained in California to recuperate by the sea. With the April 1949 general conference quickly approaching, he was hoping to return to Salt Lake City. But whenever he sat up in bed, a terrible dizziness sent the room spinning, and he had to sink back down into his pillow.[23]

Aside from the clot, the doctors could find no clear reason for the prophet's fatigue. "My biggest trouble," he had recently concluded in his journal, "is tired nerves and overwork."[24]

For much of his adult life, President Smith had struggled with health issues like poor eyesight, digestive problems, and terrible fatigue. When he was called as an apostle at age thirty-three, he knew from experience what could happen if he pushed his body too hard. But sometimes his sense of duty and desire to work kept him from slowing down.

By 1909, six years after his call to the apostleship, he was anxious and depressed. He had no energy, and for months at a time he was confined to his bed, unable to do anything. His poor eyesight prevented him from reading for any great length of time. He felt useless and hopeless, and there were times when he wished for death. For three years, he had to step away from his regular duties in the Quorum of the Twelve Apostles.[25]

President Smith found that prayer, fresh air, a nutritious diet, and regular exercise helped him regain energy. Although he was still not completely cured of his health challenges, those difficult early years as an apostle convinced him that the Lord had a plan for his life. He found solace in a letter from his father, the apostle John Henry Smith. "The bitter experience through which you are going," it read, "is but designed for your purification and uplifting and qualification for an extended life work."[26]

President Smith had since thrown his energies into alleviating suffering, injustice, and hardship. He arranged for the first printing of the Book of Mormon in braille and organized the first Church branch for the deaf. After learning that Helmuth Hübener, the young German Saint executed by the Nazis, had been wrongly excommunicated from the Church, he and his counselors reversed the action and directed local authorities to note this fact on Helmuth's membership record. As Church president, he gave new attention to Native Americans in the United States, seeking to improve living conditions and education among them.[27]

The prophet's sympathetic heart often added to his emotional burden, though. "When things are normal, my nerves are not very strong," he once told a friend.

"And when I see other people in sorrow and depressed, I am easily affected."[28]

Doctors at the time did not understand long-term physical and mental illnesses well, often using terms like "nervous exhaustion" to describe conditions like chronic fatigue or depression. Still, President Smith did his best to manage his health, taking advantage of periods of increased energy and stamina and resting when needed. Although he had never again suffered the kind of collapse he had experienced decades earlier, old age and immense responsibilities were taxing him.[29]

On March 20, the prophet sent a letter by airmail to his counselors, recommending that they hold general conference without him. President J. Reuben Clark telephoned the next day, hopeful that President Smith would still recover in time for conference. "Let's wait until next Sunday and see how you are feeling," he said.

The following week, the prophet suffered bouts of dizziness, but he felt himself slowly gaining strength. On March 27, his doctors agreed that he was healthy enough to travel, so he soon boarded a train bound for Salt Lake City. He rested well during the journey, and when conference weekend came, he knew that the Lord had blessed him with strength.

On the second day of the conference, President Smith stood before the Saints, his heart full of love and appreciation. "Many times when I have been apparently ready to go to the other side," he said, "I have been kept for some other work to be done."

He then spoke words he had not planned to say until that moment. "I have had much happiness in life," he said. "I pray that we may all so adjust ourselves as we pass through life's experiences that we can reach out and feel that we hold our Father's hand."[30]

BACK IN PRAGUE, MISSION president Wallace Toronto waited to hear if seven new American missionaries called to serve in the Czechoslovak Mission would receive permission to enter the country. During the previous year, the number of missionaries in Czechoslovakia had grown to thirty-nine—the second-largest group of U.S. citizens in the country, exceeded only by the staff of the American embassy. Ten of the missionaries were scheduled to return home, however, and they needed to be replaced for the mission to keep up its momentum.[31]

The group of new missionaries had arrived in Europe in February 1949. Since the Czechoslovak government did not immediately issue them visas, the elders waited at the Swiss-Austrian Mission home in Basel as Wallace petitioned a top government official to let the missionaries enter the country. After weeks of waiting for a decision, Wallace learned that his pleas had been rejected.

"For the time being," the official response had read, "no more American citizens are to be admitted into Czechoslovakia for the purpose of taking up permanent residency."

The missionaries were soon reassigned to the Swiss-Austrian Mission, leaving Wallace shorthanded just as the communist government was intruding more and more on Church business. The regime now required all public lessons or sermons to be approved six weeks in advance, and communist officials often attended Church meetings to monitor the Saints for unapproved speech. The government also revoked permission to print the mission magazine, *Novy Hlas,* and threatened to reduce the Saints' rations or get them fired from their jobs if they continued attending church. Some felt pressured to spy on their fellow Church members.

Distraught Saints came to Wallace for advice, and he told them they should never feel obligated to put themselves at risk. If government agents pressured them to report on a Church meeting, they should offer just enough information to satisfy the interrogators.[32]

Despite all these troubles, some Czechoslovaks were still eager to hear the gospel message. Instead of limiting public meetings, Wallace expanded the mission's reach by holding dozens of lectures in towns across the country. The gatherings became very popular, often resulting in the sale of many copies of the Book of Mormon. One evening, in the city of Plzeň, nearly nine hundred people showed up to listen.

Such successes brought additional government scrutiny, however. In some areas, including Prague, officials denied requests to hold lectures. Not long after the meeting in Plzeň, the government refused to renew residency permits to four American missionaries in the country, alleging that they were "a threat to the public peace, order, and security of the state."

Wallace again petitioned regime officials, insisting that the missionaries had done nothing to endanger the public. He produced several positive articles about Czechoslovakia from the *Deseret News* to prove that the Saints were not enemies of the government. He also mentioned the Church's distribution of food and clothing throughout the country after the war and pointed out that the missionaries were contributing to the Czech economy.[33]

None of it made any difference. The government ordered the four missionaries to leave the country by May 15, 1949. Wallace wrote in his mission report that he feared all religious movements in Czechoslovakia would soon come under strict state control.

But he refused to give up. "It is our hope and prayer that the Lord will continue to bless His work in this land," he wrote, "no matter what the political tides of the future may bring."[34]

CHAPTER 34

Go and See

Emmy Cziep was not used to small-town life. Having grown up in a bustling European city, she was at first unimpressed by her new home in Raymond, Alberta, Canada. The town had a few stores, a sugar factory, dirt roads, and no sidewalk. As she looked it over, she thought, "Did I leave all that was ever dear to me for *this*?"

Her hosts, Heber and Valeria Allen, did all they could to make her feel welcome. She had her own bedroom on the upper level of their spacious home, and Heber gave her a job at his store, the Raymond Mercantile. Emmy knew he did not need her help, but the job let her pay back the money he and Valeria had spent on her emigration. The Allens were just one of many Latter-day Saint families in Canada helping Church members in Europe. Recently, the Allens' stake had sent fifteen thousand bags of cracked wheat to the German Saints.[1]

Several weeks after settling in Raymond, Emmy received a letter from Glenn Collette, a former missionary in the Swiss-Austrian Mission. She had first met Glenn while they were serving together in Switzerland, and they had quickly developed feelings for one another. At the time, though, they had remained focused on their missions. Glenn now lived in Idaho Falls in the United States, more than five hundred miles south of Raymond, but he wanted to know if he could visit Emmy during Christmas.

The Allens were not keen on the young man coming all that way to visit Emmy, but they agreed to it, and he spent the holiday with the family. Emmy enjoyed seeing Glenn again, and after he returned to Idaho, they wrote each other nearly every day and talked on the telephone every Saturday night.[2]

On Valentine's Day, Glenn proposed to Emmy over the phone, and she accepted. A few days later, she started to worry that they needed more time to get to know each other. She knew he was a good man who had been a hardworking missionary. He also had many friends and seemed to like children. But was it wise to marry a man she had dated mostly over the phone?

Glenn's letters were reassuring, and they helped her become better acquainted with him. "I love you with my whole being," he told her in one letter. "Whatever the future may hold for me, if I have you to share it with me, happiness and joy shall be my lot."[3]

On May 24, 1949, six months after Emmy arrived in Canada, she and Glenn said a prayer before traveling to the Cardston Temple together. Glenn was nervous and forgot the marriage license, delaying them a little. And Emmy, for her part, was missing her parents in Austria. Yet she knew they were thinking of her and that they understood the importance of the covenants she was making that day.[4]

Later, as she and Glenn knelt across the altar in the sealing room, Emmy was full of gratitude. Moving to western Canada had given her a chance to be near a temple and attend it with someone she loved. Without the restored gospel, and their commitment to its teachings, she and Glenn would have never found each other.

After a honeymoon in a nearby national park, Glenn returned to Idaho Falls while Emmy remained in Raymond to wait for approval to emigrate to the United States. One evening, about a month after her marriage, she had the chance to attend the temple with a group of missionaries.

"When I go through the temple this evening, I will think of you constantly," she told Glenn in a letter. She looked forward to the day when they would return to the house of the Lord together. "Until then," she wrote, "know that I thank you, that I love you."[5]

AROUND THIS TIME, IN Nagoya, Japan, twenty-nine-year-old Toshiko Yanagida was afraid for her life. She had just suffered a miscarriage, and afterward, her doctor had found a tumor and needed to operate. Since medical equipment was still scarce in Japan after the Second World War, the procedure was dangerous. Unsure if she would survive, Toshiko worried about her sons, three-year-old Takao and five-year-old Masashi. She wanted them to have faith in God, but she and her husband, Tokichi, had never taught them about spiritual things.[6]

Even though Toshiko was not especially religious, she believed in a higher power watching over her. Growing up, she had gone to a Protestant school and studied Shinto and Buddhism, the two most common religions in Japan. She also remembered attending a meeting of The Church of Jesus Christ of Latter-day Saints once with her father, Tomigoro Takagi, who had joined the Church in 1915. Her father did not often speak about his faith, however, because Toshiko's grandparents, who had lived with the family at the time, disapproved of the Church. And after the Japanese Mission closed in 1924, when Toshiko was five years old, Tomigoro had rarely had a chance to meet with other Saints.[7]

Toshiko's surgery was a success, and when she was strong enough to travel, she went to her parents' home near Tokyo and talked to her father about religion. "I want to go to some church," she told him.[8]

Tomigoro encouraged her to attend a Latter-day Saint service. He himself had begun attending Church meetings again. After the war, Church leaders in Salt Lake City had reached out to Japanese Saints, sending them much-needed shipments of food and clothing. The

servicemember groups also continued to provide opportunities for Japanese Church members to meet with
American Latter-day Saint soldiers. In 1948, the success
of these meetings prompted the First Presidency to once
again send missionaries to the Japanese mainland.

In fact, Tomigoro knew a missionary named Ted
Price who was serving in Narumi, two hours from
Toshiko's home. "Go and see," he said. "If you tell Elder
Price you are the daughter of Tomigoro Takagi, it will
make his day."[9]

Toshiko was a little skeptical of her father's church.
She did not know anything about its teachings and did
not like the name "Mormon." But one Sunday, a few
months after her surgery, she traveled to a small meeting
hall along a hillside in Narumi. Arriving late, she found
Elder Price teaching a large group of people about the
Book of Mormon. As she listened to their discussion,
she began to think differently about the Church. She
believed what she heard, and it gave her hope.[10]

When the meeting ended, she met Elder Price and
his companion, Danny Nelson. She liked both young
men and looked forward to hearing them speak again.
Attending church in Narumi would be difficult, though,
since traveling to and from the meeting took so much
time. And her husband was not likely to go with her.
Sunday was his only day off from work, and he refused
to take part in any religion.

But what she heard that day had kindled her faith
in the restored gospel. "If I want to give my boys the

same, my husband must change," she told herself. "So how can I do that?"[11]

WHILE TOSHIKO YANAGIDA PONDERED the future of her family, Primary general president Adele Cannon Howells was looking for a way to help little children learn about the Book of Mormon. For many years, general conference talks and Church lesson materials referenced the book only occasionally. Primary lessons also tended to emphasize Bible stories and the values the Saints shared with other Christian religions. Lately, however, Church leaders and teachers had begun using the Book of Mormon more and more, and some Saints wanted the Primary to revise its lessons to make better use of the Book of Mormon and other unique Latter-day Saint teachings.

Knowing pictures could be a powerful tool for teaching the gospel, Adele wrote to apostle Spencer W. Kimball and several Church organizations about producing an illustrated Book of Mormon storybook for children.[12]

"Your proposition is very interesting," Elder Kimball responded. But he worried that the project would be too expensive.[13]

Adele was not ready to give up on the idea yet. Since her call as Primary general president in 1943, she had carried out several ambitious projects, including two innovative children's programs. The first, *Children's Friend of the Air,* was a fifteen-minute radio show based on stories from the Primary's official magazine. The second was *Junior Council,* a weekly television program that debuted in 1948, the same year the Church televised general conference for the first time. *Junior Council* featured a panel of children who responded to a series of questions submitted by readers of the *Children's Friend* and by a live studio audience.[14]

For many years, Adele had also worked on plans to construct a new children's hospital in Salt Lake City. The Primary had been operating a hospital in the city since 1922, but the institution now needed larger, updated facilities. Church leaders broke ground for the new hospital in April 1949 on a hilltop overlooking the Salt Lake Valley. To raise the necessary funds, and to help Primary children feel involved in the building's construction, Adele devised a "buy a brick" program. For every ten cents a child donated, she or he could claim one brick in the hospital's walls.[15]

As Adele thought more about illustrating the Book of Mormon, she considered the possibility of commissioning a series of beautiful paintings for the fiftieth anniversary of the *Children's Friend.* Since the anniversary was in 1952, only three years away, she needed to find the right artist quickly for the paintings to be finished in time.[16]

Several Latter-day Saint artists had illustrated scenes from the Book of Mormon before. Decades earlier, George Reynolds, a secretary to the First Presidency, published a Book of Mormon storybook with high-quality illustrations by local artists. A short time later, he published a number of articles about the life of Nephi, illustrated by Danish artist C. C. A. Christensen.

More recently, illustrator Phil Dalby had begun drawing a series of dramatic Book of Mormon comic strips for the *Deseret News*. And Minerva Teichert, who had studied at some of the best art schools in the United States, had started an ambitious series of Book of Mormon paintings shortly after completing murals for an ordinance room in the Manti Temple. Minerva wanted her paintings to bring the Book of Mormon to life, and many of them featured brightly colored scenes of the women who often went unnamed in the work of scripture.[17]

As Adele searched for an artist, she learned about the work of Arnold Friberg, a thirty-six-year-old Latter-day Saint illustrator who had recently moved to Utah. One of his religious paintings impressed her. It depicted Richard Ballantyne, the founder of the Sunday School, sitting in front of a crackling fire, leaning forward as he taught a group of raptly attentive children. The details in the painting were meticulous, from the wood grain of the plank floor to the firelight shining on the children's faces.[18]

After further investigation, Adele decided that Arnold would be the perfect choice. He was undoubtedly talented, and he was clearly passionate about creating religious paintings. Although his commission would be expensive, Adele had the means to help pay for the paintings herself, if necessary.[19]

Convinced the project would be of great value, she described the Primary board's efforts in her diary, hoping their dream would become a reality. "May the Lord help us," she wrote.[20]

BACK IN JAPAN, TOSHIKO Yanagida was attending every Church meeting she could. On Sunday mornings, she traveled to Narumi for Sunday School. The class was taught by Tatsui Sato, a former Protestant who had been baptized with his wife, Chiyo, about a year after the war ended. Toshiko then attended sacrament meeting in the evening in another part of town. The branch held MIA meetings on Mondays for anyone who wanted to study the scriptures and play games, and soon she was attending those as well. After her operation, Toshiko had felt physically, emotionally, and financially drained. Being with the Saints lifted her spirits and gave her a new purpose in life.

Her husband, Tokichi, was not happy about her long absences. When she began leaving home more often, sometimes on short notice, he demanded that she choose between her home and her faith. "If you want to go to church that much, let's divide the children up between us," he said. "I'll take our eldest son and you can take the younger one—and you can just leave this house."[21]

Toshiko had started going to church for the sake of her sons, so she was not about to let it break up her family. But she did not want to return to her old life either. Instead, she decided to work harder at home to show Tokichi that she could devote herself to the Church without damaging their family. "Please let me keep doing this just a little longer," she pleaded with him. And both day and night she prayed that he too would come to church and share in her faith.[22]

One day, Toshiko invited Elder Price and Elder Nelson to her son Takao's birthday party. The missionaries were happy to come, despite the distance, and arrived with a gift of candy for Takao.[23]

At the party, Elder Nelson sat next to Tokichi and talked to him about the Church and missionary work. He explained that he and Elder Price paid for their missions themselves and received no money from the Church. The elders also testified of the restored gospel and what it could mean for the family. After the meal, they all played games together, and the young men prayed with the Yanagidas before returning to Narumi.[24]

"These missionaries are different," Tokichi told Toshiko later. He disliked priests who took money for their services, so he was impressed that the missionaries were willing to sacrifice so much to serve God. "They are wonderful men," he said.[25]

Two months later, in August 1949, Toshiko decided to be baptized. She traveled eight hours to Tokyo so her father could be present. Elder Price performed the baptism, and the mission president, Edward Clissold, confirmed her. Toshiko was overjoyed to finally be a member of the Church, and she could see that her father was happy too.[26]

Not long after the baptism, Tokichi had to go to Tokyo for business, so Toshiko suggested he visit the mission office and say hello to Elder Nelson, who had recently been transferred there. "If I have time" was all Tokichi said.[27]

With no telephone in their home, Toshiko had to wait three days for her husband to return with news about his trip. She wanted to know right away if he had gone to the mission home. "Did you see Nelson?" she asked.

"Yes," Tokichi said. "I was baptized by him, and the person named Elder Goya laid his hands on my head." Toshiko did not know Koojin Goya, who was one of several Japanese American missionaries from Hawaii who had been called to serve in Japan.[28]

Toshiko was astonished. Tokichi had never once gone to church with her in Narumi, but somehow the Lord had led him to be baptized.

"Banzai!" she thought. *Yes!*[29]

After Tokichi was baptized, he and Toshiko decided to attend church with the Satos at an American service-members group on a military base near their home in Nagoya. Toshiko was happy that her family could now attend church together, but their meetings were in English. Although Tatsui knew English well and could translate for the Yanagidas, Toshiko wished her family could learn about the gospel in their own language.

Before long, she wrote a letter to the new mission president, Vinal Mauss, asking if Japanese meetings could be held in Nagoya.[30]

ON NOVEMBER 6, 1949, PAUL Bang baptized his eight-year-old daughter, Sandra. It had been twenty-two years since Paul's baptism in the nearby Ohio River. During that time, he had watched the Cincinnati Branch grow into one of the strongest Latter-day Saint congregations in that region of the United States. Now he and his wife, Connie, were passing on the legacy of faith they inherited to Sandra and her younger siblings.[31]

Around a hundred Saints met each week in Cincinnati for sacrament meeting. When constructing a new meetinghouse during the war proved impossible, the branch had purchased a former Jewish synagogue and, with the help of branch president Alvin Gilliam's construction company, renovated it inside and out. The Saints had also hired an art student to paint a mural of the Savior on the wall behind the pulpit.[32]

The new chapel gave the branch plenty of space to grow. After the war, many young branch members— especially those with strong family ties to the area—had chosen to stay in Cincinnati, start families, and serve in the Church.[33] For a time, Paul had been a counselor in the branch presidency, and he was now on the district high council with his father, Christian Bang. Connie, meanwhile, led the Gleaner Girls in the branch's YWMIA.[34]

The size of the Cincinnati Branch, as well as the experience of its members, allowed it to support smaller branches in the area. Every Sunday, families from Cincinnati drove to Georgetown, a village forty miles to the east, to support a small group of Saints there.[35]

As strong as the Cincinnati Branch was, its members remained divided over racial segregation. Len and Mary Hope, the only African American couple in the branch, continued to hold monthly meetings in their home because some branch members still did not want them attending regular Church services. The gatherings had grown to as many as thirty people, including the Bangs and their extended family. Mary never knew how many people would come, but she always seemed to prepare enough food for everyone. Len conducted the meetings and chose the hymns. One of his favorites was "We Thank Thee, O God, for a Prophet."[36]

Sometimes Len's friends criticized him for belonging to a church where he could not hold the priesthood or attend services, but he and Mary remained true to their faith. Their friends in the branch watched out for them, providing priesthood blessings for family members and helping with home repairs and improvements.[37] When one of the Hopes' African American friends, Mary Louise Cates, accepted the gospel, Paul baptized her. A few years later, a member of the branch gave the Hopes' granddaughter a baby blessing.[38]

After nearly a quarter century of steadfast faith, Len and Mary had taken a trip to Utah in 1947. They stayed in the home of former Cincinnati missionary Marion Hanks, who showed them around Salt Lake City and took them to general conference. They were also welcomed into the home of Abner and Martha Howell, another Black couple in the Church. The trip and the kind treatment they received delighted the Hopes. Now, two years later, Len's health was declining, and he wanted to move to Utah and be buried there someday.[39]

Not long after Sandra Bang's baptism, the district presidency called Paul to serve as president of a small branch in Hamilton, a city north of Cincinnati. A short time later, Connie was called to be the Cincinnati Branch Relief Society secretary. Her patriarchal blessing had urged her to be a willing worker in the kingdom of God, and she and Paul had tried to be just that. All along the way, they had seen the Lord's blessings.[40]

Through the patriarch, the Lord had also promised Connie that her father, George Taylor, would share in the joy of the gospel. For many years, Connie had no reason to think her father would ever embrace the Church. Then, after the war, cancer attacked his already failing body. He began attending church with Connie's mother, Adeline, worshipping with the Saints until his death in 1947.

After he died, George appeared to Adeline in a dream. He looked sickly and downhearted, and he still walked with the limp he had carried for years. The dream confused Adeline, and she asked a Church leader what it meant. He told her that George wanted his temple work done.

So Adeline traveled to Utah to receive her temple blessings and arrange for George to receive his. She was sealed to him by proxy on September 28, 1949, in the Salt Lake Temple. Sometime after that, George came again to her in a dream. This time he was happy and healthy, free of the maladies that had hampered him in life.

He took her in his arms, and they danced.[41]

CHAPTER 35

We Cannot Fail

As 1950 dawned, the Cold War between the United States and the Soviet Union was intensifying. Under Soviet influence, new communist governments across central and eastern Europe were closing their borders and changing their social and economic ways of life. At the same time, several western European countries were aligning with the United States and Canada to defend themselves against possible attacks from communist countries. And a race to build and stockpile weapons had begun after the Soviet Union carried out its first successful nuclear weapons test, startling the world with the detonation of a bomb like those the United States had used against Japan in the war.[1]

In Czechoslovakia, mission leaders Wallace and Martha Toronto prepared for possible expulsion. The country's communist government, which continued to keep a close eye on them and their missionaries, had recently passed a law restricting religious freedom and forbidding foreigners from serving as religious leaders in the nation. The number of Latter-day Saint missionaries forced out of the country had now grown to twelve, and it was only a matter of time before the regime expelled the rest.

Wallace wrote to the First Presidency about the crisis, and they advised him to send his family and most of the remaining missionaries out of Czechoslovakia. Yet President George Albert Smith and his counselors still hoped that Wallace and one or two elders serving as assistants might get permission to remain.

"You have been loyal and fearless," the First Presidency told him. "For your divine guidance we shall continue to petition the Lord and rely upon His over-ruling power to protect and prosper His Church in that choice land."[2]

On Monday, January 30, members of the Prostějov Branch informed Wallace that two missionaries serving in their city, Stanley Abbott and Aldon Johnson, had not shown up for Sunday School the previous day. At first the Saints assumed the missionaries had either missed their train or were delayed by heavy snow. But the branch members had since learned that the elders' apartment had been searched and that the secret police had interrogated a local Latter-day Saint. Now everyone feared the worst.

Wallace contacted the American embassy and immediately left for Prostějov. Through diplomatic channels, he learned that the elders had been imprisoned for trying to visit a Church member in a labor camp.

As days turned to weeks, the Czechoslovak government refused to communicate directly with Wallace. Local police in Prostějov forbade the Saints from holding meetings in town, and some members of the branch were questioned and harassed. By February 20, Wallace had overseen the evacuation of eleven more missionaries, but no one from the mission had been allowed to visit or speak with Elder Abbott or Elder Johnson.

The imprisoned missionaries were kept separate from each other, with Elder Abbott held in solitary confinement. The prison gave the missionaries a chunk of black bread in the morning and a bowl of soup at night. They could not bathe or change their clothes. During interrogations, the secret police threatened to beat them with iron rods and imprison them for years if they did not confess to being spies.[3]

On February 24, Martha answered a telephone call from the American ambassador. The Czechoslovak government had relocated the imprisoned missionaries to Prague and was willing to release them if they promised to leave the country within two hours. Martha quickly booked two tickets on an airplane bound for Switzerland. She then contacted Wallace, and they agreed to meet at the airport, where the missionaries would be delivered.

At the airport, Wallace only had time to give the missionaries their tickets and some instructions. Martha, meanwhile, stood on an observation deck nearby. When she saw the police escort the two young men to a plane, she waved to them. The elders looked thin and unkempt, and she called out to ask if they were all right.

"Yes," they replied, waving back. They then boarded the aircraft, and Martha watched as the plane disappeared into the bleak clouds hanging over the city.[4]

In the days that followed, Martha hurried to prepare for her family's evacuation. She planned to travel alone with the six children, including an infant son, while Wallace remained in Czechoslovakia as long as the government allowed it.

The day before their departure, the family was eating lunch when men in leather jackets came to the mission home and demanded to speak with Wallace. Right away Martha knew they were the secret police. She was already sick and emotionally exhausted, and their presence only made her feel worse. After what had happened to the missionaries, and to many Czechoslovak citizens, she had no idea what the police might do to her husband.

"Martha, I have to go with these men," Wallace said. He was sure they wanted to question him about the recently expelled missionaries. "In case I don't come back," he said, "take the children as planned tomorrow morning and get them home."

The hours ticked by with no word from Wallace, and it seemed that Martha would have to leave without knowing what happened to her husband. Then, seven hours after the police had taken him away, Wallace returned home in time to take his family to the train.

At the station, a crowd of Church members gathered, carrying packages filled with fruit, baked goods, and sandwiches for Martha and the children. Some Saints handed the food through the windows of the train as it began to pull away. Others ran along the platform and threw kisses. Martha watched them, her eyes full of tears, until the train rounded a bend and they were out of sight.[5]

"PRESIDENT MAUSS IS COMING to Nagoya. Can you go and meet him?"

The missionaries' question surprised Toshiko Yanagida. She had been waiting to hear from the new president of the Japanese Mission ever since she wrote him about bringing a Japanese-language branch to her hometown of Nagoya. President Mauss had never written back, so she was unsure if he had received the letter.[6]

Toshiko agreed to go, and she and the missionaries met President Mauss at the railway station a short time later. As soon as he arrived, she asked him if he had read her letter. "I have," he said. "That is why I came." He wanted her to help him find a place to hold Church meetings in town. Toshiko was thrilled.[7]

They began their search at once. There were not many Saints in Nagoya—only the missionaries, Toshiko's family, and a woman named Yoshie Adachi in a city of six hundred thousand people—so they did not need much space to meet. Yet President Mauss decided to rent a lecture hall in a large school in the city.

The Nagoya Saints held their first Sunday School meeting in January 1950. To attract more people, Toshiko and the missionaries placed flyers in a local newspaper. The next Sunday, 150 people showed up at the lecture hall. Latter-day Saint meetings often drew crowds in postwar Japan as many people sought hope and meaning after the trauma they had experienced.[8] But for most, interest in the Church was temporary, especially as the country grew more economically stable. As fewer people felt a need to turn to faith, attendance at the meetings declined.[9]

For their part, Toshiko and her husband, Tokichi, struggled with aspects of being Latter-day Saints—especially paying tithing. Tokichi did not make much money, and sometimes they wondered if they had enough to pay for their son's school lunch. They were also hoping to buy a house.

After one Church meeting, Toshiko asked a missionary about tithing. "Japanese people are very poor now after the war," she said. "Tithing is so hard for us. Must we pay?"[10]

The elder replied that God commanded everyone to pay tithes, and he spoke of the blessings of obeying the principle. Toshiko was skeptical—and a little angry. "This is American thinking," she told herself.

Other missionaries encouraged her to have faith. One sister missionary promised Toshiko that paying tithing could help her family reach their goal of owning their own house. Wanting to be obedient, Toshiko and Tokichi decided to pay their tithing and trust that blessings would come.[11]

Around this time, the sister missionaries began holding informal Relief Society meetings in their apartment for Toshiko and other women in the area. They shared gospel messages, discussed practical ways to care for their homes, and learned to cook inexpensive foods. Like Relief Societies in other parts of the world, they held bazaars, where they sold chocolate and other goods to raise money for their activities. About a year after the Nagoya Saints started holding meetings, a Relief Society was formally organized, with Toshiko as president.[12]

She and Tokichi also began to see blessings come from paying tithing. They purchased an affordable lot in the city and drew up blueprints for a house. They then applied for a home loan through a new government program, and once they received approval to build, they started work on a foundation.

The process went smoothly until a building inspector noticed that their lot was inaccessible to firefighters. "This land is not land that is suitable for building a house," he told them. "You cannot proceed any further with the construction."

Unsure what to do, Toshiko and Tokichi spoke to the missionaries. "The six of us will fast and pray for you," an elder told them. "You do the same."

For the next two days, the Yanagidas fasted and prayed with the missionaries. Another inspector then came out to reassess their lot. He had a reputation for being strict, and at first he gave the Yanagidas little hope of passing the inspection. But as he looked over the lot, he noticed a solution. In an emergency, the fire department could get to the property simply by removing a nearby fence. The Yanagidas could build their house after all.

"I guess you two must have done something exceptionally good in the past," the inspector told them. "In all my years I have never been so accommodating."

Toshiko and Tokichi were overjoyed. They had fasted and prayed and paid their tithing. And just as the sister missionary had promised, they would have a home of their own.[13]

IN EARLY 1951, DAVID O. McKay was grappling with challenges facing the Church's missionary program. During the past six months, he had watched from afar as another worldwide conflict erupted, this time in eastern Asia. Backed by China and the Soviet Union, communist North Korea was at war with South Korea. Fearing the spread of communism, the United States and other allies had sent troops to support the South Koreans in their fight.[14]

At the time, the Church had about five thousand full-time missionaries, nearly all of whom came from the United States, and hundreds of new missionaries were being called every month.[15] But the war in Korea had created a new demand for soldiers, and the U.S. government was once again drafting young men nineteen to twenty-six years old—the very age group from which the Church drew most of its missionaries. After careful consideration, the First Presidency temporarily lowered the missionary age from twenty to nineteen, giving young men a chance to serve a mission before they faced the temptations found in military life, should they be drafted.[16]

As the counselor in the First Presidency who oversaw missionary work, President McKay soon faced pressure from many sides. He sometimes received letters from Saints who accused leaders of showing favoritism by recommending some young men for missions, thus allowing them to defer military service, while leaving others to be drafted. Local citizens and draft boards, meanwhile, accused the Church of neglecting its patriotic duty by continuing to call young men as missionaries.[17]

Church leaders did not see it that way. They had long encouraged Saints to answer the call of their country whenever it came.[18] Still, after consulting with draft officials in Utah, the First Presidency made further changes to the existing policy. For the duration of the war, they decided, young men eligible for military service would no longer be called on full-time missions. Calls would be limited to unmarried women and older men, married couples, veterans, and young men ineligible for military service. The Church also called more senior couples to serve missions.[19]

That winter, while President McKay negotiated with draft board officials, President George Albert Smith's health began to fail. President McKay visited the prophet on his birthday, April 4, and found him near death, surrounded by family. Full of emotion, President McKay blessed the prophet only hours before he passed away.[20]

Two days later, President McKay opened the first session of April 1951 general conference. Standing at the Tabernacle podium, he spoke of President Smith's exemplary life. "His was a noble soul," he told the congregation, "happiest when he could make others happy."

Later in the conference, the Saints sustained David O. McKay as the president of the Church, with Stephen L Richards and J. Reuben Clark as his counselors. "No one can preside over this Church without first being in tune with the head of the Church, our Lord and Savior, Jesus Christ," President McKay told the Saints as he closed the conference. "Without His divine guidance and constant inspiration, we cannot succeed. With His guidance, with His inspiration, we cannot fail."[21]

As the new prophet looked to the future, he had decades of experience to guide him. Many people believed his tall, dignified bearing, piercing eyes, and white hair helped him look like a prophet. His sense of humor, love of people, and closeness to the Spirit also endeared him to men and women in and out of the Church. His years as a teacher and school principal were still evident in his personality. He was calm and decisive under pressure and an engaging speaker who often quoted poetry in his sermons. When he was not on Church assignments, he was usually working on his family farm in Huntsville, Utah.

Many matters weighed on President McKay's mind as his presidency began. During his apostolic ministry, he had often spoken about the sacredness of marriage, family, and education, and his ongoing attention to these priorities helped him guide the Church down the right path. The end of the Second World War had brought about a "baby boom" in the United States as soldiers returned home, married, and settled into domestic life. With the help of government aid, many of these men had enrolled in universities to gain an education and receive vital career training. President McKay was eager to offer them support.[22]

He was also concerned about the horrors of the Korean War and the spread of communism in certain parts of the world. At the time, many government and religious leaders were speaking out against communism. Like them, President McKay believed communist regimes suppressed religion and curtailed liberty.

"The Church of Christ stands for the influence of love," he declared shortly after general conference, "which is eventually the only power that will bring to mankind redemption and peace."[23]

THAT SPRING, IN SALT Lake City, Primary general president Adele Cannon Howells knew her health was giving out. She was only sixty-five years old, but a bout with rheumatic fever as a child had damaged her heart. Despite her condition, she refused to stop working.[24]

Her plan to commission a series of Book of Mormon paintings for the fiftieth anniversary of the *Children's Friend* was finally moving forward. While not everyone thought hiring a professionally trained artist like Arnold Friberg was the best use of time or money, Adele believed the paintings would spark children's interest in the Book of Mormon and be well worth the expense.[25]

Over the last two years, she had gained support from the Sunday School and convinced members of the Quorum of the Twelve Apostles that the paintings would be worthwhile. Adele and Sunday School officials put together a committee to oversee the project and forwarded some of Arnold's sketches to President McKay and his counselors.[26]

In January 1951, Adele and a representative from the Sunday School met with the First Presidency to discuss the proposal.[27] Both she and Arnold wanted to depict Book of Mormon stories that were full of spiritual power and compelling action, such as Helaman's stripling warriors marching off to battle and Samuel the Lamanite prophesying of the Savior's birth. Arnold did not want the paintings done in a childish style. He believed children needed to see the word of God as powerful and majestic. He wanted the Book of Mormon heroes to appear physically powerful, almost larger than life. "The muscularity in my paintings is only an expression of the spirit within," he later explained.[28]

The First Presidency agreed with Adele that Arnold was the right artist for the job.[29] The Sunday School and the Church-owned Deseret Book Company committed to pay two-thirds of the initial cost, and Adele covered the other third out of her own pocket.[30] In the months that followed, she and Arnold made plans for the paintings as her health continued to deteriorate. Before long, she was confined to a bed.[31]

On the night of April 13, Adele arranged to sell some of her property to pay for the paintings.[32] She also called Marion G. Romney, an assistant to the Quorum of the Twelve Apostles, to discuss the Book of Mormon and the children of the Church. She spoke about the paintings and her desire to have them finished in the coming year. She said she hoped all the children in the Church would begin reading the Book of Mormon early in life.

The following afternoon, Adele passed away. At her funeral, Elder Romney paid tribute to the creative and energetic woman who had given so freely to the Primary organization. "She greatly loved the Primary work," he said. "Every person she touched felt the depth of her love for them individually."[33]

A short time later, Arnold Friberg began his first Book of Mormon painting: *The Brother of Jared Sees the Finger of the Lord.*[34]

NEAR THE CITY OF Valence in southeast France, Jeanne Charrier went on a walk with her cousin. Nestled alongside the Rhône River, Valence was a beautiful place with a centuries-old Roman Catholic cathedral. While many of the people in the city were Catholic, Jeanne's family members were among the few Protestants. Going back generations, they had risked their reputations and even their lives for their beliefs.[35]

Jeanne had grown up a devoted Christian, but more recently, during her university studies in mathematics and philosophy, she encountered ideas that led her to doubt her faith. She pondered the famous words of French philosopher René Descartes—"I think, therefore I am." The insight only brought more questions. She thought, "I am where, how, and why?"

Some time before Jeanne's hillside walk, her questions had led her to kneel and seek the Lord. "God," she prayed, "if you exist, I'm waiting for an answer."[36]

Jeanne and her cousin had not brought anything to drink on their walk and soon became thirsty. They saw a small group of people and decided to ask for some water. An older man and woman were glad to help, and they introduced themselves as Léon and Claire Fargier. They were members of The Church of Jesus Christ of

Latter-day Saints, and the two young men with them were missionaries. The group offered Jeanne and her cousin a pamphlet about the Church, and Léon invited them to an upcoming mission conference and a concert by a string quartet from Brigham Young University.[37]

Jeanne was curious and decided to attend. At the conference, someone gave her a Book of Mormon. Once she returned home and started reading it, she could not stop. "This is really something," she thought.[38]

After that, Jeanne began to spend more time with the Fargiers. Léon and Claire had been married for thirteen years when they were baptized into the Church in 1932. Before the Second World War, Léon had served as a missionary and led Sunday meetings for the tiny group of Saints from Valence and Grenoble, a town over forty miles away.[39] Once the war began and the American missionaries evacuated, Léon had overseen a much larger area. He traveled all over France, blessing the sick and administering the sacrament. Some days he managed to catch a train between towns, but most often he walked or rode his bicycle, sometimes for hours a day.[40]

When they met Jeanne, Léon and Claire were local missionaries in the Valence Branch. Struggling to rebuild after the war's devastation, the small congregation met in a boardinghouse. Despite the humble circumstances, Jeanne was drawn to the meetings and eager to learn more about the gospel. She asked for more books and was given a copy of the Doctrine and Covenants. As she read the book, she could not deny the power of its words.

"This is true," she concluded. "It is not possible otherwise."[41]

Before long, Jeanne wanted to be baptized, but she worried about how her family would react. They were bitterly opposed to the Church, and she knew they would never support her choice. For a time, she felt torn between her faith and her family, and she put off committing to baptism. Then she remembered what Peter and the other New Testament apostles had said on the day of Pentecost: "We ought to obey God rather than men."

Their words rang in her head, and she knew what she had to do. On a beautiful day in May 1951, she waded into a hot spring in the Cévennes mountains and was baptized by Léon Fargier. She wanted her parents to be there with her, but their hostility to the restored gospel was too strong, and she decided to keep the baptism a secret.[42]

Her family soon found out, however, and wanted nothing more to do with her. Jeanne took their rejection hard. She was young—only twenty-five years old—and she wondered if she might be better off moving to the United States and joining the Saints there.[43] But the Fargiers implored her to stay. There were only nine hundred Saints in all of France, Belgium, and French-speaking Switzerland, and they needed her help to build up the Church in Valence.[44]

EIGHT HUNDRED AND FIFTY miles away, in Brno, Czechoslovakia, Terezie Vojkůvková opened a package from her friend Martha Toronto, who had arrived safely home in the United States. Inside, Terezie found clothes for her family, and she was immensely grateful. Her family was barely getting by ever since her husband, Otakar Vojkůvka, had lost his bookbinding business two years earlier. Communist officials had seized the company and arrested Otakar, who was a successful businessman and the president of the Brno Branch. After enduring six months in a labor camp, he now earned a pitiful wage as a factory worker.

Terezie wrote Martha to thank her for the package. "Rent is high, and the upkeep of our place costs a great deal," she told her friend. "Sickness has taken its share of the income, and so there has been little left with which to clothe the family."[45]

In the same letter, Terezie mentioned the new restrictions she and other Czechoslovak Saints endured under the communist government. A few weeks after Martha fled the country, her husband, Wallace, had been forced to follow her. Soon after that, the communist government ordered the acting mission president, a Czechoslovak Saint named Rudolf Kubiska, to dissolve the mission. Saints across the country were also ordered to stop holding public meetings.

Unsure how to respond to the government's actions, some Saints wondered if they should allow the government to appoint Church leaders so they could continue holding meetings, as was happening in other denominations. The mission presidency, however, felt that such an arrangement was out of the question.

Terezie missed attending weekly Church meetings. "The Sundays are long and without spirit when we cannot share our feelings and testimonies with others," she wrote Martha.

Still, she did not feel forsaken. As a member of the Communist Party, President Kubiska had political connections, which shielded the Czechoslovak Saints from the extreme harassment and persecution some other religious groups suffered. With some final instructions from President Toronto, he and his counselors had also quietly carried out a simple plan to continue worship services.[46]

They instructed the Saints how to worship at home. Every individual and family was to pray, study the scriptures, set aside tithes and offerings, and learn the gospel from whatever Church materials they had available, including recent issues of the *Improvement Era* that the Torontos had carefully censored to remove any criticism of communism. Once a month, small groups of Saints could gather at someone's home to take the sacrament. When possible, priesthood quorums were to meet privately, and branch and mission leaders would try to visit the Saints.

As a precaution, the mission presidency did not write these instructions down but instead spread them by word of mouth. Going without public meetings helped many of the Czechoslovak Saints realize how precious their Church membership was. They grew spiritually, and, despite the risk, a few of them continued to share the gospel with their friends. Some people were even baptized amid the oppression.[47]

With the help of Saints in the United States, Terezie arranged for her parents' temple work to be done. She wished that she and her family could go to the temple themselves and be sealed together. "The members of the Church in Zion, I dare venture to say, do not appreciate the great privilege they have to live so close to the temple of the Lord," she wrote to Martha.

"Will there ever be the much-desired peace among men on the face of the earth?" she further reflected in the letter. "If we could only love one another—all of us—and if only war and hate could cease!"[48]

CHAPTER 36

Carefully and Prayerfully

Clemencia Pivaral glanced at a clock as her train pulled out of Guatemala City Central Station. It was eight o'clock in the morning on October 10, 1951. Far off in the distance, gray clouds darkened the sky, threatening rain. But above the station, the skies were clear and sunny. It was a good day, Clemencia thought. She and her twelve-year-old son, Rodrigo, were starting a two-thousand-mile journey with two other Guatemalan Saints. Their destination was a large conference of Spanish-speaking Saints at the temple in Mesa, Arizona.[1]

For the last seven years, hundreds of Saints from Mexico, Central America, and the western United States had gathered annually in Mesa to attend a conference and do temple work. Most of the Saints who came to the event had saved for years to have enough money for the trip. Three Arizona stakes hosted them when they arrived, with local members housing the visitors and preparing meals so their guests could spend more time in the temple. To offset the cost of the conference, the Spanish-speaking Saints charged admission to two performances of a talent show and *The Time Is Come,* a genealogy-themed play written by Ivie Jones, the wife of the Spanish-American Mission president.[2]

This was Clemencia's first time attending the conference. She had met the missionaries in early 1950, shortly after district president John O'Donnal sent a pair of elders to her hometown, Quetzaltenango, Guatemala's second-largest city. Clemencia was a twenty-nine-year-old widow, and the elders and sisters who taught her were happy when she quickly embraced their lessons on baptisms for the dead, temples, and other gospel principles. A few months later, she found work as a teacher of blind, deaf, and nonverbal students in Guatemala City, so she and her son moved there and began attending church with the O'Donnals and other members of the Guatemala City Branch.[3]

One day, while Clemencia was studying the Doctrine and Covenants at the branch meetinghouse, Mexican Mission president Lucian Mecham asked her if she was a member of the Church. "No," she replied. "The missionaries have not yet asked me if I want to be baptized."

President Mecham interviewed her immediately, asking her if she believed in everything the missionaries had taught her. She told him she did.

"If you are ready to be baptized," he said, "how about tomorrow?"

"Yes!" she replied.[4]

Now, more than a year later, she was on her way to the temple to receive her endowment. The Church in Guatemala was still small, with fewer than seventy members. Only a few Guatemalans had received their temple blessings, including Carmen O'Donnal, who had been endowed and sealed in the Salt Lake Temple the year after her baptism.[5] Clemencia was glad to be making the trip. The oppressive heat on the train made her drowsy, but as she watched the lush scenery of Guatemala's coast outside her window, nothing could dampen her spirits.

She and the other Saints on the train passed the time by reading their scriptures and discussing the gospel. Clemencia also met a woman who seemed eager to talk about religion. After they shared their beliefs with one another, Clemencia gave her a copy of *La verdad restaurada,* a missionary pamphlet by apostle John A. Widtsoe. She invited her to attend church the next time she was in Guatemala City.[6]

After arriving in Mexico City, Clemencia and the other Guatemalan Saints joined a group of Mexican Church members on their way to the conference. They traveled north for three days in a van, singing as they went, and finally arrived in Mesa on October 20. There the Guatemalan Saints met up with John and Carmen O'Donnal, who had traveled to the United States earlier in the month for a vacation.[7]

The first days of the conference were filled with meetings and temple preparation. Ordinance work began on October 23, the third day of the conference. A huge crowd turned out for the first endowment session of the day, and the ordinance took six hours to complete. Clemencia received her endowment and then, on the following day, she received the ordinance for her maternal grandmother, who had died when Clemencia was a little girl. Later that day, Clemencia and Ralph Brown, the missionary who had baptized her, acted as proxies in the sealing of her grandparents.[8]

After the conference, Clemencia and her son traveled to Salt Lake City with the O'Donnals. They visited Temple Square, and Clemencia and the O'Donnals attended more endowment sessions. John also met with Church leaders about building a chapel and mission home in Guatemala City.[9]

The work of the Lord was expanding in Central America, and soon Guatemala and its neighboring countries would have a mission of their own.

ON JANUARY 15, 1952, JOHN Widtsoe submitted a report to the First Presidency on European Latter-day Saint emigration. Thousands of Saints had fled their homelands since the end of the war, and the presidency had asked John to keep track of the movement and well-being of the emigrants. While some of these Saints had moved to South America, Africa, or Australia, most had settled in the United States or Canada, often with the encouragement and help of missionaries and other Saints.

Although it was good news that the emigrating Church members had found safe harbors, John and other leaders were concerned about how the loss of these Saints would affect Europe's struggling branches. If the Church was to grow on the continent, it needed the Saints to remain in their own countries. But what could persuade them to stay—especially when so many challenges surrounded them?

Eighteen months earlier, John had raised this question at a conference of European mission leaders in Copenhagen, Denmark. During the meeting, several mission presidents agreed that the European Saints were emigrating because they were terrified of another war breaking out, and they longed for the stability and support they could find in the Church in North America.

"We lost twenty-eight members during the air raids in Hamburg alone, and the people remember that," one mission president had told John. "I don't know how we can stop the people from wanting to go to America."

"You can't," another mission president said. "The people would swim the ocean if they could."

John was surprised that Saints were leaving even Denmark, which had experienced fewer hardships than many other European countries during the war. He asked the presidents what could be done.

"I think if we had a temple in Europe," a mission president suggested, "we could stop it quite a bit."

The idea was inspired. With John's endorsement, the mission presidents recommended that the First Presidency approve plans for a temple in Europe. "One thing is certain," John told the men. "We can't convert the whole world and bring them to America." Instead, the Church could bring temples to the world.[10]

At the time John submitted his report on emigration, the First Presidency had not made any announcements about building a temple in Europe. But they had already authorized John to oversee a committee on translating the temple endowment into several European languages. Since the ordinance was available only in English and Spanish, Saints who spoke other languages participated without fully understanding the words of the ceremony.

The committee had recruited several European Saints, including Pieter Vlam from the Netherlands, to do the translations, which would be used in special sessions in the existing temples. But if the Church built a temple in Europe, it could provide ordinances in multiple languages to Saints from many nations.[11]

A few months after receiving John's report, President McKay spoke to the Quorum of the Twelve Apostles about emigration. After acknowledging the need to strengthen the European branches, the prophet mentioned that the president of the British Mission had recently urged him to build a temple in Great Britain.

"The brethren of the First Presidency considered it carefully and prayerfully," President McKay told the

Twelve, "and have now come to the conclusion that if we build a temple in Great Britain, we should at the same time build one in Switzerland." During the two world wars, Switzerland had remained neutral, giving it political stability. The country was also near the center of western Europe.

After President McKay finished speaking, John said, "The people in Great Britain and foreign-speaking missions are dreaming of a time when a temple will be erected in Europe." He voiced his full support for the First Presidency's plan, and everyone in the room agreed that the Church should proceed with building the temples.[12]

MEANWHILE, ACROSS THE ATLANTIC, the city of Berlin was at the center of the Cold War. In 1949, Germany had split into two nations. The Soviet-occupied eastern region had become a new communist state, the German Democratic Republic (GDR) or East Germany. The remainder of the country became the Federal Republic of Germany, or West Germany. Although Berlin was in the GDR, the west side of the city had been under the control of France, Great Britain, and the United States when the country split. Now the city was divided as well, east and west, between communist and democratic powers.[13]

Traveling between East and West Berlin did not normally pose a problem. But that spring, border officials stopped twenty-one-year-old Henry Burkhardt on his way to the headquarters of the East German Mission in the Allied Zone. Henry was a missionary from the GDR serving as a district president in Thuringia, a state southwest of Berlin. He had entered West Berlin many times before, but this time the officials found that he was carrying his district's yearly reports, including tithing lists. And the sight of the financial records alarmed them. The East German economy was sluggish, and the country's leaders had forbidden its citizens from sending or carrying money into West Germany.

As a mission leader in the GDR, Henry knew he had to follow the new restrictions carefully, so he always deposited tithing money in an East German bank. His effort to carry the reports out of the country was enough to raise the officers' suspicions, though, and they detained him at once.

Henry remained in custody for three days before the officers determined that he had done nothing wrong. They released him, but not before forbidding him from delivering the reports to the mission office.[14]

About a month later, Henry returned to West Berlin to attend a Church conference. Although East German citizens were technically free to worship as they pleased, the government was wary of outside influences on its people, including foreign religions. Since the GDR had expelled non-German religious leaders from its borders, North American missionaries in the East German Mission were confined to West Berlin. All other mission work in the country fell to East Germans like Henry.

After the conference ended, the mission president, Arthur Glaus, asked Henry to be the Church's official recordkeeper in the GDR and to serve as a liaison between mission headquarters and the East German branches. Henry understood that he would be released as the district president in Thuringia soon after the conference so he could devote himself to these new duties. But he also learned from the mission office that he might be called as the district president in Berlin or maybe a counselor in the mission presidency.

"Well," he thought, "whatever happens, it is the will of the Lord."[15]

Henry was still serving as district president in Thuringia two months later when President David O. McKay came to Europe on his first international tour since becoming Church president. The prophet and his wife, Emma Ray McKay, were spending six weeks in Great Britain, the Netherlands, Denmark, Sweden, Norway, Finland, Switzerland, France, and Germany. Although one former mission president had advised him not to come to Berlin, fearing it would be dangerous to travel through the GDR, he came anyway. The city was a place where Saints from both sides of divided Germany could meet together.[16]

President McKay arrived in Berlin on June 27, 1952, and during his visit, he and President Glaus asked to meet with Henry. President McKay started the interview by asking him a few questions about himself. Then the prophet said, "Are you willing to serve as a counselor in the mission presidency?"[17]

Although Henry was expecting new responsibilities, the request hit him like a thunderclap. He would be the only East German counselor in the mission presidency, not just a liaison between the mission president and the Saints in the GDR. With the government refusing to recognize the legitimacy of foreign religious leaders, he would be, in effect, the presiding Church authority over more than sixty branches in the country. If East German officials had any issues with the Church, they would come to him.

The call made Henry anxious. He had been a member of the Church all his life, but he was still young and inexperienced. He was also shy around others. Yet he did not voice these concerns. The Lord's prophet had just issued him a calling, so he accepted it.

Less than two weeks later, Henry moved to the city of Leipzig to open a small mission office. The work kept him busy, and he tried hard to build relationships with local government and priesthood leaders. But the new responsibilities were a strain, and he soon began losing sleep.

"Why was I the person called to do this work?" he asked himself.[18]

AFTER SPENDING A WEEK with the Saints and missionaries in Germany, President and Sister McKay traveled to

Switzerland for a second time on their tour. Unbeknownst to most Saints, the prophet had come to Europe to select sites for the British and Swiss temples. In England, he had selected a site in Newchapel, Surrey, just south of London. He had then gone to Bern, the capital of Switzerland, and chosen a site for a temple there. After continuing on to the Netherlands, however, he had learned that his choice for the Swiss Temple site had been purchased by another party. Now they had to start their search over again.[19]

On July 3, Samuel and Lenora Bringhurst, the Swiss-Austrian Mission leaders, met the McKays at the Zurich airport. The party drove to Bern, where they looked over several properties for sale. On the outskirts of town, in a village called Zollikofen, they stopped at a train station. President McKay looked to his left and pointed to the crest of a hill near a forest. Could that property be obtained? he wondered. Samuel replied that it was not for sale.[20]

The next morning President McKay continued his search. He found a large plot not far from the Bern Branch meetinghouse. It was a good setting for a temple, and he authorized Samuel to purchase the property at once. His work accomplished, the prophet left Bern the next day, moving on to the last leg of his tour. He spoke to large crowds in Basel and Paris before returning home to Salt Lake City in late July.[21]

Soon after President McKay's return, the First Presidency announced the plan to build a temple in Switzerland. French and Swiss Saints were ecstatic. "It gives tangible and convincing proof," read one article in *L'Étoile,* the Church's French periodical, "that the Church wishes to remain in Europe and continually develop the branches of the European missions."[22]

But there was trouble in Bern. Samuel was unable to finalize the purchase of the temple site. The property was part of an estate controlled by thirty heirs, some of whom objected to the sale. In mid-November, Samuel wrote President McKay to say that the property was no longer available.

The prophet called Samuel the next day on the telephone. "President Bringhurst," he said, "is there a sinister force opposing us?"

Samuel did not know the answer. "They merely told us they have changed their minds," he said.

Samuel described two other properties. One of them was the property near Zollikofen that President McKay had pointed to during his visit. Samuel said it was an ideal location, tucked away from noise and traffic and yet just a four-minute walk from the streetcar. And it had recently been put on the market for sale.

During the conversation, Samuel was silent about his own spiritual impressions. He and Lenora had been praying about which of the two properties to recommend to President McKay. Earlier that week, they visited the property near Zollikofen one last time. As they walked across the land, they had a peaceful feeling that the Lord wanted the site for a temple.

"Surely this is the place," Samuel had said to Lenora.

"I feel the same way about it," she agreed.[23]

After speaking with Samuel, President McKay consulted with his counselors, who recommended that the Church buy the property. He then called Samuel back and authorized the purchase.

A week later, after the transaction was completed, President McKay wrote the mission president, thanking him for his efforts.

"After five months' negotiations for the former site, all efforts failed, and when this property came on the market the deal was closed within one week!" the prophet marveled. "Surely the Lord has had a directing hand in this."[24]

AROUND THIS TIME, JOHN Widtsoe published *In a Sunlit Land,* a memoir spanning his birth in Norway to his recent service in the Quorum of the Twelve Apostles. He had written the book for his family, but at his friends' urging, he had reluctantly agreed to publish it for a wider audience. He dedicated the book to his posterity and to "the courageous youth" of the Church.[25]

John, now eighty years old, was starting to feel his age. A few years earlier, a small hemorrhage in his eye had damaged his sight, forcing him to read with a magnifying glass. He continued to keep a busy schedule until he started having severe lower back pain. He began meeting regularly with his doctor, who diagnosed him with cancer.

Because of his age, doctors did not want to operate on him. John knew he was dying, but he did not stop working. He started relying more and more on his wife, Leah. "I have enjoyed a rich life," he told G. Homer Durham, his daughter Eudora's husband, "and I am willing to live and serve as long as the Lord permits."[26]

John was now ten years older than his mother, Anna, had been when she passed away. If he had achieved any distinction in his long life, it was because of her choice to join the Church in Norway, encourage his education, and nurture his faith. Anna too had rarely slowed down. In the years before her death, she had frequently counseled other immigrants as they settled in Zion.

John still remembered how one newly arrived convert had come to her complaining bitterly about the Church and Saints in Utah. "We have come here to build up Zion," Anna promptly reminded him, "not to tear it down." The convert had taken Anna's words to heart, and they changed the course of his life.

John himself had spent much of his life building up the Church, with Leah at his side. Their efforts to strengthen the Church in Europe and train its leaders had helped the European Saints weather the Second World War and navigate its tumultuous aftermath. Now the faith and diligence of those Saints would be rewarded with the construction of two temples.[27]

The new temples would anchor the Church in Europe and advance another work John loved:

genealogy. After the war, in fact, the Church had begun an ambitious program of photographing birth and death records in European archives and parishes, making available millions of new names for temple work.[28]

Since returning from their mission, John and Leah had also built up the Church through writing. Together they published *The Word of Wisdom: A Modern Interpretation,* which drew on their faith in revelation and their scientific understanding of nutrition to promote greater health among readers. Beginning in 1935, John became editor of the *Improvement Era* and wrote a regular column called "Evidences and Reconciliations," which answered gospel questions submitted by readers. He eventually collected the columns into several popular books.[29]

John's health worsened as the year progressed. Leah bore his illness with dignity, although it was hard for her to believe that her husband of more than fifty years would soon be gone. She and John had been loving companions and the best of friends. As she watched his health fade, her testimony of the restored gospel gave her strength, as it had when their son Marsel died.

"I don't know what people do who do not have our understanding of life hereafter, with its continuation of family relations and joys," she wrote a friend.

On November 19, John had the opportunity to hold his first great-grandchild, Kari Widtsoe Koplin, a few days after she was born. He was confined to bed by that time, but he was grateful to see a new generation of Widtsoes enter the world. A few days later, his doctor informed him his kidneys were failing.

"So that's how it is going to be," John said. Outside was a beautiful fall day, bright with sunshine.

He passed away at home on November 29, 1952, with his doctor and family beside him. At the funeral, President McKay observed, "A man who makes the greatest contribution to humanity is he who loves and follows truth at all costs." He then quoted John's final words from *In a Sunlit Land*: "I hope it will be said of me, I have tried to live unselfishly, to serve God and help my fellow men, and use my time and talents industriously for the advancement of human good."

Later, as Leah rode to the cemetery for John's burial, she saw snowflakes out her window. The sight cheered her. "John was born in a severe storm," she thought, "so now his body's interment receives the benediction of a beautiful white blanket of snow."[30]

CHAPTER 37

With Real Intent

In March 1953, twenty-one-year-old Inge Lehmann stepped out the door of her home into the chilly air in Bernburg, GDR. She knew her parents did not approve of where she was going. Joining a new church was bad enough. But going into the icy waters of the Saale River? Inge was still weak from a bout of tuberculosis, and her parents feared for her health.

She could not be dissuaded, though. She had been meeting with the Latter-day Saints of the Bernburg Branch for years. It was finally time to be baptized.

Dusk was fading into night as Inge gathered with the small group preparing for the baptismal service. She recognized one of them—Henry Burkhardt, a missionary who had served in the Bernburg Branch a couple of years earlier. He made an impression on almost everyone he met, but Inge had not yet gotten to know him.[1]

Since receiving his new calling in the mission presidency, Henry had become a person of interest for the Stasi, the GDR's secret police. Although the East German government had officially recognized the Church, officials insisted that Henry stop using the name "East German Mission" and cease all proselytizing activities. Henry agreed to these demands, but because he frequently traveled back and forth between East and West Germany to communicate with Church leaders, the government still kept a close eye on him. Already the Stasi suspected him of spying and had labeled him an "enemy of the state."[2]

One of Inge's friends, a young woman named Erika Just, was also being baptized that night. Inge and Erika were neighbors. In the difficult years after the Second World War, several people in their neighborhood had shown interest in the Church. But as time passed and people were no longer in urgent need of the food and supplies the Church provided, many of them stopped attending. Inge and Erika were among a small group of young people who remained, growing closer at MIA activities during the week and sacrament meetings on Sunday evenings.

The fading sunlight disappeared completely when the group arrived at the banks of the Saale. Clouds obscured the moon, and here and there clumps of ice broke the river's dark surface. A German missionary,

Wolfgang Süss, waded into the water. As the first of the five candidates for baptism entered after him, the moon emerged from behind the clouds. Its reflection shimmered on the river's surface as if to signal God's approval. On the riverbank, a few people waited, ready to wrap each new member in a blanket.[3]

Soon Inge stepped into the river. When Elder Süss brought her up out of the water, she was a new person.

After the baptisms, the small group returned to the branch meetinghouse, a hat shop that had been remodeled to hold sacrament meetings and Sunday School classes. When Inge's turn came to be confirmed a member of the Church and receive the Holy Ghost, Henry Burkhardt placed his hands on her head and spoke the words of the blessing.

Henry had not taken special notice of Inge during the time he served in her branch. But a few days later, he made a note about her in his journal.

He recounted that five people had made covenants with their Father in Heaven that night. "I knew them all to some degree from my work in Bernburg," he wrote. "I have particular confidence in Inge Lehmann."[4]

LATER THAT YEAR, IN the fall of 1953, thirty-six-year-old Nan Hunter started every weekday the same way. At six o'clock each morning she was at her ward meetinghouse in San Diego, California, teaching seminary to about twenty-five teenagers. On the outside, Nan was talkative and self-assured. Inside she felt unsteady. She was teaching a course on the Book of Mormon and wasn't certain if the book was true.[5]

Nan, a mother with children in high school, was thrilled when the early-morning seminary program was launched for the first time. The Church in the western United States had been blossoming since the end of the war. The conflict had given Americans a new perspective on the value of family and faith, and Saints in California, many of whom had come from Utah, wanted their children to benefit from all the programs of the Church. In April 1950, ten stakes in Southern California had asked the Church Board of Education to help them start a seminary program for high school students in their area. Ray Jones, a seminary teacher in Logan, Utah, agreed to move to Los Angeles and get the program started.

Ray's students in Utah had attended seminary during the day in a building near their school. In California, where there were fewer Saints living near each other, such an arrangement was impractical. After surveying parents and Church leaders, Ray found that the only time seminary could be held was before school. Local Saints would have to teach most classes since the Church could not employ many full-time seminary teachers in California.

"It will never work!" some parents predicted, certain their children would not wake up before sunrise to attend a religion class at their church building. But early-morning seminary thrived in Southern California. After just three years, over fifteen hundred students were enrolled in fifty-seven classes.[6]

As enthusiastic as Nan was about the early-morning seminary program, she was not pleased when David Milne, a counselor in the bishopric, invited her to teach the class.

"I can't possibly do it," she replied. She had enjoyed seminary as a young woman growing up in central Utah, but she had no formal training and no college education.[7]

David asked her to talk to Ray Jones, who recommended that she speak with William Berrett, vice president in the Church Department of Education. William reassured her that she was indeed dedicated and qualified—just the person they were looking for to teach the Book of Mormon.

"That boring thing?" Nan said, surprised. "No way could I teach that. I haven't even finished reading it because I always get stuck in Isaiah."

William looked her in the eye. "Sister Hunter, I'd like to make you a promise. If you will read that book with real intent and if you'll pray about it as you read it, then I guarantee that you'll gain a testimony of that book." He assured her it would become her favorite work of scripture to teach, and Nan finally agreed to try.[8]

Nan held class in the Relief Society room, where she had access to a piano and a blackboard. Soon the youth started bringing their friends who were not members of the Church. She loved the enthusiasm and testimony of her students, but she felt the burden of not knowing for sure if the Book of Mormon was scripture. How could she testify of truths she did not know herself?

Every night she would pray about the book, just as William Berrett had suggested, but no answer came. Then one night she decided she could not go on as she had before. She had to know. She skipped ahead to read 3 Nephi and afterward knelt at her bed. "Is this book really true, Father?" she asked. "Do you really want me to teach these kids?"

A glorious, heavenly feeling came over her, as though someone was embracing her. "Yes, it's true," a still, small voice whispered.

Nan was a different person after that. At the beginning of the school year, she had taken a test on the Book of Mormon and scored just 25 percent. At the end of the year, she took another test and scored 98 percent. By then, six nonmembers who had been attending her class had joined the Church.[9]

MEANWHILE, IN SALT LAKE City, forty-three-year-old Gordon B. Hinckley rarely had a moment to rest. He had spent most of his working life as a Church employee, having begun his career as executive secretary of the Church's Radio, Publicity, and Mission Literature Committee. For the past two years, he had served as executive secretary of the Church's Missionary Committee. He was now involved in almost every aspect of the

Church's efforts to spread the gospel, from missionary training to public relations—and he had a hard time leaving his work at the office.[10]

Gordon's wife, Marjorie, was expecting their fifth child, but when Gordon came home to his family, he scarcely had a chance to see them before the phone started ringing. Sometimes the call was about a homesick missionary halfway around the world. Other times it would be someone upset about the Church's policy on mission calls and the military draft.[11]

Although an armistice had recently halted the war between North and South Korea, the United States continued to draft young men of missionary age. The Church adapted its wartime policy so that some young men could receive draft deferments and serve missions. The opportunity was not guaranteed, however, creating some disappointment and hurt. Still, for young men who were drafted, there were often opportunities to share the gospel in the nations where they were stationed. In Seoul, South Korea, for instance, Latter-day Saint soldiers regularly met with a small group of Korean Saints, many of them refugees who had learned about the restored gospel from American servicemen after the war.[12]

In October 1953, President David O. McKay arranged to speak with Gordon about taking on another responsibility. "As you know, we are going to construct a temple in Switzerland," he said. "I want you to find a way to present the temple instruction in the various languages of Europe while using a minimum number of temple workers."[13]

The temples in Europe would be unlike any others. In each of the Church's eight operating temples, several trained ordinance workers guided patrons through a series of rooms decorated with murals representing stages of the plan of salvation. But ordinance workers would be hard to find with European Saints spread so thin across the continent, so the First Presidency wanted to use modern technologies to reduce the number of ordinance workers and the space needed for the endowment.[14]

"You've had vast experience in preparation of films and materials of that kind," President McKay said to Gordon. "I'm putting on your shoulders the responsibility of finding a way to do this." And Gordon would have to start right away. The Swiss Temple would be finished in less than two years.

"Well, President," Gordon said, "we'll do what we can."[15]

EARLY THE NEXT YEAR, President McKay again left the United States with Emma Ray to visit Saints in Europe, South Africa, and South America. His first tour of the Church's worldwide missions, taken in 1920–21 with Hugh Cannon, had opened his eyes to the needs and concerns of Saints across the globe. Now, as he set out on this new tour, he was especially concerned about the South African Mission. Although the Church had been in the country for more than a hundred years, it was facing a shortage of leadership there because of the restriction keeping people of Black African descent from holding the priesthood or receiving temple ordinances.

The restrictions had always presented particular challenges in South Africa, where missionaries often encountered men who were unsure or unaware if they had mixed African and European ancestry, raising questions about their eligibility for priesthood ordination. Ultimately, the First Presidency requested that all prospective priesthood holders in the country confirm their eligibility by proving that their earliest South African ancestors had migrated to Africa rather than originated there.[16]

This process was time-consuming and often frustrating. Some potential branch or district leaders belonged to families that had been in South Africa since before good genealogical records were kept. Others spent considerable money researching their family lines only to become stuck in their search. As a result, mission president Leroy Duncan had decided to call missionaries to lead congregations where worthy men could not prove their ancestries.

"There have been only five men ordained to the Melchizedek Priesthood in the past five years," Leroy informed the First Presidency. "The work would progress more rapidly if more of our good, faithful brethren could hold the priesthood."[17]

President McKay hoped to address the problem directly when he arrived in South Africa. But he was also mindful of the country's tense racial divisions. South Africa was governed by its white minority population, which had recently begun passing oppressive laws designed to treat Black and "Coloured" (or mixed-race) residents as second-class citizens, wholly separate from whites.

This system of laws, known as apartheid, had made strict racial segregation central to South African society. As President McKay pondered the problem, he had to consider the Church's practice of operating within the existing laws of a nation. He also understood that even an inspired change to the priesthood and temple restrictions might draw the ire of white Church members and others outside the faith.[18]

The McKays arrived in South Africa in January 1954 and spent the next several days meeting with Saints across the country. President McKay took time to visit with as many people as he could, particularly those who seemed timid or on the edges of the crowd.[19] In Cape Town, he shook hands with Clara Daniels and her daughter, Alice, who had been founding members of the Branch of Love years earlier. William Daniels, Clara's husband and the branch president, had passed away in 1936. Since then, Clara and Alice had continued faithfully as some of the few Saints of mixed race in South Africa.[20]

During his travels, President McKay prayed sincerely to know how to address the priesthood restriction in the country. He observed the Saints carefully and pondered the difficulties they faced. He understood that if the Church continued to require prospective priesthood holders in South Africa to trace their ancestries off the continent, then the branches might not have enough local leaders to carry on the work of the Church.[21]

On Sunday, January 17, he spoke about the priesthood and temple restrictions at a missionary meeting in Cape Town. While he offered no definitive statement on the origin of the practice, he acknowledged that several Black men had held the priesthood during the presidencies of Joseph Smith and Brigham Young. He also spoke of his past struggle to uphold the restrictions during his 1921 world tour, recounting the time he petitioned President Grant in behalf of a Black Saint in Hawaii who wished to receive the priesthood.

"I sat down and talked to the brother," President McKay told the missionaries, "and gave him the assurance that someday he will receive every blessing to which he is entitled, for the Lord is just, and no respecter of persons."

President McKay did not know when that day would come, and he affirmed that the restriction would remain in place until the Lord revealed otherwise. Yet he felt that something needed to change.

"There are worthy men in the South African Mission who are being deprived of the priesthood simply because they are unable to trace their genealogy out of this country," he stated. "I am impressed that an injustice is being done to them." From that time forward, he declared, Saints whose ancestry was in question would no longer have to prove their lineage to receive the priesthood.[22]

Before leaving South Africa, President McKay reiterated that the day would come when people of Black African descent would receive every blessing of the priesthood. Already, Black individuals from other countries were showing greater interest in the restored gospel. A few years earlier, several residents of the western African nation of Nigeria had written to Church headquarters for information. Other requests would soon come.[23]

At the same time, many Black people throughout the world were seeking equality, often by challenging the legality of segregation. As their actions rippled through society, more and more people were asking Church leaders heartfelt questions about the restrictions.[24]

LATER THAT YEAR, IN the German Democratic Republic, a small ship lazily steamed up the Elbe, a wispy, white plume rising from the vessel's lone smokestack. A single word was written on the ship's side: *Einheit*. Unity.

Aboard the ship, Henry Burkhardt greeted other Saints from around the GDR who had gathered for a conference of the Mutual Improvement Associations. Although Henry was around the same age as many of the young adults in the crowd, as the leader of the Church in the GDR he was overseeing the event rather than simply enjoying it.[25]

The scenic boat ride was just one of many activities planned for the five hundred or so young adults at the conference. Since the 1930s, missions across the world had held MIA conferences to help strengthen faith and foster courtship and marriage within the Church. Lately, however, the East German police had begun forbidding church groups from holding any recreational activities, like ball games or hikes. Such restrictions made it difficult to be a Church member in the GDR, and already many East German Saints had fled to West Germany or to the United States. Henry knew many young people who dreamed of emigrating, but he hoped activities like these would encourage some of them to stay, ensuring the Church's continued presence in the nation.[26]

The steamer continued gliding upriver, passing tree-covered hills and tall columns of gray sandstone. Among the crowd, Henry noticed Inge Lehmann, the young woman he had confirmed in Bernburg the previous year. He had seen Inge a few times since then, and they had talked with each other at an MIA activity on Easter.

Henry often felt tongue-tied and self-conscious around young women. When he was a nineteen-year-old missionary, he had been expected to focus on his work. Now that he had settled into his new Church responsibilities, some Saints in the mission had begun wondering when, and whom, he might marry.

As Henry talked with Inge, he felt something quite different from the awkwardness he had felt in the past. He decided he wanted to see her again.[27]

Over the next few months, Henry did what he could to visit Inge. He drove around the mission in an old Opel Olympia, and since cars were rare in the GDR, Latter-day Saints noticed whenever he drove through her neighborhood. Henry's duties in the mission kept him busy, so he had few opportunities to see Inge. Still, it was not long before their relationship blossomed.

When winter came, Henry and Inge decided to get married. Over the Christmas holiday, Inge's parents invited Henry and his parents to their home in Bernburg to announce their engagement. Although the Lehmanns had been unhappy with their daughter's decision to join the Church, their attitude had begun to soften. They had even developed a friendship with Henry.[28]

As Henry and Inge celebrated their engagement, however, their future remained uncertain. Henry's Church service made it difficult for him to earn a living, and he wondered how he could support a family. There was also the question of marriage in the temple—something Henry and Inge both wanted.

With the Swiss Temple less than a year away from completion, their dream was not entirely out of reach. It was not as easy as simply saving money for the journey, though. Policies governing who could travel outside the GDR were becoming stricter. Henry and Inge knew there was little chance the government would allow them to leave the country together.[29]

CHAPTER 38

More Power,
More Light

One day in mid-1954, Jeanne Charrier made her way along the road leading to the hillside village of Privas, France. Ever since Jeanne's baptism three years before, she had been making frequent trips to the home of Eugenie Vivier. A widow whose children had long since moved away, Madame Vivier had been studying about the Church for nearly a decade without committing to baptism, but Jeanne did not mind visiting her. Time with the widow was more of a pleasure than a duty.

When Jeanne arrived at Madame Vivier's home, the woman's face broke into a welcoming smile. She ushered Jeanne inside and took her seat by an open window.[1]

As usual, Jeanne came to the house with a lesson. Her scholarly mind and love of ideas had led her to study the gospel deeply.² A few months earlier, she had written an article for *L'Étoile* about that year's MIA theme, Doctrine and Covenants 88:86: "Abide ye in the liberty wherewith ye are made free; entangle not yourselves in sin, but let your hands be clean, until the Lord comes."³

"In obeying the laws," Jeanne had written, "we get more power, more light." She quoted from the New Testament and several ancient and modern thinkers to make her point. "To be free is to shake off sin, ignorance, and error," she continued, "and dwell in the freedom of the gospel of Jesus Christ."⁴

Along with serving as the president of the MIA in her small branch in Valence, Jeanne taught Sunday School and Relief Society lessons. She took her responsibilities as a teacher seriously. She had a burning testimony of the restored gospel and longed to share it.⁵

Unfortunately, few of Jeanne's friends and none of her family members wanted to hear anything about the Church. Jeanne still lived at home, but her relationship with her family had deteriorated ever since her baptism. Her parents rarely spoke to her, and when they did, it was to express their disapproval or accuse her of betraying their family's Protestant heritage.⁶

Most of her friends and professors at the university, meanwhile, were dismissive of all religion. If she tried to tell them about Joseph Smith, they scoffed at the idea that any person could see a vision.⁷

In Madame Vivier, however, Jeanne had found a kindred spirit. One of the reasons the elderly woman had put off baptism for so long was that her family opposed it. But she, like Jeanne, enjoyed studying the scriptures. Madame Vivier was also an example of how a person could live a contented, simple life. She did not have much material wealth besides her small home, some fruit trees, and a few chickens, but every time Jeanne visited, Madame Vivier pulled fresh eggs out of her apron pockets and pressed Jeanne to accept them.[8]

Jeanne knew that, like Madame Vivier, she might have to learn to be content with a more solitary life. There were few young men in France who were Latter-day Saints, and Jeanne had decided she would not marry outside the Church. Nor was she willing to marry a Church member she did not love or who did not love her. Even if she were to remain single, she decided, the restored gospel was worth it. The truths she was learning—of the plan of salvation, the restoration of the priesthood, and the reality of a living prophet—filled her soul with joy.[9]

After finishing her gospel lesson and reminding Madame Vivier to read the Book of Mormon, Jeanne ended their visit by bringing up baptism—something she had talked about many times with her friend. This time, however, Madame Vivier was not wary of the subject, and she agreed to be baptized.

A rush of happiness filled Jeanne's heart. After nearly ten years of study, this faithful woman was ready to join the Church.[10]

NOT LONG AFTER RECEIVING the assignment to help modify the presentation of the endowment, Gordon B. Hinckley assembled a team of professionals to produce a motion picture for the European temples. But by the spring of 1955, the film was still far from finished, and the Swiss Temple dedication was only a few months away.[11]

Sensitive to the sacred nature of the endowment, President McKay authorized Gordon to shoot the film in the large assembly hall of the Salt Lake Temple—the same room where, more than sixty years before, Wilford Woodruff had dedicated the building.[12]

Although temple workers normally performed the endowment wearing white suits and dresses, Gordon received permission to film the ceremony with actors in costumes. The committee hung a massive gray backdrop in the assembly room and positioned lights to illuminate the set, where artificial rocks dotted the ground amid large trees that had been hoisted through the temple windows with pulleys. To help portray the creation of the world, Gordon received permission from the Walt Disney Company to insert a short clip from the film *Fantasia* into the production.[13]

Everyone involved in the temple film, from the actors and crew to the editor and Gordon himself, worked on it in addition to their regular full-time jobs, giving up nights and weekends. By the end of May 1955, Gordon and the production team had put together an initial cut of the film, but Gordon was not satisfied with what he saw. The flow of the film seemed rough and choppy, and some of the acting and costuming needed work.[14]

He reached out to Winnifred Bowers, the costumer who had been working on the film, to get advice on improving the production. She suggested ways to smooth out the transitions and recommended making small changes to the costumes. And she was sure the director, Harold Hansen, could help the actors adjust their performances after seeing what it looked like on-screen. "But with all this, Brother Hinckley," Winnifred noted, "I think you've got it more figured out than you thought you had."[15]

Gordon and his team worked for several more weeks to refine the film. On June 23, they showed it to the general authorities, and President McKay was pleased with their work. "You've done a fine job," he told Gordon and his team. "I think this is the way things should go."[16]

But their work was not yet done. Since the Church did not have the equipment necessary to dub motion pictures into other languages, Gordon and his team decided to reshoot the film in German, French, Danish, Dutch, Norwegian, and Swedish. Fortunately, the translations had already been done, but completing six more versions of the film would take months, even for a seasoned director.[17]

Gordon did not have a lot of time. President McKay and all the Saints waiting to receive their temple blessings in Switzerland were depending on him. He could not rest until every film was complete and had arrived safely in Europe.[18]

IN THE GDR, MEANWHILE, Helga Meyer played hymns on a small organ in her living room to welcome family and friends to Sunday school. Nine years had passed since she had left Berlin to live with her husband, Kurt, in the small village of Cammin. Despite the challenges of living in the GDR, the Meyers had made a comfortable home for their three young children. Their door was always open to anyone who wanted to visit.[19]

Many of Helga's neighbors had attended Sunday school meetings enthusiastically. After an opening hymn and a prayer, Kurt would take the adults aside for a lesson while Helga sang hymns and shared Bible stories with dozens of eager children.[20]

But these large gatherings had recently shrunk. When a Lutheran pastor heard about the Meyers' Sunday school, he forbade his parishioners from attending. Now only a handful of Latter-day Saints living in and around Cammin came on Sunday mornings—a much smaller class than what Helga had attended as a girl in the Tilsit Branch Sunday School. Yet Helga could always count on Elise Kuhn, a widow from a nearby village, to make the long walk to the Meyer home, even in rain or snow. The family of Edith Tietz, Helga's good friend who had joined the Church a few years before, also attended faithfully.[21]

In the class, Helga and Kurt usually taught directly from the scriptures, since they had few other lesson materials to draw from.[22] For English-speaking parts of the world, the Church's magazine for Sunday Schools, the *Instructor,* supplied plenty of resources for teachers, from articles on using flannel boards effectively to maps, charts, and illustrations. One recent issue included full-color reproductions of some of Arnold Friberg's newest Book of Mormon paintings, *Abinadi Delivers His Message to King Noah* and *Alma Baptizes in the Waters of Mormon.*[23]

German-language lesson materials, by contrast, had been in short supply after the war, and strict censorship in the GDR had made them almost impossible to acquire.[24] For the East German Saints, Church headquarters now seemed more distant than ever.[25] Helga still longed to emigrate to the United States, as her aunt Lusche and other loved ones had done since the end of the war. But she knew how dangerous it would be for a whole family to try to leave the GDR. And apart from the danger, she would never go without her parents. Her mother's health, which had always been poor, had only gotten worse after years of waiting in vain for Helga's brother Henry to return from the war.[26]

In difficult times throughout their lives, Helga and her family had found strength and comfort in the Church. After Sunday School, they and the handful of Saints in Cammin would catch the train for sacrament meeting with the Neubrandenburg Branch, a little over ten miles away. Sometimes strangers would appear at the meeting, and Helga feared they were spies who had come to listen in on their talks and testimonies.

The Saints in Neubrandenburg did their best to ignore such threats and continued on, teaching one another from the scriptures and singing the songs of Zion.[27]

EARLY IN SEPTEMBER 1955, about a week before the Swiss Temple dedication, Gordon B. Hinckley carefully placed two suitcases in the hands of airline employees at the Salt Lake City airport. The bags contained the completed temple film in all seven languages. He hated to let the thirty thousand feet of film out of his sight, but the suitcases were too bulky to bring into the cabin of the airplane that he and his wife, Marjorie, would take on the first leg of their trip to Switzerland. At least the accompanying audio tracks, stored separately in two compact canisters, were small enough that he could carry them himself.[28]

Gordon had been anxious about protecting the sacred content of the film from the moment he sent it off to a lab in California for final processing. He had asked a close friend who worked in Hollywood to take the film to the lab and stay there to ensure its privacy while it was processed. Gordon now needed to see the film safely through airports in New York and London before delivering it personally to the Swiss Temple.[29]

William Perschon, the new president of the Swiss-Austrian Mission, greeted the Hinckleys as they stepped off the plane in Basel. They retrieved the film, and Gordon filled out a customs declaration form, noting the film materials among his possessions. A customs official looked over the form and said, "I can't let this in. We don't permit the entry of film into Switzerland without clearance through the federal film board."

"I have to get it in some way," Gordon said. "You certainly permit film to come into Switzerland?"

"With proper clearance, yes," the official replied. He then explained that the Swiss film board needed to review and approve the film before releasing it back into Gordon's care. The official, meanwhile, would send it to the customs office in Bern. Since it was Saturday, Gordon would not be able to retrieve the film from customs until the office opened on Monday morning.[30]

Gordon thought about trying to persuade the official to simply let him take the film to Bern himself, but he worried that an argument would make matters worse. So he and Marjorie left with President Perschon for the mission home, deeply concerned about the safety of the temple film. The following day, they fasted and prayed that the film would not fall into the wrong hands.[31]

Early on Monday, Gordon and President Perschon picked up the reels at the customs office and took them directly to the film board. There a man ushered Gordon into a private room. "What is the title of this film?" he asked.

"It doesn't have a title," Gordon replied. "It's just music and instruction to be used in this temple out here." He offered to let the man listen to the audio track. As a precaution, he had put a long recording of organ music at the beginning of the film to deter any unauthorized person from accessing its sacred contents.[32]

The man listened to the music for a while. "Well," he finally said, "what is it?"

"It's just church instruction," Gordon repeated. "It's church music, dull organ music."

A look of friendly understanding then came over the man. "All right," he said. Without asking to hear or see more, he took out a stamp and approved the film.[33]

CHAPTER 39

A New Era

On Tuesday, September 6, 1955, Helga Meyer boarded a train for West Berlin. She and other members of the Neubrandenburg Branch had recently learned that the Tabernacle Choir was coming to the city to give a concert. The choir had been touring Europe since mid-August, performing in cities from Glasgow to Copenhagen ahead of the dedication of the Swiss Temple. It was the choir's most momentous undertaking since its performance at the Chicago World's Fair six decades earlier. For many who attended the concerts, hearing the choir sing was the experience of a lifetime.[1]

It had long seemed impractical to bring over 350 choir members across the ocean, but President David O. McKay believed it was time for the choir to venture beyond North America. "There is no more potent force for missionary work than the Tabernacle Choir," he had said when plans were announced.[2]

The entire tour was the product of much work, preparation, and prayer, but the choir's presence in West Berlin was especially remarkable. High-level negotiations between the United States and the Soviet Union had taken place to allow such a large group of Americans to travel through the German Democratic Republic into the western sector of the city.[3]

Once Helga and other East German Saints heard about the choir's upcoming visit, they sought and received permission to travel to West Berlin. While the choir would perform for a paying audience in the evening, it would also give a free "rehearsal concert" in the daytime for residents of the GDR and East German refugees who now lived in West Germany. The Meyers did not have much money, but Kurt's fishing business and Helga's work as a kindergarten teacher had brought in just enough income for her to travel on her own to West Berlin and purchase a ticket for the evening concert.[4]

When Helga's train arrived in West Berlin, she exited the station and made her way to the spacious Schöneberg sports arena for the free afternoon concert. The auditorium was nearly full of people, but she was able to find a seat near the stage.

Helga, Kurt, and their children had spent many evenings huddled around the radio, listening to Tabernacle Choir broadcasts. Since the program came from the

United States, the family kept the volume low so that no one on the street would overhear the music and report them. But today she could listen without fear, letting the words and music flow all around her.[5]

The choir began with music by famed German composers Bach, Handel, and Beethoven. Then the concert transitioned to the beloved Latter-day Saint hymns "O My Father" and "Come, Come, Ye Saints." Helga did not understand the English words of the hymns, but as the singers' voices filled the space with joyous sound, her heart soared.

These were her people, Helga realized, come from far away.[6]

A few hours later, she returned to the hall for the choir's evening concert. This time West German Saints, American servicemembers, and government officials occupied most of the seats in the packed hall. The concert was being recorded so that Radio Free Europe, an American-sponsored station in West Germany, could broadcast it to the people living in the GDR, Czechoslovakia, Poland, and other communist countries in central and eastern Europe.[7]

Once again, Helga was delighted as she listened to the music. The Spirit of the Lord enveloped her, and she and those around her could not stop the tears from flowing. It felt like heaven on earth.

After the concert, the choir exited the hall and began boarding their buses. Helga and a group of German Saints followed them outside and sang "God Be with

You Till We Meet Again." They waved handkerchiefs in the air until the last bus was out of sight.[8]

A FEW DAYS LATER, on Sunday, September 11, 1955, President McKay pulled into a crowded parking lot on the outskirts of Bern, Switzerland. For the past several years, he had followed the progress on the two European temples from afar. Recently, he had broken ground for the temple in London. And today he had arrived to dedicate the newly completed Swiss Temple.[9]

It was a triumphant moment for President McKay. Europe had been a source of strength to the Church for generations. Both of the prophet's parents had been born on European soil. His father's family joined the Church in Scotland, and his mother's family were among the early converts in Wales. Now European Saints would no longer have to cross an ocean to enjoy the blessings of the temple, as his parents and grandparents had.[10]

For days, rain had fallen on Bern. But on this morning, blue skies and sunshine greeted President McKay. The temple's simple, modern exterior stood out against a backdrop of evergreen trees. The building was cream-colored, with rows of white pilasters and tall windows gracing its sides. A single gilded spire, supported by a brilliant white base, reached high above the brass front doors. And in the distance, clearly visible from the temple grounds, rose the Jura Mountains and majestic Swiss Alps.[11]

As President McKay entered the temple, he passed beneath large block letters above the door. *Das Haus des Herrn,* the message read in German. The House of the Lord. For the first time, the words appeared on a Latter-day Saint temple in a language other than English.[12]

A few minutes later, at ten o'clock, the prophet stood at a pulpit in the third-floor assembly room. An audience of about six hundred people, more than half of them members of the Tabernacle Choir, looked on. Another nine hundred people sat in other rooms in the temple while listening to the proceedings over loudspeakers.[13]

After singing by the choir and a prayer, President McKay welcomed all who were in attendance and remarked that past presidents of the Church were there in spirit. Among them, he said, was Joseph F. Smith, who had prophesied in Bern a half century before that temples would one day be built in countries across the world.[14]

Samuel Bringhurst, who had recently been called as president of the Swiss Temple, spoke next. He recounted the difficulty in finding the property and testified of the Lord's guidance in locating the current site.[15]

Apostle Ezra Taft Benson followed. He told the audience of his paternal grandmother, Louisa Ballif, whose parents had joined the Church in Switzerland in the 1850s and emigrated to Utah. As a young man growing up in Idaho, Ezra had listened to his grandmother recount her family's conversion and her affection for the old country.

"I assure you," the apostle said, "I loved Switzerland long before I ever saw it."

Elder Benson then reflected on his mission to the Saints in Europe after the Second World War. He mentioned going to Vienna and Zełwągi. And he remembered fondly the kindness of Swiss government officials who helped the Church distribute aid.[16]

After Elder Benson sat down, President McKay returned to the stand to dedicate the house of the Lord. "O God, our Eternal Father," he prayed. "On this sacred occasion, the completion and dedication of the first temple to be erected by the Church in Europe, we give our hearts and lift our voices to Thee in praise and gratitude." He thanked the Lord for the restored gospel, for modern revelation, and for the Swiss people, who had for centuries honored the right to worship as conscience dictated.

During his prayer, the prophet seemed burdened by the unbelief of people in lands where the gospel of Jesus Christ could not now be preached. "Bless the leaders of nations," he pleaded, "that their hearts may be cleared of prejudices, suspicion, and avarice and filled with a desire for peace and righteousness."

President McKay closed the morning dedicatory session by leading the assembly in the Hosanna Shout.[17] During the service, he asked Ewan Harbrecht, a young soprano with the Tabernacle Choir whose German-born grandmother had been an early member of the Cincinnati Branch, to stand and sing.

Everywhere they had performed in Europe, Ewan and the choir had been greeted to loud applause. But in the *Haus des Herrn,* a peaceful reverence befitting the occasion settled over the room. "Bless this house," she sang.

> *Bless the people here within*
> *Keep them pure and free from sin*
> *Bless us all that we may be*
> *Fit O Lord to dwell with thee.*[18]

THE FOLLOWING THURSDAY, JEANNE Charrier entered the Swiss Temple to attend the last of the nine dedicatory sessions. Surrounded by fellow Saints from the French Mission, including Léon and Claire Fargier, Jeanne was honored to be in the Lord's house, numbered among the Europeans who would soon make eternal covenants.[19]

President McKay spoke, as he had done at each of the previous sessions. Jeanne felt a special connection to the prophet, whom she had met at a conference in Paris during his 1952 European tour. She had been a member of the Church for only a year at the time, and the pain of being rejected by her parents was still fresh. President McKay had paused to ask about her baptism and what her life had been like since. Rather than simply shaking her hand, he had given her a warm, grandfatherly hug, helping to dispel her inner turmoil.[20]

As President McKay welcomed the Saints of the French Mission to the temple, his words were translated by Robert Simond, a longtime Swiss member of the Church who served in the mission presidency. "This dedication marks an epoch in the history of the Church," the prophet told the Saints. "In several ways it begins a new era."[21]

He then spoke to those who would soon be receiving the initiatory and endowment ordinances. He wanted them to be prepared to comprehend the great principles of life contained in the temple experience.

"Seeing or visualizing the glory of the temple work is somewhat like obtaining a testimony of the divinity of Christ's work," he said. "To some, the glory of the truth of the restored gospel comes immediately. To others it comes more slowly, but surely."[22]

The first endowment sessions in the Swiss Temple were scheduled to begin the following week. But after learning how many Saints needed to return to their home countries before then, President McKay asked Gordon B. Hinckley if his team could work through the night to ready the temple for endowment work Friday morning.[23]

On Friday afternoon, Jeanne returned to the temple with other French-speaking Saints. The first two endowment sessions of the day had been in German, and since the endowment was a new experience for most participants, everything took longer than expected. By the time the French session began, the sun had set, and there were sessions in other languages to follow.[24]

After listening to apostle Spencer W. Kimball speak at a special meeting in the temple chapel, Jeanne and other French Saints participated in the initiatory and endowment ordinances. Together in one room, they watched the new French-language temple film and learned more about the earth's creation, the Fall of Adam and Eve, and the Atonement of Jesus Christ. They made covenants with God and in turn received the promise of great blessings in this life and in the life to come.[25]

When Jeanne's session finished, it was the middle of the night. Saints from Sweden, Finland, the Netherlands, Denmark, and Norway went on to receive their endowment in sessions that continued around the clock until late Saturday night.[26]

Having participated in the ordinances of the temple, Jeanne understood it was a place of faith and hope that would prepare her to someday enter God's presence. And although her earthly family was not yet ready to hear the gospel message, she was eager to do work for deceased ancestors who were waiting to receive temple blessings.

"No one will be forgotten," she thought.[27]

IT HAD BEEN QUITE a week for Gordon B. Hinckley. Once the endowment film cleared customs, he had overseen the installation of the temple's projection and sound equipment, synchronized the sound and film in each language to assure that they were working properly, and trained the new temple engineer, Hans Lutscher, who would take on the full-time responsibility after he was endowed himself.[28]

Gordon and his team enjoyed a brief reprieve from their hectic schedule during the five days of the dedication, but as soon as President McKay announced his desire to begin ordinance work in the temple immediately, they went right back to work.

Since early Friday morning, Gordon had spent nearly two days operating the projector and sound system. Sleep was hardly an option. And Bern's damp fall climate had aggravated a case of the flu Gordon had caught. His eyes and nose would not stop running, his head felt heavy, and his body ached.[29]

Still, as the sessions went on hour after hour, Gordon was amazed by how well the filmed endowment functioned. The temple workers experienced few problems with the new process, despite the challenges of accommodating people from so many different countries. Watching the ordinance unfold, Gordon realized how difficult it would have been to present it in seven languages in the traditional manner.[30]

When the final endowment session ended late Saturday, Gordon was exhausted. But beyond his red eyes and sore throat, he felt a rush of something far more significant. Since coming to Bern, he had seen hundreds of Saints from the nations of Europe enter the temple. Many of them had made great sacrifices to come to the dedication. Some of them, he could see, were very poor. Others had borne the loss of family and other loved ones during the two world wars. They shed tears as they received the endowment and witnessed their families sealed together for eternity.

More than ever before, Gordon knew with certainty that the Lord had inspired President McKay to bring temple blessings to the women and men of Europe. Seeing their joy was worth all the long nights and stressful days Gordon had experienced over the past two years.[31]

LIKE MOST SAINTS LIVING in the GDR, Henry Burkhardt was not able to go to Bern for the temple dedication or the first endowment sessions. Instead, he was preparing an attic room in his parents' house where he and Inge would live after their upcoming wedding. He had applied for an apartment of his own, but he had no idea when or if the government would grant one. He decided they could make do in this small, unheated space, which he hoped Inge would find a little more cheerful after he put up new wallpaper.

Henry and Inge had seen each other only a few times in the nine months since their engagement, usually when Henry was near Bernburg for a district conference. They planned to have a civil wedding on October 29, and they were determined to be sealed in the temple as soon as possible after that.[32]

Although the East German government allowed its citizens to travel to West Germany, Henry and Inge could not alert anyone that they were traveling out of the country together, since authorities might assume that they were leaving permanently. They secured their visas to West Germany in different cities and worked with the mission office in West Berlin to obtain their visas to Switzerland. According to the plan, the Swiss visas would be sent to the West German Mission office in Frankfurt. If the papers failed to arrive, the couple would have to return to the GDR without being sealed.[33]

The day after their wedding in Bernburg, Henry and Inge traveled without incident to West Germany and found their visas to Switzerland waiting for them. They soon purchased round-trip tickets to Bern and spent some time with friends in West Germany. Everywhere they went, people were polite and friendly to them. They marveled at how wonderful it felt to move around freely without any restrictions.[34]

Henry and Inge arrived in Bern on the evening of November 4 and spent the last of the money they had saved for the trip to rent a small room near the train station. The next morning, the couple ascended the steps to the temple doors and entered the Lord's house. Soon they sat in the temple's endowment room and received the ordinance as the German-language film flickered on a screen in front of them.

After the ordinance, they entered a sealing room and knelt across the altar from one another. They learned of the glorious promises given to those who entered into the sealing covenant. Then they themselves were joined together forever.[35]

"How beautiful it is to now belong to each other for eternity," Henry reflected. "What a great responsibility, with many blessings, has been given us."[36]

The next evening, Henry and Inge walked to the train station for their trip back to their attic room in the GDR. They knew they did not have to return there if they did not want to. They had friends who could help them stay in West Germany. They could even try to emigrate to the United States, as so many other European Saints had.

The couple did not want to leave their homeland, though. Life in the GDR was not always easy, but their families were there, and God had work for them to do.[37]

The train soon came, and they climbed aboard. Leaving Switzerland, neither Henry nor Inge had any idea when, or if, they would be able to return to the temple. Yet they trusted in God to guide their future. Bound together for time and eternity, they were more committed than ever to serving Him. And they knew He would never leave them.[38]

NOTE ON SOURCES

This volume is a work of narrative nonfiction based on hundreds of historical sources. Utmost care has been taken to ensure its accuracy. Readers should not assume, however, that the narrative presented here is perfect or complete. The records of the past, and our ability to interpret them in the present, are limited.

All sources of historical knowledge contain gaps, ambiguities, and biases. They often convey their creator's point of view, and witnesses of the same events experience, remember, interpret, and record them differently. The challenge of the historian is to assemble known points of view and piece together an accurate understanding of the past.

Saints is a true account of the history of The Church of Jesus Christ of Latter-day Saints, based on what we know and understand at the present time from existing historical records. It is not a comprehensive history, nor is it the only possible telling of the Church's sacred history. But the scholars who researched, wrote, and edited this volume know the historical sources well, used them thoughtfully, and documented them in the endnotes and list of sources cited. Readers are invited to evaluate the sources themselves, many of which have been digitized and linked to the endnotes. It is probable that the discovery of more sources, or new readings of existing sources, will in time yield other meanings, interpretations, and possible points of view.

The narrative in *Saints* draws on historical sources of two kinds: primary and secondary. Primary sources contain information about events from those who witnessed them firsthand. Some primary sources, like letters, journals, and reports or recordings of discourses, were produced at the time of the events they describe. These contemporaneous sources reflect what people thought, felt, and did in the moment, revealing how the past was interpreted when it was the present. Other primary sources, like autobiographies and oral history interviews, were written after the fact. These reminiscent sources reveal what the past came to mean to the writer over time, often making them better than contemporary sources at recognizing the significance of past events. Since they rely on memory, however, reminiscent sources can include inaccuracies and be influenced by the author's later understandings and beliefs.

Secondary historical sources contain information from people who did not witness the events described firsthand. Such sources include later family histories and academic works. This volume is indebted to many such sources, which proved valuable for the broader contextual and interpretive work they provided.

Every source in *Saints* was evaluated for credibility, and each sentence was repeatedly checked for consistency with the sources. Lines of dialogue and other quotations come directly from historical sources. Spelling, capitalization, and punctuation in direct quotations have been silently modernized for clarity. In some instances, more significant modifications, like shifting from the past tense to present tense or standardizing grammar, have been made to quotations to improve readability. In these cases, endnotes describe the changes made. Choices about which sources to use and how to use them were made by a team of historians, writers, and editors who based decisions on both historical integrity and literary quality.

As the story of the Church becomes more global, *Saints* increasingly relies on sources created in languages other than English. At times, the writers of this volume relied on volunteer or machine translation to craft the narrative. All quotations from translated sources come from professional translators.

Some antagonistic sources were used to write this volume and are cited in the notes. These sources were primarily used to characterize opposition to the Church during the late nineteenth and early twentieth centuries. Though hostile to the Church, these documents sometimes contain details that were not recorded elsewhere. Some of these details were used when other records confirmed their general accuracy. Facts from these antagonistic records were used without adopting their hostile interpretations, and citing a source in the endnotes does not signal Church endorsement.

As a narrative history written for a general audience, this volume presents a history of the Church in a coherent, accessible format. While drawing on the techniques of popular storytelling, it does not go beyond information found in historical sources. When the text includes even minor details, such as facial expressions or weather conditions, it is because these details are found in or reasonably deduced from the historical record.

To maintain the readability of the narrative, the volume rarely addresses challenges in or to the historical record in the text itself. Instead, such source-based discussions are found in topical essays on saints.ChurchofJesusChrist.org and are referenced in endnotes under the bolded heading "Topic." Readers are encouraged to consult these essays as they read *Saints*.

NOTES

Some sources are referred to with a shortened citation. The "Sources Cited" section provides full citation information for all sources. Many sources are available digitally and are linked from the electronic version of the book, available at saints.ChurchofJesusChrist.org and in Gospel Library. The abbreviation CHL stands for Church History Library, The Church of Jesus Christ of Latter-day Saints, Salt Lake City.

Text in bold in the notes points to topical articles with additional information online at saints.ChurchofJesusChrist.org and in Gospel Library under "Church History Topics."

CHAPTER 1: A BRIGHTER AND A BETTER DAY

1. Evan Stephens, "The World's Fair Gold Medal," *Children's Friend,* Sept. 1920, 19:374; "The Tabernacle Choir," *Deseret Weekly,* Sept. 1, 1894, 340–41; Handy, *Official Directory of the World's Columbian Exposition,* 42, 191–92, 194, 197; Emmeline B. Wells, "World's Congress and World's Fair," *Deseret Evening News,* June 17, 1893, 7. **Topic: Columbian Exposition of 1893**

2. Evan Stephens, "The World's Fair Gold Medal," *Children's Friend,* Sept. 1920, 19:372–74; George Q. Cannon, "The Tabernacle Choir at the World's Fair," *Juvenile Instructor,* Sept. 15, 1893, 28:566–67; "The Tabernacle Choir," *Deseret Weekly,* Sept. 1, 1894, 340–41; Neilson, *Exhibiting Mormonism,* 109–14. **Topics: Tabernacle Choir; Wales**

3. *Saints,* volume 2, chapters 1, 10, 26–27, 29, 32–35, 37, and 39–41; Neilson, *Exhibiting Mormonism,* 46–48. **Topics: Manifesto; Plural Marriage after the Manifesto**

4. Evan Stephens, "The World's Fair Gold Medal," *Children's Friend,* Sept. 1920, 19:372–74; "The Tabernacle Choir," *Deseret Weekly,* Sept. 1, 1894, 340–41.

5. Evan Stephens, "The World's Fair Gold Medal," *Children's Friend,* Sept. 1920, 19:372–74; Oct. 1920, 19:420; "To the World's Fair," *Standard* (Ogden, UT), June 7, 1893, 1. **Topic: George Q. Cannon**

6. Neilson, *Exhibiting Mormonism,* 92–102, 144–49; Wells, Diary, volume 16, May 10 and 12, 1893; "World's Fair Exodus," *Salt Lake Herald,* May 11, 1893, 2; Evan Stephens, "The World's Fair Gold Medal," *Children's Friend,* Sept. 1920, 19:374; Oct. 1920, 19:420–21; George Q. Cannon, "The Tabernacle Choir at the World's Fair," *Juvenile Instructor,* Sept. 15, 1893, 28:566.

7. "A Groundless Apprehension," *Deseret Evening News,* July 14, 1888, [2]; "Taking of Testimony," *Deseret Evening News,* Oct. 20, 1891, 5; George Q. Cannon, Journal, Apr. 5, 1895; Walker, "Crisis in Zion," 115–17; Arrington, *Great Basin Kingdom,* 386–93, 401; *Saints,* volume 2, chapters 35 and 37. **Topics: Antipolygamy Legislation; Salt Lake Temple**

8. Joseph F. Smith to Heber J. Grant, July 12, 1893, Heber J. Grant Collection, CHL; Talmage, Journal, Aug. 23, 1893; Dean, Journal, July 1, 3, and 5, 1893; Aug. 2, 3, and 5, 1893; "Another Bank Gone," *Deseret Evening News,* June 30, 1893, 5; "Prices of Farm Products," *Standard* (Ogden, UT), Dec. 31, 1893, 6; Walker, "Crisis in Zion," 129. **Topic: Church Finances**

9. George Q. Cannon, Journal, May 10, 1893; Grant, Journal, May 10, 1893. **Topic: Heber J. Grant**

10. George Q. Cannon, Journal, May 10, 1893; Francis Marion Lyman, Journal, May 10, 1893; Joseph F. Smith to Heber J. Grant, July 12, 1893, Heber J. Grant Collection, CHL; Grant, Journal (press copy), May 31, 1893.

11. Grant, Journal (press copy), May 19, 1893; Walker, "Crisis in Zion," 123–25.

12. Grant, Journal, May 31–June 30, 1893.

13. Wells, Diary, volume 16, May 19, 1893; Emmeline B. Wells, "Utah Women in Chicago," *Deseret Evening News,* June 24, 1893, 7; Sewall, *World's Congress of Representative Women,* 1:81–82. **Topic: Emmeline B. Wells**

14. "Editor's Department," *Young Woman's Journal,* Apr. 1893, 4:326; *Deseret News, 1989–90 Church Almanac,* 204; Plewe, *Mapping Mormonism,* 96–97, 206–7; "Remarks," *Deseret Evening News,* Aug. 19, 1893, [9]; "Sunday Services," *Deseret Evening News,* July 31, 1893, 9; Abraham H. Cannon, Diary, Jan. 13, 1892; Neilson, *Exhibiting Mormonism,* 17–18, 81–83, 90–91; Givens, *Viper on the Hearth,* 105–64; Shipps, *Sojourner in the Promised Land,* 62–66.

15. Emmeline B. Wells, "Utah Women in Chicago," *Deseret Evening News,* June 24, 1893, 7.

16. [Rosetta Luce Gilchrist], *Apples of Sodom: A Story of Mormon Life* (Cleveland: William W. Williams, 1883); Etta L. Gilchrist, "The Ballot as a Measure of Reform," *Woman's Exponent,* Nov. 15, 1891, 20:75, 78–79; see also Wells, Diary, volume 14, Apr. 20, 1891; May 3, 1891; June 16 and 19, 1891. **Topic: Women's Suffrage**

17. Emmeline B. Wells, "Utah Women in Chicago," *Deseret Evening News,* June 24, 1893, 7; Etta L. Gilchrist, "The World's Fair," *Woman's Exponent,* June 15, 1893, 21:177–78; "Tell of Their Western Life," *Chicago Tribune,* May 20, 1893, [2]; Committees on the Grain Movement, Minutes, Nov. 17, 1876, in Derr and others, *First Fifty Years of Relief Society,* 399–404. **Topic: Relief Society**

18. Etta L. Gilchrist, "The World's Fair," *Woman's Exponent,* June 15, 1893, 21:177–78.

19. Leah Dunford to Susa Young Gates, July 2, 1893, Family Correspondence, Susa Young Gates Papers, CHL; Susa Young Gates to Leah Dunford, June 30, 1893; July 1, 1893; July 6, 1893; July 12, 1893; July 22, 1893, Widtsoe Family Papers, CHL; Widtsoe, *In a Sunlit Land,* 38–39; Handlin, "Making Men of the Boys," 62.

20. Widtsoe, Oral History Interview, 4; Susa Young Gates to Leah Dunford, July 10, 1892; June 30, 1893; July 1, 1893; July 12, 1893, Widtsoe Family Papers, CHL; Simpson, *American Universities and the Birth of Modern Mormonism,* 28–53; *Saints,* volume 2, chapter 42.

21. Leah Dunford to Susa Young Gates, July 2, 1893, Family Correspondence, Susa Young Gates Papers, CHL; "The Editor's Department," *Young Woman's Journal,* Mar. 1891, 2:283–84; Mary Howe, "Professional and Business Opportunities for Women," *Young Woman's Journal,* Oct. 1891, 3:24–25.

22. Mintz, *Huck's Raft,* 197; Mary Howe, "Professional and Business Opportunities for Women," *Young Woman's Journal,* Oct. 1891–Apr. 1892, 3:24–25, 77–78, 132–33, 228–29, 259–60; "Y. L. Conference," *Young Woman's Journal,* Apr. 1891, 2:331; "Be Ye Not Unequally Yoked Together," *Young Woman's Journal,* Feb. 1891, 2:236–39; Susa Young Gates to Leah Dunford, July 12, 1893, Widtsoe Family Papers, CHL.

23. Widtsoe, Oral History Interview, 17; John A. Widtsoe to Leah Dunford, Jan. 10, 1893; Susa Young Gates to Leah Dunford, July 15, 1893, Widtsoe Family Papers, CHL; Leah Dunford to Susa Young Gates, July 22, 1893, Family Correspondence, Susa Young Gates Papers, CHL; Widtsoe, *In a Sunlit Land,* 228–29; see also *Saints,* volume 2, chapter 30.

24. Widtsoe, Oral History Interview, 31–32; Widtsoe, *In a Sunlit Land,* 38–39, 228–29.

25. Widtsoe, *In a Sunlit Land,* 229–30; Leah Dunford to Susa Young Gates, July 18, 1893, Family Correspondence, Susa Young Gates Papers, CHL. **Topic: John and Leah Widtsoe**

26. Widtsoe, *In a Sunlit Land,* 229, 231–32; John A. Widtsoe to Anna Gaarden Widtsoe, July 24, 1893, Widtsoe Family Papers, CHL; see also Parrish, *John A. Widtsoe,* 95–103.

27. Widtsoe, Diary, Sept. 30 and Oct. 15, 1891; Anna Gaarden Widtsoe to John A. Widtsoe, May 11, 1893; John A. Widtsoe to Anna Gaarden Widtsoe, June 21, 1893, Widtsoe Family Papers, CHL.

28. John A. Widtsoe to Anna Gaarden Widtsoe, May 21, 1893, Widtsoe Family Papers, CHL; see also John A. Widtsoe to Anna Gaarden Widtsoe, June 21, 1893, Widtsoe Family Papers, CHL; and Simpson, *American Universities and the Birth of Modern Mormonism,* 50–51.

29. John A. Widtsoe to Anna Gaarden Widtsoe, July 24, 1893, Widtsoe Family Papers, CHL. Quotation edited for readability; "had" in original changed to "have."

30. Leah Dunford to Susa Young Gates, July 22, 1893, Family Correspondence, Susa Young Gates Papers, CHL.

31. Heber J. Grant to Joseph F. Smith, May 11, 1905, Heber J. Grant Collection, CHL; Grant, Journal, Sept. 2 and Oct. 3, 1893; Heber J. Grant to Rachel Ivins Grant, Sept. 9, 1893; Heber J. Grant to Heber M. Wells, Sept. 9, 1893, Letterpress Copybook, volume 17, 375, 377, 402–3, Heber J. Grant Collection, CHL; George Q. Cannon, Journal, May 10, 1893.

32. Heber J. Grant to Joseph F. Smith, May 11, 1905, Heber J. Grant Collection, CHL; Grant, Journal, Oct. 3, 1893, and Jan. 29, 1942; Abraham H. Cannon, Diary, Feb. 14, 1895.

33. Heber J. Grant to Joseph F. Smith, May 11, 1905, Heber J. Grant Collection, CHL; Grant, Journal, Oct. 3, 1893; Jan. 8, 1916; Jan. 29, 1942; Woodruff, Journal, Sept. 4, 1893; Walker, "Crisis in Zion," 133–34.

34. Grant, Journal, Oct. 3, 1893; Heber J. Grant to Heber M. Wells, Sept. 9, 1893, Letterpress Copybook, volume 17, 402, Heber J. Grant Collection, CHL. **Topic: Church Finances**

35. Grant, Journal (press copy), Sept. 4, 1893, 623; Heber J. Grant to Heber M. Wells, Sept. 7, 1893, Letterpress Copybook, volume 17, 370, Heber J. Grant Collection, CHL; George Q. Cannon, Journal, Sept. 4, 1893.

36. "The Tabernacle Choir," *Deseret Weekly,* Sept. 1, 1894, 340–41; Evan Stephens, "The World's Fair Gold Medal," *Children's Friend,* Oct. 1920, 19:420–21.

37. Evan Stephens, "The World's Fair Gold Medal," *Children's Friend,* Oct. 1920, 19:421; George Q. Cannon, Journal, Sept. 3, 1893; George Q. Cannon, "The Tabernacle Choir at the World's Fair," *Juvenile Instructor,* Sept. 15, 1893, 28:567; Pugsley, Autobiography, 5.

38. George Q. Cannon, Journal, Aug. 28–29, 1893; "Choir Arrangement," *Deseret Evening News,* June 7, 1893, 1; "The Choir Goes," *Deseret Evening News,* Aug. 18, 1893, 1; Neilson, *Exhibiting Mormonism,* 121–24.

39. Evan Stephens, "The World's Fair Gold Medal," *Children's Friend,* Oct. 1920, 19:421; "The Tabernacle Choir," *Deseret Weekly,* Sept. 1, 1894, 340; Handy, *Official Directory of the World's Columbian Exposition,* 104.

40. Evan Stephens, "The World's Fair Gold Medal," *Children's Friend,* Oct. 1920, 19:421–22. Quotation edited for readability; two instances of "His" in original changed to "Thy," and "deemed" changed to "deems."

41. George Q. Cannon, Journal, Sept. 8, 1893; Evan Stephens, "The World's Fair Gold Medal," *Children's Friend,* Oct. 1920, 19:422; "The Tabernacle Choir," *Deseret Weekly,* Sept. 1, 1894, 340; Woodruff, Journal, Sept. 8, 1893; Revelation 5:12; W. S. B. M., "The Welsh Eisteddfod," *Music,* Sept. 1893, 4:545; "Close of the Eisteddfod," *Dixon (IL) Evening Telegraph,* Sept. 9, 1893, 2.

42. "The Tabernacle Choir," *Deseret Weekly,* Sept. 1, 1894, 341; Woodruff, Journal, Sept. 8, 1893; George Q. Cannon, Journal, Sept. 8, 1893; "Hail to the Choir!," *Deseret Evening News,* Sept. 9, 1893, 4; see also Neilson, *Exhibiting Mormonism,* 135–37; and George Q. Cannon, "The Tabernacle Choir at the World's Fair," *Juvenile Instructor,* Sept. 15, 1893, 28:566.

43. "Utah's Singing Children," *Salt Lake Tribune,* Sept. 14, 1893, 8; Evan Stephens, "The World's Fair Gold Medal," *Children's Friend,* Oct. 1920, 19:422–23; "Attractions," *Los Angeles Times,* Sept. 9, 1893, 2; "Welsh Singing Competition," *Edinburgh Evening News,* Sept. 9, 1893, [2]; "Choral Contest at Chicago," *Manchester Evening News,* Sept. 9, 1893, [3]; "Great Choral Contest," *Queensland (Australia) Times,* Dec. 7, 1893, 6; "World's Fair Eisteddfod," *Western Mail* (Cardiff, Wales), Sept. 11, 1893, 5.

44. "Utah at the Fair," *Journal* (Logan, UT), Sept. 13, 1893, 1; "Utah Day at the Fair," *Salt Lake Herald,* Sept. 10, 1893, 1; Woodruff, Journal, Sept. 9, 1893; George Q. Cannon, Journal, Sept. 9, 1893.

45. "Cache Conference," *Journal* (Logan, UT), Nov. 1, 1893, 1; "Religious," *Deseret Weekly,* Sept. 30, 1893, 469; Woodruff, Journal, Sept. 16–19, 1893; Neilson, "B. H. Roberts," 53–84. **Topics: Columbian Exposition of 1893; B. H. Roberts**
46. "Discourse," *Deseret Evening News,* Oct. 28, 1893, [9]; "General Conference," *Deseret Evening News,* Oct. 6, 1893, 5; Oct. 7, 1893, 5.
47. George Q. Cannon, Journal, Oct. 5, 1893. Quotation edited for readability; "felt" and "was" in original changed to "feel" and "is."

CHAPTER 2: AS WE PROVE OURSELVES READY

1. James, Journal, 18–28; Howard, "William Jarman," 61–66, 70–79.
2. Howard, "William Jarman," 70–79; James, Journal, 28; "From Various Missionary Fields," *Latter-day Saints' Millennial Star,* Sept. 18, 1893, 55:609.
3. "From Various Missionary Fields," *Latter-day Saints' Millennial Star,* Sept. 11, 1893, 55:603. **Topic: England**
4. Anthon Lund to Sarah Ann Peterson Lund, Aug. 16, 1893, Letterbooks, volume 1, 40–41, Anthon H. Lund Papers, CHL; Anthon Lund to Wilford Woodruff, Mar. 20, 1895, First Presidency Mission Administration Correspondence, CHL; Howard, "William Jarman," 84–85; Rasmussen, *Mormonism and the Making of a British Zion,* 117–19; see also "Abstract of Correspondence," *Latter-day Saints' Millennial Star,* July 17, 1893, 55:471; Aug. 7, 1893, 55:520.
5. J. M. Sjodahl, "Apostle Anthon H. Lund," in *Lives of Our Leaders,* 202–10; "Why We Gather," *Latter-day Saints' Millennial Star,* Mar. 13, 1893, 55:180–82; "Statistical Report of the European Mission," *Latter-day Saints' Millennial Star,* Apr. 9, 1894, 56:230–31; Rasmussen, *Mormonism and the Making of a British Zion,* 101–2, 117–19; *Saints,* volume 2, chapter 39.
6. Anthon Lund to Sarah Ann Peterson Lund, Aug. 16, 1893; Aug. 25, 1893, Letterbooks, volume 1, 40–41, 53, Anthon H. Lund Papers, CHL; Anthon Lund to First Presidency, Nov. 10, 1893, First Presidency Mission Administration Correspondence, CHL; James, Journal, 21.
7. Anthon Lund to First Presidency, Nov. 10, 1893, First Presidency Mission Administration Correspondence, CHL; "The Mission in Denmark," *Latter-day Saints' Millennial Star,* Nov. 13, 1893, 55:740–42; "The Mission in Sweden and Norway," *Latter-day Saints' Millennial Star,* Nov. 20, 1893, 55:756–59; "The Netherlands Mission," *Latter-day Saints' Millennial Star,* Nov. 27, 1893, 55:773–74; "A Brief History of the Church in the Netherlands," Global Histories, ChurchofJesusChrist.org/study/history/global-histories; Mulder, *Homeward to Zion,* 96; see also Lund, Journal, Sept. 24–Oct. 25, 1893.
8. "Why We Gather," *Latter-day Saints' Millennial Star,* Mar. 13, 1893, 55:180–82; Firmage and Mangrum, *Zion in the Courts,* 241–42; Anthon Lund to First Presidency, Nov. 10, 1893; Anthon Lund to Wilford Woodruff, Sept. 12, 1893, First Presidency Mission Administration Correspondence, CHL; Anthon Lund to Sarah Ann Peterson Lund, Aug. 25, 1893, Letterbooks, volume 1, 53, Anthon H. Lund Papers, CHL; Lund, Journal, July 23, 1893; Jan. 3, 1894; July 2, 1894.
9. Anthon Lund to Wilford Woodruff, Sept. 12, 1893, First Presidency Mission Administration Correspondence, CHL; Strong, *Our Country,* 111–18; First Presidency to Brigham Young Jr., Feb. 11, 1892; First Presidency to Anthon Lund, May 29, 1894, First Presidency Letterpress Copybooks, volume 28.
10. Lund, Journal, Nov. 30, 1893. **Topic: Emigration**
11. Leah Dunford to John A. Widtsoe, Sept. 26, 1893, Widtsoe Family Papers, CHL; see also Leah Dunford to John A. Widtsoe, Aug. 21, 1893; Sept. 10, 1893; Sept. 18, 1893; Nov. 3–4, 1893, Widtsoe Family Papers, CHL.

12. Leah Dunford to John A. Widtsoe, Sept. 10, 1893; Sept. 18, 1893; Sept. 26, 1893; Nov. 3, 1893; John A. Widtsoe to Leah Dunford, Nov. 10, 1893, Widtsoe Family Papers, CHL. **Topic: Church Academies**

13. Leah Dunford to John A. Widtsoe, Dec. 20, 1893, Widtsoe Family Papers, CHL; Gates, *History of the Young Ladies' Mutual Improvement Association,* 101–2, 124–25, 181–83, 301; *L.D.S. Young Men's Mutual Improvement Association Manual; Guide to the First Year's Course of Study in the Young Ladies' Mutual Improvement Association.* **Topics: Young Men Organizations; Young Women Organizations; Church Periodicals**

14. Leah Dunford to John A. Widtsoe, Nov. 3, 1893; Jan. 4, 1894, Widtsoe Family Papers, CHL; Leah Dunford to Susa Young Gates, Mar. 26, 1893; Mar. 12, 1896, Family Correspondence, Susa Young Gates Papers, CHL.

15. George Q. Cannon, Journal, Jan. 1, 1894. **Topic: George Q. Cannon**

16. Woodruff, Journal, Dec. 13 and 31, 1893; Lyman, *Political Deliverance,* 7; *Saints,* volume 2, chapters 10, 21, 36, and 37; George Q. Cannon, Journal, Dec. 14, 1893. **Topic: Utah**

17. Woodruff, Journal, Jan. 9 and 13, 1894; George Q. Cannon, Journal, Jan. 12 and 15, 1894; Feb. 4, 1896; Jan. 6, 1898; Abraham H. Cannon, Diary, Jan. 10 and 12, 1894. **Topic: Antipolygamy Legislation**

18. Alexander, *Things in Heaven and Earth,* 308–9; Alexander, *Mormonism in Transition,* 3; Joseph F. Smith, "True Economy," *Deseret Evening News,* Dec. 16, 1893, 9; Arrington, *Great Basin Kingdom,* 380–412; Quinn, *Wealth and Corporate Power,* 109–11. **Topic: Church Finances**

19. George Q. Cannon, Journal, Mar. 15, 1894.

20. Stapley, "Adoptive Sealing Ritual," 56–104; Irving, "Law of Adoption," 303–10; see also Anthon Lund to Heber J. Grant, June 19, 1894, Letterbooks, volume 1, 323, Anthon H. Lund Papers, CHL; and Heber J. Grant to Anthon Lund, July 14, 1894, Letterpress Copybook, volume 18, 281, Heber J. Grant Collection, CHL. **Topic: Sealing**

21. George Q. Cannon, Journal, Mar. 15, 1894; George Q. Cannon, Journal, Oct. 15, 1890; Abraham H. Cannon, Diary, Oct. 15, 1890; Stapley, "Adoptive Sealing Ritual," 104–5. **Topic: Jane Elizabeth Manning James**

22. George Q. Cannon, Journal, Mar. 15, 1894; Abraham H. Cannon, Diary, Dec. 18, 1890; see also Stapley, "Adoptive Sealing Ritual," 104–8.

23. George Q. Cannon, Journal, Mar. 15, 1894.

24. "Jarman and Jarman," *Deseret Evening News,* Mar. 24, 1894, 5; Howard, "William Jarman," 84.

25. Albert Jarman to Maria Bidgood Barnes, before Feb. 19, 1894, Jarman Family Papers, Huntington Library, San Marino, CA; Anthon Lund to Wilford Woodruff, Mar. 20, 1895, First Presidency Mission Administration Correspondence, CHL.

26. Albert Jarman to Maria Bidgood Barnes, before Feb. 19, 1894; Mar. 9, 1894, Jarman Family Papers, Huntington Library, San Marino, CA; "Jarman and Jarman," *Deseret Evening News,* Mar. 24, 1894, 5.

27. Albert Jarman to Maria Bidgood Barnes, Feb. 19, 1894; Feb. 23, 1894; Apr. 27, 1894, Jarman Family Papers, Huntington Library, San Marino, CA; "Jarman and Jarman," *Deseret Evening News,* Mar. 24, 1894, 5.

28. George Q. Cannon, Journal, Apr. 5, 1894; Abraham H. Cannon, Diary, Apr. 5, 1894. **Topic: Wilford Woodruff**

29. "The Law of Adoption," *Deseret Evening News,* Apr. 14, 1894, 9; Doctrine and Covenants 128:18; Bennett, *Temples Rising,* 298–301.

30. "The Law of Adoption," *Deseret Evening News,* Apr. 14, 1894, 9; Doctrine and Covenants 137:7; Bennett, *Temples Rising,* 299–300; Stapley, *Power of Godliness,* 42–44. **Topics: Adjustments to Temple Work; Family History and Genealogy; Temple Building**

CHAPTER 3: THE PATH OF RIGHT

1. Anthon H. Lund to Heber J. Grant, June 19, 1894, Letterbooks, volume 1, 323, 326, Anthon H. Lund Papers, CHL.

2. Allen, Embry, and Mehr, *Hearts Turned to the Fathers,* 17–24, 33–41; *Saints,* volume 1, chapters 35 and 39; see also, for example, James, Journal, 1; and Albert Jarman to Maria Bidgood Barnes, before Feb. 19, 1894; Feb. 19, 1894; Feb. 23, 1894, Jarman Family Papers, Huntington Library, San Marino, CA.

3. Allen, Embry, and Mehr, *Hearts Turned to the Fathers,* 33–34, 42–47. **Topic: Family History and Genealogy**

4. Anthon H. Lund to Sarah Peterson Lund, Aug. 25, 1893, Letterbooks, volume 1, 53; James E. Talmage to Anthon H. Lund, Aug. 16, 1894, Anthon H. Lund Papers, CHL; First Presidency to Anthon H. Lund, July 5, 1894, First Presidency Letterpress Copybooks, volume 28; George Q. Cannon, Journal, Sept. 28, 1893.

5. First Presidency to Anthon H. Lund, July 5, 1894, First Presidency Letterpress Copybooks, volume 28. **Topic: Emigration**

6. *Saints,* volume 2, chapters 10–14; see also Thirteenth General Epistle, Oct. 1855, in Neilson and Waite, *Settling the Valley,* 242–44, 248–49.

7. First Presidency to Anthon H. Lund, July 5, 1894, First Presidency Letterpress Copybooks, volume 28. **Topic: Gathering of Israel**

8. Anthon H. Lund to First Presidency, Aug. 4, 1894, First Presidency Mission Administration Correspondence, CHL; Lund, Journal, July 30, 1894.

9. An Act to Enable the People of Utah to Form a Constitution and State Government, and to Be Admitted into the Union [July 16, 1894], *Statutes at Large* [1895], 53rd Cong., 2nd Sess., chapter 138, 107–12; George Q. Cannon, Journal, July 17, 1894; "Utah's Bill Is Law," *Deseret Evening News,* July 17, 1894, 1. **Topic: Utah**

10. *Saints,* volume 2, chapters 10, 17, and 26. **Topic: American Legal and Political Institutions**

11. "Steps Leading to Statehood," *Deseret Evening News,* July 30, 1894, 4; "Convention and Woman Suffrage," *Woman's Exponent,* Apr. 1, 1895, 23:241–42; *Saints,* volume 2, chapters 25, 30, and 35. **Topic: Women's Suffrage**

12. *Saints,* volume 2, chapters 37 and 41; Emmeline B. Wells, "A Glimpse of Washington," Mar. 1, 1891, in Derr and others, *First Fifty Years of Relief Society,* 579–81.

13. Emmeline B. Wells, "Letter to the Sisters at Home," *Woman's Exponent,* Apr. 1, 1886, 14:164; [Emmeline B. Wells], "Editorial Thoughts," *Woman's Exponent,* May 1, 1888, 16:180; Doctrine and Covenants 26:2; 28:13.

14. George Q. Cannon, Journal, Apr. 4, 7, and 11, 1895; "President B. H. Roberts," *Juvenile Instructor,* June 15, 1901, 36:354; "Ex. Governor Thomas," *Woman's Exponent,* May 1, 1895, 23:261; "Is Still the Theme," *Deseret Evening News,* Apr. 5, 1895, 1.

15. Harrison, *Separate Spheres,* 80; Roberts, "Life Story of B. H. Roberts," 369–70.

16. George Q. Cannon, Journal, Apr. 4, 7, and 11, 1895; "President B. H. Roberts," *Juvenile Instructor,* June 15, 1901, 36:354; "Ex. Governor Thomas," *Woman's Exponent,* May 1, 1895, 23:261; "Is Still the Theme," *Deseret Evening News,* Apr. 5, 1895, 1.

17. An Act to Enable the People of Utah to Form a Constitution and State Government, and to Be Admitted into the Union [July 16, 1894], *Statutes at Large* [1895], 53rd Cong., 2nd Sess., chapter 138, 107–12; "Convention and Woman Suffrage," *Woman's Exponent,* Apr. 1, 1895, 23:241; [Emmeline B. Wells], "Utah and Statehood," *Woman's Exponent,* Aug. 1 and 15, 1894, 23:172; Wells, Diary, volume 19, Mar. 25, 1895; *Official Report of the Proceedings and Debates,* Mar. 14–15, 1895, 142, 163; Mar. 18–19, 1895, 197, 216.

18. Roberts, "Life Story of B. H. Roberts," 369–71; *Official Report of the Proceedings and Debates,* Mar. 28, 1895, 424. **Topic: B. H. Roberts**

19. Whitney, *Through Memory's Halls,* 105, 239; *Official Report of the Proceedings and Debates,* Mar. 30, 1895, 508.

20. "Woman Suffrage," *Woman's Exponent,* Apr. 1, 1895, 23:244. **Topic: Emmeline B. Wells**

21. Relief Society General Board, Minutes, volume 1, Apr. 4, 1895, 94–96; Wells, Diary, volume 19, Apr. 4, 1895.

22. Albert Jarman to Maria Bidgood Barnes, before Feb. 19, 1894; Apr. 27, 1894, Jarman Family Papers, Huntington Library, San Marino, CA; "Jarman and Jarman," *Deseret Evening News,* Mar. 24, 1894, 5.

23. Albert Jarman to Maria Bidgood Barnes, Nov. 16, 1894; Feb. 16, 1895, Jarman Family Papers, Huntington Library, San Marino, CA; Eleventh Ward, General Minutes, June 30, 1895, 219–20; "Albert Edward Jarman Meets with His Father, William Jarman," Photograph, available at familysearch.org; Howard, "William Jarman," 66, 69; "Albert Jarman Interviewed," *Deseret Evening News,* July 22, 1899, 3.

24. "Albert Jarman Interviewed," *Deseret Evening News,* July 22, 1899, 3; "Jarman's Lurid Murder Tales," *Deseret Evening News,* July 22, 1899, 3; Anthon H. Lund to Wilford Woodruff, Mar. 20, 1895, First Presidency Mission Administration Correspondence, CHL.

25. Eleventh Ward, General Minutes, June 30, 1895, 219–20; Albert Jarman to Maria Bidgood Barnes, Dec. 8, 1894, Jarman Family Papers, Huntington Library, San Marino, CA.

26. Anthon H. Lund to Wilford Woodruff, Mar. 20, 1895, First Presidency Mission Administration Correspondence, CHL; "Albert Jarman Interviewed," *Deseret Evening News,* July 22, 1899, 3.

27. Albert Jarman to Maria Bidgood Barnes, Dec. 8, 1894; Dec. 21, 1894; Jan. 5, 1895; Feb. 12, 1895; Feb. 16, 1895, Jarman Family Papers, Huntington Library, San Marino, CA.

28. Albert Jarman to Maria Bidgood Barnes, Mar. 12, 1895, Jarman Family Papers, Huntington Library, San Marino, CA; Anthon H. Lund to Wilford Woodruff, Mar. 20, 1895, First Presidency Mission Administration Correspondence, CHL.

29. William Jarman to Albert Jarman, Mar. 1, 1895, copy in Anthon H. Lund to Wilford Woodruff, Mar. 20, 1895, First Presidency Mission Administration Correspondence, CHL.

30. Albert Jarman to Maria Bidgood Barnes, Feb. 16, 1895; Mar. 5, 1895, Jarman Family Papers, Huntington Library, San Marino, CA; "Albert Edward Jarman and William Jarman," Photograph, available at familysearch.org; "Albert Edward Jarman Meets with His Father, William Jarman," Photograph, available at familysearch.org; "Mormonism Exposed by Mr. William Jarman," *East Anglian Daily Times* (Ipswitch, England), May 27, 1909, 4.

31. Statehood Constitutional Convention [1895] State Constitution, article 4, section 1, 7, 60; Wells, Diary, volume 19, Apr. 18, 1895; Emmeline B. Wells, "Equal Suffrage in the Constitution," *Woman's Exponent,* May 1, 1895, 23:260.

32. Roberts, "Life Story of B. H. Roberts," 392; *Proceedings before the Committee,* 1:927; "Rawlins, Thatcher and Roberts," *Salt Lake Herald,* Sept. 6, 1895, 3; "Roberts' Tour of Triumph," *Salt Lake Herald,* Oct. 8, 1895, 1.

33. *Saints,* volume 2, chapters 10 and 27; Lyman, *Political Deliverance,* 150–81; Woodruff, Journal, Oct. 4, 1892; "Declaration," *Deseret Evening News,* Mar. 17, 1892, 4. **Topic: Political Neutrality**

34. Franklin D. Richards, Journal, Sept. 14, 1894; "Roberts' Strong Position," *Salt Lake Herald,* Oct. 14, 1895, 1; "Talk with Thatcher," *Salt Lake Tribune,* Nov. 11, 1896, 8; Lyman, *Political Deliverance,* 259.

35. Abraham H. Cannon, Diary, Oct. 7, 1895; Grant, Journal, Oct. 7, 1895; Francis Marion Lyman, Journal, Oct. 7, 1895. **Topic: Joseph F. Smith**

36. Francis Marion Lyman, Journal, Oct. 7 and 10, 1895; "The Crisis in Utah," *Salt Lake Herald,* Oct. 18, 1895, 4; "Roberts' Strong Position," *Salt Lake Herald,* Oct. 14, 1895, 1; Roberts, "Life Story of B. H. Roberts," 393–94.

37. "Roberts' Strong Position," *Salt Lake Herald,* Oct. 14, 1895, 1; "Masterful Roberts," *Salt Lake Herald,* Nov. 2, 1895, 5; Roberts, "Life Story of B. H. Roberts," 395–96.

38. "Not a Democratic Year," *Salt Lake Tribune,* Nov. 6, 1895, 7; "Democratic Leaders Talk," *Salt Lake Herald,* Nov. 8, 1895, 1; Francis Marion Lyman, Journal, Nov. 7, 1895; Roberts, "Life Story of B. H. Roberts," 399; see also White, *Republic for Which It Stands,* 849–51.

39. "Utah a State," *Deseret Evening News,* Jan. 4, 1896, 1; Woodruff, Journal, Jan. 4, 1896; Wells, Diary, volume 20, Jan. 4, 1896; Salt Lake Tabernacle Decorated for Utah Statehood Celebration, Photograph, CHL. **Topic: Utah**

40. Grant, Journal, Jan. 8, 1896; George Q. Cannon, Journal, Mar. 5 and 19, 1896.

41. Grant, Journal, Feb. 13, 1896; Francis Marion Lyman, Journal, Feb. 13, 1896; Brigham Young Jr., Journal, Feb. 13, 1896; George Q. Cannon, Journal, Feb. 13, 1896.

42. Woodruff, Journal, Mar. 5, 1896; George Q. Cannon, Journal, Mar. 5, 1896; Francis Marion Lyman, Journal, Mar. 5, 1896; Grant, Journal, Mar. 5, 1896. **Topics: Church Discipline; Quorums of the Seventy**

43. Grant, Journal, Mar. 12, 1896; Francis Marion Lyman, Journal, Mar. 12, 1896. B. H. Roberts quotation edited for readability; original source has "he wanted us to know that the action that was to be taken against him was causing him the deepest sorrow" and "he did not want us to think that he failed to appreciate all that he was going to lose."

44. B. H. Roberts to Francis Marion Lyman and Heber J. Grant, Mar. 13, 1896, in Francis Marion Lyman, Journal, Mar. 13, 1896; Grant, Journal, Mar. 13, 1896.

45. George Q. Cannon, Journal, Mar. 26, 1896.

46. George Q. Cannon, Journal, Apr. 5 and 6, 1896.

47. "To the Saints," *Deseret Weekly,* Apr. 11, 1896, 532–34; see also "To the Saints," in Clark, *Messages of the First Presidency,* 3:271–77. **Topic: Political Neutrality**

48. "Sixty-Sixth Annual Conference," *Deseret Weekly,* Apr. 11, 1896, 531. First sentence of quotation edited for readability; "had been pledged" in original changed to "has been pledged." **Topic: B. H. Roberts**

CHAPTER 4: A GREAT AMOUNT OF GOOD

1. "Mutual Improvement," *Salt Lake Herald,* June 1, 1896, 6; Gates, *History of the Young Ladies' Mutual Improvement Association,* 132, 221–22; [Thomas Hull], "Should the Mutual Improvement Associations Unite?," *Young Woman's Journal,* Aug. 1896, 7:503–5; see also Thomas Hull, Letter to Editor, *Contributor,* Oct. 1896, 17:741.

2. [Thomas Hull], "Should the Mutual Improvement Associations Unite?," *Young Woman's Journal,* Aug. 1896, 7:504; Gates, *History of the Young Ladies' Mutual Improvement Association,* 128, 138–39, 221; Young Women General Board, Minutes, Apr. 8, 1896, 68–70. **Topics: Young Men Organizations; Young Women Organizations**

3. "Mutual Improvement," *Salt Lake Herald,* June 1, 1896, 6; "General Conference of the Young Men's and Young Ladies' Mutual Improvement Associations," A. Elmina Shepard Taylor Collection, CHL; Hartley, *My Fellow Servants,* 349, 421; Walker, "'Going to Meeting' in Salt Lake City's Thirteenth Ward," 142. **Topic: Sacrament Meetings**

4. "The Old B. Y. Academy," *Young Woman's Journal,* May 1892, 3:337; Widtsoe, *In a Sunlit Land,* 39, 42, 49, 232; Susa Young Gates to Leah Dunford, June 22, 1896; John A. Widtsoe to Leah Dunford, Feb. 14, 1894; Apr. 28, 1894; Leah Dunford to John A. Widtsoe, Mar. 25, 1894; Apr. 4, 1896, Widtsoe Family Papers, CHL; Leah Dunford, "A Visit to Pratt Institute," *Young Woman's Journal,* Mar. 1897, 8:249–59.

5. John A. Widtsoe to Leah Dunford, Apr. 1896, Widtsoe Family Papers, CHL.

6. Leah Dunford to John A. Widtsoe, Apr. 20, 1896, Widtsoe Family Papers, CHL.

7. Leah Dunford to Susa Young Gates, June 22, 1896; July 7, 1896; July 11, 1896; [Sept. 21 and 22, 1896], Family Correspondence, Susa Young Gates Papers, CHL; *Annual of the University of Utah,* 7, 96; Susa Young Gates to Leah Dunford, Sept. 14, 1896, Widtsoe Family Papers, CHL; Kesler, *Reminiscences,* 34–36, 161.

8. Embry, "Women's Life Cycles," 396–97, 410; Arrington, "Pioneer Midwives," 57–61; Mulvay, "Zion's Schoolmarms," 67–72; Buchanan, "Education among the Mormons," 439–40, 445–46. **Topic: Pioneer Women and Medicine**

9. Leah Dunford to Susa Young Gates, [Sept. 21 and 22, 1896], Family Correspondence, Susa Young Gates Papers, CHL; Kesler, *Reminiscences,* 36.

10. Leah Dunford to Susa Young Gates, Oct. 18, 1896, Family Correspondence, Susa Young Gates Papers, CHL. Quotation edited for readability; "the force of Bro Smith's blessing" in original changed to "the force of Brother Smith's blessing."

11. "Institute Records of June, 1897," *Pratt Institute Monthly,* Oct. 1897, 6:26; Leah Dunford to Susa Young Gates, Oct. 25, 1896, Family Correspondence, Susa Young Gates Papers, CHL; Donnette Smith to Julina Lambson Smith, Oct. 18, 1896, Family Correspondence, Joseph F. Smith Papers, CHL.

12. Salt Lake Temple, Baptisms for the Dead, 1896–97, volume H, 153–54, microfilm 183,417; Endowments for the Dead, 1896–97, volume E, 108, 112–13, 116, microfilm 184,088; Sealings of Couples, Deceased, May 27, 1896–Mar. 24, 1898, volume C, 80, microfilm 1,239,575, U.S. and Canada Record Collection, FHL; Ezra Stevenson, "Zion's Maori Association," *Deseret Evening News,* Apr. 8, 1896, 1; Oct. 8, 1896, 2; Newton, *Tiki and Temple,* 84.

13. "Temple List," available at ChurchofJesusChrist.org/temples; George Reynolds to Ezra F. Richards, Feb. 27, 1897, First Presidency Letterpress Copybooks, volume 31; Whaanga, "From the Diary of Mere Whaanga," Mar. 7, [1902].

14. Whaanga, "From the Diary of Mere Whaanga," Feb. 8, 1902, and Mar. 7, [1902]; "Hirini Whaanga Is Here," *Salt Lake Tribune,* July 20, 1894, 8. **Topic: New Zealand**

15. Douglas, "Latter-day Saints Missions and Missionaries in Polynesia," 92–94; First Presidency to William T. Stewart, Oct. 14, 1893, William T. Stewart Papers, CHL; First Presidency to Anthon H. Lund, July 5, 1894, First Presidency Letterpress Copybooks, volume 28; William T. Stewart to First Presidency, Aug. 12, 1893, First Presidency Mission Administration Correspondence, CHL; Newton, *Tiki and Temple,* 78–79.
Topic: Emigration

16. "Hirini Whaanga Is Here," *Salt Lake Tribune,* July 20, 1894, 8; Whaanga, "From the Diary of Mere Whaanga," Feb. 8, 1902; Apr. 30, 1902; Mar. 15, 1903; Newton, *Tiki and Temple,* 81.

17. Whaanga, "From the Diary of Mere Whaanga," Mar. 15, 1903; George F. Gibbs to William Paxman, Sept. 23, 1895; George F. Gibbs to James L. Bunting, Oct. 11, 1895, First Presidency Letterpress Copybooks, volume 29; Benjamin Goddard to William Paxman, Jan. 17, 1895, in Gardner, Journal, Apr. 2, 1895.

18. "To the Maori Saints," *Deseret Evening News,* Feb. 20, 1897, 11; "Zion's Maori Association," *Deseret Evening News,* Oct. 8, 1896, 2; First Presidency to William T. Stewart, Oct. 14, 1893; First Presidency to Ezra F. Richards, Feb. 27, 1897, First Presidency Letterpress Copybooks, volumes 27 and 31.

19. Whaanga, "From the Diary of Mere Whaanga," Feb. 8, 1902; "To the Maori Saints," *Deseret Evening News,* Feb. 20, 1897, 11; Newton, *Tiki and Temple,* 42–76, 84–86; "The Australasian Mission," *Deseret Evening News,* Mar. 4, 1896, 8; "From Australasia," *Deseret Evening News,* Oct. 9, 1896, 8.

20. Benjamin Goddard to William Paxman, Jan. 17, 1895, in Gardner, Journal, Apr. 2, 1895.

21. Susa Young Gates, "Biographical Sketches," *Young Woman's Journal,* Aug. 1898, 9:340–41; McBride, "I Could Have Gone into Every House," Church History website, history.ChurchofJesusChrist.org. Quotation edited for readability; original source has "Oh de-ah! Oh de-ah! what a ho'wible noise they do make in ou'h Pa-ak—to be suah!"

22. Susa Young Gates, "Biographical Sketches," *Young Woman's Journal,* Aug. 1898, 9:339, 341.

23. Susa Young Gates, "Biographical Sketches," *Young Woman's Journal,* Aug. 1898, 9:339–43; "From Various Missionary Fields," *Latter-day Saints' Millennial Star,* July 9, 1896, 58:441–42; Aug. 27, 1896, 58:555; Nottingham Conference, Manuscript History and Historical Reports, Aug. 25, 1896, CHL.

24. Susa Young Gates, "Biographical Sketches," *Young Woman's Journal,* Aug. 1898, 9:340–41.

25. Susa Young Gates, "Biographical Sketches," *Young Woman's Journal,* Aug. 1898, 9:342; "London Conference," *Latter-day Saints' Millennial Star,* Oct. 28, 1896, 59:684–85.

26. Susa Young Gates, "Biographical Sketches," *Young Woman's Journal,* Aug. 1898, 9:342.

27. "London Conference," *Latter-day Saints' Millennial Star,* Oct. 28, 1896, 59:684.

28. Susa Young Gates, "Biographical Sketches," *Young Woman's Journal,* Aug. 1898, 9:342; see also McBride, "I Could Have Gone into Every House," Church History website, history.ChurchofJesusChrist.org. Quotation edited for readability; "nowhere had I found" in original changed to "nowhere have I found."

29. Susa Young Gates, "Biographical Sketches," *Young Woman's Journal,* Aug. 1898, 9:343. **Topic: Growth of Missionary Work**

30. Leah Dunford to Lillian Hamlin, Sept. 25, 1897, Family Correspondence, Susa Young Gates Papers, CHL; John A. Widtsoe to Leah Dunford, Aug. 14, 1897, Widtsoe Family Papers, CHL; Widtsoe, *In a Sunlit Land,* 49–50, 232.

31. John A. Widtsoe to Leah Dunford, Oct. 4, 1897, Widtsoe Family Papers, CHL; Widtsoe, *In a Sunlit Land,* 232; Jacob Gates to Susa Young Gates, Sept. 15, 1897, Family Correspondence, Susa Young Gates Papers, CHL; "Alonzo Pratt Kesler," Missionary Database, history.ChurchofJesusChrist.org/missionary; see also Dunford and Widtsoe correspondence, Sept. 1, 1896–July 25, 1897, Widtsoe Family Papers, CHL.

32. Leah Dunford to Susa Young Gates, Sept. 12, 1897, Family Correspondence, Susa Young Gates Papers, CHL. Quotations edited for readability; original source has "I told him he couldn't see me at all as I would be busy until 5 o'clock. Well he might just as well go home in the morning then if he could not see me. Why certainly, he could suite himself about that. Well he guessed he would stay over if he might see me in the evening."

33. Leah Dunford to Susa Young Gates, Sept. 12, 1897; Leah Dunford to Lillian Hamlin, Sept. 25, 1897, Family Correspondence, Susa Young Gates Papers, CHL. **Topic: John and Leah Widtsoe**

34. Presidency of YLNMIA to "Sisters Visiting the Stakes," [Aug.] 1897, Young Woman's Journal Files, Susa Young Gates Papers, CHL; Susa Young Gates to Leah Dunford, Sept. 16, 1897; John A. Widtsoe to Leah Dunford, Sept. 13, 1897, Widtsoe Family Papers, CHL.

35. Susa Young Gates to Leah Dunford, Sept. 16, 1897, Widtsoe Family Papers, CHL.

36. John A. Widtsoe to Leah Dunford, Nov. 14, 1897, Widtsoe Family Papers, CHL; Susa Young Gates to John A. Widtsoe, Nov. 22, 1897, Widtsoe Family Papers, CHL. **Topic: Susa Young Gates**

37. John A. Widtsoe to Leah Dunford, Oct. 18, 1897; Nov. 14, 1897, Widtsoe Family Papers, CHL; Widtsoe, *In a Sunlit Land,* 37, 51–52.

38. Woodruff, Journal, May 14, 1843; Pratt, *Autobiography,* 86–87; John A. Widtsoe to Leah Dunford, Nov. 29, 1897, Widtsoe Family Papers, CHL.

39. John A. Widtsoe to Leah Dunford, Nov. 29, 1897, Widtsoe Family Papers, CHL.

40. Leah Dunford to John A. Widtsoe, Nov. 7, 1897; John A. Widtsoe to Leah Dunford, Nov. 29, 1897; Susa Young Gates to John A. Widtsoe, Nov. 22, 1897, Widtsoe Family Papers, CHL.

41. Susa Young Gates to John A. Widtsoe, Jan. 20, 1898, Widtsoe Family Papers, CHL.

CHAPTER 5: AN ESSENTIAL PREPARATION

1. Allen, Diary, 12; "Our First Lady Missionaries," *Latter-day Saints' Millennial Star,* July 28, 1898, 60:472; Maki, "They Can Bear Testimony, They Can Teach," Church History website, history.ChurchofJesusChrist.org.

2. "Our First Lady Missionaries," *Latter-day Saints' Millennial Star,* July 28, 1898, 60:472; Historical Department, Journal History of the Church, Mar. 11, 1898, 2; Susa Young Gates, "Biographical Sketches," *Young Woman's Journal,* Aug. 1898, 9:342; McBride, "I Could Have Gone into Every House," Church History website, history. ChurchofJesusChrist.org.

3. George Q. Cannon, in *Sixty-Eighth Annual Conference,* 6–8; *Saints,* volume 2, chapters 25 and 29; *Saints,* volume 3, chapter 1.

4. Watt and Godfrey, "Old 42," 87–99; Allen, Diary, 13–14. Quotation edited for readability; original source has "Bro McMurrin said in his remarks he wanted each of us to understand that we had been called here by the Lord."

5. Allen, Diary, 16–18.

6. Allen, Diary, 18–23; "A Letter from Bristol," *Latter-day Saints' Millennial Star,* July 28, 1898, 60:476–77.

7. "Editorial Notes," *Latter-day Saints' Millennial Star,* June 23, 1898, 60:393; July 14, 1898, 60:443; "Programme of Dr. Talmage's Lecture Tour," *Latter-day Saints' Millennial Star,* July 21, 1898, 60:460; "The Stereopticon versus Prejudice," and "Lime-Light Views," *Latter-day Saints' Millennial Star,* Aug. 11, 1898, 60:504–5, 507–11.

8. "A Letter from Bristol," *Latter-day Saints' Millennial Star,* July 28, 1898, 60:477. **Topic: Growth of Missionary Work**

9. New Zealand Auckland Mission, Manuscript History, volume 3, part 2, Apr. 11, 1898; Hirini Whaanga to Wilford Woodruff, Jan. 8, 1898, First Presidency Missionary Calls and Recommendations, CHL.

10. Historical Department, Journal History of the Church, Dec. 17, 1897, 2; New Zealand Auckland Mission, Manuscript History, volume 3, part 2, Apr. 3, 1898; "In New Zealand," *Lehi (UT) Banner,* Aug. 2, 1898, [7]; Edward H. Anderson, "Lesson of the Life of Hirini Whaanga," *Improvement Era,* Jan. 1906, 9:260; Newton, *Tiki and Temple,* 37, 60, 87–88; Ezra Stevenson to George Reynolds, Jan. 11, 1899, First Presidency Mission Administration Correspondence, CHL.

11. Ezra Stevenson to Wilford Woodruff, June 9, 1898, First Presidency Mission Administration Correspondence, CHL; Gardner, Journal, Apr. 2, 1895; "New Zealand Mission," *Deseret Evening News,* Jan. 14, 1899, 17; Ezra Stevenson to George Reynolds, Jan. 11, 1899, First Presidency Mission Administration Correspondence, CHL; Newton, *Tiki and Temple,* 87–88.

12. "Dramatic and Lyric," *Salt Lake Herald,* Feb. 20, 1898, 11; "A Fine Entertainment," *Salt Lake Herald,* Feb. 26, 1898, 8; "Society," *Salt Lake Herald,* Feb. 27, 1898, 13; George Q. Cannon, Journal, Feb. 25, 1898; Dean, Journal, Feb. 26, 1898; Newton, *Tiki and Temple,* 87–88.

13. "Utahn in New Zealand," *Deseret Weekly,* May 14, 1898, 692; "An Enjoyable Affair," *Deseret Evening News,* Apr. 9, 1898, 5; Stevenson, Mission Journal, July 26, 1898; "Ezra Thompson DuFresne Stevenson," Missionary Database, history.ChurchofJesusChrist.org/missionary; Ezra Richards, Journal, Apr. 4, 1898.

14. Ezra Richards to Wilford Woodruff, Mar. 25, 1898, First Presidency Mission Administration Correspondence, CHL; Ezra Richards, Journal, Mar. 25 and Apr. 4, 1898; New Zealand Auckland Mission, Manuscript History, volume 3, part 2, Apr. 11, 1898.

15. Ezra Richards, Journal, Apr. 5, 1898.

16. New Zealand Auckland Mission, Manuscript History, volume 3, part 2, Apr. 11, 1898; Newton, *Tiki and Temple,* 88. **Topic: New Zealand**

17. See, for example, "It Was Spanish Work," *Boston Evening Journal,* Mar. 31, 1898, 6; and "War May Be Declared within the Next Ten Days," *San Francisco Call,* Mar. 26, 1898, 1; see also Musicant, *Empire by Default,* 143–45, 151–52; and Miller, *From Liberation to Conquest,* 55–60, 69, 116–17, 140–46.

18. Wells, Diary, volume 22, May 10, 1898; George Q. Cannon, Journal, Apr. 24, 1898; Brigham Young Jr., Journal, Feb. 22 and Apr. 25–27, 1898; Lydia D. Alder, "Hispania," *Woman's Exponent,* May 1, 1898, 26:275; "The War with Spain," and "Utah Patriotism," *Woman's Exponent,* May 1, 1898, 26:276; "Mrs. Henrotin's Letter," *Woman's Exponent,* May 1, 1898, 26:277–78; "Women's Council on War," and "Anna Garlin Spencer on the War," *Woman's Exponent,* May 15, 1898, 26:283. **Topics: Mormon Battalion; Mexican-American War**

19. Brigham Young Jr., Journal, Feb. 22 and Apr. 24, 1898; Wells, Diary, volume 22, Apr. 24, 1898; "Services at the Tabernacle," *Deseret Evening News,* Apr. 25, 1898, 8; George Q. Cannon, Journal, Apr. 26, 1898. First quotation edited for readability; "was peace" in original changed to "is peace."

20. "Apostle Young Repudiated," *Salt Lake Tribune,* Apr. 26, 1898, 4; Woodruff, Journal, Apr. 25, 1898; George Q. Cannon, Journal, Apr. 26, 1898; see also Brigham Young Jr., Journal, Apr. 25–27, 1898. Quotation edited for readability; two instances of "were" in original changed to "are."

21. "No Disloyalty Here," *Deseret Evening News,* Apr. 25, 1898, 4; Reeves, "Utah and the Spanish-American War," 97–107. **Topic: Spanish-American War**

22. Woodruff, Journal, June 9 and Aug. 9–28, 1898; Alexander, *Things in Heaven and Earth,* 329; "His Death Came Suddenly," *Deseret Evening News,* Sept. 2, 1898, 1; George Q. Cannon, Journal, Aug. 24–31, 1898.

23. George Q. Cannon, Journal, Aug. 29 and Sept. 2, 1898; *Saints,* volume 1, chapters 27 and 34. Quotation edited for readability; "had had" in original changed to "have had."

24. Woodruff, Journal, Sept. 1–2, 1898; Joseph F. Smith, Journal, Sept. 2, 1898; "President Woodruff Is Dead," *Deseret Evening News,* Sept. 2, 1898, 1; see also Bitton, *George Q. Cannon,* 422–23. **Topic: Wilford Woodruff**

25. LeRoi C. Snow, "An Experience of My Father's," *Improvement Era,* Sept. 1933, 36:677; Lorenzo Snow, "An Account of a Private Interview with President Woodruff."

26. LeRoi C. Snow, "An Experience of My Father's," *Improvement Era,* Sept. 1933, 36:677; George Q. Cannon, Journal, Jan. 6, 1898; John Henry Smith, Diary, Sept. 6, 1898; Clawson, Journal, Dec. 1, 1898, and Apr. 21, 1899; see also Walker, "Crisis in Zion," 115–42. **Topic: Church Finances**

27. Joseph F. Smith, Journal, Sept. 6 and 9, 1898; Historical Department, Journal History of the Church, Sept. 9, 1898, 2; Sept. 13, 1898, 2. **Topic: Quorum of the Twelve**

28. Historical Department, Journal History of the Church, Sept. 13, 1898, 5; Joseph F. Smith, Journal, Sept. 13, 1898; George Q. Cannon, Journal, Sept. 13, 1898; compare LeRoi C. Snow, "An Experience of My Father's," *Improvement Era,* Sept. 1933, 36:677. **Topics: Lorenzo Snow; Succession of Church Leadership; Salt Lake Temple**

29. Historical Department, Journal History of the Church, Sept. 13, 1898, 2–5; George Q. Cannon, Journal, Sept. 13, 1898; Joseph F. Smith, Journal, Sept. 13, 1898; Francis Marion Lyman, Journal, Sept. 13, 1898; Cowley, Journal, Sept. 13, 1898. Quotation edited for readability; "He felt that it was for him to do the very best he could" in original changed to "It is for me to do the very best I can."

30. "The Conference," *Deseret Evening News,* Oct. 10, 1898, 5; Winter, Journal, volume 4, Oct. 9, 1898; "Conference Talks to Big Crowds," *Salt Lake Herald,* Apr. 8, 1901, 5. **Topics: First Presidency; Common Consent**

31. John Henry Smith, Diary, July 29, 1898; Francis Marion Lyman, Journal, July 12 and Dec. 1, 1898; Clawson, Journal, Nov. 10, 1898; Dec. 1, 1898; Mar. 9, 1899; Historical Department, Journal History of the Church, Dec. 1, 1898, 2; Jan. 5, 1899, 4–6; Clawson, "Reorganization of Financial System," 1–6; Clawson, "Memoirs of the Life of Rudger Clawson," 372–74; Franklin D. Richards, Journal, Nov. 7, 10, and 14, 1898; see also Horne, *Latter Leaves in the Life of Lorenzo Snow,* 308–12; and Bell, "Windows of Heaven Revisited," 56.

32. Bell, "Windows of Heaven Revisited," 55–57; Franklin D. Richards, Brigham Young Jr., George Q. Cannon, Joseph F. Smith, in *Sixty-Ninth Annual Conference,* 46–47, 48–50, 65–66, 67–70; Historical Department, Journal History of the Church, Apr. 8, 1899, 2–3; Joseph F. Smith, Journal, Apr. 8, 1899.

33. Historical Department, Journal History of the Church, Apr. 10, 1899, 2. Quotation edited for readability; "were" and "was" in original changed to "are" and "is."

34. LeRoi C. Snow, "From Despair to Freedom through Tithing," *Deseret News,* Church section, Mar. 29, 1941, 6; see also Bell, "Windows of Heaven Revisited," 57–58; and Horne, *Latter Leaves in the Life of Lorenzo Snow,* 314–15.

35. LeRoi C. Snow, "The Lord's Way Out of Bondage," *Improvement Era,* July 1938, 41:401; Bell, "Windows of Heaven Revisited," 58.

36. Winter, Journal, volume 4, May 15 and 16, 1899; "Tour of President Snow," *Salt Lake Herald,* May 21, 1899, 1; Bell, "Windows of Heaven Revisited," 59–60; LeRoi C. Snow, "The Lord's Way Out of Bondage," *Improvement Era,* July 1938, 41:401; McArthur, Oral History Interview, [00:15:16].

37. LeRoi C. Snow, "From Despair to Freedom through Tithing," *Deseret News,* Church section, Mar. 29, 1941, 6; LeRoi C. Snow, "The Lord's Way Out of Bondage," *Improvement Era,* July 1938, 41:439; Brooks, *Uncle Will Tells His Story,* 64; see also Bell, "Windows of Heaven Revisited," 60–63.

38. St. George Utah Stake, General Minutes, May 17, 1899; "Pres. Snow in Sunny St. George," *Deseret Evening News,* May 17, 1899, 2. First quotation edited for readability; original source has "We could scarcely express the reason why we came, yet he presumed the Lord would have somewhat to say to us."

39. LeRoi C. Snow, "The Lord's Way Out of Bondage," *Improvement Era,* July 1938, 41:439.

40. St. George Utah Stake, General Minutes, May 17, 1899; Clawson, Journal, July 2, 1899; Bell, "Windows of Heaven Revisited," 63; see also Horne, *Latter Leaves in the Life of Lorenzo Snow,* 319.

41. "Discourse by President Lorenzo Snow," *Latter-day Saints' Millennial Star,* Aug. 24, 1899, 61:533; St. George Utah Stake, General Minutes, May 18, 1899; Bell, "Windows of Heaven Revisited," 71–72; see also Historical Department, Journal History of the Church, May 18, 1899, 6; and Horton, "Wherein Shall We Return?," 32–35. **Topic: Tithing**

42. Francis Marion Lyman, Journal, May 22–27, 1899; Winter, Journal, volume 4, May 22 and 26, 1899; see also "The Party Enroute," *Deseret Evening News,* May 17, 1899, 2; "Good Prospects Down at Beaver," *Deseret Evening News,* May 25, 1899, 5; Horne, *Latter Leaves in the Life of Lorenzo Snow,* 328–36; Doctrine and Covenants 119 (Revelation, 8 July 1838–C, at josephsmithpapers.org); and Horton, "Wherein Shall We Return?," 37–39.

43. Bell, "Windows of Heaven Revisited," 70; "From Proceedings of Solemn Assembly," 5:180–82, Church Manuscripts, BYU.

44. Clawson, Journal, July 2, 1899; Cowley, Autobiography, July 2, 1899; LeRoi C. Snow, "The Lord's Way Out of Bondage," *Improvement Era,* July 1938, 41:400–401, 439–42. **Topics: Tithing; Consecration and Stewardship**

CHAPTER 6: OUR WISH AND OUR MISSION

1. George T. Judd, "New Zealand Mission," *Deseret Evening News,* Jan. 14, 1899, 15.

2. George T. Judd, "New Zealand Mission," *Deseret Evening News,* Jan. 14, 1899, 15; "Mission Fields," *Deseret Evening News,* Jan. 7, 1899, 15; Stevenson, Mission Journal, Oct. 29 and 30, 1898.

3. Stevenson, Mission Journal, Nov. 10, 1898; George T. Judd, "New Zealand Mission," *Deseret Evening News,* Jan. 14, 1899, 15.

4. George T. Judd, "New Zealand Mission," *Deseret Evening News,* Jan. 14, 1899, 15; Stevenson, Mission Journal, Nov. 25, 1898.

5. "Maori Chief Returns Home," *Deseret Evening News,* May 13, 1899, [17]; Ezra T. Stevenson to Wilford Woodruff, June 9, 1898, First Presidency Mission Administration Correspondence, CHL; Stevenson, Mission Journal, Mar. 5 and 26, 1899.

6. "Maori Chief Returns Home," *Deseret Evening News,* May 13, 1899, [17]; Stevenson, Mission Journal, Apr. 17, 1899. **Topic: New Zealand**

7. Widtsoe, *In a Sunlit Land,* 53–58; "A Union of Art and Science," *Young Woman's Journal,* July 1898, 9:332; "In the European Mission," *Deseret Weekly,* Sept. 17, 1898, 437; Kertz-Welzel, "The Singing Muse?," 8; Coray, "Emma Lucy Gates (Bowen)," 4, 12–13; John A. Widtsoe to Anna Gaarden Widtsoe, Apr. 2, 1899; Leah Dunford Widtsoe to Anna Gaarden Widtsoe, Apr. 21, 1899, Widtsoe Family Papers, CHL.

8. Widtsoe, *In a Sunlit Land,* 53–55, 63–64, 67; "A Union of Art and Science," *Young Woman's Journal,* July 1898, 9:332. **Topic: John and Leah Widtsoe**

9. "Statistical Report of the European Mission," *Latter-day Saints' Millennial Star,* Feb. 15, 1900, 62:103; Arnold H. Schulthess to Conference Presidents and Presiding Elders, June 21, 1899, Arnold H. Schulthess Papers, CHL; *Der Stern,* Jan. 1, 1898, 1; Scharffs, *Mormonism in Germany,* 46–51.

10. Swiss-German Mission, Office Journal, Apr. 14, 1899, 4; Peter Loutensock to George Reynolds, Mar. 4, 1898; Peter Loutensock to Wilford Woodruff, Apr. 24, 1898, First Presidency Mission Administration Correspondence, CHL; Widtsoe, *In a Sunlit Land,* 67–68; Scharffs, *Mormonism in Germany,* 46–51. **Topic: Germany**

11. Coray, "Emma Lucy Gates (Bowen)," 12–13; Leah Dunford Widtsoe to Anna Gaarden Widtsoe, July 1899; John A. Widtsoe to Leah Dunford Widtsoe, Aug. 24, 1899; Leah Dunford Widtsoe to John A. Widtsoe, Sept. 5–9, 1899, Widtsoe Family Papers, CHL; Leah Dunford Widtsoe to Susa Young Gates, Sept. 10–Oct. 19, 1899, Family Correspondence, Susa Young Gates Papers, CHL.

12. John A. Widtsoe to Leah Dunford Widtsoe, Sept. 16, 1899, Widtsoe Family Papers, CHL.

13. John A. Widtsoe to Leah Dunford Widtsoe, Nov. 20, 1899; Leah Dunford Widtsoe to John A. Widtsoe, [Nov. 21, 1899], Widtsoe Family Papers, CHL; Widtsoe, *In a Sunlit Land,* 57.

14. Widtsoe, *In a Sunlit Land,* 57; John A. Widtsoe to Leah Dunford Widtsoe, Telegram, Nov. 20, 1899; Leah Dunford Widtsoe to John A. Widtsoe, [Nov. 21, 1899], Widtsoe Family Papers, CHL. Quotation edited for readability; original source has "magda by gods grace."

15. "Objections Made to Mr. Roberts," *Deseret Evening News,* Dec. 4, 1899, 1; Roberts, "Life Story of B. H. Roberts," 418; Brackenridge, "William R. Campbell," 140.

16. "Roberts and Baskin Sweep Everything," *Salt Lake Herald,* Nov. 9, 1898, 1; Francis Marion Lyman, Journal, Aug. 4 and Sept. 14, 1898; Bitton, *Ritualization of Mormon History,* 157–59.

17. "What the Nation Thinks on the Roberts Case," *Salt Lake Tribune,* Dec. 4, 1898, 17; "Opposition to Roberts Because He Is a Mormon," *Salt Lake Herald,* Dec. 13, 1898, 1; Roberts, "Life Story of B. H. Roberts," 418; Brackenridge, "William R. Campbell," 106–15. **Topic: B. H. Roberts**

18. Brackenridge, "William R. Campbell," 113–19, 137–40; see also, for example, "Roberts's Election to Congress," *New York Journal and Advertiser,* Jan. 2, 1899, 4; "Mormon Apostle Reveals the Truth," *New York Journal and Advertiser,* Jan. 5, 1899, 6; and "Crush the Harem," *New York Journal and Advertiser,* Jan. 27, 1899, 7.

19. "Objections Made to Mr. Roberts," *Deseret Evening News,* Dec. 4, 1899, 1; *Congressional Record* [1900], volume 33, 3–5.

20. *Congressional Record* [1900], volume 33, 47–49.

21. "Before the Committee," *Evening Times* (Washington, DC), Dec. 9, 1899, 2; "Roberts Excluded," *Evening Times,* Jan. 26, 1900, 1; "The Roberts Case," *National Tribune* (Washington, DC), Dec. 28, 1899, 2; "The Manifesto and the End of Plural Marriage," Gospel Topics Essays, ChurchofJesusChrist.org/study/manual/gospel-topics-essays; *Congressional Record* [1900], volume 33, 1075, 1215–16. **Topic: American Legal and Political Institutions**

22. Joseph F. Smith, Journal, Jan. 24, 1900; George Q. Cannon, Journal, Feb. 6, 1900; Lund, Journal, Dec. 28, 1899; Wells, Diary, volume 24, Nov. 19, 1899; see also, for example, "Roberts Excluded," *Evening Star* (Washington, DC), Jan. 26, 1900, 1; "Exclude," *Wichita (KS) Daily Eagle,* Jan. 26, 1900, 1; and "Roberts Excluded from the House," *Seattle (WA) Post-Intelligencer,* Jan. 26, 1900, 1.

23. "The Manifesto and the End of Plural Marriage," Gospel Topics Essays, ChurchofJesusChrist.org/study/manual/gospel-topics-essays; Hardy, *Solemn Covenant,* 285.

24. Cannon, "Beyond the Manifesto," 30–36; Hardy, *Solemn Covenant,* 182–88, 206–27, appendix 2; "The Manifesto and the End of Plural Marriage," note 36, Gospel Topics Essays, ChurchofJesusChrist.org/study/manual/gospel-topics-essays. The four apostles were John W. Taylor, Abraham H. Cannon, George Teasdale, and Matthias F. Cowley. Four additional apostles married new plural wives between 1900 and 1904: Brigham Young Jr., Marriner W. Merrill, Abraham O. Woodruff, and Rudger Clawson. **Topic: Plural Marriage after the Manifesto**

25. "The Manifesto and the End of Plural Marriage," Gospel Topics Essays, ChurchofJesusChrist.org/study/manual/gospel-topics-essays; Cannon, "Beyond the Manifesto," 30–36; Hardy, *Solemn Covenant,* 206–32; see also Alexander, *Things in Heaven and Earth,* 326–28.

26. Lund, Journal, Dec. 28, 1899; Wells, Diary, volume 24, Nov. 19, 1899; Francis Marion Lyman, Journal, Jan. 26, 1900. **Topic: Political Neutrality**

27. Zina Young Card to Susa Young Gates, Apr. 22, 1900, General Correspondence, Susa Young Gates Papers, CHL; "Logan," *Deseret Evening News,* Mar. 31, 1900, 7; "Oneida Stake Conference," *Woman's Exponent,* May 15, 1900, 28:135–36. **Topic: Zina D. H. Jacobs Young**

28. *Saints,* volume 2, chapter 36; Doig and Stone, "The Alberta Settlement," 58–61, 69–71, 79–85, 99; Sherlock, "Mormon Migration and Settlement after 1875," 64–65. **Topic: Canada**

29. Cardston Ward, Relief Society Minutes and Records, July 5, 1900, 73; Oct. 4, 1900, 87; Jan. 3, 1901, 95.

30. Daynes, *More Wives Than One,* 92–94; Daynes, "Single Men in a Polygamous Society," 90–93.

31. Cardston Ward, Young Women's Mutual Improvement Association Minutes, May 6, 1900, 372.

32. Cardston Ward, Young Women's Mutual Improvement Association Minutes, May 6–Sept. 26, 1900, 371–85.

33. "Ethics for Young Girls," *Young Woman's Journal,* Jan.–Dec. 1900. **Topic: Church Periodicals**

34. Cardston Ward, Young Women's Mutual Improvement Association Minutes, May 6, 1900, 372; June 6, 1900, 377–78. Quotation edited for readability; "own that we are a Mormon" in original changed to "own that we are Mormons."

35. "Oneida Stake Conference," *Woman's Exponent,* May 15, 1900, 28:136; Cardston Ward, Relief Society Minutes and Records, July 5, 1900, 73.

36. George Q. Cannon, Journal, Nov. 22 and Dec. 10, 1900; *Saints,* volume 2, chapters 9–11. **Topic: Hawaii**

37. George Q. Cannon, Journal, Dec. 10 and 11, 1900; Jan. 5, 1901; Walker, "Abraham Kaleimahoe Fernandez," [2]; "Pres. Cannon and Party Return," *Deseret Evening News,* Jan. 16, 1901, 8.

38. *Saints,* volume 2, chapters 9–11, 39, and 44; George Q. Cannon, Journal, Nov. 22 and Dec. 12, 1900; George Q. Cannon to Lorenzo Snow and Joseph F. Smith, Dec. 14, 1900, First Presidency General Authorities Correspondence, CHL.

39. George Q. Cannon, Journal, Dec. 12, 1900; Angell, *Theaters of Hawai'i,* 16–17; "President Cannon Celebrates Semi-centennial in Hawaii," *Salt Lake Herald,* Dec. 25, 1900, 6; "Pres. Cannon and Party Return," *Deseret Evening News,* Jan. 16, 1901, 8.

40. George Q. Cannon to Lorenzo Snow and Joseph F. Smith, Dec. 14, 1900, First Presidency General Authorities Correspondence, CHL; "President Cannon Celebrates Semi-centennial in Hawaii," *Salt Lake Herald,* Dec. 25, 1900, 6.

41. George Q. Cannon, Journal, Dec. 12, 1900; George Q. Cannon to Lorenzo Snow and Joseph F. Smith, Dec. 14, 1900, First Presidency General Authorities Correspondence, CHL; "Pres. Cannon and Party Return," *Deseret Evening News,* Jan. 16, 1901, 8. **Topic: Gift of Tongues**

42. "President Cannon Celebrates Semi-centennial in Hawaii," *Salt Lake Herald,* Dec. 25, 1900, 6; George Q. Cannon, Journal, Dec. 13, 1900.

43. George Q. Cannon, Journal, Dec. 28, 1900; "Napela, Jonathan (Ionatana) Hawaii," and "Napela, Kitty Richardson," Biographical Entries, Journal of George Q. Cannon website, churchhistorianspress.org; *Saints,* volume 2, chapters 10–11 and 31. **Topic: Jonathan Napela**
44. Takagi, *Trek East,* 19–20; George Q. Cannon, Journal, Dec. 30, 1900, and Jan. 4, 1901.
45. George Q. Cannon, Journal, Jan. 5, 1901; "Pres. Cannon and Party Return," *Deseret Evening News,* Jan. 16, 1901, 8. **Topic: George Q. Cannon**
46. Snow, *Greeting to the World by President Lorenzo Snow,* [1]; "Special New Century Services," *Deseret Evening News,* Jan. 1, 1901, 5.
47. "Special New Century Services," *Deseret Evening News,* Jan. 1, 1901, 5.
48. "Special New Century Services," and "Greeting to the World," *Deseret Evening News,* Jan. 1, 1901, 5; Snow, *Greeting to the World by President Lorenzo Snow,* [1]–[3].

CHAPTER 7: ON TRIAL

1. Joseph F. Smith, Journal, Feb. 18, 1901; George Q. Cannon, Journal, Mar. 13–Apr. 7, 1901; Bitton, *George Q. Cannon,* 447; Joseph F. Smith to George Q. Cannon, Apr. 7, 1901, Letterpress Copybooks, 503, Joseph F. Smith Papers, CHL.
2. Joseph F. Smith, Journal, Apr. 12, 1901; see also, for example, "Mr. Cannon Improving," *Salt Lake Herald,* Apr. 4, 1901, 2; "Mr. Cannon Better," *Salt Lake Herald,* Apr. 5, 1901, 7; and "President Cannon Worse," *Salt Lake Herald,* Apr. 9, 1901, 3. **Topic: George Q. Cannon**
3. Horne, "Joseph F. Smith's Succession to the Presidency," 270–73; "Life Sketch of Joseph F. Smith," *Deseret Evening News,* Oct. 17, 1901, 1.
4. "Opening of a Mission in Japan," *Deseret Evening News,* Apr. 6, 1901, part 2, 9; "Personal Mention," *Salt Lake Herald,* Apr. 24, 1901, 8; "Mexico Welcomes the Mormons," *Deseret Evening News,* June 24, 1901, 1; Lund, Journal, Oct. 1–2, 1901; Clawson, Journal, Oct. 1–3, 1901. **Topic: Growth of Missionary Work**
5. "Passed into the Repose of Death," *Deseret Evening News,* Aug. 28, 1901, 8; "'Aunt' Zina Laid to Rest," *Deseret Evening News,* Sept. 2, 1901, 8.
6. Cardston Ward, Relief Society Minutes and Records, Aug. 15, 1901, 132. **Topic: Zina D. H. Jacobs Young**
7. Clawson, Journal, Oct. 10, 1901; "President Snow Dead," *Salt Lake Tribune,* Oct. 11, 1901, 1; "In the Tabernacle," *Deseret Evening News,* Oct. 14, 1901, 5. **Topic: Lorenzo Snow**
8. Lund, Journal, Oct. 17, 1901; Clawson, Journal, Oct. 17, 1901; Historical Department, Journal History of the Church, Oct. 17, 1901, 2; "The General Authorities," *Seventy-First Annual Conference,* 45. **Topics: Joseph F. Smith; First Presidency; Succession of Church Leadership; Bishop**
9. "Reorganization of the First Presidency," *Deseret Evening News,* Nov. 16, 1901, 23; *Saints,* volume 1, chapter 32.
10. "Authorities of the Church Sustained," *Deseret Evening News,* Nov. 11, 1901, 23; Wells, Diary, volume 27, Nov. 10, 1901; Relief Society General Board, Minutes, Nov. 10, 1901, 31. **Topic: Common Consent**
11. "Bathsheba Wilson Bigler Smith," Biographical Entry, First Fifty Years of Relief Society website, churchhistorianspress.org; Nauvoo Relief Society Minute Book, Mar. 17, 1842, in Derr and others, *First Fifty Years of Relief Society,* 30; *General Relief Society,* 32–52; see also Swinton, "Bathsheba Wilson Bigler Smith," 349–65.
12. *General Relief Society,* 27–28.
13. *General Relief Society,* 20, 52–59, 91–92, 96. **Topic: Church Headquarters**
14. Relief Society General Board, Minutes, June 20, 1902, 51; *General Relief Society,* 59–60; Derr, Cannon, and Beecher, *Women of Covenant,* 161–63. **Topic: Relief Society**

15. Derr, Cannon, and Beecher, *Women of Covenant,* 154–61; *General Relief Society,* 86–87; see also, for example, "Timely Suggestions," *Woman's Exponent,* Dec. 1 and 15, 1902, 31:51; "Lectures for Mothers," *Woman's Exponent,* Mar. 1, 1903, 31:75; and "Mother's Work," *Woman's Exponent,* Oct. 1, 1903, 32:35. **Topic: Church Periodicals**

16. Cardston Alberta Stake Relief Society, Minutes, Aug. 24, 1903, 25–28; Derr, Cannon, and Beecher, *Women of Covenant,* 157–59.

17. "Smoot Chosen Senator by Majority of Thirty," *Salt Lake Herald,* Jan. 21, 1903, 1; John Henry Smith, Diary, Jan. 24, 1902; Clawson, Journal, Nov. 13, 1902; Lund, Journal, Nov. 14, 1902.

18. Allie Smoot to Reed Smoot, Feb. 24, 1904, Reed Smoot Papers, BYU.

19. See, for example, "Smoot Question Considered," *Deseret Evening News,* Feb. 2, 1903, 8; "Reed Smoot's Case," *Evening Star* (Washington, DC), Mar. 2, 1904, 1; and *Proceedings before the Committee,* 1:26–30; see also Heath, "First Modern Mormon," 1:95–99.

20. Edward H. Anderson, "The Bureau of Information," *Improvement Era,* Dec. 1921, 25:131–39; Lund, "Joseph F. Smith and the Origins of the Church Historic Sites Program," 346–47. **Topic: Public Relations**

21. "Nineteen Citizens of Utah Sign Protest," *Salt Lake Herald,* Feb. 10, 1903; *Proceedings before the Committee,* 1:26–30. **Topic: First Presidency**

22. Flake, *Politics of American Religious Identity,* 34–35, 38; Clawson, Journal, Mar. 5, 1903; First Presidency to Reed Smoot, Mar. 9, 1903, Reed Smoot Papers, BYU.

23. Charles W. Nibley, "Reminiscences of President Joseph F. Smith," *Improvement Era,* Jan. 1919, 22:195; Joseph F. Smith to Reed Smoot, Jan. 8, 1904, First Presidency Letterpress Copybooks, volume 39.

24. Reed Smoot to Joseph F. Smith, Feb. 5, 1904, Reed Smoot Papers, BYU; *Proceedings before the Committee,* 1:26–30; Riess, "Heathen in Our Fair Land," 298; Reed Smoot to Joseph F. Smith, Dec. 16, 1903; Jan. 8, 1904; Jan. 9, 1904, Reed Smoot Papers, BYU.

25. "Reed Smoot's Fate Is Sealed in the Senate," *Salt Lake Tribune,* Nov. 18, 1903, 1; "Senator Smoot Files His Reply," *Salt Lake Herald,* Jan. 5, 1904, 1; Reed Smoot to Joseph F. Smith, Jan. 9, 1904; Jan. 18, 1904, Reed Smoot Papers, BYU. **Topic: Reed Smoot Hearings**

26. Lund, Journal, Feb. 25, 1904; Francis Marion Lyman, Journal, Feb. 24–27, 1904; Reed Smoot to First Presidency, Jan. 18, 1904, Reed Smoot Papers, BYU; Joseph F. Smith to Reed Smoot, Jan. 8, 1904, First Presidency Letterpress Copybooks, volume 39.

27. "Smith Expounds the Tenets of Mormon Church," *Washington (DC) Times,* Mar. 2, 1904, 1; *Proceedings before the Committee,* 1:476; Bray, "Joseph F. Smith's Beard," 462. **Topic: Hyrum Smith**

28. Flake, *Politics of American Religious Identity,* 61; *Proceedings before the Committee,* 1:80–96. Quotation edited for clarity; "the first president of the church" in original changed to "the president of the Church."

29. *Proceedings before the Committee,* 1:96–98. **Topic: Common Consent**

30. *Proceedings before the Committee,* 1:98, 483–84. **Topic: Plural Marriage in Utah**

31. *Proceedings before the Committee,* 1:99, 483–84; Salt Lake Stake, Minutes of the Quarterly Conference, volume 9, Mar. 19, 1905, 40–41; Flake, *Politics of American Religious Identity,* 95–96.

32. *Proceedings before the Committee,* 1:100–128; Flake, *Politics of American Religious Identity,* 75–79.

33. *Proceedings before the Committee,* 1:129–31; Lorenzo Snow, "Polygamy and Unlawful Cohabitation," *Deseret Evening News,* Jan. 8, 1900, 4; "The Manifesto and the End of Plural Marriage," Gospel Topics Essays, ChurchofJesusChrist.org/study/manual/gospel-topics-essays.

34. *Proceedings before the Committee,* 1:129–30; "A Frank, Honest Declaration," *Deseret Evening News,* Mar. 3, 1904, 1.

35. *Proceedings before the Committee,* 1:129–31; see also Philip Loring Allen, "The Mormon Church on Trial," *Harper's Weekly,* Mar. 26, 1904, 469. **Topic: Antipolygamy Legislation**

36. *Proceedings before the Committee,* 1:138–43, 150, 158, 173–74, 177–78; "The Manifesto and the End of Plural Marriage," Gospel Topics Essays, ChurchofJesusChrist. org/study/manual/gospel-topics-essays. **Topics: Joseph F. Smith; Reed Smoot Hearings; Plural Marriage after the Manifesto; Church Discipline**

37. *Proceedings before the Committee,* 1:79–350; Paulos, "Under the Gun at the Smoot Hearings," 205–7; Joseph F. Smith to Franklin S. Bramwell, Mar. 21, 1904, Letterpress Copybooks, 461, Joseph F. Smith Papers, CHL.

38. Carlos A. Badger to Edward E. Jenkins, Mar. 16, 1904, Carlos A. Badger Letterbooks, volume 1, 454, CHL; Reed Smoot to Joseph F. Smith, Mar. 23, 1904, Reed Smoot Papers, BYU; see also, for example, "Utah Plague Spot," *National Tribune* (Washington, DC), Mar. 10, 1904, 8; "Gives History of Mormonism," *San Francisco Call,* Mar. 12, 1904, 2; and "Mormons at W.C.T.U. Session," *New York Times,* Mar. 15, 1904, 5.

39. George F. Gibbs to Harry J. Boswell, Mar. 22, 1904, First Presidency Letterpress Copybooks, volume 39; see also Merrill, *Apostle in Politics,* 50–51. **Topic: Public Relations**

40. *Proceedings before the Committee,* 1:178; Reed Smoot to Joseph F. Smith, Mar. 23, 1904, Reed Smoot Papers, BYU; Flake, *Politics of American Religious Identity,* 91–92.

41. Hardy, *Solemn Covenant,* appendix 2, [426]; Joseph F. Smith, in *Seventy-Fourth Annual Conference,* 75; "The Manifesto and the End of Plural Marriage," Gospel Topics Essays, ChurchofJesusChrist.org/study/manual/gospel-topics-essays.

42. Joseph F. Smith, in *Seventy-Fourth Annual Conference,* 75–76; "President Lyman Very Emphatic," *Deseret Evening News,* Oct. 31, 1910, 1; Flake, *Politics of American Religious Identity,* 91–92.

43. Joseph F. Smith, in *Seventy-Fourth Annual Conference,* 76.

Chapter 8: The Rock of Revelation

1. "George R. Francis" [Joseph M. Tanner] to John A. Widtsoe, Apr. 28, 1904, John A. Widtsoe Papers, CHL; see also Clarence Snow to John A. Widtsoe, Mar. 29, 1904, John A. Widtsoe Papers, CHL; John A. Widtsoe to Anna Gaarden Widtsoe, Apr. 20, 1904, Widtsoe Family Papers, CHL; Flake, *Politics of American Religious Identity,* 51; and Ward, *Joseph Marion Tanner,* 39–41, 49–50.

2. John A. Widtsoe to Anna Gaarden Widtsoe, Apr. 20, 1904, Widtsoe Family Papers, CHL.

3. Widtsoe, *In a Sunlit Land,* 235; "Local Points," *Journal* (Logan, UT), Feb. 11, 1902, [8]; "Anna Karine Pedersdatter," and "Petroline Jorgine Pedersdatter Gaarden," Missionary Database, history.ChurchofJesusChrist.org/missionary; Anna Gaarden Widtsoe to Leah D. Widtsoe, Feb. 8, 1904, Widtsoe Family Papers, CHL.

4. "Osborne John Peter Widtsoe," Missionary Database, history.ChurchofJesusChrist. org/missionary; Osborne Widtsoe to John A. Widtsoe, Oct. 10–11, 1903; Oct. 12, 1903; Oct. 21, 1903, Widtsoe Family Papers, CHL; *Harvard University Catalogue,* 1903–4, 121.

5. Logan Fifth Ward, Young Women's Mutual Improvement Association Minutes and Records, volume 4, Mar. 25, 1903; Sept. 2, 1903; Sept. 28, 1904; see also, for example, Leah Dunford Widtsoe, "Lessons in Cookery," *Young Woman's Journal,* Jan. 1901, 12:33–36; Leah Dunford Widtsoe, "Furnishing the Home," *Young Woman's Journal,* Jan. 1902, 13:25–29; and Leah D. Widtsoe, "The Cook's Corner," and "Accidents and Sudden Illness," *Young Woman's Journal,* Jan. 1903, 14:32–36.

6. Widtsoe, *In a Sunlit Land,* 42, 66–67; *Saints,* volume 2, chapter 44.

7. John A. Widtsoe, "Geological Time," *Improvement Era,* July 1904, 7:699–705; John A. Widtsoe, "The Law of Evolution," *Improvement Era,* Apr. 1904, 7:401–9. **Topics: Organic Evolution; Church Periodicals**

8. John A. Widtsoe to Anna Gaarden Widtsoe, Nov. 24, 1903, Widtsoe Family Papers, CHL; Joseph F. Smith to John A. Widtsoe, Sept. 24, 1903, John A. Widtsoe Papers, CHL.

9. Francis Marion Lyman, Journal, Mar. 10 and 26, 1904; Apr. 10, 1906; Reed Smoot to Joseph F. Smith, Mar. 23, 1904, Reed Smoot Papers, BYU; Flake, *Politics of American Religious Identity,* 91–92; Miller, *Apostle of Principle,* 411–14, 431, 442–43, 463, 502; Tanner, *A Mormon Mother,* 173, 268, 314; Hardy, *Solemn Covenant,* 206–7. **Topics: Plural Marriage after the Manifesto; Matthias F. Cowley**

10. Francis Marion Lyman, Journal, Mar. 31, 1904; Apr. 6, 1904; May 3, 1904; July 9, 16, and 21, 1904; see also 3 Nephi 11:28.

11. Francis Marion Lyman, Journal, Aug. 18 and Sept. 29, 1904; Clawson, Journal, Sept. 29 and Oct. 4, 1904; John Henry Smith, Diary, Sept. 21 and 29, 1904; Miller, *Apostle of Principle,* 432–33; Alexander, *Mormonism in Transition,* 67–68; "The Manifesto and the End of Plural Marriage," Gospel Topics Essays, ChurchofJesusChrist.org/study/manual/gospel-topics-essays. **Topic: Sealing**

12. Francis Marion Lyman, Journal, Dec. 29, 1904, and Jan. 4–5, 1905; Lund, Journal, Dec. 30, 1904; Mouritsen, "George Franklin Richards," 274–76; Miller, *Apostle of Principle,* 454–57, 503–4. John Henry Smith undertook a similar mission to speak with Matthias Cowley in Mexico. Matthias declined to testify. John Henry Smith, Diary, Jan. 8, 1905; Cowley, Journal, Jan. 7 and 20, 1905; Cowley, Autobiography, Jan. 20, 1905.

13. Francis Marion Lyman, Journal, Jan. 12, 1905; Mouritsen, "George Franklin Richards," 274; Account of Meetings, Oct. 1905, Francis M. Lyman Papers, CHL; Flake, *Politics of American Religious Identity,* 102–5.

14. Francis M. Lyman to George Teasdale, July 8, 1904, in Francis Marion Lyman, Journal, July 9, 1904; Reed Smoot to Joseph F. Smith, Dec. 8, 1905; Reed Smoot to George Gibbs, Telegram, Dec. 8, 1905, Reed Smoot Papers, BYU; Jorgensen and Hardy, "The Taylor-Cowley Affair," 4–36.

15. John W. Taylor to Council of the Twelve Apostles, Oct. 28, 1905; Matthias F. Cowley to Council of the Twelve Apostles, Oct. 29, 1905, Reed Smoot Papers, BYU; Mouritsen, "George Franklin Richards," 274–76.

16. Mouritsen, "George Franklin Richards," 275–76; Francis Marion Lyman, Journal, Oct. 28, 1905; Miller, *Apostle of Principle,* 464–67. **Topics: Matthias F. Cowley; Quorum of the Twelve**

17. "The Centennial Memorial Company," in [Smith], *Proceedings at the Dedication,* 7; Susa Young Gates, "Memorial Monument Dedication," *Improvement Era,* Feb. 1906, 9:313–14; Mar. 1906, 9:388; Susa Young Gates, "Watchman, What of the Hour?," *Young Woman's Journal,* Feb. 1906, 17:51; "Ceremonies at the Unveiling," *Deseret Evening News,* Dec. 23, 1905, 2; Erekson, "American Prophet, New England Town," 314–15. **Topics: Historic Sites; Joseph Smith Jr.**

18. Susa Young Gates, "Memorial Monument Dedication," *Improvement Era,* Feb. 1906, 9:313–14; Mar. 1906, 9:388; Susa Young Gates, "Watchman, What of the Hour?," *Young Woman's Journal,* Feb. 1906, 17:51; Flake, *Politics of American Religious Identity,* 95–98, 109–11; "Why Sustain Him?," *Salt Lake Tribune,* Mar. 9, 1905, 4; "People Talk about Joseph F.'s Shame," *Salt Lake Tribune,* Mar. 21, 1905, 1; "Joseph F. Does Not Understand," *Salt Lake Tribune,* Mar. 22, 1905, 4; "The Church Disavows Itself," *Salt Lake Tribune,* Mar. 30, 1905, 4.

19. Flake, *Politics of American Religious Identity,* 94–102.

20. "Introduction," "The Centennial Memorial Company," and "Dedication Exercises," in [Smith], *Proceedings at the Dedication,* [1], [5], 7, 9–17; Susa Young Gates, "Watchman, What of the Hour?," *Young Woman's Journal,* Feb. 1906, 17:51.

21. "The Centennial Memorial Company," and "Description of the Monument," in [Smith], *Proceedings at the Dedication,* 7, 26–27; Wells, "Report on Joseph Smith's Birthplace," 23–25; Susa Young Gates, "Watchman, What of the Hour?," *Young Woman's Journal,* Feb. 1906, 17:52.

22. "Dedication Exercises," in [Smith], *Proceedings at the Dedication,* 9–17; Susa Young Gates, "Memorial Monument Dedication," *Improvement Era,* Feb. 1906, 9:310; Susa Young Gates, "Watchman, What of the Hour?," *Young Woman's Journal,* Feb. 1906, 17:55; see also Joseph Smith Centennial Photograph Album, CHL.

23. [Smith], *Proceedings at the Dedication,* 30–31; Francis Marion Lyman, Journal, Dec. 23, 1905; "Full Text of President Smith's Prayer in Dedication of Memorial," *Deseret Evening News,* Dec. 30, 1905, 5; see also Ephesians 2:20; and Matthew 16:18.
24. Lund, Journal, Dec. 26, 1905; Lund, "Joseph F. Smith and the Origins of the Church Historic Sites Program," 342–55. **Topic: Historic Sites**
25. Harper, *First Vision,* 71–73, 93–99, 131–34; Allen, "Emergence of a Fundamental," 44–58; see also, for example, Pratt, *An Interesting Account,* 4–5, in *JSP,* H1:523; and Hyde, *Ein Ruf aus der Wüste,* 14–16.
26. Susa Young Gates, "Memorial Monument Dedication," *Improvement Era,* Mar. 1906, 9:381–83, 388; Susa Young Gates, "Watchman, What of the Hour?," *Young Woman's Journal,* Feb. 1906, 17:56–61. Quotation edited for readability; "Here had the boy kneeled" in original changed to "Here the boy kneeled." **Topic: Sacred Grove and Smith Family Farm**
27. Francis Marion Lyman, Journal, Dec. 30, 1905; Susa Young Gates, "Memorial Monument Dedication," *Improvement Era,* Mar. 1906, 9:383, 388.
28. Widtsoe, *In the Gospel Net,* 101–2. **Topic: Norway**
29. Widtsoe, *In the Gospel Net,* 104–5, 113–14; Anthon Skanchy to First Presidency, Feb. 4, 1904, First Presidency Mission Administration Correspondence, CHL; *Saints,* volume 2, chapters 32–33.
30. Widtsoe, *In the Gospel Net,* 113–14.
31. Anna Gaarden Widtsoe to John A. Widtsoe, Nov. 2, 1903, John A. Widtsoe Papers, CHL.
32. Widtsoe, *In the Gospel Net,* 115; Anna Gaarden Widtsoe to John A. Widtsoe, Apr. 19, 1904, Widtsoe Family Papers, CHL.
33. Anna Gaarden Widtsoe to John A. Widtsoe, June 6, 1904, Widtsoe Family Papers, CHL; John A. Widtsoe to Anna Gaarden Widtsoe, Aug. 18, 1905, Widtsoe Family Papers, CHL; Widtsoe, *In a Sunlit Land,* 83–87; Woodworth, "Financial Crisis at Brigham Young Academy," 73, 105–6; "Widtsoe, Osborne John Peder," in Jenson, *Latter-day Saint Biographical Encyclopedia,* 2:403–4. **Topic: Church Academies**
34. Anna Gaarden Widtsoe to John A. Widtsoe, Dec. 9, 1904, Widtsoe Family Papers, CHL.
35. Widtsoe, *In the Gospel Net,* 105, 115.
36. LeGrand Richards, "President Joseph F. Smith in Europe," *Latter-day Saints' Millennial Star,* Aug. 23, 1906, 68:532–33; Roothoff, Autobiography, 4.
37. Osborne J. P. Widtsoe, "The Little Blind Boy of Holland," *Juvenile Instructor,* Nov. 15, 1907, 42:679–81.
38. Osborne J. P. Widtsoe, "The Little Blind Boy of Holland," *Juvenile Instructor,* Nov. 15, 1907, 42:679–81; LeGrand Richards, "President Joseph F. Smith in Europe," *Latter-day Saints' Millennial Star,* Aug. 23, 1906, 68:533.
39. LeGrand Richards, "Discourse by President Joseph F. Smith," *Latter-day Saints' Millennial Star,* Aug. 30, 1906, 68:546.
40. Osborne J. P. Widtsoe, "The Little Blind Boy of Holland," *Juvenile Instructor,* Nov. 15, 1907, 42:679–81; Roothoff, Autobiography, 4. **Topics: Healing; Netherlands**
41. "Saints Gather at Conference," *Deseret Evening News,* Oct. 5, 1906, 1–2; Mitchell, "Mormons in Wilhelmine Germany," 152; Scharffs, *Mormonism in Germany,* 51–53; Swiss-German Mission, Office Journal, Apr. 22, 1900, 4–5; Aug. 1, 1900, 4–5; Apr. 9, 1909, 92–94; Hugh J. Cannon to George Reynolds, Aug. 11, 1904; Sept. 13, 1904, First Presidency Mission Administration Correspondence, CHL; Thomas McKay to Reed Smoot, Mar. 17, 1909, First Presidency Mission Administration Correspondence, CHL. **Topic: Germany**
42. "Saints Gather at Conference," *Deseret Evening News,* Oct. 5, 1906, 1–2; Ballif, Journal, Aug. 16–17, 1906; Ashby D. Boyle, "Prest. Smith in Switzerland," *Deseret Evening News,* Sept. 29, 1906, 30; "The Gospel of Doing," *Der Stern,* Oct. 15, 1906, 38:305–8.
43. "The Gospel of Doing," *Der Stern,* Nov. 1, 1906, 38:331–32; see also Isaiah 11:9. Quotation edited for readability; "when temples of God that are dedicated to the holy ordinances of the gospel and not to idol worship will be established" in original changed to "when temples of God that are dedicated to the holy ordinances of the gospel will be established." **Topics: Temple Building; Switzerland**

CHAPTER 9: STRUGGLE AND FIGHT

1. "Joseph F. Smith Is Now in Zion," *Salt Lake Tribune,* Sept. 30, 1906, 1; Francis Marion Lyman, Journal, Apr. 8, 1906; "J. M. Tanner Dropped from Two Boards," *Salt Lake Telegram,* Apr. 10, 1906, 6; Church Board of Education, Minutes, Apr. 25, 1906, 51. Joseph Tanner was asked to complete his contractual obligation to the Church through the end of the school year.
2. John Henry Smith, Diary, Apr. 8, 1906; Francis Marion Lyman and George Albert Smith, in *Seventy-Sixth Annual Conference,* 79–80, 93–94. **Topic: Quorum of the Twelve**
3. Reed Smoot to Charles Penrose, Apr. 30, 1906, Reed Smoot Papers, BYU.
4. "Senator Smoot's Case," *Evening Star* (Washington, DC), June 11, 1906, 6.
5. Flake, *Politics of American Religious Identity,* 5; Paulos, *Mormon Church on Trial,* xxiv–xxxiii; Heath, "First Modern Mormon," 1:179, 184–87; Winder, "Theodore Roosevelt and the Mormons," 12–13; "Smoot Keeps His Seat," *Evening Star* (Washington, DC), Feb. 21, 1907, 9; "Senator Smoot Seated," *Washington (DC) Times,* Feb. 21, 1907, 10. **Topics: Reed Smoot Hearings; American Legal and Political Institutions**
6. Joseph F. Smith to Reed Smoot, Feb. 23, 1907, Reed Smoot Papers, BYU.
7. Joseph F. Smith, in *Seventy-Seventh Annual Conference,* 7. **Topics: Tithing; Church Finances**
8. "Address to the World," and "An Address," in *Seventy-Seventh Annual Conference,* 8–9, 3–16 (second numbering).
9. "Address to the World," in *Seventy-Seventh Annual Conference,* 9.
10. "Death of Jane Manning James," *Deseret Evening News,* Apr. 16, 1908, 1; "First Negroes to Join Mormon Church," *Salt Lake Herald,* Oct. 2, 1899, 5; *Saints,* volume 2, chapters 5 and 6; "James, Jane Elizabeth," Pioneer Database, history.ChurchofJesusChrist.org/overlandtravel; see also "James, Jane Elizabeth Manning," Biographical Entry, Century of Black Mormons website, exhibits.lib.utah.edu. **Topic: Jane Elizabeth Manning James**
11. "Death of Jane Manning James," *Deseret Evening News,* Apr. 16, 1908, 1; James, Autobiography, [8]; Newell, *Your Sister in the Gospel,* 128; see also, for example, "Old Folks' Day at the Lagoon," *Salt Lake Herald,* June 27, 1902, 5; and "Salt Lake Observes Day of the Pioneers," *Salt Lake Tribune,* July 26, 1904, 1.
12. "'Aunt Jane' Laid to Rest," *Deseret Evening News,* Apr. 21, 1908, 2; "James, Jane Elizabeth Manning," Biographical Entry, Century of Black Mormons website, exhibits. lib.utah.edu; James, Autobiography, [1], [6]. **Topics: Joseph and Emma Hale Smith Family; Slavery and Abolition**
13. James, Autobiography, [8]; Newell, *Your Sister in the Gospel,* 72–73; "James, Jane Elizabeth Manning," Biographical Entry, Century of Black Mormons website, exhibits. lib.utah.edu.
14. "'Aunt Jane' Laid to Rest," *Deseret Evening News,* Apr. 21, 1908, 2; Jane James to Joseph F. Smith, Feb. 7, 1890, Joseph F. Smith Papers, CHL; Jane James to Joseph F. Smith, Aug. 31, 1903, First Presidency Temple Ordinance Files, CHL; Quorum of the Twelve Apostles, Minutes, Jan. 2, 1902, George Albert Smith Family Papers, J. Willard Marriott Library, University of Utah, Salt Lake City.
15. "Race and the Priesthood," Gospel Topics Essays, ChurchofJesusChrist.org/study/manual/gospel-topics-essays; *Saints,* volume 2, chapters 12 and 28.
16. Newell, *Your Sister in the Gospel,* 97–100, 106–8, 114, 119; *Saints,* volume 2, chapter 39; "James, Jane Elizabeth Manning," Biographical Entry, Century of Black Mormons website, exhibits.lib.utah.edu; Reiter, "Black Saviors on Mount Zion," 105–13. **Topics: Priesthood and Temple Restriction; Baptism for the Dead**
17. Zina D. Young to Joseph F. Smith, Jan. 15, 1894, First Presidency Temple Ordinance Files, CHL; Salt Lake Temple, Sealings for the Dead, Couples, 1893–1942, volume A, May 18, 1894, microfilm 184,587, U.S. and Canada Record Collection, FHL; Newell, *Your Sister in the Gospel,* 114–15.

18. Quorum of the Twelve Apostles, Minutes, Jan. 2, 1902, George Albert Smith Family Papers, J. Willard Marriott Library, University of Utah, Salt Lake City; James, Autobiography, [8].
19. Clawson, Journal, Nov. 13, 1902; Jane James to Joseph F. Smith, Aug. 31, 1903, First Presidency Temple Ordinance Files, CHL. Vicarious temple ordinances were performed for Jane Manning James in 1979.
20. "'Aunt Jane' Laid to Rest," *Deseret Evening News,* Apr. 21, 1908, 2; "Death of Jane Manning James," *Deseret Evening News,* Apr. 16, 1908, 1.
21. "But One of Many Cases," *Salt Lake Tribune,* July 28, 1909, 4; "Some New Polygamists," *Salt Lake Tribune,* Nov. 13, 1909, 6; George F. Richards, Journal, July 14, 1909; Francis Marion Lyman, Journal, July 14 and 21–22, 1909; John Henry Smith, Diary, July 14, 1909. **Topic: Plural Marriage after the Manifesto**
22. Francis Marion Lyman, Journal, Jan. 7, 1910; Feb. 9–10, 1910; Sept. 28, 1910; Oct. 3, 1910; George F. Richards, Journal, July 21–22, 1909; Sept. 22, 1909; "Excommunication," *Deseret Evening News,* Sept. 28, 1910, 1; "Excommunication," *Deseret Evening News,* Oct. 3, 1910, 1; First Presidency to Presidents and Counselors, Oct. 5, 1910, in Clark, *Messages of the First Presidency,* 4:216–18; Hales, *Modern Polygamy and Mormon Fundamentalism,* 95–105.
23. Richard Barry, "The Political Menace of the Mormon Church," *Pearson's,* Sept. 1910, 24:319–30; "The Mormon Evasion of Anti-polygamy Laws," *Pearson's,* Oct. 1910, 24:443–51; "The Mormon Method in Business," *Pearson's,* Nov. 1910, 24:571–78; Cannon, "Magazine Crusade against the Mormon Church," 4, 6–8; Smoot, Diary, Oct. 18, 1910, Reed Smoot Papers, BYU.
24. Cannon, "Cannon's National Campaign," 65, 105; Cannon, "Wives and Other Women," 83.
25. Joseph F. Smith and Anthon H. Lund to John O'Hara Cosgrave, Oct. 20, 1910, First Presidency Cumulative Correspondence, CHL; Tichi, *Exposés and Excess,* 65–72, 76–83; Frank J. Cannon and Harvey J. O'Higgins, "Under the Prophet in Utah," *Everybody's Magazine,* Dec. 1910, 23:722–37, 99–104 [second numbering]; Jan. 1911, 24:29–35; Feb. 1911, 24:189–205; Mar. 1911, 24:383–99; Apr. 1911, 24:513–28; May 1911, 24:652–64; June 1911, 24:825–35; Frank J. Cannon and Harvey J. O'Higgins, "The New Polygamy," *Everybody's Magazine,* July 1911, 25:94–107; Frank J. Cannon and Harvey J. O'Higgins, "The Prophet and Big Business," *Everybody's Magazine,* Aug. 1911, 25:209–22; Cannon, "Cannon's National Campaign," 65–74.
26. *Saints,* volume 1, chapters 13 and 39; *Saints,* volume 2, chapters 25 and 27; Howard, "William Jarman," 61.
27. Lucy Gates to "Dearest Ones," Apr. 6, 1909, Emma Lucy Gates Bowen Papers, BYU; Horace G. Whitney to the Burtons and others, Apr. 18, 1909, Susa Young Gates Papers, CHL; Horace G. Whitney, "Emma Lucy Gates Scores a Big Hit," *Deseret Evening News,* Apr. 26, 1909, 1; "Emma Lucy Gates Sings in the Berlin Royal Opera House," *Deseret Evening News,* May 8, 1909, 26.
28. Horace G. Whitney, "Emma Lucy Gates Sings in the Berlin Royal Opera House," *Deseret Evening News,* May 8, 1909, 26; Horace G. Whitney, "Emma Lucy Gates Scores a Big Hit," *Deseret Evening News,* Apr. 26, 1909, 1; Horace G. Whitney to the Burtons and others, Apr. 18, 1909, Susa Young Gates Papers, CHL.
29. Lucy Gates to "Dearest Ones," Apr. 6, 1909, Emma Lucy Gates Bowen Papers, BYU; Horace G. Whitney, "Emma Lucy Gates Sings in the Berlin Royal Opera House," *Deseret Evening News,* May 8, 1909, 26; Alexander, *Mormonism in Transition,* 227–30; Mitchell, "Mormons in Wilhelmine Germany," 152–56, 163–70; Allen, *Danish but Not Lutheran,* 161–76.
30. Lucy Gates to "Dearest Ones," Apr. 6, 1909, Emma Lucy Gates Bowen Papers, BYU; Horace G. Whitney to the Burtons and others, Apr. 18, 1909, Susa Young Gates Papers, CHL; Arthur M. Abell, "Enrico Caruso," *Musical Courier,* Nov. 18, 1908, 57:6.
31. Susa Young Gates to Lucy Gates, Apr. 12, 1910; Jacob Gates to Lucy Gates, Apr. 13, 1910, Susa Young Gates Papers, CHL. Quotation edited for readability; "shamed" in original changed to "ashamed."

32. Thomas McKay, "Concerning the Banishment from Berlin," *Latter-day Saints' Millennial Star,* Aug. 11, 1910, 72:508–9; Swiss-German Mission, Office Journal, July 21–23, 1910, 111; Lucy Gates to "Dearest Ones," Sept. 27 and Oct. 2, 1910, Emma Lucy Gates Bowen Papers, BYU; "Salt Lake Boy in Berlin Jail," *Deseret Evening News,* Aug. 8, 1910, 5.

33. Lucy Gates to "Dearest Ones," Sept. 27 and Oct. 2, 1910, Emma Lucy Gates Bowen Papers, BYU, emphasis in original.

34. Burton Hendrick, "The Mormon Revival of Polygamy," *McClure's Magazine,* Jan. 1911, 36:245–61; Feb. 1911, 36:449–64; Cannon, "Magazine Crusade against the Mormon Church," 2–4; Wilson, *McClure's Magazine and the Muckrakers,* 56, 190–200; Miraldi, *Muckraking and Objectivity,* 57–60.

35. Burton Hendrick, "The Mormon Revival of Polygamy," *McClure's Magazine,* Feb. 1911, 36:458; Hardy, *Solemn Covenant,* 183.

36. Cannon, "Mormon Muckraker," 47–52; Cannon, "Magazine Crusade against the Mormon Church," 27, note 100; "Benjamin Erastus Rich," Missionary Database, history. ChurchofJesusChrist.org/missionary; Isaac Russell to D. B. Turney, Apr. 28, 1911, B. H. Roberts Collection, CHL.

37. Burton Hendrick, "The Mormon Revival of Polygamy," *McClure's Magazine,* Feb. 1911, 36:457; Isaac Russell, "Mr. Roosevelt to the Mormons," *Collier's,* Apr. 15, 1911, 47:28; "Authorities Sustained," in *Eighty-First Semi-annual Conference,* 114; "The Manifesto and the End of Plural Marriage," Gospel Topics Essays, ChurchofJesusChrist.org/study/ manual/gospel-topics-essays; *Deseret News Church Almanac* [1974], 133–34.

38. Isaac Russell to B. H. Roberts, Jan. 16, 1911; Feb. 8, 1911, B. H. Roberts Collection, CHL; Burton Hendrick, "The Mormon Revival of Polygamy," *McClure's Magazine,* Feb. 1911, 36:457; Cannon, "Mormon Muckraker," 57–59; 57, note 31.

39. Isaac Russell to Joseph F. Smith, Feb. 11, 1913; Isaac Russell to Theodore Roosevelt, Feb. 2, 1911, First Presidency Mission Administration Correspondence, CHL; Richard Barry, "The Political Menace of the Mormon Church," *Pearson's,* Sept. 1910, 24:327.

40. 24 Parliamentary Debate, House of Commons, 5th series, Apr. 20, 1911, 1044–45; Arthur L. Beeley, "Government Investigation of the 'Mormon' Question," *Improvement Era,* Nov. 1914, 18:57; Bennett and Jensen, "Nearer, My God to Thee," 118–20; Thorp, "Crusade against the Saints in Britain," 79–81.

41. Rasmussen, *Mormonism and the Making of a British Zion,* 117–19; "Mormonism Exposed by Mr. William Jarman," *East Anglian Daily Times* (Ipswich, England), May 27, 1909, 4; "Jarman," *Nuneaton (England) Observer,* July 12, 1912, 3; Thorp, "Crusade against the Saints in Britain," 74–77.

42. Rudger Clawson to Winston Churchill, Jan. 12, 1911, copy, First Presidency Mission Administration Correspondence, CHL; 22 Parliamentary Debate, House of Commons, 5th series, Mar. 6, 1911, 811, 989.

43. "Anti-Mormon Crusade," *Evening Express* (Liverpool), Apr. 3, 1911, 7; "The Mormons," *Evening Express,* Apr. 19, 1911, 5; "Anti-Mormon Riots," *Evening Express,* Apr. 21, 1911, 4; "Anti-Mormon Riots at Birkenhead," *Liverpool Daily Post and Liverpool Mercury,* May 4, 1911, 5; Rudger Clawson to First Presidency, Apr. 25, 1911, First Presidency Mission Administration Correspondence, CHL. Quotation edited for readability; "he would give no heed to it" in original changed to "I will give no heed to it."

44. "The Mormons," *Evening Express* (Liverpool), Apr. 19, 1911, 5; "Anti-Mormon Campaign," *Manchester Guardian,* Apr. 24, 1911, 12; Rudger Clawson to First Presidency, Apr. 25, 1911, First Presidency Mission Administration Correspondence, CHL.

45. Rudger Clawson to First Presidency, Apr. 25, 1911, First Presidency Mission Administration Correspondence, CHL; "Anti-Mormonism," *Evening Express* (Liverpool), Apr. 24, 1911, 4; "Anti-Mormon Campaign," *Manchester Guardian,* Apr. 24, 1911, 12; see also "Anti-Mormon Riots," *Evening Express,* Apr. 21, 1911, 4.

46. Rudger Clawson to First Presidency, Apr. 7, 1911, First Presidency Mission Administration Correspondence, CHL; Beeley, *Summary Statement,* 13; Thorp, "British Government and the Mormon Question," 308–11.

47. Theodore Roosevelt to Isaac Russell, Feb. 4, 1911, First Presidency Mission Administration Correspondence, CHL.

48. Smoot, Diary, Mar. 14, 16, and 22, 1911; Apr. 2, 1911, Reed Smoot Papers, BYU; Cannon, "Magazine Crusade against the Mormon Church," 27; Reed Smoot to First Presidency, Apr. 1, 1911, First Presidency General Authorities Correspondence, CHL.

49. Smoot, Diary, Apr. 7, 1911, Reed Smoot Papers, BYU; Isaac Russell, "Mr. Roosevelt to the Mormons," *Collier's,* Apr. 15, 1911, 47:28; *Theodore Roosevelt Refutes Anti-Mormon Falsehoods,* 1911; Isaac Russell, "Mr. Roosevelt to the 'Mormons,'" *Improvement Era,* June 1911, 14:713–18; Joseph F. Smith to Isaac Russell, Apr. 25, 1911; B. H. Roberts to Isaac Russell, May 15, 1911, Isaac Russell Papers, Special Collections, Cecil H. Green Library, Stanford University, Stanford, CA.

50. Alfred Henry Lewis, "Viper on the Hearth," *Cosmopolitan,* Mar. 1911, 50:439–50; "The Trail of the Viper," *Cosmopolitan,* Apr. 1911, 50:693–703; "The Viper's Trail of Gold," *Cosmopolitan,* May 1911, 50:823–33; see also Givens, *Viper on the Hearth,* 97–120.

51. Francis Marion Lyman, Journal, Jan. 5, 1911; Feb. 15 and 22, 1911; Mar. 28, 1911; Cowley, Journal, May 2, 1911; Miller, *Apostle of Principle,* 540–51; Hardy, *Solemn Covenant,* appendix 2, [422].

52. Francis Marion Lyman, Journal, May 10–11, 1911; George F. Richards, Journal, May 11, 1911; Cowley, Journal, May 10–12, 1911; Joseph F. Smith to Isaac Russell, June 15, 1911, Letterpress Copybooks, 505, Joseph F. Smith Papers, CHL; "Excommunication," *Deseret Evening News,* May 2, 1911, 2; "Official Action," *Deseret Evening News,* May 12, 1911, 1. **Topics: Church Discipline; Matthias F. Cowley**

53. "No Polygamy Now," *Washington (DC) Post,* June 30, 1911, 1–2. Quotation edited for readability; "How it could be shown" in original changed to "How could it be shown."

54. Theodore H. Tiller, "Mormon Head Says Work and Thrift Are First Teachings of His Religion," *Washington (DC) Times,* June 29, 1911, 8; "Gives Mormon View," *Evening Star* (Washington, DC), June 30, 1911, 10; Reed Smoot to Joseph F. Smith, July 2, 1911, First Presidency General Authorities Correspondence, CHL.

55. Joseph F. Smith to Isaac Russell, July 13, 1911, Letterpress Copybooks, 540–41, Joseph F. Smith Papers, CHL. **Topic: Public Relations**

CHAPTER 10: GIVE ME STRENGTH

1. Alma Richards, Statement, Oct. 14, 1954, Alma Richards Papers, BYU; Alma Richards, "Alma W. Richards, Olympic Champion," *Salt Lake Herald-Republican,* Aug. 25, 1912, sporting section, [1]; Eugene L. Roberts, "Something about Utah's Great Athlete," *Salt Lake Evening Telegram,* July 13, 1912, 16. Quotation edited for readability; original source has "I promised him that if he would train consistently for a year and a half he would make the team." **Topic: Sweden**

2. Alma Richards, Statement, Oct. 14, 1954, Alma Richards Papers, BYU; Alma Richards, "Alma W. Richards, Olympic Champion," *Salt Lake Herald-Republican,* Aug. 25, 1912, sporting section, [1]; Eugene L. Roberts, "Something about Utah's Great Athlete," *Salt Lake Evening Telegram,* July 13, 1912, 16; Gerlach, *Alma Richards,* 32–38.

3. Szymanski, "Theory of the Evolution of Modern Sport," 1–32; Young Men's Mutual Improvement Association, Board Minutes, Jan. 30, 1907; Feb. 20, 1907; Mar. 20, 1907; Apr. 17 and 24, 1907; May 1, 1907.

4. Mead, "Denominationalism," 305; Young Men's Mutual Improvement Association, Board Minutes, Dec. 18, 1907; Feb. 26, 1908; Mar. 10 and 30, 1910; Sept. 7 and 21, 1910; Kimball, *Sports in Zion,* 58–63, 66–68, 101. Deseret Gymnasium later moved to the block north of Temple Square.

5. Young Men's Mutual Improvement Association, Board Minutes, Jan. 30, 1907; July 29, 1907; Dec. 2, 1908. **Topics: Young Men Organizations; Young Women Organizations; Correlation**

6. Eugene L. Roberts, "The Boy Pioneers of Utah," *Improvement Era,* Oct. 1911, 14:1084–92; Lears, *No Place of Grace,* 66–83; Putney, *Muscular Christianity,* 1–10.

7. Young Men's Mutual Improvement Association, Board Minutes, Nov. 29, 1911; Eugene L. Roberts, "The Boy Pioneers of Utah," *Improvement Era,* Oct. 1911, 14:1090–92; Lyman R. Martineau, "Athletics," *Improvement Era,* Sept. 1911, 14:1014–16; Lyman R. Martineau, "M. I. A. Scouts," *Improvement Era,* Mar. 1912, 15:354–61; see also Kimball, *Sports in Zion,* 125–45. Quotation edited for readability; final "and" added.

8. Alexander, *Mormonism in Transition,* 273–76; "Alma Richards—His Record and Testimony," *Improvement Era,* Nov. 1942, 45:731; "'Mormon Giant' Writes to E. L. Roberts," *Provo (UT) Herald,* July 26, 1912, 1; Doctrine and Covenants 89:18–21; Kimball, *Sports in Zion,* 115–16. **Topic: Word of Wisdom**

9. Alma Richards, Statement, Oct. 14, 1954, Alma Richards Papers, BYU; Eugene L. Roberts, "Something about Utah's Great Athlete," *Salt Lake Evening Telegram,* July 13, 1912, 16. Quotation edited for readability; "Mr. Roberts told me in the Spring of 1912 that I was one of the 15 best" in original changed to "You are one of the fifteen best."

10. "B.Y.U. Athlete Member of American Team," *Provo (UT) Herald,* June 12, 1912, 1; "Beaver Boy on American Team," *Salt Lake Tribune,* June 11, 1912, 9; "Utah Boy on Olympic Team," *Evening Standard* (Ogden, UT), June 11, 1912, 6.

11. Tullis, *Mormons in Mexico,* 87–91; Garner, *Porfirio Díaz,* 218–20; Gonzales, *Mexican Revolution,* 73–111.

12. First Presidency to Reed Smoot, Feb. 27, 1912; First Presidency to Junius Romney, Mar. 13, 1912, First Presidency Letterpress Copybooks, volume 49; Junius Romney to First Presidency, Feb. 6, 1912, First Presidency, Joseph F. Smith Stake Correspondence, CHL; Hardy and Seymour, "Importation of Arms and the 1912 Mormon 'Exodus' from Mexico," 297, 299–300.

13. Hardy and Seymour, "Importation of Arms and the 1912 Mormon 'Exodus' from Mexico," 298–306; Romney, "Junius Romney and the 1912 Mormon Exodus," 231–42; Stover, "Exodus of 1912," 45–69; First Presidency to Junius Romney, Mar. 13, 1912, First Presidency Letterpress Copybooks, volume 49.

14. Romney, Affidavit, 28–29. Quotation edited for readability; "we did not feel justified" in original changed to "we do not feel justified."

15. Romney, Affidavit, 28–31; Romney, Special Tributes, 12–14. **Topics: Mexico; Colonies in Mexico**

16. Junius Romney to Joseph F. Smith, Telegram, Aug. 7, 1912, First Presidency, Joseph F. Smith Stake Correspondence, CHL; Kimball, Oral History Interview, 22; Kimball, *Autobiography,* 10; Miner and Kimball, *Camilla,* 1, 28, 30; Mexico Northwestern Railway Company, *Road to Wealth,* [2].

17. Miner and Kimball, *Camilla,* 1–3, 15–17, 21, 25, 28; Hatch, *Colonia Juarez,* 44–45, 159–60, 243–51; Romney, *Mormon Colonies in Mexico,* 93–94, 142–43.

18. Kimball, Oral History Interview, 22; Kimball, *Autobiography,* 10; Miner and Kimball, *Camilla,* 6, 12–13, 28; Eyring, Autobiography, 23.

19. Kimball, *Autobiography,* 10; Kimball, Oral History Interview, 22; Miner and Kimball, *Camilla,* 28–30; Brown, "1910 Mexican Revolution," 28–29.

20. Kimball, *Autobiography,* 10–11; Kimball, Oral History Interview, 22–23; Miner and Kimball, *Camilla,* 30–31; Kimball, *Writings of Camilla Eyring Kimball,* 38; "Collection of Stories and Events in the Life of Anson Bowen Call," 13.

21. "'Mormon Giant' Writes to E. L. Roberts," *Provo (UT) Herald,* July 26, 1912, 1; Alma Richards, Statement, Oct. 14, 1954, Alma Richards Papers, BYU; "Memories of the Last Olympic Games," *Literary Digest,* July 3, 1920, 66:98; "Horine Can't Jump," *Salt Lake Evening Telegram,* Aug. 19, 1912, 10; Bergvall, *Fifth Olympiad,* 178–87, 392–93; Gerlach, *Alma Richards,* 56, 140.

22. "'Mormon Giant' Writes to E. L. Roberts," *Provo (UT) Herald,* July 26, 1912, 1; Alma Richards, Statement, Oct. 14, 1954, Alma Richards Papers, BYU; "Memories of the Last Olympic Games," *Literary Digest,* July 3, 1920, 66:98; Sullivan, "What Happened at Stockholm," 30; "Horine Can't Jump," *Salt Lake Evening Telegram,* Aug. 19, 1912, 10; Paul Ray, "Utah's Big Athlete Talks of Olympiad," *Salt Lake Tribune,* Aug. 20, 1912, 9; Bergvall, *Fifth Olympiad,* 392–94.

23. Alma Richards, Statement, Oct. 14, 1954, Alma Richards Papers, BYU; "Memories of the Last Olympic Games," *Literary Digest,* July 3, 1920, 66:98. Quotation edited for clarity; "was" and "would" in original changed to "is" and "will."

24. Alma Richards, Statement, Oct. 14, 1954, Alma Richards Papers, BYU; "Memories of the Last Olympic Games," *Literary Digest,* July 3, 1920, 66:98; Sullivan, "What Happened at Stockholm," 30; Bergvall, *Fifth Olympiad,* 394.

25. Bergvall, *Fifth Olympiad,* 393; Alma Richards, Statement, Oct. 14, 1954, Alma Richards Papers, BYU; "'Mormon Giant' Writes to E. L. Roberts," *Provo (UT) Herald,* July 26, 1912, 1; Paul Ray, "Utah's Big Athlete Talks of Olympiad," *Salt Lake Tribune,* Aug. 20, 1912, 9.

26. "Puny Lad Becomes World's Best Jumper," *Pittsburgh Press,* July 12, 1912, 23; "Puny Lad Becomes World's Best Jumper," *Wichita (KS) Beacon,* July 12, 1912, 4; "Something about the Unknown Who Won the Olympic High Jump," *Sacramento Star,* July 13, 1912, 9.

27. Paul Ray, "Utah's Big Athlete Talks of Olympiad," *Salt Lake Tribune,* Aug. 20, 1912, 9; "'Mormon Giant' Writes to E. L. Roberts," *Provo (UT) Herald,* July 26, 1912, 1; "Memories of the Last Olympic Games," *Literary Digest,* July 3, 1920, 66:98.

28. Monroy, History of the San Marcos Branch, 7–[7b]; Tullis, *Martyrs in Mexico,* 91; Tullis, "Reopening the Mexican Mission in 1901," 441–53. Translated quotation edited for readability; "were" in original changed to "are."

29. Monroy, History of the San Marcos Branch, 7–[7b]; Villalobos, Oral History Interview, 2; Tullis, *Martyrs in Mexico,* 20–21. Translated quotation edited for readability; "came" in original changed to "come," "their house" changed to "our house," and "they could" changed to "we can."

30. Monroy, History of the San Marcos Branch, 8–[9b]; Villalobos, Oral History Interview, 2–3; Tullis, *Martyrs in Mexico,* 22–25; Walter Young, Diary, Mar. 30, 1913.

31. Monroy, History of the San Marcos Branch, [9b]–[10b]; Villalobos, Oral History Interview, 3; Tullis, *Martyrs in Mexico,* 25–32; Walter Young, Diary, May 24, 1913, and June 10–11, 1913; *Diary of W. Ernest Young,* 98–99.

Chapter 11: Too Heavy

1. Herwig, *The Marne, 1914,* 110; Junius F. Wells and Arthur Horbach, "The Liege Branch during the Great War," *Latter-day Saints' Millennial Star,* Nov. 6, 1919, 81:712; Chas. Arthur Horbach entry, Liege Branch, Belgian Conference, French Mission, no. 44, in Belgium (Country), part 1, Record of Members Collection, CHL. **Topic: Belgium**

2. Sheffield, *Short History of the First World War,* 12–27; Clark, *Sleepwalkers,* 367–403, 469–70, 526–27. **Topic: World War I**

3. Herwig, *The Marne, 1914,* 108–17; Zuber, *Ten Days in August,* 13, 155, 188–98; Junius F. Wells and Arthur Horbach, "The Liege Branch during the Great War," *Latter-day Saints' Millennial Star,* Nov. 6, 1919, 81:712.

4. Anne Matilde Horbach entry, Liege Branch, Belgian Conference, French Mission, no. 43, in Belgium (Country), part 1, Record of Members Collection, CHL; Junius F. Wells and Arthur Horbach, "The Liege Branch during the Great War," *Latter-day Saints' Millennial Star,* Nov. 6, 1919, 81:712; Willey, Memoirs, 19, 27; J. Moyle Gray to Heber J. Grant, Aug. 15, 1919, Heber J. Grant Collection, CHL.

5. Junius F. Wells and Arthur Horbach, "The Liege Branch during the Great War," *Latter-day Saints' Millennial Star,* Nov. 6, 1919, 81:712–13; J. Moyle Gray to Heber J. Grant, Aug. 15, 1919, Heber J. Grant Collection, CHL; Tonia V. Deguée entry, Liege Branch, Belgian Conference, French Mission, no. 8, in Belgium (Country), part 1, Record of Members Collection, CHL; Kahne, *History of the Liège District,* 14–15.

6. Willey, Memoirs, 31, 33, 35; Hall, Autobiography, [6]; Junius F. Wells and Arthur Horbach, "The Liege Branch during the Great War," *Latter-day Saints' Millennial Star,* Nov. 6, 1919, 81:712–13; J. Moyle Gray to Heber J. Grant, Aug. 15, 1919, Heber J. Grant Collection, CHL.

7. "Missionary Journal of Myrl Lewis," Sept. 3, 1914; "List of Names of Missionaries Transferred from European Mission to British Mission," 1914; Hyrum Smith to First Presidency, Aug. 29, 1914, First Presidency Mission Administration Correspondence, CHL.

8. Junius F. Wells and Arthur Horbach, "The Liege Branch during the Great War," *Latter-day Saints' Millennial Star,* Nov. 6, 1919, 81:712–13; J. Moyle Gray to Heber J. Grant, Aug. 15, 1919, Heber J. Grant Collection, CHL; Chas. Arthur Horbach, Anne Matilde Horbach, and Charles Jean Devignez entries, Liege Branch, Belgian Conference, French Mission, nos. 43, 44, 77, in Belgium (Country), part 1, Record of Members Collection, CHL.

9. Junius F. Wells and Arthur Horbach, "The Liege Branch during the Great War," *Latter-day Saints' Millennial Star,* Nov. 6, 1919, 81:712–13; J. Moyle Gray to Heber J. Grant, Aug. 15, 1919, Heber J. Grant Collection, CHL. **Topic: Sacrament Meetings**

10. Hyrum M. Smith, Diary, Oct. 2, 1914; "Hyrum Mack Smith," Missionary Database, history.ChurchofJesusChrist.org/missionary; Smith, Salt Lake Tabernacle Address, 1.

11. Smith, Salt Lake Tabernacle Address, 1–2; "'Mormon' Women in Great Britain," *Deseret Evening News,* Oct. 13, 1914, 5; McGreal, *Liverpool in the Great War,* 28–29.

12. Smith, Salt Lake Tabernacle Address, 2.

13. Smith, Salt Lake Tabernacle Address, 2–3; "'Mormon' Women in Great Britain," *Deseret Evening News,* Oct. 13, 1914, 5.

14. Smith, Salt Lake Tabernacle Address, 3; "'Mormon' Women in Great Britain," *Deseret Evening News,* Oct. 13, 1914, 5. Quotation edited for readability; "had" in original changed to "have."

15. Smith, Salt Lake Tabernacle Address, 3–4. Quotation edited for readability; "We would do the best that we could" in original changed to "We will do the best that we can."

16. Smith, Salt Lake Tabernacle Address, 4–6; Amy Brown Lyman, "Notes from the Field," *Relief Society Magazine,* Nov. 1915, 2:504–6; "Daughters of Zion," *Relief Society Magazine,* Oct. 1916, 3:543; "'Mormon' Women in Great Britain," *Deseret Evening News,* Oct. 13, 1914, 5.

17. Smith, Salt Lake Tabernacle Address, 5; "Daughters of Zion," *Relief Society Magazine,* Oct. 1916, 3:543; Nottingham Branch Relief Society Minutes, Oct. 1915, 151; Hyrum M. Smith, Diary, Mar. 9–10, 1915. **Topics: England; Relief Society**

18. Joseph F. Smith to Hyrum M. Smith, Nov. 7, 1914, Letterpress Copybooks, 6, Joseph F. Smith Papers, CHL; Sheffield, *Short History of the First World War,* 34–37; Audoin-Rouzeau, "1915: Stalemate," 66–69.

19. Audoin-Rouzeau, "1915: Stalemate," 70–71; Hiery, *Neglected War,* 22–30; Doctrine and Covenants 87:3, 6.

20. "To Presidents of Stakes and Bishops of Wards," *Deseret Evening News,* Jan. 13, 1915, 4; "Donations for Church Members in Europe," *Deseret Evening News,* Jan. 22, 1915, 3.

21. "Donation to War Sufferers," *Improvement Era,* Mar. 1915, 18:455; Charles W. Nibley, Orrin P. Miller, and David A. Smith to First Presidency, Oct. 11, 1915, First Presidency General Administration Files, CHL; Hyrum M. Smith to Mission Presidents, Mar. 23, 1915, First Presidency Mission Files, CHL.

22. "Church Leader Returns Home," *Salt Lake Herald-Republican,* June 17, 1915, 12; *Saints,* volume 2, chapters 13 and 27; Joseph F. Smith, Journal, May 22, 1915; "From Far Away Hawaii," *Latter-day Saints' Millennial Star,* July 8, 1915, 77:417–18. **Topic: Hawaii**

23. Joseph F. Smith, Journal, May 21 and 22, 1915; Heath, *Diaries of Reed Smoot,* xxxiv; Smoot, Diary, Mar. 11 and 13, 1915, Reed Smoot Collection, BYU; "Leave for Islands Trip," *Salt Lake Herald-Republican,* Apr. 25, 1915, [32]; Walker, "Abraham Kaleimahoe Fernandez," [2].

24. Joseph F. Smith, Journal, May 23–26, 1915; "From Far Away Hawaii," *Latter-day Saints' Millennial Star,* July 8, 1915, 77:418; Britsch, *Moramona,* 227–31.

25. Britsch, *Unto the Islands of the Sea,* 31–32, 43, 278–80, 384. **Topic: French Polynesia**

26. Moffat, Woods, and Anderson, *Saints of Tonga,* 54–57; Britsch, *Unto the Islands of the Sea,* 289–94; Newton, *Southern Cross Saints,* 179–82; Historical Department, Journal History of the Church, June 1913, 20; Newton, *Tiki and Temple,* 66–69, 95–96, 121–28. **Topics: Australia; New Zealand; Samoa; Tonga; Church Academies**

27. Smoot, Diary, June 1–2, 1915, Reed Smoot Collection, BYU; Dowse, "The Laie Hawaii Temple," 68–69; I Hemolele, Photograph, Joseph F. Smith Library, Brigham Young University–Hawaii, Laie; Holiness to the Lord inscription tablet detail, Architect's Office, Salt Lake Temple Architectural Drawings, CHL; see also Exodus 28:36; 39:30; and Psalm 93:5.

28. Smoot, Diary, June 1, 1915, Reed Smoot Collection, BYU.

29. Smoot, Diary, May 27 and June 1, 1915, Reed Smoot Collection, BYU; "President Smith and Party Return," *Liahona, the Elders' Journal,* July 6, 1915, 13:24; "Dedication of the Temple Site at Cardston, Canada," *Liahona, the Elders' Journal,* Sept. 16, 1913, 11:206; "Cardston Temple Site Dedicated by Church Leaders," *Salt Lake Herald-Republican,* July 28, 1913, 1. **Topics: Temple Building; Canada**

30. Smoot, Diary, June 1, 1915, Reed Smoot Collection, BYU; Joseph F. Smith, Journal, June 1, 1915; Reed Smoot, in *Ninety-First Semi-annual Conference,* 137. **Topic: Hawaii**

31. Romney, *Mormon Colonies in Mexico,* 235; Kimball, *Autobiography,* 14–18.

32. Rey L. Pratt, "A Latter-day Martyr," *Improvement Era,* June 1918, 21:720–21; Grover, "Execution in Mexico," 9; Monroy, History of the San Marcos Branch, [12b], [15b], 19, [22b], 25, [31b]–32; Tullis, *Martyrs in Mexico,* 7, 34–35.

33. Monroy, History of the San Marcos Branch, [31b]; Jesus M. de Monroy to Rey L. Pratt, Aug. 27, 1915, CHL; Grover, "Execution in Mexico," 13–15; Tullis, *Mormons in Mexico,* 103. **Topic: Mexico**

34. Monroy, History of the San Marcos Branch, 7, [10b]–11, 19; *Diary of W. Ernest Young,* 98–99, 106–7; "Rey Lucero Pratt," Missionary Database, history.ChurchofJesusChrist.org/missionary; Tullis, *Martyrs in Mexico,* 23, 28, 32–41, 92–96.

35. Monroy, History of the San Marcos Branch, 23, 25, [31b]; Tullis, *Martyrs in Mexico,* 9, 32–33.

36. Monroy, History of the San Marcos Branch, [31b]–32; Jesus M. de Monroy to Rey L. Pratt, Aug. 27, 1915, CHL; Rey L. Pratt, "A Latter-day Martyr," *Improvement Era,* June 1918, 21:723; Tullis, *Martyrs in Mexico,* 10–12. Translated quotations edited for readability; "if he had" in original changed to "if it weren't so," and "if they didn't give them their weapons that they would hang them from the highest tree" changed to "If you do not give us your weapons we will hang you from the highest tree."

37. Monroy, History of the San Marcos Branch, 32.

38. Monroy, History of the San Marcos Branch, 32–33; Jesus M. de Monroy to Rey L. Pratt, Aug. 27, 1915, CHL; Rey L. Pratt, "A Latter-day Martyr," *Improvement Era,* June 1918, 21:723–24.

39. Monroy, History of the San Marcos Branch, [32b]–[33b]; Villalobos, Oral History Interview, 4.

40. Hyrum M. Smith to First Presidency, Aug. 29, 1914; "List of Names of Missionaries Transferred from European Mission to British Mission," 1914, First Presidency Mission Administration Correspondence, CHL; First Presidency to Hyrum M. Smith, Sept. 9, 1914, First Presidency Letterpress Copybooks, volume 53.

41. Hyrum M. Smith, Diary, Sept. 25 and 26; Nov. 29, 1914; Hyrum M. Smith to First Presidency, Sept. 30, 1914, First Presidency Mission Administration Correspondence, CHL.

42. Hyrum M. Smith to First Presidency, May 12, 1915; May 25, 1915; Aug. 20, 1915, First Presidency Mission Files, CHL; Hyrum M. Smith, Diary, Aug. 18–21, 1915.
43. Hyrum M. Smith to First Presidency, Aug. 20, 1915; Oct. 15, 1915; First Presidency to Hyrum M. Smith, Sept. 11, 1915, First Presidency Mission Files, CHL; "Releases and Departures," *Latter-day Saints' Millennial Star,* Sept. 23, 1915, 77:608.
44. First Presidency to Hyrum M. Smith, Sept. 11, 1915, First Presidency Mission Files, CHL.
45. Hyrum M. Smith, Diary, Sept. 10, 1915, emphasis in original; Hyrum M. Smith to First Presidency, Oct. 15, 1915, First Presidency Mission Files, CHL.
46. "Releases and Departures," *Latter-day Saints' Millennial Star,* Sept. 23, 1915, 77:608; Hyrum M. Smith to First Presidency, Oct. 15, 1915, First Presidency Mission Files, CHL.

CHAPTER 12: THIS TERRIBLE WAR

1. "Steamship Movements," *Gazette* (Montreal, Quebec), Sept. 27, 1915, 11; Scandinavian manifest, in "Passenger Lists, 1865–1922"; Hyrum M. Smith, Diary, Mar. 15, 1916; Hyrum M. Smith to Joseph F. Smith and Counselors, Oct. 15, 1915; Dec. 10, 1915, First Presidency Mission Files, CHL; "Emigration Book, 1914–24," Oct. 22, 1915; Nov. 26, 1915; Dec. 31, 1915; Halpern, *Naval History of World War I,* 302–4.
2. J. Moyle Gray to Heber J. Grant, Aug. 15, 1919, Heber J. Grant Collection, CHL; Junius F. Wells and Arthur Horbach, "The Liège Branch during the Great War," *Latter-day Saints' Millennial Star,* Nov. 6, 1919, 81:713; "He Did All He Could," *Latter-day Saints' Millennial Star,* Dec. 3, 1931, 93:792–93; Kahne, *History of the Liège District,* 10; Schaepdrijver, *Bastion,* 35–36; Veranneman, *Belgium in the Great War,* 37–42.
3. J. Moyle Gray to Heber J. Grant, Aug. 15, 1919, Heber J. Grant Collection, CHL; Junius F. Wells and Arthur Horbach, "The Liège Branch during the Great War," *Latter-day Saints' Millennial Star,* Nov. 6, 1919, 81:713–14; Kahne, *History of the Liège District,* 14–17; Hyrum M. Smith, Diary, Mar. 8, 1915; Hyrum M. Smith, letter sent to mission presidents, Mar. 23, 1915, First Presidency Mission Files, CHL.
4. Junius F. Wells and Arthur Horbach, "The Liège Branch during the Great War," *Latter-day Saints' Millennial Star,* Nov. 6, 1919, 81:714. **Topic: World War I**
5. Charles W. Penrose, in *Eighty-Sixth Annual Conference,* 15–16; Joseph F. Smith to Hyrum M. Smith, July 1, 1916, Letterpress Copybooks, 322, Joseph F. Smith Papers, CHL; Joseph F. Smith to Edward Bunker, Feb. 27, 1902, Letterpress Copybooks, 26–27, Joseph F. Smith Papers, CHL; Joseph F. Smith to Lillie Golsan, July 16, 1902, Letterpress Copybooks, 93, Joseph F. Smith Papers, CHL; Lund, Journal, Apr. 8, 1912.
6. Historical Department, Office Journal, Mar. 14, 1852; Brigham Young, Apr. 9, 1852, in *Journal of Discourses,* 1:50–51; Woodruff, Journal, Apr. 9, 1852; Dec. 11, 1869; Clayton, Diary, Oct. 3, 1852; Brigham Young, "Adam, Our Father and God," *Latter-day Saints' Millennial Star,* Nov. 26, 1853, 15:769–70; George Q. Cannon, Journal, Nov. 18, 1882; Abraham H. Cannon, Diary, Mar. 10, 1889; Francis Marion Lyman, Journal, Feb. 20, 1894, and July 13, 1898; Joseph F. Smith, Anthon H. Lund, and Charles W. Penrose to Samuel O. Bennion, Feb. 20, 1912, First Presidency Letterpress Copybooks, volume 49; George F. Richards, Journal, Apr. 6, 1915.
7. Lund, Journal, Sept. 16, 1902; "What Is Mormonism?," *Missionary Review of the World,* Nov. 1905, 28:854; Burton J. Hendrick, "The Mormon Revival of Polygamy," *McClure's Magazine,* Jan. 1911, 36:246.
8. Joseph F. Smith, John R. Winder, and Anthon H. Lund, "The Origin of Man," *Improvement Era,* Nov. 1909, 13:75–81; Whitney, Journal, Sept. 27 and 30, 1909; Grant, Journal, June 18, 1925.
9. "Priesthood Quorums' Table," *Improvement Era,* Feb. 1915, 18:366; Jan. 1916, 19:274; "Theological Department," *Juvenile Instructor,* Mar. 1916, 51:181; Widtsoe, *Rational Theology,* 46–56, 62–64; Talmage, *Jesus the Christ,* 18–23, 32–41; Parrish, *John A. Widtsoe,* 205; Talmage, *Talmage Story,* 181–82; Alexander, *Mormonism in Transition,* 295–97.

10. Charles W. Penrose, in *Eighty-Sixth Annual Conference,* 15–23.
11. Talmage, Journal, July 1, 1916; Lund, Journal, June 29, 1916; Francis Marion Lyman, Journal, June 29, 1916; George F. Richards, Journal, June 29, 1916. **Topic: First Presidency**
12. "The Father and the Son," *Deseret Evening News,* July 1, 1916, 4; "The Father and the Son," *Improvement Era,* Aug. 1916, 19:934–42.
13. Joseph F. Smith to Hyrum M. Smith, July 1, 1916, Letterpress Copybooks, 322, Joseph F. Smith Papers, CHL; "The Father and the Son," *Deseret Evening News,* July 1, 1916, 4; "The Father and the Son," *Improvement Era,* Aug. 1916, 19:934–42; see also "The Father and the Son," *Latter-day Saints' Millennial Star,* Aug. 3, 1916, 78:481–85; Aug. 10, 1916, 78:497–500.
14. Prior, "1916: Impasse," 89–98; Sheffield, *Short History of the First World War,* 64–66.
15. Schwarz, Autobiography, 8–9. In 1929, Barmen and four adjoining towns were combined to form a new town later called Wuppertal.
16. Prior, "1916: Impasse," 93–98; Sheffield, *Short History of the First World War,* 64–66.
17. Schwarz, Autobiography, 9–10.
18. "Ehre ihrem Andenken," *Der Stern,* June 15, 1915, 47:192.
19. Schwarz, Autobiography, 3, 8–10; "Frei vom Irrtum," *Der Stern,* Sept. 1, 1916, 48:269.
20. See, for example, Anton Ernst to Hyrum W. Valentine, Apr. 24, 1916, in "Feldpostbriefe," *Der Stern,* June 1, 1916, 48:172–73; George Sadler, Letter to the Editor, July 14, 1916, in "A Letter from the Front," *Latter-day Saints' Millennial Star,* Aug. 17, 1916, 78:527–28; John Henry Moore, Letter to the Editor, in "A Testimony from the Front," *Latter-day Saints' Millennial Star,* Nov. 2, 1916, 78:702–3; and Anderson, "Brothers across Enemy Lines," 127–39.
21. Monroy, History of the San Marcos Branch, 33–35; Jesus M. de Monroy to Rey L. Pratt, Aug. 27, 1915, CHL; Grover, "Execution in Mexico," 16–18.
22. Jesus M. de Monroy to Rey L. Pratt, Aug. 27, 1915, CHL.
23. Rey L. Pratt to Jesus M. de Monroy, Oct. 21, 1915, copy in Monroy, History of the San Marcos Branch, 40–[42b]; Jesus M. de Monroy to Rey L. Pratt, Aug. 27, 1915, CHL. Translated quotation edited for readability; "the faith" in original changed to "your faith."
24. Tullis, *Martyrs in Mexico,* 88–89.
25. Monroy, History of the San Marcos Branch, 44–[44b].
26. Monroy, History of the San Marcos Branch, 38, [44b]; Tullis, *Martyrs in Mexico,* 77.
27. Monroy, History of the San Marcos Branch, [44b]. Translated quotation edited for readability; "her" in original changed to "my."
28. *Diary of W. Ernest Young,* 121; Tullis, *Martyrs in Mexico,* 78, 80. **Topic: Mexico**
29. George F. Richards, Journal, Aug. 25, 1916; Joseph F. Smith to Hyrum M. Smith, July 1, 1916, Letterpress Copybooks, [320b], Joseph F. Smith Papers, CHL.
30. Ida B. Smith, "A Word of Farewell to the Sisters," *Latter-day Saints' Millennial Star,* Aug. 24, 1916, 78:540–42; Smith, Salt Lake Tabernacle Address, 5–9. **Topic: Relief Society**
31. George F. Richards, Journal, Oct. 22 and 27, 1916; Nov. 4 and 29, 1916; George F. Richards to Joseph F. Smith and Counselors, Oct. 26, 1916, First Presidency Mission Files, CHL. **Topic: Sacrament Meetings**
32. Amy Brown Lyman, "Notes from the Field," *Relief Society Magazine,* Mar. 1916, 3:160; Isabella Blake, "Interesting Items from Glasgow," *Latter-day Saints' Millennial Star,* Nov. 16, 1916, 78:727; "Lady Missionaries," *Latter-day Saints' Millennial Star,* Jan. 25, 1917, 79:60. **Topic: Scotland**
33. Isabella Blake, "Interesting Items from Glasgow," *Latter-day Saints' Millennial Star,* Nov. 16, 1916, 78:727; Blake family entries, Glasgow Branch, nos. 257, 258, 284, 325, 358, 375, 459, 505, in Scotland, part 3, Record of Members Collection, CHL.
34. Isabella Blake, "Home," *Latter-day Saints' Millennial Star,* July 1, 1915, 77:403; Isabella Blake, "Interesting Items from Glasgow," *Latter-day Saints' Millennial Star,* Nov. 16, 1916, 78:727; Amy Brown Lyman, "Notes from the Field," *Relief Society Magazine,* Mar. 1916, 3:160; Isabella Thomson Blake, entry, Twentieth Ward, Ensign Stake, in Twentieth Ward (old), part 3, segment 1, Record of Members Collection, CHL.

35. Isabella Blake, "Interesting Items from Glasgow," *Latter-day Saints' Millennial Star,* Nov. 16, 1916, 78:727. **Topic: Growth of Missionary Work**

CHAPTER 13: HEIRS OF SALVATION

1. Susa Young Gates, Journal, Jan. 10–11, 14, 17, and 19, 1917; Susa Young Gates to Jacob Gates, Jan. 20, 1917, Susa Young Gates Papers, CHL; "Susa Young Gates," *Utah Genealogical and Historical Magazine,* July 1933, 24:98–100.
2. "Susa Young Gates," *Utah Genealogical and Historical Magazine,* July 1933, 24:99–100; Susa Young Gates, "Genealogy in the Relief Society," *Utah Genealogical and Historical Magazine,* Jan. 1916, 7:41–42; Susa Young Gates, "The history of the work," 1–4; Susa Young Gates, "One of the most interesting phases," 1–4, Relief Society, Susa Young Gates Files, CHL; Allen, Embry, and Mehr, *Hearts Turned to the Fathers,* 41–47, 60–70; Derr, Cannon, and Beecher, *Women of Covenant,* 189–93; Susa Young Gates, "Genealogy in the Relief Society," *Utah Genealogical and Historical Magazine,* Jan. 1916, 7:41–45; see also, for example, "Genealogy and Art," *Relief Society Magazine,* Apr. 1916, 3:230–31.
3. Susa Young Gates, Journal, Jan. 19 and 25, 1917; Susa Young Gates to Jacob Gates, Jan. 20, 1917, Susa Young Gates Papers, CHL.
4. Susa Young Gates, Journal, Jan. 27–Feb. 4, 1917, Susa Young Gates Papers, CHL, emphasis in original. Quotation edited for readability; "He said he always enjoys" and "loved" in original changed to "I always enjoy" and "love." **Topics: Family History and Genealogy; Susa Young Gates**
5. Joseph F. Smith, in *Eighty-Seventh Annual Conference,* 2–12; *Salt Lake Telegram,* Apr. 5–6, 1917; *Salt Lake Tribune,* Apr. 5–6, 1917; *Ogden (UT) Standard,* Apr. 5–6, 1917; *Provo (UT) Herald,* Apr. 5, 1917.
6. O'Toole, *The Moralist,* 233–61; DiNunzio, *Woodrow Wilson,* 397–403.
7. Joseph F. Smith, in *Eighty-Seventh Annual Conference,* 3–8.
8. Alford, "Joseph F. Smith and the First World War," 438–40; Roberts, "Utah National Guard in the Great War," 313–14. **Topic: B. H. Roberts**
9. "War Is upon Us," *Relief Society Magazine,* May 1917, 4:284–85; "Red Cross Work in the Relief Society," *Relief Society Magazine,* Aug. 1917, 4:430; Janette A. Hyde, "Home Science Department," *Relief Society Magazine,* Oct. 1917, 4:572–75; "Liberty Bonds," *Relief Society Magazine,* Nov. 1917, 4:643–44; "A Utah Girl in France," *Relief Society Magazine,* Dec. 1917, 4:690–91; "Will Serve Nation on French Front," *Salt Lake Tribune,* July 14, 1917, 16; Sillito, "Drawing the Sword of War against War," 100–115; see also Murphy, "Utah Women in World War I," 335–37.
10. Joseph F. Smith, Journal, May 14, 1917; "President Smith Back from Hawaii," *Ogden (UT) Standard,* May 25, 1917, 9; Christensen, *Stories of the Temple in La'ie,* 20–25; Anderson, "Jewel in the Gardens of Paradise," 170–76. **Topic: Temple Building**
11. Joseph F. Smith, in *Eighty-Eighth Semi-annual Conference,* 6–7.
12. Joseph F. Smith, Journal, Jan. 1–23, 1918.
13. Whitaker, Journal, Jan. 27, 1918.
14. Joseph F. Smith, Journal, Jan. 20, 21, and 23, 1918. Elder M. Russell Ballard, a maternal grandson of Hyrum Mack Smith, later spoke about his grandfather's death; see M. Russell Ballard, "The Vision of the Redemption of the Dead," *Ensign* or *Liahona,* Nov. 2018, 71–74.
15. Joseph Fielding Smith, Journal, Jan. 24, 1918; Whitaker, Journal, Jan. 27, 1918.
16. Joseph F. Smith, Journal, Jan. 24, 1918; Joseph Fielding Smith, Journal, Jan. 24, 1918; "May Not Live in Beehive," *Salt Lake Tribune,* Nov. 1, 1901, 8; "The Bee-Hive House," *Salt Lake Tribune,* Aug. 10, 1902, 2; "Joseph F. Smith's Birthday," *Salt Lake Tribune,* Nov. 15, 1905, 12.

17. Jenson, "Hyrum M. Smith"; Whitaker, Journal, Jan. 27, 1918; "Report of Funeral Services in Honor of Ida B. Smith," 9; "Apostle H. M. Smith," *Ogden (UT) Standard,* Jan. 24, 1918, 1; Smith, "Remember Who You Are," 331.
18. "Report of Funeral Services in Honor of Ida B. Smith," 15–17; "Sometime," in Smith, *Sometime and Other Poems,* 11–14.
19. Smith, "Remember Who You Are," 302, 331.
20. Heber J. Grant to Richard W. Young, Oct. 1, 1918, Heber J. Grant Collection, CHL.
21. Jenson, "Hyrum M. Smith."
22. "Report of Funeral Services in Honor of Ida B. Smith," 9.
23. Smith, "Remember Who You Are," 331; Heber J. Grant to Richard W. Young, Oct. 1, 1918, Heber J. Grant Collection, CHL; Death Certificate for Ida Elizabeth Smith, Sept. 24, 1918, Utah Department of Health, Office of Vital Records and Statistics, Utah State Archives and Records Service, Salt Lake City.
24. Whitney, Journal, Oct. 3, 1918; Heber J. Grant to Reed Smoot, Sept. 25, 1918; Heber J. Grant to George F. Richards, Sept. 27, 1918; Heber J. Grant to Richard W. Young, Oct. 1, 1918, Heber J. Grant Collection, CHL.
25. Tate, "Great World of the Spirits of the Dead," 5–40; Alford, "Calvin S. Smith," 254–69; Madsen, *Defender of the Faith,* 301–14; Dehner, *Influenza,* 42–50; Brown, *Influenza,* 43–58; "Preparing Here for Spanish Influenza," *Salt Lake Tribune,* Oct. 4, 1918, 20; "State Board of Health Issues Drastic Order," *Salt Lake Telegram,* Oct. 9, 1918, 1. **Topic: Influenza Pandemic of 1918**
26. 1 Peter 3:18–20; 4:6; Doctrine and Covenants 138:1–24; Bennett, "Joseph F. Smith, World War I, and His Visions of the Dead," 126.
27. Doctrine and Covenants 138:25–28.
28. Doctrine and Covenants 138:29–48; see also Doctrine and Covenants 110:13–15; and Malachi 4:5–6.
29. Doctrine and Covenants 138:49–59; see also Abraham 3:22. **Topics: Joseph F. Smith; Vision of the Redemption of the Dead**
30. "Prest. Joseph F. Smith Greets Thousands at Semi-annual Conference," *Deseret Evening News,* Oct. 4, 1918, 1; Joseph F. Smith, in *Eighty-Ninth Semi-annual Conference,* 2; Wells, Diary, volume 44, Oct. 4, 1918.
31. Joseph F. Smith, in *Eighty-Ninth Semi-annual Conference,* 2; Susa Young Gates to Elizabeth Claridge McCune, Nov. 14, 1918, Susa Young Gates Papers, CHL.
32. Susa Young Gates, Journal, Nov. 5, 1918; Susa Young Gates to Elizabeth Claridge McCune, Nov. 14, 1918, Susa Young Gates Papers, CHL; Tait, "Susa Young Gates and the Vision of the Redemption of the Dead," 315–22.
33. Tait, "Susa Young Gates and the Vision of the Redemption of the Dead," 315–22; Susa Young Gates, "Genealogy in the Relief Society," *Utah Genealogical and Historical Magazine,* Jan. 1916, 7:42; "Donations to the Society," *Utah Genealogical and Historical Magazine,* July 1917, 8:143. **Topic: Genealogy and Family History**
34. Susa Young Gates to Elizabeth Claridge McCune, Nov. 14, 1918, Susa Young Gates Papers, CHL. Quotation edited for readability; "was" in original changed to "am."
35. Susa Young Gates, Journal, Nov. 5, 1918; Susa Young Gates to Elizabeth Claridge McCune, Nov. 14, 1918, Susa Young Gates Papers, CHL; Joseph Fielding Smith, Journal, Oct. 31, 1918; Tait, "Susa Young Gates and the Vision of the Redemption of the Dead," 319. **Topic: Vision of the Redemption of the Dead**
36. **Topics: World War I; Influenza Pandemic of 1918**
37. David A. Smith, Statement, Nov. 19, 1918, Letterpress Copybook, volume 54, 6, Heber J. Grant Collection, CHL. Quotation edited for clarity; "You had better wait and see him" in original changed to "You had better see him."
38. David A. Smith, Notes, 22, Heber J. Grant Collection, box 177, folder 14, CHL.
39. Lund, Journal, Nov. 18, 1918; Heber J. Grant to "Family of President Joseph F. Smith," Nov. 20, 1918, Joseph F. and Alice K. Smith Family Correspondence, CHL. **Topic: Joseph F. Smith**

CHAPTER 14: FOUNTAINS OF LIGHT AND HOPE

1. Heber J. Grant to "Family of President Joseph F. Smith," Nov. 20, 1918, Joseph F. and Alice K. Smith Family Correspondence, CHL; Frank W. Otterstrom, "Tributes of Honor," *Deseret Evening News,* Nov. 30, 1918, section 4, vii; Heber J. Grant, Remarks at YMMIA Board Meeting, Jan. 29, 1919, Letterpress Copybook, volume 54, 585–87; Heber J. Grant Collection, CHL; Death Certificate for Joseph Fielding Smith, Nov. 19, 1918, Utah Department of Health, Office of Vital Records and Statistics, Utah State Archives and Records Service, Salt Lake City; see also Heber J. Grant, Remarks, Jan. 29, 1919, Letterpress Copybook, volume 54, 586; Heber J. Grant to Homer Durham and Eudora Widtsoe Durham, Dec. 30, 1941, Letterpress Copybook, volume 80, 706; Heber J. Grant to Reed Smoot, Aug. 28, 1918, Heber J. Grant Collection, CHL; and Heber J. Grant, in *One Hundredth Annual Conference,* 22.
2. Lund, Journal, Nov. 19–22, 1918; "Prest. Joseph F. Smith Followed to Grave by Magnificent Cortege," *Deseret Evening News,* Nov. 22, 1918, section 2, [1]; "State Board of Health Issues Drastic Order," *Salt Lake Telegram,* Oct. 9, 1918, 1.
3. "Prest. Joseph F. Smith Followed to Grave by Magnificent Cortege," *Deseret Evening News,* Nov. 22, 1918, section 2, [1]; Frank W. Otterstrom, "Tributes of Honor," *Deseret Evening News,* Nov. 30, 1918, section 4, vii; "Thousands Pay Last Honor to Church Leader," *Salt Lake Herald,* Nov. 23, 1918, 3.
4. Lund, Journal, Nov. 23, 1918; Talmage, Journal, Nov. 23, 1918. **Topic: Heber J. Grant**
5. Heber M. Wells to Heber J. Grant, Nov. 27, 1918; John A. Widtsoe to Heber J. Grant, Nov. 23, 1918; Heber J. Grant to Charles A. Callis, Jan. 14, 1919, Letterpress Copybook, volume 54, 84; Heber J. Grant to Isaac A. Russell, Jan. 12, 1922, Letterpress Copybook, volume 58, 806; Heber J. Grant to Edward H. Felt, Mar. 4, 1919, Letterpress Copybook, volume 54, 245; Heber J. Grant to Samuel Woolley, Apr. 24, 1919, Letterpress Copybook, volume 54, 726, Heber J. Grant Collection, CHL.
6. **Topic: Adjustments to Priesthood Organization**
7. *Deseret News 1989–90 Church Almanac,* 204; Alexander, *Mormonism in Transition,* 114–19; Lund, "Joseph F. Smith and the Origins of the Church Historic Sites Program," 342–58; First Presidency, *To the Presidents of Stakes, Bishops and Parents in Zion.* **Topic: Family Home Evening**
8. Heber J. Grant to George Romney, Nov. 24, 1918; Heber J. Grant to James Lawry, June 21, 1919, Heber J. Grant Collection, CHL; "Many Offices Were Held by Joseph Smith," *Salt Lake Herald,* Nov. 20, 1918, 6; Church Board of Education, Minutes, Nov. 27, 1918; Lund, Journal, Nov. 27, 1918. **Topic: David O. McKay**
9. "Grant Is Bank President," *Salt Lake Tribune,* Dec. 6, 1918, 16; "New Head of the Utah-Idaho Sugar," *Ogden (UT) Standard,* Dec. 12, 1918, 4; Zion's Cooperative Mercantile Institution, Minutes, Dec. 19, 1918, 236–37. **Topic: Church Finances**
10. Frank W. Otterstrom, "Tributes of Honor," *Deseret Evening News,* Nov. 30, 1918, section 4, vii; Charles W. Penrose to Heber J. Grant, Dec. 5, 1918; Heber J. Grant to Joshua F. Grant, Dec. 14, 1918; Heber J. Grant to Junius F. Wells, Dec. 12, 1918; Heber J. Grant to S. A. Whitney, Dec. 24, 1918, Heber J. Grant Collection, CHL.
11. "Spring Session of Conference Is Called Off," *Salt Lake Herald,* Mar. 21, 1919, [16]; "Conference Is to Be Held in Salt Lake," *Ogden (UT) Standard,* Apr. 19, 1919, 2; Heber J. Grant to Augusta Winters Grant, Mar. 20, 1919, Heber J. Grant Collection, CHL; "Spirit of the Lord Attends Elders of Church," *Deseret Evening News,* Mar. 15, 1919, section 4, vii; Heber J. Grant, in *Eighty-Ninth Annual Conference,* 74; Bray, "The Lord's Supper during the Progressive Era," 88–104. **Topic: Sacrament Meetings**
12. Heber J. Grant to "My Dearly Beloved Daughters," Dec. 1, 1919, Letterpress Copybook, volume 55, 259, Heber J. Grant Collection, CHL. **Topic: Influenza Pandemic of 1918**

13. Christensen, *Stories of the Temple in La'ie,* 33; Heber J. Grant to "My Dearly Beloved Daughters," Dec. 1, 1919, Letterpress Copybook, volume 55, 259; Heber J. Grant to Augusta Winters Grant, Nov. 29, 1919, Heber J. Grant Collection, CHL; *Saints,* volume 1, chapter 21; volume 2, chapter 44; Britsch, *Moramona,* 241–44.

14. Heber J. Grant, "The Dedicatory Prayer in the Hawaii Temple," *Improvement Era,* Feb. 1920, 23:281–88; Christensen, *Stories of the Temple in La'ie,* 35–38.

15. Heber J. Grant to "My Dearly Beloved Daughters," Dec. 1, 1919, Letterpress Copybook, volume 55, 259, Heber J. Grant Collection, CHL. Quotation edited for clarity; "he" in original changed to "President Smith." **Topics: Hawaii; Temple Dedications and Dedicatory Prayers**

16. Relief Society General Board, Minutes, Nov. 20, 1919, 292; Lyman, "Social Service Work in the Relief Society," 3–8; Hall, *Faded Legacy,* 79–82; McDannell, *Sister Saints,* 46–47. **Topic: Amy Brown Lyman**

17. McGerr, *Fierce Discontent,* xiii–xvi, 79–80, 256–59; Flanagan, *America Reformed,* 283–86; Lyman, *In Retrospect,* 30; Hall, *Faded Legacy,* 48–50.

18. Lyman, "Social Service Work in the Relief Society," 1–2, 6; Alexander, "Latter-day Saint Social Advisory Committee," 19–39. **Topics: Relief Society; Welfare Programs**

19. Relief Society General Board, Minutes, Oct. 23, 1919, 267–71; Susa Young Gates, "Address to the Relief Society Board," 3–7, Relief Society Files, Susa Young Gates Papers, CHL; Derr, Cannon, and Beecher, *Women of Covenant,* 222.

20. Cannon and Derr, "Resolving Differences/Achieving Unity," 130–31; Derr, Cannon, and Beecher, *Women of Covenant,* 241–42. **Topics: Fasting; Bishop**

21. Lyman, "Social Service Work in the Relief Society," 8–11; Amy Brown Lyman, "Class in Charities and Relief Work," *Relief Society Magazine,* Aug. 1920, 7:437–40; Amy Brown Lyman, "In Retrospect," *Relief Society Magazine,* July 1942, 29:464; Derr, "History of Social Services," 30–31; see also, for example, "Guide Lessons," *Relief Society Magazine,* Jan. 1920, 7:59–62; Feb. 1920, 7:118–24.

22. "Two Church Workers Will Tour Missions of Pacific Islands," *Deseret News,* Oct. 15, 1920, 5; Hugh J. Cannon, Journal, Dec. 4, 1920. **Topic: David O. McKay**

23. Hugh J. Cannon, Journal, Dec. 4, 1920–Feb. 7, 1921; McKay, Journal, Jan. 9, 1921, and Feb. 7, 1921; Neilson, *To the Peripheries of Mormondom,* xix–xxxii; Neilson and Teuscher, *Pacific Apostle,* xxvi–xxx, xl, 78; Britsch, *From the East,* 60–61; Plewe, *Mapping Mormonism,* 141.

24. McKay, Journal, Feb. 7, 1921, in Neilson and Teuscher, *Pacific Apostle,* 77–80.

25. Church Board of Education, Minutes [1919–25], Feb. 24, 1920; Mar. 3, 1920; Church Board of Education, Minutes [1888–2006], Mar. 18, 1926; *By Study and Also by Faith,* 33, 36–38, 597–99; Taylor, "Report of Sermons of Elder David O. McKay," 12; Hatch, *Colonia Juarez,* 229–38. **Topics: Church Academies; Seminaries and Institutes**

26. McKay, Journal, Apr. 21–22, 1921, in Neilson and Teuscher, *Pacific Apostle,* 103–11, 113, 118; Newton, *Tiki and Temple,* 162; David O. McKay, "Hui Tau," *Improvement Era,* July 1921, 24:769–77.

27. Newton, *Tiki and Temple,* 164; McKay, Journal, Apr. 23, 1921, in Neilson and Teuscher, *Pacific Apostle,* 123.

28. McKay, Journal, Apr. 23, 1921, in Neilson and Teuscher, *Pacific Apostle,* 123; Taylor, "Report of Sermons of Elder David O. McKay," 1–3; Young, Oral History Interview, 9–10; Cowan, "An Apostle in Oceania," 193–95. **Topic: Gift of Tongues**

29. Taylor, "Report of Sermons of Elder David O. McKay," 12. **Topic: New Zealand**

30. Widtsoe, *In the Gospel Net,* 127; Widtsoe, *In a Sunlit Land,* 85–87, 97–98, 124–27, 156.

31. Widtsoe, *In the Gospel Net,* 127–30; Widtsoe, Diary, May 28, 1919; June 12–July 11, 1919.

32. Widtsoe, Diary, Mar. 13–17, 1920.

33. Widtsoe, *In a Sunlit Land,* 156. Quotation edited for readability; original source has "He asked me to come to his office without delay."

34. **Topic: Church Headquarters**

35. John A. Widtsoe to James E. Addicott, Oct. 3, 1921, John A. Widtsoe Papers, CHL; Widtsoe, *In a Sunlit Land,* 156–57. Quotation edited for readability; "Was I willing to accept the call?" in original changed to "Are you willing to accept the call?"
36. Widtsoe, *In a Sunlit Land,* 156–57; Grant, Journal, Mar. 17, 1921.
37. Widtsoe, *In a Sunlit Land,* 157, 161–62; Joseph F. Smith, in *Seventy-Seventh Annual Conference,* 7–8. **Topic: Church Finances**
38. Leah D. Widtsoe to Heber J. Grant, June 30, 1921, Heber J. Grant Collection, CHL. **Topics: John and Leah Widtsoe; Quorum of the Twelve**
39. Grant, Journal, Mar. 17, 1921; Susa Young Gates to John A. Widtsoe, Mar. 31, 1921, Susa Young Gates Papers, CHL.
40. Heber J. Grant to Isaac Russell, Feb. 17, 1922, Isaac Russell Papers, Special Collections, Green Library, Stanford University, Stanford, CA; Heber J. Grant to Annie Wells Cannon, Apr. 25, 1921; Heber J. Grant to Frances Grant, May 18, 1921, Heber J. Grant Collection, CHL; Susa Young Gates to Elizabeth Claridge McCune, Feb. 10, 1921; May 6, 1921, Relief Society, Susa Young Gates Files, CHL; Madsen, *Emmeline B. Wells,* 480–81, 484–86, 488–90.
41. Heber J. Grant to Isaac Russell, Feb. 17, 1922, Isaac Russell Papers, Special Collections, Cecil H. Green Library, Stanford University, Stanford, CA; Annie Wells Cannon, Journal, Apr. 2, 1921; Madsen, *Emmeline B. Wells,* 490–91.
42. Relief Society General Board, Minutes, Apr. 2, 1921, 42–43; "Is Chosen by Head Church Official," *Salt Lake Telegram,* Apr. 2, 1921, 2. **Topic: Relief Society**
43. Relief Society General Board, Minutes, Apr. 14, 1921, 51; Susa Young Gates to Elizabeth Claridge McCune, Apr. 20, 1921; May 6, 1921, Relief Society, Susa Young Gates Files, CHL; Susa Young Gates, Journal, 1921–22, undated entry after Feb. 3, 1932. **Topic: Amy Brown Lyman**
44. Annie Wells Cannon, Journal, Apr. 2–20, 1921.
45. Annie Wells Cannon, Journal, Apr. 24–25, 1921; Susa Young Gates, "President Emmeline B. Wells," *Improvement Era,* June 1921, 24:718–21. **Topic: Emmeline B. Wells**

CHAPTER 15: NO GREATER REWARD

1. Neilson, *To the Peripheries of Mormondom,* xxix–xxx; David O. McKay and Hugh J. Cannon, "Summary and Report," 2–3, First Presidency Miscellaneous Correspondence, CHL.
2. David O. McKay, Diary, Nov. 8–10, 1921 [University of Utah]; David O. McKay and Hugh J. Cannon, "Summary and Report," 6–7; First Presidency to Joseph W. Booth, Sept. 23, 1919, First Presidency Miscellaneous Correspondence, CHL; Goldberg, "Armenian Exodus," Church History website, history.ChurchofJesusChrist.org. **Topics: Turkish Mission; Fasting**
3. Booth, Journal, volume 10, Nov. 30–Dec. 18, 1921; Goldberg, "Armenian Exodus," Church History website, history.ChurchofJesusChrist.org.
4. David O. McKay and Hugh J. Cannon, "Summary and Report," 4–5, 7; David O. McKay and Hugh J. Cannon to "First Presidency and Members of the Twelve," June 11, 1921, 3, First Presidency Miscellaneous Correspondence, CHL.
5. Alexander, *Mormonism in Transition,* 305–6; Presiding Bishopric Office Journal, Aug. 2, 1921; Johnson and Johnson, "Twentieth-Century Mormon Outmigration," 43–47; Shipps, "Scattering of the Gathered," 72–76; Beecher, "Post-Gathering Expansion of Zion," 103–6. **Topic: Outmigration**
6. Heber J. Grant, in *Ninety-Second Annual Conference,* 9–10; Orton, *Los Angeles Stake Story,* 40–62; Cowan and Homer, *California Saints,* 264–72. **Topic: Wards and Stakes**
7. Grant, Journal, Feb. 7, 1917, and Apr. 9, 1924; Heber J. Grant, in *Ninety-Second Annual Conference,* 165; Heber J. Grant to Stephen L. Richards, May 5, 1920, First Presidency Letterpress Copybooks, volume 59; see also *Saints,* volume 2, chapter 28.

8. Heber J. Grant, "Significant Counsel to the Young People," *Improvement Era,* Aug. 1921, 24:865–79; see also, for example, Heber J. Grant, in *Ninetieth Semi-annual Conference,* 10; and "Conference of Cache Stake Well Attended," *Logan (UT) Republican,* Sept. 20, 1921, 1.

9. Heber J. Grant, "Significant Counsel to the Young People," *Improvement Era,* Aug. 1921, 24:867. **Topics: Young Women Organizations; Young Men Organizations**

10. "Address by Prest. Grant First Sent," *Deseret News,* May 8, 1922, section 2, [1]; "The Vacuum Tube Amplifier," *Improvement Era,* Mar. 1922, 25:457; Wolsey, "History of Radio Station KSL," 51–67. **Topic: Broadcast Media**

11. Susa Young Gates, Journal, 1921–22, May 1922, image 13, Susa Young Gates Papers, CHL; [Susa Young Gates], "Editorial," *Relief Society Magazine,* Jan. 1915, 2:37–38; Mann, "History of the Relief Society Magazine," 30. The *Relief Society Magazine* began in 1914 as the *Relief Society Bulletin.* Its name was changed one year later. **Topic: Church Periodicals**

12. Susa Young Gates to Clarissa Williams, June 1922, copy, John A. Widtsoe Papers, CHL; Susa Young Gates to Elizabeth McCune, May 6, 1921, Research Notes, Susa Young Gates Files, CHL; Susa Young Gates, Journal, 1921–22, May 1922, image 13, Susa Young Gates Papers, CHL; Hall, *Faded Legacy,* 82–83.

13. Susa Young Gates, Journal, 1921–22, May 1922, image 13, Susa Young Gates Papers, CHL; Relief Society General Presidency to First Presidency, Dec. 21, 1921, First Presidency General Administration Files, CHL; Blumell, "Welfare before Welfare," 98–99. **Topic: Amy Brown Lyman**

14. Hall, *Faded Legacy,* 87–103; Derr, Cannon, and Beecher, *Women of Covenant,* 227–32. **Topics: Relief Society; Welfare Programs**

15. Relief Society General Board, Minutes, June 28, 1922, 66–67; Susa Young Gates to First Presidency, June 6, 1922; Susa Young Gates to Clarissa Williams, June 1922, copy, John A. Widtsoe Papers, CHL; Susa Young Gates to Elizabeth McCune, May 6, 1921, Research Notes, Susa Young Gates Files, CHL. Quotation edited for readability; original source has "Sister Gates said she was leaving her work with a love for her co-laborers and trusted they would extend the same love to her." **Topic: Susa Young Gates**

16. Susa Young Gates, Journal, 1921–22, Feb. 13, 1922, 4, Susa Young Gates Papers, CHL; Gates, *History of the Young Ladies' Mutual Improvement Association.*

17. Susa Young Gates, Journal, 1915–25, Oct. 30, 1922, image 124; Susa Young Gates, Journal, 1921–22, Dec. 28, 1922, 3, Susa Young Gates Papers, CHL.

18. Lee, Autobiography, 1–8, 12; William O. Lee Life Sketch, [1]–[2].

19. Lee, Autobiography, 7–8.

20. Cardston Alberta Stake Young Women's Mutual Improvement Association, Minutes and Records, Nov. 17, 1912, 1–3; Lee, Autobiography, 10–11.

21. Emily H. Higgs, May W. Cannon, and Sadie G. Pack, "Liberty Glen Camp," *Young Woman's Journal,* Jan. 1913, 24:31–34; Josephson, *History of the YWMIA,* 44–47, 135–37; "Summer Work," *Young Woman's Journal,* July 1914, 25:449–50. **Topic: Young Women Organizations**

22. Young Women General Board, Minutes, Oct. 8, 1914, 84; Jan. 28, 1915, 121; Feb. 18, 1915, 126–28; Josephson, *History of the YWMIA,* 48–55; "Mormon Girls Organize 'Bee Hive,'" *Salt Lake Telegram,* Apr. 18, 1915, 6; *Hand Book for the Bee-Hive Girls of the Y. L. M. I. A.* [1st ed.], 4–14; Elen Wallace, "The Bee-Hive Symbolism," *Young Woman's Journal,* July 1916, 27:390–95.

23. *Hand Book for the Bee-Hive Girls of the Y. L. M. I. A.* [1st ed.], 4–5; Cardston Alberta Stake Young Women's Mutual Improvement Association, Minutes and Records, July 4, 1915, 91; Apr. 1, 1916, 107; Nov. 6, 1916, 118.

24. Wood, *Alberta Temple,* 35–67; Prete and Prete, *Canadian Mormons,* 95–98. **Topic: Canada**

25. John A. Widtsoe to Leah D. Widtsoe, July 12, 1923, Widtsoe Family Papers, CHL.

26. Thomas, "Apostolic Diplomacy," 130–39; Widtsoe, *In a Sunlit Land,* 186; Parrish, *John A. Widtsoe,* 327–30; Merrill, *Apostle in Politics,* 154. **Topics: Denmark; Sweden; Norway**

27. John A. Widtsoe to Leah D. Widtsoe, July 12, 1923, Widtsoe Family Papers, CHL.
28. "Karl Marsel Widtsoe," Missionary Database, history.ChurchofJesusChrist.org/ missionary; John A. Widtsoe to Leah D. Widtsoe, July 12, 1923, Widtsoe Family Papers, CHL; Widtsoe, *In a Sunlit Land,* 236.
29. Thomas, "Apostolic Diplomacy," 137, 148–57.
30. Reed Smoot and John A. Widtsoe to First Presidency, Aug. 8, 1923, John A. Widtsoe Papers, CHL. **Topic: Growth of Missionary Work**
31. John A. Widtsoe to Leah D. Widtsoe, July 24, 1923, Widtsoe Family Papers, CHL; Widtsoe, *In a Sunlit Land,* 157–63.
32. Wood, Journal, Aug. 26, 1923; Grant, Journal, Aug. 25, 1923; George F. Richards, Journal, Aug. 25, 1923; Wood, *Alberta Temple,* 74; Prete and Prete, *Canadian Mormons,* 99. **Topic: Canada**
33. Lee, Autobiography, 8–9, 14; Wood, *Alberta Temple,* 116; Mouritsen, "George Franklin Richards," 210. Quotation edited for readability; "would" in original changed to "will."
34. Lee, Autobiography, 14; Alberta Temple Dedication Services, Aug. 26, 1923, 1, 12; "Great Mormon Temple at Cardston Dedicated," *Lethbridge (AB) Daily Herald,* Aug. 27, 1923, [1]. **Topic: Temple Dedications and Dedicatory Prayers**
35. George F. Richards, Journal, June 1, 1921; Feb. 8, 1922; May 29, 1922; Jan. 12–13, 1923; Apr. 6, 1923; Lund, Journal, Apr. 27, 1916, and July 22, 1920; Stapley and Wright, "History of Baptism for Health," 108–9; Alexander, *Mormonism in Transition,* 316–17; Mouritsen, "George Franklin Richards," 199–206. **Topic: Healing**
36. First Presidency to Presidents of Stakes and Presidents of Temples, June 12, 1923, First Presidency Letterpress Copybooks, volume 65; Mouritsen, "George Franklin Richards," 211–12; Alexander, *Mormonism in Transition,* 316–17. **Topics: Adjustments to Temple Work; Temple Endowment**
37. Lee, Autobiography, 14; "New Year's Greetings from Some of Our Stake Presidents," *Young Woman's Journal,* Jan. 1924, 35:41.
38. "New Year's Greetings from Some of Our Stake Presidents," *Young Woman's Journal,* Jan. 1924, 35:41. **Topic: Young Women Organizations**

CHAPTER 16: WRITTEN IN HEAVEN

1. Kullick, "Life of Herta"; Anna Kullick, Hamburg Passenger List, Apr. 20, 1922, 499; Ernst Biebersdorf, Hamburg Passenger List, Mar. 27, 1923, 689, available at ancestry .com. **Topic: Argentina**
2. Wilhelm Friedrichs to Charles W. Nibley, Dec. 15, 1924; Apr. 15, 1925, Argentine Mission Correspondence, CHL.
3. Palmer and Grover, "Parley P. Pratt's 1851 Mission to Chile," 115; Williams and Williams, *From Acorn to Oak,* 13–15, 17–20; Newton, *German Buenos Aires,* 75–85. **Topic: Chile**
4. Wilhelm Friedrichs to Charles Nibley, Mar. 2, 1924; Mar. 5, 1924; May 2, 1924; Dec. 15, 1924; Apr. 15, 1925; Wilhelm Friedrichs to Sylvester Q. Cannon, June 29, 1925, Argentine Mission Correspondence, CHL.
5. Wilhelm Friedrichs to Charles Nibley, Dec. 15, 1924; Apr. 15, 1925; Wilhelm Friedrichs to Sylvester Q. Cannon, June 29, 1925, Argentine Mission Correspondence, CHL.
6. Sylvester Q. Cannon to Wilhelm Friedrichs, June 24, 1925, Argentine Mission Correspondence, CHL. Quotation edited for clarity; "the Presidency" in original changed to "the First Presidency."
7. Wilhelm Friedrichs to Sylvester Q. Cannon, June 29, 1925, Argentine Mission Correspondence, CHL.
8. Schrag, *Not Fit for Our Society,* 70, 123, 144–45; Pegram, "Ku Klux Klan, Labor, and the White Working Class during the 1920s," 373–96; Smith, *Managing White Supremacy,* 73–75; Jackson, *Ku Klux Klan in the City,* 5–23; Higham, *Strangers in the Land,* 285–99.

9. Grant, Journal, Feb. 6, 1923; Seferovich, "History of the LDS Southern States Mission," 122–24; Mason, *Mormon Menace,* 145–47, 159–60; Charles A. Callis to First Presidency, Jan. 31, 1924; First Presidency to Charles A. Callis, Feb. 5, 1924, First Presidency Mission Files, CHL; see also Helaman 2:12–13; 6:16–32.

10. Gerlach, *Blazing Crosses in Zion,* 1–16; Bornstein, *Colors of Zion,* 34–39; Thomas, *Plessy v. Ferguson,* 3–4, 29–31; Jackson, "Race and History in Early American Film," 27–51; First Presidency to Joseph W. McMurrin, Nov. 23, 1920, First Presidency Mission Files, CHL. **Topic: Racial Segregation**

11. Marie Graves to Heber J. Grant, Nov. 10, 1920, First Presidency Mission Files, CHL.

12. Doctrine and Covenants 58:64; Mark 16:15; *Saints,* volume 1, chapter 46; volume 2, chapters 13, 31, and 32; First Presidency to Joseph W. McMurrin, Nov. 23, 1920, First Presidency Mission Files, CHL.

13. David O. McKay to Stephen L. Richards and J. Reuben Clark Jr., Jan. 19, 1954, David O. McKay Scrapbook, CHL.

14. Bush, "Mormonism's Negro Doctrine," 37–38; "Ritchie, Nelson Holder," Biographical Entry, Century of Black Mormons website, exhibits.lib.utah.edu; Salt Lake Temple Records, Living Sealings Previously Married, Book A, 1893–1902, microfilm 186,213; Salt Lake Temple Records, Sealings for the Living, Book A, 1893–1905, microfilm 186,206, Special Collections, FHL; Nelson H. Ritchie and Annie C. Ritchie, Sugar House Ward, Granite Stake, nos. 483 and 484, in Sugar House Ward, part 1, Record of Members Collection, CHL; Whitaker, Journal, Dec. 10, 1909. **Topic: Priesthood and Temple Restriction**

15. Gerlach, *Blazing Crosses in Zion,* 23–53, 55–101, 104–5; Grant, Journal, Mar. 6, 1924.

16. Grant, Journal, Apr. 4, 1925.

17. "Passing Events," *Improvement Era,* Aug. 1925, 28:1013; "William Jennings Bryan," *Improvement Era,* Sept. 1925, 28:1092–93.

18. Larson, *Summer for the Gods,* 31–59, 112, 116–21, 155, 168, 263; Marsden, *Fundamentalism and American Culture,* 175–77, 184–85; Numbers, *Creationists,* 51–68. **Topic: Organic Evolution**

19. Grant, Journal, Apr. 11, 1924; Heber J. Grant to Charles W. Lovett, Aug. 25, 1919, Letterpress Copybook, volume 54, 994; Heber J. Grant to Henry W. Beyers, June 28, 1933, Heber J. Grant Collection, CHL; Heber J. Grant to Fred W. Shibley, Jan. 21, 1930, Letterpress Copybook, volume 67, 646, Heber J. Grant Collection, CHL.

20. Grant, Journal, Apr. 11, 1924; 3 Nephi 9:1; Heber J. Grant to George T. Odell, Mar. 17, 1925, Letterpress Copybook, volume 63, 8; Heber J. Grant to Eva G. Moss, Nov. 26, 1925, Letterpress Copybook, volume 63, 612, Heber J. Grant Collection, CHL; Heber J. Grant to Earl Foote, Nov. 27, 1925, First Presidency Letterpress Copybooks, volume 65.

21. Grant, Journal, June 18, 1925.

22. "The Origin of Man," *Improvement Era,* Nov. 1909, 13:75–81; "'Mormon' View of Evolution," *Deseret News,* July 18, 1925, section 3, 5.

23. Larson, *Summer for the Gods,* 191–92.

24. Heber J. Grant to Tenney McFate, Aug. 5, 1925, First Presidency Letterpress Copybooks, volume 65; Heber J. Grant to Martha Geddes, Sept. 23, 1925, First Presidency Miscellaneous Correspondence, CHL; Heber J. Grant to Arne Arnesen, Aug. 15, 1925, First Presidency Letterpress Copybooks, volume 65; see also Matthew 7:16–20. **Topic: Organic Evolution**

25. Testimony of Len R. Hope and Mary Hope, 1–[2]; "Hope, Len," Biographical Entry, Century of Black Mormons website, exhibits.lib.utah.edu.

26. Testimony of Len R. Hope and Mary Hope, 1–[2]; "Hope, Len," Biographical Entry, Century of Black Mormons website, exhibits.lib.utah.edu; Len Hope entry, Genealogical Record, Alabama Conference, Southern States Mission, 70, in Alabama (State), part 1, segment 1, Record of Members Collection, CHL; John Matthew Tolbert entry, Genealogical Record, Alabama Conference, Southern States Mission, 149, in Alabama (State), part 1, segment 1, Record of Members Collection, CHL.

27. Testimony of Len R. Hope and Mary Hope, [2]; DuRocher, "Violent Masculinity," 49–60.

28. Testimony of Len R. Hope and Mary Hope, [2]; Stephenson, "Short Biography of Len, Sr. and Mary Hope," [9]; Flynt, *Alabama in the Twentieth Century,* 227–28, 317–31, 446–49; Feldman, *Sense of Place,* 12–15, 26–28, 73–76. **Topic: Racial Segregation**
29. Testimony of Len R. Hope and Mary Hope, 1–[2]; "Hope, Len," Biographical Entry, Century of Black Mormons website, exhibits.lib.utah.edu. Len Hope quotation edited for clarity; "I was investigating" in original changed to "I was investigating the Church."
30. Testimony of Len R. Hope and Mary Hope, 1–[2]; "Hope, Len," Biographical Entry, Century of Black Mormons website, exhibits.lib.utah.edu; Joseph Hancock to Gloria Gunn, Dec. 31, 1949, Joseph P. Hancock Mission Letters and Autobiography, CHL.
31. Joseph Hancock to Gloria Gunn, Dec. 31, 1949, Joseph P. Hancock Mission Letters and Autobiography, CHL; Testimony of Len R. Hope and Mary Hope, [2], [3]; "Hope, Len," and "Hope, Mary Lee Pugh," Biographical Entries, Century of Black Mormons website, exhibits.lib.utah.edu; Stephenson, "Short Biography of Len, Sr. and Mary Hope," [9].
32. Testimony of Len R. Hope and Mary Hope, [3]. Quotation edited for readability; "I could see" in original changed to "I can see."
33. Rey L. Pratt, Diary, Dec. 6, 1925; Melvin J. Ballard to First Presidency, Jan. 26, 1926, First Presidency Mission Files, CHL; Melvin J. Ballard, in *Ninety-Seventh Semi-annual Conference,* 35; Wilhelm Friedrichs to Sylvester Q. Cannon, June 29, 1925, Argentine Mission Correspondence, CHL.
34. Melvin J. Ballard to First Presidency, Jan. 26, 1926, First Presidency Mission Files, CHL; Melvin J. Ballard, in *Ninety-Seventh Semi-annual Conference,* 35.
35. Melvin J. Ballard to First Presidency, Dec. 15, 1925, First Presidency Mission Files, CHL; Rey L. Pratt, Diary, Dec. 10, 1925; South American Mission Index, in South American Mission, Manuscript History, [1]–7; South American Mission, Manuscript History, Dec. 13, 1925, [17].
36. "Dedicatorial Prayer, Dedicating the Lands of South America to the Preaching of the Gospel," First Presidency Mission Files, CHL; Melvin J. Ballard, "Prayer Dedicating the Lands of South America to the Preaching of the Gospel," *Improvement Era,* Apr. 1926, 29:575–77.
37. Melvin J. Ballard to First Presidency, Dec. 15, 1925; Mar. 15, 1926, First Presidency Mission Files, CHL; Melvin J. Ballard, in *Ninety-Seventh Semi-annual Conference,* 35–36; "The Missions: The Sunday School in South America," *Instructor,* Dec. 1939, 74:539; "Elder Ballard Dedicated South American Nations," South American Mission, Manuscript History, [19].
38. Melvin J. Ballard, in *Ninety-Seventh Semi-annual Conference,* 34–36; Rey L. Pratt, Diary, Jan. 1–2, 3, and 14, 1926; Rey L. Pratt to Family, Feb. 8, 1926, Rey L. Pratt Papers, CHL.
39. Rey L. Pratt to Family, Feb. 14, 1926, Rey L. Pratt Papers, CHL; "The Missions: The Sunday School in South America," *Instructor,* Dec. 1939, 74:539; Melvin J. Ballard to First Presidency, Mar. 22, 1926, First Presidency Mission Files, CHL.
40. Melvin J. Ballard, in *Ninety-Seventh Semi-annual Conference,* 36; Melvin J. Ballard to First Presidency, Mar. 1, 1926, First Presidency Mission Files, CHL.
41. First Presidency to Melvin J. Ballard, Mar. 23, 1926; Melvin J. Ballard to First Presidency, Mar. 22, 1926; June 16, 1926, First Presidency Mission Files, CHL; Curbelo, *History of the Mormons in Argentina,* 38–39; Williams and Williams, *From Acorn to Oak Tree,* 29; Melvin J. Ballard, in *Ninety-Seventh Semi-annual Conference,* 37.
42. Sharp, Oral History Interview, 10; see also Sharp, Autobiography, 48; and Sharp, Journal, July 4, 1926, and index card inserted in journal. **Topic: Argentina**

CHAPTER 17: SPARED FOR EACH OTHER

1. Secretary of the General Church Board of Education to Joseph F. Smith, Nov. 30, 1901, Centennial History Project Records, BYU; Church Board of Education, Minutes, Feb. 3, 1926; Mar. 3 and 10, 1926.

2. Church Board of Education, Minutes, Feb. 3, 1926.
3. Church Board of Education, Minutes, Mar. 3, 1926. **Topic: Church Academies**
4. Greene, Interview; Greene, *A Life Remembered,* 33; Wright, "Beginnings of the First LDS Institute of Religion at Moscow, Idaho," 68–70.
5. Greene, *A Life Remembered,* 33; *By Study and Also by Faith,* 64; Wright, "Beginnings of the First LDS Institute of Religion at Moscow, Idaho," 70–72. Quotation edited for readability; original source has "The university could never attract L.D.S. students unless there were better facilities."
6. Church Board of Education, Minutes, Mar. 23, 1926; June 25, 1926; Sept. 1, 1926; Oct. 12, 1926; Grant, Journal, Mar. 24, 1926; *By Study and Also by Faith,* 64–65. **Topic: Seminaries and Institutes**
7. Grant, Journal, Sept. 13, 1926; Heber J. Grant to Marriner W. Eccles and Henry H. Rolapp, Sept. 13, 1926, First Presidency Miscellaneous Correspondence, CHL; Sessions, Oral History Interview [1972], 4; Griffiths, "First Institute Teacher," 175–82; Tomlinson, "History of the Founding of the Institutes of Religion," 151–59.
8. Widtsoe, Diary, Jan. 1, 1927.
9. Widtsoe, Diary, Nov. 21 and Dec. 14, 1926; Widtsoe, *In a Sunlit Land,* 236; Thomas Hull to John A. Widtsoe and Leah D. Widtsoe, June 15, 1927, Widtsoe Family Papers, CHL.
10. Widtsoe, Diary, Oct. 7 and 9, 1926; Dec. 8 and 14, 1926; Jan. 1, 1927; "Anne Widtsoe and Lewis Wallace Married," *Ogden (UT) Standard-Examiner,* Oct. 10, 1926, section 2, [1]; Leah D. Widtsoe to John A. Widtsoe, Feb. 20, 1927, Widtsoe Family Papers, CHL.
11. See Widtsoe, Diary, Jan. and Feb. 1927; Leah D. Widtsoe to John A. Widtsoe, Feb. 20, 1927, Widtsoe Family Papers, CHL.
12. Leah D. Widtsoe, "I Remember Brigham Young," *Improvement Era,* June 1961, 64:385; Widtsoe, Oral History Interview, 11–12; Susa Young Gates to Heber J. Grant and Counselors, Dec. 5, 1922; Susa Young Gates to James Kirkham and Albert Hooper, Nov. 12, 1929, Susa Young Gates Papers, CHL. Quotation edited for readability; original source has "'Nevertheless,' said I, 'you have it to do.'"
13. Widtsoe, Oral History Interview, 11–12; Leah D. Widtsoe to John A. Widtsoe, Feb. 20, 1927; Susa Young Gates to Leah D. Widtsoe, July 28, 1928; Lucy G. Bowen to Leah D. Widtsoe and John A. Widtsoe, Nov. 25, 1930, Widtsoe Family Papers, CHL; "Mrs. Susa Young Gates," *Deseret News,* May 27, 1933, 4. **Topic: Brigham Young**
14. J. E. Fisher to John A. Widtsoe and Leah D. Widtsoe, May 22, 1927, Widtsoe Family Papers, CHL; Widtsoe, Diary, May 23, 1927; Susa Young Gates, draft of obituary for Marsel Widtsoe, Widtsoe Family Papers, CHL; "Karl M. Widtsoe Dies of Pneumonia," *Deseret News,* May 30, 1927, section 2, [1].
15. Widtsoe, Diary, May 23–28, 1927; Widtsoe, *In a Sunlit Land,* 29, 236.
16. Leah D. Widtsoe to First Presidency, Sept. 16, 1933, First Presidency Mission Files, CHL; Widtsoe, Oral History Interview, 33; Widtsoe, *In a Sunlit Land,* 235–37.
17. Fish, "My Life Story," [1]–[2]; Paul Bang, "My Life Story," 1, 7–8; U.S. Department of Commerce, Bureau of the Census, *Fifteenth Census of the United States: 1930,* volume 1, 836.
18. Christian Bang Sr., "My Story," [1]–[3]; Fish, "My Life Story," [1]; Fish, Kramer, and Wallis, *History of the Mormon Church in Cincinnati,* 52–54.
19. Fish, Kramer, and Wallis, *History of the Mormon Church in Cincinnati,* 21–42, 45–50; "Mormons Baptize Child in the Ohio," *Commercial Tribune* (Cincinnati), Sept. 16, 1912, 12.
20. Christian Bang Sr., "My Story," [3]; Alexander, *Mormonism in Transition,* 105–6.
21. Anderson, "My Journey through Life," volume 4, 117–18; Christian Bang Sr., "My Story," [5]; Anderson, *Twenty-Three Years in Cincinnati,* 2–3, 13, 45; Johnson and Johnson, "Twentieth-Century Mormon Outmigration," 43–47; Plewe, *Mapping Mormonism,* 144–47. **Topic: Outmigration**
22. "World-Wide Attack on Mormonism Now Planned," *Commercial Tribune* (Cincinnati), June 30, 1912, [16]; "Fight on Mormonism to Start in Cincinnati," *Commercial Tribune,* Jan. 26, 1915, 3; "Cannon Makes Severe Attack on Mormonism," *Commercial Tribune,* Feb. 3, 1915, 10.

23. Fish, "My Life Story," [3], [6]; Christian Bang Sr., "My Story," [5]; Paul Bang, "My Life Story," 6, 8.

24. Bang family entries, South Ohio District, Northern States Mission, nos. 27–33, 324, 334, in Ohio (State), part 2, Record of Members Collection, CHL.

25. "News from the Missions," *Liahona, the Elders' Journal,* July 12, 1927, 25:42; Paul Bang entry, South Ohio District, Northern States Mission, no. 334, in Ohio (State), part 2, Record of Members Collection, CHL; Paul Bang, "My Life Story," 7; *Picturesque Cincinnati,* 77. The *Liahona* misspelled his name "Paul Bancy."

26. Sessions, Oral History Interview [1972], 4–5; Sessions and Sessions, Oral History Interview [1965], 12; Wright, "Beginnings of the First LDS Institute of Religion at Moscow, Idaho," 66–68; Tomlinson, "History of the Founding of the Institutes of Religion," 159–61.

27. J. Wyley Sessions to Heber J. Grant, Nov. 13, 1926, First Presidency Miscellaneous Correspondence, CHL; Sessions and Sessions, Oral History Interview [1965], 10; Tomlinson, "History of the Founding of the Institutes of Religion," 154–55.

28. Sessions and Sessions, Oral History Interview [1965], 10–11; Tomlinson, "History of the Founding of Institutes of Religion," 161, 183–86.

29. Sessions, Oral History Interview [1972], 5; Tomlinson, "History of the Founding of Institutes of Religion," 161–62; Griffiths, "First Institute Teacher," 182.

30. Sessions and Sessions, Oral History Interview [1965], 11–13; Sessions, Oral History Interview [1972], 8–9; Tomlinson, "History of the Founding of Institutes of Religion," 159–68; Griffiths, "First Institute Teacher," 182–85.

31. Sessions and Sessions, Oral History Interview [1965], 11–12; Tomlinson, "History of the Founding of Institutes of Religion," 168–73. Wyley Sessions quotation edited for readability; "didn't" and "hadn't" in original changed to "don't" and "haven't."

Topic: Seminaries and Institutes

32. Leah D. Widtsoe to John A. Widtsoe, Sept. 20, 1927, Widtsoe Family Papers, CHL; John A. Widtsoe to Heber J. Grant, Oct. 17, 1927, First Presidency General Administration Files, CHL; Leah D. Widtsoe to First Presidency, Sept. 16, 1933, First Presidency Mission Files, CHL.

33. Widtsoe, Diary, May 31–June 7, 1927; Widtsoe, *In a Sunlit Land,* 236–37.

34. Leah D. Widtsoe to John A. Widtsoe, Telegram, Aug. 31, 1927; Leah D. Widtsoe to John A. Widtsoe, Sept. 20, 1927, Widtsoe Family Papers, CHL; Widtsoe, Diary, June 21–Sept. 21, 1927.

35. Widtsoe, Diary, Aug. 8, 1927.

36. Widtsoe, Oral History Interview, 12–13; Widtsoe, Diary, Sept. 16 and 24, 1927; Harold Shepstone to Susa Young Gates, Oct. 25, 1927; Dec. 2, 1927, Susa Young Gates Papers, CHL. Quotation edited for readability; two instances of "would" in original changed to "will."

37. Hal and Bichette Gates to Susa Young Gates, Telegram, Sept. 24, 1927, Family Correspondence, Susa Young Gates Papers, CHL; Leah D. Widtsoe to John A. Widtsoe, Sept. 20, 1927, Widtsoe Family Papers, CHL.

38. Widtsoe, Diary, Sept. 29–30, 1927; Widtsoe, *In a Sunlit Land,* 189; John A. Widtsoe to James E. Talmage and Merry B. Talmage, Nov. 1, 1927, John A. Widtsoe Papers, CHL; Van Orden, *Building Zion,* 93–94; "Mission Presidents in Convention," *Latter-day Saints' Millennial Star,* Sept. 20, 1928, 38:600–602.

39. Leah D. Widtsoe to First Presidency, Sept. 16, 1933, First Presidency Mission Files, CHL; Leah D. Widtsoe to John A. Widtsoe, July 12, 1927; Leah D. Widtsoe to Louisa Hill, May 11, 1928, Widtsoe Family Papers, CHL; Widtsoe, *In a Sunlit Land,* 189; John A. Widtsoe to James E. Talmage and Merry B. Talmage, Nov. 1, 1927, John A. Widtsoe Papers, CHL.

40. See Widtsoe, Diary, Oct.–Nov. 1927.

41. Widtsoe, Oral History Interview, 13; Susa Young Gates to Harold J. Shepstone, Oct. 5, 1927, Susa Young Gates Papers, CHL.

42. Widtsoe, Diary, Nov. 21, 1927; Widtsoe, *In the Gospel Net,* 102–5, 133, 135; Susa Young Gates to Leah D. Widtsoe and John A. Widtsoe, Nov. 21, 1927, Widtsoe Family Papers, CHL.

CHAPTER 18: ANY PLACE ON EARTH

1. Reinhold Stoof to First Presidency, Nov. 2, 1927; Dec. 13, 1927, First Presidency Mission Files, CHL; Grover, "Sprechen Sie Portugiesisch?," 116–17; Sharp, Oral History Interview, 7–8, 10.
2. Melvin J. Ballard to First Presidency, June 16, 1926; Reinhold Stoof to First Presidency, Nov. 2, 1927; Nov. 16, 1927, First Presidency Mission Files, CHL; Grover, "Sprechen Sie Portugiesisch?," 118–19, 125–27.
3. Reinhold Stoof to First Presidency, Nov. 2, 1927; Jan. 24, 1928, First Presidency Mission Files, CHL; Grover, "Sprechen Sie Portugiesisch?," 120.
4. South American Mission, Manuscript History, volume 1, Feb. 29, 1928; Reinhold Stoof to First Presidency, Jan. 24, 1928, First Presidency Mission Files, CHL; Stoddard, Oral History Interview, 19–20; Grover, "Sprechen Sie Portugiesisch?," 120. **Topics: Argentina; Brazil**
5. Widtsoe, Diary, Dec. 23, 1927–Jan. 14, 1928; John A. Widtsoe to Heber J. Grant, Jan. 18, 1928, First Presidency Mission Files, CHL; Leah Dunford Widtsoe to [Louisa] Hill, May 11, 1928; Leah Dunford Widtsoe to Mary Booth Talmage, Oct. 30, 1929; Leah Dunford Widtsoe to Libby Ivins, Nov. 1, 1929, Widtsoe Family Papers, CHL.
6. Presiding Bishopric, Financial, Statistical, and Historical Reports for Stakes and Missions, volume 10, 1927; John A. Widtsoe to First Presidency, May 1, 1928, First Presidency Mission Files, CHL; Alexander, *Mormonism in Transition,* 243.
7. John A. Widtsoe to First Presidency, Feb. 28, 1928; July 2, 1928, First Presidency Mission Files, CHL. **Topic: Emigration**
8. Missionary Department, Missionary Registers, 1860–1925; John A. Widtsoe to First Presidency, Feb. 28, 1928; Oct. 16, 1928; Oct. 16, 1929; Aug. 24, 1932, First Presidency Mission Files, CHL.
9. Leah Dunford Widtsoe, "Greeting to the Sisters," *Latter-day Saints' Millennial Star,* Jan. 5, 1928, 90:10–11; "Book of Mormon Studies," *Latter-day Saints' Millennial Star,* Jan. 12, 1928, 90:22–23; Leah Dunford Widtsoe to Brother Morton, June 26, 1928, Widtsoe Family Papers, CHL; Doctrine and Covenants 97:21. **Topic: Zion/New Jerusalem**
10. Widtsoe, Diary, Jan. 28–29, 1928; John A. Widtsoe to Heber J. Grant, Oct. 17, 1927, First Presidency General Administration Files, CHL; Leah Dunford Widtsoe to [Louisa] Hill, May 11, 1928, Widtsoe Family Papers, CHL.
11. John A. Widtsoe to Heber J. Grant, Oct. 17, 1927, First Presidency General Administration Files, CHL; Leah Dunford Widtsoe to [Louisa] Hill, May 11, 1928, Widtsoe Family Papers, CHL. **Topic: John and Leah Widtsoe**
12. Sell, Transcrito, 1; Brazilian Mission, History of Mission Work, [9b]; Sell, Oral History Interview, 1.
13. Sell, Transcrito, 1; Sell, Oral History Interview, 1.
14. Sell, Transcrito, 1; Brazilian Mission, History of Mission Work, 2–[9b]; Sell, Oral History Interview, 1–2.
15. Sell, Oral History Interview, 2; Brazilian Mission, History of Mission Work, [9b].
16. Sell, Oral History Interview, 2–4; Sell, Transcrito, 1; Brazilian Mission, History of Mission Work, [9b], 21. **Topic: Brazil**
17. Cincinnati Branch, Minutes, Mar. 29, 1929, 2; Fish, Kramer, and Wallis, *History of the Mormon Church in Cincinnati,* 55; *One Hundred Years of Presbyterianism,* 182; "Joseph Smith's Prophecy of Mormon Church in Cincinnati," *Commercial Tribune* (Cincinnati), Sept. 16, 1929, [1].

18. Cincinnati Branch, Minutes, Mar. 29, 1929, 1–2; Anderson, "My Journey through Life," volume 4, 118, 124; Jackson, *Places of Worship,* 175, 189, 205; see also Fish, "My Life Story," [2].

19. Anderson, "My Journey through Life," volume 4, 122–23, 126–30, 133; Cincinnati Branch member entries, South Ohio District, Northern States Mission, in Ohio (State), part 2, Record of Members Collection, CHL; *Williams' Cincinnati Directory* [1927–28]; Fish, "My Life Story," [6]; Paul Bang, "My Life Story," 7, 10.

20. Cincinnati Branch, Minutes, Apr. 1929, 3; Noah S. Pond to Heber J. Grant, Apr. 16, 1929; Heber J. Grant to Noah S. Pond, Apr. 16, 1929; Charles V. Anderson to Heber J. Grant, Apr. 16, 1929; Heber J. Grant to Charles V. Anderson, Apr. 17, 1929, First Presidency Mission Files, CHL.

21. Cincinnati Branch, Minutes, Apr.–June 1929, 3; Anderson, "My Journey through Life," volume 4, 134; see also, for example, "Changes in Law of the Land," *Cincinnati Enquirer,* Feb. 3, 1915, 10; "To Talk on Mormonism," *Commercial Tribune* (Cincinnati), Mar. 10, 1916, 10; and "Antimormon Meeting," *Commercial Tribune,* May 4, 1916, 10.

22. "News from the Missions," *Liahona, the Elders' Journal,* May 14, 1929, 26:574.

23. German-Austrian Mission, Manuscript History and Historical Reports, volume 1, May 31, 1929; Meyer and Galli, *Under a Leafless Tree,* 58; Naujoks and Eldredge, *Shades of Gray,* 35; Clayson, Oral History Interview, 4. The town of Tilsit, Germany, is now Sovetsk, Russia. **Topic: Russia**

24. German-Austrian Mission, Manuscript History and Historical Reports, volume 1, May 31, 1929; Melvin O. Allen, Journal, Mar. 10 and Apr. 17, 1929; Worlton, Journal, Apr. 17, 1929.

25. Obituary for Friedrich W. Schulzke, *Der Stern,* Feb. 15, 1937, 69:60–61; Schulzke, "Story of Friedrich Schulzke," 13–14; Schulzke family entries, Tilsit Branch, Königsberg Conference, Swiss-German Mission, in Germany (Country), part 30, Record of Members Collection, CHL.

26. Obituary for Friedrich W. Schulzke, *Der Stern,* Feb. 15, 1937, 69:60–61; Schulzke, "Story of Friedrich Schulzke," 15–16; see also Parshall, "Friedrich Schulzke," [2].

27. German-Austrian Mission, Branch Histories, 137–38; Tilsit Branch, Manuscript History and Historical Reports, 1914–20.

28. Tilsit Branch, Manuscript History and Historical Reports, 1921–23; see also, for example, German-Austrian Mission, Manuscript History and Historical Reports, volume 1, May 31, 1929; July 31, 1929; Dec. 31, 1929.

29. Naujoks and Eldredge, *Shades of Gray,* 29, 35; German-Austrian Mission, Branch Histories, 138; Meyer and Galli, *Under a Leafless Tree,* 58; George H. Neuenschwander to Genevieve Bramwell, Sept. 16, 1931, George H. Neuenschwander Correspondence, CHL; Clayson, Oral History Interview, 4. **Topic: Germany**

CHAPTER 19: THE GOSPEL OF THE MASTER

1. "Fire in Church," *Cincinnati Enquirer,* Sept. 10, 1929, 13; Horace Karr, "Joseph Smith's Prophecy of Mormon Church in Cincinnati," *Commercial Tribune* (Cincinnati), Sept. 16, 1929, 1–2; Cincinnati Branch, Minutes, Jan. 16, 1932, 3–4; Orson F. Whitney to "The Council of the First Presidency and the Twelve," Oct. 2, 1929, in Whitney, Journal, 88; Brown, Journal, Sept. 11, 1929.

2. Anderson, "My Journey through Life," volume 4, 134; "First Mormon Church Is to Be Dedicated Here," *Commercial Tribune* (Cincinnati), Sept. 13, 1929, 12; *Williams' Cincinnati Directory* [1929–30], 220, 2020. **Topic: Public Relations**

3. "First Mormon Church Is to Be Dedicated Here," *Commercial Tribune* (Cincinnati), Sept. 13, 1929, 12. Quotation edited for readability; "The church had outgrown" in original changed to "The Church has outgrown." **Topic: Church Finances**

4. Horace Karr, "Joseph Smith's Prophecy of Mormon Church in Cincinnati," *Commercial Tribune* (Cincinnati), Sept. 16, 1929, 1–2; Northern States Mission, General Minutes, Sept. 14–15, 1929, 571–72; Northern States Mission, Manuscript History and Historical Reports, volume 6, Sept. 15, 1929; Orson F. Whitney to "The Council of the First Presidency and the Twelve," Oct. 2, 1929, in Whitney, Journal, 88; "Chapel Fulfills Prophecy of 1831," *Deseret News*, Sept. 25, 1929, 7.

5. Cincinnati Branch, Minutes, Jan. 16, 1932, 1–4; Anderson, *Twenty-Three Years in Cincinnati,* 45; Horace Karr, "Joseph Smith's Prophecy of Mormon Church in Cincinnati," *Commercial Tribune* (Cincinnati), Sept. 16, 1929, 1–2.

6. Northern States Mission, General Minutes, Sept. 14–15, 1929, 571–72; Horace Karr, "Joseph Smith's Prophecy of Mormon Church in Cincinnati," *Commercial Tribune* (Cincinnati), Sept. 16, 1929, 1; Cincinnati Branch, Minutes, Jan. 16, 1932, 4. Quotation edited for readability; "he felt" in original changed to "I feel."

7. Grant, Journal, Nov. 1, 1929; George Atkin, "By Telegraph," *Deseret Evening News,* Nov. 5, 1880, [4]; Heber J. Grant to Richard R. Lyman, Dec. 6, 1930, Letterpress Copybook, volume 68, 187, Heber J. Grant Collection, CHL; "Tooele Stake Conference," *Deseret News,* Nov. 10, 1880, 652.

8. Heber J. Grant to June and Isaac Stewart, Dec. 2, 1929, Letterpress Copybook, volume 67, 432, Heber J. Grant Collection, CHL; Grant, Journal, Nov. 22, 1928, and Oct. 31, 1929; "Daughter L. D. S. Leader Dies at Local Hospital," *Salt Lake Tribune,* Aug. 1, 1929, 26.

9. *Saints,* volume 2, chapter 31; Plewe, *Mapping Mormonism,* 127, 132; "President Udall of Mormon Temple Is Back from Utah," *Arizona Republican* (Phoenix), Oct. 16, 1927, 4; "President Grant Invokes Divine Blessings on All," *Deseret News,* Oct. 29, 1927, section 3, ix; see also Arizona Temple, Dedication Services, Oct. 23–24, 1927, 21–22, 84–88.

10. Heber J. Grant, Rudger Clawson, in *One Hundredth Annual Conference,* 3–13, 33; Pusey, *Builders of the Kingdom,* 281–82; Rudger Clawson to First Presidency, Sept. 21, 1928, copy; Minutes, Jan. 17, 1930, Council of the Twelve Apostles, General File, CHL; see also "Members of Church Everywhere Join in Fete," *Deseret News,* Apr. 5, 1930, [section 5], 3; "Pageant Takes Gospel History through Ages," *Deseret News,* Apr. 5, 1930, [section 3], 9; and "The Centennial Pageant," *Improvement Era,* May 1930, 33:460–61, 503–4.

11. Grant, Journal, Nov. 15–25, 1929; Heber J. Grant to W. C. Orem, Dec. 30, 1918, Heber J. Grant Collection, CHL; Heber J. Grant to David O. McKay, Feb. 6, 1919, Letterpress Copybook, volume 54, 1450, Heber J. Grant Collection, CHL.

12. George F. Richards, Journal, Oct. 7, 1923; Dec. 21, 1924; Feb. 1, 1925; Jan. 9, 1927; Feb. 10, 1929; Heber J. Grant to Grace Grant Evans, Oct. 10, 1924, Heber J. Grant Collection, CHL; Baker and Mott, "From Radio to the Internet," 342–43; Grant, Journal, Feb. 14, 1929; Sunday Evening Radio Addresses, 1924–29.

13. "Entire U.S. Will Hear Them," *Deseret News,* July 11, 1929, section 2, 1; Newell, "Seventy-Five Years of the Mormon Tabernacle Choir's *Music and the Spoken Word,"* 128–29; Hicks, *Mormon Tabernacle Choir,* 71–74. **Topics: Tabernacle Choir; Broadcast Media**

14. Walker, " 'Going to Meeting' in Salt Lake City's Thirteenth Ward," 138–61; Shipps, May, and May, "Sugar House Ward," 310, 329–33; Hartley, "Church Activity during the Brigham Young Era," 249–67; George F. Richards, Journal, Mar. 15, 1925; "Ogden Tabernacle Too Small," *Ogden (UT) Standard-Examiner,* Apr. 19, 1920, 6. **Topics: Wards and Stakes; Sacrament Meetings**

15. "Boise Stake Plans Special Missionary Work in Its District," *Deseret News,* Jan. 8, 1921, 11; "Nebo Stake Organizes Home Missionaries," *Deseret News,* Jan. 23, 1922, section 2, 1.

16. George F. Richards, Journal, Oct. 31, 1921; Nov. 14, 1921; May 8, 1922; "Junior Excursions," *Deseret News,* May 13, 1922, section 4, viii; "Boxelder Junior Excursion," *Deseret News,* May 20, 1922, section 4, viii. **Topic: Baptism for the Dead**

17. Heber J. Grant to J. L. Cotter, Nov. 23, 1922, First Presidency Miscellaneous Correspondence, CHL; Heber J. Grant to John Baxter, Dec. 8, 1925, First Presidency Letterpress Copybooks, volume 71; Peterson, "Historical Analysis of the Word of Wisdom," 90–94; Heber J. Grant, in *Ninety-Second Semi-annual Conference,* 6–7; "M. I. A. and Primary Conferences Close in Joint Sessions," *Deseret News,* June 12, 1922, section 2, 6. **Topics: Word of Wisdom; Prohibition; Tithing**

18. "Young Folks of Uintah," *Deseret Weekly,* June 5, 1897, 799; Grant, Journal, Feb. 4, 1900; Nov. 16, 1907; Nov. 28, 1909; Feb. 4, 1912; Jan. 18, 1914; Feb. 11, 1917; Nov. 22, 1929; Heber J. Grant to Mary Wikoff, Jan. 31, 1930, Letterpress Copybook, volume 67, 665, Heber J. Grant Collection, CHL.

19. Grant, Journal, Nov. 21, 1929; David O. McKay to Augusta Winters Grant, Nov. 28, 1929, in Grant, Journal, Nov. 22, 1929. **Topic: Heber J. Grant**

20. Meyer and Galli, *Under a Leafless Tree,* 58; Helga Meischus entry, Königsberg Conference, Swiss-German Mission, Births and Blessings, 1921, 854–55, in Germany (Country), part 32; Königsberg District, German-Austrian Mission, Ordinations to the Priesthood, 1929, 1580, in Germany (Country), part 34, segment 1, Record of Members Collection, CHL; see also Tilsit Branch, Sunday School Minutes and Records, Jan. 2, 1927–Dec. 15, 1929. Helga's last name is spelled Meizsus or Meischus in some records.

21. Meyer and Galli, *Under a Leafless Tree,* 3–5, 12, 25–27; Königsberg District, German-Austrian Mission, Emigration Record, 1928, 67, in Germany (Country), part 34, segment 1, Record of Members Collection, CHL; see also Tilsit Branch, Sunday School Minutes and Records, May 1, 1927–Aug. 5, 1928.

22. *Circular of the First Presidency,* 5; see also Tilsit Branch, Sunday School Minutes and Records, Dec. 30, 1928; Jan. 6, 1929; Feb. 24, 1929; June 9, 1929.

23. See Tilsit Branch, Sunday School Minutes and Records, Jan. 2, 1927–Dec. 29, 1929. **Topics: Sunday School; Hymns**

24. Meyer and Galli, *Under a Leafless Tree,* 16, 25–27; see also Tilsit Branch, Sunday School Minutes and Records, Jan. 2, 1927–Dec. 29, 1929.

25. Naujoks and Eldredge, *Shades of Gray,* 29; Allen, Journal, Mar. 10, 1929; see also Tilsit Branch, Sunday School Minutes and Records, Jan. 6–Dec. 29, 1929.

26. Tilsit Branch, Sunday School Minutes and Records, June 2, 1929; Nov. 24, 1929; Dec. 1, 8, 15, and 22, 1929; Meyer and Galli, *Under a Leafless Tree,* 32.

27. See Tilsit Branch, Sunday School Minutes and Records, Jan. 2, 1927–Dec. 29, 1929.

28. Leah Dunford Widtsoe to Louise Stanley, Dec. 21, 1929, Widtsoe Family Papers, CHL.

29. See Leah Dunford Widtsoe to Libby Snow Ivins, Nov. 1, 1929; and Leah Dunford Widtsoe to Ethel Johnson, Feb. 5, 1929, Widtsoe Family Papers, CHL.

30. Danish Mission, French Mission, German-Austrian Mission, Netherland Mission, Report of the Mission President, 1929, volume 11, Presiding Bishopric Financial, Statistical, and Historical Reports, CHL; German-Austrian Mission, Manuscript History and Historical Reports, 1886–1911, volume 1, Apr. 27 and July 14, 1929; "Story of Only Church Owned Chapel in Germany," *Deseret News,* Dec. 24, 1938, Church section, 4; Phillip Jensen, "President Widtsoe and Party in Denmark," *Latter-day Saints' Millennial Star,* July 25, 1929, 91:476; Mehr, "Czechoslovakia and the LDS Church," 112–17; see also John A. Widtsoe to First Presidency, Jan. 24, 1930, First Presidency Mission Files, CHL. The town of Selbongen, Germany, is now Zełwągi, Poland. **Topics: Germany; Belgium; Denmark; Czechoslovakia; Poland**

31. Leah Dunford Widtsoe to Cornelia Groesbeck Snow, Nov. 30, 1928; Leah Dunford Widtsoe to Mrs. Haeberle, Dec. 23, 1929; Leah Dunford Widtsoe to Louise Stanley, Dec. 21, 1929, Widtsoe Family Papers, CHL; Leah Dunford Widtsoe, "Relief Society Course of Study for 1929," and "Word of Wisdom Lessons (No. 1)," *Latter-day Saints' Millennial Star,* Jan. 17, 1929, 91:35–39; Heber J. Grant, "Addresses by Members of First Presidency," *Deseret News,* June 23, 1928, section 3, v; Wendell Johnson, "Why I Believe I Should Obey the Word of Wisdom," *Juvenile Instructor,* Mar. 1929, 64:148–49; "Special Lesson," *Juvenile Instructor,* June 1929, 64:335; see also Leah Dunford Widtsoe, "Word of Wisdom Lessons (No. 9)," *Latter-day Saints' Millennial Star,* Aug. 15, 1929, 91:518–19, 521–23; and Leah Dunford Widtsoe, "Word of Wisdom Lessons (No. 12)," *Latter-day Saints' Millennial Star,* Nov. 21, 1929, 91:741–43, 745–46. **Topic: Word of Wisdom**

32. John A. Widtsoe, "A European Program for Genealogical Study, Research and Exchange," *Latter-day Saints' Millennial Star,* Sept. 19, 1929, 91:596–97; Susa Young Gates to Leah Dunford Widtsoe, Feb. 2, 1929, Widtsoe Family Papers, CHL. **Topic: Family History and Genealogy**

33. Susa Young Gates to Leah Dunford Widtsoe, Sept. 16, 1929; Oct. 3, 1929; Susa Young Gates to John A. Widtsoe, Telegram, Sept. 15, 1929, Widtsoe Family Papers, CHL; Widtsoe, Diary, Dec. 6, 1929; Harold Shepstone to Susa Young Gates, Dec. 11, 1929, Susa Young Gates Papers, CHL; see also Susa Young Gates to Leah Dunford Widtsoe, Oct. 7, 1930, Widtsoe Family Papers, CHL; and Susa Young Gates and Leah Dunford Widtsoe, *The Life Story of Brigham Young* (New York: Macmillan, 1930).

34. Widtsoe, Diary, Dec. 31, 1929; Leah Dunford Widtsoe to Ethel Johnson, Feb. 5, 1929; Leah Dunford Widtsoe to Libby Snow Ivins, Nov. 1, 1929, Widtsoe Family Papers, CHL. **Topic: John and Leah Widtsoe**

35. Grant, Journal, Apr. 6, 1930; "City Dresses Up Leading Streets for Centennial," *Deseret News,* Apr. 3, 1930, 1; "S. L. Appears in Gala Attire for Celebration of Centennial," *Deseret News,* Apr. 5, 1930, [section 3], 5.

36. "Centennial Crowd Begins to Pour In as Opening Nears," *Deseret News,* Apr. 4, 1930, 1; "Church Centennial Arrives," *Deseret News,* Apr. 5, 1930, [section 5], 1, 3; "Rails, Airlines, Autos Bring Crowds to S. L.," *Deseret News,* Apr. 5, 1930, [section 4], 3; "Church Had Only Seven Elders at First Conference," *Deseret News,* Apr. 5, 1930, [section 4], 4.

37. "News of Centennial Reaches 75,000,000 Persons in America," *Deseret News,* Apr. 5, 1930, [section 4], 4; "A Comprehensive History of the Church," *Deseret News,* Apr. 5, 1930, [section 3], 11; "Mormon Centenary," *Time,* Apr. 7, 1930, 26–28, 30; see also *Saints,* volume 1, chapters 8 and 9; and Publicity Committee Scrapbook, 1930.

38. Grant, Journal, Apr. 6, 1930; "First Day, Morning Meeting," *One Hundredth Annual Conference,* 2; "White Ticket Must Be Used on Sunday," *Deseret News,* Apr. 4, 1930, 1; "Centennial Crowd Begins to Pour In as Opening Nears," *Deseret News,* Apr. 4, 1930, 1; "Saints All Over World Join in Centenary Fete," and "800,000 to Hear Centennial over Radio Hook-Ups," *Deseret News,* Apr. 5, 1930, [section 3], 2–3; "News of Centennial Reaches 75,000,000 Persons in America," *Deseret News,* Apr. 5, 1930, [section 4], 4. **Topic: Broadcast Media**

39. Heber J. Grant, in *One Hundredth Annual Conference,* 3–13; First Presidency to Stakes and Mission Presidents, Mar. 3, 1930, in Clark, *Messages of the First Presidency,* 5:273.

40. "First Day, Morning Meeting," and Heber J. Grant, in *One Hundredth Annual Conference,* 2, 21–22; see also "Hosanna Shouts Mark Mormons' Centennial Here," *Milwaukee (MN) Journal,* Apr. 7, 1930, 4; and William Callister, "Members of L. D. S. Church in Europe Celebrate Centennial," *Deseret News,* May 10, 1930, section 3, vi.

41. *The Message of the Ages: A Sacred Pageant* . . . (Salt Lake City: The Church of Jesus Christ of Latter-day Saints, 1930); "God and Man's Story Retold in Allegory," *Salt Lake Tribune,* Apr. 7, 1930, 1, 8–9; "Pageant Takes Gospel History through Ages," "Greatest Music of World Woven into Big Pageant," and "History and Relics Studied to Make Costumes Perfect," *Deseret News,* Apr. 5, 1930, [section 3], 9; "The Centennial Pageant," *Improvement Era,* May 1930, 33:460–61, 503–4.

42. "New Floodlights Illuminate All 7 Temples of Church," *Deseret News,* Apr. 5, 1930, [section 3], 5; William Callister, "Centennial Celebrations in Salt Lake," *Latter-day Saints' Millennial Star,* May 15, 1930, 92:372. **Topic: Angel Moroni**

CHAPTER 20: HARD TIMES

1. "Large Class of Graduates at U.S.A.C.," *Journal* (Logan, UT), May 25, 1929, 8; Lewis, Oral History Interview, 1–2.

2. Lewis, Oral History Interview, 1–2, 25. **Topic: Relief Society**

3. Lewis, Oral History Interview, 2. **Topic: Amy Brown Lyman**

4. Lewis, Oral History Interview, 2–3.

5. Lewis, Oral History Interview, 3; see also, for example, "Relief Society Social Service Department Report for January 1930," [1]–[4], Presiding Bishopric General Files, 1872–1948, CHL.

6. *Ward Charity,* [3]–6; Derr, "History of Social Services," 40–41; Lewis, Oral History Interview, 3; Bell family entry, Relief Society Family Welfare Department Budget, Nov. 24, 1928, Presiding Bishopric General Files, 1872–1948, CHL. **Topics: Bishop; Welfare Programs**
7. Lewis, Oral History Interview, 6; Payne, *Crash!,* 5, 83–84; Shlaes, *Forgotten Man,* 85–93, 101; Kennedy, *Freedom from Fear,* 56–58. **Topic: Great Depression**
8. Payne, *Crash!,* 84–85; Shlaes, *Forgotten Man,* 95–104; Kennedy, *Freedom from Fear,* 58–69.
9. Bluth and Hinton, "Great Depression," 481–85; Alexander, *Utah, the Right Place,* 310–11; Orval W. Adams to John A. Widtsoe, May 26, 1930, Widtsoe Family Papers, CHL; Lewis, Oral History Interview, 6; Heber J. Grant to Reed Smoot, Jan. 14, 1932, First Presidency Miscellaneous Correspondence, CHL.
10. Love Branch, Miscellaneous Minutes, May 19, 1930. **Topic: South Africa**
11. Mowbray Branch, Cottage Meeting Minutes, Apr. 25–Dec. 12, 1921; Stevenson, *Global History of Blacks and Mormonism,* 49–50; Bickford-Smith, *Ethnic Pride and Racial Prejudice in Victorian Cape Town,* 210–11; Chidester, *Religions of South Africa,* 81–83; Adhikari, *Not White Enough, Not Black Enough,* 2–5. **Topic: Racial Segregation**
12. Wright, *History of the South African Mission,* 2:252–54; Philles Jacoba Elizabeth February Sampson entry, Cape Town Conference, South African Mission, no. 153, in South Africa (Country), part 1, Record of Members Collection, CHL; see also William P. Daniels, "My Testimony," *Cumorah's Southern Messenger,* Feb. 20, 1935, 9:28. Spellings of the name "Phyllis Sampson" are inconsistent in the records.
13. Wright, *History of the South African Mission,* 2:252–55; Love Branch, Miscellaneous Minutes, Dec. 14, 1931; Okkers, Oral History Interview, 3–4. **Topics: Joseph F. Smith; Priesthood and Temple Restriction**
14. Stevenson, *Global History of Blacks and Mormonism,* 50; Mowbray Branch, General Minutes, July 24, 1921–Jan. 1, 1928; Nicholas G. Smith, Diary, Nov. 5, 1920.
15. Wright, *History of the South African Mission,* 2:253, 256; South Africa Mission, Manuscript History and Historical Reports, Jan. 4, 1923; Martin, Autobiography, Jan. 1, 1927; see also, for example, Love Branch, Miscellaneous Minutes, Feb. 20, 1929–Apr. 28, 1930; and Mowbray Branch, Cottage Meeting Minutes, Aug. 29, 1921.
16. Stevenson, *Global History of Blacks and Mormonism,* 49–50; Don M. Dalton to First Presidency, Apr. 11, 1930, First Presidency Mission Files, CHL.
17. Okkers, Oral History Interview, 4. Quotation edited for readability; original source has "You've been over to Salt Lake City and baptized."
18. Love Branch, Miscellaneous Minutes, May 19, 1930; Talmage, *Jesus the Christ,* 308–9.
19. Widtsoe, Diary, June 18–24, 1930; "Conference on Womans Activity in European Missions," June 18–24, 1930, 1–2, Susa Young Gates Papers, CHL; European Mission Presidents Conference, June 18–24, 1930.
20. Leah D. Widtsoe to Anna W. Wallace and Eudora Widtsoe, Apr. 8, 1930, Widtsoe Family Papers, CHL; "Conference on Womans Activity in European Missions," June 25–28, 1930, 2–7, Susa Young Gates Papers, CHL; Presiding Bishopric, Office Journal, Sept. 3, 1929, 244. **Topic: The Gathering of Israel**
21. "Conference on Womans Activity in European Missions," June 28, 1930, 8–11, Susa Young Gates Papers, CHL; see also, for example, German-Austrian Mission, General Minutes, May 1930, 130.
22. "Conference on Womans Activity in European Missions," June 27, 1930, 3, 13, Susa Young Gates Papers, CHL; European Mission Relief Society Presidents' Conference, Minutes, [Aug. 21], 1929, 28–29; Eudora Widtsoe, "The Bee-Hive Girl," *Latter-day Saints' Millennial Star,* Apr. 3, 1930, 92:273. **Topic: Young Women Organizations**
23. "Conference on Womans Activity in European Missions," June 27, 1930, 3, 12–13, Susa Young Gates Papers, CHL; *Hand Book for the Bee-Hive Girls of the Y. L. M. I. A.* [10th ed.], 9; *Handbook for the Bee-Hive Girls of the Young Ladies' Mutual Improvement Association,* [5]; Leah D. Widtsoe to First Presidency, Sept. 16, 1933, First Presidency Mission Files, CHL.

24. Leah D. Widtsoe to First Presidency, Oct. 8, 1930, First Presidency Mission Files, CHL.
25. Meyer and Galli, *Under a Leafless Tree,* 36; German-Austrian Mission, General Minutes, Sept. 1930, 143.
26. Meyer and Galli, *Under a Leafless Tree,* 32, 34; Scharffs, *Mormonism in Germany,* xiv, table 1; Naujoks and Eldredge, *Shades of Gray,* 30. **Topic: Germany**
27. Meyer and Galli, *Under a Leafless Tree,* 34.
28. Meyer and Galli, *Under a Leafless Tree,* 34–36.
29. Meyer and Galli, *Under a Leafless Tree,* 34; see also Evan Stephens, "The 'Mormon' Boy," *Deseret Sunday School Songs,* no. 269.
30. Lewis, Oral History Interview, 8; "Unemployed Plan to Ask State Aid," *Salt Lake Tribune,* Jan. 29, 1931, 9; "Idle Workers March upon Utah Capitol," *Salt Lake Tribune,* Jan. 31, 1931, 7. **Topic: Church Headquarters**
31. Lewis, Oral History Interview, 8; "Unemployed March on Utah Capitol," *Salt Lake Telegram,* Jan. 30, 1931, 8B; Alexander, *Utah, the Right Place,* 312.
32. Derr, "History of Social Services," 42; Lewis, Oral History Interview, 7, 15.
33. Lewis, Oral History Interview, 16.
34. Derr, "History of Social Services," 39; Lewis, Oral History Interview, 6–8, 15–16; Presiding Bishopric to Louise Y. Robison, Feb. 4, 1930; Amy Brown Lyman to Presiding Bishopric, Mar. 5, 1930; Presiding Bishopric to Amy Brown Lyman, [Mar. 1930], Presiding Bishopric General Files, 1872–1948, CHL; Hall, *Faded Legacy,* 112–13.
35. Relief Society, Minutes of Meetings with the Presiding Bishopric, Jan.–Dec. 1930; May 24, 1932; Nov. 2, 1932; Derr, Cannon, and Beecher, *Women of Covenant,* 251; Hall, *Faded Legacy,* 113; Bluth and Hinton, "Great Depression," 484–85. **Topics: Great Depression; Welfare Programs**
36. Lewis, Oral History Interview, 8–9; Bluth and Hinton, "Great Depression," 484.

CHAPTER 21: A KEENER UNDERSTANDING

1. Widtsoe, Diary, Mar. 16–18, 1931; "Mission Head Sees Europe Going 'Dry,'" *Salt Lake Tribune,* Mar. 17, 1931, 22; "U.S. Immigration Laws Force Church to Open Permanent Europe Branches," *Deseret News,* Mar. 17, 1931, section 2, [1]; Parrish, *John A. Widtsoe,* 475–76.
2. Lucy Gates Bowen to Leah D. Widtsoe and John A. Widtsoe, Apr. 11, 1929; John A. Widtsoe to Anna Widtsoe Wallace, May 4, 1929; Lucy Gates Bowen to John, Leah, and Eudora Widtsoe, June 10, 1929, Widtsoe Family Papers, CHL.
3. Allen, "Story of *The Truth, The Way, The Life,*" 704–7; John W. Welch, "Introduction," in Roberts, *The Truth, The Way, The Life,* xi–xii. **Topic: B. H. Roberts**
4. Joseph Fielding Smith, "Faith Leads to a Fulness of Truth and Righteousness," *Utah Genealogical and Historical Magazine,* Oct. 1930, 21:145–58.
5. Roberts, *The Truth, The Way, The Life,* 297–306.
6. Joseph Fielding Smith, "Faith Leads to a Fulness of Truth and Righteousness," *Utah Genealogical and Historical Magazine,* Oct. 1930, 21:147–48; "Pre-Adam Race Denied by Member of Twelve," *Deseret News,* Apr. 5, 1930, 8; B. H. Roberts to First Presidency, Dec. 15, 1930, B. H. Roberts Collection, CHL.
7. Allen, "Story of *The Truth, The Way, The Life,*" 720–24.
8. Widtsoe, *In Search of Truth,* 70–80, 109–11, 114–20; John A. Widtsoe to Melvin J. Ballard, Jan. 27, 1931, John A. Widtsoe Papers, CHL.
9. Widtsoe, Diary, Apr. 7, 1931; First Presidency to Council of the Twelve, First Council of Seventy, and Presiding Bishopric, Apr. 7, 1931, First Presidency Miscellaneous Correspondence, CHL; Grant, Journal, Jan. 25, 1931.
10. Joseph Smith, Discourse, Apr. 8, 1843, in *JSP,* D12:192.
11. First Presidency to Council of the Twelve, First Council of Seventy, and Presiding Bishopric, Apr. 7, 1931, First Presidency Miscellaneous Correspondence, CHL.

12. First Presidency to Council of the Twelve, First Council of Seventy, and Presiding Bishopric, Apr. 7, 1931, First Presidency Miscellaneous Correspondence, CHL; Talmage, Journal, Apr. 7, 1931; Joseph F. Smith, John R. Winder, and Anthon H. Lund, "The Origin of Man," *Improvement Era,* Nov. 1909, 13:80. **Topic: Organic Evolution**

13. John A. Widtsoe to Joseph Fielding Smith, Sept. 15, 1931; John A. Widtsoe to Rudger Clawson and Council of the Twelve, Sept. 9, 1931, John A. Widtsoe Papers, CHL; Widtsoe, Diary, Apr. 7, 1931; George F. Richards, Journal, Apr. 7, 1931; Talmage, Journal, Apr. 7, 1931; Smoot, Diary, Apr. 7, 1931, Reed Smoot Papers, BYU; George Albert Smith, Journal, Apr. 7, 1931, George Albert Smith Family Papers, J. Willard Marriott Library, University of Utah, Salt Lake City.

14. Allen, "Story of *The Truth, The Way, The Life,*" 726–31. The manuscript was published in 1994 as *The Truth, The Way, The Life: An Elementary Treatise on Theology* (Provo, UT: BYU Studies, 1994).

15. Love Branch, Miscellaneous Minutes, Dec. 14, 1931; Stevenson, *Global History of Blacks and Mormonism,* 50. Quotation edited for readability; "the Book of Mormon Ready Reference" in original changed to "*Book of Mormon Ready References,*" and "he has" changed to "I have."

16. Love Branch, Miscellaneous Minutes, Dec. 14, 1931. Quotation edited for readability; original source has "Hopes that the Lord will help them to remain steadfast."

17. Love Branch, Miscellaneous Minutes, Dec. 14, 1931. Quotation edited for readability; "He feels" in original changed to "I feel," and "Knows that if he is faithful that he will see" changed to "I know that if I am faithful, I will see."

18. Don Dalton to First Presidency, Apr. 11, 1930; First Presidency to Don Dalton, May 15, 1930, First Presidency Mission Files, CHL.

19. Love Branch, Miscellaneous Minutes, Dec. 14, 1931.

20. Love Branch, Miscellaneous Minutes, Feb. 22, 1932. Quotation edited for readability; original source has "she found it a bit difficult and knows the Lord will help her in her work."

21. Love Branch, Miscellaneous Minutes, Feb. 29, 1932, and Aug. 21, 1933. **Topic: South Africa**

22. Cincinnati Branch, Minutes, Feb. 14, 1932; Paul Bang, "My Life Story," 7; *Circular of the First Presidency,* 4; Hartley, "From Men to Boys," 109–10, 112–18. **Topic: Adjustments to Priesthood Organization**

23. "Practical Duties for Members of the Lesser Priesthood," *Improvement Era,* July 1916, 19:847; Hartley, "From Men to Boys," 118.

24. Presiding Bishopric, Minutes of the Aaronic Priesthood Convention, Apr. 8, 1932, 5; Criteria for Aaronic Priesthood Advancement, May 17, 1928, Presiding Bishopric General Files, 1889–1956, CHL.

25. Hartley, "From Men to Boys," 121; Cincinnati Branch, Minutes, Jan. 10–May 15, 1932. **Topic: Sacrament Meetings**

26. Fish, "My Life Story," [4]; Paul Bang, "My Life Story," 3–6.

27. Feck, *Yesterday's Cincinnati,* 101–2; Stradling, *Cincinnati,* 103–10.

28. Paul Bang, "My Life Story," 1, 5, 28; "Seek Relief in Bankruptcy," *Cincinnati Enquirer,* Apr. 23, 1932, 10. **Topic: Great Depression**

29. "Aaronic Priesthood Day," *Deseret News,* Apr. 27, 1927, 4; Sylvester Q. Cannon, David A. Smith, and John Wells, "Aaronic Priesthood Day," Presiding Bishopric, Bulletin no. 126, circa Mar. 1927; Cincinnati Branch, Minutes, May 15, 1932; Henry Bang, Thomas Harry Large, Julius Conrad Blackwelder, and William Carl Schnarrenberg, in Cincinnati Branch, Record of Members and Children, nos. 18, 202, 204, 210; Presiding Bishopric, Bulletin no. 186, circa Apr. 1932. **Topic: Restoration of the Aaronic Priesthood**

30. For examples, see Cincinnati Branch, Minutes, 1931–32.

31. Cincinnati Branch, Minutes, Jan. 10, 17, 24, and 31, 1932.

32. Lewis, Oral History Interview, 7, 25; Hall, *Faded Legacy,* 111–13; McCormick, "Great Depression," 136. Last quotation edited for clarity; "L.A." in original changed to "Los Angeles." **Topic: Great Depression**

33. Lewis, Oral History Interview, 6; Hall, *Faded Legacy,* 115; Derr, "Changing Relief Society Charity," 251. **Topic: Welfare Programs**

34. Lewis, Oral History Interview, 2, 11. **Topic: Amy Brown Lyman**

35. Lewis, Oral History Interview, 4, 13–15, 18–19, 25–26; Hall, *Faded Legacy,* 115–16; Derr, "Changing Relief Society Charity," 251–53; Darowski, "Utah's Plight," 12.

36. Evelyn Hodges, "Emotional Reactions to Unemployment and Relief," *Relief Society Magazine,* July 1934, 21:391.

37. Goates, *Harold B. Lee,* 90, 94; Lee, "Remarks of Elder Harold B. Lee," 3.

38. Drury, "For These My Brethren," [5]; Doctrine and Covenants 42:34.

39. Rudd, *Pure Religion,* 4.

40. *Saints,* volume 2, chapter 30; Derr and others, *First Fifty Years of Relief Society,* xxxv, 399; Alexander, *Mormonism in Transition,* 132. **Topics: Bishop; Consecration and Stewardship**

41. Drury, "For These My Brethren," [5]–[7], [15], [17]–[19]; Goates, *Harold B. Lee,* 94; "Pioneer Stake Launches Barter Employment Plan," *Salt Lake Telegram,* July 25, 1932, 12.

42. Drury, "For These My Brethren," [5]–[6]; Presiding Bishopric, Office Journal, June 20, 1932; Grant, Journal, June 20, 1932.

43. Drury, "For These My Brethren," [2], [7], [19]; Rudd, *Pure Religion,* 9.

44. Drury, "For These My Brethren," [2]–[4]; Rudd, Oral History Interview, 38–40; "100 Needy Families to Get Vegetables," *Salt Lake Telegram,* Dec. 5, 1932, [7].

45. Drury, "For These My Brethren," [8]; "Pioneer Stake Launches Barter Employment Plan," *Salt Lake Telegram,* July 25, 1932, 12; "Exchange Idea Assures Many Jobs for Idle," *Salt Lake Tribune,* July 25, 1932, 14.

46. Rudd, *Pure Religion,* 13; Drury, "For These My Brethren," [8]–[9]; Lee, "Remarks of Elder Harold B. Lee," 2; Goates, *Harold B. Lee,* 94, 96.

47. Harold B. Lee to John D. Pearmain, June 30, 1933, First Presidency Miscellaneous Correspondence, CHL; "Pioneer Stake Launches Barter Employment Plan," *Salt Lake Telegram,* July 25, 1932, 12; Drury, "For These My Brethren," [16]; Finck, "Early Days of the Welfare Plan," 3; Statistical Report, Dec. 31, 1932, in Thirty-Second Ward, Relief Society Minutes and Records, 123; "Model Community Routs Unemployment," *Salt Lake Tribune,* Aug. 6, 1933, Magazine section, 4.

48. Salt Lake Pioneer Stake, Confidential Minutes, Oct. 24, 1932, and Jan. 8, 1933.

CHAPTER 22: ETERNAL REWARD

1. Widtsoe, Diary, May 23–June 4, 1931, and May 17, 1933; Widtsoe, *In a Sunlit Land,* 207–8; Leah Dunford Widtsoe to Merle Colton Bennion, Apr. 14, 1933, Widtsoe Family Papers, CHL; Palestine-Syrian Mission, Minutes, May 21, 1933, John A. Widtsoe Papers, CHL; "President Widtsoe Visits Palestine," *Deseret News,* June 24, 1933, Church section, 2.

2. Mission Annual Report, 1933, Presiding Bishopric Financial, Statistical, and Historical Reports, CHL; John A. Widtsoe to First Presidency, July 11, 1933, First Presidency Mission Files, CHL; Widtsoe, *In a Sunlit Land,* 204–5, 208; Bertha Walser Piranian and Badwagan Piranian entries, Zürich Conference, Swiss-German Mission, nos. 274, 514, in Switzerland (Country), part 7, segment 2, Record of Members Collection, CHL.

3. Leah Dunford Widtsoe to Heber J. Grant, June 5, 1933, First Presidency Mission Files, CHL; Moser, *Global Great Depression,* chapter 5. **Topic: John and Leah Widtsoe**

4. Widtsoe, Diary, May 17, 1933; Ausdrig Piranian entry, Zürich Conference, Swiss-German Mission, no. 450, in Switzerland (Country), part 7, segment 2, Record of Members Collection, CHL; John A. Widtsoe to First Presidency, July 11, 1933, First Presidency Mission Files, CHL.

5. Leah Dunford Widtsoe to First Presidency, Sept. 1, 1933; Sept. 16, 1933, First Presidency Mission Files, CHL; Palestine-Syrian Mission, Minutes, May 21, 1933, John A. Widtsoe Papers, CHL. Quotation edited for clarity; "R.S." in original changed to "Relief Society."

6. Widtsoe, Diary, May 26–30, 1933; Widtsoe, *In a Sunlit Land,* 212; Parrish, *John A. Widtsoe,* 503; Widtsoe, Journal, May 30, 1933; John A. Widtsoe, "The Promised Land," *Latter-day Saints' Millennial Star,* July 6, 1933, 95:441; Leah Dunford Widtsoe to Heber J. Grant, June 5, 1933, First Presidency Mission Files, CHL.

7. Leah Dunford Widtsoe to Susan McCrindle, Sept. 23, 1933, Widtsoe Family Papers, CHL; Leah Dunford Widtsoe to Heber J. Grant, June 5, 1933, First Presidency Mission Files, CHL; Widtsoe, Journal, May 30, 1933; "Karl M. Widtsoe Dies of Pneumonia," *Deseret News,* May 30, 1927, section 2, 1.

8. Widtsoe, Journal, May 30–31, 1933; John A. Widtsoe to Heber J. Grant, June 9, 1933; Leah Dunford Widtsoe to Heber J. Grant, June 5, 1933, First Presidency Mission Files, CHL. **Topic: Susa Young Gates**

9. William P. Daniels, "My Testimony," *Cumorah's Southern Messenger,* Feb. 20, 1935, 9:29; Love Branch, Miscellaneous Minutes, Aug. 21, 1933. Quotations edited for readability; "I" added to the beginning of both sentences. **Topic: Healing**

10. William P. Daniels, "My Testimony," *Cumorah's Southern Messenger,* Feb. 20, 1935, 9:28–29; Okkers, "I Would Love to Touch the Door of the Temple," 177–78.

11. Heber J. Grant to John A. Widtsoe, May 17, 1933; John A. Widtsoe to Heber J. Grant, June 9, 1933, First Presidency Mission Files, CHL; Parrish, *John A. Widtsoe,* 474; Heber J. Grant to John A. Widtsoe and Leah Dunford Widtsoe, June 27, 1933, Letterpress Copybook, volume 70, 801, Heber J. Grant Collection, CHL.

12. John A. Widtsoe to Heber J. Grant, June 9, 1933; Leah Dunford Widtsoe to First Presidency, Sept. 16, 1933, First Presidency Mission Files, CHL; see also *Handbook for the Bee-Hive Girls of the Young Ladies' Mutual Improvement Association* (London: British Mission, 1933).

13. German-Austrian Mission, Swedish Mission, Netherlands Mission, Report of the Mission President, 1932, Presiding Bishopric Financial, Statistical, and Historical Reports, CHL; Cowan, *Church in the Twentieth Century,* 162–63; Parrish, *John A. Widtsoe,* 498; John A. Widtsoe to Heber J. Grant, June 9, 1933, First Presidency Mission Files, CHL.

14. Widtsoe, Diary, July 18, 1933; Parrish, *John A. Widtsoe,* 508–9; Heber J. Grant to John A. Widtsoe, Telegram, July 18, 1933; John A. Widtsoe to First Presidency, July 20, 1933, First Presidency Mission Files, CHL; Leah Dunford Widtsoe to "Dear Jack," Sept. 8, 1933, Widtsoe Family Papers, CHL.

15. Wilson, *Hitler,* 77–88; Evans, *Coming of the Third Reich,* 298–349; Noakes and Pridham, *Nazism,* 123–26; First Presidency to John A. Widtsoe, July 20, 1933, First Presidency Letterpress Copybooks, volume 89; John A. Widtsoe to First Presidency, Aug. 8, 1933, First Presidency Mission Files, CHL; Naujoks and Eldredge, *Shades of Gray,* 32. **Topics: Germany; World War II**

16. John A. Widtsoe to First Presidency, July 11, 1933; Sept. 28, 1933, First Presidency Mission Files, CHL; Carter, "Rise of the Nazi Dictatorship," 57–59; see also McDonough, *Gestapo,* chapter 3. **Topic: Political Neutrality**

17. John A. Widtsoe to First Presidency, July 11, 1933; Sept. 28, 1933, First Presidency Mission Files, CHL; Widtsoe, Diary, Sept. 20–22, 1933.

18. Hope family entries, Cincinnati Branch, South Ohio District, Northern States Mission, nos. 441–45, 691, in Ohio (State), part 2, Record of Members Collection, CHL; Hanks, Oral History Interview, 6, 12; 1930 U.S. Census, Woodlawn, Sycamore Township, Hamilton County, Ohio, 1B; Fish, Kramer, and Wallis, *History of the Mormon Church in Cincinnati,* 59; Obituary for Len Hope, *Deseret News and Salt Lake Telegram,* Sept. 15, 1952, 4B; Vernon Hope entry, Cincinnati Branch, South Ohio District, Northern States Mission, Births and Blessings, 1934, no. 258, in Ohio (State), part 4, Record of Members Collection, CHL.

19. Stradling, *Cincinnati,* 110–11; Taylor, "City Building, Public Policy," 163–64; Bunch-Lyons, *Contested Terrain,* 77–81, 96, 114; Fairbanks, "Cincinnati Blacks," 193–94; "Go to Church Tomorrow," *Cincinnati Enquirer,* Mar. 15, 1930, 10.

20. Stephenson, "Short Biography of Len, Sr. and Mary Hope," [10]; Anderson, *Twenty-Three Years in Cincinnati,* 2, 17; Duffin, Mission Journal, Dec. 1, 1935; Hanks, Oral History Interview, 2–3, 13; Henry Layton to Richard Layton and Annie Horn Layton, Mar. 3, 1931, Henry Layton Correspondence, CHL; see also "Leggroan, Edward," "Leggroan, Alice Weaver Boozer," and "Ritchie, Nelson Holder," Biographical Entries, Century of Black Mormons website, exhibits.lib.utah.edu.

21. Hanks, Oral History Interview, 3, 14, 18; see also Herman Huenefeld, Rogers Love, Rosalea Moore, Ethel Wyatt, in Cincinnati Branch, Record of Members and Children, nos. 61, 84, 96, 139. **Topic: Racial Segregation**

22. Stephenson, "Short Biography of Len, Sr. and Mary Hope," [10]; Hanks, Oral History Interview, 2, 6; Duffin, Mission Journal, Dec. 1, 1935, and Dec. 25, 1936; Holt, Mission Journal, July 27, 1931; Sept. 2, 1931; Oct. 5, 1931. First quotation edited for readability; original source has "He told them that this was the hardest visit that he had ever made to anyone in his life."

23. Essie Holt, "Hope's Home," Photograph, Essie H. Wheadon Mission Papers, CHL; Taylor, "City Building, Public Policy," 175; Holt, Mission Journal, July 27, 1931; Gibson, Mission Journal, Aug. 6, 1930.

24. Hanks, Oral History Interview, 6, 11; Gowers, Mission Journal, Nov. 15, 1934; Gibson, Mission Journal, July 7, 1930; Lyman, *As I Saw It,* 73–74; Duffin, Mission Journal, Dec. 1, 1935; Jan. 5, 1936; Feb. 7, 1937; Croshaw, Mission Journal, Apr. 30 and June 23, 1932; Holt, Mission Journal, July 27, 1931; Sept. 2, 1931; Oct. 5, 1931.

25. South Ohio District, General Minutes, Oct. 29, 1932; Cincinnati Branch, Minutes, Apr. 16, 1933; June 3 and 17, 1934; Duffin, Mission Journal, Dec. 1, 1935, and Oct. 31, 1936; Butler, Interview, 1.

26. Litster, Mission Journal, Sept. 11 and 20, 1932; Oct. 5 and 11–12, 1932; Gibson, Mission Journal, Mar. 22 and 26, 1932; Apr. 26 and 30, 1932; May 3–4, 1932; Holt, Mission Journal, July 27, 1931; Sept. 2 and 7, 1931; Oct. 5, 1931; Bang, Diary, Jan. 18, 1936.

27. Vernon Hope entry, Cincinnati Branch, South Ohio District, Northern States Mission, Births and Blessings, 1934, no. 258, in Ohio (State), part 4, Record of Members Collection, CHL; Hope family entries, in Cincinnati Branch, Record of Members and Children, nos. 50–52, 197, 214; Cincinnati Branch, Minutes, June 3, 1934.

28. Fish, Kramer, and Wallis, *History of the Mormon Church in Cincinnati,* 58–59; Stephenson, "Short Biography of Len, Sr. and Mary Hope," [12]; Lyman, *As I Saw It,* 74; Hanks, Oral History Interview, 15–16. Quotation edited for readability; original source has "Bro. Hope said he knew he chould not have the priesthood, but that he felt in the justice of God that some day this would be given to him, and he would be allowed to go on to his eternal reward with the faithful who held it." **Topic: Priesthood and Temple Restriction**

29. Meyer and Galli, *Under a Leafless Tree,* 49–52; Johnson and Reuband, *What We Knew,* 137, 230, 337–44; Koonz, *Nazi Conscience,* 20–25, 75, 100–104, 215, 253–54; Mühlberger, *Hitler's Followers,* 202–9; Tobler, "Jews, the Mormons, and the Holocaust," 80–81.

30. *Handbuch für die Bienenkorbmädchen,* 2–16, 28–29, 36, 45; "Comments on Church News of the Week," *Deseret News,* June 2, 1934, Church section, 8; Meyer and Galli, *Under a Leafless Tree,* 50–52. **Topic: Young Women Organizations**

31. Meyer and Galli, *Under a Leafless Tree,* 50; Reese, *Growing Up Female in Nazi Germany,* 30–40; Kater, *Hitler Youth,* 70–112; Lepage, *Hitler Youth,* 73, 78.

CHAPTER 23: ALL THAT IS NECESSARY

1. Taylor, Diary, Feb. 6, 1935; Bates, "Patriarchal Blessings and the Routinization of Charisma," 25–26; Heber J. Grant to Mrs. Wilford J. Allen, Sept. 12, 1932, First Presidency Miscellaneous Correspondence, CHL. **Topic: Patriarchal Blessings**
2. Taylor, Diary, Feb. 6, 1935; Wallis, Journal, Feb. 4–6, 1935; Rytting, *James H. Wallis,* 6–7, 154, 177, 189–91. **Topic: Outmigration**
3. Taylor, Diary, Feb. 6, 1935; Cornelia Taylor, Patriarchal Blessing, Feb. 6, 1935, 1–2, Paul and Cornelia T. Bang Papers, CHL.
4. Bang, Autobiography, 4–6, 8–9; Taylor, Diary, Apr. 12, 1936; Charles Anderson to Adeline Yarish Taylor, Apr. 18, 1936; Oct. 26, 1936, Paul and Cornelia T. Bang Papers, CHL.
5. Taylor, Diary, Feb. 10 and 17, 1935; Mar. 3 and 24, 1935; June 2, 1935.
6. Danish Mission, French Mission, Northern States Mission, Annual Reports, 1932, Presiding Bishopric, Financial, Statistical, and Historical Reports, CHL; Northern States Mission, Manuscript History and Historical Reports, Dec. 31, 1930, and Dec. 31, 1931; Anthony W. Ivins to Preal George, Feb. 5, 1932, First Presidency Miscellaneous Correspondence, CHL; First Presidency to John A. Widtsoe, Aug. 1, 1933, John A. Widtsoe Papers, CHL; Cincinnati Branch, Minutes, Jan. 16, 1932, 4.
7. South Ohio District, General Minutes, Nov. 1931; Taylor, Diary, Feb. 3, 10, and 17, 1935.
8. Taylor, Diary, Jan. 20, 1935; Feb. 3, 10, and 15–17, 1935; Fish, "My Life Story," [6].
9. Taylor, Diary, Feb. 15 and Mar. 22–23, 1935; Paul Bang, "My Life Story," 10–11; Bang, Autobiography, 7. Quotation edited for clarity; rather than "Paul," the original source has "Pete" (a nickname Paul Bang sometimes went by).
10. Taylor, Diary, May 26, 1935; Cornelia Taylor, Patriarchal Blessing, Feb. 6, 1935, 1, Paul and Cornelia T. Bang Papers, CHL. Quotation edited for readability; "thou will" in original changed to "thou wilt," and "thy eye" changed to "thine eye."
11. Cornelia Taylor Bang, "Youth Meeting," circa 1944, 1, Paul and Cornelia T. Bang Papers, CHL.
12. Harold B. Lee, in *One Hundred Forty-Second Semi-annual Conference,* 123–24; Gibbons, *Harold B. Lee,* 25–85; Harold B. Lee, Journal, Apr. 20, 1935; Grant, Journal, Apr. 20, 1935. Quotation edited for readability; "he wanted" in original changed to "I want."
13. Lee, "Remarks of Elder Harold B. Lee," 3; Rudd, *Pure Religion,* 14.
14. Salt Lake Pioneer Stake, Confidential Minutes, Nov. 5–6, 1932; Salt Lake Pioneer Stake Manuscript History, Mar. 26, 1933; June 30, 1933; Nov. 28, 1933; "Exchange Idea Assures Many Jobs for Idle," *Salt Lake Tribune,* July 25, 1932, 14; Goates, *Harold B. Lee,* 99; Harold B. Lee, Charles S. Hyde, and Paul Child to Heber J. Grant, May 23, 1933, J. Reuben Clark Jr. Papers, BYU; Eugene Middleton, "Personality Portraits of Prominent Utahns," *Deseret News,* Oct. 24, 1934, 16.
15. Lee, "Remarks of Elder Harold B. Lee," 2–3; Drury, "For These My Brethren," [5]–[11].
16. Heber J. Grant to Grace Evans, Sept. 12, 1933, Letterpress Copybook, volume 70, 931–32, Heber J. Grant Collection, CHL; J. Reuben Clark Jr. to Richard M. Robinson and H. M. Robinson, Oct. 26, 1934, enclosed in J. Reuben Clark Jr. to David O. McKay, Oct. 26, 1934, David O. McKay Papers, CHL; Heber J. Grant to Bessie Clark Elmer, Jan. 5, 1934; Heber J. Grant to J. N. Heywood, Oct. 23, 1934, First Presidency Miscellaneous Correspondence, CHL; Arrington and Hinton, "Origin of the Welfare Plan," 67, 76–77; Mangum and Blumell, *Mormons' War on Poverty,* 110–11.
17. Hall, *Faded Legacy,* 124; Presiding Bishopric, Office Journal, June 3, 1935; Cannon, "What a Power We Will Be in This Land," 68; J. Reuben Clark Jr. to Richard M. Robinson and H. M. Robinson, Oct. 26, 1934, enclosed in J. Reuben Clark Jr. to David O. McKay, Oct. 26, 1934, David O. McKay Papers, CHL.
18. Arrington and Hinton, "Origin of the Welfare Plan," 74–76; Mangum and Blumell, *Mormons' War on Poverty,* 114. **Topic: Welfare Programs**

19. Lee, "Remarks of Elder Harold B. Lee," 3; J. Reuben Clark to Heber J. Grant and David O. McKay, Apr. 16, 1935, David O. McKay Papers, CHL; J. Reuben Clark, in *One Hundred Fifth Semi-annual Conference,* 96–100; Cannon, "What a Power We Will Be in This Land," 66–68; Mangum and Blumell, *Mormons' War on Poverty,* 119–29; Doctrine and Covenants 104:15–18; J. Reuben Clark Jr., in *One Hundred Fourth Semi-annual Conference,* 102–3.

20. Heber J. Grant to Mrs. Claude Orton, Mar. 3, 1932; Heber J. Grant to Mrs. C. M. Whitaker, June 9, 1932; Heber J. Grant to Pauline Huddlestone, Sept. 14, 1935; Heber J. Grant to Mrs. Lee Thurgood, Jan. 29, 1932; Heber J. Grant to B. B. Brooks, Dec. 16, 1932; Heber J. Grant to Geo. W. Middleton, Aug. 5, 1931, First Presidency Miscellaneous Correspondence, CHL; Heber J. Grant to Grace Evans, Dec. 19, 1931, Heber J. Grant Collection, CHL.

21. Harold B. Lee, Journal, Apr. 20, 1935; Heber J. Grant and David O. McKay to J. Reuben Clark, Mar. 15, 1935, J. Reuben Clark Jr. Papers, BYU. Quotation edited for readability; "was" in original changed to "is."

22. Harold B. Lee, in *One Hundred Forty-Second Semi-annual Conference,* 124; Harold B. Lee, Journal, Apr. 20, 1935. Quotations edited for readability; "How could I do it" in original changed to "How can I do it," and two instances of "His" changed to "Thy."

23. Harold B. Lee, in *One Hundred Forty-Second Semi-annual Conference,* 124.

24. Harold B. Lee, Journal, Apr. 20, 1935.

25. Harold B. Lee, Journal, Apr. 20, 1935; David O. McKay to J. Reuben Clark, May 6, 1935, First Presidency General Administration Files, CHL. Quotation edited for readability; original source has "he was not going to move until he felt certain of what the Lord wanted."

26. "Grant to Organize New Hawaii Stake," *Salt Lake Telegram,* May 31, 1935, 13; Grant, Journal, June 20, 1935.

27. Historical Department, Journal History of the Church, June 30, 1935, 10. **Topic: Hawaii**

28. J. Reuben Clark, "The Outpost in Mid-Pacific," *Improvement Era,* Sept. 1935, 38:530; *Saints,* volume 2, chapter 9; Hawaiian Mission, Annual Report, 1934, Presiding Bishopric Financial, Statistical, and Historical Reports, CHL; Castle Murphy to First Presidency, Feb. 28, 1934; Apr. 3, 1934; Nov. 30, 1934, First Presidency Mission Files, CHL; Historical Department, Journal History of the Church, June 30, 1935, 5–6. **Topic: Wards and Stakes**

29. Clark, Diary, June 28–30, 1935; "Woolley Heads New LDS Stake Formed Locally," *Honolulu Advertiser,* July 1, 1935, 1; "Woolley, Ralph Edwin," in Jenson, *Latter-day Saint Biographical Encyclopedia,* 4:173–74.

30. Britsch, *Moramona,* 279–81, 299; "First Offshore Stake Organized at Honolulu," *Deseret News,* July 1, 1935, [9].

31. Grant, Journal, June 29–30, 1935; "Organization of LDS Stake Nearly Ready," *Honolulu Star-Bulletin,* July 4, 1935, 2.

32. Grant, Journal, June 25, 1935; Heber J. Grant to Frances Bennett, July 3, 1935, Heber J. Grant Collection, CHL.

33. Britsch, *Moramona,* 257–59.

34. Grant, Journal, July 3, 1935; John A. Widtsoe, "The Japanese Mission in Action," *Improvement Era,* Feb. 1939, 42:88.

35. J. Reuben Clark, "The Outpost in Mid-Pacific," *Improvement Era,* Sept. 1935, 38:533; Grant, Journal, July 3, 1935; Clark, Diary, July 3, 1935; Takagi, *Trek East,* 16–22; Parshall, "Tsune Ishida Nachie," 122–30; John A. Widtsoe, "The Japanese Mission in Action," *Improvement Era,* Feb. 1939, 42:88, 125.

36. Heber J. Grant, in *Seventy-Fourth Semi-Annual Conference,* 7, 11; Walker, "Strangers in a Strange Land," 231–32, 240–41, 247–48, 253; Britsch, "Closing of the Early Japan Mission," 263–81. **Topics: Japan; Growth of Missionary Work**

37. Heber J. Grant to Matthias F. Cowley, May 12, 1903, Letterpress Copybook, volume 36, 239, Heber J. Grant Collection, CHL; Walker, "Strangers in a Strange Land," 250. Quotation edited for clarity; "He" in original changed to "the Lord," and "here" changed to "there."

38. J. Reuben Clark, "The Outpost in Mid-Pacific," *Improvement Era,* Sept. 1935, 38:533; Grant, Journal, June 30, 1935; Ikegami, "We Had Good Examples among the Members," 228–29; Ikegami, "Brief History of the Japanese Members of the Church," 3; Kichitaro Ikegami and Tokuichi Tsuda entries, Oahu District Baptisms and Confirmations, 1935, nos. 42 and 43, in Hawaiian Islands, part 22, Record of Members Collection, CHL.

39. Britsch, *Moramona,* 282.

40. J. Reuben Clark, "The Outpost in Mid-Pacific," *Improvement Era,* Sept. 1935, 38:533; Ikegami, "Brief History of the Japanese Members of the Church," 3–4.

41. Müller, *Hitler's Wehrmacht,* 7–12; Naujoks and Eldredge, *Shades of Gray,* 44–45; Wijfjes, "Spellbinding and Crooning," 166–70.

42. Nelson, *Moroni and the Swastika,* 123–34; Naujoks and Eldredge, *Shades of Gray,* 35; German-Austrian Mission, General Minutes, Jan. 1934, 315–16; Apr. 1934, 327–28; Carter, "Rise of the Nazi Dictatorship," 59–63.

43. Carter, "Rise of the Nazi Dictatorship," 59–63; Nelson, *Moroni and the Swastika,* 167–84.

44. Naujoks and Eldredge, *Shades of Gray,* 35; Tobler, "Jews, the Mormons, and the Holocaust," 80.

45. Meyer and Galli, *Under a Leafless Tree,* 10–12.

46. Meyer and Galli, *Under a Leafless Tree,* 57–59; Naujoks and Eldredge, *Shades of Gray,* 35–37. Quotation edited for readability; "the" in original changed to "a."

47. Meyer and Galli, *Under a Leafless Tree,* 44.

48. Harold B. Lee, Journal, Feb. 1936; "Summary of Relief Survey of the Church of Jesus Christ of Latter-day Saints," Apr. 1, 1936, First Presidency General Administration Files, CHL; Olson, *Saving Capitalism,* 14–15; Derr, "History of Social Services," 49–50.

49. Harold B. Lee, Journal, Feb. 1936; Cannon, "What a Power We Will Be in This Land," 69.

50. Harold B. Lee, Journal, Mar. 15, 1936; David O. McKay, Diary, Mar. 18, 1936 [University of Utah].

51. Mangum and Blumell, *Mormons' War on Poverty,* 134; Henry A. Smith, "Church-Wide Security Program Organized," *Improvement Era,* June 1936, 39:334, 337; "Detailed Instructions on Questions Arising out of the Development of the Church Security Program," [1936], 1–5, Presiding Bishopric Welfare Files, CHL.

52. Henry A. Smith, "Church-Wide Security Program Organized," *Improvement Era,* June 1936, 39:333; "Detailed Instructions on Questions Arising out of the Development of the Church Security Program," [1936], 3–4, Presiding Bishopric Welfare Files, CHL; Arrington and Hinton, "Origin of the Welfare Plan," 78.

53. Harold B. Lee, Journal, Mar. 15, 1936. **Topic: Welfare Programs**

CHAPTER 24: THE AIM OF THE CHURCH

1. Harold B. Lee, Journal, Apr. 6, 15, and 21–28, 1936; Schedule of Regional Meetings, Apr. 24, 1936, David O. McKay Papers, CHL; Grant, Journal, Apr. 20–21 and 23, 1936.

2. First Presidency, *Important Message on Relief,* [2]–[3]; David O. McKay to Edward I. Rich, May 1, 1936, David O. McKay Papers, CHL.

3. Grant, Journal, May 2–3, 1936; "Church Officials Form New L.D.S. Stake on Coast," *Salt Lake Tribune,* May 5, 1936, 24.

4. Orton, *Los Angeles Stake Story,* 40–42; Johnson and Johnson, "Twentieth-Century Mormon Outmigration," 47; Cowan and Homer, *California Saints,* 264, 274; Candland, *History of the Oakland Stake,* 26–27; "Temple Is a Challenge to California Mormons," *Ensign* (Los Angeles), Mar. 18, 1937, 1. **Topic: Outmigration**

5. Grant, Journal, May 2–4, 1936; Cowan and Homer, *California Saints,* 267–69; Groberg, *Idaho Falls Temple,* 49–51.

6. Alexander, *Utah, the Right Place,* 318–19; Heber J. Grant to Russell B. Hodgson, Aug. 24, 1935, First Presidency Miscellaneous Correspondence, CHL; Heber J. Grant to Bayard W. Mendenhall, Nov. 27, 1935, Letterpress Copybook, volume 73, 81, Heber J. Grant Collection, CHL; Presiding Bishopric, Office Journal, June 16, 1936. **Topics: Church Finances; Temple Building**

7. "Tentative Program for Group Meetings with Stake Presidents," Oct. 1–3, [1936], David O. McKay Papers, CHL.

8. Lee, "Remarks of Elder Harold B. Lee," 3–4; "A Message from the President of the Church," *Improvement Era,* June 1936, 39:332; First Presidency, *Important Message on Relief,* [3].

9. Tullis, *Mormons in Mexico,* 111–14, 138. **Topic: Mexico**

10. Tullis, *Mormons in Mexico,* 116; *Informe de la Mesa Directiva de la 3a Convención,* [June 25, 1936], 31. **Topic: Colonies in Mexico**

11. Martin F. Sanders to J. Reuben Clark Jr., Sept. 30, 1933; Oct. 29, 1933; Harold W. Pratt to J. Reuben Clark Jr., Apr. 10, 1934, J. Reuben Clark Jr. Papers, BYU; Pulido, *Spiritual Evolution of Margarito Bautista,* 162.

12. Gomez Páez, *Lamanite Conventions,* 25–27; *Informe de la Mesa Directiva de la 3a Convención,* [June 25, 1936], 19–20; Tullis, *Mormons in Mexico,* 112, 116–17; *Acta de la Convención de Tecalco,* Apr. 26, 1936, 14–15; Pulido, "Margarito Bautista," 48–56.

13. Tullis, *Mormons in Mexico,* 117–18; Gomez Páez, *Lamanite Conventions,* 25–27.

14. Tullis, *Mormons in Mexico,* 119–21, 127; Harold W. Pratt to First Presidency, May 1, 1936, First Presidency Mission Files, CHL; Dormady, *Primitive Revolution,* 76; Pulido, *Spiritual Evolution of Margarito Bautista,* 162.

15. Tullis, *Mormons in Mexico,* 121, 125–26; *Acta de la Convención de Tecalco,* Apr. 26, 1936, 14–15; Pulido, *Spiritual Evolution of Margarito Bautista,* 108–35, 165–70. **Topic: Lamanite Identity**

16. Tullis, *Mormons in Mexico,* 138–39; Harold W. Pratt to First Presidency, Apr. 25, 1936, First Presidency Mission Files, CHL; *Acta de la Convención de Tecalco,* Apr. 26, 1936, 18. First quotation edited for readability; "was not based" in original changed to "is not based."

17. *Acta de la Convención de Tecalco,* Apr. 26, 1936, 14–18; Harold W. Pratt to First Presidency, Apr. 28, 1936, First Presidency Mission Files, CHL; Tullis, *Mormons in Mexico,* 139–40; Pulido, *Spiritual Evolution of Margarito Bautista,* 167–70. **Topic: Third Convention**

18. *Informe de la Mesa Directiva de la 3a Convención,* [June 25, 1936], 20, 21–22, 27–29, 36–37; First Presidency to Harold Pratt, July 22, 1936, First Presidency Mission Files, CHL; Tullis, *Mormons in Mexico,* 140–41. Quotation edited for clarity; "president" in original changed to "mission president."

19. Heber J. Grant, "The Message of the First Presidency to the Church," in *One Hundred Seventh Semi-annual Conference,* 2–4; see also "Tabulation of Church-Wide Survey to October 1st, 1936," [1], David O. McKay Papers, CHL.

20. Heber J. Grant, "The Message of the First Presidency to the Church," in *One Hundred Seventh Semi-annual Conference,* 3–5; "Tabulation of Church-Wide Survey to October 1st, 1936," [1]–[3], David O. McKay Papers, CHL.

21. General Church Welfare Committee, Minutes, Dec. 3, 1936; *The March of Time: Salt Lake City!,* CHL; "Church Film at Orpheum," *Deseret News,* Feb. 4, 1937, 8. **Topics: Broadcast Media; Public Relations**

22. Presiding Bishopric, Office Journal, June 2, 1936; Sept. 8, 1936; Nov. 24, 1936; Jan. 5, 1937.

23. Don Howard, "The Mormon Fathers Discard the Dole," *Los Angeles Times,* Nov. 22, 1936, Sunday magazine, 7; General Church Welfare Committee, Minutes, Dec. 3, 1936; "Three Opportunities," *California Inter-mountain Weekly News* (Los Angeles), May 14, 1936, [2].

24. "Ballard Address Enthuses Local C.S.P. Committees," *California Inter-mountain Weekly News* (Los Angeles), Dec. 3, 1936, 1; "The Church Security Program in Southern California Stakes," *California Inter-mountain Weekly News,* Dec. 10, 1936, 2; "Honest Fast Offer Will Supply L.D.S. Needy, Says Pres. Grant," *Ensign* (Los Angeles), Feb. 4, 1937, 1. **Topic: Fasting**

25. Heber J. Grant to June Stewart, Feb. 17, 1937; Heber J. Grant to Tom C. Peck, Feb. 17, 1937, Heber J. Grant Collection, CHL; "Pres. Grant Confers with Local Leaders on Temple Site," *California Inter-mountain Weekly News* (Los Angeles), Jan. 21, 1937, 1.

26. Heber J. Grant to Ethel Grant Riggs, Feb. 20, 1937, Heber J. Grant Collection, CHL; David Howells to Heber J. Grant, Feb. 17, 1937, First Presidency Miscellaneous Correspondence, CHL; Heber J. Grant to J. H. Paul, Feb. 20, 1937, Letterpress Copybook, volume 75, 80, Heber J. Grant Collection, CHL; Cowan, *Los Angeles Temple,* 18, 21.

27. "S.L. 'March of Time' Opening at Studio," *Salt Lake Telegram,* Feb. 11, 1937, 15; "Far Reaching," *Deseret News,* Feb. 20, 1937, Church section, 2.

28. "Time Turned Back on Screen to Depict Story of Church," *Salt Lake Telegram,* Jan. 26, 1937, 26; David O. McKay to J. Reuben Clark, Jan. 26, 1937, First Presidency General Administration Files, CHL.

29. Harold W. Pratt to First Presidency, July 2, 1936; Sept. 18, 1936; First Presidency to Harold W. Pratt, Sept. 18, 1936; Antoine Ivins to First Presidency, July 3, 1936, First Presidency Mission Files, CHL.

30. First Presidency to Third Convention Committee and Followers, Nov. 2, 1936, 3–4, First Presidency Mission Files, CHL.

31. First Presidency to Third Convention Committee and Followers, Nov. 2, 1936, 5–7, First Presidency Mission Files, CHL. Second sentence of quotation edited for readability; original source begins "Nothing in the foregoing is to be understood as saying or even implying that the time may not come when a President of the Mission of your own race will be appointed."

32. Mora, Oral History Interview, 36.

33. Third Convention Directive Committee to First Presidency, Dec. 7, 1936, First Presidency Mission Files, CHL; Pulido, *Spiritual Evolution of Margarito Bautista,* 165–78; Mora, Oral History Interview, 36–37; Tullis, *Mormons in Mexico,* 147.

34. Mora, Oral History Interview, 37, 39; Tullis, *Mormons in Mexico,* 147; Pulido, *Spiritual Evolution of Margarito Bautista,* 174–78.

35. Mora, Oral History Interview, 39; Pulido, *Spiritual Evolution of Margarito Bautista,* 174; Third Convention Directive Committee to First Presidency, Dec. 7, 1936, First Presidency Mission Files, CHL; Tullis, *Mormons in Mexico,* 145. **Topics: Church Discipline; Third Convention**

36. Paul Bang, "My Life Story," 17, 21; Paul Bang, Northern States Mission Certificate of Appointment, Nov. 3, 1936, Paul and Cornelia T. Bang Papers, CHL; Gus Mason entry, Cincinnati Branch, South Ohio District, Northern States Mission, no. 789, in Ohio (State), part 2, Record of Members Collection, CHL.

37. Paul Bang, "My Life Story," 11–13, 27; Bang, Diary, Jan. 5, 7–8, and 10, 1936.

38. Paul Bang, "My Life Story," 10–11, 17–19, 23; see also, for example, Taylor, Diary, [June 2, 1937]; [July 30, 1937]; [Aug. 6, 1937].

39. Cincinnati Branch, Minutes, Jan. 15, 1936; Cincinnati Branch member entries, South Ohio District, Northern States Mission, in Ohio (State), part 2, Record of Members Collection, CHL; Bang, Diary, Jan. 15, 1936; Paul Bang, "My Life Story," 19. **Topic: Outmigration**

40. McKay, Notebook, June 6, 1937, David O. McKay Papers, Special Collections, J. Willard Marriott Library, University of Utah, Salt Lake City; Taylor, Diary, [spring 1937]; [June 1 and 6, 1937]; Paul Bang, "My Life Story," 18, 23, 28; "News from the Missions," *Liahona, the Elders' Journal,* July 13, 1937, 35:62.

41. Taylor, Diary, [June 24 and July 18, 1937]; Paul Bang, "My Life Story," 19–20.

42. Paul Bang, "My Life Story," 19–20; Cowan, *Church in the Twentieth Century,* 162–63.

43. Taylor, Diary, [July 30 and Aug. 1, 1937]; Cornelia Taylor, Northern States Mission Certificate of Appointment, Dec. 12, 1937, Paul and Cornelia T. Bang Papers, CHL; Paul Bang, "My Life Story," 19.

44. Paul Bang, "My Life Story," 19, 21, 27; Taylor, Diary, Oct. 18, 1937.

CHAPTER 25: NO TIME TO LOSE

1. Collette, *Collette Family History,* 148; Hatch, *Cziep Family History,* 51, 54; Luza, *Resistance in Austria,* 6–7; Wright, "Legality of the Annexation," 631–32; Suppan, *National Conflicts,* 367–68. Quotation edited for readability; original source has "Now we weren't Austria anymore. She said that it was Satan's work and that force begets force and what the Nazis have is not good." **Topic: Austria**

2. Suppan, *National Conflicts,* 368; Luza, *Resistance in Austria,* 13–15; Cziep and Cziep, Interview, 42.

3. Hatch, *Cziep Family History,* 64, 77, 81, 200; German-Austrian Mission, Manuscript History and Historical Reports, volume 2, Nov. 5, 1933; Cziep and Cziep, Interview, 21–22, 34; Collette, *Collette Family History,* 170–72.

4. Collette, *Collette Family History,* 154, 157; Hatch, *Cziep Family History,* 45, 47, 62.

5. Cziep and Cziep, Interview, 20, 34; Hatch, *Cziep Family History,* 78, 203.

6. Bukey, *Hitler's Austria,* 28–31; Suppan, *National Conflicts,* 368; Overy, *Third Reich,* 172–75; Cziep and Cziep, Interview, 40; Hatch, *Cziep Family History,* 64–70.

7. Cziep and Cziep, Interview, 40; Hatch, *Cziep Family History,* 81.

8. Chiye Terazawa entry, Pasadena Ward, no. 477, in Pasadena Ward, Record of Members Collection, CHL; Terazawa, Mission Journal, Feb. 7, 10, 17, and 24, 1938; David Kawai to Nadine Kawai, Apr. 1, 2013, CHL.

9. J. Reuben Clark, "The Outpost in Mid-Pacific," *Improvement Era,* Sept. 1935, 38:533; Britsch, "Closing of the Early Japan Mission," 276; Alma O. Taylor to First Presidency, Mar. 21, 1936, First Presidency Mission Files, CHL.

10. Britsch, "Closing of the Early Japan Mission," 263; David O. McKay to Hilton A. Robertson, Nov. 27, 1936; Hilton A. Robertson, Japanese Mission Annual Report [1937], First Presidency Mission Files, CHL.

11. Terazawa, Mission Journal, Jan. 13 and 16, 1938; Feb. 7, 1938; John A. Widtsoe, "The Japanese Mission in Action," *Improvement Era,* Feb. 1939, 42:89; David Kawai to Nadine Kawai, Apr. 1, 2013, CHL.

12. "Japanese Church Worker Bid Adieu," *Pasadena (CA) Post,* Dec. 10, 1937, 3.

13. Terazawa, Mission Journal, Feb. 7–Mar. 10, 1938; Robertson, Diary, Feb. 8, 1938; Marion L. Lee, Mission Journal, Mar. 8, 1938.

14. Terazawa, Mission Journal, Mar. 22, 1938; Marion L. Lee, Mission Journal, Mar. 22, 1938. First quotation edited for readability; original source has "the Lord would provide."

15. Esplin, "Charting the Course," 104–5; "A Pertinent Message to Youth," Historical Department, Journal History of the Church, June 9, 1937, 5; "Preserve the Gospel in Simplicity and Purity," Historical Department, Journal History of the Church, June 13, 1937, 6; Quinn, *Elder Statesman,* 208. **Topic: Seminaries and Institutes**

16. *By Study and Also by Faith,* 599–603; Church Board of Education, Minutes, Mar. 3, 1926; Merrill Van Wagoner to J. Reuben Clark, Aug. 22, 1938; J. Reuben Clark to Merrill Van Wagoner, Aug. 22, 1938, First Presidency Miscellaneous Correspondence, CHL; "Preserve the Gospel in Simplicity and Purity," Historical Department, Journal History of the Church, June 13, 1937, 6; Quinn, *Elder Statesman,* 208; Esplin, "Charting the Course," 105.

17. Esplin, "Charting the Course," 105; J. Reuben Clark, "The Charted Course of the Church in Education," *Improvement Era,* Sept. 1938, 41:520–21.

18. J. Reuben Clark, "The Charted Course of the Church in Education," *Improvement Era,* Sept. 1938, 41:521.

19. J. Reuben Clark, "The Charted Course of the Church in Education," *Improvement Era,* Sept. 1938, 41:571–73.

20. Esplin, "Charting the Course," 106–8.

21. Church Board of Education, Minutes, Feb. 2, 1938; *The Doctrines of the Church* (Salt Lake City: The Church of Jesus Christ of Latter-day Saints, 1939).

22. Terazawa, Mission Journal, Feb. 23–24 and Feb. 28–Mar. 1, 1939.

23. Terazawa, Mission Journal, July 20, 1938, and Feb. 22–Mar. 7, 1939; Hilton A. Robertson, Japanese Mission Annual Report [1938], [1]–2; Hilton A. Robertson, Japanese Mission Annual Report [1939]; Hilton A. Robertson to First Presidency, Jan. 11, 1939, First Presidency Mission Files, CHL; Robertson, Diary, Jan. 11, 1939; Walton, *Mending Link*, 21–24.

24. Terazawa, Mission Journal, Mar. 3 and 7, 1939; Beckstead, Journal, Mar. 7, 1939.

25. Terazawa, Mission Journal, Dec. 3–4, 1939; Japanese Mission, Hawaii District Missionary Journal, Oct. 18, 1938; Parshall, "Tsune Ishida Nachie," 129–30; John A. Widtsoe, "The Japanese Mission in Action," *Improvement Era,* Feb. 1939, 42:89.

26. Terazawa, Mission Journal, Mar. 8–9, 1939; Beckstead, Journal, Mar. 7, 1939; Barrus, "The Joy of Being Inez B. Barrus," 11; Japanese Mission, Hawaii District Missionary Journal, Mar. 8, 1939; Hilton A. Robertson, Japanese Mission Annual Report [1938], [1]–2; Hilton A. Robertson to First Presidency, Jan. 11, 1939, First Presidency Mission Files, CHL.

27. Barrus, "The Joy of Being Inez B. Barrus," 11–12; Terazawa, Mission Journal, Mar. 10, 22, and 29, 1939; John A. Widtsoe to First Presidency, Nov. 7, 1938; Hilton A. Robertson, Japanese Mission Annual Report [1938], [1], First Presidency Mission Files, CHL; John A. Widtsoe, "The Japanese Mission in Action," *Improvement Era,* Feb. 1939, 42:89; "News from the Missions," *Liahona, the Elders' Journal,* Mar. 1, 1932, 29:450. **Topic: Primary**

28. Beckstead, Journal, Apr. 12, 1939; Japanese Mission, Hawaii District Missionary Journal, Apr. 15–May 20, 1939; Woolsey and Pettit, *Happy Hearts,* 1, 4; "The Primary Page," *Children's Friend,* Sept. 1939, 38:405.

29. Beckstead, Journal, Apr. 12–May 20, 1939; Terazawa, Mission Journal, May 3–20, 1939; Japanese Mission, Hawaii District Missionary Journal, Apr. 15–May 20, 1939.

30. Terazawa, Mission Journal, May 11, 1939.

31. Terazawa, Mission Journal, May 17–19, 1939; "Entertainment Will Be Given," *Hilo (HI) Tribune Herald,* May 19, 1939, 2; Japanese Mission, Hawaii District Missionary Journal, May 18–20, 1939.

32. Terazawa, Mission Journal, May 20, 1939; Beckstead, Journal, May 20, 1939; Japanese Mission, Hawaii District Missionary Journal, May 20, 1939.

33. Woolsey and Pettit, *Happy Hearts,* 28.

34. Collette, *Collette Family History,* 157–59. **Topic: Czechoslovakia**

35. Overy, *Third Reich,* 175–82, 187–88; Heimann, *Czechoslovakia,* 78–81.

36. Collette, *Collette Family History,* 157, 159–61.

37. Collette, *Collette Family History,* 161, 162–64; Hatch, *Cziep Family History,* 54, 77–80.

38. Botz, "Jews of Vienna," 320–27; Offenberger, "Jewish Responses," 60–80; Collette, *Collette Family History,* 163; Hatch, *Cziep Family History,* 80.

39. Hatch, *Cziep Family History,* 77, 81, 200.

40. Hatch, *Cziep Family History,* 79; Overy, *Third Reich,* 197. **Topic: World War II**

CHAPTER 26: WAR'S FOUL BROOD

1. First Presidency to Douglas Wood, Telegram, Aug. 24, 1939; First Presidency to Joseph Fielding Smith, Telegrams, Aug. 24, 1939; Aug. 25, 1939, First Presidency Mission Files, CHL; U.S. State Department, Memorandum, Aug. 25, 1939, U.S. State Department Correspondence regarding Mormons and Mormonism, CHL; Grant, Journal, Aug. 27, 1939; Boone, "Evacuation of the Czechoslovak and German Missions," 123, 136; see also Minert, *Under the Gun,* 27–28; and British Mission, Manuscript History and Historical Reports, Sept. 1–2, 1939. Missionaries in the British Mission evacuated directly to the United States.

2. Joseph Fielding Smith to First Presidency, May 6, 1939; Aug. 1, 1939; Joseph Fielding Smith and Jessie Evans Smith to Heber J. Grant, June 21, 1939, First Presidency Miscellaneous Correspondence, CHL; Joseph Fielding Smith to First Presidency, Aug. 28, 1939, First Presidency Mission Files, CHL.

3. Seibold, Oral History Interview, 2–3; Douglas Wood, in *One Hundred Tenth Annual Conference,* 78–79; Joseph Fielding Smith to First Presidency, Telegram, Aug. 26, 1939, First Presidency Mission Files, CHL; Boone, "Evacuation of the Czechoslovak and German Missions," 137.

4. Douglas Wood, in *One Hundred Tenth Annual Conference,* 79–81; Boone, "Evacuation of the Czechoslovak and German Missions," 143. Last part of quotation edited for readability; original source has "We had told him to follow his impressions entirely as we had no idea what towns these 31 Elders would be in."

5. Boone, "Evacuation of the Czechoslovak and German Missions," 144; Douglas Wood, in *One Hundred Tenth Annual Conference,* 79–80; Seibold, Oral History Interview, 3, 12; Montague, *Mormon Missionary Evacuation,* 83.

6. Seibold, Oral History Interview, 4–5, 12; Montague, *Mormon Missionary Evacuation,* 84–86; Boone, "Evacuation of the Czechoslovak and German Missions," 144. Quotation edited for readability; "he'd" in original changed to "you'd."

7. Seibold, Oral History Interview, 6.

8. Boone, "Evacuation of the Czechoslovak and German Missions," 146; Seibold, Oral History Interview, 10; Montague, *Mormon Missionary Evacuation,* 97–100; Overy, *Third Reich,* 197–98; Ellis Rasmussen and John Kest, "Border Incident," *Improvement Era,* Dec. 1943, 46:793, 797. **Topic: World War II**

9. Heber J. Grant, in *One Hundred Tenth Semi-annual Conference,* 8–9; Heber J. Grant to Walter Day, Sept. 8, 1939, Letterpress Copybook, volume 78, 99, Heber J. Grant Collection, CHL.

10. Grant, Journal, Dec. 6, 1939; Heber J. Grant to Rachel Grant Taylor, Dec. 14, 1939, Heber J. Grant Collection, CHL.

11. Grant, Journal, Feb. 4–5, 1940; Heber J. Grant to Charles Zimmerman, June 20, 1940, Letterpress Copybook, volume 79, 61, Heber J. Grant Collection, CHL; Clark, Office Diary, Feb. 5, 1940; Heber J. Grant to Isaac Stewart, May 10, 1940, Letterpress Copybook, volume 78, 962; Heber J. Grant to Henry Link, Aug. 2, 1941, Letterpress Copybook, volume 80, 230, Heber J. Grant Collection, CHL.

12. Grant, Journal, Apr. 27, 1940; Heber J. Grant to Grace Grant Evans, May 1, 1940; Willard [Smith] to "'Grant' Family," Feb. 22, 1940, Heber J. Grant Collection, CHL. **Topic: Heber J. Grant**

13. Bang, Autobiography, 7–8; [Bang], Wedding Day Story, [1].

14. Paul Bang, "My Life Story," 22, 27; see also Charles Anderson to Adeline Yarish Taylor, July 30, 1940, Paul and Cornelia T. Bang Papers, CHL.

15. Bang, Autobiography, 7; Cornelia Taylor, Patriarchal Blessing, Feb. 6, 1935, 1–2, Paul and Cornelia T. Bang Papers, CHL; Taylor, Diary, Apr. 12, 1936.

16. Bang, Autobiography, 7–8; Leo Muir to Presiding Bishopric, Apr. 15, 1940; Marvin O. Ashton, Memorandum, May 22, 1940, Presiding Bishopric General Files, 1889–1956, CHL; Fish, Kramer, and Wallis, *History of the Mormon Church in Cincinnati,* 67.

17. **Topics: Kirtland Temple; Other Latter Day Saint Movements**

18. [Bang], Wedding Day Story, [1]; [Bang], Honeymoon Diary, 23–24; Howlett, *Kirtland Temple,* 53–56, 60–61; Bang, "Personal History of Paul and Connie Bang—1942 Forward," 2–3.

19. Lund, "Joseph F. Smith and the Origins of the Church Historic Sites Program," 345, 352–55; Packer, "Study of the Hill Cumorah," 75, 92–94, 122–26, 135–38; Argetsinger, "Hill Cumorah Pageant," 58–59. **Topics: Church Historic Sites; Palmyra and Manchester; Sacred Grove and Smith Family Farm**

20. [Bang], Honeymoon Diary, 25; Bang, "Personal History of Paul and Connie Bang—1942 Forward," 3; Gerritsen, "Hill Cumorah Monument," 133; Paul Bang and Cornelia Taylor Bang, Hill Cumorah, 1940, Photograph, Paul and Cornelia T. Bang Papers, CHL.

21. [Bang], Honeymoon Diary, 25; "Leaders in Church Speak at Opening of Capital Chapel," *Deseret News,* Nov. 11, 1933, Church section, 1; "Will Link Parks by One Great Highway," *Deseret Evening News,* June 5, 1920, section 2, 8; "Church Forms Stakes in U.S. Capital and Denver," *Deseret News,* July 1, 1940, 11.

22. [Bang], Honeymoon Diary, 25–26; Bang, "Personal History of Paul and Connie Bang—1942 Forward," 3–5; *Williams' Cincinnati City Directory,* 70.
23. United Kingdom Air Ministry, *Daily Weather Report,* Ross-on-Wye, Dec. 11, 1940; "Victims Trapped in Wrecked Homes," *Cheltenham (England) Chronicle and Gloucestershire Graphic,* Dec. 14, 1940, 2; Overy, *Third Reich,* 224–30; Donnelly, *Britain in the Second World War,* 92–93. **Topic: England**
24. Jennifer Middleton Mason, "Sisters of Cheltenham," *Ensign,* Oct. 1996, 59–60; Mason, Oral History Interview, 4–7, 9–10, 17–18.
25. "Victims Trapped in Wrecked Homes," *Cheltenham (England) Chronicle and Gloucestershire Graphic,* Dec. 14, 1940, 2; Elder, *Secret Cheltenham,* 55; Mason, Oral History Interview, 16; Hasted, *Cheltenham Book of Days,* 347; "Over 600 Homeless after Raid," *Cheltenham Chronicle and Gloucestershire Graphic,* Dec. 21, 1940, 3.
26. British Mission, Manuscript History and Historical Reports, Sept. 1–2, 1939; Jan. 10 and 18, 1940; Jennifer Middleton Mason, "Sisters of Cheltenham," *Ensign,* Oct. 1996, 59; Mason, Oral History Interview, 10–12, 21, 26–27; Arthur Fletcher entry, Stroud Branch, Bristol District, British Mission, no. 11, in England (Country), part 42, Record of Members Collection, CHL.
27. Mason, Oral History Interview, 4–6, 13–14, 22, 24; Jennifer Middleton Mason, "Sisters of Cheltenham," *Ensign,* Oct. 1996, 59.
28. "Air Raid Danger, Warning Signals, and Blackout Instructions," file MEPO-4-489; Jennifer Middleton Mason, "Sisters of Cheltenham," *Ensign,* Oct. 1996, 59; Mason, Oral History Interview, 14.
29. Collette, *Collette Family History,* 205; Scharffs, *Mormonism in Germany,* 107; Minert, *Under the Gun,* 17, 465; Collette, *Collette Family History,* 210; Bukey, *Hitler's Austria,* 188, 196–200, 206.
30. Minert, *Under the Gun,* 463, 474; Hatch, *Cziep Family History,* 31, 64, 81, 202–3.
31. Hatch, *Cziep Family History,* 81; Collette, *Collette Family History,* 171–72.
32. Hatch, *Cziep Family History,* 81; Botz, "Jews of Vienna," 321–22; 330, note 49; Egon Weiss to "Dear Brother," Nov. 23, 1938, First Presidency Miscellaneous Correspondence, CHL.
33. Tobler, "Jews, the Mormons, and the Holocaust," 81; Heber J. Grant, in *Ninety-First Annual Conference,* 124; Heber J. Grant to Willard Smith, June 24, 1933, Letterpress Copybook, volume 70, 788; Heber J. Grant to Wesley King, Jan. 24, 1920, Letterpress Copybook, volume 55, 515, Heber J. Grant Collection, CHL.
34. Tobler, "Jews, the Mormons, and the Holocaust," 81; Egon Weiss to "Dear Brother," Nov. 23, 1938; First Presidency to "Mrs. A. Goddard," Nov. 23, 1920; Heber J. Grant to S. Sipkema, Jan. 29, 1926; Heber J. Grant, Anthony W. Ivins, and Charles W. Nibley to Cornelia van der Meide, Jan. 29, 1930, First Presidency Miscellaneous Correspondence, CHL; see also Jensen and Javadi-Evans, "Senator Elbert D. Thomas," 223–39. **Topic: Emigration**
35. See, for example, Joseph Anderson to Paula Stemmer, Oct. 13, 1938; Joseph Anderson to Max Safran, Nov. 7, 1938; and J. Reuben Clark Jr. and David O. McKay to Richard Siebenschein, Jan. 27, 1939, First Presidency Miscellaneous Correspondence, CHL.
36. Botz, "Jews of Vienna," 330; Hatch, *Cziep Family History,* 81, 200, 202; see also Tobler, "Jews, the Mormons, and the Holocaust," 85–86.

Chapter 27: God Is at the Helm

1. Schnibbe, *The Price,* 20, 24; Holmes and Keele, *When Truth Was Treason,* 29; Dewey, *Hübener vs Hitler,* 44–47. **Topic: Helmuth Hübener**
2. Schnibbe, *The Price,* 25; Holmes and Keele, *When Truth Was Treason,* 30; Dewey, *Hübener vs Hitler,* 86–87; Nelson, *Moroni and the Swastika,* 296.

3. Holmes and Keele, *When Truth Was Treason,* 29; Gellately, *Backing Hitler,* 184–86; Nelson, *Moroni and the Swastika,* 296.
4. Holmes and Keele, *When Truth Was Treason,* 30; Schnibbe, *The Price,* 25–26.
5. Schnibbe, *The Price,* 20–23, 26–27.
6. Ikegami, "Brief History of the Japanese Members of the Church," 3, 5; Ikegami, "We Had Good Examples among the Members," 229; Britsch, *Moramona,* 284; Japanese Mission President's 1940 Annual Report, Feb. 17, 1941; Jay C. Jensen to First Presidency, Dec. 16, 1941, First Presidency Mission Files, CHL; Jay C. Jensen, "L.D.S. Japanese Aid U.S. Soldiers," *Deseret News,* Nov. 28, 1942, Church section, [1]. **Topic: Sunday School**
7. Jay C. Jensen, Journal, Dec. 7, 1941; Britsch, *Moramona,* 284, 286; Jay C. Jensen, "L.D.S. Japanese Aid U.S. Soldiers," *Deseret News,* Nov. 28, 1942, Church section, [1]. Quotation edited for readability; "Japan was attacking Pearl Harbor" in original changed to "Japan is attacking Pearl Harbor."
8. Ikegami, "We Had Good Examples among the Members," 228; *Tosa Maru* manifest, in "Washington, Seattle, Passenger Lists, 1890–1957"; 1940 U.S. Census, Honolulu, Oahu, Hawaii Territory, 970; Jay C. Jensen, "L.D.S. Japanese Aid U.S. Soldiers," *Deseret News,* Nov. 28, 1942, Church section, [1]. **Topics: Hawaii; Japan; World War II**
9. Jay C. Jensen, "L.D.S. Japanese Aid U.S. Soldiers," *Deseret News,* Nov. 28, 1942, Church section, [1]; Jay C. Jensen, Journal, Dec. 7, 1941.
10. Israel, "Military Justice in Hawaii," 243–67; "Schools, Now Closed, Being Used for Defense Purposes," *Honolulu Star-Bulletin,* Dec. 8, 1941, 7; Scheiber and Scheiber, "Constitutional Liberty in World War II," 347, 354; Allen, *Hawaii's War Years,* 90–91, 112–13, 360–61; "8 P.M. Curfew in Effect for Pedestrians," *Honolulu Advertiser,* Feb. 4, 1942, 2; Wyatt Olson, "Exhibit Details Martial Law in Hawaii Following Pearl Harbor Attack," *Stars and Stripes,* Jan. 11, 2017, https://www.stripes.com; Kimura, *Issei,* 225.
11. "Family Air Raid Shelter," *Honolulu Advertiser,* Jan. 21, 1942, [1]; Yukino N. Fukabori, "Neighbors Pool Efforts, Build Air Raid Shelter," *Hilo (HI) Tribune Herald,* Jan. 26, 1942, [1]; Ikegami, Journal, Dec. 11–25, 1941. First quotation edited for readability; "I wish there is school once again" in original changed to "I wish there was school once again."
12. Central Pacific Mission, General Minutes, Dec. 7, 1941, 67.
13. Dewey, *Hübener vs Hitler,* 158–59.
14. Holmes and Keele, *When Truth Was Treason,* 33–39, 191.
15. Schnibbe, *The Price,* 27–37; Holmes and Keele, *When Truth Was Treason,* 13, 49.
16. Schnibbe, *The Price,* 39; Holmes and Keele, *When Truth Was Treason,* 49; Doctrine and Covenants 134:5; Articles of Faith 1:12.
17. Schnibbe, *The Price,* 39–40; Holmes and Keele, *When Truth Was Treason,* 38, 50; McDonough, *Gestapo,* 57–58.
18. Schnibbe, *The Price,* 41; Holmes and Keele, *When Truth Was Treason,* 50. Quotation edited for readability; original source has "They told me if I lied, they would beat me to a pulp."
19. Holmes and Keele, *When Truth Was Treason,* 51–52; Schnibbe, *The Price,* 41, 43–44.
20. Schnibbe, *The Price,* 44.
21. Amy Brown Lyman, "In Retrospect," *Relief Society Magazine,* Dec. 1942, 29:840; Hall, *Faded Legacy,* 126, 144.
22. Derr, Cannon, and Beecher, *Women of Covenant,* 277; Heber J. Grant to Dessie Grant Boyle, Apr. 21, 1941, Letterpress Copybook, volume 79, 969; Heber J. Grant to Frank W. Simmonds, Dec. 31, 1941, Letterpress Copybook, volume 80, 709, Heber J. Grant Collection, CHL.
23. Dickinson, *World in the Long Twentieth Century,* 163, 168–70, 175. **Topic: Amy Brown Lyman**
24. "Notice to Church Officers," *Deseret News,* Jan. 17, 1942, 1; "Bulletin No. 24," Feb. 19, 1942, 1–2, Relief Society Bulletins, CHL.

25. Amy Brown Lyman, "In Retrospect," *Relief Society Magazine,* Dec. 1942, 29:840; Hall, *Faded Legacy,* 158–59; Derr, Cannon, and Beecher, *Women of Covenant,* 283. **Topics: Relief Society; Female Relief Society of Nauvoo**
26. "Bulletin No. 24," Feb. 19, 1942, 5–6, Relief Society Bulletins, CHL.
27. Relief Society General Board, Minutes, Feb. 25, 1942, 27–28; Vera White Pohlman, "Relief Society Celebrates Its Centennial," *Relief Society Magazine,* Apr. 1942, 29:229.
28. "Relief Society Centennial Radio Broadcast," *Relief Society Magazine,* Apr. 1942, 29:248–50.
29. Amy Brown Lyman, "In Retrospect," *Relief Society Magazine,* Dec. 1942, 29:838–40; "Relief Society Centennial Radio Broadcast," *Relief Society Magazine,* Apr. 1942, 29:250.
30. Meyer and Galli, *Under a Leafless Tree,* 63–65, 78–80.
31. Minert, *In Harm's Way,* 399, 407; Meyer and Galli, *Under a Leafless Tree,* 81–84.
32. Overy, *Third Reich,* 248–50, 259–60; Meyer and Galli, *Under a Leafless Tree,* 84–85; Winter, *Great War and the British People,* 250–53; Pavalko and Elder, "World War II and Divorce," 1214–15.
33. Meyer and Galli, *Under a Leafless Tree,* 63, 71, 84–91; 86, note 1; Minert, *In Harm's Way,* 410–11.
34. J. Reuben Clark Jr., in *One Hundred Twelfth Annual Conference,* 94; First Presidency, "Notice to Church Officers," Jan. 17, 1942; First Presidency to Stake Presidents, Mar. 14, 1942, First Presidency Letterpress Copybooks, volume 117; Quinn, *Elder Statesman,* 97.
35. J. Reuben Clark Jr. to Henry B. Armes, Dec. 24, 1941; J. Reuben Clark Jr. to Gordon S. Rentschler, Jan. 2, 1942; J. Reuben Clark Jr. to Gordon Clark, Jan. 5, 1942, J. Reuben Clark Jr. Papers, BYU.
36. J. Reuben Clark Jr., in *One Hundred Twelfth Annual Conference,* 91, 94.
37. First Presidency to Mission Presidents, Jan. 14, 1942; First Presidency, "Notice to Church Officers," Jan. 17, 1942; First Presidency to Stake Presidencies, Ward Bishoprics, Presidents of Branches, and Presidents of Missions, Mar. 23, 1942, First Presidency Letterpress Copybooks, volume 117; Mount Graham Stake, Confidential Minutes, volume 2, Dec. 28, 1941, and Feb. 8, 1942; Cowan, *Church in the Twentieth Century,* 182.
38. J. Reuben Clark Jr., in *One Hundred Twelfth Annual Conference,* 93, 95; Fox, *J. Reuben Clark,* xiii–xv, 293–95.

CHAPTER 28: OUR UNITED EFFORTS

1. Kennedy, *Freedom from Fear,* 615–27; Miller, *World War II Cincinnati,* 51–56; Knepper, *Ohio and Its People,* 384–87.
2. "Mormons to Build Church on Old Herrmann Homesite," *Cincinnati Enquirer,* Jan. 8, 1941, 10; Fish, Kramer, and Wallis, *History of the Mormon Church in Cincinnati,* 66–68; Cincinnati Branch, Building Committee Minutes, Mar. 14, 1941–Apr. 23, 1941.
3. Bang, "Personal History of Paul and Connie Bang—1942 Forward," 4; May, "Rosie the Riveter Gets Married," 128–30; Paul Bang, Draft Registration Card, Oct. 16, 1940, Paul and Cornelia T. Bang Papers, CHL; Milton Yarish Taylor, Draft Registration Card, Oct. 16, 1940, U.S. World War II Draft Cards Young Men, available at ancestry.com.
4. Bang, "Personal History of Paul and Connie Bang—1942 Forward," 4–5; Vaughn William Ball, in Cincinnati Branch, Record of Members and Children, no. 403; Ball, Reminiscences, part 3, section 4, [00:07:38]–[00:08:38].
5. Bang, "Personal History of Paul and Connie Bang—1942 Forward," 4; Janet Taylor, in Cincinnati Branch, Record of Members and Children, no. 375; Ball, Reminiscences, part 3, section 4, [00:08:38].
6. Ball, Reminiscences, part 3, section 4, [00:08:38]–[00:09:08]; "The Fixers," Photograph, Paul and Cornelia T. Bang Papers, CHL.

7. Bang, "Personal History of Paul and Connie Bang—1942 Forward," 4; Miller, *World War II Cincinnati,* 55–56.
8. Hugill, "Good Roads," 331–39, 342–43; Jakle and Sculle, *Gas Station,* 49, 58, 131–33; Ball, Reminiscences, part 3, section 4, [00:09:57]–[00:10:49].
9. Bang, "Personal History of Paul and Connie Bang—1942 Forward," 4–5; Taylor, Autobiography, 2–3; Utah Trip, Photographs; Charles V. Anderson to Milton Taylor, Jan. 13, 1936; Charles V. Anderson to Milton Taylor, Feb. 24, 1937; Charles V. Anderson to George and Adeline Taylor, July 30, 1940, Paul and Cornelia T. Bang Papers, CHL. **Topic: Church Headquarters**
10. Bang, "Personal History of Paul and Connie Bang—1942 Forward," 4–5; Taylor, Autobiography, 2; Salt Lake Temple, Endowments of the Living, 1893–1956, volumes H, I, May 1, 1942, microfilms 184,075 and 184,082; Sealings of Living Couples, 1893–1956, volume E, May 1, 1942, microfilm 1,239,572; Sealings of Couples and Children, 1942–70, volume 3E/3F, May 1, 1942, microfilm 1,063,709, U.S. and Canada Record Collection, FHL.
11. Salt Lake Temple, Endowments for the Dead, 1893–1970, volumes 6U, 6Y, May 4, 1942, microfilms 184,248 and 1,239,528, U.S. and Canada Record Collection, FHL; Bang, "Personal History of Paul and Connie Bang—1942 Forward," 5. **Topics: Salt Lake Temple; Temple Endowment; Sealing**
12. Vlam, *Our Lives,* 95; Vlam, "Life History of Grace Alida Hermine Vlam," 7; Weinberg, *World at Arms,* 122–27.
13. Vlam, *Our Lives,* 87–89; Weinberg, *World at Arms,* 122.
14. Vlam, *Our Lives,* 87, 91, 95; Netherlands Amsterdam Mission, Manuscript History and Historical Reports, 1939, 1941–42, 1, 9–12. **Topic: Netherlands**
15. Vlam, *Our Lives,* 64, 81, 91–95; Vlam, Interview [May 2020], [01:00:25].
16. Vlam, "Life History of Grace Alida Hermine Vlam," 8; Vlam, *Our Lives,* 95.
17. Vlam, "Life History of Grace Alida Hermine Vlam," 8; Vlam, *Our Lives,* [94]–95, 158; Vlam, Interview [May 2020], [01:15:10]; Vlam, "Answers to the Questions Posed," 1–2.
18. Central Pacific Mission, General Minutes, July 5, 1942, 144.
19. Ikegami, Memories, 1; Allen, *Hawaii's War Years,* 90, 112–13, 360–61; Ikegami, Journal, Jan. 14, 1942; Feb. 19, 1942; May 5 and 6, 1942; June 25, 1942; July 5, 1942.
20. Okihiro, *Cane Fires,* 210–11; Jay C. Jensen, "L.D.S. Japanese Aid U.S. Soldiers," *Deseret News,* Nov. 28, 1942, Church section, [1]; Kennedy, *Freedom from Fear,* 748–51; Heimburger, "Remembering Topaz and Wendover," 148–50.
21. Knaefler, *Our House Divided,* 6; Odo, *No Sword to Bury,* 2–3; Scheiber and Scheiber, "Constitutional Liberty in World War II," 344, 350; Allen, *Hawaii's War Years,* 134–37, 351.
22. Allen, *Hawaii's War Years,* 91; Ikegami, Journal, June 24, 1942; Jay C. Jensen, "L.D.S. Japanese Aid U.S. Soldiers," *Deseret News,* Nov. 28, 1942, Church section, [1], 6; "We're United for Victory," in Central Pacific Mission, General Minutes, Summer 1942, 149; see also Akinaka, Diary, Dec. 7–8, 1941, and June 16, 1942.
23. Ikegami, Journal, July 5, 1942; John A. Widtsoe, in *One Hundred Twelfth Annual Conference,* 33.
24. "We're United for Victory," in Central Pacific Mission, General Minutes, Summer 1942, 149; Jay C. Jensen, "L.D.S. Japanese Aid U.S. Soldiers," *Deseret News,* Nov. 28, 1942, Church section, 6, 8.
25. "We're United for Victory," in Central Pacific Mission, General Minutes, Summer 1942, 149.
26. Schnibbe, *The Price,* 45, 47–48; Holmes and Keele, *When Truth Was Treason,* 55–56.
27. Schnibbe, *The Price,* 41–47; Holmes and Keele, *When Truth Was Treason,* 57.
28. Holmes and Keele, *When Truth Was Treason,* 61–62, 66–67.
29. Schnibbe, *The Price,* 36, 51–52; Document 52, in Holmes and Keele, *When Truth Was Treason,* 67–68, 221.
30. Schnibbe, *The Price,* 52; Holmes and Keele, *When Truth Was Treason,* 69.

31. Document 52, in Holmes and Keele, *When Truth Was Treason,* 69, 219; Schnibbe, *The Price,* 54.

32. Holmes and Keele, *When Truth Was Treason,* 69–71; Schnibbe, *The Price,* 55. **Topic: Helmuth Hübener**

33. Document 72, in Holmes and Keele, *When Truth Was Treason,* 273–75; Dewey, *Hübener vs Hitler,* 239.

34. Sommerfeld, Interview, 2; Document 72, in Holmes and Keele, *When Truth Was Treason,* 273–74.

35. Nelson, *Moroni and the Swastika,* 308–9; Sommerfeld, Interview, 9–10; Document 72, in Holmes and Keele, *When Truth Was Treason,* 274; Schnibbe, *The Price,* 31.

36. Document 72, in Holmes and Keele, *When Truth Was Treason,* 274; Sommerfeld, Interview, 4–5.

37. Sommerfeld, Interview, 11; Document 65, in Holmes and Keele, *When Truth Was Treason,* 257–58; Nelson, *Moroni and the Swastika,* 281, 307–9.

38. Documents 65, 71, and 72, in Holmes and Keele, *When Truth Was Treason,* 258, 272, 275; Keele and Tobler, "Mormons in the Third Reich," 23; Sommerfeld, Interview, 11–12.

39. Dewey, *Hübener vs Hitler,* 239; Document 61, in Holmes and Keele, *When Truth Was Treason,* 240. The original letter was lost. Helmuth's words are Marie Sommerfeld's re-creation from memory.

40. Vlam, *Our Lives,* 95–97, 107.

41. Vlam, *Our Lives,* 97, 99.

42. Vlam, *Our Lives,* 99; Vlam, "Life History of Grace Alida Hermine Vlam," 9.

43. Vlam, "Life History of Grace Alida Hermine Vlam," 9; Vlam, "Answers to the Questions Posed," 1–2; Vlam, *Our Lives,* 99, 101.

44. Vlam, *Our Lives,* 99, 101. Quotation edited for readability; original source has "he did not want to be converted, he only came to hear the story from Piet."

45. Vlam, *Our Lives,* 101. Quotation edited for readability; original source has "if they could not sleep in the night, they should pray to God and ask Him, if the things they heard from Mr. Vlam were true."

46. Vlam, *Our Lives,* 101. Quotation edited for readability; "That last night" in original changed to "That night," "him" changed to "me," and four instances of "he" changed to "I." **Topic: Fasting**

CHAPTER 29: 'TIS EVENTIDE

1. Mason, Oral History Interview, 10–11, 14–15; Hermansen, Oral History Interview, 46; Jennifer Middleton Mason, "Sisters of Cheltenham," *Ensign,* Oct. 1996, 60.

2. Mason, Oral History Interview, 12–13; Jennifer Middleton Mason, "Sisters of Cheltenham," *Ensign,* Oct. 1996, 59–60.

3. Donnelly, *Britain in the Second World War,* 103; Jennifer Middleton Mason, "Sisters of Cheltenham," *Ensign,* Oct. 1996, 60.

4. Jennifer Middleton Mason, "Sisters of Cheltenham," *Ensign,* Oct. 1996, 60; Mason, Oral History Interview, 11–12.

5. Jennifer Middleton Mason, "Sisters of Cheltenham," *Ensign,* Oct. 1996, 60; Mason, Oral History Interview, 11–12; Nellie Middleton to Carol C. Seal, Mar. 26, 1945, Nellie Middleton and Jennifer M. Mason Papers, CHL; Ray Jay Hermansen entry, Stratford Ward, Grant Stake, in Stratford Ward, part 1, segment 1, Record of Members Collection, CHL; Cheltenham Branch, Minutes, Nov. 20, 1943.

6. Jennifer Middleton Mason, "Sisters of Cheltenham," *Ensign,* Oct. 1996, 60; "Apostle Vacancies Filled," *Millennial Star,* Oct. 1943, 105:506; Kimball and Kimball, *Spencer W. Kimball,* 187–205; *Saints,* volume 1, chapter 24; Dew, *Ezra Taft Benson,* 49–65, 49–65, 171–82. **Topics: Quorum of the Twelve; Church Periodicals**

7. Jennifer Middleton Mason, "Sisters of Cheltenham," *Ensign,* Oct. 1996, 60; Mason, Oral History Interview, 11–12, 24–25.
8. Nellie Middleton to Carol C. Seal, Mar. 26, 1945, Nellie Middleton and Jennifer M. Mason Papers, CHL.
9. Santos, Memories of Claudio M. dos Santos, [1]; Woodworth, "Claudio Martins dos Santos," 1–2; Santos, Interview, 1.
10. Humphreys, *Latin America and the Second World War,* 62–63; Grover, "Sprechen Sie Portugiesisch?," 133–37; Grover, "Mormon Church and German Immigrants in Southern Brazil," 302–3; J. Alden Bowers to First Presidency, Dec. 19, 1938; July 23, 1941, First Presidency Mission Files, CHL. **Topic: Brazil**
11. J. Alden Bowers to First Presidency, Jan. 23, 1939; July 23, 1941, First Presidency Mission Files, CHL; Grover, "Sprechen Sie Portugiesisch?," 135–37; William W. Seegmiller, Annual Report of the President, Brazilian Mission, 1942, Presiding Bishopric Financial, Statistical, and Historical Reports, CHL.
12. Mission President's Annual Report, 1940, First Presidency Mission Files, CHL; Humphreys, *Latin America and the Second World War,* 59–68; Lochery, *Fortunes of War,* 165–79; J. Alden Bowers to First Presidency, Feb. 25, 1942, First Presidency Mission Files, CHL; Brazilian Mission, Annual Report, 1942, Presiding Bishopric Financial, Statistical, and Historical Reports, CHL.
13. Sorensen, Oral History Interview, 12; Sorensen, "Personal History," 80; Brazil São Paulo North Mission, Manuscript History, volume 1, part 2, Porto Alegre District, Aug. 19, 1942; Howells, Oral History Interview, 37; Grover, "Mormonism in Brazil," 61.
14. Woodworth, "Claudio Martins dos Santos," 3.
15. Grover, "Mormonism in Brazil," 62; Brazil São Paulo North Mission, Manuscript History, volume 1, part 1, Rio de Janeiro District, July 7, 1941; William W. Seegmiller to Sailor and Bonnie Seegmiller, Jan. 12, 194[3], William Seegmiller Correspondence, CHL; William W. Seegmiller to First Presidency, Jan. 28, 1944, Brazilian Mission Correspondence, CHL.
16. Woodworth, "Claudio Martins dos Santos," 1–2; Santos, Interview, 2; Santos, Memories of Claudio M. dos Santos, [2]; Claudio Martins dos Santos, Baptism Certificate, Jan. 16, 1944; Mary José Daniel Martins, Baptism Certificate, Jan. 16, 1944, São Paulo District, Brazilian Mission, Claudio and Mary dos Santos Baptismal Certificates, CHL; William W. Seegmiller to First Presidency, Jan. 28, 1944, Brazilian Mission Correspondence, CHL.
17. Meyer and Galli, *Under a Leafless Tree,* 95–96, 100.
18. Meyer and Galli, *Under a Leafless Tree,* 97–100.
19. Meyer and Galli, *Under a Leafless Tree,* 101–2; Meyer, Interview [2016], 20.
20. Meyer and Galli, *Under a Leafless Tree,* 92–93.
21. Meyer and Galli, *Under a Leafless Tree,* 16, 102; "Abide with Me; 'Tis Eventide," *Hymns,* no. 165; Meyer, Interview [2016], 20–22.
22. Meyer, Interview [2016], 22–23; Meyer and Galli, *Under a Leafless Tree,* 102.
23. Meyer and Galli, *Under a Leafless Tree,* 44, 103–4, 105.
24. Santos, Memories of Claudio M. dos Santos, [2]; Woodworth, "Claudio Martins dos Santos," 2; Santos, Interview, 2.
25. Woodworth, "Claudio Martins dos Santos," 2; Santos, Memories of Claudio M. dos Santos, [2]; Santos, Interview, 2; Claudio Martins dos Santos, Ordination Certificate, Jan. 30, 1944, São Paulo District, Brazilian Mission, Claudio and Mary dos Santos Baptismal Certificates, CHL.
26. Woodworth, "Claudio Martins dos Santos," 2; Santos, Memories of Claudio M. dos Santos, [2]–[3]; Santos, Interview, 2, 5; William W. Seegmiller to First Presidency, Jan. 11, 194[3], Brazilian Mission Correspondence, CHL.
27. Santos, Memories of Claudio M. dos Santos, [3]–[4]; Woodworth, "Claudio Martins dos Santos," 2–3; Santos, Interview, 2–3, 5.
28. Mary Jennifer Middleton entry, Cheltenham Branch, Bristol Conference, in England (Country), part 12, Record of Members Collection, CHL; Jennifer Middleton Mason, "Sisters of Cheltenham," *Ensign,* Oct. 1996, 59–60; Mason, Oral History Interview, 31, 33.

29. Mason, Oral History Interview, 33–35, 41, 43, 46, 54; Andre K. Anastasion Sr., "Survival of the British Mission during World War II," *Improvement Era,* Apr. 1969, 72:63; Brown, *Abundant Life,* 101–2.

30. Mason, Oral History Interview, 35–36; Campbell and Poll, *Hugh B. Brown,* 120–40, 164–76, 235.

31. Mason, Oral History Interview, 36–37; Jennifer Middleton Mason to Dallin Morrow, Email, June 28, 2017, Nellie Middleton and Jennifer M. Mason Papers, CHL.

32. *Missionary's Hand Book,* 134.

33. Mason, Oral History Interview, 33, 36–37; Jennifer Middleton Mason to Dallin Morrow, Email, June 28, 2017, Nellie Middleton and Jennifer M. Mason Papers, CHL.

34. Maxwell, Personal History, box 1, folder 2, 7; Maxwell, Oral History Interview [1976–77], 112, 114; Maxwell, Oral History Interview [1999–2000], 27; Hafen, *Disciple's Life,* 96–97.

35. Weinberg, *World at Arms,* 676–702; Overy, *Third Reich,* 328–29; Maxwell, Oral History Interview [1999–2000], 27–28. **Topic: World War II**

36. Hafen, *Disciple's Life,* 97.

37. Maxwell, Oral History Interview [1999–2000], 28; "Servicemen's Book Ready," *Deseret News,* Apr. 17, 1943, Church section, 1–2; *Principles of the Gospel,* ii. Quotation edited for clarity; "We pray that He will give" in original changed to "We pray that the Lord will give."

38. Maxwell, Oral History Interview [1976–77], 112–13, 115; Maxwell, Personal History, box 1, folder 2, 6; folder 3, 9; Hafen, *Disciple's Life,* 89–91.

39. Allison, *Destructive Sublime,* 61–94; Neal A. Maxwell to Clarence Maxwell and Emma Ash Maxwell, Sept. 18, 1944; Nov. 2, 1944, Neal A. Maxwell World War II Correspondence, CHL.

40. Maxwell, Personal History, box 1, folder 3, 9; Maxwell, Oral History Interview [1976–77], 116; Maxwell, Oral History Interview [1999–2000], 28–29; Neal A. Maxwell to Clarence Maxwell and Emma Ash Maxwell, Sept. 18, 1944, Neal A. Maxwell World War II Correspondence, CHL.

41. Maxwell, Oral History Interview [1976–77], 116; Hafen, *Disciple's Life,* 98.

CHAPTER 30: SUCH GRIEF

1. See Kershaw, *The End,* 129–34, 155–61, 167–82; and Weinberg, *World at Arms,* 765–71.

2. Minert, *In Harm's Way,* 17, 20–21, 25, 27–33; Meyer and Galli, *Under a Leafless Tree,* 107, 110; Meyer, Interview [2016], 16.

3. Meyer, Interview [2016], 8–13; Meyer and Galli, *Under a Leafless Tree,* 108; Kershaw, *The End,* 172–76; Minert, *In Harm's Way,* 328.

4. Mawdsley, *World War II,* 403; Weinberg, *World at Arms,* 819–24; Meyer and Galli, *Under a Leafless Tree,* 105, 110–12; Meyer, Interview [2016], 15; Matthew 18:20.

5. Minert, *In Harm's Way,* 44–45, 52; Meyer, Interview [2016], 4, 15–17; Meyer and Galli, *Under a Leafless Tree,* 112, 187–88.

6. Meyer and Galli, *Under a Leafless Tree,* 188–91; Birth, Mission Journal, Apr. 21, 1945; Minert, *In Harm's Way,* 70; Large, *Berlin,* 374–76; Moorhouse, *Berlin at War,* 375–79; see also Naimark, *Russians in Germany,* 10–17, 20–21, 78–85, 92–93, 100–101. **Topic: Fasting**

7. Meyer and Galli, *Under a Leafless Tree,* 191; Weinberg, *World at Arms,* 825; Overy, *Third Reich,* 359–65; Antill, *Berlin 1945,* 80–81; Large, *Berlin,* 364.

8. Meyer and Galli, *Under a Leafless Tree,* 108, 117–18, 191. Part of quotation edited for readability; original source has "I didn't have any particular feelings in my heart. We had imagined something quite different in connection with the word peace—like joy and celebration, but nothing of the kind was evident."

9. Meyer and Galli, *Under a Leafless Tree,* 114, 194–95; Doctrine and Covenants 78:19.
10. Overy, *Third Reich,* 365; Maxwell, Personal History, box 1, folder 3, 10. Quotation edited for readability; original source has "this was real war." **Topic: World War II**
11. Spector, *Eagle against the Sun,* 532–40; Costello, *Pacific War,* 554–61; Hafen, *Disciple's Life,* 103–5.
12. Maxwell, Personal History, box 1, folder 3, 10; Hafen, *Disciple's Life,* 102, 105.
13. Maxwell, Personal History, box 1, folder 3, 10–11; Maxwell, Oral History Interview [1976–77], 117; Hafen, *Disciple's Life,* 106–7.
14. Maxwell, Oral History Interview [1976–77], 117; Maxwell, Personal History, box 1, folder 3, 11–12; Hafen, *Disciple's Life,* 107–9, 112; Freeman and Wright, *Saints at War,* 358.
15. Hafen, *Disciple's Life,* 109–10; Maxwell, Personal History, box 1, folder 3, 10, 12; Maxwell, Dictation, 3. **Topic: Patriarchal Blessings**
16. Hafen, *Disciple's Life,* 112; Neal A. Maxwell to Clarence Maxwell and Emma Ash Maxwell, June 1, [1945], Neal A. Maxwell World War II Correspondence, CHL.
17. Wachsmann, *Nazi Concentration Camps,* 595–97; Bischof and Stelzl-Marx, "Lives behind Barbed Wire," 330–31, 338–39; Vlam, *Our Lives,* 107, 109.
18. Vlam, *Our Lives,* 105, 108; Vlam, "Life History of Grace Alida Hermine Vlam," 9, 11; Gordon B. Hinckley, "War Prisoner Teaches Truth to Officers," *Deseret News,* Mar. 30, 1949, Church section, 14.
19. Vlam, *Our Lives,* 107.
20. Maxwell, Personal History, box 1, folder 3, 13; Spector, *Eagle against the Sun,* 540; Mawdsley, *World War II,* 412; Weinberg, *World at Arms,* 882. **Topic: Philippines**
21. Hafen, *Disciple's Life,* 114.
22. Maxwell, Oral History Interview [1999–2000], 31; Maxwell, Personal History, box 1, folder 3, 13. **Topic: Servicemember Branches**
23. See Heber J. Grant to Francesca Hawes, Dec. 6, 1944, Letterpress Copybook, volume 83, 271, Heber J. Grant Collection, CHL; Heber J. Grant to M. J. Abbey, Jan. 22, 1945, First Presidency General Correspondence Files, CHL; Clark, Diary, Feb. 4 and 25, 1945; Mar. 11, 1945; Heber J. Grant, in *One Hundred Eleventh Semi-annual Conference,* 95–97, 130–34; *One Hundred Twelfth Annual Conference,* 2–11, 97; *One Hundred Fourteenth Annual Conference,* 3–12; and *One Hundred Fifteenth Annual Conference,* 4–10.
24. Death Certificate for Heber J. Grant, May 14, 1945, Utah Department of Health, Office of Vital Records and Statistics, Utah State Archives and Records Service, Salt Lake City. **Topics: Heber J. Grant; George Albert Smith**
25. Costello, *Pacific War,* 589–93; Spector, *Eagle against the Sun,* 554–56; Maxwell, Oral History Interview [1999–2000], 30–31; Hafen, *Disciple's Life,* 118.
26. Spector, *Eagle against the Sun,* 559–60; Hafen, *Disciple's Life,* 117–18. Quotation edited for readability; "hung" in original changed to "hangs." **Topic: World War II**
27. J. Reuben Clark Jr., Heber J. Grant, in *One Hundred Fifteenth Annual Conference,* 3–4, 6–7.

CHAPTER 31: THE RIGHT TRACK

1. George Albert Smith, in *One Hundred Sixteenth Semi-annual Conference,* 169–70; "Pres. Smith Gives Keynote to Sessions," *Deseret News,* Sept. 29, 1945, Church section, [1]. **Topic: George Albert Smith**
2. Bryant S. Hinckley, "Greatness in Men," *Improvement Era,* Mar. 1932, 35:269–72, 295–96; Whitney, *Through Memory's Halls,* 309; Preston Nibley, "President George Albert Smith," *Relief Society Magazine,* July 1945, 32:390–91.

3. First Presidency to Marion G. Romney, July 12, 1945, First Presidency Letterpress Copybooks, volume 131; George Albert Smith, Journal, Oct. 18, 1945; Widtsoe, Diary, Oct. 18, 1945; Gibbons, *George Albert Smith,* 296.

4. "Pres. Smith in East on Mission of Mercy," *Deseret News,* Nov. 10, 1945, Church section, [1].

5. George Albert Smith, Journal, Nov. 2–7, 1945; Widtsoe, Diary, Nov. 2–7, 1945; George Albert Smith, in *One Hundred Eighteenth Semi-annual Conference,* 5–6; Gibbons, *George Albert Smith,* 298.

6. Gibbons, *George Albert Smith,* 298; George Albert Smith, in *One Hundred Eighteenth Semi-annual Conference,* 6.

7. George Albert Smith, in *One Hundred Eighteenth Semi-annual Conference,* 6; "Pres. Smith Returns from Successful Trip to Capital," *Deseret News,* Nov. 17, 1945, Church section, [1], 7; "Trademarks of Elder Anderson," *Deseret News,* Apr. 25, 1970, Church section, 3; Anderson, *Prophets I Have Known,* 103.

8. George Albert Smith, Journal, Nov. 2 and 3, 1945; George Albert Smith, in *One Hundred Eighteenth Semi-annual Conference,* 6.

9. Meyer and Galli, *Under a Leafless Tree,* 108, 113, 117, 118, 123, 139; Minert, *In Harm's Way,* 523–25; Minert, *Under the Gun,* 495, 503–4; Scharffs, *Mormonism in Germany,* 117; Minert, "Succession in German Mission Leadership," 556, 558–61; Paul Langheinrich, Statement, Feb. 21, 1971, in Germany Hamburg Mission, Manuscript History and Historical Reports, volume 1, Feb. 20, 1943; Slaveski, *Soviet Occupation of Germany,* 151; Gross, *Myth and Reality of German Warfare,* 19–20. **Topic: Germany**

10. Meyer and Galli, *Under a Leafless Tree,* 101–3, 123.

11. Meyer and Galli, *Under a Leafless Tree,* 113, 115–16, 117; Paul Langheinrich, Statement, Feb. 21, 1971, in Germany Hamburg Mission, Manuscript History and Historical Reports, volume 1, Feb. 20, 1943.

12. Birth, Mission Journal, Jan. 14 and 21, 1946; Meyer and Galli, *Under a Leafless Tree,* 118; Kuehne, *Mormons as Citizens of a Communist State,* 365.

13. Ranglack, Langheinrich, and Neuman, "First Trip thru the Mission," 1–3; Ranglack, Langheinrich, and Neuman, "Second Trip thru the Mission," 1–4; "Report on the East German Mission as of 10 August 1945," 1–4; Kuehne, *Mormons as Citizens of a Communist State,* 360–66; Birth, Mission Journal, Jan. 22, 1946.

14. Meyer and Galli, *Under a Leafless Tree,* 120; Birth, Mission Journal, Jan. 26, 1946; Kuehne, *Mormons as Citizens of a Communist State,* 365.

15. Maxwell, Personal History, box 1, folder 3, 14; Takagi, *Trek East,* 292; Clapson, *Blitz Companion,* 97–118; Maxwell, Oral History Interview [1999–2000], 32.

16. Maxwell, Personal History, box 1, folder 3, 14; Maxwell, Oral History Interview [1999–2000], 32–34.

17. Neal A. Maxwell to Clarence Maxwell and Emma Ash Maxwell, May 2, 1946, Neal A. Maxwell World War II Correspondence, CHL.

18. Maxwell, Oral History Interview [1999–2000], 33–34; Neal A. Maxwell to "Dearest Family," Mar. 27, 1946, Neal A. Maxwell World War II Correspondence, CHL.

19. Takagi, *Trek East,* 294–95; Boone, "Roles of The Church of Jesus Christ of Latter-day Saints in Relation to the United States Military," 655–65; "Reunions Slated during Conference," *Deseret News,* Oct. 2, 1946, 12; "Okinawa Gathering in Castle," *Deseret News,* July 21, 1945, Church section, 1; William Mulder, "Okinawa Conference," *Improvement Era,* Dec. 1945, 48:734, 769; "Servicemen Report Okinawa Activities," *Deseret News,* Feb. 16, 1946, Church section, 9; Maxwell, Oral History Interview [1999–2000], 32; Ricks, "Chaplain's Diary," 461–65.

20. Takagi, *Trek East,* 293; Britsch, *From the East,* 82–85; Allred, "Missionary Role of LDS Servicemen in Occupied Japan," 63–65; Maxwell, Oral History Interview [1999–2000], 31–32. **Topics: Japan; Servicemember Branches**

21. Maxwell, Oral History Interview [1999–2000], 31, 35; Maxwell, Personal History, box 1, folder 3, 12–13; Hafen, *Disciple's Life,* 125.

22. Neal A. Maxwell to "Dearest Ones," Oct. 31, 1945, Neal A. Maxwell World War II Correspondence, CHL.

23. Slaveski, *Soviet Occupation of Germany,* xii, 37; [Paul Langheinrich] to Georgy K. Zhukov, Aug. 9, 1945, copy, in Germany Hamburg Mission, Manuscript History and Historical Reports, volume 1, Aug. 9, 1945; "Report on the East German Mission as of 10 August 1945," 1; Kuehne, *Mormons as Citizens of a Communist State,* 384; Allen, Embry, and Mehr, *Hearts Turned to the Fathers,* 225; Paul Langheinrich, "Yesterday and Today," *Improvement Era,* Sept. 1946, 49:569.

24. Vasily D. Sokolovsky to Richard Ranglack, Aug. 16, 1945, in Germany Hamburg Mission, Manuscript History and Historical Reports, volume 1, Aug. 16, 1945.

25. Paul Langheinrich, "Report of Procurement of Church Records, Films and Photocopies," Germany Hamburg Mission, Manuscript History and Historical Reports, volume 1, Aug. 16, 1945; Kahlile Mehr, "Langheinrich Legacy," *Ensign,* June 1981, 23–24; Allen, Embry, and Mehr, *Hearts Turned to the Fathers,* 226; Kuehne, *Mormons as Citizens of a Communist State,* 386.

26. Paul Langheinrich, "Report of Procurement of Church Records, Films and Photocopies," Germany Hamburg Mission, Manuscript History and Historical Reports, volume 1, Aug. 16, 1945; Corbett, "Records from the Ruins," 12–13.

27. Allen, Embry, and Mehr, *Hearts Turned to the Fathers,* 226–27.

28. Paul Langheinrich, "Report of Procurement of Church Records, Films and Photocopies," Germany Hamburg Mission, Manuscript History and Historical Reports, volume 1, Aug. 16, 1945; Allen, Embry, and Mehr, *Hearts Turned to the Fathers,* 226.

29. Paul Langheinrich, "Report of Procurement of Church Records, Films and Photocopies," Germany Hamburg Mission, Manuscript History and Historical Reports, volume 1, Aug. 16, 1945; Kuehne, *Mormons as Citizens of a Communist State,* 385–87; Kahlile Mehr, "Langheinrich Legacy," *Ensign,* June 1981, 23.

30. Corbett, "Records from the Ruins," 16; Paul Langheinrich, "Report of Procurement of Church Records, Films and Photocopies," Germany Hamburg Mission, Manuscript History and Historical Reports, volume 1, Aug. 16, 1945. **Topic: Family History and Genealogy**

31. George Albert Smith, Journal, May 22, 1946; Pierce, "Story of the Third Convention," 4–5; Pérez de Lara, "Temple of the Sun," 36–41; "An American Pyramid," *Brooklyn (NY) Daily Eagle,* Aug. 25, 1935, B11.

32. Pierce, "Story of the Third Convention," 5; Carmen Richardson, "1,200 Mexican Members Return to Church during Pres. Smith's Visit," *Deseret News,* June 15, 1946, Church section, [1]; "The Life and Ministry of George Albert Smith," in *Teachings of Presidents of the Church: George Albert Smith,* xxxiii–xxxiv; Tullis, *Mormons in Mexico,* 139, 145, 150–51, 157. **Topic: Third Convention**

33. Pierce, "Story of the Third Convention," [1]; Arwell L. Pierce, Blessing, Aug. 13, 1942, First Presidency Mission Files, CHL.

34. Pulido, "Solving Schism in *Nepantla,"* 92, 95–96; Tullis, *Mormons in Mexico,* 148, 150–52; Arwell L. Pierce to First Presidency, Nov. 9, 1942, First Presidency Mission Files, CHL.

35. Arwell L. Pierce to First Presidency, Mar. 8, 1943–A; Mar. 8, 1943–B; Apr. 9, 1945; Oct. 10, 1945; First Presidency to Arwell L. Pierce, Apr. 19, 1943–A; Apr. 19, 1943–B; Nov. 29, 1943, First Presidency Mission Files, CHL; Pulido, "Solving Schism in *Nepantla,"* 97; Mexican Mission Manuscript History, Mar. 31, 1943.

36. Pulido, "Solving Schism in *Nepantla,"* 96–97.

37. Arwell L. Pierce to First Presidency, Apr. 10, 1946; First Presidency to Abel Páez, May 9, 1946, First Presidency Mission Files, CHL; Tullis, "Shepherd to Mexico's Saints," 139–46.

38. George Albert Smith, Journal, May 21 and 22, 1946; Pierce, "Story of the Third Convention," 5; Lozano Herrera, *Historia del Mormonismo en Mexico,* 80–81.

39. Arwell L. Pierce to J. Reuben Clark and David O. McKay, June 6, 1946, First Presidency Mission Files, CHL; Bravo, Oral History Interview, 28; George Albert Smith, Journal, May 25, 1946; Carmen Richardson, "1,200 Mexican Members Return to Church during Pres. Smith's Visit," *Deseret News,* June 15, 1946, Church section, [1].

40. Arwell L. Pierce to J. Reuben Clark and David O. McKay, June 6, 1946, First Presidency Mission Files, CHL.

CHAPTER 32: BROTHERS AND SISTERS

1. Ezra Taft Benson, "European Mission Report #19," Aug. 7, 1946, 1, 3, First Presidency Mission Files, CHL; Benson, Journal, Aug. 1 and 4, 1946; Babbel, Oral History Interview, 6; "Elder Benson Reports First Visit to Poland," *Deseret News,* Aug. 17, 1946, Church section, 1, 8, 12; Minert, *In Harm's Way,* 310; "Selbongen during World War II," Global Histories, ChurchofJesusChrist.org/study/history/global-histories.
2. Ezra Taft Benson, "Report on the European Mission #1," Jan. 26–Feb. 11, 1946, 1–2, First Presidency Mission Files, CHL; "Elder Benson Prepares to Preside in European Mission," *Deseret News,* Jan. 19, 1946, Church section, [1]; Dew, *Ezra Taft Benson,* 198.
3. Ezra Taft Benson, "Report on the European Mission #7," Mar. 24, 1946, 1–3, First Presidency Mission Files, CHL; Bergera, "Ezra Taft Benson's 1946 Mission," 82, table 2.
4. Ezra Taft Benson to First Presidency, Mar. 23, 1946, First Presidency Mission Files, CHL; Corbett, "Records from the Ruins," 13–16; Ezra Taft Benson, "Report on the European Mission #5," Mar. 20, 1946, 1–3, First Presidency Mission Files, CHL; Genealogical Society of Utah Board of Trustees, Minutes, Apr. 15, 1947; Kuehne, *Mormons as Citizens of a Communist State,* 14–16, 33.
5. Relief Society General Board, Minutes, Dec. 12, 1945; Relief Society General Presidency to Ward Presidents, Nov. 21, 1945, in First Presidency and Welfare Committee Minutes, CHL; First Presidency and Welfare Committee, Minutes, Nov. 16, 1945; Dec. 14 and 21, 1945; Jan. 11 and 31, 1946. **Topic: Welfare Programs**
6. "Continued War Services," *Relief Society Magazine,* Aug. 1945, 32:484; see also "Church Welfare Service," *Relief Society Magazine,* Sept. 1946, 33:620. **Topic: Relief Society**
7. European Mission History, Oct. 22, 1946, 83; Ezra Taft Benson to First Presidency, Mar. 16, 1946, 1–2; Ezra Taft Benson, "European Mission Report #19," Aug. 7, 1946, 2–5, First Presidency Mission Files, CHL; Minert, *In Harm's Way,* 314–16.
8. Babbel, *On Wings of Faith,* 131–34; Benson, Journal, July 29 and 30, 1946; Aug. 1 and 4, 1946; see also Frederick Babbel, "'And None Shall Stay Them,'" *Instructor,* Aug. 1969, 104:268–69. **Topic: Poland**
9. Ezra Taft Benson, "European Mission Report #19," Aug. 7, 1946, 1, First Presidency Mission Files, CHL; Benson, Journal, Aug. 4, 1946; Babbel, *On Wings of Faith,* 149; Ezra Taft Benson, "European Mission Report #19," Aug. 7, 1946, 1, First Presidency Mission Files, CHL; "Selbongen during World War II," Global Histories, ChurchofJesusChrist.org/study/history/global-histories.
10. Benson, Journal, Aug. 4, 1946; Ezra Taft Benson, "European Mission Report #19," Aug. 7, 1946, 1–2, First Presidency Mission Files, CHL; Minert, *In Harm's Way,* 314–16.
11. Benson, Journal, Aug. 4, 1946; Ezra Taft Benson, "European Mission Report #19," Aug. 7, 1946, 1, First Presidency Mission Files, CHL; Ezra Taft Benson to First Presidency, Aug. 7, 1946, 2, Ezra Taft Benson Correspondence Files, CHL; Selbongen Branch, General Minutes, Aug. 4, 1896.
12. Ezra Taft Benson, "European Mission Report #20," Aug. 24, 1946, 2, First Presidency Mission Files, CHL; see also "Red Cross to Cooperate in Distribution of Supplies," *Deseret News,* Sept. 7, 1946, Church section, 1, 9.
13. Collette, *Collette Family History,* 232, 235, 245, 250; Babbel, *On Wings of Faith,* 71.
14. Minert, *Under the Gun,* 456, 467–70, 473; Hatch, *Cziep Family History,* 87, 98, 202, 303–5; Collette, *Collette Family History,* 202–26; Lewis, *Workers and Politics in Occupied Austria,* chapter 3; Taggart, "Notes on the Life of Scott Taggart," 31–32. **Topic: Austria**
15. Collette, *Collette Family History,* 256–57.

16. Marion G. Romney to First Presidency, Oct. 24, 1946, First Presidency General Administration Files, CHL; Annual Church Welfare Plan, 1946, 259, Welfare Department Northern Utah Region Documents, CHL; European Mission, Historical Reports, 92; Collette, *Collette Family History,* 257–58.
17. "President Benson Dedicates Finland for Preaching Gospel," *Deseret News,* Aug. 10, 1946, Church section, 1, 9, 12; "Letter Tells of Activity and Progress in Finland," *Deseret News,* Mar. 8, 1947, Church section, 6; "Wartime Swedish Mission Head Sees Bright Future in Finland," *Deseret News,* July 5, 1947, Church section, 1; Eben Blomquist to First Presidency, Jan. 30, 1947, First Presidency Mission Files, CHL. **Topics: Finland; Sweden**
18. Collette, *Collette Family History,* 258–61, 320; Taggart, Oral History Interview, 61, 63, 73; appendix, 25–26; "20 Austrian Children Sent to Swiss Saints," *Deseret News,* May 17, 1947, Church section, 9; see also Switzerland Zurich Mission, Manuscript History and Historical Reports, volume 12, May 17, 1947.
19. Collette, *Collette Family History,* 320, 322; Taggart, Journal, Apr. 3, 9, and 11, 1947. Quotations edited for readability; "the Lord needed me" in original changed to "the Lord needs you," and "if the Lord wanted me to stay, I would" changed to "if the Lord wants me to stay, I will." **Topic: Switzerland**
20. Meyer and Galli, *Under a Leafless Tree,* 127–30, 135.
21. Meyer and Galli, *Under a Leafless Tree,* 127, 130, 142; Meyer, Interview [2017], 2.
22. Meyer and Galli, *Under a Leafless Tree,* 129, 135–38; Meyer, Interview [2017], 2.
23. Meyer and Galli, *Under a Leafless Tree,* 132.
24. Meyer and Galli, *Under a Leafless Tree,* 132–34; Meyer, Interview [2017], 1. **Topic: Word of Wisdom (D&C 89)**
25. Hatch, *Cziep Family History,* 104–5; "Austrian Saints Hold Centennial Fete," *Deseret News,* Sept. 20, 1947, Church section, 9; Minert, *Against the Wall,* ix–xiv, 42, 187.
26. Hatch, *Cziep Family History,* 104; "Austrian Saints Hold Centennial Fete," *Deseret News,* Sept. 20, 1947, Church section, 9; "Come, Come, Ye Saints," *Hymns,* no. 30. **Topics: Pioneer Trek; Austria**
27. Vlam, *Our Lives,* 117–19, 121, 123; De Wolff and Driehuis, "Description of Post War Economic Developments," 13; Ruurd Hut entry, Amsterdam Branch, no. 240, in Netherlands (Country), part 2, Record of Members Collection, CHL.
28. De Wolff and Driehuis, "Description of Post War Economic Developments," 13; William G. Hartley, "War and Peace and Dutch Potatoes," *Ensign,* July 1978, 19; Vlam, Interview [2013], 5, 7; *That We Might Be One: The Story of the Dutch Potato Project,* Video, [00:00:16]–[00:01:09]; Minutes of the European Mission Presidents' Meeting, July 5, 1950, 6, John A. Widtsoe Papers, CHL. **Topic: Netherlands**
29. William G. Hartley, "War and Peace and Dutch Potatoes," *Ensign,* July 1978, 19–20; European Mission, Historical Reports, 169; Vlam, Interview [June 2020], [00:01:12]–[00:02:48].
30. Vlam, *Our Lives,* 121; Stam, Oral History Interview, 27; William G. Hartley, "War and Peace and Dutch Potatoes," *Ensign,* July 1978, 20; "Dutch Mission Head Tells Story," *Deseret News,* Dec. 6, 1947, Church section, 1.
31. William G. Hartley, "War and Peace and Dutch Potatoes," *Ensign,* July 1978, 20–21; Babbel, *On Wings of Faith,* 76; Vlam, *Our Lives,* 121; Vlam, Interview [2013], 5–6, 8; Allart, Autobiography, 19.
32. Vlam, Interview [2013], 6, 8, 11; "Dutch Mission Leader Tells of Welfare Potatoes," *Deseret News,* Dec. 6, 1947, Church section, 6–7; Vlam, *Our Lives,* 121; Allart, Autobiography, 19; Stam, Oral History Interview, 32; Minutes of the European Mission Presidents' Meeting, July 5, 1950, 6, John A. Widtsoe Papers, CHL.
33. William G. Hartley, "War and Peace and Dutch Potatoes," *Ensign,* July 1978, 21; "Dutch Mission Leader Tells of Welfare Potatoes," *Deseret News,* Dec. 6, 1947, Church section, 6–7; European Mission, Historical Reports, 169; Netherlands Amsterdam Mission, Manuscript History and Historical Reports, Nov. 6, 1947; Stover, Oral History Interview [1975], 1–2; Stover, Oral History Interview [1976], 56. Quotation edited for

readability; original source has "these potatoes belonged to the Lord, and if it be His will, the Lord would see that they came to Germany."

34. "Dutch Mission Head Tells Story," *Deseret News,* Dec. 6, 1947, Church section, 1.

CHAPTER 33: OUR FATHER'S HAND

1. Anderson, *Cherry Tree behind the Iron Curtain,* 1, 43–50; Mehr, "Czechoslovakia and the LDS Church," 140–41; Heimann, *Czechoslovakia,* 171–75; Woodger, *Mission President or Spy,* 158, 161, 175–77; Dunbabin, *Cold War,* 142–59; "Historical Report of the Czechoslovak Mission," June 30, 1949, 13–14, Czechoslovak Mission, Manuscript History and Historical Reports, CHL.
2. Anderson, *Cherry Tree behind the Iron Curtain,* 13, 15; Mehr, "Czechoslovakia and the LDS Church," 116, 132, 134–37; "Historical Report of the Czechoslovak Mission," Dec. 31, 1939, 8–12, Czechoslovak Mission, Manuscript History and Historical Reports, CHL.
3. Mehr, "Czechoslovakia and the LDS Church," 137–39; Hoyt Palmer, "Salt of the Earth," *Deseret News,* Feb. 14, 1951, Church section, 7, 13; Wallace F. Toronto to Josef Roubíček, Sept. 21, 1939; Josef Roubíček to Wallace F. Toronto, May 1, 1940; Sept. 10, 1941, Josef and Martha Roubíček Papers, CHL; Josef Roubíček to Wallace F. Toronto, May 29, 1945; Aug. 23, 1945; Oct. 10, 1945, Czechoslovak Mission President's Records, CHL.
4. First Presidency to Wallace F. Toronto, May 24, 1945, First Presidency Mission Files, CHL; Anderson, *Cherry Tree behind the Iron Curtain,* 38; Wallace Felt Toronto, Blessing, May 24, 1946, First Presidency Mission Files, CHL; Woodger, *Mission President or Spy,* 131; Martha Toronto to Wallace Toronto, Nov. 10, 1946; Dec. 1, 1946, Martha S. Anderson Letters to Wallace F. Toronto, CHL.
5. Anderson, *Cherry Tree behind the Iron Curtain,* 47–48; Woodger, *Mission President or Spy,* 167; Martha Sharp Toronto, Blessing, May 16, 1947, First Presidency Mission Files, CHL.
6. O'Donnal, "Personal History," 4–31, 43–48, 70–71; O'Donnal, *Pioneer in Guatemala,* 2–26, 60. **Topic: Colonies in Mexico**
7. O'Donnal, "Personal History," 49–53, 71; O'Donnal and O'Donnal, Oral History Interview, 8–13, 19.
8. O'Donnal, "Personal History," 53, 71; O'Donnal, *Pioneer in Guatemala,* 33–34; O'Donnal and O'Donnal, Oral History Interview, 11–13, 16, 19.
9. O'Donnal, "Personal History," 66–68; O'Donnal, *Pioneer in Guatemala,* 55–57; Williams and Williams, *From Acorn to Oak Tree,* 201–3; Frederick S. Williams to First Presidency, Sept. 30, 1946, First Presidency Mission Files, CHL; J. Forres O'Donnal to George Albert Smith, Dec. 31, 1946; First Presidency to J. Forres O'Donnal, Jan. 13, 1947, First Presidency General Authorities Correspondence, CHL. **Topic: Guatemala**
10. O'Donnal, "Personal History," 69–71; O'Donnal, *Pioneer in Guatemala,* 58–60; O'Donnal and O'Donnal, Oral History Interview, 12–13, 17–19; Hansen, Journal, Apr. 3–4, 1948.
11. Collette, *Collette Family History,* 261–67, 320, 324–25, 328–29.
12. Collette, *Collette Family History,* 351; see also Proverbs 3:5.
13. Collette, *Collette Family History,* 351; Olsen, Plewe, and Jarvis, "Historical Geography," 107; "Varied Church Activity during 1946," *Deseret News,* Jan. 11, 1947, Church section, 6; Bader, *Austria between East and West,* 184–95.
14. Collette, *Collette Family History,* 351–55. Quotation edited for readability; original source has "wherever I was going I was never alone—that there was my Heavenly Father to watch over me."
15. Collette, *Collette Family History,* 359. Quotation edited for readability; original source has "I told them both that they just hadn't been around girls for two years and as soon as they get home they'll find a real nice one and settle down."
16. Gellately and Stoltzfus, "Social Outsiders," 3–19; Hilberg, *Destruction of the European Jews,* 993, 1000, 1030–44; Gilbert, *Holocaust,* 824; Gigliotti and Lang, "Introduction," 1; Fates of Olga and Egon Weiss, 1–5. **Topic: World War II**

17. Collette, *Collette Family History,* 359, 363–64. Quotation edited for readability; "was" in original changed to "am." **Topics: Emigration; Canada**
18. O'Donnal, "Personal History," 71; O'Donnal and O'Donnal, Oral History Interview, 12–13; Hansen, Reminiscence, [2].
19. Guatemala Branch Manuscript History, July 2–Aug. 22, 1948; O'Donnal, "Personal History," 70–71; Arwell L. Pierce to First Presidency, Aug. 4, 1948, First Presidency Mission Files, CHL; Lingard, Journal, July 9–Aug. 25, 1948; Hansen, Journal, July 9–Aug. 22, 1948.
20. O'Donnal, "Personal History," 71; O'Donnal and O'Donnal, Oral History Interview, 12–13; Photographs of Carmen G. O'Donnal baptismal service, Nov. 13, 1948, John F. and Carmen G. O'Donnal Papers, CHL; Huber, Oral History Interview, [00:04:20]–[00:05:15].
21. Jensen, "Faces: A Personal History," 69–71; O'Donnal, "Personal History," 72; O'Donnal and O'Donnal, Oral History Interview, 30; Guatemala Branch Relief Society, Minutes, Dec. 2, 1948–Feb. 24, 1949; Antoni[a] Morales and Alicia de Cáceres entries, Baptisms and Confirmations, 1949, Guatemala, Combined Mission Report, Mexican Mission, 474, in Guatemala (Country), part 1, Record of Members Collection, CHL; Bean, Mission Journal, Nov. 20, 1948; Dec. 2, 1948; Feb. 24, 1949. **Topic: Guatemala**
22. George Albert Smith, Journal, Jan. 17–21, 1949; Mar. 9 and 19, 1949; Cowan, *Los Angeles Temple,* 29–36; Gibbons, *George Albert Smith,* 346. **Topic: George Albert Smith**
23. George Albert Smith, Journal, Feb. 7–8, 1949; Mar. 5–11 and 19–21, 1949; Apr. 3, 1949.
24. George Albert Smith, Journal, Jan. 29, 1949.
25. Woodger, "Cheat the Asylum," 115–19; Gibbons, *George Albert Smith,* 11, 30, 60–69, 77.
26. Gibbons, *George Albert Smith,* 68–74; Woodger, "Cheat the Asylum," 144–46.
27. James R. Kennard, "Book of Mormon Now Available for Blind," *Deseret News,* Mar. 30, 1936, 1; Edwin Ross Thurston, "Salt Lake Valley Branch for the Deaf," *Improvement Era,* Apr. 1949, 52:215, 244; Pusey, *Builders of the Kingdom,* 324; Anderson, *Prophets I Have Known,* 109–11; Jean Wunderlich to First Presidency, Dec. 15, 1947; First Presidency to Jean Wunderlich, Jan. 24, 1948, First Presidency General Administration Files, 1908, 1915–49, CHL. **Topics: Helmuth Hübener; American Indians**
28. Woodger, "Cheat the Asylum," 124–25.
29. Schaffner, *Exhaustion,* 91, 106–7; Gibbons, *George Albert Smith,* 54–55, 60–61, 78; Woodger, "Cheat the Asylum," 117–19, 125–28.
30. George Albert Smith, Journal, Mar. 20–30, 1949; George Albert Smith, in *One Hundred Nineteenth Annual Conference,* 87.
31. "Historical Report of the Czechoslovak Mission," June 30, 1949, 6, Czechoslovak Mission, Manuscript History and Historical Reports, CHL; Mehr, "Czechoslovakia and the LDS Church," 140.
32. "Historical Report of the Czechoslovak Mission," June 30, 1949, 2, 6, Czechoslovak Mission, Manuscript History and Historical Reports, CHL; Mehr, "Czechoslovakia and the LDS Church," 141; Anderson, *Cherry Tree behind the Iron Curtain,* 49–50. Quotation edited for readability; "were" in original changed to "are."
33. "Historical Report of the Czechoslovak Mission," June 30, 1949, 2–3, 6–7, Czechoslovak Mission, Manuscript History and Historical Reports, CHL.
34. Historical Report of the Czechoslovak Mission, June 30, 1949, 7, 13–14, Czechoslovak Mission, Manuscript History and Historical Reports, CHL.

CHAPTER 34: GO AND SEE

1. Collette, *Collette Family History,* 366, 370, emphasis in original; "1948 Sees First Welfare Supplies Headed for Czechoslovakia," *Deseret News,* Jan. 31, 1948, 10.
2. Collette, *Collette Family History,* 305, 340–41, 373; Scott A. Taggart, "Conference Held in Swiss Mission," *Deseret News,* Sept. 13, 1947, Church section, 9.

3. Collette, *Collette Family History,* 373–77.
4. Emmy Cziep Collette to Glenn Collette, June 29, 1949, in Collette, *Collette Family History,* 391–92; Collette, *Collette Family History,* 342, 364, 385.
5. Alberta Temple, Sealings of Living Couples, 1923–56, May 24, 1949, microfilm 170,738, U.S. and Canada Record Collection, FHL; Collette, *Collette Family History,* 388, 390; Emmy Cziep Collette to Glenn Collette, June 29, 1949, in Collette, *Collette Family History,* 391–92.
6. Yanagida, Oral History Interview [1996], 1, 8.
7. Yanagida, Oral History Interview [1996], 2–7; Yanagida, Oral History Interview [2001], 1; Yanagida, "Ashiato," 2; Yanagida, "Takagi and Nikichi Takahashi, Two of the Very Early Baptisms," 22; Takagi, *Trek East,* 152; Britsch, "Closing of the Early Japan Mission," 263–83.
8. Yanagida, Oral History Interview [1996], 8.
9. Yanagida, Oral History Interview [1996], 7–8; Yanagida, Oral History Interview [2001], 3; General Church Welfare Committee, Minutes, Sept. 20, 1946; Dec. 18 and 20, 1946; Oct. 10, 1947; Takagi, *Trek East,* 315–17; Britsch, *From the East,* 82–85. **Topic: Japan**
10. Yanagida, Oral History Interview [1996], 7–8; Yanagida, Oral History Interview [2001], 4; Price, Mission Journal, Apr. 24, 1949; Yanagida, "Ashiato," 7; Yanagida, "Relief Society President Experiences."
11. Price, Mission Journal, Apr. 24, 1949; Yanagida, Oral History Interview [1996], 8–9; Yanagida, Oral History Interview [2001], 3–5; Yanagida, "Banzai," 188.
12. Reynolds, "Coming Forth of the Book of Mormon," 10, 18–19, 26; Primary Association General Board, Minutes, Mar. 31, 1949; Parmley, Oral History Interview, 46; Marion G. Romney, Remarks at Adele Cannon Howells funeral, Apr. 17, 1951, Primary Association General Board, Minutes, CHL; Peterson and Gaunt, *Children's Friends,* 63, 71; Adele Cannon Howells to Velma Hill, undated; Spencer W. Kimball to Adele Cannon Howells, Counselors, and Primary Association, Aug. 18, 1949, Primary Association General Records, CHL. **Topic: Primary**
13. Spencer W. Kimball to Adele Cannon Howells, Counselors, and Primary Association, Aug. 18, 1949, Primary Association General Records, CHL. Quotation edited for readability; "was" in original changed to "is."
14. Peterson and Gaunt, *Children's Friends,* 69; Madsen and Oman, *Sisters and Little Saints,* 119–20; "2 Conference Broadcasts Will Be Open," *Deseret News,* Mar. 31, 1948, [1]. **Topics: Broadcast Media; Church Periodicals**
15. Howells, Diary, June 10, 1947; Minutes of the Board of Trustees of the Primary Children's Hospital Meeting with the First Presidency, Jan. 17, 1948; Adele Cannon Howells and others to First Presidency, Jan. 12, 1949, First Presidency Mission Files, CHL; Mandleco and Miller, "History of Children's Hospitals in Utah," 340–41; George Albert Smith, Journal, Apr. 1, 1949; "Primary Breaks Ground for Hospital Friday," *Deseret News,* Apr. 1, 1949, [1]; Peterson and Gaunt, *Children's Friends,* 73.
16. Howells, Diary, July 27, 1950; Sunday School General Presidency, Minutes, Jan. 24, 1950; Andersen, "Arnold Friberg," 248; Madsen and Oman, *Sisters and Little Saints,* 121.
17. Reynolds, *Story of the Book of Mormon;* Gutjahr, *The Book of Mormon: A Biography,* 153–64; George Reynolds, "Lessons from the Life of Nephi," *Juvenile Instructor,* Apr. 15–Oct. 1, 1891, 26:233–35, 282–84, 297–90, 348–51, 373–76, 406–9, 437–40, 475–77, 502–4, 536–38, 574–77, 585–87; Parshall, "John Philip Dalby"; Welch and Dant, *Book of Mormon Paintings,* 10–12, 162; Dant, "Minerva Teichert's Manti Temple Murals," 6–32.
18. Andersen, "Arnold Friberg," 248; Madsen and Oman, *Sisters and Little Saints,* 121; Barrett and Black, "Setting a Standard in LDS Art," 31–32; Swanson, "Book of Mormon Art of Arnold Friberg," 28.
19. Madsen and Oman, *Sisters and Little Saints,* 121; Howells, Diary, Mar. 10, 1950; Barrett and Black, "Setting a Standard in LDS Art," 32; A. H. Reiser and others to First Presidency, Oct. 4, 1950, Primary Association General Records, CHL.

20. Howells, Diary, July 27, 1950.
21. Yanagida, "Ashiato," 7–8; Yanagida, Oral History Interview [2001], 4; "Tatsui Sato: Translator for Life," Global Histories, ChurchofJesusChrist.org/study/history/global-histories.
22. Yanagida, "Banzai," 188; Yanagida, "Ashiato," 7–8.
23. Yanagida, "Ashiato," 8; Yanagida, "Banzai," 188; Price, Mission Journal, June 16, 1949.
24. Yanagida, "Banzai," 188; Yanagida, Oral History Interview [2001], 5; Price, Mission Journal, June 16, 1949.
25. Yanagida, Oral History Interview [1996], 5; Yanagida, Oral History Interview [2001], 9–10. Translated quotation edited for clarity; "They are different" in original changed to "These missionaries are different."
26. Yanagida, Oral History Interview [1996], 9; Yanagida, Oral History Interview [2001], 4; Japanese Mission, Manuscript History and Historical Reports, Aug. 18, 1949; Yanagida, "Banzai," 188.
27. Yanagida, Oral History Interview [1996], 9.
28. Yanagida, Oral History Interview [1996], 9; Yanagida, Oral History Interview [2001], 5; Yanagida, "Ashiato," 8–9; Yanagida, "Banzai," 189; Japanese Mission, Manuscript History and Historical Reports, Sept. 30, 1949; "Six Japanese Leave for Mission," *Deseret News,* Sept. 15, 1948, Church section, 14C. Toshiko Yanagida quotation edited for clarity; original source has "Did you see Nelson-san?"
29. Yanagida, "Banzai," 189; Yanagida, Oral History Interview [1996], 9; Yanagida, "Ashiato," 9.
30. Yanagida, Oral History Interview [2001], 5–6; Yanagida, "Memoirs of the Relief Society in Japan," 145; "Tatsui Sato: Translator for Life," Global Histories, ChurchofJesusChrist.org/study/history/global-histories. **Topic: Servicemember Branches**
31. Cincinnati Branch, Minutes, Nov. 6, 1949; Jones and Prince, Oral History Interview, [0:36:13]; Paul Bang, "My Life Story," 7; Fish, Kramer, and Wallis, *History of the Mormon Church in Cincinnati,* 65–78.
32. Cincinnati Branch, Minutes, July 10 and Sept. 4–Dec. 11, 1949; Fish, Kramer, and Wallis, *History of the Mormon Church in Cincinnati,* 68, 71–74; Fish, "My Life Story," [9]; Cannon, Interview, 1; Jones and Prince, Oral History Interview, [0:26:13].
33. Fish, Kramer, and Wallis, *History of the Mormon Church in Cincinnati,* 74, 76; Cincinnati Branch, Minutes, Feb. 2, 1947.
34. Fish, Kramer, and Wallis, *History of the Mormon Church in Cincinnati,* 76–77; Cincinnati Branch, Minutes, Oct. 9, 1949; Georgetown Branch, Minutes, May 2, 1948; Cincinnati Branch, YWMIA Minute Book, Attendance Roll, 1949–50.
35. Fish, Kramer, and Wallis, *History of the Mormon Church in Cincinnati,* 77; Georgetown Branch, Minutes, May 2, 1948; Oct. 1948–Feb. 1949; July–Dec. 1949; Cannon, Interview, 1.
36. Blackham, History, 6–7; Cannon, Interview, 3; Jones and Prince, Oral History Interview, [1:05:38]; see also, for example, Summers, Mission Journal, Nov. 7, 1937; Feb. 6, 1838; Mar. 6, 1938; and Jones, Mission Journal, July 3, 1949; Nov. 6, 1949; Apr. 9, 1950. **Topic: Racial Segregation**
37. Jones, Mission Journal, Sept. 3, 1949; Mar. 28, 1950; May 21, 1950; Blackham, History, 7.
38. Cincinnati Branch, Minutes, Oct. 5, 1941, and Oct. 3, 1948; Mary Louise Cates, in Cincinnati Branch, Record of Members and Children, no. 396.
39. "Cincinnati Pair to Attend Conference for First Time," *Deseret News,* Sept. 26, 1947, 9; Hanks, Oral History Interview, 3, 7–9; Blackham, History, 8; Obituary for Len Hope, *Deseret News and Salt Lake Telegram,* Sept. 15, 1952, 4B.
40. South Ohio District Presidency to Hamilton and Middleton Members, Jan. 18, 1950, Paul and Cornelia T. Bang Papers, CHL; Fish, Kramer, and Wallis, *History of the Mormon Church in Cincinnati,* 77; Cincinnati Branch, Minutes, Feb. 12, 1950; Cornelia Taylor, Patriarchal Blessing, 2, Paul and Cornelia T. Bang Papers, CHL.

41. Cornelia Taylor, Patriarchal Blessing, Feb. 6, 1935, 2, Paul and Cornelia T. Bang Papers, CHL; Ludlow, Interview, [0:00:41]–[0:04:05]; Bang, Autobiography, 7–9; Salt Lake Temple, Sealings for the Dead, Couples, 1943–70, Sept. 27, 1949, microfilm 456,528, U.S. and Canada Record Collection, FHL.

CHAPTER 35: WE CANNOT FAIL

1. Dunbabin, *Cold War,* 142–55, 162–65, 168–69; Fassmann and Münz, "European East-West Migration," 521–24, 529–32; Fink, *Cold War,* 72–76.
2. Wallace Toronto to First Presidency, Dec. 16, 1949; Dec. 21, 1949; First Presidency to Wallace Toronto, Jan. 30, 1950, First Presidency Mission Correspondence, CHL; Heimann, *Czechoslovakia,* 185–89; Bottoni, *Long Awaited West,* 66.
3. Anderson, *Cherry Tree behind the Iron Curtain,* 57; Wallace Toronto to First Presidency, Feb. 2, 1950, David O. McKay Papers, CHL; Abbott, "My Mission to Czechoslovakia," 11–12, 14–16; Wallace Toronto to First Presidency, Feb. 20, 1950, First Presidency Mission Correspondence, CHL.
4. Anderson, *Cherry Tree behind the Iron Curtain,* 59–60; Abbott, "My Mission to Czechoslovakia," 16; Czechoslovak Mission, "Missionary Bulletin," Apr. 25, 1950.
5. Anderson, *Cherry Tree behind the Iron Curtain,* 55, 60–62; Czechoslovak Mission, "Missionary Bulletin," Apr. 25, 1950; see also Wallace Toronto to First Presidency, Apr. 2, 1950, First Presidency Mission Correspondence, CHL.
6. Yanagida, Oral History Interview [2001], 6; Takagi, *Trek East,* 336; Britsch, *From the East,* 91.
7. Yanagida, Oral History Interview [2001], 6. Translated quotation edited for readability; original source has "He said he had and that was why he came to Nagoya."
8. Yanagida, Oral History Interview [2001], 6; Yanagida, "Memoirs of the Relief Society in Japan," 145. **Topic: Japan**
9. Yanagida, "Relief Society President Experiences"; Takagi, *Trek East,* 332–33.
10. Yanagida, Oral History Interview [1996], 12–13. Quotation edited for readability; "is" in original changed to "are," and "is" added to second sentence. **Topic: Tithing**
11. Yanagida, Oral History Interview [1996], 12–13.
12. Yanagida, "Memoirs of the Relief Society in Japan," 145–48; Yanagida, "Relief Society President Experiences"; Derr, Cannon, and Beecher, *Women of Covenant,* 318; Margaret C. Pickering, "Notes from the Field," *Relief Society Magazine,* Jan. 1949, 36:200–208.
13. Yanagida, Oral History Interview [1996], 12–13; Yanagida, "Ashiato," 10–14. **Topic: Fasting**
14. Stueck, *Rethinking the Korean War,* 61–82; Hwang, *Korea's Grievous War,* 70; Patterson, *Grand Expectations,* 206–15.
15. Joseph Fielding Smith, Journal, Dec. 14, 1949; Sept. 26, 1950; Nov. 13–15, 1950; Dec. 13, 1950.
16. Joseph Fielding Smith, Journal, Aug. 6, 1950; First Presidency to Stake and Mission Presidents and Ward Bishops, Oct. 20, 1950; [Franklin J. Murdock], Memorandum, Jan. 30, 1951, 1, David O. McKay Papers, CHL; Flynn, *Draft,* 116–18; Joseph Anderson to Charles Shockey, Nov. 13, 1950, First Presidency General Correspondence Files, CHL. **Topic: Growth of Missionary Work**
17. Clark, Diary, Jan. 15, 1951; David O. McKay, Diary, Mar. 30, 1950; Jan. 9–11 and 13, 1951 [CHL]; A. Duncan Mackay to David O. McKay, Jan. 10, 1951; Marion Jensen to First Presidency, circa Jan. 1951; John W. Taylor to David O. McKay, Jan. 30, 1951; Meeting of Selective Service and Church Officials, Minutes, Jan. 11, 1951, David O. McKay Papers, CHL.

18. J. Reuben Clark, in *One Hundred Twelfth Annual Conference*, 93–94; First Presidency to Stake and Mission Presidencies, Nov. 18, 1948; First Presidency to Stake and Mission Presidents and Ward Bishops, Oct. 20, 1950, David O. McKay Papers, CHL; "Church Members Warned to Eschew Communism," *Deseret News*, July 3, 1936, [1]; David O. McKay, in *One Hundred Twentieth Annual Conference*, 175–76.

19. David O. McKay, Diary, Jan. 11, 13, and 30–31, 1951 [CHL]; David O. McKay to John W. Taylor, Feb. 6, 1951, David O. McKay Papers, CHL; "Calls to Mission Must Be Cleared by Draft Boards," *Deseret News*, Jan. 16, 1951, section 2, [1]; Meeting of Mission Presidents and General Authorities, Minutes, Apr. 2, 1952, 2, 8, 11, Quorum of the Twelve Apostles Miscellaneous Minutes, CHL.

20. David O. McKay, Diary, Apr. 2 and 4, 1951 [CHL]; Gibbons, *George Albert Smith*, 366–68. **Topic: George Albert Smith**

21. David O. McKay, Diary, Apr. 6, 1951 [CHL]; David O. McKay, in *One Hundred Twenty-First Annual Conference*, 3, 157; David O. McKay, in *One Hundred Twenty-First Annual Conference*, 138–41.

22. Anderson, *Prophets I Have Known*, 119–26; Woodger, *David O. McKay*, 172–84, 189–90; McKay, *My Father*, 220–21; Allen, "David O. McKay," 302–3; Allen, "McKay, David O.," 870–75; Prince and Wright, *David O. McKay*, 3–5, 14–17; Frejka and Westoff, "Religion, Religiousness and Fertility," 7–9; Patterson, *Grand Expectations*, 68–69, 76–79. **Topic: David O. McKay**

23. David O. McKay, in *One Hundred Twenty-First Annual Conference*, 96; David O. McKay, Diary, Apr. 25, 1951 [CHL]; "LDS President Concerned over Red Attitude toward Christianity," *Salt Lake Telegram*, Apr. 26, 1951, 21; Patterson, *Grand Expectations*, 165–205. Quotation edited for readability; "stands for influence of love" in original changed to "stands for the influence of love."

24. Peterson and Gaunt, *Children's Friends*, 75.

25. Spencer W. Kimball to Adele Cannon Howells, Counselors, and Primary Association, Aug. 18, 1949; Adele Cannon Howells to David O. McKay, Dec. 6, 1950, Primary Association General Records, CHL.

26. Sunday School General Presidency, Minutes, Jan. 24, 1950; Harold B. Lee and Marion G. Romney to Adele Cannon Howells, Aug. 10, 1950; A. H. Reiser to First Presidency, Nov. 8, 1950; Book of Mormon Pictures Project Committee to Church Union Board, Jan. 8, 1951; A. Hamer Reiser to Elbert R. Curtis, Jan. 13, 1951, Primary Association General Records, CHL.

27. Book of Mormon Pictures Project Committee to Church Union Board, Jan. 8, 1951; Book of Mormon Pictures Committee to the First Presidency, Jan. 6, 1951, Primary Association General Records, CHL.

28. Adele Cannon Howells to Harold B. Lee and Marion G. Romney, Sept. 21, 1950, Primary Association General Records, CHL; Swanson, "Book of Mormon Art of Arnold Friberg," 29; Barrett and Black, "Setting a Standard in LDS Art," 33.

29. Book of Mormon Pictures Committee of the Church Union Board to the First Presidency, Jan. 6, 1951; First Presidency to A. Hamer Reiser and Adele Cannon Howells, Jan. 10, 1951, Primary Association General Records, CHL.

30. A. H. Reiser and others to First Presidency, Oct. 4, 1950; Book of Mormon Pictures Committee of the Church Union Board to the First Presidency, Jan. 6, 1951, Primary Association General Records, CHL.

31. Andersen, "Arnold Friberg," 249–50; "Adele Cannon Howells," *Cannon Chronicle*, Dec. 1952, [4].

32. Swanson, "Book of Mormon Art of Arnold Friberg," 29; "High Tribute Paid Primary President," *Deseret News*, Apr. 18, 1951, Church section, 4; David O. McKay, Diary, Feb. 15, 1952 [CHL].

33. Marion G. Romney, Remarks at Adele Cannon Howells Funeral, Apr. 17, 1951, Primary Association General Board, Minutes, CHL; Romney, Journal, Apr. 14, 1951.

34. Swanson, "Book of Mormon Art of Arnold Friberg," 29–30; Agreement Signed by Arnold Friberg, June 1, 1951, Primary Association General Records, CHL; see also Arnold Friberg, *The Brother of Jared Sees the Finger of the Lord,* in *Children's Friend,* Jan. 1953, volume 52, insert.

35. Charrier, Oral History Interview [2001], 2–3; Jeanne Esther Charrier, "Demeurez dans la liberté," *Liahona,* Dec. 2020, Local Pages of French-Speaking Europe, 4.

36. Descartes, *Discourse on Method,* 24; Charrier, Oral History Interview [2001], 2; Jeanne Esther Charrier, "Demeurez dans la liberté," *Liahona,* Dec. 2020, Local Pages of French-Speaking Europe, 3–4.

37. Jeanne Esther Charrier, "Demeurez dans la liberté," *Liahona,* Dec. 2020, Local Pages of French-Speaking Europe, 4; Charrier, Oral History Interview [2001], 2–3, 9.

38. Charrier, Oral History Interview [2001], 3.

39. Euvrard, Histoire de Léon Fargier, 4–5, 8–9; Léon Fargier, "Famille Fargier," *L'Étoile,* Sept. 1979, 1.

40. Euvrard, Histoire de Léon Fargier, 10, 13–14, 16–17, 22–24.

41. Léon Fargier, "Famille Fargier," *L'Étoile,* Nov. 1979, 15; Jeanne Esther Charrier, "Demeurez dans la liberté," *Liahona,* Dec. 2020, Local Pages of French-Speaking Europe, 4; Charrier, Oral History Interview [2001], 3.

42. Charrier, Email Interview with John Robertson, Feb. 21, 2021; Jeanne Esther Charrier, "Demeurez dans la liberté," *Liahona,* Dec. 2020, Local Pages of French-Speaking Europe, 4; Léon Fargier, "Famille Fargier," *L'Étoile,* Nov. 1979, 16; see also Acts 5:29.

43. Charrier, Oral History Interview [2001], 18; Eldredge, Mission Journal, Sept. 6, 1954; Carlson, Mission Journal, Mar. 30, 1951.

44. Charrier, Oral History Interview [2001], 29; French Mission, Monthly Mission Progress Report, Apr. 30, 1951; "Addresses of French Missionaries as of January 1, 1949," [1]–[3], Missionary Department, Franklin Murdock Files, CHL. **Topic: France**

45. Terezie Vojkůvková entry, Prague District, Czechoslovak Mission, no. 116, in Czechoslovakia, Record of Members Collection, CHL; Wallace Toronto to First Presidency, July 18, 1951, Czechoslovak Mission, Manuscript History and Historical Reports, CHL; Vrba, "History of the Brno Branch," 2. Quotation edited for clarity; "on which" in original changed to "with which."

46. Wallace Toronto to First Presidency, July 18, 1951, Czechoslovak Mission, Manuscript History and Historical Reports, CHL; Czechoslovak Mission, "Missionary Bulletin," Apr. 25, 1950; Wallace Toronto to First Presidency, Apr. 15, 1950, Missionary Department, Franklin Murdock Files, CHL; Mehr, "Czechoslovakia and the LDS Church," 143–44, 146; Vrba, "History of the Brno Branch," 3–4; Vrba, "Czechoslovak Mission," 1–2.

47. Vrba, "History of the Brno Branch," 4–5; Vrba, "Czechoslovak Mission," 2–3; Wallace Toronto to First Presidency, Apr. 15, 1950; Jan. 10, 1951, Missionary Department, Franklin Murdock Files, CHL; Wallace Toronto to First Presidency, July 18, 1951, Czechoslovak Mission, Manuscript History and Historical Reports, CHL. **Topic: Czechoslovakia**

48. Wallace Toronto to First Presidency, July 18, 1951, Czechoslovak Mission, Manuscript History and Historical Reports, CHL; Salt Lake Temple, Endowments for the Dead, 1893–1970, Mar. 17, 1950, microfilm 445,725; June 29, 1953, microfilm 445,847, U.S. and Canada Record Collection, FHL.

CHAPTER 36: CAREFULLY AND PRAYERFULLY

1. Pivaral, Journal, 2–3.

2. Mecham, Oral History Interview, 57–58; "Lamanite Saints Assemble in Mesa," *Deseret News,* Oct. 24, 1951, Church section, 14–15; "Lamanites Assemble in Mesa for Temple Session," *Deseret News,* Oct. 31, 1951, Church section, 5.

3. Ralph G. Brown, "Quetzaltenango-Guatemala," 4; Ralph G. Brown to "Clemencia, Linda and Family," Apr. 10, 2004, Ralph G. Brown Mission Papers, CHL; Golithon, "Clemencia Pivaral's Baptism Story," 1; Christofferson, Mission Journal, Feb. 19, 21, and 28, 1950; Mar. 1, 5, 7, and 12, 1950.

4. Golithon, "Clemencia Pivaral's Baptism Story," 1. Quotations edited for readability; original source has "the missionaries had not yet asked her if she wanted to be baptized" and "Pres. Mecham asked her if she was ready to be baptized, how about tomorrow?"

5. O'Donnal, *Pioneer in Guatemala*, 66–68; O'Donnal, "Personal History," 72–73. **Topic: Guatemala**

6. Pivaral, Journal, 4–5; see also John A. Widtsoe, *La verdad restaurada* ([Buenos Aires, Argentina]: Misión Argentina, [1935]).

7. Pivaral, Journal, 10–18; O'Donnal, "Personal History," 76; "Guatemalan Saints Attend S. L. Temple," *Deseret News,* Nov. 14, 1951, Church section, [12].

8. "Lamanites Assemble in Mesa for Temple Session," *Deseret News,* Oct. 31, 1951, Church section, 5; Spanish American Mission, Manuscript History, Oct. 21–23, 1951; Arizona Temple, Endowments of the Living, 1927–57, volume 120, 1944–57, no. 3570, image 363, microfilm 962,067, Special Collections, U.S. and Canada Record Collection, FHL; Arizona Temple, Endowments for the Dead, 1927–70, Heir Indexes, 1927–72, Baptisms for the Dead, 1943–79, Oct. 2, 1951, no. 23524, image 2454, microfilm 450,994, Special Collections, U.S. and Canada Record Collection, FHL; Arizona Temple, Sealings for the Dead, Couples, and Children, 1942–70, June 27, 1951, Mercedes de Jesus Orillana and Ponciano Pardo, image 1112, microfilm 456,259, Special Collections, U.S. and Canada Record Collection, FHL; Golithon, "Clemencia Pivaral's Baptism Story," 1.

9. O'Donnal, "Personal History," 77; "Guatemalan Saints Attend S. L. Temple," *Deseret News,* Nov. 14, 1951, Church section, [12].

10. Emigration Report, Jan. 15, 1952, First Presidency General Administration Files, 1930–60, CHL; Minutes of the European Mission Presidents' Meeting, July 5–6, 1950, 1, 64–68, John A. Widtsoe Papers, CHL; David O. McKay, Diary, Dec. 27, 1951 [CHL]. **Topics: Emigration; Temple Building**

11. Minutes of the European Mission Presidents' Meeting, July 6, 1950, 67; John A. Widtsoe to David O. McKay, Nov. 9, 1950, copy; May 21, 1951, John A. Widtsoe Papers, CHL; Memorandum, Dec. 7, 1950, David O. McKay Papers, CHL; see also Summary of Minutes of the Conference of the Presidents of the European Mission, July 4–10, 1950, First Presidency Mission Correspondence, CHL.

12. David O. McKay, Diary, Nov. 30, 1951; Dec. 18–20, 1951; Jan. 3, 1952; Feb. 13, 1952; Apr. 17, 1952 [CHL]; Romney, Journal, Apr. 17, 1952; Cowan, "Pivotal Swiss Temple," 133–35. **Topic: Temple Building**

13. Fink, *Cold War,* 72–76; Large, *Berlin,* 402–18.

14. Germany Hamburg Mission, Manuscript History and Historical Reports, Mar. 31, 1952; Kuehne, *Henry Burkhardt,* 1; Fassmann, *Walter K. Fassmann,* 133.

15. Kuehne, *Henry Burkhardt,* 10–11, 13; Kuehne, *Mormons as Citizens of a Communist State,* 63; Hall, "The Church of Jesus Christ of Latter-day Saints in the Former East Germany," 490, 494–95.

16. Kuehne, *Henry Burkhardt,* 11–12; David O. McKay, Diary, May 28 and June 6, 1952 [CHL]; "Pres. and Mrs. McKay to Tour Missions throughout Europe," *Deseret News,* May 28, 1952, Church section, 2; "1500 Berliners Out to Greet President," *Deseret News,* July 23, 1952, Church section, 4. **Topic: Germany**

17. "1500 Berliners Out to Greet President," *Deseret News,* July 23, 1952, Church section, 4; Burkhardt, Oral History Interview, 1. Translated quotation edited for readability; original source has "President McKay . . . then asked if I would be willing to serve as a counselor in the mission presidency."

18. Burkhardt, Oral History Interview, 1–2; Burkhardt, "Henry Johannes Burkhardt," 26; Kuehne, *Henry Burkhardt,* 13–15; Kuehne, *Mormons as Citizens of a Communist State,* 358.

19. David O. McKay to Stephen L Richards, J. Reuben Clark Jr., and the Quorum of the Twelve Apostles, June 13, 1952; July 5, 1952, First Presidency General Administration Files, 1930–60, CHL; David O. McKay, Diary, May 26, 1952 [CHL]; Morning Session, English language, Sept. 11, 1955, 2, Swiss Temple Dedicatory Addresses, CHL.

20. Bringhurst, Mission President Journal, 6; David O. McKay, Diary, Nov. 18, 1952 [CHL]; David O. McKay to Samuel Bringhurst, Nov. 19, 1952, volume 151, David O. McKay Scrapbooks, CHL.

21. David O. McKay to Stephen L Richards, J. Reuben Clark Jr., and the Quorum of the Twelve Apostles, July 5, 1952, First Presidency General Administration Files, 1930–60, CHL; David O. McKay, Diary, July 5–22 and 28, 1952 [CHL]; "McKay Finishes Tour, Lauds LDS Missions," *Salt Lake Tribune,* July 15, 1952, 12.

22. "Pres. McKay Interview Covers Many Subjects," *Deseret News,* July 30, 1952, Church section, 2; Golden L. Woolf, "Un temple en Europe," *L'Étoile,* Oct. 1952, 220.

23. Samuel Bringhurst to David O. McKay, Nov. 14, 1952, copy; David O. McKay to Samuel Bringhurst, Nov. 19, 1952, volume 151, David O. McKay Scrapbooks, CHL; David O. McKay, Diary, Nov. 18, 1952 [CHL]; Bringhurst, "Acquisition of Property of the Swiss Temple," 198–99; Bringhurst, Mission President Journal, 6, 8; Morning Session, English language, Sept. 11, 1955, 3, Swiss Temple Dedicatory Addresses, CHL.

24. David O. McKay to Samuel Bringhurst, Nov. 19, 1952; Nov. 24, 1952, volume 151, David O. McKay Scrapbooks, CHL. **Topics: Temple Building; Switzerland**

25. John A. Widtsoe, *In a Sunlit Land* (Salt Lake City: Milton R. Hunter and G. Homer Durham, 1952); John A. Widtsoe to "the Brethren of the General Authorities of the Church," Oct. 10, 1952, John A. Widtsoe Papers, CHL.

26. Durham, "Death of John A. Widtsoe," 1–5; Leah Dunford Widtsoe to Ann Rees, Dec. 19, 1952, John A. Widtsoe Papers, CHL. Quotation edited for readability; original source has "he had enjoyed a rich life and was willing to live and serve as long as the Lord permitted."

27. Durham, "Death of John A. Widtsoe," 1–5; Leah Dunford Widtsoe to Ann Rees, Dec. 19, 1952, John A. Widtsoe Papers, CHL; *Saints,* volume 2, chapters 32, 33, and 36; Widtsoe, *In the Gospel Net,* 119–20.

28. Parrish, *John A. Widtsoe,* chapter 23; Allen, Embry, and Mehr, *Hearts Turned to the Fathers,* 222–29; Genealogical Society of Utah Board of Trustees, Minutes, Oct. 14, 1947; May 17 and Oct. 24, 1950. **Topic: Family History and Genealogy**

29. John A. Widtsoe and Leah Dunford Widtsoe, *The Word of Wisdom: A Modern Interpretation* (Salt Lake City: Deseret Book, 1937); John A. Widtsoe, *Evidences and Reconciliations: Aids to Faith in a Modern Day,* 3 vols. (Salt Lake City: Bookcraft, 1951).

30. Durham, "Death of John A. Widtsoe," 3–10; Leah Dunford Widtsoe to Ann Rees, Dec. 19, 1952, John A. Widtsoe Papers, CHL; Parrish, *John A. Widtsoe,* 662–63; *In Memoriam: John A. Widtsoe,* 25, 27. Last quotation edited for readability; "had been" in original changed to "was," and "received" changed to "receives." **Topic: John and Leah Widtsoe**

CHAPTER 37: WITH REAL INTENT

1. Linford and Linford, Oral History Interview, 3–6; Kuehne, *Henry Burkhardt,* 38, 40; Burkhardt, "Henry Johannes Burkhardt," 28; see also Kuehne, *Mormons as Citizens of a Communist State,* 356–58.

2. Kuehne, *Henry Burkhardt,* 14; Arthur Glaus to First Presidency, Mar. 9, 1953, First Presidency Mission Correspondence, CHL; Hall, "The Church of Jesus Christ of Latter-day Saints in the Former East Germany," 487.

3. Linford and Linford, Oral History Interview, 3–5, 7, 12; Kuehne, *Henry Burkhardt,* 38–39.

4. Linford and Linford, Oral History Interview, 12–13; Kuehne, *Henry Burkhardt,* 38–39; Burkhardt, "Henry Johannes Burkhardt," 28. Quotation edited for readability; "had" in original changed to "have."

5. Hunter, Interview, 1–3; Fairmont Ward, Manuscript History and Historical Reports, Sept. 15, 1952; "Southern California Latter-day Saint Seminaries, Teacher's Handbook," William E. Berrett copy, 31. Seminary began in San Diego in the fall of 1952, and Nan Hunter began teaching in 1953.

6. Plewe, *Mapping Mormonism,* 144–45; Wright, "Beginning of the Early Morning Seminary Program," 223–26; "Church Announces Seminary Program in L. A. Area," *California Intermountain News,* June 27, 1950, 1; *By Study and Also by Faith,* 122–26, 129; Hunter, Interview, 11; "Enrollment Report, Southern California L. D. S. Seminaries," Sept. 30, 1953, Church Educational System, Southern California Area Files, CHL; Cowan, *Church in the Twentieth Century,* 251; Rimington, *Vistas on Visions,* 28–29. **Topic: Seminaries and Institutes**

7. Hunter, Interview, 1–3.

8. Hunter, Interview, 2.

9. Hunter, Interview, 2–3.

10. Hinckley, Journal, Nov. 12, 1951, and Dec. 5, 1951; *Teachings of Presidents of the Church: Gordon B. Hinckley,* 10–12, 15–16; Dew, *Go Forward with Faith,* 143–46, 150–51.

11. Dew, *Go Forward with Faith,* 150–51, 153, 159.

12. Dew, *Go Forward with Faith,* 150–51; Britsch, *From the East,* 173–78; "LDS Servicemen in Korea Area Set Conference," *Deseret News and Salt Lake Telegram,* Nov. 22, 1952, Church section, 11; Choi, "History of The Church of Jesus Christ of Latter-day Saints in Korea," 85–92. **Topic: South Korea**

13. David O. McKay, Diary, Oct. 29, 1953 [CHL]; Hinckley, Oral History Interview, 2; Dew, *Go Forward with Faith,* 176; "President McKay Dedicates Two European Temple Sites," *Improvement Era,* Sept. 1953, 56:655.

14. "Pres. M'Kay Approves Berne Temple Plans," *Deseret News,* Apr. 11, 1953, Church section, 7; "First Presidency Meeting," Aug. 20, 1953, David O. McKay Scrapbooks, CHL; David O. McKay, Diary, Oct. 29, 1953 [CHL]; Wise, "New Concept in Temple Building and Operation," 1–2. **Topic: Adjustments to Temple Work**

15. Hinckley, Oral History Interview, 2; Dew, *Go Forward with Faith,* 176.

16. David O. McKay, Diary, Jan. 1–3, 1954 [CHL]; Henry A. Smith, "Pres. McKay on 32,000 Mile Foreign Mission Tour," *Deseret News,* Jan. 2, 1954, Church section, 1, 4; Neilson and Teuscher, *Pacific Apostle,* xl–xliv; Anderson, *Prophets I Have Known,* 123–24; *Saints,* volume 2, chapter 12; Reiser, Oral History Interview, 166–67; Leroy H. Duncan to First Presidency, July 14, 1953, First Presidency Mission Correspondence, CHL; Wright, "History of the South African Mission," 3:419–20, 432, 439; Stevenson, *Global History of Blacks and Mormonism,* 54–56; Monson, "History of the South African Mission," 42–45. **Topics: South Africa; Priesthood and Temple Restriction**

17. J. Reuben Clark Jr. to Leroy H. Duncan, Apr. 21, 1953; Leroy H. Duncan to First Presidency, Jan. 2, 1953; Leroy H. Duncan to First Presidency, July 14, 1953, First Presidency Mission Correspondence, CHL.

18. Reiser, Oral History Interview, 166–67; David O. McKay, "The Priesthood and the Negro Race," Address given at Cape Town, South Africa, Jan. 17, 1954, David O. McKay Scrapbooks, CHL; Wright, "History of the South African Mission," 3:419; du Pré, *Separate but Unequal,* 65–98; Bickford-Smith, "Mapping Cape Town," 15–26; "Natives Are Banned by the Mormons," *Cape Argus* (Cape Town, South Africa), Jan. 12, 1954; "Mormon Leader Visits South Africa," *Die Transvaler* (Johannesburg, South Africa), Jan. 12, 1954, copies in David O. McKay Scrapbooks, CHL. **Topic: Racial Segregation**

19. Reiser, Diary, Jan. 9–19, 1954; Emma Ray McKay, Diary, Jan. 9, 1954.

20. Jensen, "President McKay Shook This Old Black Hand," 3; McKay, Scrapbook, Jan. 17, 1954; Okkers, "I Would Love to Touch the Door of the Temple," 177–78.

21. David O. McKay to Stephen L Richards and J. Reuben Clark Jr., Jan. 19, 1954, David O. McKay Scrapbooks, CHL.

22. David O. McKay, "The Priesthood and the Negro Race," Address given at Cape Town, South Africa, Jan. 17, 1954, David O. McKay Scrapbooks, CHL.

23. David O. McKay, "The Priesthood and the Negro Race," Address given at Cape Town, South Africa, Jan. 17, 1954, David O. McKay Scrapbooks, CHL; Evan P. Wright to First Presidency, June 17, 1952, in Wright, "History of the South African Mission," 3:440; N. U. Etuk to Church of Jesus Christ of Latter-day Saints, July 6, 1953, copy; Joseph Anderson to N. U. Etuk, Aug. 14, 1953, First Presidency General Correspondence Files, CHL; Stevenson, *Global History of Blacks and Mormonism,* 74. **Topic: Nigeria**
24. Patterson, *Brown v. Board of Education,* 21–45; de Gruchy, *Church Struggle in South Africa,* 53–59, 85–88, 97–99; Alice E. Hatch to David O. McKay, undated [circa Feb. 1952]; Jacob O. Rohner to David O. McKay, Jan. 11, 1952, First Presidency General Correspondence Files, CHL; Stevenson, *Global History of Blacks and Mormonism,* 66–69.
25. "Unser Fahrzeug," circa 1954, East German Mission Photographic Record of a Youth Conference, CHL; Burkhardt, "Henry Johannes Burkhardt," 28; Kuehne, *Henry Burkhardt,* 39.
26. "This Week in Church History," *Deseret News,* June 6, 1948, Church section, 18; "Finnish MIA Holds First Conference," *Deseret News,* July 27, 1949, Church section, 12; Burkhardt, "Henry Johannes Burkhardt," 28; Burkhardt, Oral History Interview, 2–3; Arthur Glaus to First Presidency, June 11, 1953, First Presidency Mission Correspondence, CHL; Scharffs, *Mormonism in Germany,* 129–35.
27. Burkhardt, "Henry Johannes Burkhardt," 28; Kuehne, *Henry Burkhardt,* 38–40; Burkhardt, Oral History Interview, 3.
28. Kuehne, *Henry Burkhardt,* 15, 40–41; Burkhardt, "Henry Johannes Burkhardt," 28; Burkhardt, Oral History Interview, 3.
29. Kuehne, *Henry Burkhardt,* 40–42, 44; Burkhardt, Oral History Interview, 2.

CHAPTER 38: MORE POWER, MORE LIGHT

1. Charrier, Oral History Interview [2001], 2; Charrier, Email Interview with John Robertson, Feb. 16, 2021.
2. Charrier, Oral History Interview [2001], 2; Charrier, Email Interview with John Robertson, Feb. 16, 2021; Feb. 21, 2021.
3. Jeanne Esther Charrier, "Demeurez dans la liberté," *L'Étoile,* Jan. 1954, 8–10; Joseph Fielding Smith, "Entangle Not Yourselves in Sin," *Improvement Era,* Sept. 1953, 56:646; see also Jeanne Esther Charrier, "Demeurez dans la liberté," *Liahona,* Dec. 2020, Local Pages of French-Speaking Europe, 4.
4. Jeanne Esther Charrier, "Demeurez dans la liberté," *L'Étoile,* Jan. 1954, 8–10.
5. "Valence," *L'Étoile,* Feb. 1952, [24]; Charrier, Oral History Interview [2001], 2; Jeanne Esther Charrier, "Demeurez dans la liberté," *Liahona,* Dec. 2020, Local Pages of French-Speaking Europe, 4; Charrier, Oral History Interview [2014], 8.
6. Charrier, Oral History Interview [2001], 1; Charrier, Oral History Interview [2014], 5–6, 9.
7. Charrier, Oral History Interview [2001], 12, 14, 17–18.
8. Charrier, Email Interview with John Robertson, Feb. 16, 2021.
9. Charrier, Email Interview with John Robertson, Feb. 6, 2021; Jeanne Esther Charrier, "Demeurez dans la liberté," *Liahona,* Dec. 2020, Local Pages of French-Speaking Europe, 4.
10. Charrier, Email Interview with John Robertson, Feb. 16, 2021.
11. Hinckley, Oral History Interview, 2–5; Dew, *Go Forward with Faith,* 176–77.
12. Dew, *Go Forward with Faith,* 177–78; *Saints,* volume 2, chapter 44. **Topic: Salt Lake Temple**
13. Hinckley, Oral History Interview, 3–4; "Things to Be Done," Mar. 28, 1955; Gunther R. Lessing and Walt Disney Productions to First Presidency, May 26, 1955, Missionary Department Executive Secretary General Files, CHL; Wise, "New Concept in Temple Building and Operation," 3–4.

14. Hinckley, Oral History Interview, 3; Winnifred Bowers to Gordon B. Hinckley, June 2, 1955, Missionary Department Executive Secretary General Files, CHL.

15. Winnifred Bowers to Gordon B. Hinckley, June 2, 1955, Missionary Department Executive Secretary General Files, CHL; Hinckley, Oral History Interview, 4; Wise, Oral History Interview, 49. Quotation edited for clarity; "licked" in original changed to "figured out."

16. Wise, Oral History Interview, 54; David O. McKay, Diary, June 23, 1955 [CHL].

17. Hinckley, Oral History Interview, 5; "Temple Rites Printed in 7 Languages," *Salt Lake Tribune,* Aug. 1, 1953, 12; Wise, "New Concept in Temple Building and Operation," 3; Winnifred Bowers to Gordon B. Hinckley, June 2, 1955, Missionary Department Executive Secretary General Files, CHL; Wise, Oral History Interview, 49, 53.

18. Wise, Oral History Interview, 53; Dew, *Go Forward with Faith,* 178.

19. Couch, Farnsworth, and Maksymiw, Oral History Interview, 3–5, 10, 26; Meyer and Galli, *Under a Leafless Tree,* 129; Meyer, Interview [2017], 1–3.

20. Meyer, Interview [2017], 2–3; Couch, Farnsworth, and Maksymiw, Oral History Interview, 1–3, 6–7, 10.

21. Couch, Farnsworth, and Maksymiw, Oral History Interview, 5–9, 28; Meyer, Interview [2017], 3; Elise Kuhn, Membership Record, Presiding Bishopric Stake and Mission Census, CHL; Meyer and Galli, *Under a Leafless Tree,* 156.

22. Couch, Farnsworth, and Maksymiw, Oral History Interview, 5; Meyer, Interview [2017], 3.

23. See Sunday School General Board, Minutes, Jan. 25, 1955, 134–35; Feb. 1, 1955, 136; Mar. 1, 1955, 141; Mar. 8, 1955, 143; "Make Those Flannelboards Sit Up and Be Noticed," *Instructor,* Jan. 1955, 90:24–26; Arnold Friberg, *Abinadi Delivers His Message to King Noah,* and *Alma Baptizes in the Waters of Mormon,* in *Instructor,* Nov. 1954, volume 89, inserts. **Topic: Church Periodicals**

24. Richard Ranglack, Paul Langheinrich, and Max Jeske to Thomas E. McKay, Jan. 5, 1946, Thomas E. McKay Correspondence, CHL; Starke, "Memoirs," 66, 73; Gregory, Mission President Journal, 17; Kuehne, *Mormons as Citizens of a Communist State,* 69, 72–73; Kuehne, *Henry Burkhardt,* 31.

25. Starke, "Memoirs," 79–80; Gregory, Mission President Journal, 2, 4, 15, 29.

26. Couch, Farnsworth, and Maksymiw, Oral History Interview, 16–18; Meyer and Galli, *Under a Leafless Tree,* 139–41, 156–58.

27. Meyer and Galli, *Under a Leafless Tree,* 142; Couch, Farnsworth, and Maksymiw, Oral History Interview, 11; Meyer, Interview [2017], 2, 4; Neubrandenburg Branch General Minutes, 1951–54.

28. Hinckley, Oral History Interview, 5–6; Dew, *Go Forward with Faith,* 179.

29. Hinckley, Oral History Interview, 5–6.

30. Hinckley, Oral History Interview, 6; Dew, *Go Forward with Faith,* 179–80.

31. Dew, *Go Forward with Faith,* 180; Hinckley, Oral History Interview, 6.

32. Hinckley, Oral History Interview, 6–7; Dew, *Go Forward with Faith,* 180.

33. Hinckley, Oral History Interview, 7; Dew, *Go Forward with Faith,* 180.

CHAPTER 39: A NEW ERA

1. Meyer, Interview [2017], 2–4; Itinerary, Aug. 13–Sept. 18, 1955, Mormon Tabernacle Choir Tour Files, CHL; Thomas, *Tabernacle Choir Goes to Europe,* xvii–xviii. **Topic: Tabernacle Choir**

2. Cornwall, *Century of Singing,* 102–3; Henry A. Smith, "Tabernacle Choir Will Tour Europe," *Deseret News and Salt Lake Telegram,* Sept. 25, 1954, Church section, 7. Quotation edited for readability; "for that missionary work" in original changed to "for missionary work."

3. Henry A. Smith, "Tabernacle Choir Will Tour Europe," *Deseret News and Salt Lake Telegram,* Sept. 25, 1954, Church section, 7; Thomas, *Tabernacle Choir Goes to Europe,* 45–48.

4. Meyer, Interview [2017], 1, 4; Cornwall, *Century of Singing,* 130; Meyer and Galli, *Under a Leafless Tree,* 152; Couch, Farnsworth, and Maksymiw, Oral History Interview, 3–4; Hinckley, Oral History Interview, 9; Kuehne, *Mormons as Citizens of a Communist State,* 76.

5. Meyer, Interview [2017], 3; Gregory, Mission President Journal, 43; Couch, Farnsworth, and Maksymiw, Oral History Interview, 21; Thomas, *Tabernacle Choir Goes to Europe,* 138; Cornwall, "Chronological History of Salt Lake Tabernacle Choir," 366. **Topic: Broadcast Media**

6. Cornwall, "Chronological History of Salt Lake Tabernacle Choir," 368; Meyer, Interview [2017], 3–4. **Topic: Hymns**

7. Henze, "RFE's Early Years," 3–16; Cornwall, "Chronological History of Salt Lake Tabernacle Choir," 367.

8. Meyer, Interview [2017], 4; Cornwall, *Century of Singing,* 117; Cornwall, "Chronological History of Salt Lake Tabernacle Choir," 367.

9. Ted Cannon, "Pres. McKay Dedicates First Temple of Church in Europe," *Deseret News and Salt Lake Telegram,* Sept. 17, 1955, Church section, 2; David O. McKay, Diary, Apr. 17, 1952, and Jan. 14, 1953 [CHL]: "Ground Broken for British Temple," *Deseret News and Salt Lake Telegram,* Sept. 3, 1955, Church section, 6–7. **Topics: Temple Building; David O. McKay**

10. "Report Given by Pres. David O. McKay," 8, in David O. McKay, Diary, Aug. 27, 1953 [CHL].

11. Holmes, Journal, Sept. 11, 1955; Kirby, "History of The Church of Jesus Christ of Latter-day Saints in Switzerland," 126, 130; Marba C. Josephson, "A Temple Risen to Our Lord," *Improvement Era,* Sept. 1955, 58:624, 687. **Topic: Switzerland**

12. Ted Cannon, "President McKay Dedicates First LDS Temple in Europe," *Deseret News and Salt Lake Telegram,* Sept. 12, 1955, 1.

13. Ted Cannon, "President McKay Dedicates First LDS Temple in Europe," *Deseret News and Salt Lake Telegram,* Sept. 12, 1955, 1; "LDS Opens First Temple on Continent of Europe," *Salt Lake Tribune,* Sept. 12, 1955, section 2, 17.

14. Morning Session, English language, Sept. 11, 1955, 1–2, Swiss Temple Dedicatory Addresses, CHL; "The Gospel of Doing," *Der Stern,* Nov. 1, 1906, 38:331–32. **Topic: Joseph F. Smith**

15. Morning Session, English language, Sept. 11, 1955, 2–4, Swiss Temple Dedicatory Addresses, CHL; Ted Cannon, "Pres. McKay Dedicates First Temple of Church in Europe," *Deseret News and Salt Lake Telegram,* Sept. 17, 1955, Church section, 2.

16. Morning Session, English language, Sept. 11, 1955, 6–7, 9, Swiss Temple Dedicatory Addresses, CHL; see also Dew, *Ezra Taft Benson,* 8–12. **Topic: Switzerland**

17. Morning Session, English language, Sept. 11, 1955, 12–14, Swiss Temple Dedicatory Addresses, CHL. **Topic: Temple Dedications and Dedicatory Prayers**

18. Morning and Afternoon Sessions, English language, Sept. 11, 1955, 5, Swiss Temple Dedicatory Addresses, CHL; Harbrecht, "Personal History of Ewan E. Harbrecht Mitton," 1:5–7; Fish, "My Life Story," [1]; Christian Bang Sr., "My Story," [3].

19. Charrier, Email Interview with John Robertson, Feb. 18, 2021; Afternoon Session, French language, Sept. 15, 1955, 2, Swiss Temple Dedicatory Addresses, CHL; Nolan Olsen, "People from 14 Countries Attend Swiss Temple," *Herald-Journal* (Logan, UT), Sept. 25, 1955, 3; see also Ted Cannon, "Choir Boards Trains for Date in Zurich," *Deseret News,* Sept. 13, 1955, 1.

20. Charrier, Email Interview with John Robertson, Feb. 21, 2021; Jeanne Esther Charrier, "Demeurez dans la liberté," *Liahona,* Dec. 2020, Local Pages of French-Speaking Europe, 4.

21. David O. McKay, Diary, Sept. 15, 1955 [CHL]; Afternoon Session, French language, Sept. 15, 1955, 2, Swiss Temple Dedicatory Addresses, CHL.

22. Afternoon Session, French language, Sept. 15, 1955, 3, Swiss Temple Dedicatory Addresses, CHL.

23. Dew, *Go Forward with Faith,* 183; Samuel E. Bringhurst to El Ray L. Christiansen, Sept. 20, 1955, El Ray L. Christiansen Temple Correspondence Files, CHL.

24. David O. McKay, Diary, Sept. 16, 1955 [CHL]; Kimball, Journal, Sept. 16, 1955; Nolan Olsen, "People from 14 Countries Attend Swiss Temple," *Herald-Journal* (Logan, UT), Sept. 25, 1955, 3.

25. Kimball, Journal, Sept. 16, 1955; "About the Temple Endowment," Temples, ChurchofJesusChrist.org/temples. **Topic: Temple Endowment**

26. Kimball, Journal, Sept. 16, 1955; David O. McKay, Diary, Sept. 16, 1955 [CHL]; Nolan Olsen, "People from 14 Countries Attend Swiss Temple," *Herald-Journal* (Logan, UT), Sept. 25, 1955, 3.

27. Charrier, Email Interview with John Robertson, Feb. 18, 2021.

28. Hinckley, Oral History Interview, 5, 7; Dew, *Go Forward with Faith,* 181.

29. Hinckley, Oral History Interview, 7, 9–10; Dew, *Go Forward with Faith,* 181–83; Paul Evans to Gordon B. Hinckley, Aug. 14, 1955, Missionary Department Executive Secretary General Files, CHL.

30. Hinckley, Oral History Interview, 7–10; Dew, *Go Forward with Faith,* 183–84. **Topic: Adjustments to Temple Work**

31. Hinckley, Oral History Interview, 2, 9; Dew, *Go Forward with Faith,* 176, 182–83; Ted Cannon, "Pres. McKay Dedicates First Temple of Church in Europe," *Deseret News and Salt Lake Telegram,* Sept. 17, 1955, Church section, 2, 9. **Topic: Gordon B. Hinckley**

32. Kuehne, *Henry Burkhardt,* 41–42.

33. Kuehne, *Henry Burkhardt,* 42; Burkhardt, "Henry Johannes Burkhardt," 28.

34. Burkhardt, Journal, Nov. 11, 1955; Kuehne, *Henry Burkhardt,* 42.

35. Kuehne, *Henry Burkhardt,* 42; Burkhardt, Oral History Interview, 6; Burkhardt, "Henry Johannes Burkhardt," 28–29. **Topic: Sealing**

36. Kuehne, *Henry Burkhardt,* 42. Quotation edited for readability; "was" in original changed to "is," and "had" changed to "has."

37. Burkhardt, Journal, Nov. 11, 1955; Burkhardt, Oral History Interview, 6–7.

38. Burkhardt, Journal, Nov. 11, 1955; Kuehne, *Henry Burkhardt,* 42; Burkhardt, Oral History Interview, 6.

SOURCES CITED

This list serves as a comprehensive guide to all sources cited in the third volume of *Saints: The Story of the Church of Jesus Christ in the Latter Days*. In entries for manuscript sources, dates identify when the manuscript was created, which is not necessarily the time period the manuscript covers. Volumes of *The Joseph Smith Papers* are listed under "JSP." Many sources are available digitally, and links are found in the electronic version of the book, available at saints.ChurchofJesusChrist.org and in Gospel Library.

Citation of a source does not imply that it is endorsed by the Church. For more information about the types of sources used in *Saints*, see "Note on Sources."

The sources for the epigraphs found in the book are as follows:

Volume epigraph: Joseph Smith, "Church History," Mar. 1, 1842, in *JSP*, H1:499–500
Part 1 epigraph: Lorenzo Snow, in *Seventieth Annual Conference*, 3
Part 2 epigraph: Joseph F. Smith, in *Eighty-Seventh Semi-annual Conference*, 3
Part 3 epigraph: Heber J. Grant, "Personal and Family Prayer," *Improvement Era*, Dec. 1942, 45:779
Part 4 epigraph: George Albert Smith, "The Editor's Page," *Improvement Era*, July 1945, 48:387

The following abbreviations are used in notes and in this list of sources cited:

BYU: L. Tom Perry Special Collections, Harold B. Lee Library, Brigham Young University, Provo, Utah
CHL: Church History Library, The Church of Jesus Christ of Latter-day Saints, Salt Lake City
FHL: Family History Library, The Church of Jesus Christ of Latter-day Saints, Salt Lake City

Abbott, S. E., comp. "My Mission to Czechoslovakia, 1947/1950," July 1986. Czechoslovakia Histories, 1947–68. CHL.

"About the Temple Endowment." Temples. The Church of Jesus Christ of Latter-day Saints. Accessed Aug. 5, 2021. https://www.ChurchofJesusChrist.org/temples/what-is-temple-endowment.

Acta de la Convención de Tecalco, Apr. 26, 1936. In *Quejas de la Tercera Convención, enviados a la Primera Presidencia, Apr.–July, 1936*. CHL. English translation of portions in possession of editors.

An Act to Enable the People of Utah to Form a Constitution [July 16, 1894], Utah Statehood Constitutional Convention Records [1895]. Available at Utah Division of Archives and Records Service website, accessed Aug. 21, 2021, https://images.archives.utah.gov/digital/collection/3212/id/8292.

Adhikari, Mohamed. *Not White Enough, Not Black Enough: Racial Identity in the South African Coloured Community*. Athens: Ohio University Press, 2005.

"Air Raid Danger, Warning Signals, and Blackout Instructions." Metropolitan Police, Office of the Commissioner, Miscellaneous Books and Papers, 1818–1987. Records of the Office of the Commissioner and Successors, 1803–1998. Records of the Metropolitan Police Office, 1803–2012. National Archives, Kew, England.

Akinaka, Isaac Fukuo. Diary, 1941–45. Available at 100th Infantry Battalion Veterans website, accessed June 23, 2021, https://www.100thbattalion.org/archives/memoirs-and-journals/issac-akinaka-diaries/.

Alberta Temple Dedication Services: Cardston, Alberta, Aug. 26–29, 1923. CHL.

"Albert Edward Jarman and William Jarman." Photograph. Available at FamilySearch, accessed Nov. 15, 2019, https://www.familysearch.org/photos/artifacts/52722390.

"Albert Edward Jarman Meets with His Father, William Jarman." Photograph. Available at FamilySearch, accessed Nov. 15, 2019, https://www.familysearch.org/photos/artifacts/30725515.

Alexander, Thomas G. "Between Revivalism and the Social Gospel: The Latter-day Saint Social Advisory Committee, 1916–1922." *BYU Studies* 23, no. 1 (1983): 19–39.

———. *Mormonism in Transition: A History of the Latter-day Saints, 1890–1930*. 3rd ed. Salt Lake City: Greg Kofford Books, 2012. Also available as Thomas G. Alexander, *Mormonism in Transition: A History of the Latter-day Saints, 1890–1930*, 2nd ed. (Urbana: University of Illinois Press, 1986).

———. *Things in Heaven and Earth: The Life and Times of Wilford Woodruff, a Mormon Prophet*. Salt Lake City: Signature Books, 1991.

———. *Utah, the Right Place*. Salt Lake City: Gibbs Smith, 2007.

Alford, Kenneth L. "Calvin S. Smith: 'Utah's Fighting Chaplain.'" *Utah Historical Quarterly* 86, no. 3 (Summer 2018): 254–69.

———. "Joseph F. Smith and the First World War: Eventual Support and Latter-day Saint Chaplains." In *Joseph F. Smith: Reflections on the Man and His Times,* edited by Craig K. Manscill, Brian D. Reeves, Guy L. Dorius, and J. B. Haws, 434–55. Provo, UT: Religious Studies Center, Brigham Young University; Salt Lake City: Deseret Book, 2013.

Allart, Truus. Autobiography, 2013. CHL.

Allen, Gwenfread. *Hawaii's War Years, 1941–1945*. Honolulu: University of Hawaii Press, 1950.

Allen, Inez Knight. Diary, 1898–99. Mormon Missionary Diaries, 1832–circa 1960. BYU.

Allen, James B. "David O. McKay." In *The Presidents of the Church,* edited by Leonard J. Arrington, 275–313. Salt Lake City: Deseret Book, 1986.

———. "Emergence of a Fundamental: The Expanding Role of Joseph Smith's First Vision in Mormon Religious Thought." *Journal of Mormon History* 7 (1980): 43–61.

———. "McKay, David O." In *Encyclopedia of Mormonism,* edited by Daniel H. Ludlow, 2:870–75. New York: Macmillan, 1992.

———. "The Story of *The Truth, The Way, The Life.*" *BYU Studies* 33, no. 4 (1993): 690–741.

Allen, James B., Jessie L. Embry, and Kahlile B. Mehr. *Hearts Turned to the Fathers: A History of the Genealogical Society of Utah, 1894–1994*. Provo, UT: BYU Studies, 1995.

Allen, Julie K. *Danish but Not Lutheran: The Impact of Mormonism on Danish Cultural Identity, 1850–1920*. Salt Lake City: University of Utah Press, 2017.

Allen, Melvin Orson. Journals, 1929–30. Melvin O. Allen Mission Papers, 1928–2004. CHL.

Allison, Tanine. *Destructive Sublime: World War II in American Film and Media*. New Brunswick, NJ: Rutgers University Press, 2018.

Allred, William B. "Not Weary in Well-Doing: The Missionary Role of LDS Servicemen in Occupied Japan, 1945–1953." *Journal of Mormon History* 46, no. 3 (July 2020): 60–76.

Andersen, Velan Max. "Arnold Friberg, Artist: His Life, Philosophy and His Works." Master's thesis, Brigham Young University, 1970.

Anderson, Charles V. "My Journey through Life," circa 1940. 5 vols. Winston Beard Family Collection, circa 1923–2019. CHL.

———. *Twenty-Three Years in Cincinnati: A Six Months' Visit to the Old Mission Field*. Salt Lake City: Publisher unidentified, [1937].

Anderson, Jeffery L. "Brothers across Enemy Lines: A Mission President and a German Soldier Correspond during World War I." *BYU Studies* 41, no. 1 (2002): 127–39.

Anderson, Joseph. *Prophets I Have Known*. Salt Lake City: Deseret Book, 1973.

Anderson, Martha Toronto. *A Cherry Tree behind the Iron Curtain: The Autobiography of Martha Toronto Anderson*. Salt Lake City: By the author, 1977.

Anderson, Paul L. "A Jewel in the Gardens of Paradise: The Art and Architecture of the Hawai'i Temple." *BYU Studies* 39, no. 4 (2000): 164–82.

Angell, Lowell. *Images of America: Theatres of Hawai'i*. Charleston, SC: Arcadia, 2011.

Annual of the University of Utah including the Utah State Normal School, Salt Lake City. Announcements for 1896–97, with Catalogue of Students for 1895–96. Salt Lake City: Tribune Job Printing, 1896.

Antill, Peter. *Berlin 1945: End of the Thousand Year Reich*. Oxford: Osprey, 2005.

Architect's Office. Salt Lake Temple Architectural Drawings, 1853–93. CHL.

Argentine Mission. Correspondence, 1924–44, 2004. CHL.

Argetsinger, Gerald S. "The Hill Cumorah Pageant: A Historical Perspective." *Journal of Book of Mormon Studies* 13, no. 1 (2004): 58–69, 171.

Arizona Republican. Phoenix. 1890–1930.

Arizona Temple. Dedication Services, 1927. CHL.

Arrington, Chris Rigby. "Pioneer Midwives." In *Mormon Sisters: Women in Early Utah,* edited by Claudia L. Bushman, 43–65. Logan: Utah State University Press, 1997.

Arrington, Leonard J. *Great Basin Kingdom: An Economic History of the Latter-day Saints, 1830–1900.* Cambridge, MA: Harvard University Press, 1958.

Arrington, Leonard J., and Wayne K. Hinton. "Origin of the Welfare Plan of The Church of Jesus Christ of Latter-day Saints." *BYU Studies* 5, no. 2 (Winter 1964): 67–85.

Audoin-Rouzeau, Stéphane. "1915: Stalemate." In *Global War,* edited by Jay Winter, 65–88. Vol. 1 of *The Cambridge History of the First World War.* Cambridge: Cambridge University Press, 2014.

Babbel, Frederick W. *On Wings of Faith.* Salt Lake City: Bookcraft, 1972.

———. Oral History Interview by Maclyn P. Burg, Nov. 12, 1974, and Feb. 5, 1975. Oral History Collection, Dwight D. Eisenhower Library, Abilene, KS.

Bader, William B. *Austria between East and West, 1945–1955.* Stanford, CA: Stanford University Press, 1966.

Badger, Carlos A. Letterbooks, 1903–7. 4 vols. CHL.

Baker, Sherry Pack, and Elizabeth Mott. "From Radio to the Internet: Church Use of Electronic Media in the Twentieth Century." In *A Firm Foundation: Church Organization and Administration,* edited by David J. Whittaker and Arnold K. Garr, 339–60. Provo, UT: Religious Studies Center, Brigham Young University; Salt Lake City: Deseret Book, 2011.

Ball, Vaughn. Reminiscences, 1979–80. Audio recording. CHL.

Ballif, Serge F. Journals, 1905–9. CHL.

Bang, Christian, Sr. "My Story," Apr. 9, 1959. Paul and Cornelia T. Bang Papers, 1935–44, 1977–78. CHL.

Bang, Cornelia Taylor. Autobiography, 1977–78. Paul and Cornelia T. Bang Papers, 1935–44, 1977–78. CHL.

[Bang, Cornelia Taylor]. Honeymoon Diary. Paul and Cornelia T. Bang Papers, 1935–44, 1977–78. CHL.

———. Wedding Day Story. Paul and Cornelia T. Bang Papers, 1935–44, 1977–78. CHL.

Bang, Paul. Diary, Jan.–June 1936. Paul and Cornelia T. Bang Papers, 1935–44, 1977–78. CHL.

———. "My Life Story," circa 1978. Paul and Cornelia T. Bang Papers, 1935–44, 1977–78. CHL.

———. "Personal History of Paul and Connie Bang—1942 Forward." In Paul Bang, "My Life Story," circa 1978. Paul and Cornelia T. Bang Papers, 1935–44, 1977–78. CHL.

Barrett, Robert T., and Susan Easton Black. "Setting a Standard in LDS Art: Four Illustrators of the Mid-twentieth Century." *BYU Studies* 44, no. 2 (2005): 25–80.

Barrus, Inez Beckstead. "The Joy of Being Inez B. Barrus," 1989. Inez Beckstead Barrus Papers, 1939, 1989. CHL.

———. Papers, 1939, 1989. CHL.

Bates, Irene M. "Patriarchal Blessings and the Routinization of Charisma." *Dialogue: A Journal of Mormon Thought* 26, no. 3 (Fall 1993): 1–29.

Bean, Arlene. Mission Journal, 1948–49. CHL.

Beckstead, Inez. Journal, 1939. Inez Beckstead Barrus Papers, 1939, 1989. CHL.

Beecher, Dale. "The Post-gathering Expansion of Zion: Mormon Settlements of the Twentieth Century." In *Times of Transition,* edited by Thomas G. Alexander, 103–7. Provo, UT: Joseph Fielding Smith Institute for Latter-day Saint History, 2003.

Beeley, Arthur L. *A Summary Statement of the Investigation Made by the British Government of the "Mormon" Question in England.* Liverpool: Millennial Star Office, 1914.

Bell, E. Jay. "The Windows of Heaven Revisited: The 1899 Tithing Reformation." *Journal of Mormon History* 20, no. 1 (Spring 1994): 45–83.

Bennett, Richard E. "'And I Saw the Hosts of the Dead, Both Small and Great': Joseph F. Smith, World War I, and His Visions of the Dead." In *By Study and by Faith: Selections from the Religious Educator,* edited by Richard Neitzel Holzapfel and Kent P. Jackson, 113–35. Provo, UT: Religious Studies Center, Brigham Young University, 2009.

———. *Temples Rising: A Heritage of Sacrifice.* Salt Lake City: Deseret Book, 2019.

Bennett, Richard E., and Jeffrey L. Jensen. "'Nearer, My God, to Thee': The Sinking of the *Titanic.*" In *Regional Studies in Latter-day Saint Church History: The British Isles,* edited by Cynthia Doxey, Robert C. Freeman, Richard Neitzel Holzapfel, and Dennis A. Wright, 109–27. Provo, UT: Religious Studies Center, Brigham Young University, 2007.

Benson, Ezra Taft. Correspondence Files, 1946. CHL.

———. Journal, 1921–27, 1938–39, 1943–88. CHL.

Bergera, Gary James. "Ezra Taft Benson's 1946 Mission to Europe." *Journal of Mormon History* 34, no. 2 (Spring 2008): 73–112.

Bergvall, Erik, ed. *The Fifth Olympiad: The Official Report of the Olympic Games of Stockholm, 1912.* Stockholm: Wahlstrom and Widstrand, 1913.

Bickford-Smith, Vivian. *Ethnic Pride and Racial Prejudice in Victorian Cape Town: Group Identity and Social Practice, 1875–1902.* Cambridge: Cambridge University Press, 1995.

———. "Mapping Cape Town: From Slavery to Apartheid." In *Lost Communities, Living Memories: Remembering Forced Removals in Cape Town,* edited by Sean Field, 15–26. Cape Town: David Phillip, 2001.

Birth, Helga. Mission Journal, 1944–46, 1950, 1951, 1958. Helga Meyer Collection, 1944–58, 2016–18. CHL. English translation by Bertha Bockholt, Oct. 2016, in possession of editors.

Bischof, Günter, and Barbara Stelzl-Marx. "Lives behind Barbed Wire: A Comparative View of Austrian Prisoners of War during and after World War II in Soviet and American Captivity." In *Austrian Lives,* edited by Günter Bischof, Fritz Plasser, and Eva Maltschnig, 327–58. Contemporary Austrian Studies 21. New Orleans: University of New Orleans Press, 2012.

Bitton, Davis. *George Q. Cannon: A Biography.* Salt Lake City: Deseret Book, 1999.

———. *The Ritualization of Mormon History and Other Essays.* Urbana: University of Illinois Press, 1994.

Black, Susan Easton. "The Mormon Battalion, 1846–1847." In *Mapping Mormonism: An Atlas of Latter-day Saint History,* edited by Brandon S. Plewe, 78–79. Provo, UT: Brigham Young University Press, 2012.

Blackham, Lula Belle. History, 2021. CHL.

Blumell, Bruce D. "Welfare before Welfare: Twentieth Century LDS Church Charity before the Great Depression." *Journal of Mormon History* 6 (1979): 89–106.

Bluth, John F., and Wayne K. Hinton. "The Great Depression." In *Utah's History,* edited by Richard D. Poll, 481–96. Provo, UT: Brigham Young University Press, 1978.

The Book of Mormon: Another Testament of Jesus Christ. Salt Lake City: The Church of Jesus Christ of Latter-day Saints, 2013.

Boone, David F. "The Evacuation of the Czechoslovak and German Missions at the Outbreak of World War II." *BYU Studies* 40, no. 3 (2001): 122–54.

Boone, Joseph F. "The Roles of The Church of Jesus Christ of Latter-day Saints in relation to the United States Military, 1900–1975." PhD diss., Brigham Young University, 1975.

Booth, Joseph W. Journals, 1898–1928. 13 vols. Mormon Missionary Diaries, 1832–circa 1960. BYU.

Bornstein, George. *The Colors of Zion: Blacks, Jews, and Irish from 1845 to 1945.* Cambridge, MA: Harvard University Press, 2011.

Boston Evening Journal. Boston. 1872–98.

Bottoni, Stefano. *Long Awaited West: Eastern Europe since 1944.* Translated by Sean Lambert. Bloomington: Indiana University Press, 2017.

Botz, Gerhard. "The Jews of Vienna from the 'Anschluß' to the Holocaust [1987]." *Historical Social Research/Historische Sozialforschung, Supplement,* no. 28 (2016): 316–34.

Bowen, Emma Lucy Gates. Papers, 1896–1950. BYU.

Brackenridge, R. Douglas. "'About the Worst Man in Utah': William R. Campbell and the Crusade against Brigham H. Roberts, 1898–1900." *Journal of Mormon History* 39, no. 1 (Winter 2013): 69–157.

Bravo, Agricol Lozano. Oral History Interview by Gordon Irving, Aug. 8, 1974. CHL. English translation of portions by Patty Hendrickson and Bonnie Linck, June 2016, in possession of editors.

Bray, Justin R. "Joseph F. Smith's Beard and the Public Image of the Latter-day Saints." In *Joseph F. Smith: Reflections on the Man and His Times,* edited by Craig K. Manscill, Brian D. Reeves, Guy L. Dorius, and J. B. Haws, 133–58. Provo, UT: Religious Studies Center, Brigham Young University; Salt Lake City: Deseret Book, 2013.

———. "The Lord's Supper during the Progressive Era, 1890–1930." *Journal of Mormon History* 38, no. 4 (Fall 2012): 88–104.

Brazilian Mission. Correspondence, 1942–44. CHL.

———. History of Mission Work, 1928–32. CHL.

Brazil São Paulo North Mission. Manuscript History and Historical Reports, 1927–77. CHL.

"A Brief History of the Church in the Netherlands." Global Histories. The Church of Jesus Christ of Latter-day Saints. Accessed July 22, 2020. https://www.ChurchofJesusChrist.org/study/history/global-histories/netherlands/nl-overview.

Bringhurst, Samuel E. "Acquisition of Property of the Swiss Temple." In *Temples of the Most High,* compiled by N. B. Lundwall, 196–202. Salt Lake City: Bookcraft, 1993.

———. Mission President Journal, 1950–60. CHL.

British Mission. Manuscript History and Historical Reports, 1841–1971. CHL.

Britsch, R. Lanier. "The Closing of the Early Japan Mission." In *Taking the Gospel to the Japanese, 1901 to 2001,* edited by Reid L. Neilson and Van C. Gessel, 263–83. Provo, UT: Brigham Young University Press, 2006.

———. *From the East: The History of the Latter-day Saints in Asia, 1851–1996.* Salt Lake City: Deseret Book, 1998.

———. *Moramona: The Mormons in Hawai'i.* 2nd ed. Mormons in the Pacific Series. Laie: Jonathan Napela Center for Hawaiian and Pacific Islands Studies, Brigham Young University–Hawaii, 2018.

———. *Unto the Islands of the Sea: A History of the Latter-day Saints in the Pacific.* Salt Lake City: Deseret Book, 1986.

Brooklyn Daily Eagle. Brooklyn, NY. 1849–1938.

Brooks, Juanita. *Uncle Will Tells His Story.* Salt Lake City: Taggart, 1970.

Brown, Barbara Jones. "The 1910 Mexican Revolution and the Rise and Demise of Mormon Polygamy in Mexico." In *Just South of Zion: The Mormons in Mexico and Its Borderlands,* edited by Jason H. Dormady and Jared M. Tamez, 23–38. Albuquerque: University of New Mexico Press, 2015.

Brown, Hugh B. *An Abundant Life: The Memoirs of Hugh B. Brown.* Edited by Edwin B. Firmage. Salt Lake City: Signature Books, 1988.

Brown, Jeremy. *Influenza: The Hundred-Year Hunt to Cure the Deadliest Disease in History.* New York: Touchstone, 2018.

Brown, John Parley. Journal, 1927–29. John P. Brown Mission Journals, 1927–29. CHL.

Brown, Ralph G. Mission Papers, circa 1950. CHL.

Buchanan, Frederick S. "Education among the Mormons: Brigham Young and Schools of Utah." *History of Education Quarterly* 22, no. 4 (Winter 1982): 435–59.

Bukey, Evan Burr. *Hitler's Austria: Popular Sentiment in the Nazi Era, 1938–1945.* Chapel Hill: University of North Carolina Press, 2000.

Bunch-Lyons, Beverly A. *Contested Terrain: African-American Women Migrate from the South to Cincinnati, Ohio, 1900–1950.* New York: Routledge, 2002.

Burkhardt, Johannes Henry. "Henry Johannes Burkhardt." In *German Latter-day Saints and World War II: Their Personal Stories of Survival,* edited by Lynn M. Hansen and Faith D. Hansen, 25–31. Provo, UT: BYU Studies, 2012.

———. Journal, 1950–2007. J. Henry Burkhardt Collection, 1950–2007. CHL. English translation of portions in possession of editors.

702

————. Oral History Interview by Phillip Lear and Doreen Lear, Feb. 14, 2018. CHL. English translation of portions in possession of editors.

Bush, Lester E., Jr. "Mormonism's Negro Doctrine: An Historical Overview." *Dialogue: A Journal of Mormon Thought* 8, no. 1 (Spring 1973): 12–68.

Butler, Ramay Chapin Storm. Interview by Jed Woodworth, Feb. 1, 2021. CHL.

By Study and Also by Faith: One Hundred Years of Seminaries and Institutes of Religion. Salt Lake City: The Church of Jesus Christ of Latter-day Saints, 2015.

California Intermountain News. Los Angeles. 1935–85.

California Inter-mountain Weekly News. Los Angeles. 1935–37.

Campbell, Eugene E., and Richard D. Poll. *Hugh B. Brown: His Life and Thought.* Salt Lake City: Bookcraft, 1975.

Candland, Evelyn. *An Ensign to the Nations: History of the Oakland Stake.* Oakland: Oakland California Stake, 1992.

Cannon, Abraham H. Diaries, 1879–95. BYU.

Cannon, Annie Wells. Journals, 1877–1942. BYU.

Cannon, Brian Q. "'What a Power We Will Be in This Land': The LDS Church, the Church Security Program, and the New Deal." *Journal of the West* 43 (Fall 2004): 66–75.

Cannon, George Q. Journals, 1849–1901. 50 vols. CHL. Also available at churchhistorianspress.org.

Cannon, Hugh J. Journal, 1920–21. Typescript. Hugh J. Cannon Papers, 1891–1977. CHL.

Cannon, Janath R., and Jill Mulvay Derr. "Resolving Differences/Achieving Unity: Lessons from the History of Relief Society." In *As Women of Faith: Talks Selected from the BYU Women's Conferences,* edited by Mary E. Stovall and Carol Cornwall Madsen, 122–47. Salt Lake City: Deseret Book, 1989.

Cannon, Kenneth L., Jr. "'And Now It Is the Mormons': The Magazine Crusade against the Mormon Church, 1910–1911." *Dialogue: A Journal of Mormon Thought* 46, no. 1 (Spring 2013): 1–63.

————. "Beyond the Manifesto: Polygamous Cohabitation among LDS General Authorities after 1890." *Utah Historical Quarterly* 46, no. 1 (Winter 1978): 24–36.

————. "Isaac Russell: Mormon Muckraker and Secret Defender of the Church." *Journal of Mormon History* 39, no. 4 (2013): 44–98.

————. "'The Modern Mormon Kingdom': Frank J. Cannon's National Campaign against Mormonism, 1910–18." *Journal of Mormon History* 37, no. 4 (2011): 60–105.

————. "Wives and Other Women: Love, Sex, and Marriage in the Lives of John Q. Cannon, Frank J. Cannon, and Abraham H. Cannon." *Dialogue: A Journal of Mormon Thought* 43, no. 4 (Winter 2010): 71–130.

Cannon, Mildred Catherine Bang. Oral History Interview by Jed Woodworth, Jan. 15, 2021. CHL.

Cannon Chronicle. Salt Lake City. 1952.

Cardston Alberta Stake. Relief Society Minutes and Records, 1894–1973. CHL.

————. Young Women's Mutual Improvement Association Minutes and Records, 1894–1969. 2 vols. CHL.

Cardston Ward, Alberta Stake. Relief Society Minutes and Records, 1887–1911. 7 vols. CHL.

————. Young Women's Mutual Improvement Association Minutes and Records, 1887–1917. 8 vols. CHL.

Carlson, Barbara L. Mission Journal, 1950–51. Barbara L. Carlson Collection, 1950–2006. CHL.

Carter, Steve. "The Rise of the Nazi Dictatorship and Its Relationship with the Mormon Church in Germany, 1933–1939." *International Journal of Mormon Studies* 3 (Spring 2010): 56–89.

Central Pacific Mission. General Minutes, 1922–48. CHL.

Century of Black Mormons Database. J. Willard Marriott Library, University of Utah, Salt Lake City. Accessed July 24, 2021. https://exhibits.lib.utah.edu/s/century-of-black-mormons.

Charrier, Jeanne. Email Interview with John Robertson, Feb. 2021. Jeanne-Esther Charrier History, 2010–15. CHL. English translation by Yvette Longstaff in possession of editors.

————. Oral History Interview by Dominique Aujé, Apr. 16, 2014. CHL. English translation by Yvette Longstaff in possession of editors.

703

———. Oral History Interview by Scott R. Christensen, Nov. 16, 2001. CHL. English translation by Yvette Longstaff in possession of editors.

Cheltenham Branch. Minutes, 1943–45. Nellie Middleton and Jennifer M. Mason Papers, 1908–45, 1986. CHL.

Cheltenham Chronicle and Gloucestershire Graphic. Gloucestershire, England. 1901–50.

Chicago Tribune. Chicago. 1847–.

Chidester, David. *Religions of South Africa.* London: Routledge, 1992.

Children's Friend. Salt Lake City. 1902–70.

Choi, Dong Sull. "A History of The Church of Jesus Christ of Latter-day Saints in Korea, 1950–1985." PhD diss., Brigham Young University, 1990.

Christensen, Clinton D., comp. *Stories of the Temple in Lāʻie, Hawaiʻi.* Laie: Jonathan Napela Center for Hawaiian and Pacific Islands Studies, Brigham Young University–Hawaii, 2019.

Christiansen, El Ray L. Temple Correspondence Files, 1955–70. CHL.

Christofferson [Johnson], Dorothy Jane. Mission Journal and Photographs, 1950, 2017. CHL.

Church Board of Education. Minutes, 1888–2006. CHL.

———. Minutes, 1919–25. CHL.

Church Educational System. Southern California Area Files, circa 1950–77. CHL.

Church Manuscripts, 1962–65. BYU.

Cincinnati Branch. Building Committee Minutes. Cincinnati Ward, Cincinnati Stake, Miscellaneous Minutes, 1941. CHL.

———. Minutes. Cincinnati Ward, Cincinnati Stake, General Minutes, 1925–77. 10 vols. (3 supplements). CHL.

———. YWMIA Minute Book, Attendance Roll, 1949–50. Cincinnati Ward, Cincinnati Stake, Young Women's Mutual Improvement Association Minutes and Records, 1948–73. CHL.

Cincinnati Branch, Northern States Mission. Record of Members and Children, 1932–41. CHL.

Cincinnati Enquirer. Cincinnati. 1872–.

Cincinnati Ward, Cincinnati Stake. Young Women's Mutual Improvement Association Minutes and Records, 1948–73. CHL.

Circular of the First Presidency of The Church of Jesus Christ of Latter-day Saints. Salt Lake City: Publisher unidentified, 1877.

Clapson, Mark. *The Blitz Companion: Aerial Warfare, Civilians and the City since 1911.* London: University of Westminster Press, 2019.

Clark, Christopher. *The Sleepwalkers: How Europe Went to War in 1914.* New York: HarperCollins, 2013.

Clark, James R., ed. *Messages of the First Presidency of The Church of Jesus Christ of Latter-day Saints, 1833–1964.* 6 vols. Salt Lake City: Bookcraft, 1975.

Clark, J. Reuben, Jr. Diaries, 1916–61. J. Reuben Clark Jr. Papers, 1873–1962. BYU.

———. Papers, 1873–1962. BYU.

Clawson, Rudger. Journals and Diaries, 1887–1905. Rudger Clawson Papers, 1870–1943. Special Collections, J. Willard Marriott Library, University of Utah, Salt Lake City. Also available as Stan Larson, ed., *A Ministry of Meetings: The Apostolic Diaries of Rudger Clawson* (Salt Lake City: Signature Books, Smith Research Associates, 1993).

———. "Memoirs of the Life of Rudger Clawson Written by Himself," circa 1926–35. CHL.

———. "Reorganization of Financial System at President's Office, under Administration of Presidents Lorenzo Snow and Joseph F. Smith," 1923. Typescript. CHL.

Clayson, Eli K. Oral History Interview by Douglas F. Tobler, Dec. 9, 1985. CHL.

Clayton, William. Diaries, 1846–53. CHL.

"A Collection of Stories and Events in the Life of Anson Bowen Call," 1999. CHL.

Collette, Emma Esther Cziep. *Glenn and Emmy: A Collette Family History, 1920–2007.* Idaho Falls, ID: By the author, 2007.

Collier's: The National Weekly. New York City. 1905–57.

Commercial Tribune. Cincinnati. 1898–1930.

Congressional Record: Containing the Proceedings and Debates of the Fifty-Sixth Congress, First Session. Vol. 33. Washington, DC: Government Printing Office, 1900.

Contributor. Salt Lake City. 1879–96.

Coray, John Louis. "Emma Lucy Gates (Bowen), Soprano—Her Accomplishments in Opera and Concert." Master's thesis, Brigham Young University, 1956.

Corbett, Don C. "Records from the Ruins," no date. Walter H. Karl Kindt, Personal Histories of German Latter-day Saints, 1930, 1945–47, 2003. CHL.

Cornwall, J. Spencer. *A Century of Singing: The Salt Lake Mormon Tabernacle Choir.* Salt Lake City: Deseret Book, 1958.

Cornwall, Millicent D., comp. "Chronological History of Salt Lake Tabernacle Choir," 1836–1957. Chronological History of Salt Lake Tabernacle Choir, 1836–1965, 1938–65. CHL.

Cosmopolitan. Rochester, NY. 1886–1925.

Costello, John. *The Pacific War, 1941–1945.* New York: Rawson, Wade, 1981.

Couch, Heidy, Christine Farnsworth, and S. Nia Maksymiw. Oral History Interview by Jed Woodworth and Angela Hallstrom, Feb. 19, 2021. CHL.

Council of the Twelve Apostles. General File, 1928–30. CHL.

Cowan, Richard O. "An Apostle in Oceania: Elder David O. McKay's 1921 Trip around the Pacific." In *Pioneers in the Pacific: Memory, History, and Cultural Identity among the Latter-day Saints,* edited by Grant Underwood, 189–200. Provo, UT: Religious Studies Center, Brigham Young University, 2005.

———. *The Church in the Twentieth Century.* Salt Lake City: Bookcraft, 1985.

———. *The Los Angeles Temple: A Beacon on a Hill.* Provo, UT: Religious Studies Center, Brigham Young University; Salt Lake City: Deseret Book, 2018.

———. "The Pivotal Swiss Temple." In *Regional Studies in Latter-day Saint Church History: Europe,* edited by Donald Q. Cannon and Brent L. Top, 129–45. Provo, UT: Department of Church History and Doctrine, Brigham Young University, 2003.

Cowan, Richard O., and William E. Homer. *California Saints: A 150-Year Legacy in the Golden State.* Provo, UT: Religious Studies Center, Brigham Young University, 1996.

Cowley, Matthias F. Journals and Autobiography, 1877–1940. CHL.

Croshaw, Fred. Mission Journal, 1931–34. Fred Croshaw Collection, 1931–34. CHL.

Cumorah's Southern Messenger. Cape Province, South Africa. 1933–70.

Curbelo, Néstor. *The History of the Mormons in Argentina.* Translated by Erin B. Jennings. Salt Lake City: Greg Kofford Books, 2009.

Czechoslovak Mission. Manuscript History and Historical Reports, 1928–59. CHL.

———. "Missionary Bulletin," Apr. 25, 1950. Franklin Murdock Files, 1940–57. CHL.

Czechoslovak Mission President's Records, 1939–62. CHL.

Cziep, Alois, and Hermine Cziep. Interview by Douglas Tobler, Dec. 24, 1974. CHL. English translation by Sylvia Ghosh, Mar. 2017, in possession of editors.

Dant, Doris R. "Minerva Teichert's Manti Temple Murals." *BYU Studies* 38, no. 3 (1999): 6–32.

Darowski, Joseph F. "Utah's Plight: A Passage through the Great Depression." Master's thesis, Brigham Young University, 2004.

Daynes, Kathryn M. *More Wives Than One: Transformation of the Mormon Marriage System, 1840–1910.* Urbana: University of Illinois Press, 2001.

Dean, Joseph H. Journals, 1876–1944. CHL.

de Gruchy, John W. *The Church Struggle in South Africa.* Grand Rapids, MI: William B. Eerdmans, 1979.

Dehner, George. *Influenza: A Century of Science and Public Health Response.* Pittsburgh: University of Pittsburgh Press, 2012.

Derr, Jill Mulvay. "Changing Relief Society Charity to Make Way for Welfare, 1930–1944." In *New Views of Mormon History: A Collection of Essays in Honor of Leonard J. Arrington,* edited by Davis Bitton and Maureen Ursenbach Beecher, 242–72. Salt Lake City: University of Utah Press, 1987.

———. "A History of Social Services in The Church of Jesus Christ of Latter-day Saints, 1916–1984," Oct. 1988. CHL.

Derr, Jill Mulvay, Janath Russell Cannon, and Maureen Ursenbach Beecher. *Women of Covenant: The Story of Relief Society.* Salt Lake City: Deseret Book; Provo, UT: Brigham Young University Press, 1992.

Derr, Jill Mulvay, Carol Cornwall Madsen, Kate Holbrook, and Matthew J. Grow, eds. *The First Fifty Years of Relief Society: Key Documents in Latter-day Saint Women's History*. Salt Lake City: Church Historian's Press, 2016.

Der Stern: Eine Monatschrift zur Verbreitung der Wahrheit. Bern, Zürich, Hamburg, Dresden, Berlin, and Frankfurt. 1869–1999. English translation of portions in possession of editors.

Descartes, René. *Discourse on Method and Meditations*. Translated, with an introduction, by Laurence J. Lafleur. New York: Macmillan and Collier Macmillan, 1960.

Deseret News. Salt Lake City. 1850–.

Deseret News 1989–90 Church Almanac. Salt Lake City: Deseret News in cooperation with The Church of Jesus Christ of Latter-day Saints, 1988.

Deseret News and Salt Lake Telegram. Salt Lake City. 1952–64.

Deseret News Church Almanac. Salt Lake City: Deseret News, 1974.

Deseret Sunday School Songs. Salt Lake City: Deseret Sunday School Union, 1909. Copy at CHL.

Dew, Sheri L. *Ezra Taft Benson: A Biography*. Salt Lake City: Deseret Book, 1987.

———. *Go Forward with Faith: The Biography of Gordon B. Hinckley*. Salt Lake City: Deseret Book, 1996.

Dewey, Richard Lloyd. *Hübener vs Hitler: A Biography of Helmuth Hübener, Mormon Teenage Resistance Leader*. Faith in Conflict Series 1. Provo, UT: Academic Research Foundation, 2004.

De Wolff, P., and W. Driehuis. "A Description of Post War Economic Developments and Economic Policy in the Netherlands." In *The Economy and Politics of the Netherlands since 1945*, edited by Richard T. Griffiths, 13–60. The Hague: M. Nijhoff, 1980.

Dickinson, Edward Ross. *The World in the Long Twentieth Century: An Interpretive History*. Oakland: University of California Press, 2018.

DiNunzio, Mario R., ed. *Woodrow Wilson: Essential Writings and Speeches of the Scholar-President*. New York: New York University Press, 2006.

Dixon Evening Telegraph. Dixon, IL. 1885–1985.

The Doctrine and Covenants of The Church of Jesus Christ of Latter-day Saints: Containing Revelations Given to Joseph Smith, the Prophet, with Some Additions by His Successors in the Presidency of the Church. Salt Lake City: The Church of Jesus Christ of Latter-day Saints, 2013.

The Doctrines of the Church: A Guide to Study (for Student and Teacher) Prepared Especially for Week-Day Program of Religious Education. Salt Lake City: The Church of Jesus Christ of Latter-day Saints, 1939.

Doig, Rebecca J., and W. Jack Stone. "The Alberta Settlement." In *Canadian Mormons: History of The Church of Jesus Christ of Latter-day Saints in Canada*, edited by Roy A. Prete and Carma T. Prete, 55–99. Provo, UT: Religious Studies Center, Brigham Young University; Salt Lake City: Deseret Book, 2017.

Donnelly, Mark. *Britain in the Second World War*. London: Rutledge, 1999.

Dormady, Jason H. *Primitive Revolution: Restorationist Religion and the Idea of the Mexican Revolution, 1940–1968*. Albuquerque: University of New Mexico Press, 2011.

Douglas, Norman. "Latter-day Saints Missions and Missionaries in Polynesia." PhD diss., Australian National University, 1974.

Dowse, Richard J. "The Laie Hawaii Temple: A History from Its Conception to Completion." Master's thesis, Brigham Young University, 2012.

Drury, Jesse. "For These My Brethren," circa 1950. Typescript. CHL.

Duffin, Marion F. Mission Journals, 1935–37. CHL.

Dunbabin, J. P. D. *The Cold War: The Great Powers and Their Allies*. 2nd ed. Harlow, England: Pearson Longman, 2008.

du Pré, Roy H. *Separate but Unequal: The 'Coloured' People of South Africa—A Political History*. Johannesburg: Jonathan Ball, 1994.

Durham, G. Homer. "The Death of John A. Widtsoe: A Memoir," May 30, 1967. John A. Widtsoe Biographical Materials, 1948–76. CHL.

DuRocher, Kris. "Violent Masculinity: Learning Ritual and Performance in Southern Lynchings." In *Southern Masculinity: Perspectives on Manhood in the South since*

Reconstruction, edited by Craig Thompson Friend, 46–64. Athens: University of Georgia Press, 2009.

East Anglian Daily Times. Ipswich, England. 1874–1910.

East German Mission. Photographic Record of a Youth Conference, 1954. CHL.

Edinburgh Evening News. Edinburgh, Scotland. 1873–.

Eighty-Eighth Semi-annual Conference of The Church of Jesus Christ of Latter-day Saints. Held in the Tabernacle and Assembly Hall, Salt Lake City, Utah, October 5th, 6th, 7th, 1917, with a Full Report of the Discourses. Salt Lake City: Deseret News, 1917.

Eighty-First Semi-annual Conference of The Church of Jesus Christ of Latter-day Saints. Held in the Tabernacle and Assembly Hall, Salt Lake City, Utah, Oct. 6, 7, 9, 1910, with a Full Report of the Discourses. Salt Lake City: Deseret News, 1910.

Eighty-Ninth Annual Conference of The Church of Jesus Christ of Latter-day Saints. Held in the Tabernacle and Assembly Hall, Salt Lake City, Utah, June 1st, 2nd and 3rd, 1919, with a Full Report of the Discourses. Salt Lake City: Deseret News, 1919.

Eighty-Ninth Semi-annual Conference of The Church of Jesus Christ of Latter-day Saints. Held in the Tabernacle and Assembly Hall, Salt Lake City, Utah, October 4th, 5th, and 6th, 1918, with a Full Report of the Discourses. Salt Lake City: Deseret News, 1918.

Eighty-Seventh Annual Conference of The Church of Jesus Christ of Latter-day Saints. Held in the Tabernacle and Assembly Hall, Salt Lake City, Utah, April 6th, 7th and 8th, 1917, with a Full Report of the Discourses. Salt Lake City: Deseret News, 1917.

Eighty-Seventh Semi-annual Conference of The Church of Jesus Christ of Latter-day Saints. Held in the Tabernacle and Assembly Hall, Salt Lake City, Utah, October 6th, 7th and 8th, 1916, with a Full Report of the Discourses. Salt Lake City: Deseret News, 1916.

Eighty-Sixth Annual Conference of The Church of Jesus Christ of Latter-day Saints. Held in the Tabernacle and Assembly Hall, Salt Lake City, Utah, April 6, 7, and 9, 1916, with a Full Report of the Discourses. Salt Lake City: Deseret News, 1916.

Elder, David. *Secret Cheltenham.* Gloucestershire, England: Amberley, 2019.

Eldredge, Erma. Mission Journal, 1954. CHL.

Eleventh Ward, University West Stake. General Minutes, 1855–1979. CHL.

Embry, Jessie L. "Women's Life Cycles, 1850 to 1940." In *Women in Utah History: Paradigm or Paradox?,* edited by Patricia Lyn Scott and Linda Thatcher, 394–415. Logan: Utah State University Press, 2005.

"Emigration Book, 1914–24." European Mission Emigration Records, 1849–1925. CHL.

Ensign. Los Angeles. Feb.–July 1937.

Ensign. Salt Lake City. 1971–2020.

Erekson, Keith A. "American Prophet, New England Town: The Memory of Joseph Smith in Vermont." Master's thesis, Brigham Young University, 2002.

Esplin, Scott C. "Charting the Course: President Clark's Charge to Religious Educators." *Religious Educator* 7, no. 1 (2006): 103–19.

European Mission. Historical Reports, 1946–50. CHL.

———. Relief Society Presidents' Conference Minutes, 1929. CHL.

European Mission History, 1946. CHL.

European Mission Presidents Conference, 1930. CHL.

Euvrard, Christian. "Histoire de Leon Fargier," 2016. Draft. CHL. Also available in "Un phénomène assez étrange pour notre époque," in *Socio-Histoire de l'Église de Jésus-Christ des Saints des Derniers Jours en France et en Europe francophone,* vol. 2, by Christian Euvrard (forthcoming).

Evans, Richard J. *The Coming of the Third Reich.* London: Penguin Books, 2004.

Evening Express. Liverpool. 1874–1945.

Evening Standard. Ogden, UT. 1910–13.

Evening Star. Washington, DC. 1854–1972.

Evening Times. Washington, DC. 1895–1902.

Everybody's Magazine. New York City. 1899–1923.

Eyring, Emma Romney. Autobiography, 1953. Typescript. CHL.

Fairbanks, Robert B. "Cincinnati Blacks and the Irony of Low-Income Housing Reform, 1900–1950." In *Race and the City: Work, Community, and Protest in Cincinnati, 1820–1970,* edited by Henry Louis Taylor Jr., 193–208. Urbana: University of Illinois Press, 1993.

Fairmont Ward, San Diego Stake. Manuscript History and Historical Reports, 1941–83. CHL.

Fassmann, Heinz, and Rainer Münz. "European East-West Migration, 1945–1992." *International Migration Review* 28, no. 3 (Autumn 1994): 520–38.

Fassmann, Walter K. *Walter K. Fassmann: An Autobiography.* Salt Lake City: By the author, 1995.

The Fates of Olga and Egon Weiss, 2021. CHL.

Feck, Luke. *Yesterday's Cincinnati.* Seemann's Historic Cities Series 19. Miami: E. A. Seemann, 1975.

Feldman, Lynne B. *A Sense of Place: Birmingham's Black Middle-Class Community, 1890–1930.* Tuscaloosa: University of Alabama Press, 1999.

Finck, Alfons J. "The Early Days of the Welfare Plan in Pioneer Stake." Typescript, 1966. Welfare Services Department Historical Files, 1932–2008, 2014, 2019. CHL.

Fink, Carole K. *Cold War: An International History.* Boulder, CO: Westview, 2014.

Firmage, Edwin Brown, and Richard Collin Mangrum. *Zion in the Courts: A Legal History of The Church of Jesus Christ of Latter-day Saints, 1830–1900.* Urbana: University of Illinois Press, 1988.

The First Fifty Years of Relief Society. Church History Department, The Church of Jesus Christ of Latter-day Saints. https://churchhistorianspress.org.

First Presidency. Cumulative Correspondence, 1900–49. CHL.

———. General Administration Files, 1855–1955. CHL.

———. General Administration Files, 1930–60. CHL.

———. General Authorities Correspondence, 1887–1918. CHL.

———. General Correspondence Files, 1940–59. CHL.

———. *An Important Message on Relief.* Salt Lake City: The Church of Jesus Christ of Latter-day Saints, 1936. Copy at CHL.

———. Joseph F. Smith Stake Correspondence, 1901–18. CHL.

———. Letterpress Copybooks, 1877–1949. CHL.

———. Miscellaneous Correspondence, 1915–39. CHL.

———. Mission Administration Correspondence, 1877–1918. CHL.

———. Missionary Calls and Recommendations, 1877–1918. CHL.

———. Mission Correspondence, 1950–59. CHL.

———. Mission Files, 1908, 1915–49. CHL.

———. Temple Ordinance Files, 1877–1915. CHL.

———. *To the Presidents of Stakes, Bishops, and Parents in Zion.* Apr. 27, 1915. [Salt Lake City]: The Church of Jesus Christ of Latter-day Saints, 1921. Copy at CHL.

First Presidency and Welfare Committee. Meeting Minutes, 1937–63. CHL.

Fish, Judith Bang. "My Life Story," circa 1999. Paul and Cornelia T. Bang Papers, 1935–44, 1977–78. CHL.

Fish, Stanley L., Bradley J. Kramer, and William Budge Wallis. *History of the Mormon Church in Cincinnati (1830–1985).* Cincinnati: Cincinnati Ohio and Cincinnati Ohio North Stakes, 1997.

Flake, Kathleen. *The Politics of American Religious Identity: The Seating of Senator Reed Smoot, Mormon Apostle.* Chapel Hill: University of North Carolina Press, 2004.

Flanagan, Maureen A. *America Reformed: Progressives and Progressivisms, 1890–1920s.* New York: Oxford University Press, 2007.

Flynn, George Q. *The Draft, 1940–1973.* Lawrence: University Press of Kansas, 1993.

Flynt, Wayne. *Alabama in the Twentieth Century.* Tuscaloosa: University of Alabama Press, 2004.

Fox, Frank W. *J. Reuben Clark: The Public Years.* Provo, UT: Brigham Young University Press; Salt Lake City: Deseret Book, 1980.

Freeman, Robert C., and Dennis A. Wright. *Saints at War: Experiences of Latter-day Saints in World War II*. American Fork, UT: Covenant Communications, 2001.

Frejka, Tomas, and Charles F. Westoff. "Religion, Religiousness and Fertility in the US and in Europe." *European Journal of Population* 24, no. 1 (Mar. 2008): 5–31.

Gardner, William. Journal, 1894–95. William Gardner Papers, 1884–1916. CHL.

Garner, Paul. *Porfirio Díaz*. London: Longman, 2001.

Gates, Susa Young. Files, 1911–22. CHL.

———. *History of the Young Ladies' Mutual Improvement Association of The Church of Jesus Christ of Latter-day Saints from November 1869 to June 1910*. Salt Lake City: Deseret News, 1911.

———. Journals, 1870–1933. Susa Young Gates Papers, circa 1870–1933. CHL.

———. Papers, circa 1870–1933. CHL.

Gates, Susa Young, and Leah Dunford Widtsoe. *The Life Story of Brigham Young*. New York: Macmillan, 1930.

Gazette. Montreal. 1778–.

Gellately, Robert. *Backing Hitler: Consent and Coercion in Nazi Germany*. New York: Oxford University Press, 2001.

Gellately, Robert, and Nathan Stoltzfus. "Social Outsiders and the Construction of the Community of the People." In *Social Outsiders in Nazi Germany,* edited by Robert Gellately and Nathan Stoltzfus, 3–19. Princeton, NJ: Princeton University Press, 2001.

Genealogical Society of Utah. Board of Trustees Minutes, 1894–1975. CHL.

General Church Welfare Committee. Minutes, 1936–67. CHL.

The General Relief Society. Officers, Objects and Status. Salt Lake City: General Officers, 1902.

George Albert Smith Family Papers, 1731–1969. Special Collections, J. Willard Marriott Library, University of Utah, Salt Lake City.

Georgetown Branch, Minutes. Georgetown Ward, Cincinnati Stake, General Minutes, 1948–77. 4 vols. (1 supplement). CHL.

Georgetown Ward, Cincinnati Stake. General Minutes, 1948–77. 4 vols. (1 supplement). CHL.

Gerlach, Larry R. *Alma Richards: Olympian*. Salt Lake City: University of Utah Press, 2016.

———. *Blazing Crosses in Zion: The Ku Klux Klan in Utah*. Logan: Utah State University Press, 1982.

German-Austrian Mission. Branch Histories, circa 1934. CHL.

———. General Minutes, 1925–37. 2 vols. CHL.

———. Manuscript History and Historical Reports, 1925–37. 4 vols. CHL.

Germany Hamburg Mission. Manuscript History and Historical Reports, 1937–77. 12 vols. CHL. English translation of portions in possession of editors.

Gerritsen, Allen P. "The Hill Cumorah Monument: An Inspired Creation of Torleif S. Knaphus." *Journal of Book of Mormon Studies* 13, no. 1 (2004): 124–35, 173.

Gibbons, Francis M. *George Albert Smith: Kind and Caring Christian, Prophet of God*. Salt Lake City: Deseret Book, 1990.

———. *Harold B. Lee: Man of Vision, Prophet of God*. Salt Lake City: Deseret Book, 1993.

Gibson, Inez. Mission Journals, 1930–32. CHL.

Gigliotti, Simone, and Berel Lang. "Introduction." In *The Holocaust: A Reader,* edited by Simone Gigliotti and Berel Lang, 1–8. Oxford: Blackwell, 2005.

Gilbert, Martin. *The Holocaust: The Jewish Tragedy*. London: Collins, 1986.

[Gilchrist, Rosetta Luce]. *Apples of Sodom: A Story of Mormon Life*. Cleveland: William W. Williams, 1883.

Givens, Terryl L. *The Viper on the Hearth: Mormons, Myths, and the Construction of Heresy*. New York: Oxford University Press, 2013.

Goates, L. Brent. *Harold B. Lee: Prophet and Seer*. Salt Lake City: Bookcraft, 1985.

Goldberg, James. "The Armenian Exodus." Pioneers in Every Land, Church History Department, The Church of Jesus Christ of Latter-day Saints. Published 2013. https://history.ChurchofJesusChrist.org/exhibit/1921-lds-armenian-exodus.

Golithon, Clemencia Pivaral. "Clemencia Pivaral's Baptism Story." Clemencia Pivaral Golithon Papers, 1940–2011. CHL.

Gomez Páez, Fernando Rogelio. *The Church of Jesus Christ of Latter-day Saints and the Lamanite Conventions: From Darkness to Light*. Mexico: Museo de Historia del Mormonismo, 2004.

Gonzales, Michael J. *The Mexican Revolution, 1910–1940*. Albuquerque: University of New Mexico Press, 2002.

"Gospel Topics." The Church of Jesus Christ of Latter-day Saints. https://www.ChurchofJesusChrist.org/study/manual/gospel-topics.

Gowers, Ronald M. Mission Journal, 1934–36. CHL.

Grant, Heber J. Collection, 1852–1945 (bulk 1880–1945). CHL.

———. Journals, 1880–1922. Heber J. Grant Collection, 1852–1945 (bulk 1880–1945). CHL.

———. Journals, 1886–1945. Heber J. Grant Collection, 1852–1945 (bulk 1880–1945). CHL.

———. Journals (press copy), 1886–1925. Heber J. Grant Collection, 1852–1945 (bulk 1880–1945). CHL.

Greene, Norma Geddes. Interview, 1990. CHL.

———. *A Life Remembered: The Personal Memoirs of Norma Geddes Greene*. [Moscow, ID?]: By the author, [1993].

Gregory, Herold Lamar. Mission President Journal, 1953–57. Herold L. Gregory Mission Journals, 1948–51, 1953–57. CHL.

Griffiths, Casey Paul. "The First Institute Teacher." *Religious Educator* 11, no. 2 (2010): 175–201.

Groberg, Delbert V. *The Idaho Falls Temple: The First LDS Temple in Idaho*. Salt Lake City: Publishers Press, 1985.

Gross, Gerhard P. *The Myth and Reality of German Warfare: Operational Thinking from Moltke the Elder to Heusinger*. Lexington: University of Kentucky Press, 2016.

Grover, Mark L. "Execution in Mexico: The Deaths of Rafael Monroy and Vicente Morales." *BYU Studies* 35, no. 3 (1995–96): 6–28.

———. "The Mormon Church and German Immigrants in Southern Brazil: Religion and Language." *Jahrbuch für Geschichte von Staat, Wirtschaft und Gesellschaft Lateinamerikas* 26 (1989): 295–308.

———. "Mormonism in Brazil: Religion and Dependency in Latin America." PhD diss., Indiana University, 1985.

———. "Sprechen Sie Portugiesisch? Nein: The German Beginnings of the Church in Brazil." *Journal of Mormon History* 45, no. 2 (Apr. 2019): 115–43.

Guatemala Branch, Central American Mission. Manuscript History and Historical Reports, 1947–84. CHL.

———. Relief Society Minutes and Records, 1948–62. CHL.

Guide to the First Year's Course of Study in the Young Ladies' Mutual Improvement Association. Salt Lake City: George Q. Cannon and Sons, 1892.

Gutjahr, Paul C. *The Book of Mormon: A Biography*. Princeton, NJ: Princeton University Press, 2012.

Hafen, Bruce C. *A Disciple's Life: The Biography of Neal A. Maxwell*. Salt Lake City: Deseret Book, 2002.

Hales, Brian C. *Modern Polygamy and Mormon Fundamentalism: The Generations after the Manifesto*. Salt Lake City: Greg Kofford Books, 2006.

Hall, Bruce W. "And the Last Shall Be First: The Church of Jesus Christ of Latter-day Saints in the Former East Germany." *Journal of Church and State* 42, no. 3 (Summer 2000): 485–505.

Hall, Dave. *A Faded Legacy: Amy Brown Lyman and Mormon Women's Activism, 1872–1959*. Salt Lake City: University of Utah Press, 2015.

Hall, Perry C. Autobiography, circa 1976. CHL.

Halpern, Paul G. *A Naval History of World War I*. Annapolis, MD: Naval Institute Press, 1994.

Hamburg Passenger Lists, 1850–1934. Database. Ancestry.com. Accessed Feb. 3, 2021. https://www.ancestryinstitution.com/search/collections/1068/.

Hancock, Joseph P. Mission Letters and Autobiography, 1949, 2007. CHL.

Hand Book for the Bee-Hive Girls of the Y. L. M. I. A. Salt Lake City: General Board of the Young Ladies' Mutual Improvement Association, 1915.

Hand Book for the Bee-Hive Girls of the Y. L. M. I. A. 10th ed. Salt Lake City: General Board of the Young Ladies' Mutual Improvement Association, 1928.

Handbook for the Bee-Hive Girls of the Young Ladies' Mutual Improvement Association, Church of Jesus Christ of Latter-day Saints, British and South African Missions. 1st European ed. London: British Mission, 1933.

Handbuch für die Bienenkorbmädchen des Fortbildungsvereins für junge Damen. 2nd ed. [Basel, Switzerland]: Swiss-German and German-Austrian Mission of The Church of Jesus Christ of Latter-day Saints, 1928. Helga Meiszus's copy is available in Helga Meyer Collection, 1944–58, 2016–18, CHL.

Handlin, Oscar. "Making Men of the Boys." In *Glimpses of the Harvard Past,* by Bernard Bailyn, Donald Fleming, Oscar Handlin, and Stephan Thernstrom, 45–62. Cambridge, MA: Harvard University Press, 1986.

Handy, Moses P. *The Official Directory of the World's Columbian Exposition, May 1st to October 30th, 1893.* Chicago: W. B. Conkey, 1893.

Hanks, Marion D. Oral History Interview by Jessie L. Embry, May 18, 1989. Marion D. Hanks Collection, 1989. BYU.

Hansen, Earl Eugene. Journal, 1947–48. Earl E. Hansen Mission Papers, 1947–48, 2010. CHL.

——. Reminiscence, 2010. Earl E. Hansen Mission Papers, 1947–48, 2010. CHL.

Harbrecht, Ewan E. "Personal History of Ewan E. Harbrecht Mitton," 2010. 2 vols. Ewan E. Harbrecht Mitton Collection, 1955, 2003. CHL.

Hardy, B. Carmon. *Solemn Covenant: The Mormon Polygamous Passage.* Urbana: University of Illinois Press, 1992.

Hardy, B. Carmon, and Melody Seymour. "The Importation of Arms and the 1912 Mormon 'Exodus' from Mexico." *New Mexico Historical Review* 72, no. 4 (Oct. 1997): 297–318.

Harper, Steven C. *First Vision: Memory and Mormon Origins.* New York: Oxford University Press, 2019.

Harper's Weekly. New York City. 1857–1916.

Harrison, Brian. *Separate Spheres: The Opposition to Women's Suffrage in Britain.* Routledge Library Editions: Women's History 20. London: Routledge, 2012.

Hartley, William G. "Common People: Church Activity during the Brigham Young Era." In *Nearly Everything Imaginable: The Everyday Life of Utah's Mormon Pioneers,* edited by Ronald W. Walker and Doris R. Dant, 249–94. Provo, UT: Brigham Young University Press, 1999.

——. "From Men to Boys: LDS Aaronic Priesthood Offices, 1829–1996." *Journal of Mormon History* 22, no. 1 (Spring 1996): 80–136.

——. *My Fellow Servants: Essays on the History of the Priesthood.* Provo, UT: BYU Studies, 2010.

Harvard University Catalogue, 1903–04. Cambridge, MA: Harvard University, 1903.

Hasted, Michael. *The Cheltenham Book of Days.* Stroud, Gloucestershire, England: History Press, 2013.

Hatch, Gayle Collette, comp. *Alois and Hermine: A Cziep Family History, 1893–2005.* Durham, NC: By the compiler, 2005. Copy at CHL.

Hatch, Nelle Spilsbury. *Colonia Juarez: An Intimate Account of a Mormon Village.* Salt Lake City: Deseret Book, 1954.

Heath, Harvard S. "Reed Smoot: The First Modern Mormon." 2 vols. PhD diss., Brigham Young University, 1990.

——. ed. *In the World: The Diaries of Reed Smoot.* Salt Lake City: Signature Books, 1997.

Heimann, Mary. *Czechoslovakia: The State That Failed.* New Haven, CT: Yale University Press, 2009.

Heimburger, Christian. "Remembering Topaz and Wendover: Memorializing the Dark Shadows of History." *Utah Historical Quarterly* 86, no. 2 (Spring 2018): 148–53.

Henze, Paul B. "RFE's Early Years: Evolution of Broadcast Policy and Evidence of Broadcast Impact." In *Cold War Broadcasting: Impact on the Soviet Union and Western Europe,* edited by A. Ross Johnson and R. Eugene Parta, 3–16. New York: Central European University Press, 2010.

Herald-Journal. Logan, UT. 1931–.

Hermansen, Ray J. Oral History Interview by Becky B. Lloyd, June 2, 2004. Saving the Legacy: An Oral History of Utah's World War II Veterans, 2001–10. American West Center, Special Collections, J. Willard Marriott Library, University of Utah, Salt Lake City.

Herwig, Holger H. *The Marne, 1914: The Opening of World War I and the Battle That Changed the World.* New York: Random House, 2011.

Hicks, Michael. *The Mormon Tabernacle Choir: A Biography.* Urbana: University of Illinois Press, 2015.

Hiery, Hermann Joseph. *The Neglected War: The German South Pacific and the Influence of World War I.* Honolulu: University of Hawaii Press, 1995.

Higham, John. *Strangers in the Land: Patterns of American Nativism, 1860–1925.* New Brunswick, NJ: Rutgers University Press, 1955.

Hilberg, Raul. *The Destruction of the European Jews.* Rev. ed. 3 vols. New York: Holmes and Meier, 1985.

Hilo Tribune Herald. Hilo, HI. 1923–64.

Hinckley, Gordon B. Journals, 1946–2008. CHL.

———. Oral History Interview by Gordon Irving, Sept. 2, 1983. CHL.

Historical Department. Journal History of the Church, 1896–2001. CHL.

———. Office Journal, 1844–2012. CHL.

Holmes, Blair R., and Alan F. Keele. *When Truth Was Treason: German Youth against Hitler; The Story of the Helmuth Hübener Group.* Urbana: University of Illinois Press, 1995.

Holmes, Brent M. Journal, 1955–58. CHL.

Holt, Essie. Mission Journal, 1931–32. Essie H. Wheadon Mission Papers, circa 1931–40. CHL.

The Holy Bible, Containing the Old and New Testaments Translated Out of the Original Tongues: And with the Former Translations Diligently Compared and Revised, by His Majesty's Special Command. Authorized King James Version with Explanatory Notes and Cross References to the Standard Works of The Church of Jesus Christ of Latter-day Saints. Salt Lake City: The Church of Jesus Christ of Latter-day Saints, 2013.

Honolulu Advertiser. Honolulu. 1921–2010.

Honolulu Star-Bulletin. Honolulu. 1912–2010.

Horne, Dennis B. "Joseph F. Smith's Succession to the Presidency." In *Joseph F. Smith: Reflections on the Man and His Times,* edited by Craig K. Manscill, Brian D. Reeves, Guy L. Dorius, and J. B. Haws, 265–77. Provo, UT: Religious Studies Center, Brigham Young University; Salt Lake City: Deseret Book, 2013.

———. *Latter Leaves in the Life of Lorenzo Snow, 5th President of The Church of Jesus Christ of Latter-day Saints.* With material prepared in 1890 by Orson F. Whitney. Springville, UT: Cedar Fort, 2012.

Horton, Zachary Ryan. "'Wherein Shall We Return?': A Historical and Analytical Examination of Lorenzo Snow's 1899 Reemphasis of Tithing." Master's thesis, Brigham Young University, 2015.

Howard, Susan W. "William Jarman: 'That Anti-Mormon Apostle of the British Isles.'" *Journal of Mormon History* 43, no. 1 (Jan. 2017): 60–86.

Howells, Adele Cannon. Diaries, 1927–50. Adele Cannon Howells Papers, 1902–51. CHL.

Howells, Rulon S. Oral History Interview by Gordon Irving, Jan. 18, 1973. CHL.

Howlett, David J. *Kirtland Temple: The Biography of a Shared Mormon Sacred Space.* Urbana: University of Illinois Press, 2014.

Huber, Patricia O'Donnal. Oral History Interview by Clate W. Mask, June 28, 2018. Audio recording. CHL.

Hugill, Peter J. "Good Roads and the Automobile in the United States, 1880–1929." *Geographical Review* 72, no. 3 (July 1982): 327–49.

Humphreys, R. A. *Latin America and the Second World War. Vol. 2, 1942–1945.* London: Athlone, 1982.

Hunter, Nan. Interview, July 11, 1985. Church Educational System, Southern California Area Files, circa 1950–77. CHL.

Hwang, Su-kyoung. *Korea's Grievous War.* Philadelphia: University of Pennsylvania Press, 2016.

Hyde, Orson. *Ein Ruf aus der Wüste, eine Stimme aus dem Schoose der Erde: Kurzer Ueberblick des Ursprungs und der Lehre der Kirche "Jesus Christ of Latter Day Saints" in Amerika, gekannt von Manchen unter der Benennung; "Die Mormonen."* Frankfurt: Im Selbstverlage des Verfassers, 1842. Excerpts also available in German and in English translation on the Joseph Smith Papers website, josephsmithpapers.org.

Hymns of The Church of Jesus Christ of Latter-day Saints. Salt Lake City: The Church of Jesus Christ of Latter-day Saints, 1985.

I Hemolele, circa 1880–89. Photograph. Laie Plantation and Community Photo Collection, Joseph F. Smith Library, Brigham Young University–Hawaii, Laie.

Ikegami, David. Journal, 1941–42. David Ikegami Papers, circa 1930–42, 2008–20. CHL.

———. "We Had Good Examples among the Members: The Conversion Story of Kichitaro (Kay) Ikegami as Related by His Son, David Ikegami." In *Mormon Pioneers of Japanese Ancestry: Their Conversion Stories,* compiled and edited by Dennis H. Atkin and Theodocia H. Atkin, 228–30. Flagstaff, AZ: Theodocia H. Atkin, 2008.

Ikegami, Donna. "A Brief History of the Japanese Members of The Church of Jesus Christ of Latter-day Saints in Hawaii," July 3, 2020. Typescript. David Ikegami Papers, circa 1930–42, 2008–20. CHL.

———. David Ikegami Memories, no date. David Ikegami Papers, circa 1930–42, 2008–20. CHL.

Improvement Era. Salt Lake City. 1897–1970.

Informe de la Mesa Directiva de la 3a Convención a la Primera Presidencia, [June 25, 1936]. In *Informe General de la Tercera Convención de los Miembros de la Iglesia de Jesu-Cristo de los Santos de los Ultimos Días Celebrada en Tecalco, México, el 21 de abril 1936 y que fué enviado a la Primera Presidencia para su resolución.* Publication place and publisher unidentified, 1936. Copy at CHL. English translation of portions in possession of editors.

In Memoriam: John A. Widtsoe. [Salt Lake City]: Bookcraft, [1952]. Copy at CHL.

Instructor. Salt Lake City. 1930–70.

Irving, Gordon. "The Law of Adoption: One Phase of the Development of the Mormon Concept of Salvation, 1930–1980." *BYU Studies* 14, no. 3 (Summer 1974): 291–314.

Israel, Fred L. "Military Justice in Hawaii, 1941–1944." *Pacific Historical Review* 36, no. 3 (Aug. 1967): 243–67.

Jackson, Kenneth T. *The Ku Klux Klan in the City, 1915–1930.* New York: Oxford University Press, 1967.

Jackson, Richard W. *Places of Worship: 150 Years of Latter-day Saint Architecture.* Provo, UT: Religious Studies Center, Brigham Young University, 2003.

Jackson, Robert. "The Celluloid War before *The Birth:* Race and History in Early American Film." In *American Cinema and the Southern Imaginary,* edited by Deborah E. Barker and Kathryn McKee, 27–51. Athens: University of Georgia Press, 2011.

Jakle, John A., and Keith A. Sculle. *The Gas Station in America.* Baltimore: Johns Hopkins University Press, 1994.

James, Jane Manning. Autobiography, circa 1902. CHL.

James, John J. Mission Journal, 1893–95. CHL.

Japanese Mission. Manuscript History and Historical Reports, 1901–55. CHL.

Japanese Mission (Hawaii). Hawaii District Missionary Journals, 1938–44. CHL.

Jarman Family Papers. Huntington Library, San Marino, CA.

Jensen, Jay C., and Eva B. Jensen. Journal Excerpts, 1941. CHL.

Jensen, Mary White. "Faces: A Personal History," Apr. 2002. CHL.

Jensen, R. Devan, and Petra Javadi-Evans. "Senator Elbert D. Thomas: Advocate for the World." In *Latter-day Saints in Washington, DC,* edited by Kenneth L. Alford, Lloyd D. Newell, and Alexander L. Baugh, 223–39. Provo, UT: Religious Studies Center, Brigham Young University; Salt Lake City: Deseret Book, 2021.

Jensen, Royal Duane. "President McKay Shook This Old Black Hand," 1967. CHL.

Jenson, Andrew. *Latter-day Saint Biographical Encyclopedia.* 4 vols. Salt Lake City: Deseret News, 1910–36.

Jenson, Martha Smith. "Hyrum M. Smith," circa 1972. CHL.

John F. and Carmen G. O'Donnal Papers, 1878–2001, bulk 1972–98. CHL.

Johnson, Eric A., and Karl-Heinz Reuband. *What We Knew: Terror, Mass Murder, and Everyday Life in Nazi Germany: An Oral History.* London: John Murray, 2005.

Johnson, G. Wesley, and Marian Ashby Johnson. "On the Trail of the Twentieth-Century Mormon Outmigration." *BYU Studies* 46, no. 1 (2007): 41–83.

Jones, Janet L., and Diane C. Prince. Oral History Interview by Jed Woodworth and Scott Hales, Jan. 15, 2021. CHL.

Jones, Joseph Dean. Mission Journal, 1948–50. CHL.

Jorgensen, Victor W., and Carmon L. Hardy. "The Taylor-Cowley Affair and the Watershed of Mormon History." *Utah Historical Quarterly* 48, no. 1 (Winter 1980): 4–36.

Josef and Martha Roubíček Papers, 1935–57, 1970–90. CHL.

Joseph F. and Alice K. Smith Family Correspondence, 1902–20, 1955. CHL.

Joseph Smith Centennial Photograph Album, 1905. CHL.

Josephson, Marba C. *History of the YWMIA.* Salt Lake City: Deseret News Press, 1955.

Journal. Logan, UT. 1892–1931.

Journal of Discourses. 26 vols. Liverpool: F. D. Richards, 1855–86.

The Journal of George Q. Cannon. 1849–1901. Church History Department, The Church of Jesus Christ of Latter-day Saints. https://www.churchhistorianspress.org/george-q-cannon.

JSP, D12 / Grua, David W., Brent M. Rogers, Matthew C. Godfrey, Robin Scott Jensen, Christopher James Blythe, and Jessica M. Nelson, eds. *Documents, Volume 12: March–July 1843.* Vol. 12 of the Documents series of *The Joseph Smith Papers,* edited by Matthew C. Godfrey, R. Eric Smith, Matthew J. Grow, and Ronald K. Esplin. Salt Lake City: Church Historian's Press, 2021.

JSP, H1 / Davidson, Karen Lynn, David J. Whittaker, Mark Ashurst-McGee, and Richard L. Jensen, eds. *Histories, Volume 1: Joseph Smith Histories, 1832–1844.* Vol. 1 of the Histories series of *The Joseph Smith Papers,* edited by Dean C. Jessee, Ronald K. Esplin, and Richard Lyman Bushman. Salt Lake City: Church Historian's Press, 2012.

Juvenile Instructor. Salt Lake City. 1866–1929.

Kahne, Marcel. *History of the Liège District, 1889–1997.* [France]: By the author, [circa 1997]. Copy at CHL.

Kater, Michael H. *Hitler Youth.* Cambridge, MA: Harvard University Press, 2004.

Kawai, David. Letter to Nadine Kawai, Apr. 1, 2013. CHL.

Keele, Alan F., and Douglas F. Tobler. "The Fuhrer's New Clothes: Helmuth Hübener and the Mormons in the Third Reich." *Sunstone* 5, no. 6 (Nov.–Dec. 1980): 20–29.

Kennedy, David M. *Freedom from Fear: The American People in Depression and War, 1929–1945.* The Oxford History of the United States 9. New York: Oxford University Press, 1999.

Kershaw, Ian. *The End: Hitler's Germany, 1944–45.* London: Allen Lane, 2011.

Kertz-Welzel, Alexandra. "The Singing Muse? Three Centuries of Music Education in Germany." *Journal of Historical Research in Music Education* 26, no. 1 (Oct. 2004): 8–27.

Kesler, Donnette Smith. *Reminiscences by Donnette Smith Kesler: The Wife of Alonzo Pratt Kesler.* Salt Lake City: Elbert C. Kirkham, 1952.

Kimball, Camilla Eyring. *Autobiography of Camilla Eyring Kimball.* Publication place unidentified: By the author, 1975.

———. Oral History Interview by Jessie L. Embry, Apr.–June 1977. Photocopy of typescript. CHL.

Kimball, Edward L., ed. *The Writings of Camilla Eyring Kimball.* Salt Lake City: Deseret Book, 1990.

Kimball, Edward L., and Andrew E. Kimball Jr. *Spencer W. Kimball: Twelfth President of The Church of Jesus Christ of Latter-day Saints.* Salt Lake City: Bookcraft, 1977.

Kimball, Richard Ian. *Sports in Zion: Mormon Recreation, 1890–1940.* Chicago: University of Illinois Press, 2003.

Kimball, Spencer W. Journals, 1905–81. CHL.

Kimura, Yukiko. *Issei: Japanese Immigrants in Hawaii.* Honolulu: University of Hawaii Press, 1988.

Kirby, Dale Z. "History of The Church of Jesus Christ of Latter-day Saints in Switzerland." Master's thesis, Brigham Young University, 1971.

Knaefler, Tomi Kaizawa. *Our House Divided: Seven Japanese American Families in World War II*. Honolulu: University of Hawaii Press, 1991.

Knepper, George W. *Ohio and Its People*. Kent, OH: Kent State University Press, 1997.

Koonz, Claudia. *The Nazi Conscience*. Cambridge, MA: Belknap, 2003.

Kuehne, Raymond. *Henry Burkhardt and LDS Realpolitik in Communist East Germany*. Salt Lake City: University of Utah Press, 2011.

———. *Mormons as Citizens of a Communist State: A Documentary History of The Church of Jesus Christ of Latter-day Saints in East Germany, 1945–1990*. Salt Lake City: University of Utah Press, 2010.

Kullick, Edward. "Life of Herta," no date. Copy in possession of editors.

Large, David Clay. *Berlin*. New York: Basic Books, 2000.

Larson, Edward J. *Summer for the Gods: The Scopes Trial and America's Continuing Debate over Science and Religion*. Cambridge, MA: Harvard University Press, 1997.

Latter-day Saints' Millennial Star. Manchester, England, 1840–42; Liverpool, 1842–1932; London, 1932–70.

Layton, Henry. Correspondence, 1930–31. CHL.

L.D.S. Young Men's Mutual Improvement Associations Manual, Part One. Salt Lake City: [The Church of Jesus Christ of Latter-day Saints], 1891.

Lears, T. J. Jackson. *No Place of Grace: Antimodernism and the Transformation of American Culture, 1880–1920*. Chicago: University of Chicago Press, 1981.

Lee, Armenia Willey. Autobiography. Cardston Alberta Temple: An Historical Record Collection. University of Lethbridge Library, Lethbridge, Alberta, Canada.

Lee, Harold B. Journal, 1935–36. CHL.

———. "Remarks of Elder Harold B. Lee," 1959. Typescript. CHL.

Lee, Marion L. Mission Journal, 1938–39. CHL.

Lehi Banner. Lehi, UT. 1891–1917.

Lepage, Jean-Denis G. G. *Hitler Youth, 1922–1945: An Illustrated History*. Jefferson, NC: McFarland, 2009.

Lethbridge Daily Herald. Lethbridge, Alberta, Canada. 1908–26.

L'Étoile. Germany; France. 1968–99. English translation of portions in possession of editors.

Lewis, Evelyn Hodges. Oral History Interview by Loretta L. Hefner, Sept. 15, 1979. CHL.

Lewis, Jill. *Workers and Politics in Occupied Austria, 1945–55*. Manchester, England: Manchester University Press, 2007.

Liahona. Salt Lake City. 1995–.

Liahona, the Elders' Journal. Independence, MO. 1907–45.

Linford, Erika Just, and Lawrence L. Linford. Oral History Interview by Angela Hallstrom, Oct. 30, 2020. CHL.

Lingard, David D. Journal, 1947–49. David D. Lingard Mission Papers, 1947–49. CHL.

Literary Digest. New York City. 1890–1938.

Litster, Elizabeth Opal. Mission Journal, 1931–32. CHL.

Liverpool Daily Post and Liverpool Mercury. Liverpool. 1904–16.

Lives of Our Leaders: Character Sketches of Living Presidents and Apostles of The Church of Jesus Christ of Latter-day Saints; With Portraits. Salt Lake City: Deseret News, 1901.

Lochery, Neill. *Brazil: The Fortunes of War; World War II and the Making of Modern Brazil*. New York: Basic Books, 2014.

Logan Fifth Ward, Cache East Stake. Young Women's Mutual Improvement Association Minutes and Records, 1878–1973. 4 vols. CHL.

Logan Republican. Logan, UT. 1902–21.

Los Angeles Times. Los Angeles. 1886–.

Love Branch, South African Mission. Miscellaneous Minutes, 1925–34. CHL.

Lozano Herrera, Agrícol. *Historia del Mormonismo en Mexico*. Mexico: Editorial Zarahemla, 1983. English translation of portions by Elena Lowe, Aug. 2017, in possession of editors.

Ludlow, Linda Bang. Interview by Jed Woodworth, Jan. 14, 2021. Video recording. Paul and Cornelia T. Bang Papers, 1935–44, 1977–78. CHL.

Lund, Anthon H. Journals, 1860–1921. 41 vols. CHL.

———. Papers, 1869–1920. CHL.

Lund, Jennifer L. "Joseph F. Smith and the Origins of the Church Historic Sites Program." In *Joseph F. Smith: Reflections on the Man and His Times,* edited by Craig K. Manscill, Brian D. Reeves, Guy L. Dorius, and J. B. Haws, 342–58. Provo, UT: Religious Studies Center, Brigham Young University; Salt Lake City: Deseret Book, 2013.

Luza, Radomir V. *The Resistance in Austria, 1938–1945.* Minneapolis: University of Minnesota Press, 1984.

Lyman, Amy Brown. *In Retrospect: Autobiography of Amy Brown Lyman.* Salt Lake City: Deseret News Press, 1945.

———. "Social Service Work in the Relief Society, 1917–1928." A Brief History of Social Service Work in Relief Society, 1917–27. CHL.

Lyman, Edward Leo. *Political Deliverance: The Mormon Quest for Utah Statehood.* Urbana: University of Illinois Press, 1986.

Lyman, Francis Marion. Journals, 1860–1916. CHL.

———. Papers, 1849–1947. CHL.

Lyman, Karl R. *As I Saw It.* Orem, UT: By the author, 1972.

Madsen, Carol Cornwall. *Emmeline B. Wells: An Intimate History.* Salt Lake City: University of Utah Press, 2017.

Madsen, Carol Cornwall, and Susan Staker Oman. *Sisters and Little Saints: One Hundred Years of Primary.* Salt Lake City: Deseret Book, 1979.

Madsen, Truman G. *Defender of the Faith: The B. H. Roberts Story.* Salt Lake City: Bookcraft, 1980.

Maki, Elizabeth. "'They Can Bear Testimony, They Can Teach': Pioneering Efforts of the First Single Sister Missionaries," July 17, 2012. Women of Conviction, Church History Department, The Church of Jesus Christ of Latter-day Saints. Published July 17, 2012. https://history.ChurchofJesusChrist.org/article/inez-knight-missionary.

Manchester Evening News. Manchester, England. 1868–.

Manchester Guardian. Manchester, England. 1821–1959.

Mandleco, Barbara, and Carma Miller. "A History of Children's Hospitals in Utah." *Utah Historical Quarterly* 76, no. 4 (Fall 2008): 338–56.

Mangum, Garth, and Bruce Blumell. *The Mormons' War on Poverty: A History of LDS Welfare, 1830–1990.* Salt Lake City: University of Utah Press, 1993.

Mann, Patricia Ann. "A History of the Relief Society Magazine, 1914–1970." Master's thesis, Brigham Young University, 1971.

The March of Time: Salt Lake City! Motion picture. New York: RKO Pictures Distribution, Time Magazine, [1936]. Copy at CHL.

Marsden, George M. *Fundamentalism and American Culture: The Shaping of Twentieth-Century Evangelicalism, 1870–1925.* New York: Oxford University Press, 1980.

Martha S. Anderson Letters to Wallace F. Toronto, 1946–47, 1956–58, 1961. CHL.

Martin, Samuel. Autobiography, 1947. CHL.

Mason, Patrick Q. *The Mormon Menace: Violence and Anti-Mormonism in the Postbellum South.* New York: Oxford University Press, 2011.

Mawdsley, Evan. *World War II: A New History.* New York: Cambridge University Press, 2009.

Maxwell, Neal A. Dictation, Sept. 1979. CHL.

———. Oral History Interview by Gordon Irving, Nov. 1999–Feb. 2000. CHL.

———. Oral History Interview by James B. Allen, 1976–77. CHL.

———. Personal History, box 1, folders 2–4. Neal A. Maxwell Scrapbook, circa 1976–2004. CHL.

———. Scrapbook, circa 1976–2004. CHL.

———. World War II Correspondence, 1944–46. CHL.

May, Elaine Tyler. "Rosie the Riveter Gets Married." In *The War in American Culture: Society and Consciousness during World War II,* edited by Lewis A. Erenberg and Susan E. Hirsch, 128–43. Chicago: University of Chicago Press, 1996.

McArthur, Moroni. Oral History Interview by Thomas P. McArthur, Apr. 6, 1959. Moroni and Emma McArthur Oral Histories, Nellie McArthur Gubler Family Papers, 1849–2007. BYU.

McBride, Matthew S. "'I Could Have Gone into Every House': Elizabeth McCune Helped Pave the Way for Sister Missionaries," July 10, 2012. Women of Conviction, Church History Department, The Church of Jesus Christ of Latter-day Saints. Published July 10, 2012. https://history.ChurchofJesusChrist.org/article/elizabeth-mccune-missionary.

McClure's Magazine. New York City. 1893–1929.

McCormick, John S. "The Great Depression." In *Utah History Encyclopedia,* edited by Allan Kent Powell, 136–38. Salt Lake City: University of Utah Press, 1994.

McDannell, Colleen. *Sister Saints: Mormon Women since the End of Polygamy.* New York: Oxford University Press, 2019.

McDonough, Frank. *The Gestapo: The Myth and Reality of Hitler's Secret Police.* London: Coronet, 2015.

McGerr, Michael. *A Fierce Discontent: The Rise and Fall of the Progressive Movement in America, 1870–1920.* New York: Oxford University Press, 2003.

McGreal, Stephen. *Liverpool in the Great War.* Barnsley, England: Pen and Sword Books, 2014.

McKay, David Lawrence. *My Father, David O. McKay.* Edited by Lavina Fielding Anderson. Salt Lake City: Deseret Book, 1989.

McKay, David O. Diary, 1932, 1936–70. David O. McKay Papers, 1901–70. CHL.

———. Papers, 1897–1983. Special Collections, J. Willard Marriott Library, University of Utah, Salt Lake City.

———. Papers, 1901–70. CHL.

———. Scrapbooks, 1906–70. CHL.

McKay, Emma Ray. Diary, 1954. McKay Family Papers, 1897–1983. CHL.

McKay, Thomas E. Correspondence, 1939–46. CHL.

Mead, Sidney E. "Denominationalism: The Shape of Protestantism in America." *Church History* 23, no. 4 (Dec. 1954): 291–320.

Mecham, Lucian Mormon. Oral History Interview by Gordon Irving, 1974. CHL.

Mehr, Kahlile. "Enduring Believers: Czechoslovakia and the LDS Church, 1884–1990." *Journal of Mormon History* 18, no. 2 (1992): 111–54.

Merrill, Milton R. *Reed Smoot: Apostle in Politics.* Logan: Utah State University Press, 1990.

The Message of the Ages: A Sacred Pageant . . . . Salt Lake City: The Church of Jesus Christ of Latter-day Saints, 1930.

Mexican Mission. Manuscript History and Historical Reports, 1874–1977. CHL.

Mexico Northwestern Railway Company. *The Road to Wealth.* Publication place unidentified: By the author, [1909].

Meyer, Helga. Interview by Jed Woodworth, Oct. 21, 2016. Helga Meyer Collection, 1944–58, 2016–18. CHL.

———. Interview by Jed Woodworth, Aug. 30, 2017. Helga Meyer Collection, 1944–58, 2016–18. CHL.

Meyer, Helga, and Lark Evans Galli. *Under a Leafless Tree: The Story of Helga Meyer, a Mormon Girl from East Prussia.* Salt Lake City: Greg Kofford Books, 2021.

Middleton, Nellie, and Jennifer M. Mason Papers, 1908–45, 1986. CHL.

Miller, Bonnie M. *From Liberation to Conquest: The Visual and Popular Cultures of the Spanish-American War of 1898.* Amherst: University of Massachusetts Press, 2011.

Miller, Clyde Allen. *Apostle of Principle: John W. Taylor, 1858–1916.* Sandy, UT: Taylor, forthcoming.

Miller, Robert Earnest. *World War II Cincinnati: From the Front Lines to the Home Front.* Charleston, SC: History Press, 2014.

Milwaukee Journal. Milwaukee. 1882–1995.

Miner, Caroline E., and Edward L. Kimball. *Camilla: A Biography of Camilla Eyring Kimball.* Salt Lake City: Deseret Book, 1980.

Minert, Roger P. *Against the Wall: Johann Huber and the First Mormons in Austria.* Provo, UT: Religious Studies Center, Brigham Young University; Salt Lake City: Deseret Book, 2015.

———. *In Harm's Way: East German Latter-day Saints in World War II.* Provo, UT: Religious Studies Center, Brigham Young University, 2009.

———. "Succession in German Mission Leadership during World War II." In *A Firm Foundation: Church Organization and Administration,* edited by David J. Whittaker and Arnold K. Garr, 553–71. Provo, UT: Religious Studies Center, Brigham Young University; Salt Lake City: Deseret Book, 2011.

———. *Under the Gun: West German and Austrian Latter-day Saints in World War II.* Provo, UT: Religious Studies Center, Brigham Young University; Salt Lake City: Deseret Book, 2011.

Mintz, Steven. *Huck's Raft: A History of American Childhood.* Cambridge, MA: Harvard University Press, 2006.

Miraldi, Robert. *Muckraking and Objectivity: Journalism's Colliding Traditions.* Westport, CT: Greenwood, 1990.

Missionary Database. Church History Department, The Church of Jesus Christ of Latter-day Saints. https://history.ChurchofJesusChrist.org/missionary.

Missionary Department. Executive Secretary General Files, 1940–62. CHL.

———. Franklin Murdock Files, 1940–57. CHL.

———. Missionary Registers, 1860–1959. CHL.

"Missionary Journal of Myrl Lewis," 1914–15. Myrl Lewis Papers, 1913–2016. CHL.

Missionary Review of the World. New York City. 1888–1939.

The Missionary's Hand Book. Independence, MO: The Church of Jesus Christ of Latter-day Saints, 1937.

Mitchell, Michael. "The Mormons in Wilhelmine Germany, 1870–1914: Making a Place for an Unwanted American Religion in a Changing German Society." Master's thesis, Brigham Young University, 1994.

Moffat, Riley M., Fred E. Woods, and Brent R. Anderson. *Saints of Tonga: A Century of Island Faith.* Provo, UT: Religious Studies Center, Brigham Young University, 2020.

Monroy, Guadalupe. History of the San Marcos Branch, 1934–36. Copy. CHL. English translation of portions in possession of editors.

Monroy, Jesus M. Letter to Rey L. Pratt, Aug. 27, 1915. CHL.

Monson, Farrell Ray. "History of the South African Mission of The Church of Jesus Christ of Latter-day Saints, 1853–1970." Master's thesis, Brigham Young University, 1971.

Montague, Terry Bohle. *"Mine Angels Round About": Mormon Missionary Evacuation from Western Germany, 1939.* Orem, UT: Granite, 2000.

Moorhouse, Roger. *Berlin at War: Life and Death in Hitler's Capital, 1939–45.* London: Bodley Head, 2010.

Mora González, Santiago. Oral History Interview by Gordon Irving, Aug. 12, 1974. CHL. English translation of portions by Patsy Hendrickson in possession of editors.

Mormon Tabernacle Choir Tour Files, 1896–1978. CHL.

Moser, John E. *The Global Great Depression and the Coming of World War II.* Boulder, CO: Paradigm, 2015.

Mount Graham Stake. Confidential Minutes, 1938–82. CHL.

Mouritsen, Dale C. "A Symbol of New Directions: George Franklin Richards and the Mormon Church, 1861–1950." PhD diss., Brigham Young University, 1982.

Mowbray Branch, South African Mission. Cottage Meeting Minutes, 1921–25. CHL.

———. General Minutes, 1912–73. 10 vols. CHL.

Mühlberger, Detlef. *Hitler's Followers: Studies in the Sociology of the Nazi Movement.* London: Routledge, 1991.

Mulder, William. *Homeward to Zion: The Mormon Migration from Scandinavia.* Minneapolis: University of Minnesota Press, 2000.

Müller, Rolf-Dieter. *Hitler's Wehrmacht: 1935–1945.* Lexington: University Press of Kentucky, 2016.

Mulvay, Jill C. "Zion's Schoolmarms." In *Mormon Sisters: Women in Early Utah,* edited by Claudia L. Bushman, 67–83. Logan: Utah State University Press, 1997.

Murphy, Miriam B. "'If Only I Shall Have the Right Stuff': Utah Women in World War I." *Utah Historical Quarterly* 58, no. 4 (Fall 1990): 334–50.

Music. Chicago. 1891–1902.

Musical Courier. New York City. 1880–1962.

Musicant, Ivan. *Empire by Default: The Spanish-American War and the Dawn of the American Century.* New York: Henry Holt, 1998.

Naimark, Norman M. *The Russians in Germany: A History of the Soviet Zone of Occupation, 1945–1949.* Cambridge, MA: Belknap Press of Harvard University Press, 1995.

National Tribune. Washington, DC. 1877–1917.

Naujoks, Arthur O., Jr., and Michael S. Eldredge. *Shades of Gray: Memoirs of a Prussian Saint on the Eastern Front.* Salt Lake City: Mill Creek, 2004.

Neilson, Reid L. *Exhibiting Mormonism: The Latter-day Saints and the 1893 Chicago World's Fair.* New York: Oxford University Press, 2011.

———. "Mormonism's Blacksmith Orator: B. H. Roberts at the 1893 World's Parliament of Religions." *Mormon Historical Studies* 12, no. 1 (Spring 2011): 53–84.

———. *To the Peripheries of Mormondom: The Apostolic Around-the-World Journey of David O. McKay, 1920–1921.* Salt Lake City: University of Utah Press, 2011.

Neilson, Reid L., and Carson V. Teuscher, eds. *Pacific Apostle: The 1920–21 Diary of David O. McKay in the Latter-day Saint Island Missions.* Urbana: University of Chicago Press, 2020.

Neilson, Reid L., and Nathan N. Waite, eds. *Settling the Valley, Proclaiming the Gospel: The General Epistles of the Mormon First Presidency.* New York: Oxford University Press, 2017.

Nelson, David Conley. *Moroni and the Swastika: Mormons in Nazi Germany.* Norman: University of Oklahoma Press, 2015.

Netherlands Amsterdam Mission. Manuscript History and Historical Reports, 1841–1977. CHL.

Neubrandenburg Branch, Germany Dresden Mission. General Minutes, 1949–75. CHL.

Neuenschwander, George H. Correspondence with Genevieve Bramwell, 1928–33, 2004. CHL.

Newell, Lloyd D. "Seventy-Five Years of the Mormon Tabernacle Choir's *Music and the Spoken Word,* 1929–2004: A History of the Broadcast of America's Choir." *Mormon Historical Studies* 5, no. 1 (Spring 2004): 127–42.

Newell, Quincy D. *Your Sister in the Gospel: The Life of Jane Manning James, a Nineteenth-Century Black Mormon.* New York: Oxford University Press, 2019.

New Mexico Historical Review. Albuquerque. 1926–.

Newton, Marjorie. *Southern Cross Saints: The Mormons in Australia.* Laie, HI: Institute for Polynesian Studies, 1991.

———. *Tiki and Temple: The Mormon Mission in New Zealand, 1854–1958.* Salt Lake City: Greg Kofford Books, 2012.

Newton, Ronald C. *German Buenos Aires, 1900–1933: Social Change and Cultural Crisis.* Austin: University of Texas, 1977.

New York Journal and Advertiser. New York City. 1897–1901.

New York Times. New York City. 1851–.

New Zealand Auckland Mission. Manuscript History and Historical Reports, 1854–1974. CHL.

Ninetieth Semi-annual Conference of The Church of Jesus Christ of Latter-day Saints. Held in the Tabernacle and Assembly Hall, Salt Lake City, Utah, October 3rd, 4th and 5th, 1919, with a Full Report of the Discourses. Salt Lake City: Deseret News, 1919.

Ninety-First Annual Conference of The Church of Jesus Christ of Latter-day Saints. Held in the Tabernacle and Assembly Hall, Salt Lake City, Utah, April 3, 4, 5, 6, 1921, with a Full Report of the Discourses. Salt Lake City: Deseret Book, 1921.

Ninety-First Semi-annual Conference of The Church of Jesus Christ of Latter-day Saints. Held in the Tabernacle and Assembly Hall, Salt Lake City, Utah, Oct. 8, 9, 10, 1920, with a Full Report of the Discourses. Salt Lake City: Deseret Book, 1920.

Ninety-Second Annual Conference of The Church of Jesus Christ of Latter-day Saints. Held in the Tabernacle and Assembly Hall, Salt Lake City, Utah, April 6, 7 and 9, 1922, with a Full Report of All the Discourses. Salt Lake City: Deseret Book, 1922.

Ninety-Second Semi-annual Conference of The Church of Jesus Christ of Latter-day Saints. Held in the Tabernacle and Assembly Hall, Salt Lake City, Utah, October 6, 7, and 9, 1921, with a Full Report of All the Discourses. Salt Lake City: The Church of Jesus Christ of Latter-day Saints, 1921.

Ninety-Seventh Semi-annual Conference of The Church of Jesus Christ of Latter-day Saints. Held in the Tabernacle and Assembly Hall, Salt Lake City, Utah, October 3, 4 and 5, 1926, with a Full Report of All the Discourses. Salt Lake City: The Church of Jesus Christ of Latter-day Saints, 1926.

Noakes, J., and G. Pridham, eds. *Nazism, 1919–1945: A History in Documents and Eyewitness Accounts.* Vol. 1, *The Nazi Party, State and Society, 1919–1939.* New York: Schocken Books, 1983.

Northern States Mission. General Minutes, 1875–1930. CHL.

———. Manuscript History and Historical Reports, 1831–32, 1875–1977. CHL.

Nottingham Branch, British Mission. Relief Society Minutes and Records, 1895–1973. CHL.

Nottingham Conference, British Mission. Manuscript History and Historical Reports, 1852–1951. CHL.

Numbers, Ronald L. *The Creationists: From Scientific Creationism to Intelligent Design.* Cambridge, MA: Harvard University Press, 2006.

Nuneaton Observer. Nuneaton, Warwickshire, England. 1907–16.

Odo, Franklin. *No Sword to Bury: Japanese Americans in Hawai'i during World War II.* Philadelphia: Temple University Press, 2004.

O'Donnal, John Forres. "Personal History of John Forres O'Donnal," 2001. John F. and Carmen G. O'Donnal Papers, 1878–2001 (bulk 1972–98). CHL.

———. *Pioneer in Guatemala.* Yorba Linda, CA: Shumway Family History Services, 1997.

O'Donnal, John Forres, and Carmen G. O'Donnal. Oral History Interview by Gordon Irving, Aug. 28–29, 1979. CHL.

Offenberger, Ilana F. "Jewish Responses to Nazism in Vienna after the Anschluss." In *Understanding and Teaching the Holocaust,* edited by Laura J. Hilton and Avinoam Patt, 60–80. Madison: University of Wisconsin Press, 2020.

Official Report of the Proceedings and Debates of the Convention Assembled at Salt Lake City on the Fourth Day of March, 1895, to Adopt a Constitution for the State of Utah. Salt Lake City: Star Printing, 1898.

Ogden Standard. Ogden, UT. 1888–1920.

Ogden Standard-Examiner. Ogden, UT. 1920–.

Okihiro, Gary Y. *Cane Fires: The Anti-Japanese Movement in Hawaii, 1865–1945.* Philadelphia: Temple University Press, 1991.

Okkers, Alice Johanna. "I Would Love to Touch the Door of the Temple." In *"All Are Alike unto God": Fascinating Conversion Stories of African Saints,* edited by E. Dale LeBaron, 176–80. Salt Lake City: Bookcraft, 1990.

———. Oral History Interview by E. Dale LeBaron, July 29, 1988. BYU.

Olsen, Daniel H., Brandon E. Plewe, and Jonathan A. Jarvis. "Historical Geography: Growth, Distribution, and Ethnicity." In *Canadian Mormons: History of The Church of Jesus Christ of Latter-day Saints in Canada,* edited by Roy A. Prete and Carma T. Prete, 101–26. Provo, UT: Religious Studies Center, Brigham Young University, 2017.

Olson, James Stuart. *Saving Capitalism: The Reconstruction Finance Corporation and the New Deal, 1933–1940.* Princeton, NJ: Princeton University Press, 1988.

One Hundred Eighteenth Semi-annual Conference of The Church of Jesus Christ of Latter-day Saints. Held in the Tabernacle, Salt Lake City, Utah, October 3, 4 and 5, 1947, with Report of Discourses. Salt Lake City: The Church of Jesus Christ of Latter-day Saints, 1947.

One Hundred Eleventh Semi-annual Conference of The Church of Jesus Christ of Latter-day Saints. Held in the Tabernacle, Salt Lake City, Utah, October 4, 5, 6, 1940, with Report of Discourses. Salt Lake City: The Church of Jesus Christ of Latter-day Saints, 1940.

One Hundred Fifteenth Semi-annual Conference of The Church of Jesus Christ of Latter-day Saints. Held in the Tabernacle, Salt Lake City, Utah, October 6, 7 and 8, 1944, with Report of Discourses. Salt Lake City: The Church of Jesus Christ of Latter-day Saints, 1944.

One Hundred Fifth Semi-annual Conference of The Church of Jesus Christ of Latter-day Saints. Held in the Tabernacle, Salt Lake City, Utah, October 5, 6, 7, 1934, with Report of Discourses. Salt Lake City: The Church of Jesus Christ of Latter-day Saints, 1934.

One Hundred Forty-Second Semi-annual Conference of The Church of Jesus Christ of Latter-day Saints. Held in the Tabernacle, Salt Lake City, Utah, October 6, 7, 8, 1972, with Report of Discourses. Salt Lake City: The Church of Jesus Christ of Latter-day Saints, 1972.

One Hundred Fourteenth Annual Conference of The Church of Jesus Christ of Latter-day Saints. Held in the Tabernacle, Salt Lake City, Utah, April 6, 7 and 9, 1944, with Report of Discourses. Salt Lake City: The Church of Jesus Christ of Latter-day Saints, 1944.

One Hundred Fourth Semi-annual Conference of The Church of Jesus Christ of Latter-day Saints. Held in the Tabernacle, Salt Lake City, Utah, October 6, 7, 8, 1933, with Report of Discourses. Salt Lake City: The Church of Jesus Christ of Latter-day Saints, 1933.

One Hundred Nineteenth Annual Conference of The Church of Jesus Christ of Latter-day Saints. Held in the Tabernacle, Salt Lake City, Utah, April 3, 4 and 6, 1949, with Report of Discourses. Salt Lake City: The Church of Jesus Christ of Latter-day Saints, 1949.

One Hundred Seventh Semi-annual Conference of The Church of Jesus Christ of Latter-day Saints. Held in the Tabernacle, Salt Lake City, Utah, October 2, 3, 4, 1936, with Report of Discourses. Salt Lake City: The Church of Jesus Christ of Latter-day Saints, 1936.

One Hundred Sixteenth Semi-annual Conference of The Church of Jesus Christ of Latter-day Saints. Held in the Tabernacle, Salt Lake City, Utah, October 5, 6 and 7, 1945, with Report of Discourses. Salt Lake City: The Church of Jesus Christ of Latter-day Saints, 1945.

One Hundred Tenth Annual Conference of The Church of Jesus Christ of Latter-day Saints. Held in the Tabernacle, Salt Lake City, Utah, April 5, 6, 7, 1940, with Report of Discourses. Salt Lake City: The Church of Jesus Christ of Latter-day Saints, 1940.

One Hundred Tenth Semi-annual Conference of The Church of Jesus Christ of Latter-day Saints. Held in the Tabernacle, Salt Lake City, Utah, October 6, 7, 8, 1939, with Report of Discourses. Salt Lake City: The Church of Jesus Christ of Latter-day Saints, 1939.

One Hundredth Annual Conference of The Church of Jesus Christ of Latter-day Saints. Held in the Tabernacle, Salt Lake City, Utah, April 6, 7, 8, 9, 1930, with a Full Report of All the Discourses. Salt Lake City: The Church of Jesus Christ of Latter-day Saints, 1930.

One Hundred Twelfth Annual Conference of The Church of Jesus Christ of Latter-day Saints. Held in the Tabernacle, Salt Lake City, Utah, April 4, 5, 6, 1942, with Report of Discourses. Salt Lake City: The Church of Jesus Christ of Latter-day Saints, 1942.

One Hundred Twentieth Annual Conference of The Church of Jesus Christ of Latter-day Saints. Held in the Tabernacle, Salt Lake City, Utah, April 6, 8, and 9, 1950, with Report of Discourses. Salt Lake City: The Church of Jesus Christ of Latter-day Saints, 1950.

One Hundred Twenty-First Annual Conference of The Church of Jesus Christ of Latter-day Saints. Held in the Tabernacle, Salt Lake City, Utah, April 6, 7, 8 and 9, 1951, with Report of Discourses. Salt Lake City: The Church of Jesus Christ of Latter-day Saints, 1951.

One Hundred Years of Presbyterianism in the Ohio Valley. Cincinnati: Presbytery of Cincinnati, 1890.

Orton, Chad M. *More Faith Than Fear: The Los Angeles Stake Story*. Salt Lake City: Bookcraft, 1987.

O'Toole, Patricia. *The Moralist: Woodrow Wilson and the World He Made*. New York: Simon and Schuster, 2018.

Overy, Richard. *The Third Reich: A Chronicle*. London: Quercus, 2010.

Packer, Cameron J. "A Study of the Hill Cumorah: A Significant Latter-day Saint Landmark in Western New York." Master's thesis, Brigham Young University, 2002.

Palmer, Delbert A., and Mark L. Grover. "Hoping to Establish a Presence: Parley P. Pratt's 1851 Mission to Chile." *BYU Studies* 38, no. 4 (1999): 115–38.

The Parliamentary Debates. (Official Report). Fifth Series, Volume 22. First Session of the Thirtieth Parliament of the United Kingdom of Great Britain and Ireland. 1 George V. House of Commons. Second Volume of Session 1911, Comprising Period from Monday, 27th February, 1911, to Friday, 17th March, 1911. London: James Truscott and Son, 1911.

The Parliamentary Debates. (Official Report). Fifth Series, Volume 24. First Session of the Thirtieth Parliament of the United Kingdom of Great Britain and Ireland. 1 George V. House of Commons. Fourth Volume of Session 1911, Comprising Period from Monday, 10th April, 1911, to Friday, 28th April, 1911. London: James Truscott and Son, 1911.

Parmley, Martha LaVern Watts. Oral History Interview by Jill Mulvay Derr, 1974–76. CHL.

Parrish, Alan K. *John A. Widtsoe: A Biography.* Salt Lake City: Deseret Book, 2003.

Parshall, Ardis E. " 'Courage to Follow Convictions': Tsune Ishida Nachie (1856–1938)." In *1846–1870,* edited by Richard E. Turley Jr. and Brittany A. Chapman, 122–30. Vol. 3 of *Women of Faith in the Latter Days.* Salt Lake City: Deseret Book, 2012.

———. "Friedrich Schulzke: It Fell to My Lot to Guide the Little Branch," Jan. 28, 2009. CHL.

———. "John Philip Dalby: Musician, Storyteller, Artist," Sept. 2, 2009. CHL.

Pasadena Post. Pasadena, CA. 1929–45.

"Passenger Lists, 1865–1922." Database. Library and Archives Canada. Accessed July 17, 2020. https://www.bac-lac.gc.ca/eng/discover/immigration/immigration-records/passenger-lists/passenger-lists-1865-1922/Pages/introduction.aspx.

Patterson, James T. *Brown v. Board of Education: A Civil Rights Milestone and Its Troubled Legacy.* New York: Oxford University Press, 2001.

———. *Grand Expectations: The United States, 1945–1974.* The Oxford History of the United States 10. New York: Oxford University Press, 1996.

Paul and Cornelia T. Bang Papers, 1935–44, 1977–78. CHL.

Paulos, Michael Harold. "Under the Gun at the Smoot Hearings: Joseph F. Smith's Testimony." *Journal of Mormon History* 34, no. 4 (2008): 181–225.

———, ed. *The Mormon Church on Trial: Transcripts of the Reed Smoot Hearings.* Salt Lake City: Signature Books, 2008.

Pavalko, Eliza K., and Glen H. Elder Jr. "World War II and Divorce: A Life-Course Perspective." *American Journal of Sociology* 95, no. 5 (Mar. 1990): 1213–34.

Payne, Phillip G. *Crash! How the Economic Boom and Bust of the 1920s Worked.* Baltimore: Johns Hopkins University Press, 2015.

The Pearl of Great Price: A Selection from the Revelations, Translations, and Narrations of Joseph Smith, First Prophet, Seer, and Revelator to The Church of Jesus Christ of Latter-day Saints. Salt Lake City: The Church of Jesus Christ of Latter-day Saints, 2013.

Pearson's. New York City. 1903–25.

Pegram, Thomas R. "The Ku Klux Klan, Labor, and the White Working Class during the 1920s." *Journal of the Gilded Age and the Progressive Era* 17, no. 2 (2018): 373–96.

Pérez de Lara, Jorge. "Temple of the Sun: Celebrating 100 Years of Excavation at Mexico's Teotihuacan." *Archaeology* 58, no. 6 (Nov.–Dec. 2005): 36–41.

Peterson, Janet, and LaRene Gaunt. *The Children's Friends: Primary Presidents and Their Lives of Service.* Salt Lake City: Deseret Book, 1996.

Peterson, Paul H. "An Historical Analysis of the Word of Wisdom." Master's thesis, Brigham Young University, 1972.

Picturesque Cincinnati. Cincinnati: John Shillilo, [1883].

Pierce, Arwell Lee. "The Story of the Third Convention," no date. Photocopy of typescript. CHL.

Pioneer Database. Church History Department, The Church of Jesus Christ of Latter-day Saints. https://history.ChurchofJesusChrist.org/overlandtravel.

Pittsburgh Press. Pittsburgh. 1884–1992.

Pivaral, Clemencia. Journal and Photographs, 1951, 2021. Clemencia Pivaral Golithon Papers, 1940–2011. CHL.

Plewe, Brandon S., ed. *Mapping Mormonism: An Atlas of Latter-day Saint History.* Provo, UT: Brigham Young University Press, 2012.

Pratt, Orson. *A[n] Interesting Account of Several Remarkable Visions, and of the Late Discovery of Ancient American Records.* Edinburgh: Ballantyne and Hughes, 1840.

Pratt, Parley P. *The Autobiography of Parley Parker Pratt, One of the Twelve Apostles of The Church of Jesus Christ of Latter-day Saints, Embracing His Life, Ministry and Travels, with Extracts, in Prose and Verse, from His Miscellaneous Writings.* Edited by Parley P. Pratt Jr. New York: Russell Brothers, 1874.

Pratt, Rey L. Papers, 1901–59. CHL.

Pratt Institute Monthly. Brooklyn, NY. 1892–1904.

Presiding Bishopric. Bulletins, 1916–61. CHL.

———. Financial, Statistical, and Historical Reports of Wards, Stakes, and Missions, 1884–1955. CHL.

———. General Files, 1872–1948. CHL.

———. General Files, 1889–1956. CHL.

———. Minutes of the Aaronic Priesthood Convention Held in the Assembly Hall, 1930–37. CHL.

———. Office Journals, 1901–46. CHL.

———. Stake and Mission Census, 1950–60, 1962. CHL.

———. Welfare Files, 1930–46. CHL.

Prete, Roy A., and Carma T. Prete, eds. *Canadian Mormons: History of The Church of Jesus Christ of Latter-day Saints in Canada.* Provo, UT: Religious Studies Center, Brigham Young University, 2017.

Price, Harrison T. Mission Journals, 1947–50. CHL.

Primary Association. General Board Minutes, 1889–1994, 2005–14. CHL.

———. General Records, 1941–73. CHL.

Prince, Gregory A., and Wm. Robert Wright. *David O. McKay and the Rise of Modern Mormonism.* Salt Lake City: University of Utah Press, 2005.

Principles of the Gospel. [Salt Lake City]: [The Church of Jesus Christ of Latter-day Saints], 1943. Copy in O. Leslie and Dorothy C. Stone Family Papers, 1916–85. CHL.

Prior, Robin. "1916: Impasse." In *Global War,* edited by Jay Winter, 89–109. Vol. 1 of *The Cambridge History of the First World War.* Cambridge: Cambridge University Press, 2014.

Proceedings before the Committee on Privileges and Elections of the United States Senate in the Matter of the Protests against the Right of Hon. Reed Smoot, a Senator from the State of Utah, to Hold His Seat. Vol. 1. Washington, DC: Government Printing Office, 1904.

Provo Herald. Provo, UT. 1909–22.

Publicity Committee Scrapbook, 1930. CHL.

Pugsley, Nellie D. Autobiography, circa 1940. CHL.

Pulido, Elisa. "Margarito Bautista, Mexican Politics, and the Third Convention." *Mormon Studies Review* 8 (Jan. 2021): 48–56.

———. "Solving Schism in Nepantla: The Third Convention Returns to the LDS Fold." In *Just South of Zion: The Mormons in Mexico and Its Borderlands,* edited by Jason H. Dormady and Jared M. Tamez, 89–109. Albuquerque: University of New Mexico Press, 2015.

———. *The Spiritual Evolution of Margarito Bautista: Mexican Mormon Evangelizer, Polygamist Dissident, and Utopian Founder, 1878–1961.* New York: Oxford University Press, 2020.

Pusey, Merlo J. *Builders of the Kingdom: George A. Smith, John Henry Smith, George Albert Smith.* Provo, UT: Brigham Young University Press, 1981.

Putney, Clifford. *Muscular Christianity: Manhood and Sports in Protestant America, 1880–1920.* Cambridge, MA: Harvard University Press, 2001.

Queensland Times, Ipswich Herald, and General Advertiser. Ipswich, Australia. 1861–.

Quinn, D. Michael. *Elder Statesman: A Biography of J. Reuben Clark.* Salt Lake City: Signature Books, 2002.

———. *The Mormon Hierarchy: Wealth and Corporate Power.* Salt Lake City: Signature Books, 2017.

Quorum of the Twelve Apostles. Miscellaneous Minutes, 1888–1969. CHL.

Ranglack, Richard, Paul Langheinrich, and Gottfried Neuman. "The First Trip thru the Mission." European Mission, Thomas E. McKay Correspondence, 1939–46. CHL.

———. "The Second Trip thru the Mission." European Mission, Thomas E. McKay Correspondence, 1939–46. CHL.

Rasmussen, Matthew Lyman. *Mormonism and the Making of a British Zion*. Salt Lake City: University of Utah Press, 2016.

Record of Members Collection, 1836–1970. CHL.

Reese, Dagmar. *Growing Up Female in Nazi Germany*. Translated by William Templer. Ann Arbor: University of Michigan Press, 2006.

Reeves, Richard I. "Utah and the Spanish-American War." Master's thesis, Brigham Young University, 1998.

Reiser, A. Hamer. Diary, 1954. Copy in David O. McKay Scrapbooks, 1906–70. CHL.

———. Oral History Interview by William G. Hartley, July–Aug. 1974. CHL.

Reiter, Tonya. "Black Saviors on Mount Zion: Proxy Baptisms and Latter-day Saints of African Descent." *Journal of Mormon History* 43, no. 4 (Oct. 2017): 100–123.

Relief Society. Bulletins, 1935–58. CHL.

———. General Board Minutes, 1842–2007. CHL.

———. General Board Minutes, 1886–1911. 3 vols. CHL.

———. Minutes of Meetings with the Presiding Bishopric, 1918–38. CHL.

Relief Society Magazine. Salt Lake City. 1915–70.

"Report of Funeral Services in Honor of Ida B. Smith," Sept. 27, 1918. Photocopy of typescript. CHL.

"Report on the East German Mission as of 10 August 1945." European Mission, Thomas E. McKay Correspondence, 1939–46. CHL.

Reynolds, George. *The Story of the Book of Mormon*. Salt Lake City: Joseph Hyrum Parry, 1888.

Reynolds, Noel B. "The Coming Forth of the Book of Mormon in the Twentieth Century." *BYU Studies* 38, no. 2 (1999): 6–47.

Richards, Alma. Papers, 1919–72. BYU.

Richards, Ezra F. Journal, 1897–98. Ezra F. Richards Papers, 1885–1939. CHL.

Richards, Franklin D. Journals, 1844–99. 49 vols. Richards Family Collection, 1837–1961. CHL.

Richards, George F. Journals, 1880–1900. 24 vols. George F. Richards Papers, 1883–1950. CHL. Also available at churchhistorianspress.org.

Ricks, Eldin. "A Chaplain's Diary: World War 2 Experiences of Eldin Ricks." Compiled by Irene Hailes Ricks. Eldin Ricks Papers, 1944–45, Saints at War Project Records, 1847–2017. BYU.

Riess, Jana K. "Heathen in Our Fair Land: Anti-polygamy and Protestant Women's Missions in Utah, 1869–1910." PhD diss., Columbia University, 2000.

Rimington, David B. *Vistas on Visions: A Golden Anniversary History of Church Education in Southern California*. Publication place unidentified: By the author, 1988.

Roberts, B. H. Collection, 1883–1933. CHL.

———. "The Life Story of B. H. Roberts," circa 1933. CHL. Also available as Gary James Bergera, ed., *The Autobiography of B. H. Roberts* (Salt Lake City: Signature Books, 1990).

———. *The Truth, The Way, The Life: An Elementary Treatise on Theology*. Edited by John W. Welch. 2nd ed. Provo, UT: BYU Studies, 1996.

Roberts, Richard C. "The Utah National Guard in the Great War, 1917–18." *Utah Historical Quarterly* 58, no. 4 (Fall 1990): 312–33.

Robertson, Hilton A. Diary, 1936–44. Hilton A. Robertson Collection, 1921–76. CHL.

Romney, Joseph Barnard. "'The Lord, God of Israel, Brought Us out of Mexico!': Junius Romney and the 1912 Mormon Exodus." *Journal of Mormon History* 36, no. 4 (Fall 2010): 208–58.

Romney, Junius. Affidavit, Dec. 6, 1935. CHL.

———. Special Tributes, no date. Typescript. CHL.

Romney, Marion G. Journal, 1941–86. CHL.

Romney, Thomas Cottam. *The Mormon Colonies in Mexico*. Salt Lake City: Deseret Book, 2005.

Roothoff, John Johannes. Autobiography and Sound Recording, circa 1980. CHL.

Rudd, Glen L. Oral History Interview by Bruce D. Blumell, 1975. Glen L. Rudd Interviews, May–Oct. 1975. CHL.

———. *Pure Religion: The Story of Church Welfare since 1930*. Salt Lake City: The Church of Jesus Christ of Latter-day Saints, 1995.

Russell, Isaac. Papers, 1898–1927. Special Collections, Cecil H. Green Library, Stanford University, Stanford, CA.

Rytting, Gloria Wallis. *James H. Wallis: Poet, Printer and Patriarch*. Salt Lake City: R. and R. Enterprises, 1989.

Sacramento Star. Sacramento, CA. 1904–25.

Saints: The Story of the Church of Jesus Christ in the Latter Days. Vol. 1, *The Standard of Truth, 1815–1846*. Salt Lake City: The Church of Jesus Christ of Latter-day Saints, 2018.

Saints: The Story of the Church of Jesus Christ in the Latter Days. Vol. 2, *No Unhallowed Hand, 1846–1893*. Salt Lake City: The Church of Jesus Christ of Latter-day Saints, 2020.

Salt Lake Herald. Salt Lake City. 1870–1909, 1918–20.

Salt Lake Herald-Republican. Salt Lake City. 1909–18.

Salt Lake Pioneer Stake. Confidential Minutes, 1904–76. CHL.

———. Manuscript History and Historical Reports, 1904–77. CHL.

Salt Lake Stake. Minutes of the Quarterly Conference, vol. 9, 1904–6. Salt Lake Stake Confidential Minutes, 1869–1977. CHL.

Salt Lake Tabernacle Decorated for Utah Statehood Celebration, 1896. Photograph. CHL.

Salt Lake Telegram. Salt Lake City. 1902–52.

Salt Lake Tribune. Salt Lake City. 1871–.

San Francisco Call. San Francisco. 1895–1913.

Santos, Claudio Martins dos. Interview by Jeremy Talmage, July 10, 2017. CHL. English translation in possession of editors.

———. Memories of Claudio M. dos Santos, 2009. CHL.

São Paulo District, Brazilian Mission. Claudio and Mary dos Santos Baptismal Certificates, 1944. CHL.

Schaepdrijver, Sophie De. *Bastion: Occupied Bruges in the First World War*. Belgium: Hannibal, 2014.

Schaffner, Anna Katharina. *Exhaustion: A History*. New York: Columbia University Press, 2016.

Scharffs, Gilbert W. *Mormonism in Germany: A History of The Church of Jesus Christ of Latter-day Saints in Germany between 1840 and 1970*. Salt Lake City: Deseret Book, 1970.

Scheiber, Harry N., and Jane L. Scheiber. "Constitutional Liberty in World War II: Army Rule and Martial Law in Hawaii, 1941–1946." *Western Legal History* 3, no. 2 (Summer/Fall 1990): 341–78.

Schnibbe, Karl-Heinz. *The Price: The True Story of a Mormon Who Defied Hitler*. Salt Lake City: Bookcraft, 1984.

Schrag, Peter. *Not Fit for Our Society: Immigration and Nativism in America*. Berkeley: University of California Press, 2010.

Schulthess, Arnold H. Papers, 1866–1924. CHL.

Schulzke, Margot Seymour. "The Story of Friedrich Schulzke." Friedrich W. Schulzke Papers, 1908, 1915–40, circa 2016. CHL.

Schwarz, Paul. Autobiography, circa 1943. CHL. English translation by Edgar Wolferts, June 2020, available at CHL.

Seattle Post-Intelligencer. Seattle. 1888–1914.

Secretary of the General Church Board of Education. Letter to Joseph F. Smith, Nov. 30, 1901. Centennial History Project Records, 1835–1979 (bulk 1971–79). BYU.

Seegmiller, William W. Correspondence, 1926, 1939–45. CHL.

Seferovich, Heather M. "History of the LDS Southern States Mission, 1875–1898." Master's thesis, Brigham Young University, 1996.

Seibold, Norman G. Oral History Interview by David F. Boone, Aug. 30, 1978. CHL.

Selbongen Branch, Switzerland Mission. General Minutes, 1922–71. 8 vols. CHL. English translation of portions by Berta Bockholt, 2020, in possession of editors.
"Selbongen during World War II." Global Histories. The Church of Jesus Christ of Latter-day Saints. Accessed Feb. 2021. https://www.ChurchofJesusChrist.org/study/history/global-histories/poland/stories-of-faith/pl-02-selbongen-during-world-war-ii.
Sell, Acilda. Oral History Interview by Michael N. Landon, Aug. 3, 2004. CHL. English translation of portions by Scott Hales, Aug. 2020, in possession of editors.
———. Transcrito, 2003. In Relato do Histórico Pioneiros/Historical Pioneers Stories, 2001–3, Registros da Área Brasil coleção, 1965–2014. CHL. English translation of portions in possession of editors.
Sessions, J. Wyley. Oral History Interview, Aug. 12, 1972. CHL.
Sessions, J. Wyley, and Magdalene Sessions. Oral History Interview by Richard O. Cowan, June 29, 1965. Copy in possession of editors.
Seventieth Annual Conference of The Church of Jesus Christ of Latter-day Saints. Held in the Tabernacle, Salt Lake City, April 6th, 7th and 8th, 1900, with a Full Report of the Discourses. Also an Account of the General Conference of the Deseret Sunday School Union. Salt Lake City: Deseret News, 1900.
Seventy-First Annual Conference of The Church of Jesus Christ of Latter-day Saints. Held in the Tabernacle, Salt Lake City, April 5th, 6th, and 7th, 1901, with a Full Report of the Discourses. Salt Lake City: Deseret News, 1901.
Seventy-Fourth Annual Conference of The Church of Jesus Christ of Latter-day Saints. Held in the Tabernacle, Salt Lake City, April 3rd, 4th, and 6th, 1904, with a Full Report of the Discourses. Also an Account of the General Conference of the Deseret Sunday School Union. Salt Lake City: Deseret News, 1904.
Seventy-Fourth Semi-annual Conference of The Church of Jesus Christ of Latter-day Saints. Held in the Tabernacle, Salt Lake City, October 4th, 5th and 6th, 1903, with a Full Report of the Discourses. Also an Account of the General Conference of the Deseret Sunday School Union. Salt Lake City: Deseret News, 1903.
Seventy-Seventh Annual Conference of The Church of Jesus Christ of Latter-day Saints. Held in the Tabernacle, Salt Lake City, Utah, April 5, 6, 7, 1907, with a Full Report of the Discourses, Also "An Address to the World" by the Church. Salt Lake City: Deseret News, 1907.
Seventy-Sixth Annual Conference of The Church of Jesus Christ of Latter-day Saints. Held in the Tabernacle, Salt Lake City, Utah, April Sixth, Seventh, Eighth, Nineteen Hundred and Six, with a Full Report of the Discourses. Salt Lake City: Deseret News, 1906.
Sewall, May Wright, ed. *The World's Congress of Representative Women* . . . . 2 vols. Chicago: Rand, McNally, 1894.
Sharp, James Vernon. Autobiography, circa 1987. CHL.
———. Journal, 1926–27. CHL.
———. Oral History Interview by Gordon Irving, Dec. 5–7, 1972. CHL.
Sheffield, Gary. *A Short History of the First World War.* London: Oneworld, 2014.
Sherlock, Richard. "Mormon Migration and Settlement after 1875." *Journal of Mormon History* 2, no. 1 (1975): 53–68.
Shipps, Jan. "The Scattering of the Gathered and the Gathering of the Scattered: The Mormon Diaspora in the Mid-twentieth Century." In *Honoring Juanita Brooks: A Compilation of 30 Annual Presentations from the Juanita Brooks Lecture Series, 1984–2014,* 72–88. St. George, UT: Dixie State University, 2014.
———. *Sojourner in the Promised Land: Forty Years among the Mormons.* Urbana: University of Illinois Press, 2000.
Shipps, Jan, Cheryll L. May, and Dean L. May. "Sugar House Ward: A Latter-day Congregation." In *Portraits of Twelve Religious Communities,* edited by James P. Wind and James W. Lewis, 293–348. Vol. 1 of *American Congregations.* Chicago: University of Chicago Press, 1994.
Shlaes, Amity. *The Forgotten Man: A New History of the Great Depression.* New York: MJF Books and HarperCollins, 2007.

Sillito, John. "Drawing the Sword of War against War: B. H. Roberts, World War I, and the Quest for Peace." *Utah Historical Quarterly* 87, no. 2 (Spring 2019): 100–115.

Simpson, Thomas W. *American Universities and the Birth of Modern Mormonism, 1867–1940.* Chapel Hill: University of North Carolina Press, 2016.

Sixty-Eighth Annual Conference of The Church of Jesus Christ of Latter-day Saints. Held in the Tabernacle, Salt Lake City, April 6th, 7th, 8th, and 10th, 1898, with a Full Report of the Discourses. Salt Lake City: Deseret News, 1898.

Sixty-Ninth Annual Conference of The Church of Jesus Christ of Latter-day Saints. Held in the Tabernacle, Salt Lake City, April 6th, 7th, and 9th, 1899, with a Full Report of the Discourses. Salt Lake City: Deseret News, 1899.

Slaveski, Filip. Journal, 1939–51. Microfilm of typescript. CHL.

———. *The Soviet Occupation of Germany: Hunger, Mass Violence, and the Struggle for Peace, 1945–1947.* Cambridge: Cambridge University Press, 2013.

Smith, Hyrum Mack. Diaries, 1896, 1913–16. CHL.

Smith, Ida Bowman. Salt Lake Tabernacle Address, 1917. CHL.

Smith, J. Douglas. *Managing White Supremacy: Race, Politics, and Citizenship in Jim Crow Virginia.* Chapel Hill: University of North Carolina Press, 2002.

Smith, John Henry. Diaries, 1874–1911. CHL.

Smith, Joseph F. Journals, 1874–1918. CHL.

———. Papers, 1854–1918. CHL.

Smith, Joseph Fielding. Journals, 1899–1965. Joseph Fielding Smith Papers, 1893–1973. CHL.

[Smith, Joseph Fielding]. *Proceedings at the Dedication of the Joseph Smith Memorial Monument at Sharon, Windsor County, Vermont, December 23rd, 1905.* [Salt Lake City?]: Publisher unidentified, [1906?].

Smith, May Riley. *Sometime and Other Poems.* New York: Anson D. F. Randolph, 1893.

Smith, Nicholas G. Diaries, 1902–45. Nicholas G. Smith Collection, 1902–70. CHL.

Smith, Shauna. "Remember Who You Are: Recollections of the Joseph Fielding and Ruth Pingree Smith Children," 1999. Private possession.

Smoot, Reed. Papers, 1827–1967. BYU.

Snow, Lorenzo. "An Account of a Private Interview with President Woodruff," Dec. 3, 1892. CHL.

———. *Greeting to the World by President Lorenzo Snow Delivered at the Centennial Services, Latter-day Saints' Tabernacle, Salt Lake City, Jan. 1, 1901.* [Salt Lake City]: Publisher unidentified, [1901?]. Copy at CHL.

Sommerfeld, Marie. Interview by Douglas Tobler, 1974. Audio recording. CHL. English transcription, circa 1985, available at CHL.

Sorensen, Asael Taylor. "Asael T. Sorenson, Sr.: A Personal History," 2001. CHL.

———. Oral History Interview by Gordon Irving, Oct. 8, 1973. CHL.

South Africa Mission. Manuscript History and Historical Reports, 1853–1977. 5 vols. CHL.

South American Mission. Manuscript History and Historical Reports, 1925–35. 2 vols. CHL.

"Southern California Latter-day Saint Seminaries, Teacher's Handbook, 1953–1954." William E. Berrett copy. Church Educational System, Southern California Area Files, circa 1950–77. CHL.

South Ohio District, Great Lakes Mission. General Minutes, 1931–43. CHL.

South Ohio District Presidency. Letter to Hamilton and Middleton Members, Jan. 18, 1950. Paul and Cornelia T. Bang Papers, 1935–44, 1977–78. CHL.

Spanish American Mission. Manuscript History and Historical Reports, 1936–67. CHL.

Spector, Ronald H. *Eagle against the Sun: The American War with Japan.* New York: Free Press, 1985.

Stam, Symen. Oral History Interview by William G. Hartley, 1974. CHL.

Standard. Ogden, UT. 1888–1902.

Stapley, Jonathan A. "Adoptive Sealing Ritual in Mormonism." *Journal of Mormon History* 37, no. 3 (Summer 2011): 56–104.

———. *The Power of Godliness: Mormon Liturgy and Cosmology.* New York: Oxford University Press, 2018.

Stapley, Jonathan A., and Kristine L. Wright. "'They Shall Be Made Whole': A History of Baptism for Health." *Journal of Mormon History* 34, no. 4 (Fall 2008): 69–112.

Starke, Oskar Helmut. "Memoirs from the Lives of Oskar Helmut Starke and Anni Helene Piering Starke," [1999]. CHL.

Stars and Stripes. Bloomfield, MO, 1861; Paris, 1918–19; Washington, DC, 1919–; London, 1942–45.

Statehood Constitutional Convention (1895) State Constitution. Series 3214. Utah Division of Archives and Records Service, Utah State Archives, Salt Lake City.

The Statutes at Large of the United States of America, from August, 1893, to March, 1895, and Recent Treaties, Conventions, and Executive Proclamations. Vol. 28. Washington, DC: Government Printing Office, 1895.

Stephenson, Jonathan. "'I Cries Inside': A Short Biography of Len, Sr. and Mary Hope." Paper for Central Office Church History Class, no date. Marion D. Hanks Collection, 1873, 1904–2018. CHL.

Stevenson, Ezra T. Du Fresne. Mission Journals, 1887–90, 1898–1900. CHL.

Stevenson, Russell W. *For the Cause of Righteousness: A Global History of Blacks and Mormonism, 1830–2013*. Salt Lake City: Greg Kofford Books, 2014.

Stewart, William T. Papers, 1878–93. CHL.

St. George Utah Stake. General Minutes, 1864–1977. CHL.

Stoddard, Waldo Izatt. Oral History Interview by Gordon Irving, Sept. 7, 1973. CHL.

Stover, Philip R. "The Exodus of 1912: A Huddle of Pros and Cons—Mormons Twice Disposed." *Journal of Mormon History* 44 (July 2018): 45–69.

Stover, Walter. Oral History Interview by Richard L. Jensen, Aug. 1976. CHL.

———. Oral History Interview by William G. Hartley, 1975. CHL.

Stradling, David. *Cincinnati: From River City to Highway Metropolis*. Making of America Series. Charleston, SC: Arcadia, 2003.

Strong, Josiah. *Our Country: Its Possible Future and Its Present Crisis*. New York: Baker and Taylor, 1891.

Stueck, William. *Rethinking the Korean War: A New Diplomatic and Strategic History*. Princeton, NJ: Princeton University Press, 2002.

Sullivan, James E. "What Happened at Stockholm." *Outing* 61, no. 1 (Oct. 1912): 21–31.

Summers, Helen W. Mission Journal, 1937–38. Helen W. Summers Mission Papers, 1937–38. CHL.

Sunday Evening Radio Addresses, 1924–29, 1932–34. CHL.

Sunday School. General Board Minutes, 1867–1993. CHL.

———. General Presidency Meeting Agendas, Minutes, and Assignments, 1934–59, 1964–94, 1998, 2000. CHL.

Suppan, Arnold. *Hitler—Beneš—Tito: National Conflicts, World Wars, Genocides, Expulsions, and Divided Remembrance in East-Central and Southeastern Europe, 1848–2018*. Vienna: Austrian Academy of Sciences, 2019.

Swanson, Vern G. "The Book of Mormon Art of Arnold Friberg: 'Painter of Scripture.'" *Journal of Book of Mormon Studies* 10, no. 1 (2001): 26–35, 79.

Swinton, Heidi S. "Bathsheba Wilson Bigler Smith (1822–1910)." In *1821–1845*, edited by Richard E. Turley Jr. and Brittany A. Chapman, 349–65. Vol. 2 of *Women of Faith in the Latter Days*. Salt Lake City: Deseret Book, 2012.

Swiss-German Mission. Office Journal, 1898–1920. Swiss and German Mission Journal, 1898–1920. CHL.

Swiss Temple Dedicatory Addresses at Dedication of Swiss Temple: Zollikofen, Switzerland, Sept. 11–15, 1955. English transcripts. CHL.

Switzerland Zurich Mission. Manuscript History and Historical Reports, 1850–1977. CHL.

Szymanski, Stefan. "A Theory of the Evolution of Modern Sport." *Journal of Sport History* 35, no. 1 (Spring 2008): 1–32.

Taggart, Scott. Journal, 1946–48. Scott Taggart Papers, 1946–48. CHL.

———. "Notes on the Life of Scott Taggart," circa 1964. Scott Taggart Papers, 1946–48. CHL.

———. Oral History Interview by James B. Allen, 1973. CHL.

Tait, Lisa Olsen. "Susa Young Gates and the Vision of the Redemption of the Dead: D&C 138." In *Revelations in Context: The Stories behind the Sections of the Doctrine and Covenants,* edited by Matthew McBride and James Goldberg, 315–22. Salt Lake City: The Church of Jesus Christ of Latter-day Saints, 2016.

Takagi, Shinji. *The Trek East: Mormonism Meets Japan, 1901–1968.* Salt Lake City: Greg Kofford Books, 2016.

Talmage, James E. *Jesus the Christ: A Study of the Messiah and His Mission according to the Holy Scriptures Both Ancient and Modern.* Salt Lake City: Deseret News, 1915.

———. Journals, Daybooks, and Other Materials, 1879–1933. BYU.

Talmage, John R. *The Talmage Story: Life of James E. Talmage—Educator, Scientist, Apostle.* Salt Lake City: Bookcraft, 1972.

Tanner, Annie Clark. *A Mormon Mother: An Autobiography.* Salt Lake City: Deseret News Press, 1941.

Tate, George S. "'The Great World of the Spirits of the Dead': Death, the Great War, and the 1918 Influenza Pandemic as Context for Doctrine and Covenants 138." *BYU Studies* 46, no. 1 (2007): 5–40.

"Tatsui Sato: Translator for Life." Global Histories. The Church of Jesus Christ of Latter-day Saints. Accessed July 2, 2021. https://www.ChurchofJesusChrist.org/study/history/global-histories/japan/stories-of-faith/jp-07-tatsui-sato-bb.

Taylor, A. Elmina Shepard. Collection, 1844–1956. CHL.

Taylor, Cornelia. Diary, 1935–37. Paul and Cornelia T. Bang Papers, 1935–44, 1977–78. CHL.

Taylor, George Shepard. "Report of Sermons of Elder David O. McKay Delivered at the Annual Conference of the New Zealand Mission of The Church of Jesus Christ of Latter-day Saints Held at Huntly, Waikato, New Zealand, April 23rd to 25th, 1921," 1921. CHL.

Taylor, Henry Louis, Jr. "City Building, Public Policy, the Rise of the Industrial City, and Black Ghetto-Slum Formation in Cincinnati, 1850–1940." In *Race and the City: Work, Community, and Protest in Cincinnati, 1820–1970,* edited by Henry Louis Taylor Jr., 156–92. Urbana: University of Illinois Press, 1993.

Taylor, Janet L. Autobiography, 1954. CHL.

Teachings of Presidents of the Church: George Albert Smith. Salt Lake City: The Church of Jesus Christ of Latter-day Saints, 2011.

Teachings of Presidents of the Church: Gordon B. Hinckley. Salt Lake City: The Church of Jesus Christ of Latter-day Saints, 2016.

"Temple List." Temples, The Church of Jesus Christ of Latter-day Saints. Accessed Aug. 23, 2021. https://www.ChurchofJesusChrist.org/temples/list.

Terazawa, Chiye. Mission Journal, 1938–39. Chiye and Toshi Terazawa Mission Papers, 1938–39, 1952–54, 2002. CHL.

Testimony of Len R. Hope and Mary Hope, 1938. CHL.

That We Might Be One: The Story of the Dutch Potato Project. The Church of Jesus Christ of Latter-day Saints. Video, 11:57. Accessed Feb. 11, 2021. https://www.ChurchofJesusChrist.org/study/history/global-histories/netherlands/stories-of-faith/nl-04-the-dutch-potato-project.

Theodore Roosevelt Refutes Anti-Mormon Falsehoods. His Testimony as to Mormon Character. Advice concerning Polygamy. A Vigorous Arraignment of Magazine Slanderers. Publication place and publisher unidentified, [1911]. CHL.

Thirty-Second Ward, Pioneer Stake. Relief Society Minutes and Records, 1902–71. CHL.

Thomas, Brook, ed. *Plessy v. Ferguson: A Brief History with Documents.* Boston: Bedford Books, 1997.

Thomas, John C. "Apostolic Diplomacy: The 1923 European Mission of Senator Reed Smoot and Professor John A. Widtsoe." *Journal of Mormon History* 28, no. 1 (Spring 2002): 130–65.

Thomas, Warren John. *Salt Lake Mormon Tabernacle Choir Goes to Europe—1955.* Salt Lake City: Deseret News Press, 1957.

Thorp, Malcolm R. "The British Government and the Mormon Question, 1910–1922." *Journal of Church and State* 21, no. 2 (1979): 305–23.

———. "'The Mormon Peril': The Crusade against the Saints in Britain, 1910–1911." *Journal of Mormon History* 2 (1975): 69–88.

Tichi, Cecelia. *Exposés and Excess: Muckraking in America, 1900/2000.* Philadelphia: University of Pennsylvania Press, 2004.

Tilsit Branch, Berlin Mission. Manuscript History and Historical Reports, 1902–30. CHL.

———. Sunday School Minutes and Records, 1927–29. CHL.

Time. New York City. 1923–.

Tobler, Douglas F. "The Jews, the Mormons, and the Holocaust." *Journal of Mormon History* 18, no. 1 (Spring 1992): 59–92.

Tomlinson, Terry Lyn. "A History of the Founding of the Institutes of Religion, 1926–1936: A Case Study of a Religious Education Movement in American Higher Education." PhD diss., University of California Riverside, 2011.

Tullis, F. LaMond. *Martyrs in Mexico: A Mormon Story of Revolution and Redemption.* Provo, UT: Religious Studies Center, Brigham Young University, 2018.

———. *Mormons in Mexico: The Dynamics of Faith and Culture.* Logan: Utah State University Press, 1987.

———. "Reopening the Mexican Mission in 1901." *BYU Studies* 22, no. 4 (Fall 1982): 441–53.

———. "A Shepherd to Mexico's Saints: Arwell L. Pierce and the Third Convention." *BYU Studies* 37, no. 1 (1997): 127–57.

United Kingdom Air Ministry, Meteorological Office. *The Daily Weather Report, British Section, 1st October to 31st December, 1940.* London, 1940. Available at https://digital.nmla.metoffice.gov.uk/IO_e67c1eb2-e37c-4261-ac2e-6b89d379ffc3/.

U.S. and Canada Record Collection. FHL.

U.S. Bureau of the Census. Population Schedules. Microfilm. FHL.

U.S. Department of Commerce, Bureau of the Census. *Fifteenth Census of the United States: 1930.* 6 vols. Washington, DC: Government Printing Office, 1931.

U.S. State Department Correspondence regarding Mormons and Mormonism, 1910–40. CHL.

U.S. World War II Draft Cards Young Men, 1940–47. Database. Ancestry.com. Accessed Jan. 7, 2021. https://www.ancestry.com/search/collections/2238/.

Utah Department of Health. Office of Vital Records and Statistics. Utah State Archives and Records Service, Salt Lake City.

Utah Genealogical and Historical Magazine. Salt Lake City. 1910–40.

Van Orden, Bruce A. *Building Zion: The Latter-day Saints in Europe.* Salt Lake City: Deseret Book, 1996.

Veranneman, Jean-Michel. *Belgium in the Great War.* Barnsley, England: Pen and Sword Military, 2018.

Villalobos, Maria Concepcion Monroy Hernandez de. Oral History Interview by Gordon Irving, Aug. 16, 1974. CHL. English translation of portions in possession of editors.

Vlam, Grace Alida Hermine. "Answers to the Questions Posed," Apr. 3, 2001. Saints at War Project, 1847–2017. BYU.

———. Interview by Chad Carr, Sept. 20, 2013. Grace A. Vlam Papers, 2013–20. CHL.

———. Interview by James Perry, May 29 and June 10, 2020. CHL.

———, ed. *Our Lives: Pieter Vlam and Hanna Vlam-Gysler.* Salt Lake City: By the editor, 1993. CHL.

———. Papers, 2013–20. CHL.

———. "She Who Gathers for the Lord: The Life History of Grace Alida Hermine Vlam," [2015]. Copy in Grace A. Vlam Papers, 2013–20. CHL.

Vrba, Cenek H. "Czechoslovak Mission of The Church of Jesus Christ of Latter-day Saints, 1950–1968." Czechoslovakia Histories, 1947–68. CHL.

———. "History of the Brno Branch of The Church of Jesus Christ of Latter-day Saints, 1950–1968." Czechoslovakia Histories, 1947–68. CHL.

Wachsmann, Nikolaus. *KL: A History of the Nazi Concentration Camps.* New York: Farrar, Straus and Giroux, 2015.

Walker, Isaiah. "Abraham Kaleimahoe Fernandez: A Hawaiian Saint and Royalist, 1857–1915." Paper presented at the Mormon Pacific Historical Society 28th Annual Conference, Laie, HI, Mar. 17, 2007.

Walker, Ronald W. "Crisis in Zion: Heber J. Grant and the Panic of 1893." *BYU Studies* 43, no. 1 (2004): 115–42.

———. "'Going to Meeting' in Salt Lake City's Thirteenth Ward, 1849–1881: A Microanalysis." In *New Views of Mormon History: A Collection of Essays in Honor of Leonard J. Arrington*, edited by Davis Bitton and Maureen Ursenbach Beecher, 138–61. Salt Lake City: University of Utah Press, 1987.

———. "Strangers in a Strange Land: Heber J. Grant and the Opening of the Japanese Mission." *BYU Studies* 43, no. 1 (2004): 231–62.

Wallis, James H. Journals, 1932–40. 2 vols. CHL.

Walton, John H., ed. *The Mending Link: A Brief and Nostalgic History of the Japanese Mission in Hawaii as Told by Those Who Served Therein*. [Salt Lake City]: By the editor, 2002.

Ward, Margery W. *A Life Divided: The Biography of Joseph Marion Tanner, 1859–1927*. Salt Lake City: Publishers Press, 1980.

Ward Charity: Details of Administration. Salt Lake City: Presiding Bishopric, 1930.

"Washington, Seattle, Passenger Lists, 1890–1957." Database with images. FamilySearch. Accessed Dec. 3, 2020. https://www.familysearch.org/search/collection/1916081.

Washington Post. Washington, DC. 1877–.

Washington Times. Washington, DC. 1902–39.

Watt, Ronald G., and Kenneth W. Godfrey. "'Old 42': The British and European Mission Headquarters in Liverpool, England, 1855–1904." *Mormon Historical Studies* 10, no. 1 (Spring 2009): 87–99.

Weinberg, Gerhard L. *A World at Arms: A Global History of World War II*. 2nd ed. Cambridge: Cambridge University Press, 2005.

Welch, John W., and Doris R. Dant. *The Book of Mormon Paintings of Minerva Teichert*. Provo, UT: BYU Studies; Salt Lake City: Bookcraft, 1997.

Welfare Department. Northern Utah Region Documents, 1939–49. CHL.

Wells, Emmeline B. Diaries, 1844–1920. 47 vols. BYU. Also available at churchhistorianspress.org.

Wells, Junius F. "Report on Joseph Smith's Birthplace," June 1905. Junius F. Wells Papers, 1867–1930. CHL.

Western Mail. Cardiff, Wales. 1869–.

Whaanga, Mere. "From the Diary of Mere Whaanga," edited by Hyran Smith. Hyran Smith Additions to Mere Whaanga Journal Transcription, [2006]. Matthew Cowley Pacific Church History Centre, Temple View, New Zealand.

Wheadon, Essie H. Mission Papers, circa 1931–40. CHL.

Whitaker, John M. Autobiography and Journals, 1883–1960. CHL.

White, Richard. *The Republic for Which It Stands: The United States during Reconstruction and the Gilded Age, 1865–1896*. The Oxford History of the United States 7. New York: Oxford University Press, 2017.

Whitney, Orson F. Journals, 1877–79, 1881–98, 1901–3, 1905–31. CHL.

———. *Through Memory's Halls: The Life Story of Orson F. Whitney as Told by Himself*. Independence, MO: Zion's Printing and Publishing, 1930.

Wichita Beacon. Wichita, KS. 1910–60.

Wichita Daily Eagle. Wichita, KS. 1890–1906.

Widtsoe, John A. Diaries and Notebooks, 1881–1952. CHL.

———. *Evidences and Reconciliations: Aids to Faith in a Modern Day*. 3 vols. Salt Lake City: Bookcraft, 1943, 1947, 1951.

———. *In a Sunlit Land: The Autobiography of John A. Widtsoe*. Salt Lake City: Milton R. Hunter and G. Homer Durham, 1952.

———. *In Search of Truth: Comments on the Gospel and Modern Thought*. Salt Lake City: Deseret Book, 1930.

————. *In the Gospel Net: The Story of Anna Karine Gaarden Widtsoe*. Salt Lake City: Improvement Era, 1942.

————. *La verdad restaurada*. [Buenos Aires]: Misión Argentina, [1935].

————. Papers, no date. CHL.

————. *A Rational Theology: As Taught by The Church of Jesus Christ of Latter-day Saints*. [Salt Lake City]: General Priesthood Committee, 1915.

Widtsoe, John A., and Leah Dunford Widtsoe. *The Word of Wisdom: A Modern Interpretation*. Salt Lake City: Deseret Book, 1937.

Widtsoe, Leah Dunford. Journal, 1933. CHL.

————. Oral History Interview by Hollis Scott, Feb. 11, 1965. BYU.

Widtsoe Family Papers, 1824–1953. CHL.

Wijfjes, Huub. "Spellbinding and Crooning: Sound Amplification, Radio, and Political Rhetoric in International Comparative Perspective, 1900–1945." *Technology and Culture* 55, no. 1 (Jan. 2014): 148–85.

Willey, Willard Haven. Memoirs, circa 1912–77. CHL.

William O. and Henry C. Lee Life Sketches, circa 2009. CHL.

Williams, Frederick Salem, and Frederick G. Williams. *From Acorn to Oak Tree: A Personal History of the Establishment and First Quarter Century Development of the South American Missions*. Fullerton, CA: Et Cetera, Et Cetera Graphics, 1987.

Williams' Cincinnati Directory . . . . Cincinnati: Williams Directory, 1927–28.

Williams' Cincinnati Directory . . . . Cincinnati: Williams Directory, 1929–30.

Williams' Cincinnati City Directory, 1940 . . . . Cincinnati: Williams Directory, 1939–40.

Wilson, A. N. *Hitler: A Short Biography*. London: HarperPress, 2012.

Wilson, Harold S. *McClure's Magazine and the Muckrakers*. Princeton, NJ: Princeton University Press, 1970.

Winder, Michael K. "Theodore Roosevelt and the Mormons." *Theodore Roosevelt Association Journal* 31, no. 4 (Fall 2010): 11–19.

Winter, Arthur. Journals, 1883–1940. 6 vols. Arthur Winter Collection, 1833–1940. CHL.

Winter, J. M. *The Great War and the British People*. Houndmills, England: Macmillan, 1986.

Wise, Frank S. "A New Concept in Temple Building and Operation," 1978. CHL.

————. Oral History Interview by Gordon Irving, 1980–81. CHL.

Wolsey, Heber Grant. "The History of Radio Station KSL from 1922 to Television." PhD diss., Michigan State University, 1967.

Woman's Exponent. Salt Lake City. 1872–1914.

Wood, Edward J. Journals, circa 1884–1933. Edward J. Wood Collection, 1884–1982. CHL.

Wood, Vi A. *The Alberta Temple: Centre and Symbol of Faith*. Calgary, Alberta, Canada: Detselig, 1989.

Woodger, Mary Jane. "'Cheat the Asylum of a Victim': George Albert Smith's 1909–12 Breakdown." *Journal of Mormon History* 34, no. 4 (Fall 2008): 113–52.

————. *David O. McKay: Beloved Prophet*. American Fork, UT: Covenant Communications, 2004.

————. *Mission President or Spy? The True Story of Wallace F. Toronto, the Czech Mission, and World War II*. Provo, UT: Religious Studies Center, Brigham Young University; Salt Lake City: Deseret Book, 2019.

Woodruff, Wilford. Journals and Papers, 1828–98. CHL.

Woodworth, Jed L. "Claudio Martins dos Santos," 2017. Typescript. Jed Woodworth Collection on Claudio dos Santos, 2017, 2019. CHL.

————. "Refusing to Die: Financial Crisis at Brigham Young Academy, 1877–1897." *BYU Studies* 38, no. 1 (1999): 71–123.

Woolsey, Maryhale, and Mildred Tanner Pettit. *The Happy Hearts: An Operetta*. [Salt Lake City]: General Board of the Primary Association of The Church of Jesus Christ of Latter-day Saints, 1938.

Worlton, John E. Mission Journal and Scrapbook, 1927–30. CHL.

Wright, Dennis A. "The Beginnings of the First LDS Institute of Religion at Moscow, Idaho." *Mormon Historical Studies* 10, no. 1 (Spring 2009): 65–84.

—————. "Good Morning Los Angeles: The Beginning of the Early Morning Seminary Program." In *Regional Studies in Latter-day Saint Church History: California,* edited by David F. Boone, Robert C. Freeman, Andrew H. Hedges, and Richard Neitzel Holzapfel, 223–37. Provo, UT: Department of Church History and Doctrine, Brigham Young University, 1998.

Wright, Evan P. "A History of the South African Mission," 1977, 1985, 1987. 3 vols. CHL.

Wright, Herbert. "The Legality of the Annexation of Austria by Germany." *American Journal of International Law* 38, no. 4 (Oct. 1944): 621–35.

Yanagida, Toshiko Takagi. "Ashiato," no date. CHL. English translation in possession of editors.

—————. "Banzai!" In *Mormon Pioneers of Japanese Ancestry: Their Conversion Stories,* compiled and edited by Dennis H. Atkin and Theodocia H. Atkin, 188–89. Flagstaff, AZ: Theodocia H. Atkin, 2008.

—————. "Memoirs of the Relief Society in Japan, 1951–1991." *BYU Studies* 44, no. 2 (Apr. 2005): 145–54.

—————. Oral History Interview by Glenn Rowe, Richard E. Turley, and Kazuo Imai, Aug. 29, 2001. CHL. English translation in possession of editors.

—————. Oral History Interview by Ronald O. Barney, Sept. 9, 1996. CHL.

—————. "Relief Society President Experiences," 2006. DVD. CHL. English transcription by Andrew Hall in possession of the editors.

—————. "Takagi and Nikichi Takahashi, Two of the Very Early Baptisms." In *Mormon Pioneers of Japanese Ancestry: Their Conversion Stories,* compiled and edited by Dennis H. Atkin and Theodocia H. Atkin, 21–22. Flagstaff, AZ: Theodocia H. Atkin, 2008.

Young, Brigham, Jr. Journals and Papers, 1862–1902. CHL.

Young, Gordon Claridge. Oral History Interview by Lauritz G. Petersen, Aug. 28, 1972. CHL.

Young, Walter Ernest. Diaries, 1910–18. CHL.

—————. *The Diary of W. Ernest Young.* Publication place unidentified: By the author, circa 1973. CHL.

Young Men's Mutual Improvement Association. Board Minutes, 1898–1972. Young Men, Minutes, 1898–1989, 1991–97, 2001–3. CHL.

Young Woman's Journal. Salt Lake City. 1889–1929.

Young Women. General Board Minutes, 1891–97, 1914–17. CHL.

Zion's Cooperative Mercantile Institution. Minutes, 1868–1973. CHL.

Zuber, Terence. *Ten Days in August: The Siege of Liège 1914.* Stroud, England: Spellmount, 2014.

ACKNOWLEDGMENTS

Hundreds of people contributed to this new history of the Church, and we are grateful to each one of them. We are indebted to Saints who kept the records on which this book is based and to the generations of historians employed by the Church who have meticulously collected and preserved them. Special thanks to David Golding, Jessica Marie Nelson, and Ryan Saltzgiver for creating the supplemental materials online. The digitization of sources was led by Audrey Spainhower Dunshee and completed by staff of the Church History Department.

We express deep gratitude to the many family historians who have recorded and digitized and shared their records with us. Special thanks to George Durham, Shirley Eichers, Lark Evans Galli, Priscilla Hancock, Gayle Hatch, Donna Ikegami, Lyle Jensen, Kent Johnson, Janet Taylor Jones, Alan Lee, Brian Lee, Kathleen Lloyd, Linda Bang Ludlow, Jennifer Middleton Mason, Cory H. Maxwell, Helga Meyer, Matthias Miller, Ewan Harbrecht Mitton, Becka Pace, Carol Rees, Jacqueline Rich, Jan Roothoff, Karla Smith, Linda Stapley, Grace A. H. Vlam, Edgar Wolferts, and Shauna Zukle. Many thanks to the Family History Department and FamilySearch for their commitment to making genealogical records and services available to everyone. It is no exaggeration to say that without these records and FamilySearch's discovery tools, this book could not have been written. Many staff members, missionaries, and volunteers in the Church History Department contributed directly or indirectly to this book. In particular, we thank the following for their assistance: Allen Andersen, Jill Andersen, Jeff Anderson, Jay Burton, Clint Christensen, Tom Clark, Christine Cox, Jeff Crossley, Emily Crumpton, Richard Davis, Keith Erekson, Jared Feller, Seth Gardner, Matthew Godfrey, Cas Hadfield, Joan Harding, Matt Heiss, Melissa Wei-Tsing Inouye, Natalie Johnson, Jenny Lund, Brandon Metcalf, James Miller, Tarienne Mitchell, Joan Nay, Jacob Olmstead, Michelle Sayers Pollock, Elise Reynolds, Julie A. Russell, Sheridan Sylvester, Jeremy Talmage, Emily Utt, and Brian Warburton. We also thank James Goldberg for helping shape the literary structure of the book; Jenny Rollins and Laura E. Hilton for helping draft and revise scenes; Nicole Christensen Fernley, Kaytee Johnson, McKinsey Kemeny, Riley M. Lorimer, Taylor Kalia Orr, and Naomi White for editorial contributions; and Sylvia Coates for indexing the volume. The members of the Church Historian's Press Editorial Board provided ongoing support.

Many expert readers from outside the department offered feedback on parts of the book. These include Ian Barber, Jorge T. Becerra, Richard Bennett, R. Lanier Britsch, Brian Q. Cannon, Néstor Curbelo, Nancy Dance, Jill Mulvay Derr, Christian Euvrard, Kathleen Flake, Casey Paul Griffiths, Mark Grover, Steven C. Harper, Richard Ian Kimball, Carol Cornwall Madsen, Khumbulani Mdletshe, Dmitry Mikulin, Matthias Miller, Thierry K. Mutombo, Marjorie Newton, Bonnie L. Oscarson, Elisa Pulido, W. Paul Reeve, Carlos F. Rivas, Jorge L. Saldívar, Cristina Sanches, Ciro Schmeil, Cherry Silver, Ben Spackman, Jonathan Stapley, George Tate, Douglas Tobler, F. LaMond Tullis, Richard E. Turley Jr., Grace A. H. Vlam, and Gary Walton. Sarah Clement Reed, Michael Knudson, Savannah Woolsey Larson, Heather Olsen, Annie

Smith Devenport, Lucia Cathers, Quinn Preece, and Christian Patrick Wawro offered valuable assistance translating the letters of Anna and John Widtsoe.

Greg Newbold created the engaging artwork. John Heath and Debra Abercrombie contributed to the outreach effort, and Benjamin Wood helped with product management. Deborah Gates, Kiersten Olson, Jo Lyn Curtis, Cindy Pond, and Susan Henson provided administrative assistance. Mark Hales provided project management. In his role as product manager for the first three volumes, Ben Ellis Godfrey magnified his role many times over, including creating and hosting the *Saints* podcast.

Members of several Church departments contributed, including a cross-departmental team made up of Irene Caso, Drew Conrad, Irinna Danielson, David Dickson, Norm Gardner, Paul Murphy, Alan Paulsen, and Jen Ward. Katie Parker of the Publishing Services Department oversaw the final publication process, and Patric Gerber, Benson Y. Parkinson, Lindsey Maughan, Alyssa Aramaki, Preston Shewell, Josh McFadden, Cara Nickels, Wendy Jennings, Sarah Schulzke Trump, and Kat Tilby provided production assistance. Other contributors include Christopher Clark, Jon Thorup, Jake Davis, DJ Christensen, Michael Smith, Jim McKenna, Alan Blake, Jared Moon, Casey Olson, Brian D. Garner, Benjamin Peterson, Paul VanDerHoeven, and Gary Walton. Translators carefully prepared the entire text in thirteen languages.

Finally, we thank readers from all around the world who reviewed the narrative and provided feedback. Their contributions improved the book and helped ensure that it would speak to the minds and hearts of Saints everywhere.

INDEX

Aaronic Priesthood, 324–26. *See also* priesthood
Abbott, Stanley, 539–41
Abinadi Delivers His Message to King Noah (Friberg painting), 593
Adam, 182–83, 204, 319, 605
adoption sealings, 28, 31, 132–33
Agricultural College, Logan, Utah, 50, 91, 111–12, 122, 219
Alberta Temple, 171, 234–35, 237–39, 525
Allen, Heber, 512, 523–24
Allied forces
    advancing into Germany, 460
    Battle of Okinawa between Japan and, 465–68, 470
    D-Day invasion by, 457
    occupation of Japan, 471–72
    Pearl Harbor attack and U.S. joining, 413–14, 458
    "Victory in Europe Day" celebration (1945), 465
    See also France; Great Britain; Soviet Union; United States of America; World War II
Alma Baptizes in the Waters of Mormon (Friberg painting), 593
American Indians. *See* Native Americans
American South, 243–45, 249–52
Amsterdam (Netherlands) Branch, 501–4. *See also* Netherlands, Saints in
Anderson, Charles
    at baptism of Bang family, 266
    and Cincinnati Branch chapel, 281–83, 287–88
    as Cincinnati Branch president, 264–65, 377
    commemorating restoration of Aaronic Priesthood, 326
    organizing tracting society, 352
    as witness to sealing of Bang family, 429–30
Anderson, Christine, 264–65, 287–88, 429
Anderson, Edward, 232
Anderson, Nephi, 377
Anderson's Ferry, Ohio, 266
Anschluss (Nazi Germany unification, 1938), 380–81, 395
Aoki, Tamotsu, 391
apartheid, 582
Arabic sinking (1915), 176–77
Argentina, 241–43
Arizona, Saints in, 289–90
Arizona Temple, 487, 557–58, 560
Armenian Saints, 227–28
Articles of Faith, 324–25
Articles of Faith (Talmage book), 359–60, 377, 406
Atonement of Jesus Christ, 182–83, 202–3, 605
Austria, 380–83, 395

Austria, Saints in
    commemorating pioneers' arrival in Salt Lake Valley, 498–500
    Cziep family, 380–83, 394–95
    Emmy Cziep in postwar Vienna, 492–95
    Frankenburg Branch, 499
    with Jewish heritage, 395, 410
    men drafted for German army, 408
    Nazi Party members and sympathizers among, 408–9
Austro-Hungarian Empire, 163

Ball, Vaughn, 428–29
Ballantyne, Richard, 530
Ballard, Melvin J., 253–56, 273, 320, 364, 368
Ballif, Louisa, 601
Bang, Chris, 325
Bang, Christian, Sr., 263–66, 281, 287, 534
Bang, Connie (Cornelia Belle) Taylor
    on Cincinnati Branch meetinghouse building committee, 427–28
    courtship with Paul Bang, 353, 377–79
    marriage and tour of historic sites, 402–5
    missionary work of, 352, 378–79
    passing on legacy of faith to children, 534
    patriarchal blessing for, 350–53, 402, 536
    temple sealing, 428–30
    in YWMIA, 534
Bang, Henry, 325–27, 352
Bang, Judy, 352–53, 377–78
Bang, Paul
    Aaronic Priesthood responsibilities of, 324–25
    baptism, 263, 266
    courtship with Connie Taylor, 353, 377–79
    marriage and tour of historic sites, 402–5
    missionary work of, 376–79
    serving in Cincinnati Branch, 325–27, 427–28, 534–36
    temple sealing, 428–30
Bang, Rosa Kiefer, 263–66
Bang, Sandra, 428–29, 534, 536
baptism
    of Bang family members in U.S., 266, 534
    as binding together in love, 90
    of Guatemalan Saints, 515, 558–59
    for healing, 239
    of Helga Meiszus in Germany, 313
    of Inge Lehmann in GDR, 573–75
    of Jeanne Charrier in France, 553
    of Jennifer Middleton in England during World War II, 454–57
    of Len and Mary Hope in U.S., 249–52

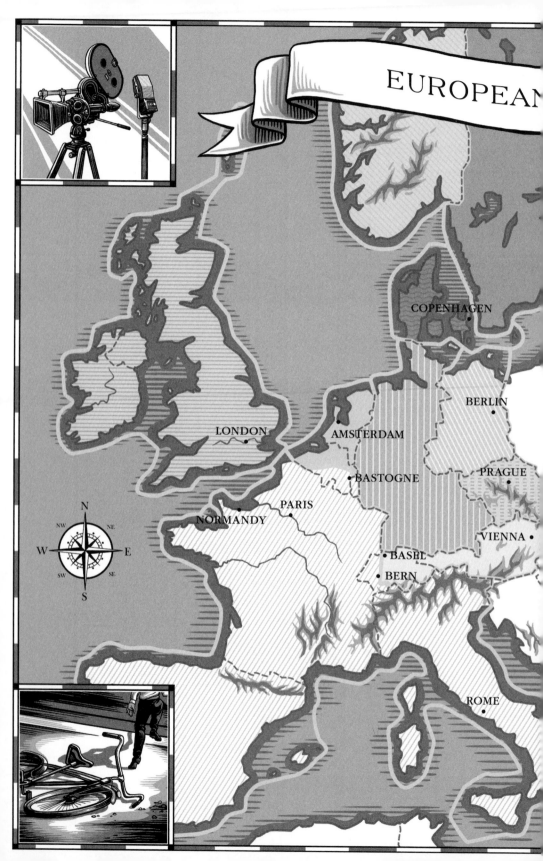

MISSIONS

MISSION BOUNDARIES 1955

	British Mission
	Czechoslovak Mission (closed in 1950)
	Danish Mission
	East German Mission
	Finnish Mission
	French Mission
	Netherlands Mission
	Norwegian Mission
	Swedish Mission
	Swiss-Austrian Mission
	West German Mission